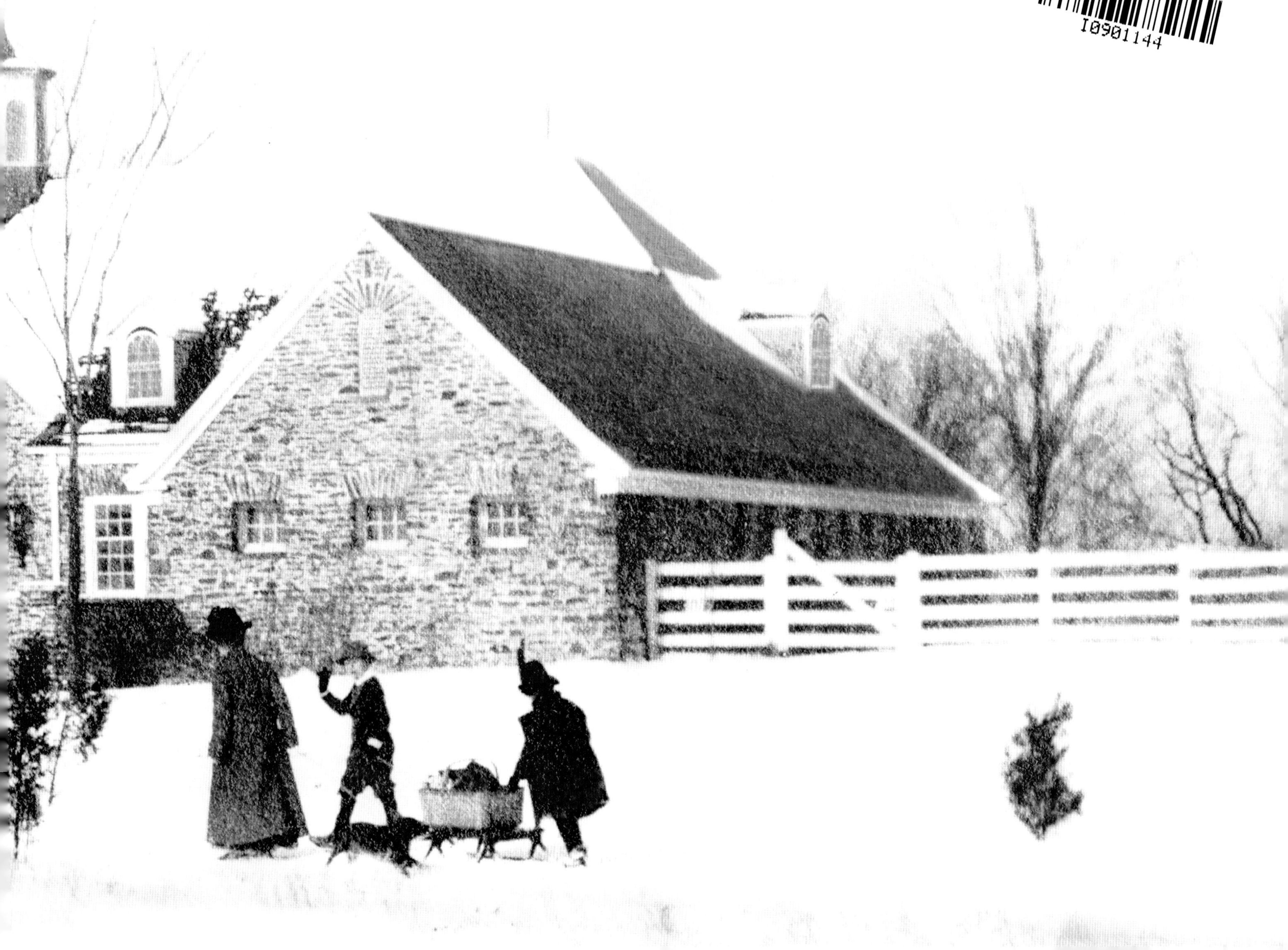

OUR TIME AT FOXHOLLOW FARM

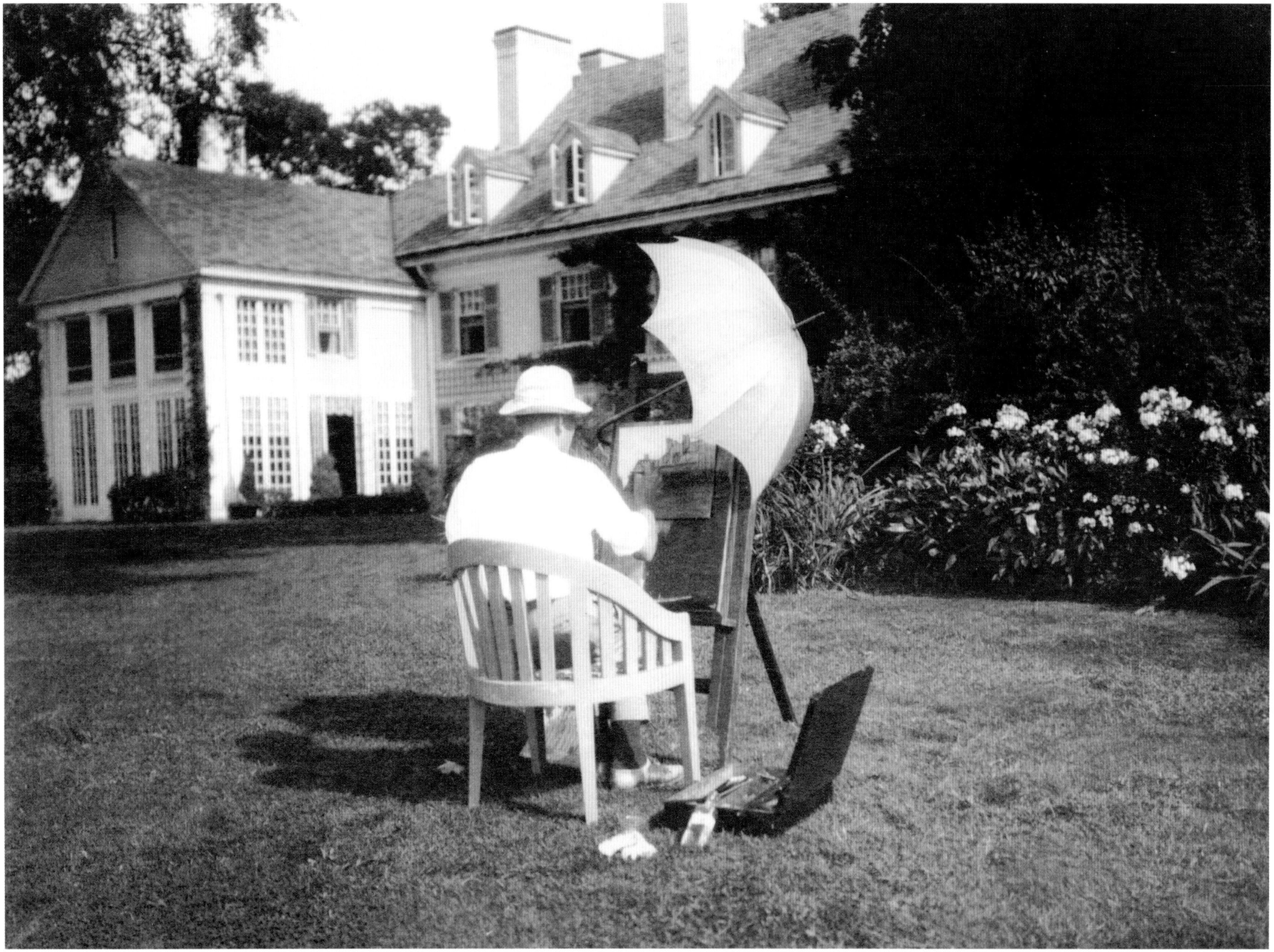

OUR TIME AT FOXHOLLOW FARM

A HUDSON VALLEY FAMILY REMEMBERED

David Byars

excelsior editions

AN IMPRINT OF STATE UNIVERSITY OF NEW YORK PRESS

www.sunypress.edu

BOOK DESIGN BY DAVID BYARS

Published by State University of New York Press, Albany

Printed in the United States of America

For information, contact State University of New York Press, Albany, NY
www.sunypress.edu

Excelsior Editions is an imprint of State University of New York Press

Production, Jenn Bennett
Marketing, Fran Keneston

Library of Congress Cataloging-in-Publication Data

Names: Byars, David- author.
Title: Our time at Foxhollow Farm : A Hudson Valley family remembered / David Byars.
Description: Albany : State University of New York Press, [2016] | Series:
Excelsior editions | Includes bibliographical references.
Identifiers: ISBN 9781438462813 (hardcover : alk. paper) | ISBN 9781438462837 (e-book)
Subjects: New York / regional. | American history--New York--history--photography.

10 9 8 7 6 5 4 3

All photographs courtesy of the Dows Collection and Dows family archives unless noted otherwise.

Page 34, 38, 39: Olmsted Photograph Album Collection, Olmsted Job #3077.
Page 36: Olmsted Photograph Album Collection, Olmsted Job #3077,
Tracy Dows, Rhinebeck, NY, Olmsted Photo #3077-01-p22, 1917.
Page 41: Olmsted Photograph Album Collection, Olmsted Job #3077,
Tracy Dows, Rhinebeck, NY, Olmsted Photo #3077-01-p13, 1917.

ENDPAPERS Olin and Margaret Dows walking with their nurse in front of the carriage house on a snowy winter day, 1912.

PREVIOUS PAGES Olin Dows painting on the back lawn of Foxhollow Farm in 1918.

FOLLOWING PAGES Tracy Dows seated in the entrance hall of the family home he created in 1926.

INTRODUCTION PAGES The entrance of the house that welcomed many guests, 1916.

Deb Dows on her horse in front of the carriage house, 1926.

Furthermore:
a program of the J. M. Kaplan Fund

Support of this book was provided by Furthermore: a program of the J. M. Kaplan Fund.

Contents

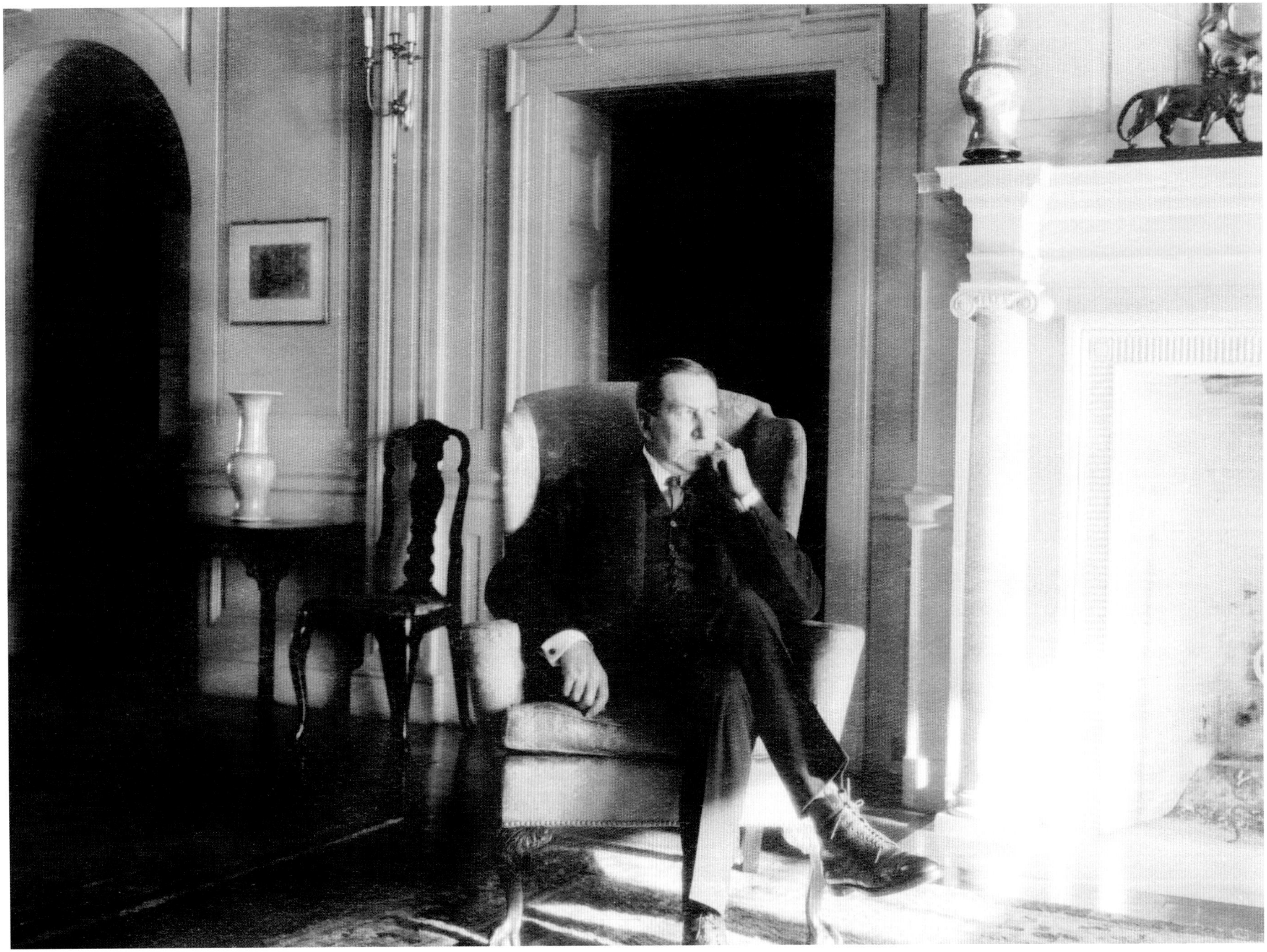

Preface

THE DOWS COLLECTION

In 1994 Hudson River Heritage, with the encouragement of its cofounder J. Winthrop Aldrich, received an extraordinary gift: Deborah Dows bequeathed her father's twenty-six family photograph albums, along with other archival material, to the nonprofit organization. The assembled images became the Dows Collection, a photographic history of Tracy Dows and his family from the early 1900s to the 1930s, while they were living at Foxhollow Farm in Rhinebeck, New York. Almost all were taken by Tracy, whose wish it was that the albums documenting his family's years at their Hudson Valley estate be preserved. *Our Time at Foxhollow Farm* provides an engaging, touching, and wonderfully well-rounded social and historical record of the privileged life of a Rhinebeck family in the early decades of the last century. We thank the Dows family profoundly for sharing it with us.

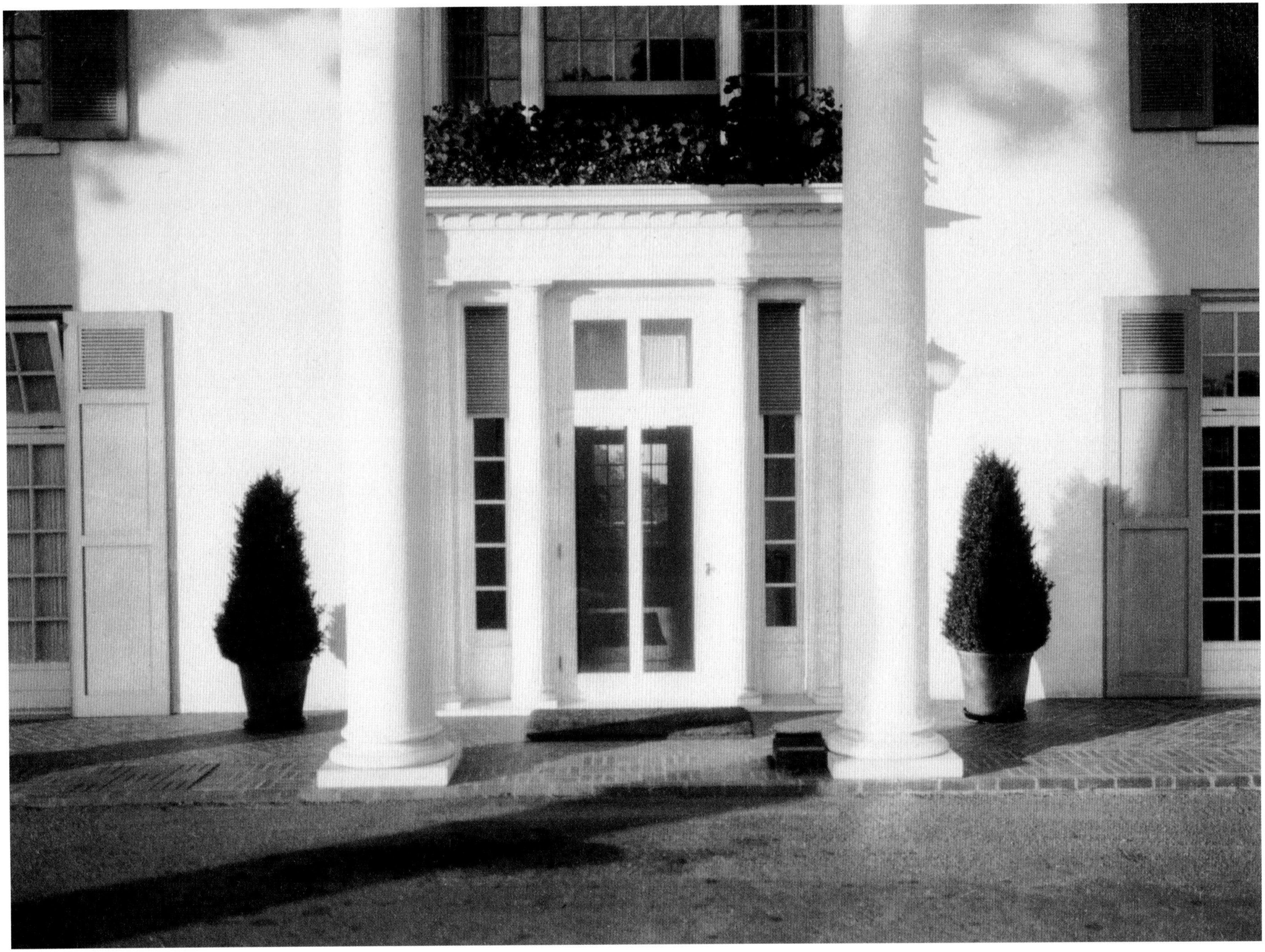

Introduction

BY DAVID BYARS

This story begins and ends with photographs, starting with a few early images, then more, and ultimately a book full of them, left behind with the intention, it appears, of telling a story. It's the story of life on a gentleman's farm in Rhinebeck, New York—its houses and stables, and all the children, friends and families who pass through it. When Tracy Dows took up photography around 1900, it was still a new medium; eventually, his hobby led him to join New York City's Camera Club. But this project—one of determined yet casual intimacy—begins around the time Tracy Dows is married, on November 11, 1903, to Alice Townsend Olin.

Like her husband, Alice was from a prominent New York City family, born, in 1881, at the height of the Gilded Age. Her father, Colonel Stephen Henry Olin, a successful trusts and estates lawyer, was a descendant of the Livingstons, who traced their settlement of the Hudson River Valley to the late 1600s. Her mother, Alice "Elsie" Wadsworth Barlow Olin, was the daughter of Samuel Latham Mitchill Barlow, a financier, railway lawyer, and noted collector of fine art. When she was a young woman, Elsie's two closest friends, Consuelo Yznaga and Jennie Jerome, married into the British aristocracy. (Conseulo became the wife of George Montagu, eighth Duke of Manchester, and Jennie married Lord Randolph Churchill and was the mother of Winston Churchill.) When Elsie married Stephen, she was said to have remarked, "I would rather have him than all the titles in Europe." Sadly, she died in 1882 while giving birth to Alice's sister, Julia. Alice, then only one-and-a-half years old, lived with her grandparents at 1 Madison Avenue, a large brownstone on Manhattan's Madison Square Park. As a child, she spent summers at Elsinore, the Barlow country estate in Glen Cove, Long Island, where her grandfather would drive the family carriage down the road to Sagamore Hill to visit his friend, Theodore Roosevelt, in nearby Oyster Bay.

In 1889, Alice's grandparents died within a few months of each other, and Stephen Henry Olin and his two daughters moved to an apartment on Gramercy Park, where Alice, as she grew older, acted as hostess for her father's dinner guests, who included such luminaries as Edith Wharton and Stanford White. Later, along with her good friend Eleanora "Nora" Iselin, Alice attended Mrs. William Astor's famous balls. Around the time they moved to Gramercy Park, Alice and her family had begun to spend summers in Rhinebeck at Glenburn, her father's ancestral Hudson River home. Ownership of the property dated to a royal grant to Henry Beekman in 1697, passing down through the Livingstons, and eventually, through marriage, to Dr. Thomas Tillotson, surgeon general during the Revolutionary War. In 1830, Tillotson's descendants named the spot Glenburn (from Scotch Gaelic meaning "brook in the glen"). Alice and Julia loved the magical ravines and waterfalls of Glenburn, where they played together as children. Alice became fond of a particular spot high on a plateau with a full view of the river. As Julia later wrote in her autobiography, *From Gaslight to Dawn*, Alice turned to her once and said, "Someday I will own that place."

Born in New York City in 1871, Tracy Dows grew up at 1 East 69th Street and spent summers at Charlton Hall, his family's country estate, in Irvington, New York. Tracy's father, David Dows, was the owner of David Dows & Company, a prosperous grain merchant business in Manhattan. He was also vice president of the Chicago, Rock Island and Pacific Railroad Company, as well as one of the successful businessmen responsible for the construction of the West Side Elevated Railway in Manhattan. One of seven siblings, Tracy attended Harvard College, taking a position in his father's business upon his graduation in 1893. He was a member of numerous clubs, including the Knickerbocker Club, the Players , the Down Town Association, the New York Yacht Club, and the Grolier Club. In 1902, he bought a sailing yacht named *Lady Godiva* and rechristened it the *Mohican*. In October 1903, he photographed Alice at the ship's wheel, steering a course seemingly right toward the photographer. One month later, they were married.

The wedding, naturally, was at Glenburn. The couple honeymooned sailing the *Mohican* down the Hudson, and, after a trip to Washington, D.C., settled in the village of Irvington, just north of New York City, where they rented a large cottage on a Hudson River overlook. Here Alice gave birth to Olin in 1904 and Margaret in 1906, and soon Tracy began planning a larger home in Rhinebeck.

In the meantime, he took the family on trips aboard the *Mohican*—both short jaunts to Manhattan or longer journeys to Newport or Maine, where they would visit Charles Dana Gibson, the well-known Gibson Girl illustrator, and his wife, Irene Langhorne Gibson, on their private island in Penobscot Bay.

In Irvington, the Dowses' social circle expanded to include such friends and neighbors as the financier J. Borden Harriman and his wife Florence "Daisy" Harriman, the suffragette, and the banker James A. Stillman and his wife, Anne (known as Fifi), who lived next to the Rockefellers in Pocantico Hills. As Tracy planned the family estate, his friends Stillman and Gibson recommended a young and talented architect, Harrie T. Lindeberg, who had trained as Stanford White's assistant at McKim, Mead & White. In 1906 Lindeberg and his fellow worker, Lewis Colt Albro, had left the firm to set up their own practice. One of their first commissions was Mondanne, the large Cotswolds-style house built for Stillman.

In the nineteenth century, the Hudson Valley, with its fertile grounds and expansive river views, became the bucolic escape for Gilded Age New Yorkers to build their country houses. When Tracy and Alice settled on Rhinebeck for their family home, Tracy purchased the land adjacent to Glenburn and began buying neighboring farms—eventually establishing the 800 acres that became Foxhollow Farm. One of these adjoining properties was Linwood Hill, the land with the high plateau that Alice had loved as a child, and it was there that the couple built their new home. Tracy and Alice knew exactly what they wanted: a sort of Mount Vernon on the Hudson. Tracy commissioned Albro & Lindeberg to design the estate's buildings, beginning with what they named Stone Cottage, a comfortable house with an exterior of fieldstone and views to the mountain ridges in the distance, into which the family moved in 1907. They lived there for three years while the larger house was under construction.

A superintendent's cottage, carriage and coachman's quarters, gate lodge, and children's cottage, were all designed by Lindeberg. Tracy hired the popular farm architects Edward Burnett and Alfred E. Hopkins to design the agricultural buildings. Tracy also hired the prestigious Olmsted Brothers to design the grounds of the property—Frederick Law Olmsted, Jr., and his stepbrother, John Charles Olmsted, who traveled back and forth from their studio in Brookline, Massachusetts, to supervise the landscaping of the estate. When the family moved into the manor house in 1910, the Foxhollow Farm estate employed over forty servants and workers. Tracy personally involved himself in the day-to-day operation of his farm and devoted himself largely to the pursuit of agricultural affairs both at home and in the county. He took pride in his Brown Swiss cows, which were milked in the estate's dairy.

The Dowses' love of country life was matched by their love of theater and opera. During the early years of living at Foxhollow Farm, they rented apartments in Manhattan hotels, often staying for a few months, to attend performances. Their third child, Deborah (known as Deb), was born in New York City in 1914. During the 1910s and 1920s, the Dowses traveled frequently around the country, spending time in such places as Jekyll Island in Georgia, and Seal Harbor in Maine, where Tracy's sisters and brothers-in-law had built cottages. In 1921, Tracy and Alice closed Foxhollow Farm and took the family on a year-long tour of France and Italy, an experience both had enjoyed themselves as children.

When they were home, the Dowses socialized with their neighbors at their estates along the Hudson River. Since she had summered in Rhinebeck as a child, Alice had known Franklin Delano Roosevelt from a young age. Years later, in 1939, she was one of the guests invited to Top Cottage on the afternoon when President Roosevelt entertained the king and queen of England at his so-called "hot dog luncheon." Alice and Tracy also knew Vincent Astor, who had spent his summers in Rhinebeck at Ferncliff, the Astor country estate—and who, in 1912, became one of the richest men in the world by inheriting a fortune after his father, John Jacob Astor IV, perished on the *Titanic*. Two years later, Vincent married Helen Dinsmore Huntington, whom Alice watched grow from a child into a lovely woman. Vincent and Helen became Tracy and Alice's dearest friends, often accompanying them on trips aboard Vincent's yachts, the *Noma* and the *Nourmahal*. Their friendship remained close throughout their lives.

Among Foxhollow Farm's many visitors and guests was Thomas Wolfe, the noted American author. Wolfe spent several summers in the Gate Lodge as a guest of Olin Dows, whom he knew from Harvard College, and wrote much of his great novel, *Look Homeward, Angel*, while staying there. Observing the life of the Dowses and other Hudson River families supplied him with material for his following novel, *Of Time and the River*. Tracy, meanwhile, involved himself in local businesses and civic organizations. (He would be instrumental in the relocation of the popular Dutchess County Fair to Rhinebeck in 1919.) In 1914, he had become an investor in the purchase of the Rhinebeck Hotel, originally a tavern built in the early 1700s. He hired his friend Lindeberg to transform the building into a Colonial Revival inn, naming it Beekman Arms. Lindeberg's design for the inn drew on his work at Foxhollow Farm. The fresh new look he produced instantly made the Beekman Arms a town attraction, and today it ranks as the oldest operating inn in the United States.

But, this was also a time of unrest: World War I was underway and it seemed that everyone, even the privileged, did their part. Alice, who had learned knitting from her paralyzed grandmother, had a goal to knit a sock a day for the soldiers, while Helen Huntington Astor set up a convalescent home near her apartment in Paris for wounded American soldiers so they would have a place to recuperate.

Throughout their lives, the Dows children established their own relationships with Foxhollow Farm. Olin, who was privately tutored as a child by C. K. Chatterton of Vassar College, was photographed by Tracy from an early age drawing at

The Family

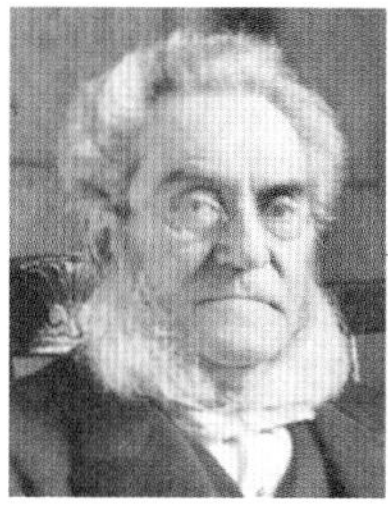

David Dows
1814–1890

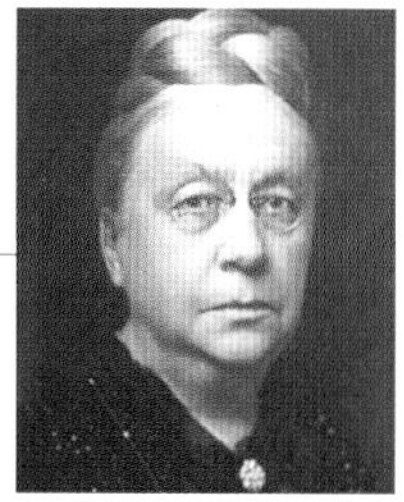

Margaret
Worcester Dows
1831–1909

Descendants of Robert Livingston, First Lord of the Manor, and Judge Henry Beekman, founder of Rhinebeck

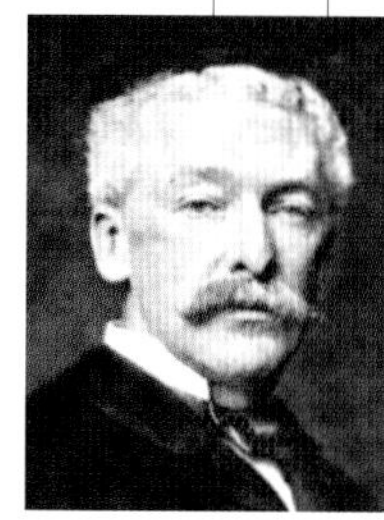

Stephen Henry
Olin
1847–1925

1. Elsie Barlow
Olin
1853–1882

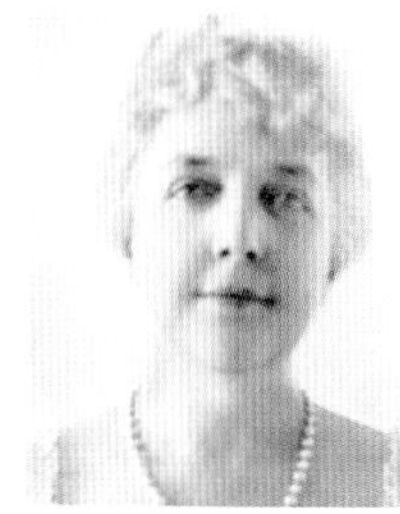

2. Emeline
Harriman Olin
1860–1938

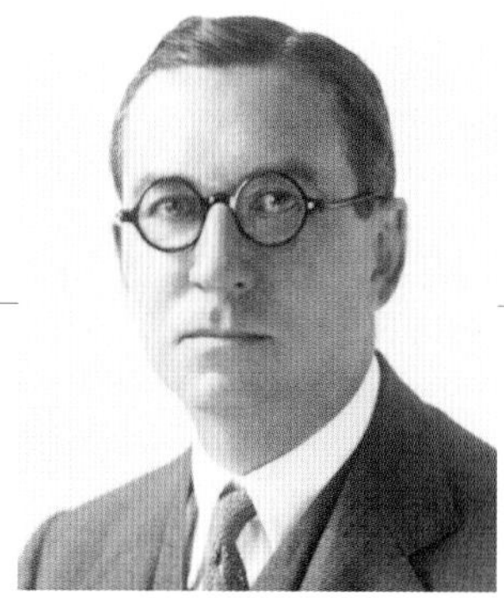

Tracy Dows
1871–1937

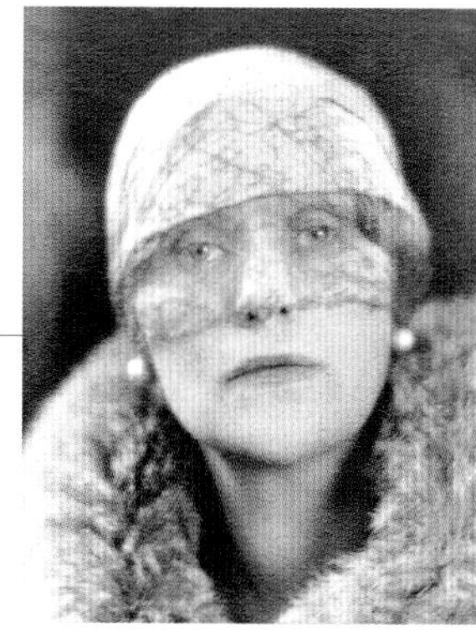

Alice Olin Dows
1881–1963

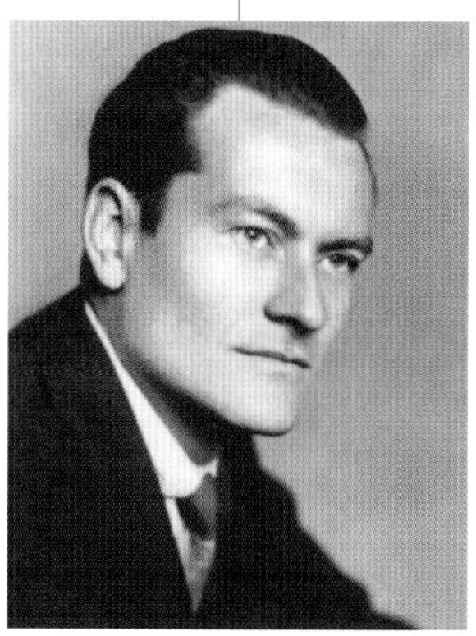

Stephen Olin Dows
1904–1981

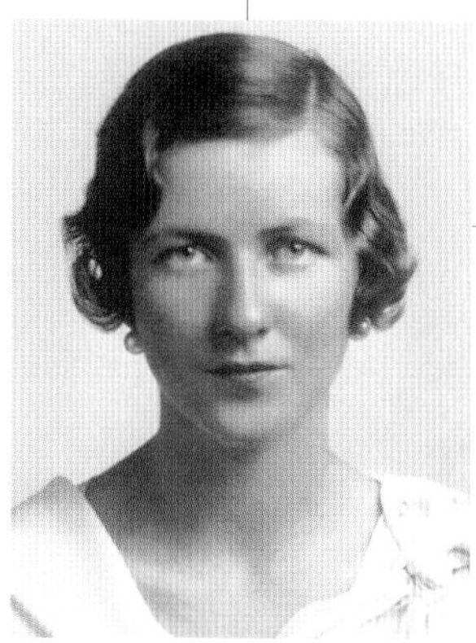

Margaret Dows Thyberg
1906–1992

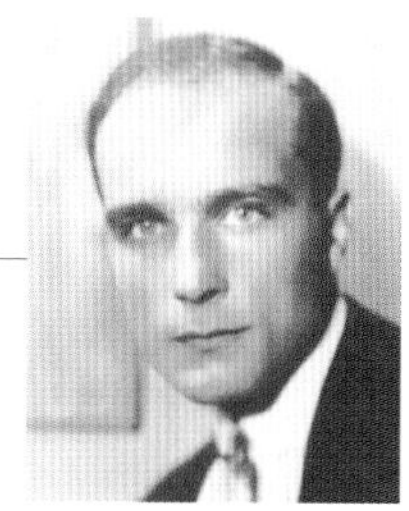

Knut Richard Thyberg
1896–1980

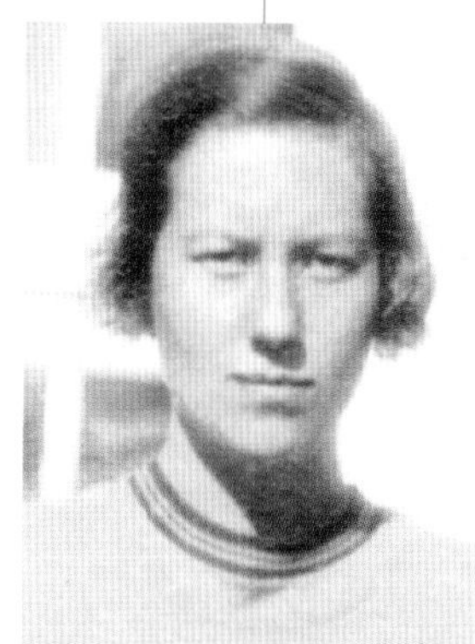

Deborah Dows
1914–1994

Olin Knut
Thyberg
1926–present

Birgitta
Thyberg Martz
1928–present

Peter Jan
Thyberg
1933–present

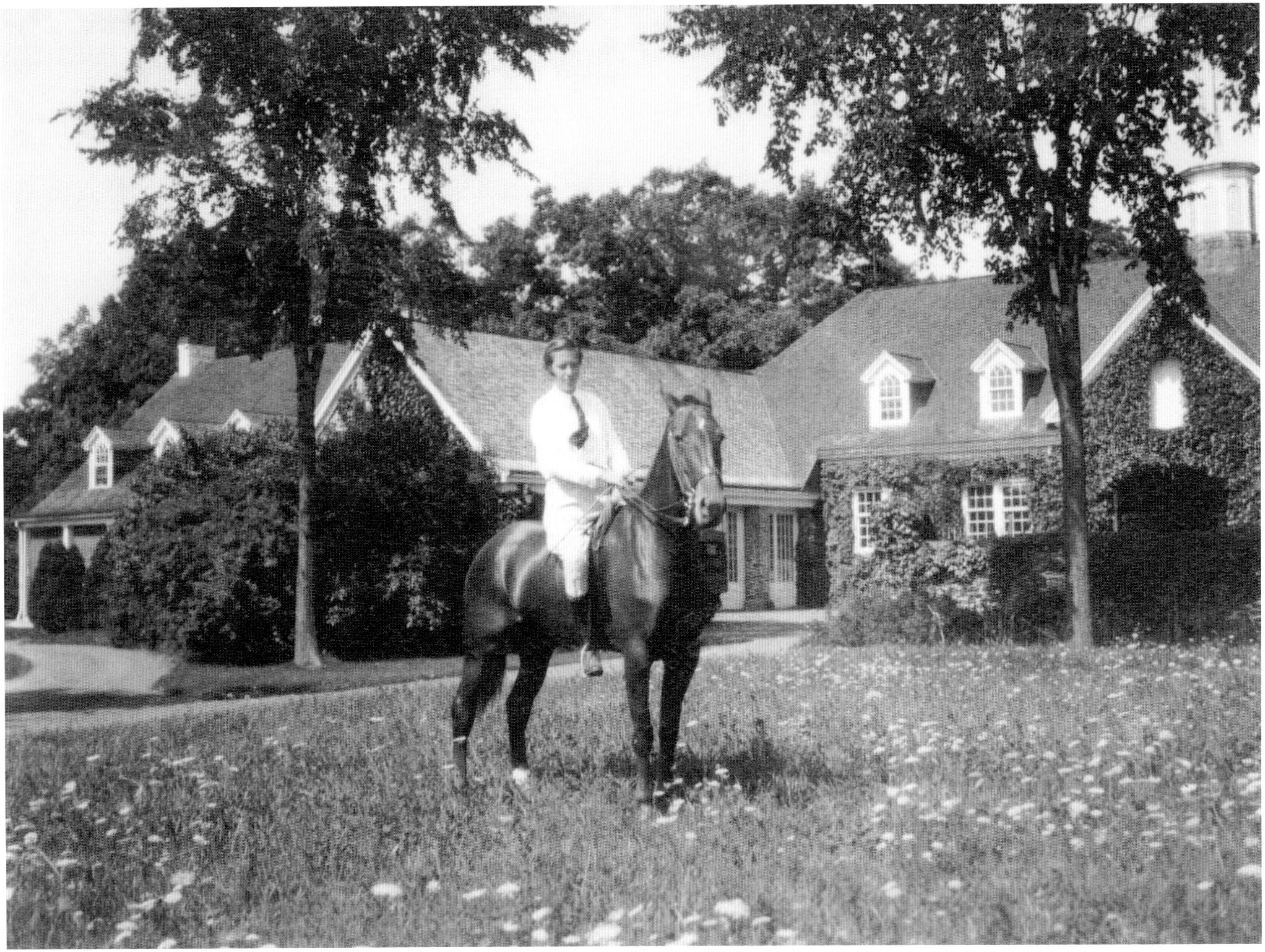

Foxhollow Farm. He studied in Paris in 1921, when the family traveled to France. He entered Harvard College in 1922 and three years later enrolled at the Yale Art School. He painted murals for the walls of Manhattan apartments and Hudson River estate owners and specialized in elaborate screens. At the request of President Franklin D. Roosevelt, Olin was commissioned by the Federal Works Agency to paint the remarkable murals along the upper walls in the newly built Rhinebeck post office in 1939 and Hyde Park post office in 1940. Olin first served as a war artist in the U.S. Army during World War II, carrying his watercolors along with his rifle. He received the Bronze Star Medal in 1944 for his meritorious service as a technical sergeant at the battle of St. Lô, Normandy, France. As part of a photographic unit, Olin made his way through a partially exposed minefield under intense German artillery fire, returning with valuable pictorial records. Deb grew up riding at Foxhollow Farm, where the most southerly area of the estate, known as Southlands, became her favorite spot. She also loved riding over the stone bridges and along the wooded trails of Glenburn. Margaret married Knut Richard Thyberg on October 3, 1925, on the back lawn at Foxhollow Farm. Knut was a Swedish diplomat, and after their wedding, they settled in Stockholm before moving to an array of diplomatic posts, including Riga, London, Copenhagen, and Cairo.

In the mid-1920s Alice decided she wanted to spend time in Washington, D.C. Her friend Daisy Harriman, who lived there, helped her find a large comfortable house to rent. A few years later, Alice persuaded Tracy to buy a former nineteenth-century schoolhouse in Georgetown that Olin decorated with rural scenes of Glenburn and Foxhollow Farm. Eventually, Alice spent most of her time in Washington, and Tracy most of his at Foxhollow Farm, while Deb and Olin divided their time between the two homes. In Washington, Alice quickly became known as a patron of the arts, her house often the scene of impromptu parties during which classical musicians performed. In 1922, while sailing back from the family trip abroad, Alice was introduced to the famous soprano Lucrezia Bori. Alice had always admired her performances at the Metropolitan Opera. Bori, as Alice called her, became and remained one of her closest friends for the rest of her life. By the late 1920s, Tracy and Alice were living apart but would travel back and forth when the family gathered for holidays and special occasions. Summers were mostly spent at Foxhollow Farm.

In 1935, Deb married John Lancaster Burling in the garden of Alice's townhouse in Washington. An unhappy situation ended in divorce two years later. Deb married a second time in 1959 and was divorced several years later. As her mother would be the first to admit, Deb struggled with her choices in life, all the while appreciating the support and love from both of her parents. She was devoted to her father, ("Pup," as she called him), who taught her how to cherish the land, and later, after traveling the world, she would eventually return to her beloved Southlands in Rhinebeck. This she would never regret.

After all the wonderful years he had spent there, Foxhollow Farm ultimately became too expensive for Tracy to maintain, especially after the stock market crash of 1929. He decided to move the family out of the estate in 1930, turning the house into a girls' preparatory school called the Foxhollow School. Tracy then moved abroad and took up residence in London at the Connaught Hotel. In 1932, he moved to the Hotel d'Angleterre in Copenhagen, to be near Margaret, who had transferred there from Stockholm. In the early 1930s, Alice also spent time abroad, living in France and Germany, taking Deb and Olin with her. In 1936, Margaret and her family were posted to Egypt, and all five Dows family members assembled there for the Christmas and New Year's holidays. It was to be their last time together. On July 3, 1937, Tracy died unexpectedly at the Connaught Hotel, where he had once again been staying. After Tracy's death, Foxhollow Farm eventually sold. Alice kept the house in Washington, however, she, Deb, and Olin decided in 1938 to return to Glenburn. In 1950, Olin married Carmen Vial de Senoret Browne, a Chilean delegate to the United Nations. Along with her son, Luis Fernando Browne, they lived half of the year in Rhinebeck, half in Chile. Olin made the Glenburn carriage house his studio, continuing to paint until his death in 1981.

After Olin married, Alice decided to renovate and enlarge a cottage next to Glenburn where she lived until her death in 1963. Margaret's husband Knut died in 1980 and Margaret in 1992. In 1938, Deb built her own house next to Southlands, the area of her father's property she loved the most, devoting herself, until her death in 1994, to the property and her animals, and living a much simpler life than the one in which she had grown up. She had established a riding school in the 1930s, and in 1983 The Southlands Foundation was formed—an organization dedicated to the understanding of the environment and horsemanship.

In 2007, I left Manhattan, where I had lived for twenty-five years, and moved up the Hudson River to Riverdale, in the Bronx, next to an estuary named Spuyten Duyvil Creek. Its name is thought to come from Old Dutch, meaning "spout of the devil," a description of the wild currents in that part of the Lower Hudson. I began to wander up the river to the north—the larger views and the great old estates seemed to beckon one north, to explore. One day I found myself at a party held by Hudson River Heritage at The Locusts, the delightful 1941 villa built for Helen Huntington Hull in Staatsburg. The event—and the house—left a lasting impression on me. Shortly afterward I joined the organization and became a board member. In 2009, I was shown the Dows Collection, the family photograph albums of Tracy Dows that had been in storage since 1994, and I was mesmerized. It was a treasure trove of historical and social images, a photo-diary of the past. With these thousands of photographs, I knew that a book should be published on the lives of this remarkable family. Tracy Dows would have wanted it that way.

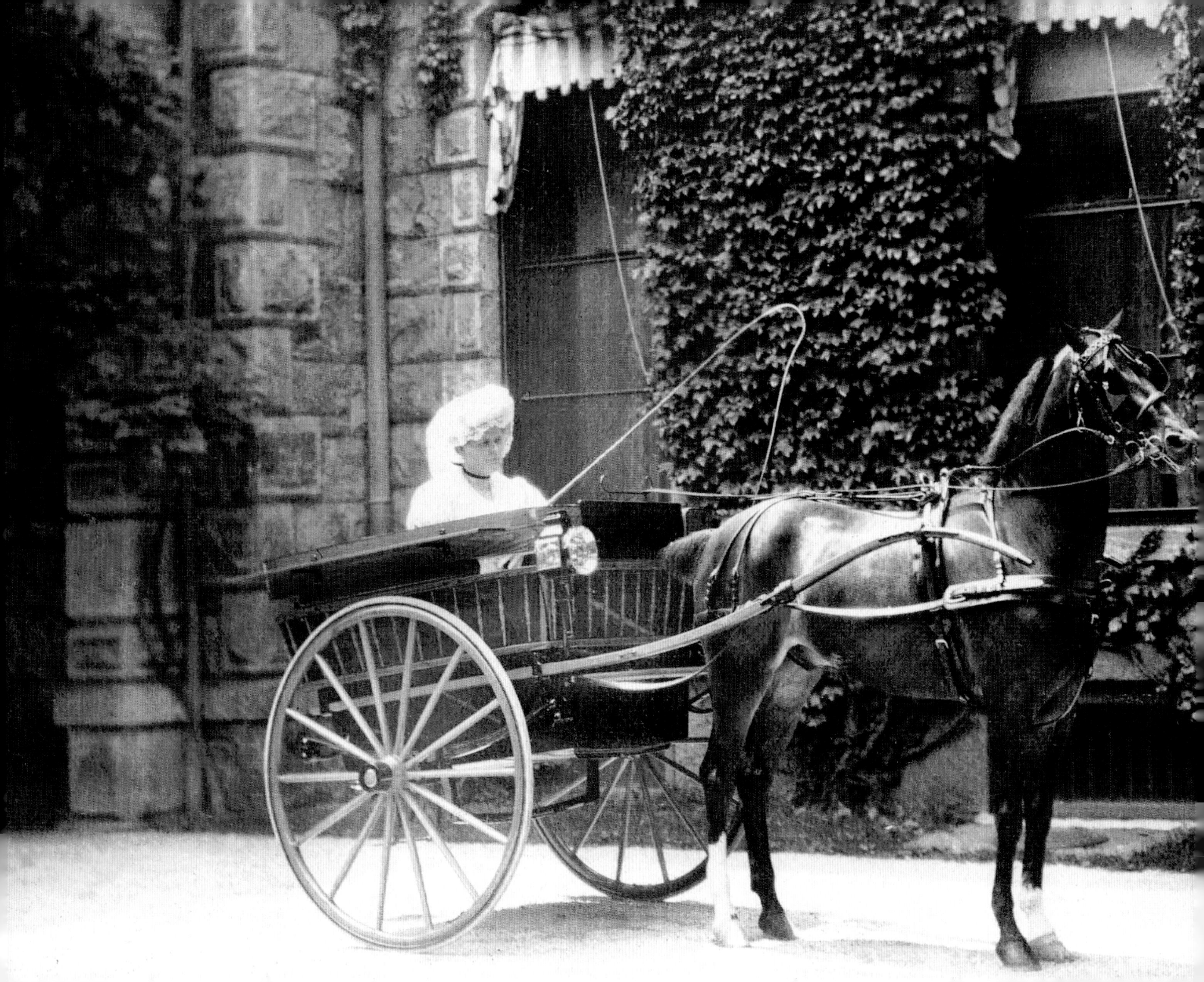

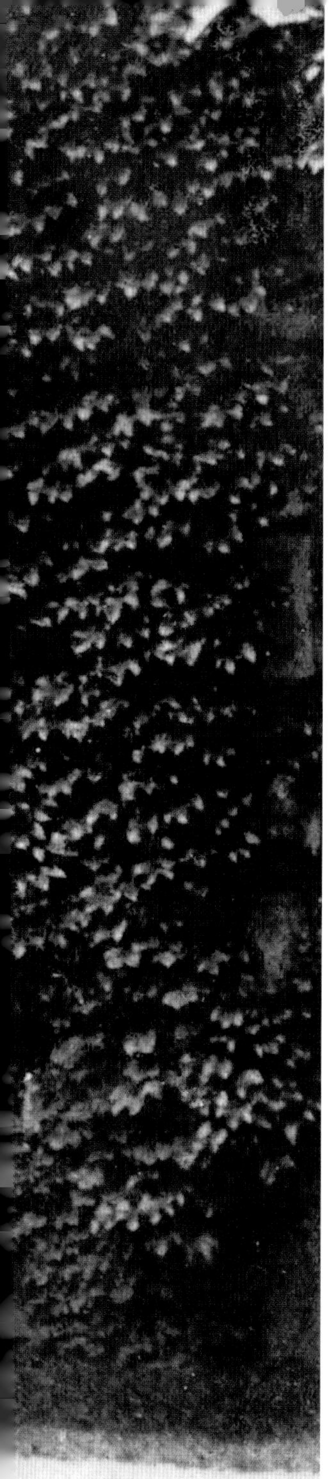

CHAPTER ONE

The EARLY YEARS

1903–1906

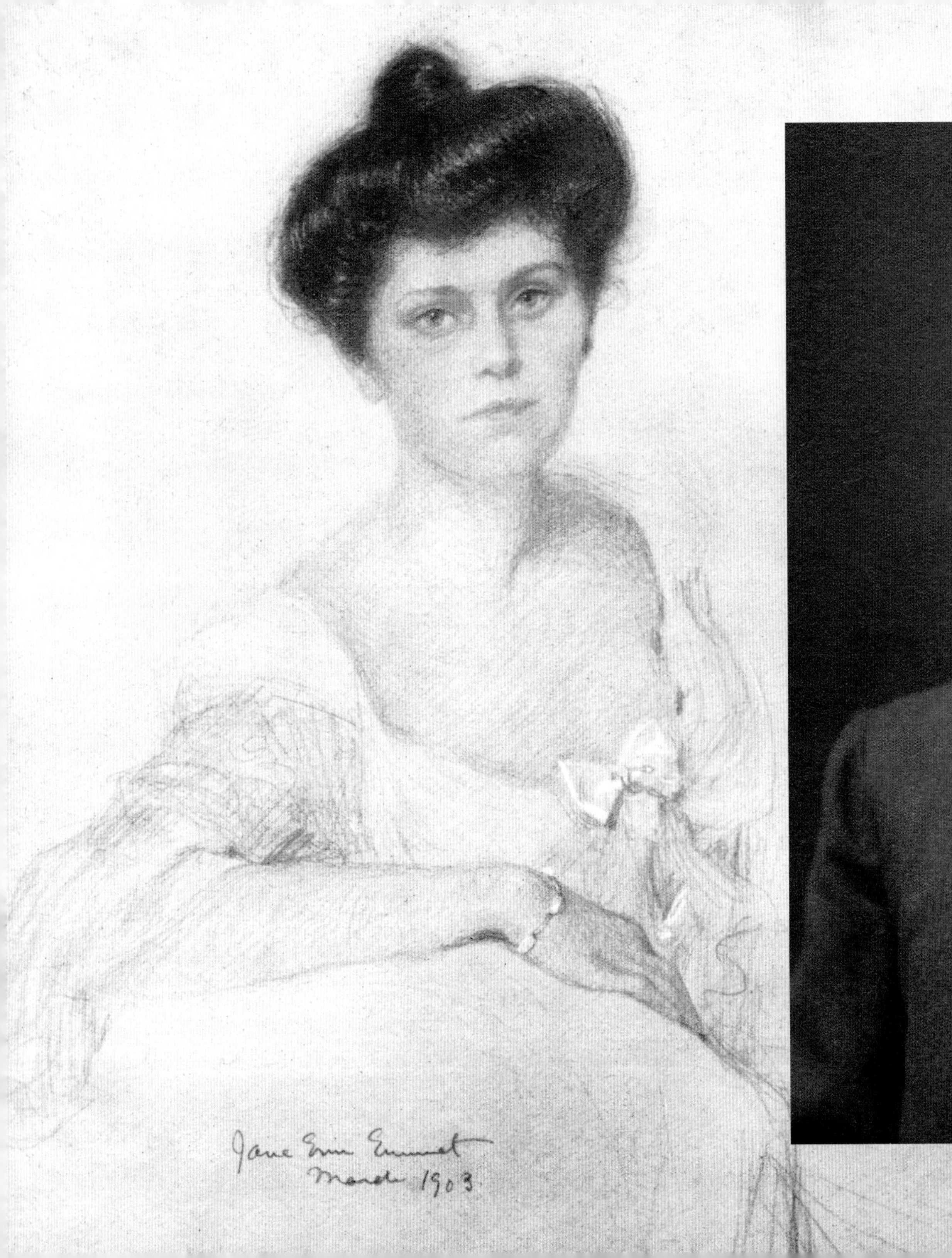
Jane Erin Emmet
March 1903

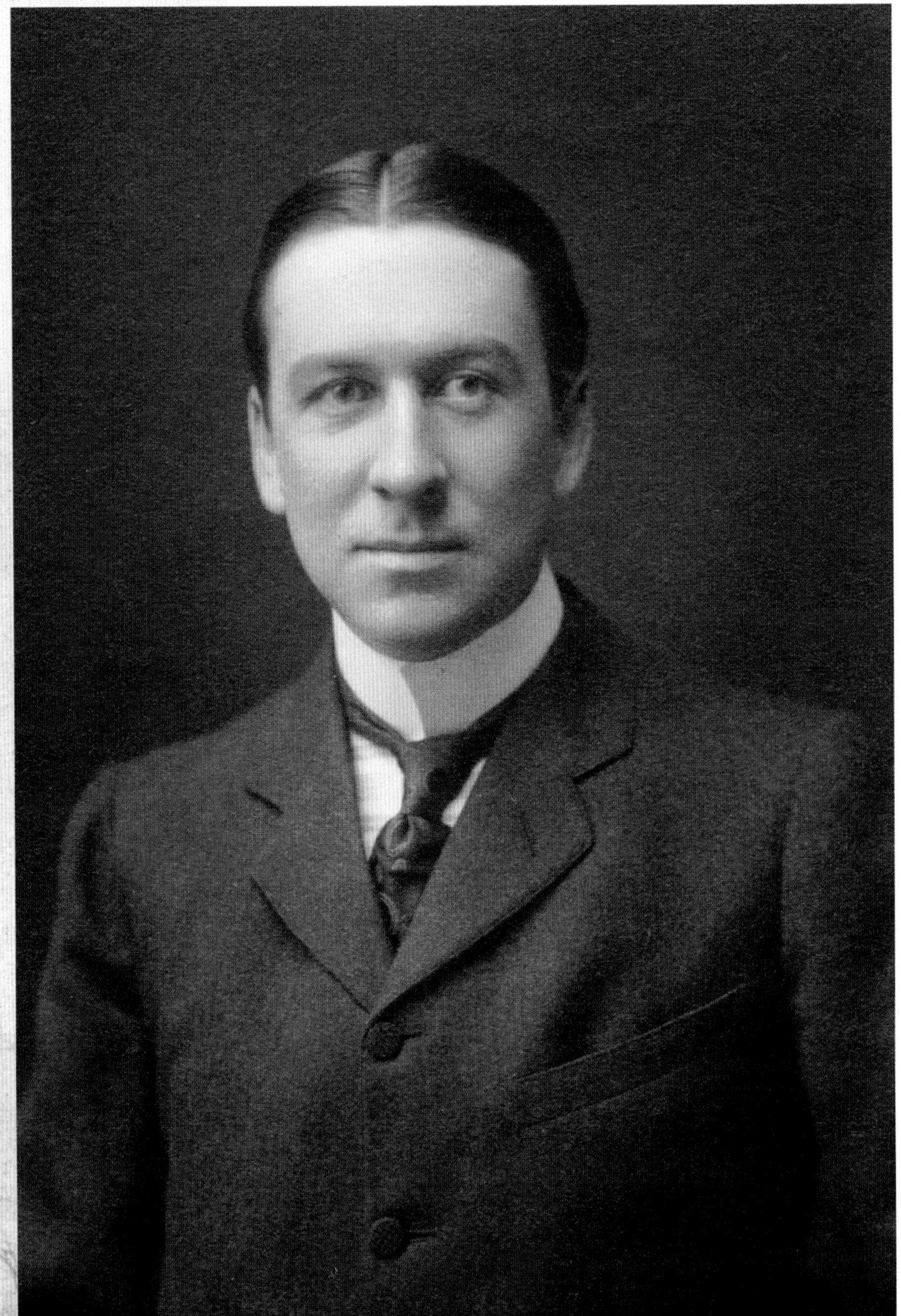

PREVIOUS PAGES Alice Olin Dows with her horse and cart while living in Irvington, New York, 1906.

OPPOSITE A 1903 portrait of Alice Townsend Olin by American painter Jane Erin Emmet de Glehn; Tracy Dows as a young man photographed by Ferdinand Stark around 1900.

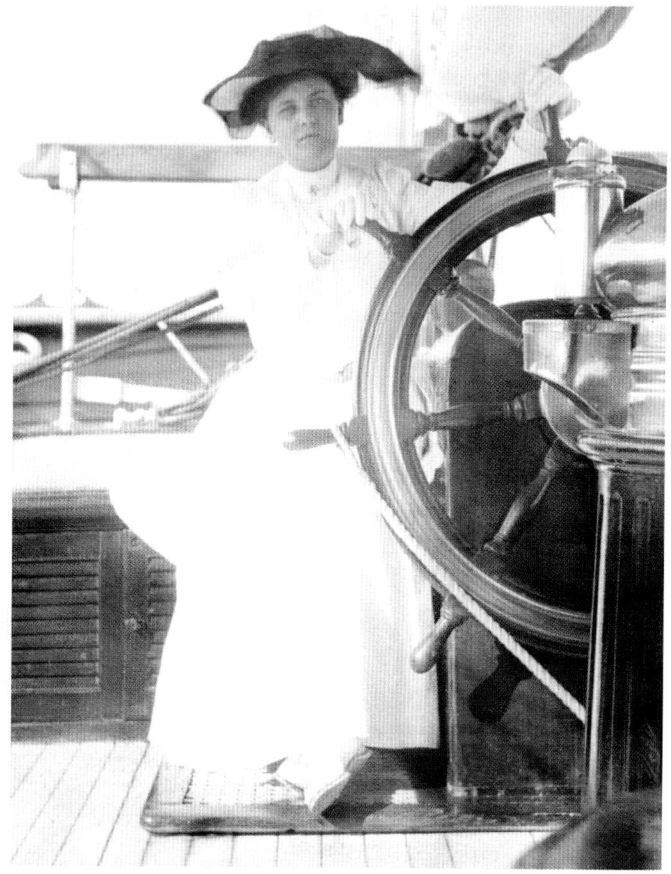

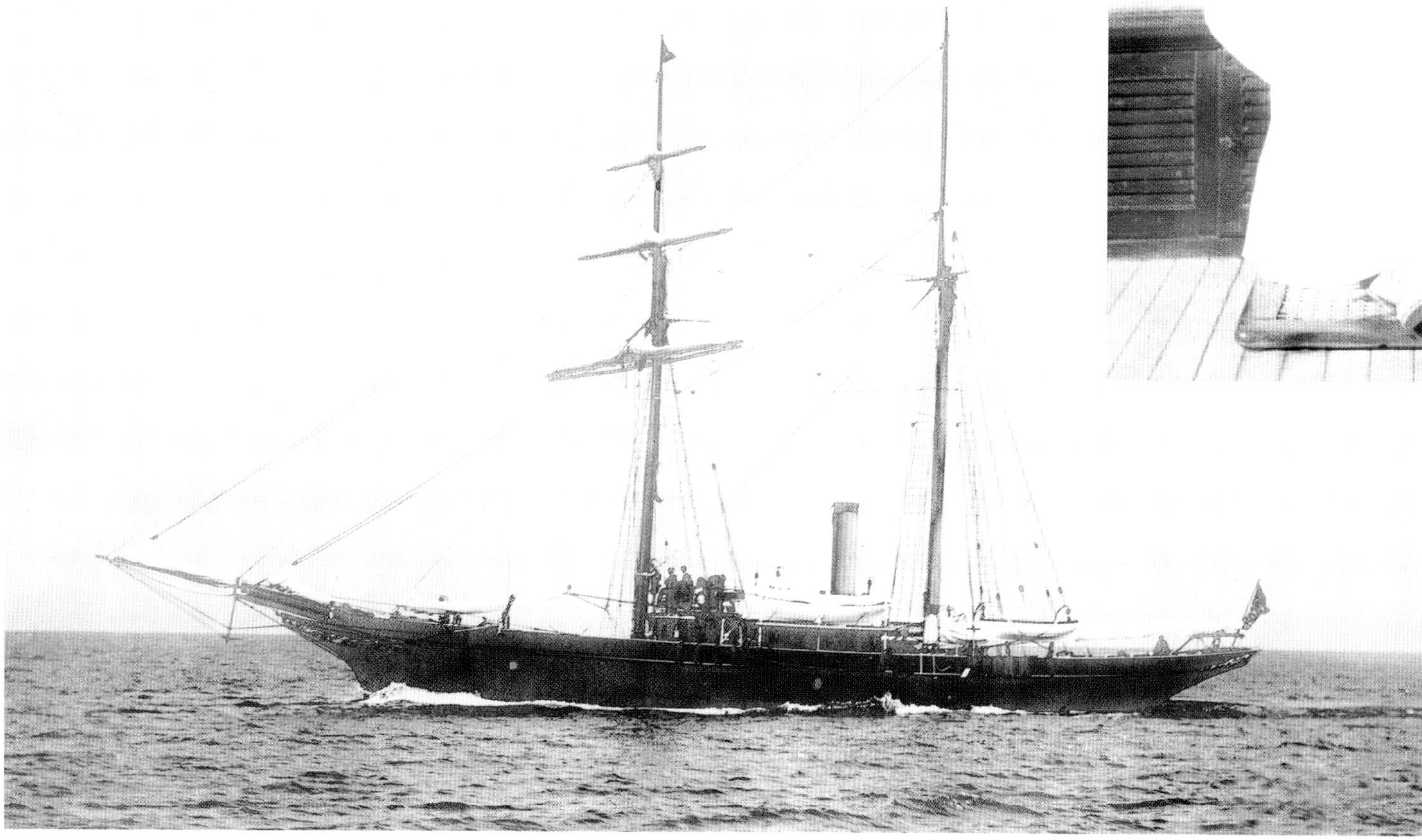

LEFT Tracy's yacht, the *Mohican*, in 1902. Originally built as the *Lady Godiva* in 1890 by Laird Brothers in Scotland, the yacht was purchased by Tracy twelve years later, who had it converted to steam and its hull painted black.

ABOVE Alice at the wheel of the *Mohican* on a sailing trip with Tracy along the coast of Long Island in October 1903, a month before their wedding.

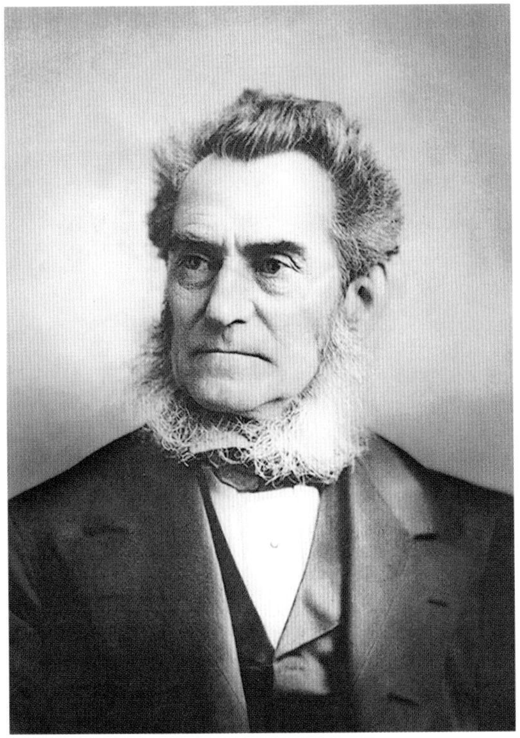

ABOVE Tracy's father, David Dows, with his distinctive beard, in a portrait taken in the 1870s. The youngest of twelve children, in 1828 he became a clerk in a dry goods store in Albany, New York, and later received mercantile training with his brother, John, in his firm of Dows & Carey in New York City. After the deaths of his brother and Mr. Carey, David continued with the firm, which ultimately became his, establishing David Dows & Company in 1854. The business boomed and David became one of the most successful grain merchants in the world, amassing a fortune of millions. He was a leading member of the Produce Exchange in New York and vice president of the Chicago, Rock Island and Pacific Railroad, as well as the owner of the Eden Musée, a popular waxworks and entertainment center in Manhattan. At the time of his death in 1890, it was reported that each of David's seven children received $400,000 from his will.

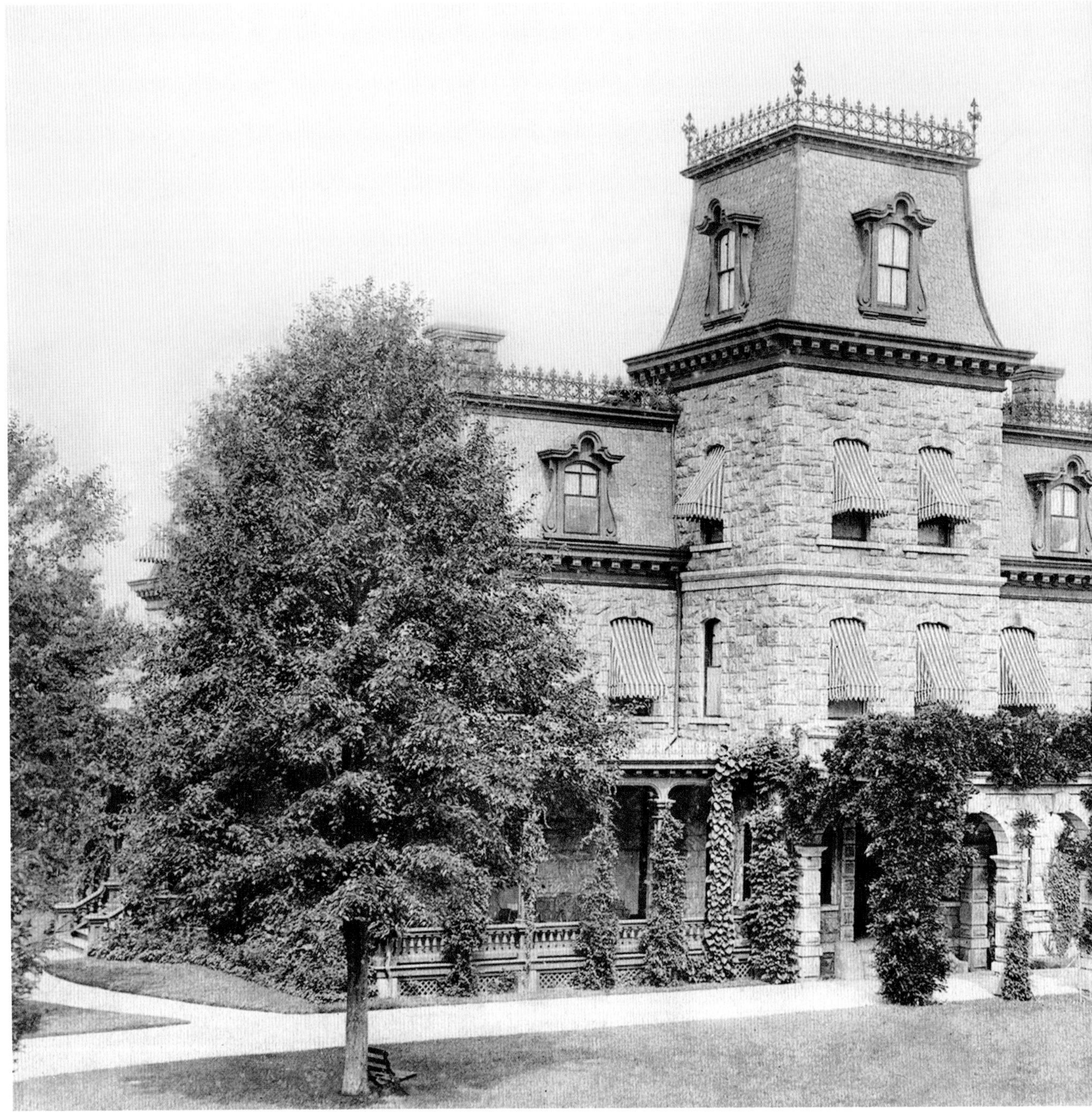

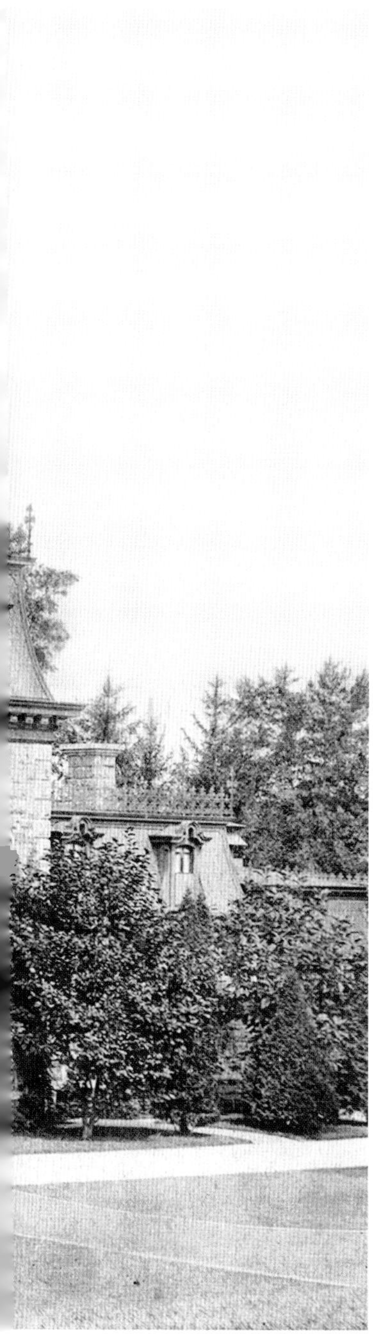

LEFT Charlton Hall, David Dows's country estate, as seen around 1903. The stately thirty-one-room mansion, built in 1868 with exterior marble-granite walls two feet thick, had extensive gardens, a reflecting pool, a greenhouse, carriage house, gate house, and sweeping views of the Hudson River. As a child, Tracy spent summers here with his family. After his father's death in 1890, his mother, Margaret Worcester Dows, continued to live in the house until her death in 1909. It was then bought by Tracy's nephew, David Dows III. In 1913 the estate was sold out of the Dows family and the house was eventually demolished in the 1940s.

BELOW Three generations of Dowses in 1889: David Dows, age 74; David Dows, Jr. (Tracy's brother), age 32; and David Dows III, age 4.

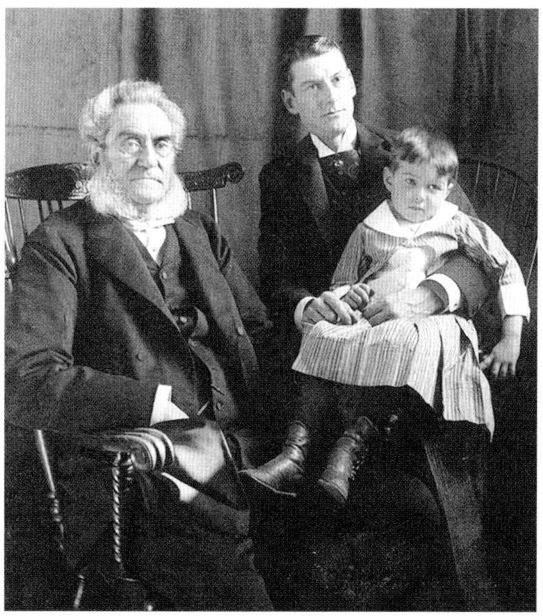

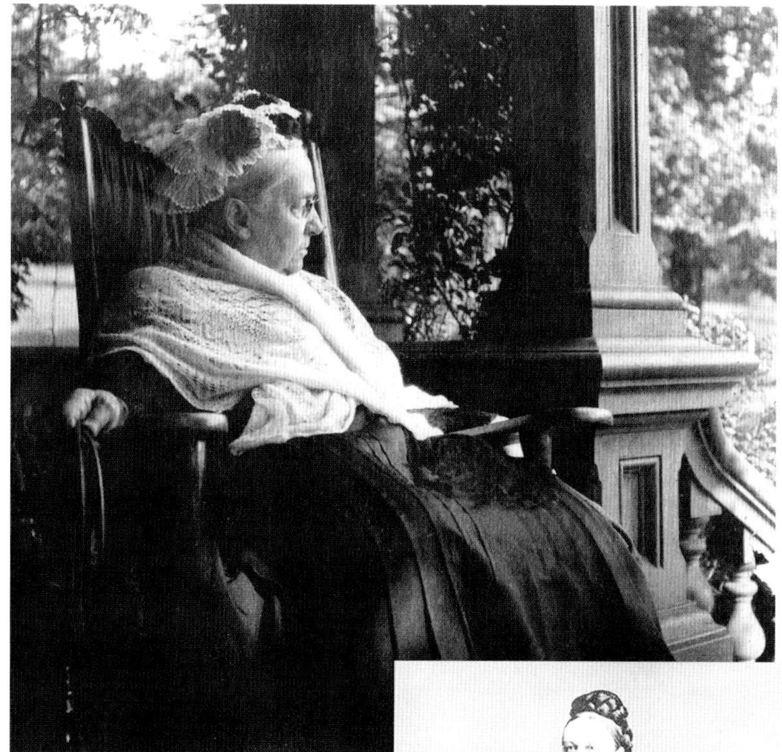

ABOVE Margaret Worcester Dows on the porch at Charlton Hall in 1907. Said to have been irascible and a tyrant to her servants, she was nonetheless always kind to Alice. Upon her death in 1909, she bequeathed *Heart of the Andes*, painted by Frederic Edwin Church in 1859, to the Metropolitan Museum of Art in New York City. When first sold in 1859 for $10,000, it was said to be the highest price ever paid for an American landscape painting. David Dows purchased it in 1876.

RIGHT A studio photograph of Margaret Worcester Dows taken in the 1880s. Many compared her looks to those of Queen Victoria.

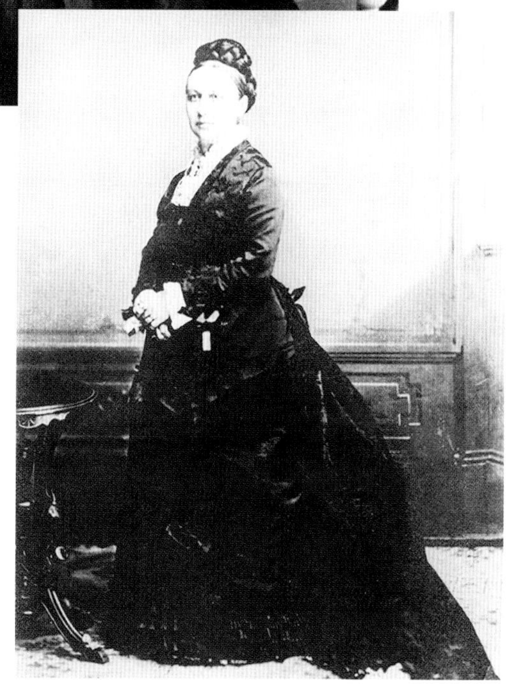

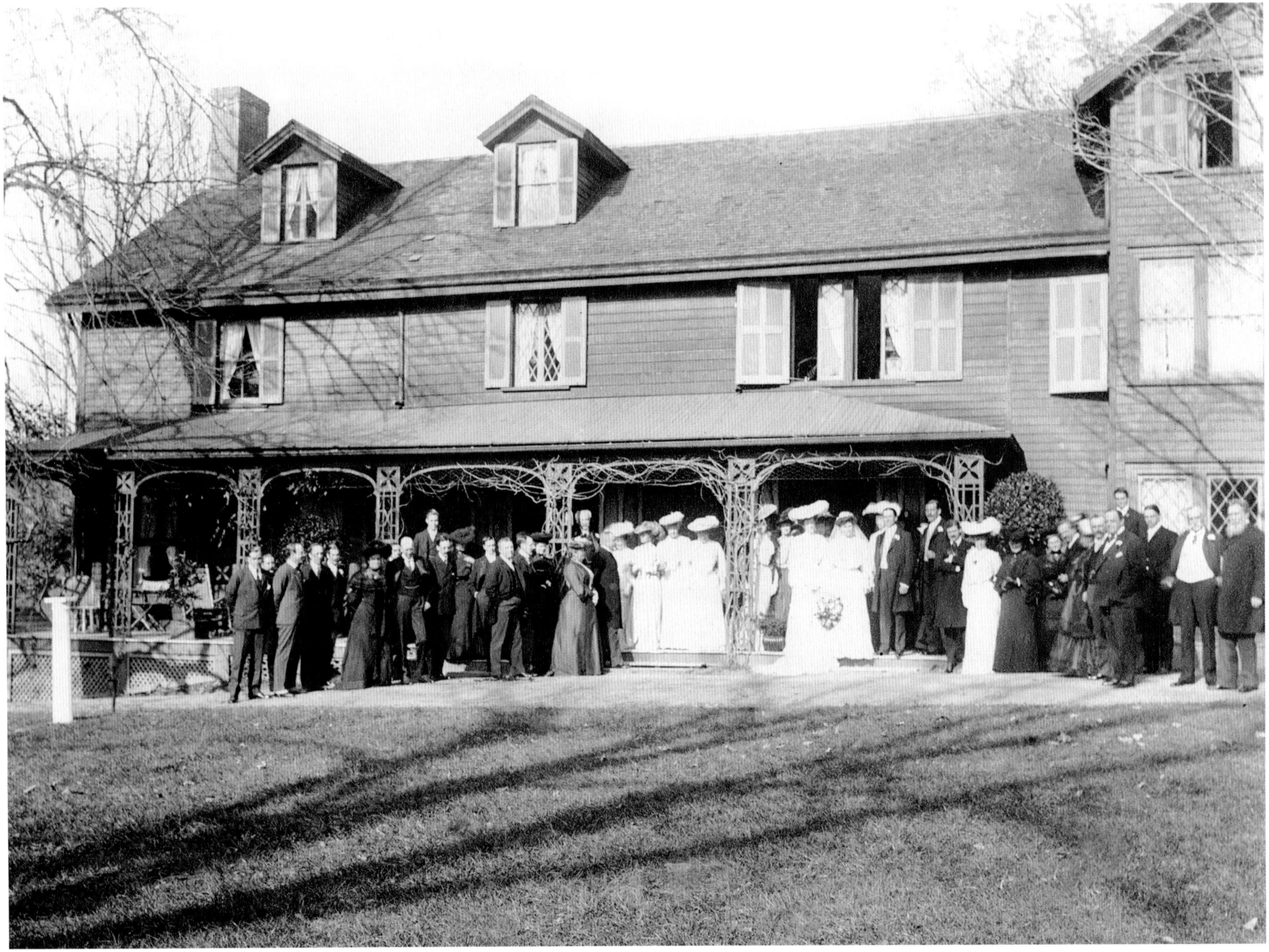

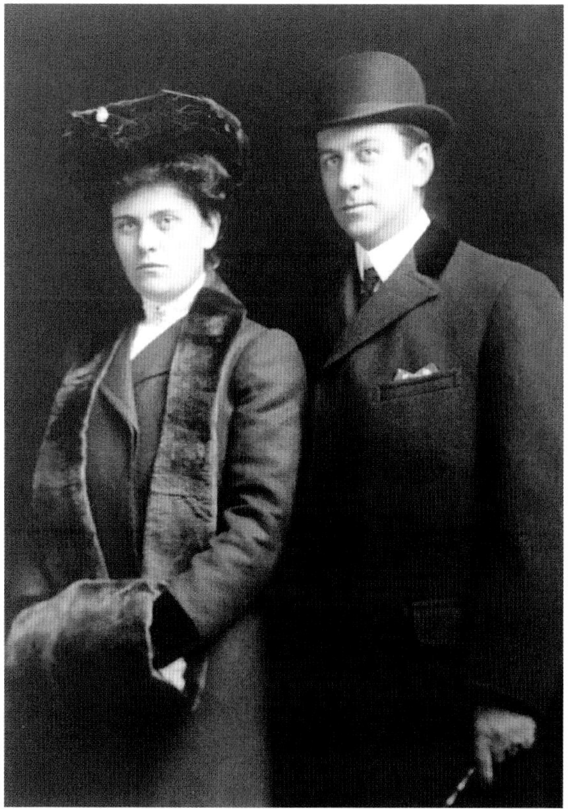

ABOVE A studio portrait of Alice and Tracy taken in 1903 in Washington, D.C., the year they were married.

OPPOSITE The wedding took place on November 11, 1903, at Glenburn, the country home of Alice's father, Stephen Henry Olin, in Rhinebeck, New York. Reverend Ernest C. Saunders, rector of Rhinebeck's Church of the Messiah, performed the ceremony. The bridesmaid was Miss Nora Iselin and the best man was Henry G. Barbey, both from New York City. Guests traveled on a special train on the New York Central & Hudson River Railroad to Staatsburg, and from there by horse-drawn carriages to Glenburn.

BELOW Photographed at the wedding, from left, Henry G. Barbey, Emeline Harriman Olin (Alice's stepmother who had married her father earlier that year), Nora Iselin, Alice, Tracy, and Stephen Henry Olin, seated.

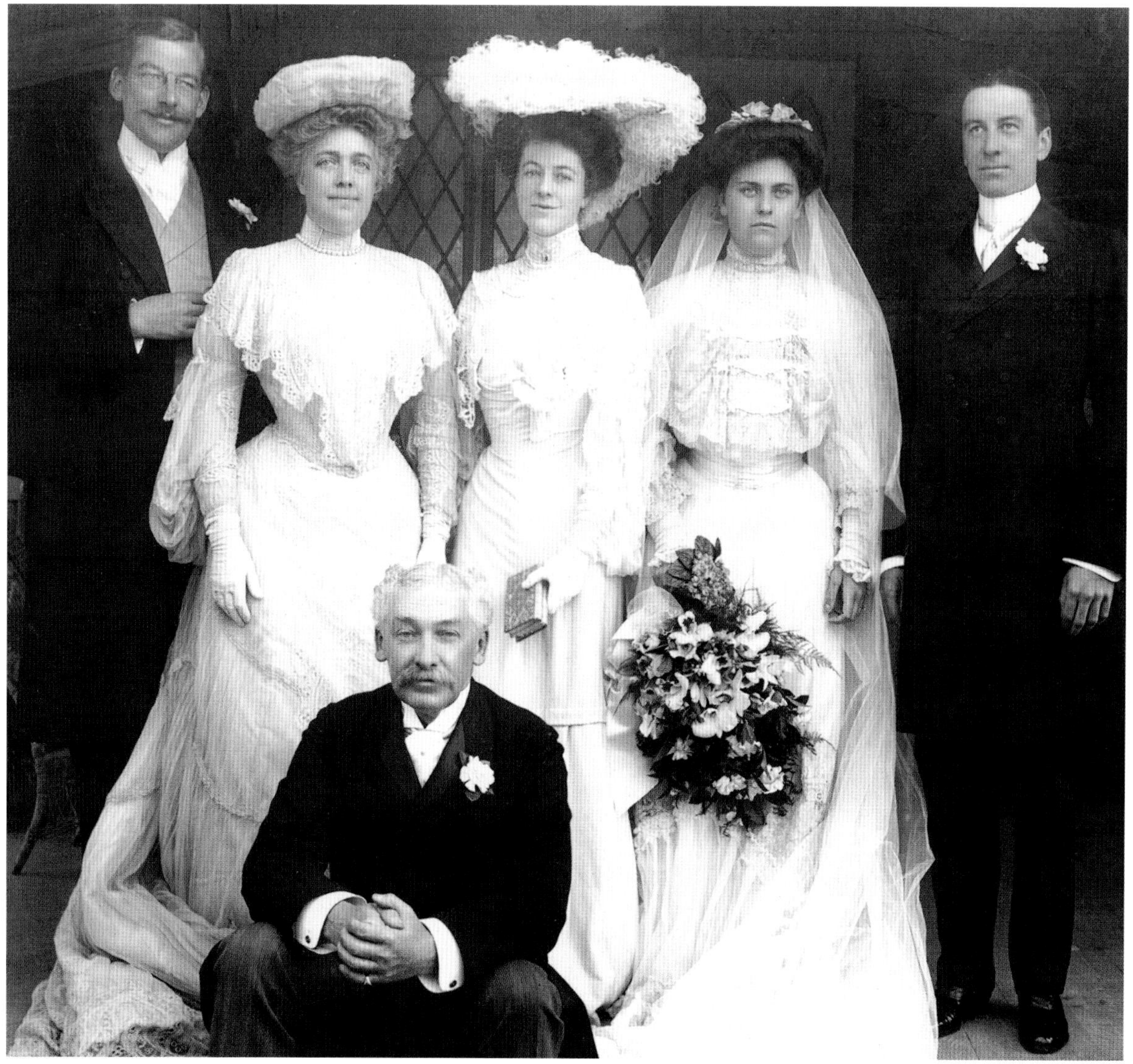

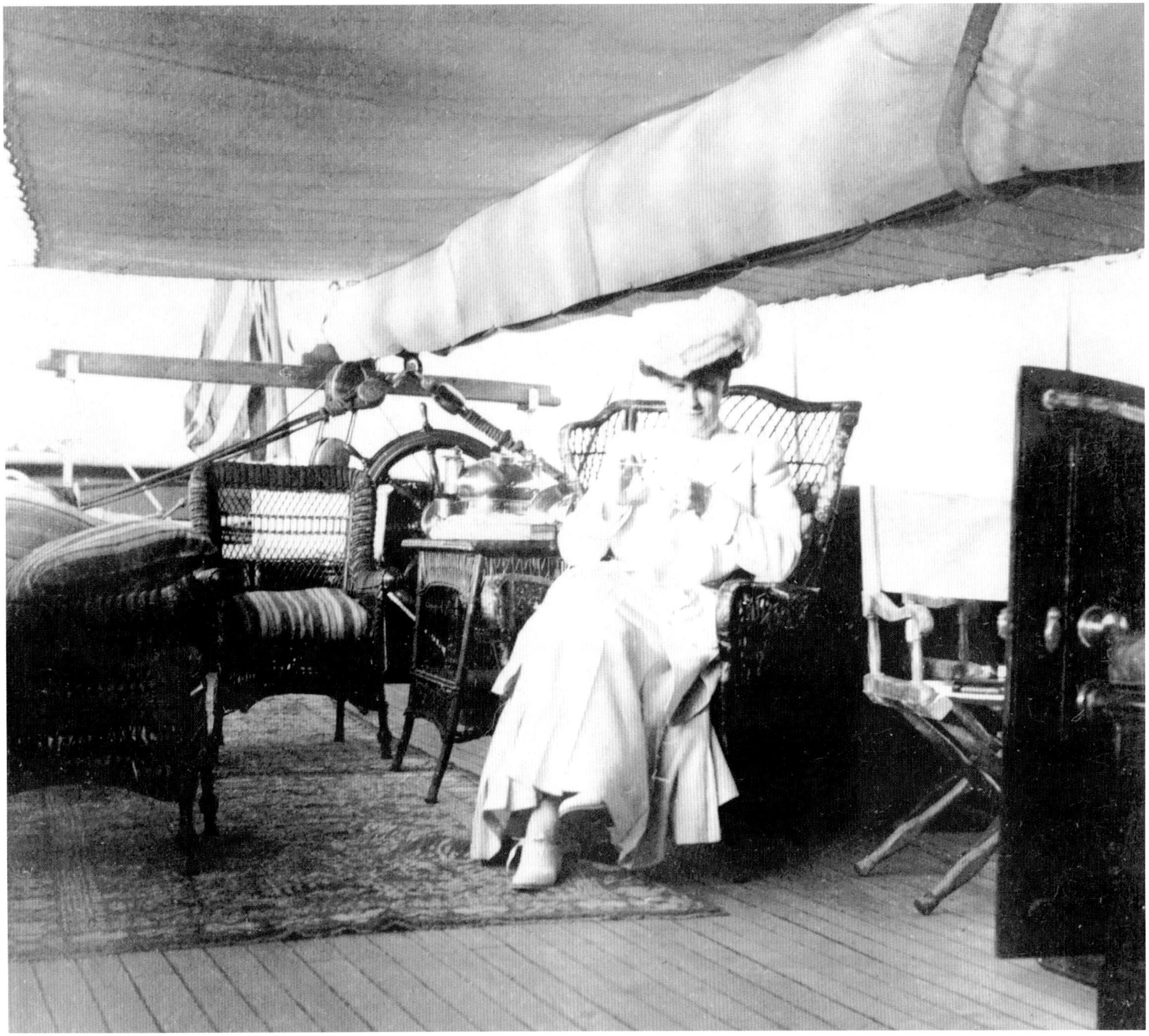

LEFT After their wedding, Tracy and Alice spent their honeymoon on the Hudson River aboard the *Mohican*. Alice relaxed knitting on deck—it was to be a lifelong occupation.

OPPOSITE Tracy at the Battle Monument, designed by Stanford White, at West Point Academy, one of the stops on their trip where the couple took photographs of themselves against a lovely view of the Hudson River.

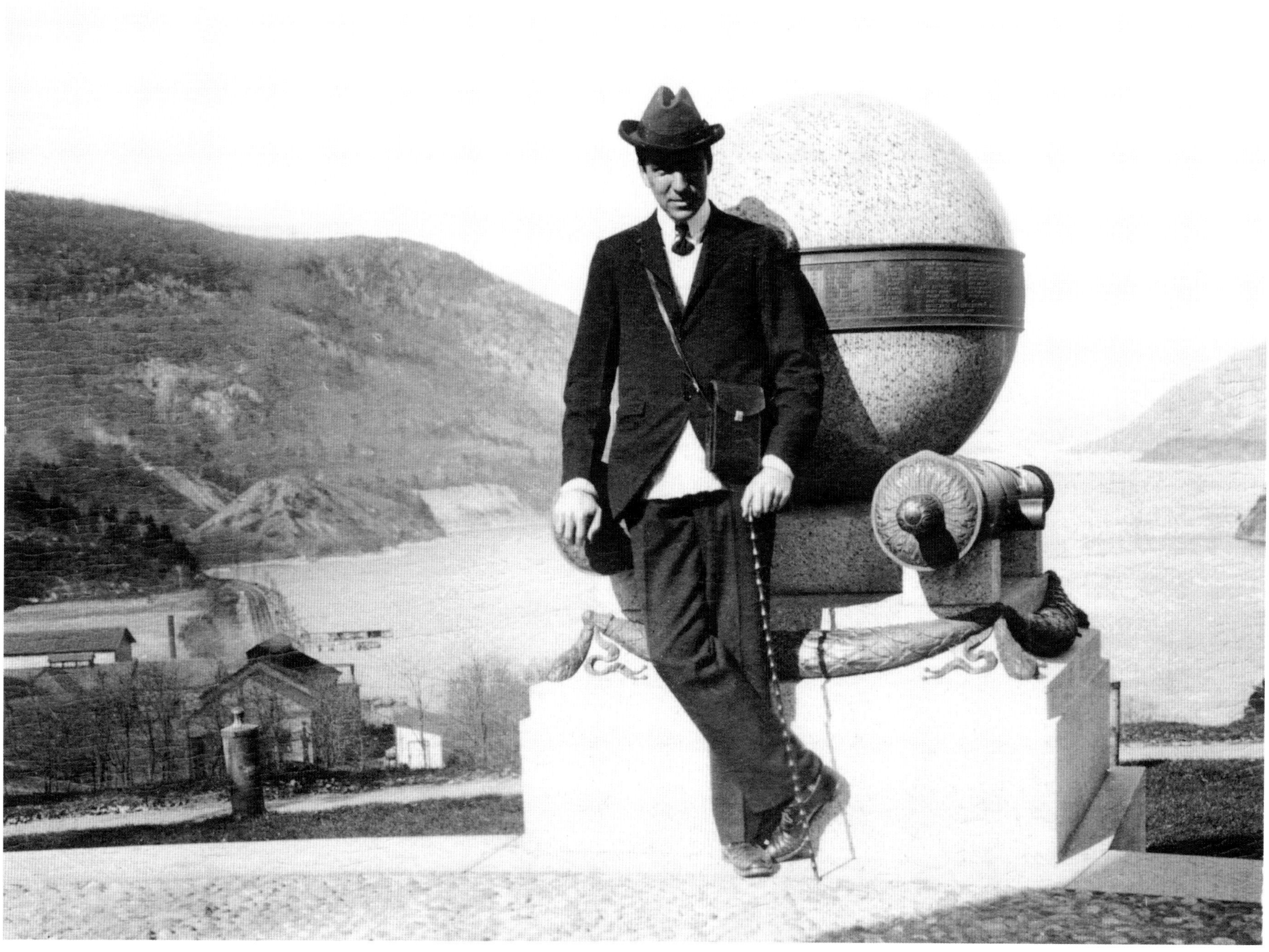

RIGHT In 1904, Tracy and Alice began their married life in Irvington, New York, where they rented Woodland Cottage from Tracy's cousin, George Mairs, for three years. The first two of their children, Olin and Margaret, were born there.

BELOW A twenty-four-year-old Alice posing among the lush vines at Woodland Cottage, 1905.

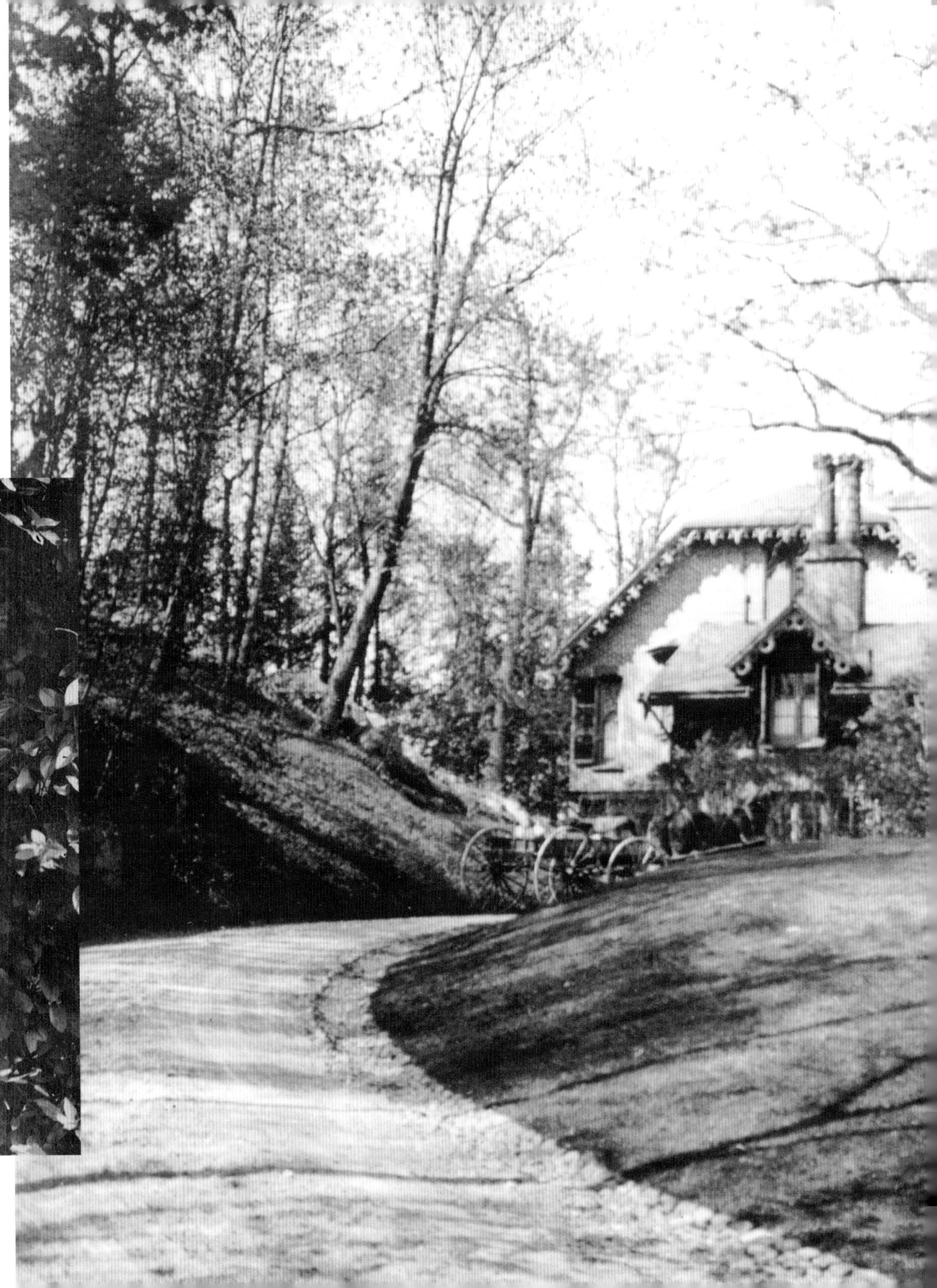

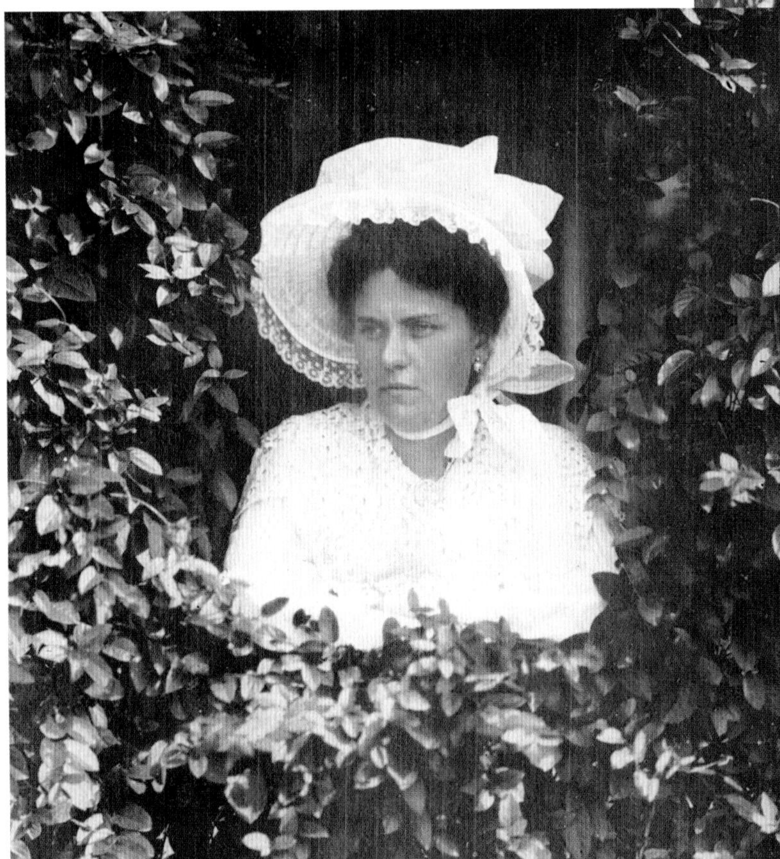

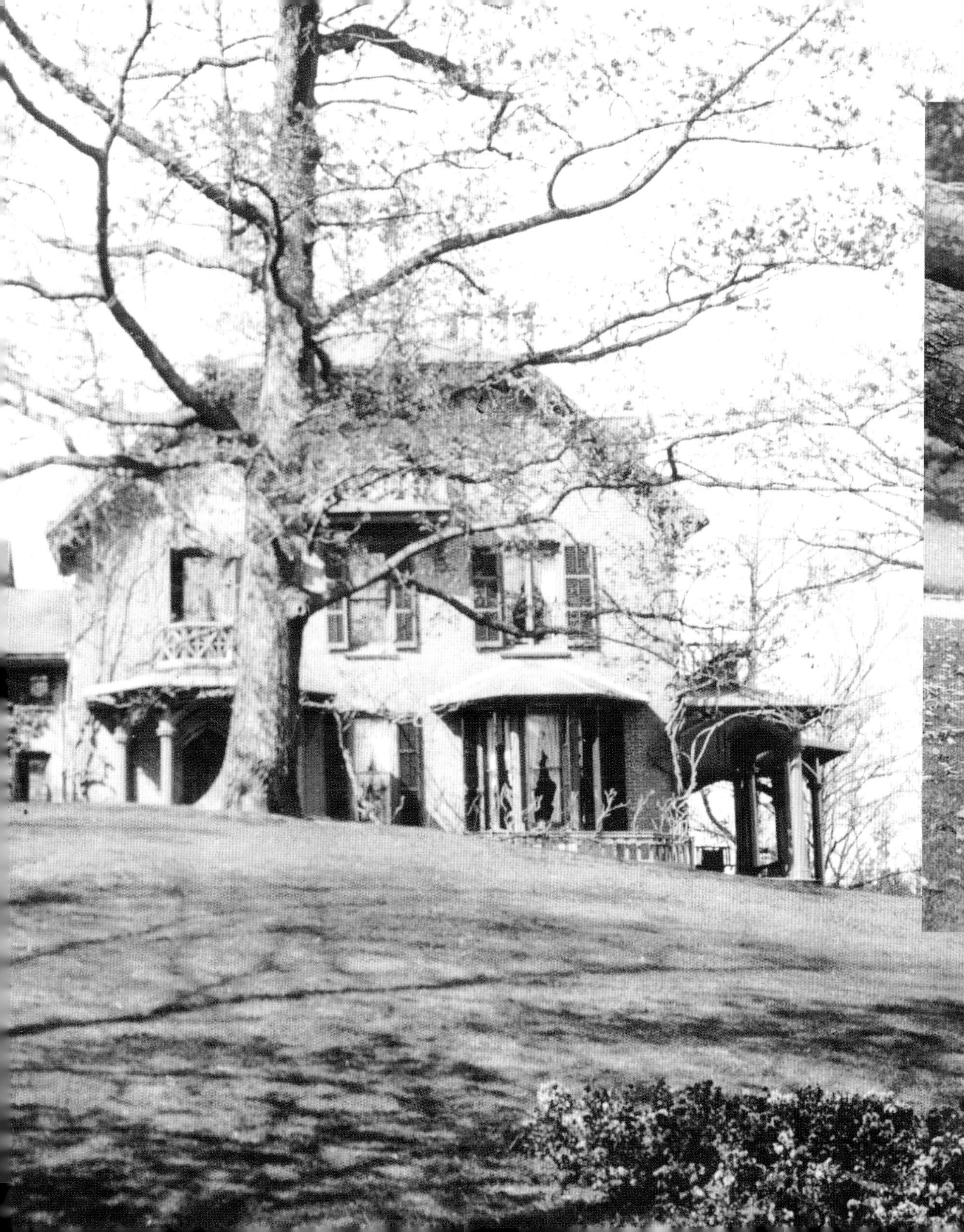

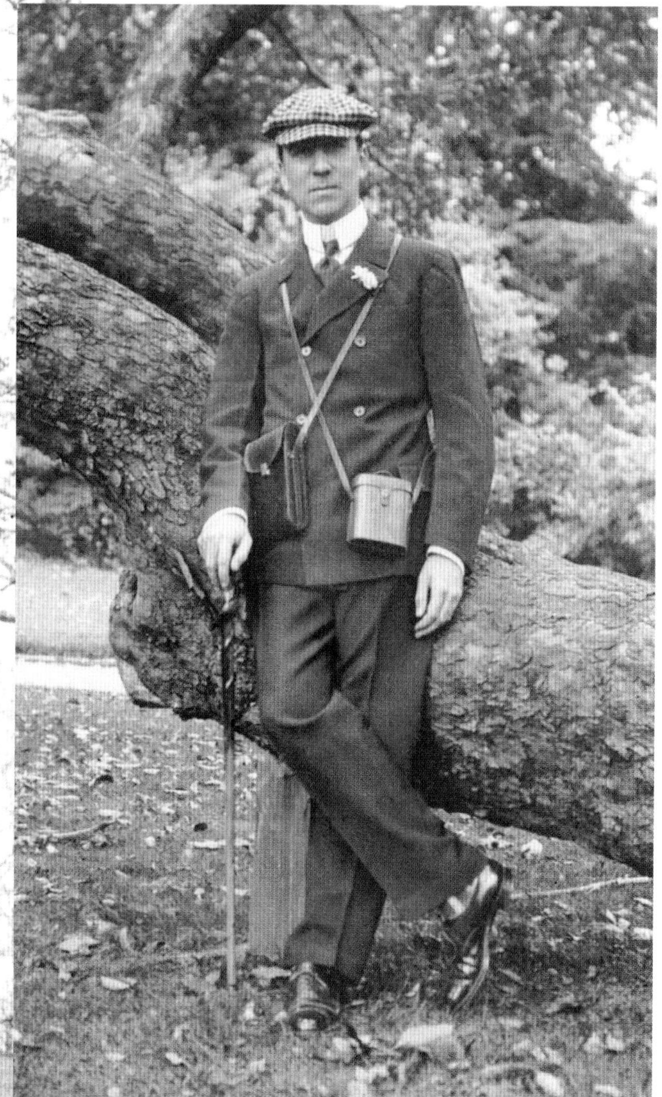

ABOVE Tracy, age 33, with his binoculars and Kodak Folding Pocket camera on the grounds of Woodland Cottage in 1904. He later purchased a Graflex Speed Graphic camera in 1912, the first year it was produced.

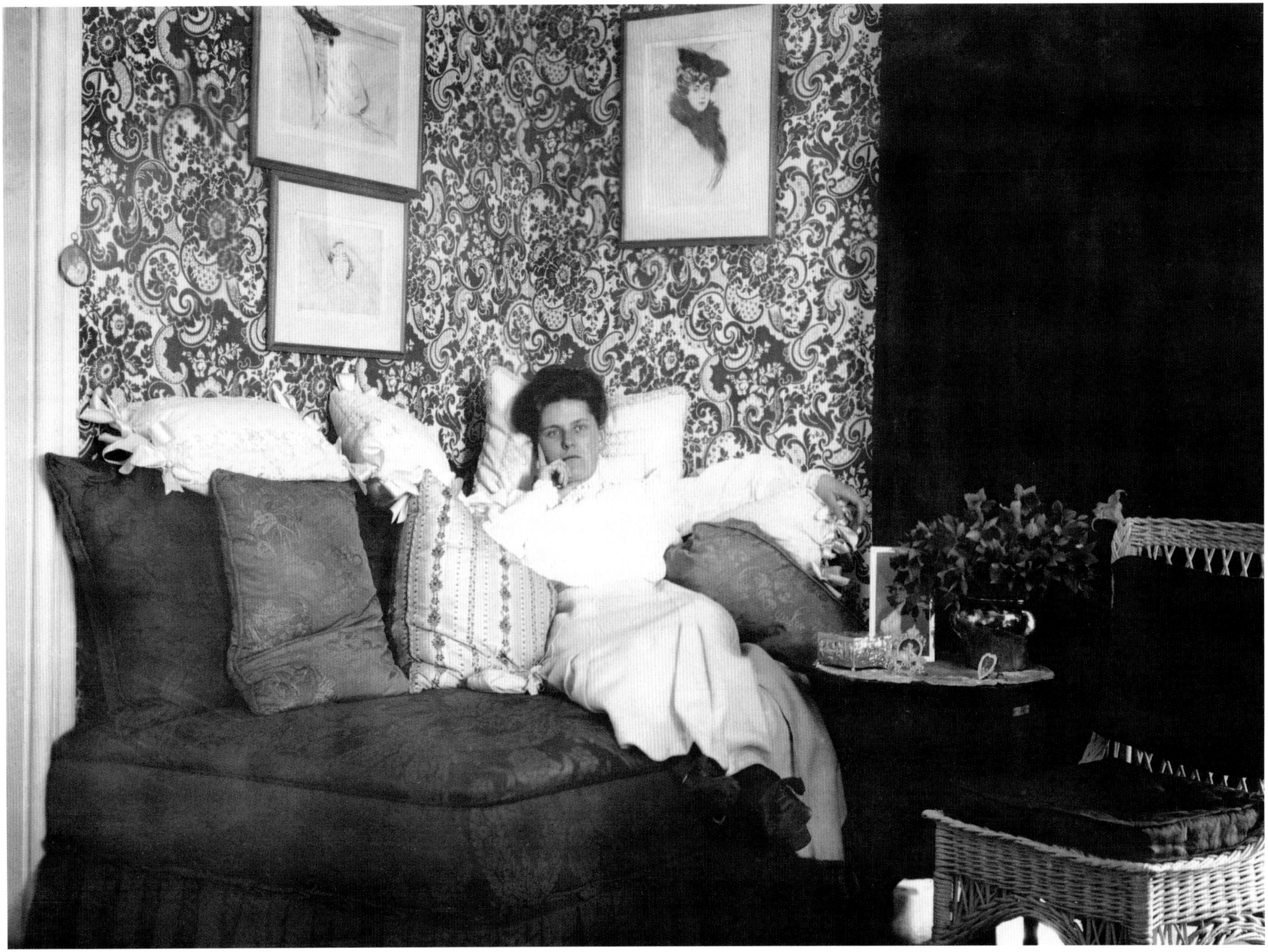

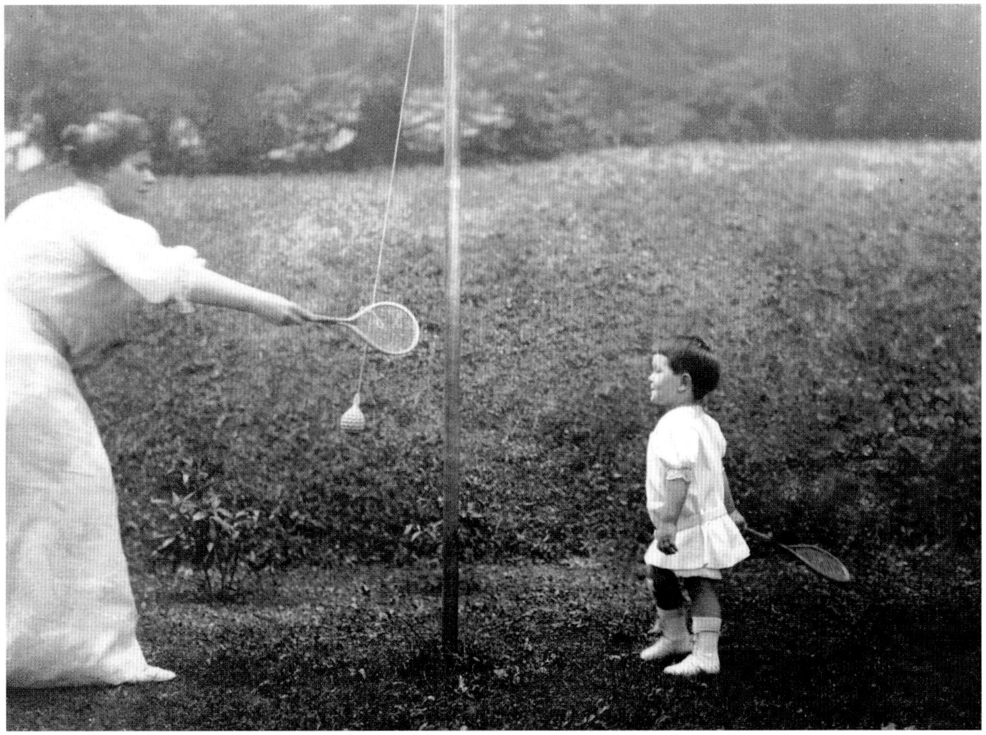

ABOVE Alice and a two-year-old Olin playing tether tennis in 1906.

OPPOSITE Alice in the parlor of Woodland Cottage. The wicker furniture and bold pattern wallpaper were fashionable at the time. The drypoint etchings on the wall were by the French artist Paul César Helleu, whose work closely resembles that of Charles Dana Gibson, a good friend of the Dowses. In 1912, Helleu designed the marvelous zodiac ceiling mural in New York City's Grand Central Terminal.

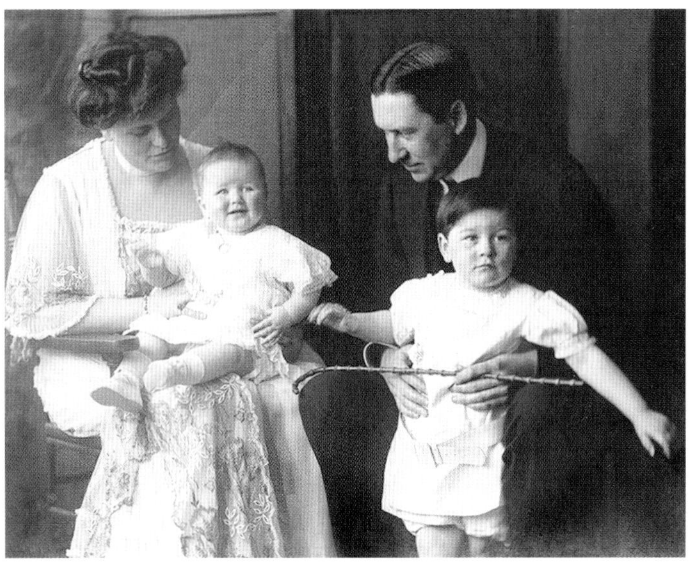

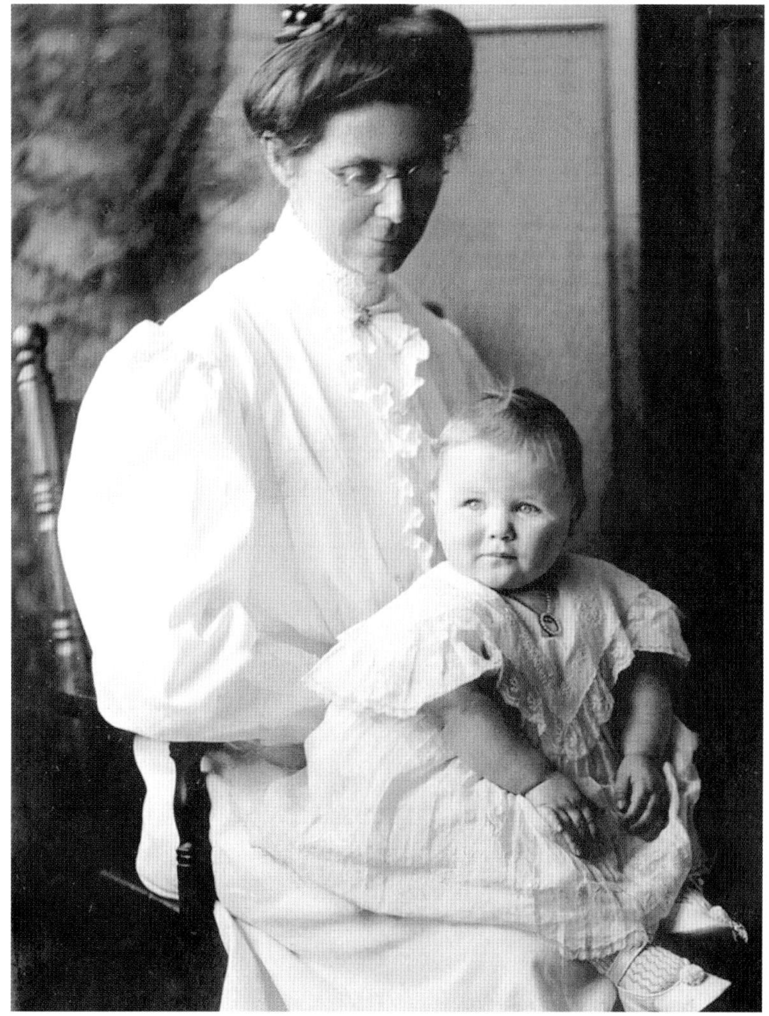

LEFT AND ABOVE Photographs of the family taken in 1907 by E. B. Core, who specialized in children's portraits. Their devoted Norwegian nurse, Greta Heyerdahl, has one-year-old Margaret on her lap. All three Dows children were raised by Greta, whom they loved dearly. She remained with the family for over fifty years, until her death, and is buried in the Dows family plot at the Rhinebeck cemetery.

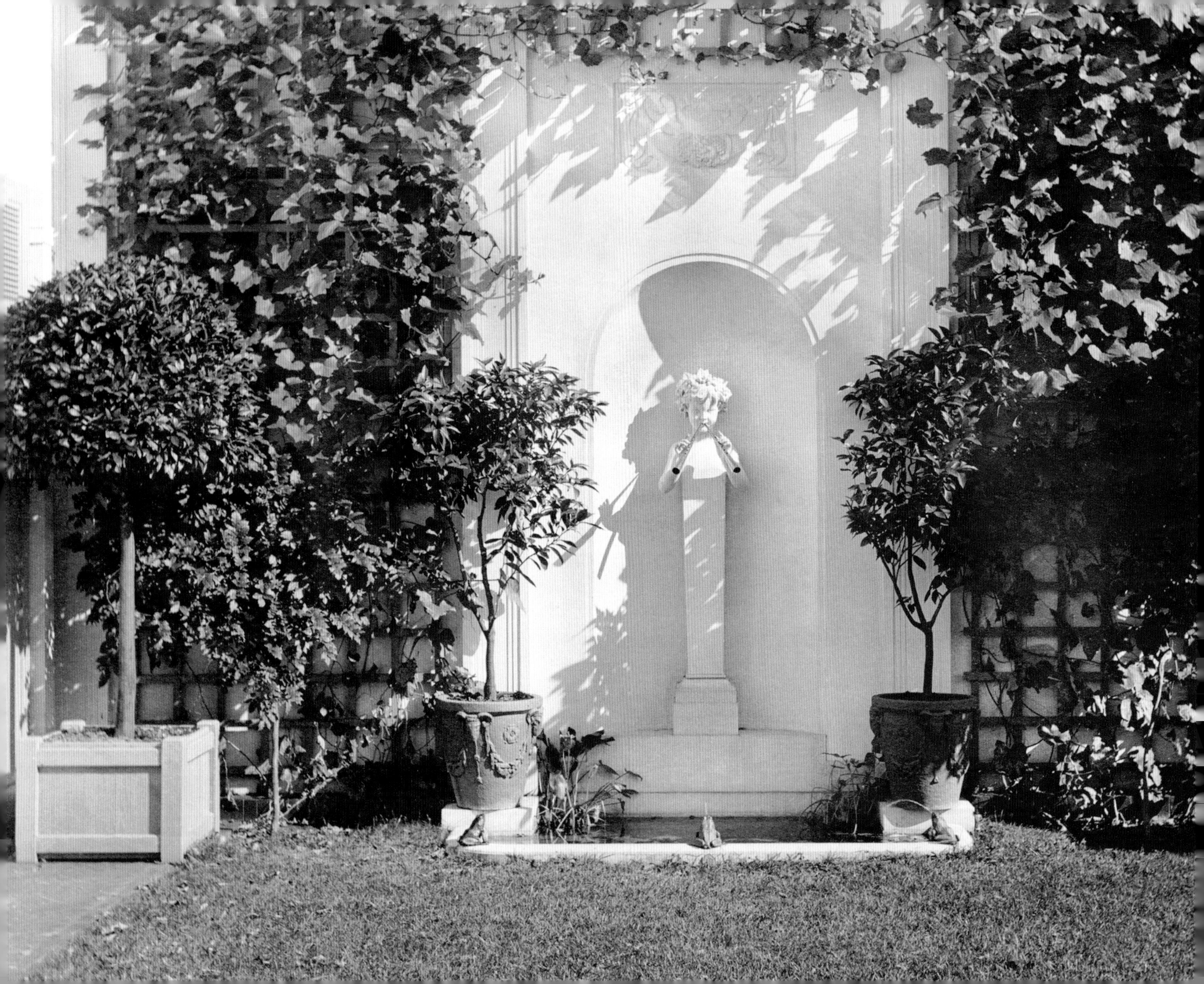

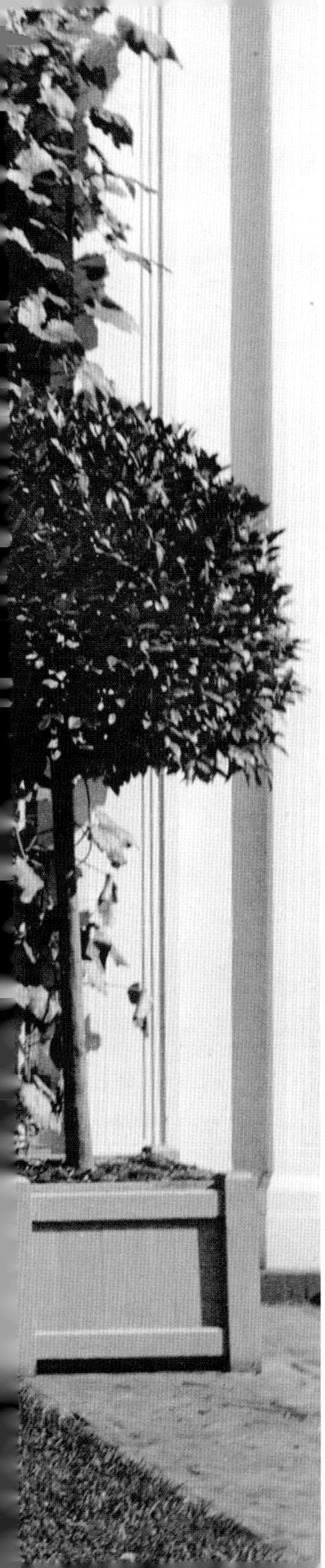

CHAPTER TWO

MR. DOWS Builds His DREAM HOUSE

PREVIOUS PAGES The wall fountain at Foxhollow Farm, photographed by Harry Coutant ca. 1917.

RIGHT Linwood Hill in 1905, five years before it became the site of the Foxhollow Farm house. It was designed in the Gothic Revival style by the noted architect Alexander Jackson Davis in 1842 for Dr. Federal Vanderburgh, a homeopathic doctor. Tracy purchased Linwood Hill from George Holliday in 1906, along with adjoining farms, to complete the Foxhollow Farm estate, which totaled approximately 800 acres.

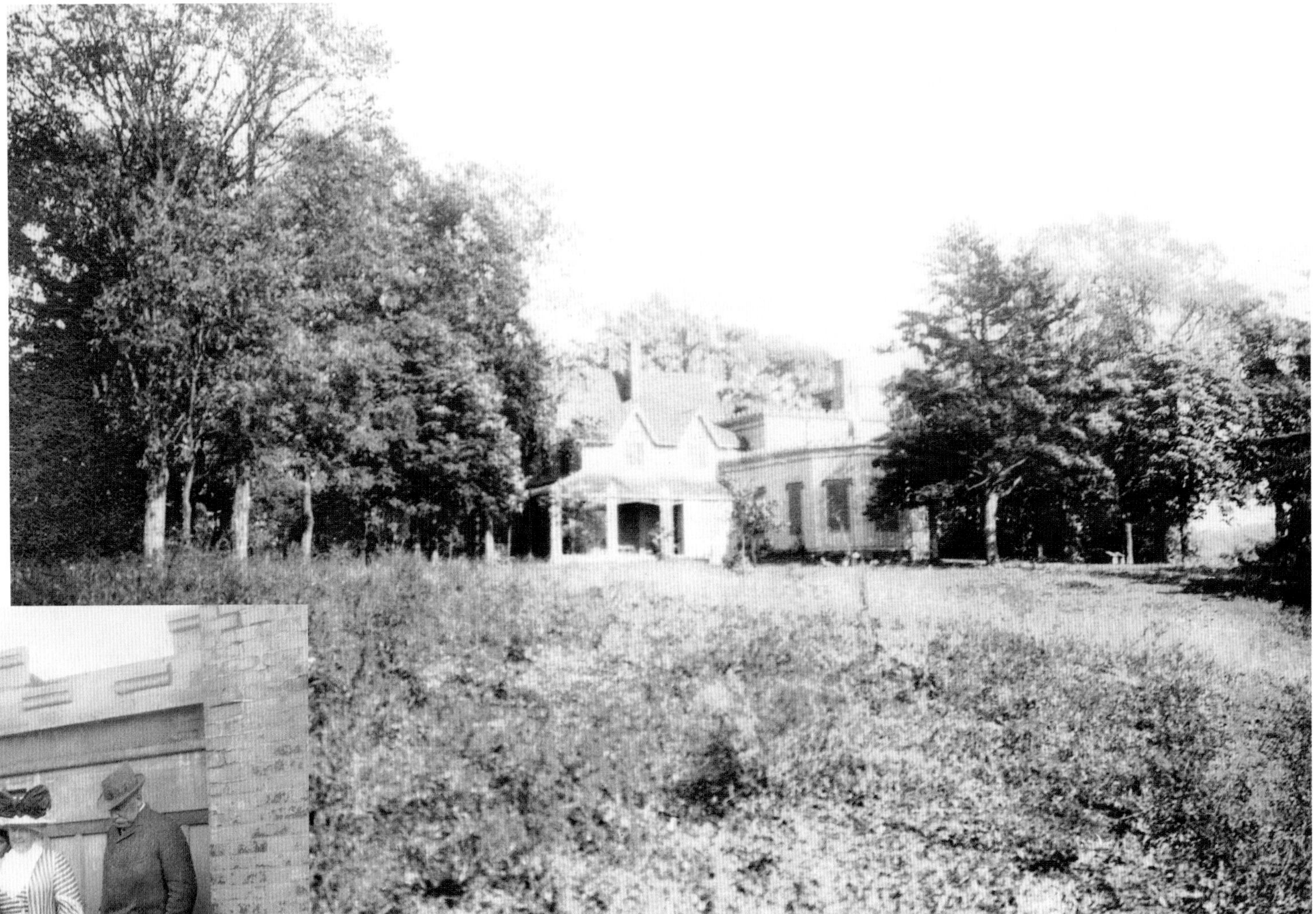

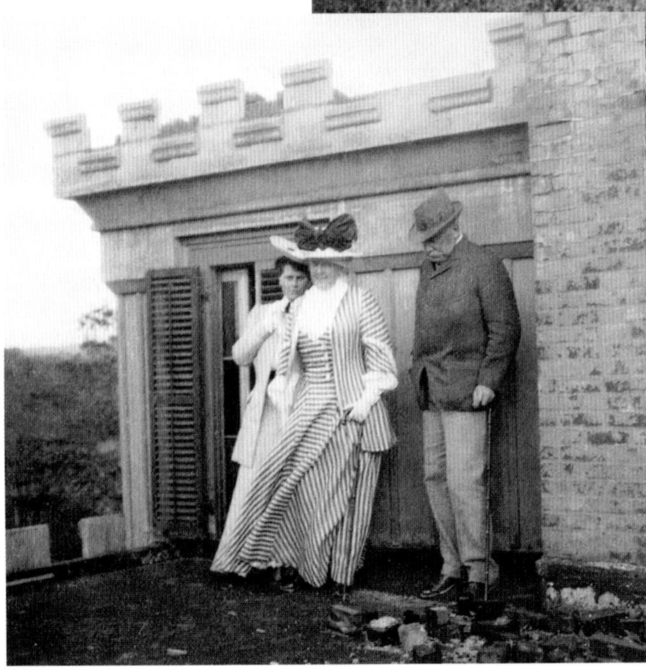

LEFT Alice on site with Mr. and Mrs. Stephen Olin in 1907, as the original house was being razed.

OPPOSITE Olin, Margaret, and their sleigh driver in front of a dismantled wing of Linwood Hill.

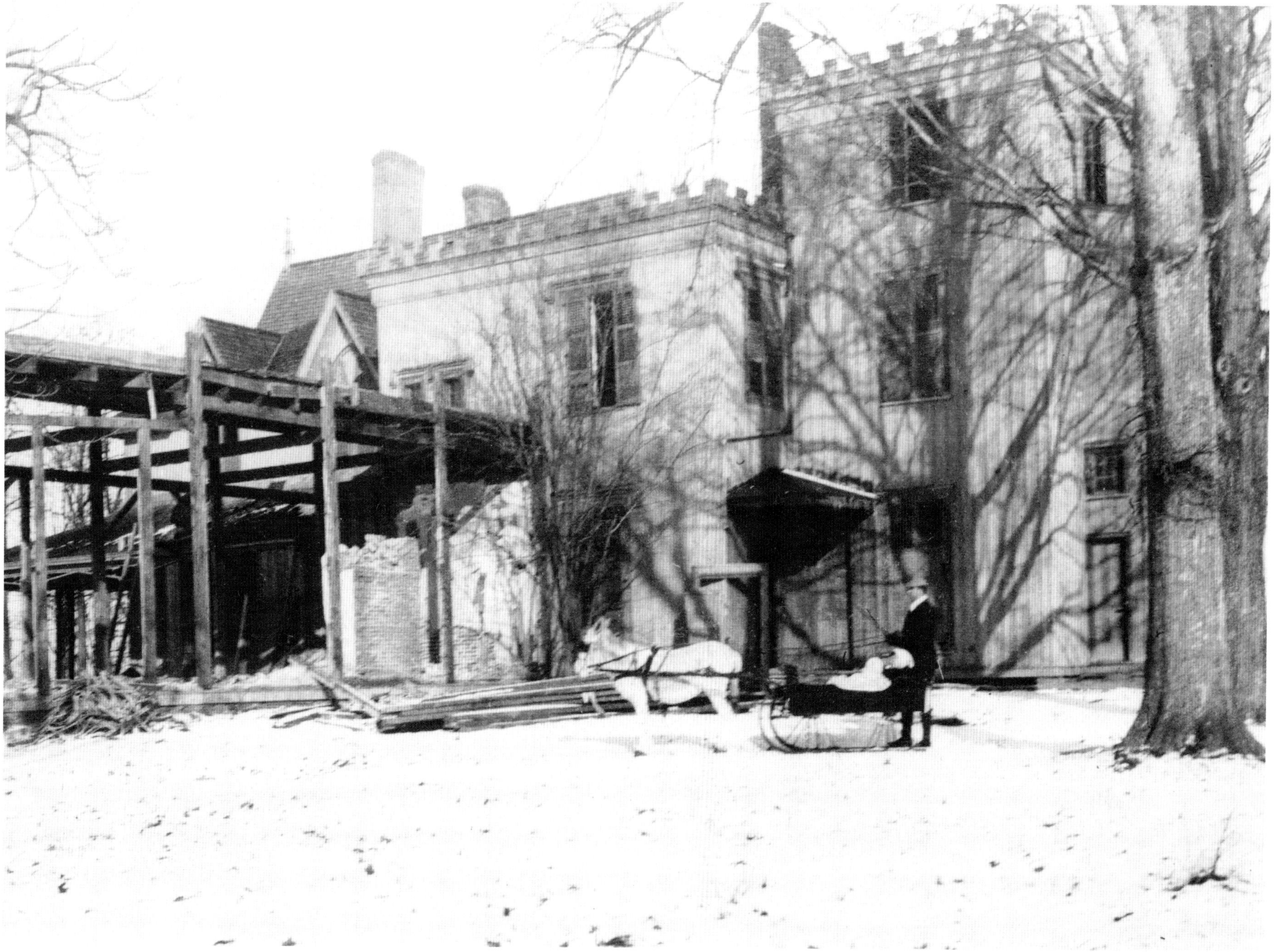

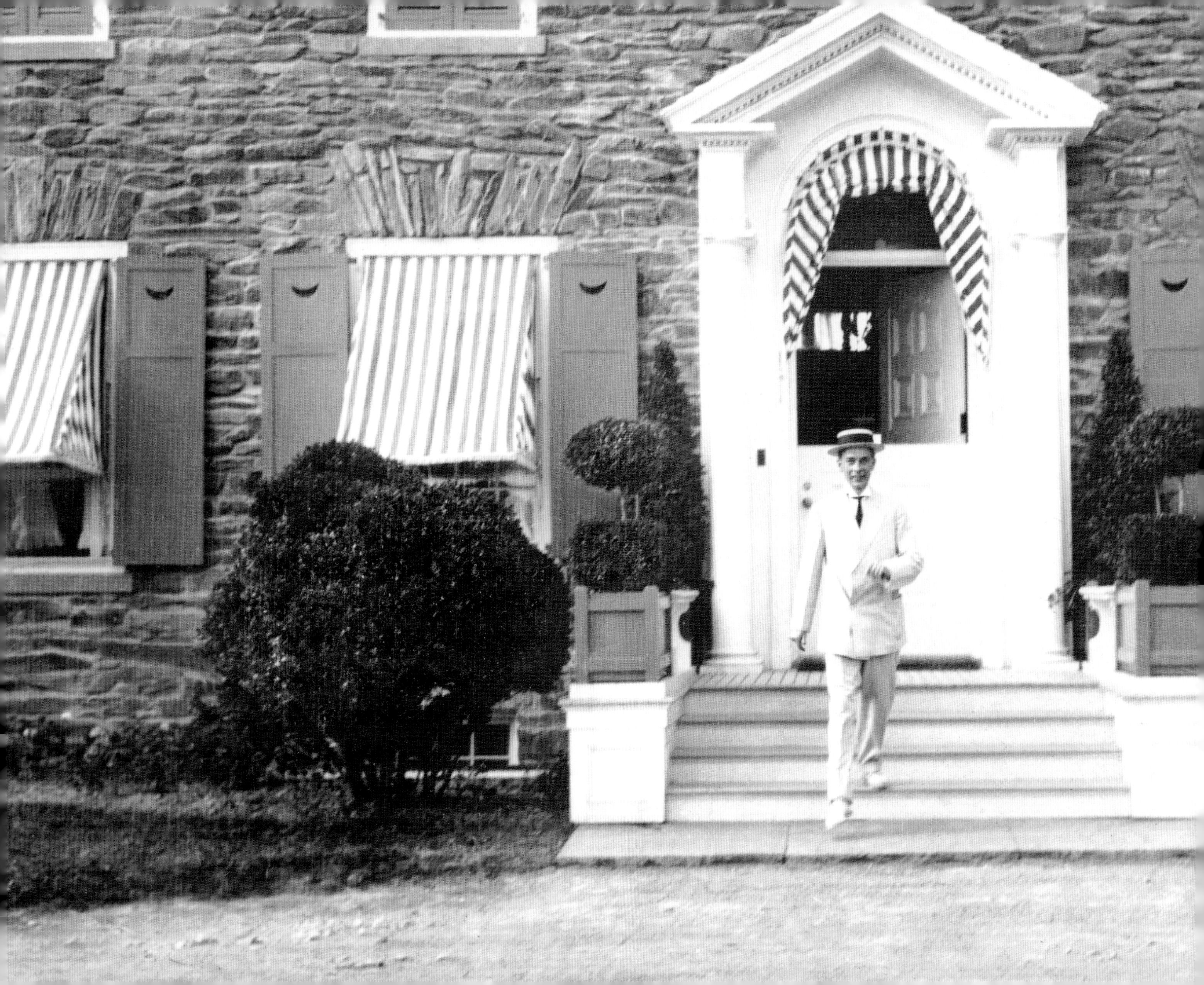

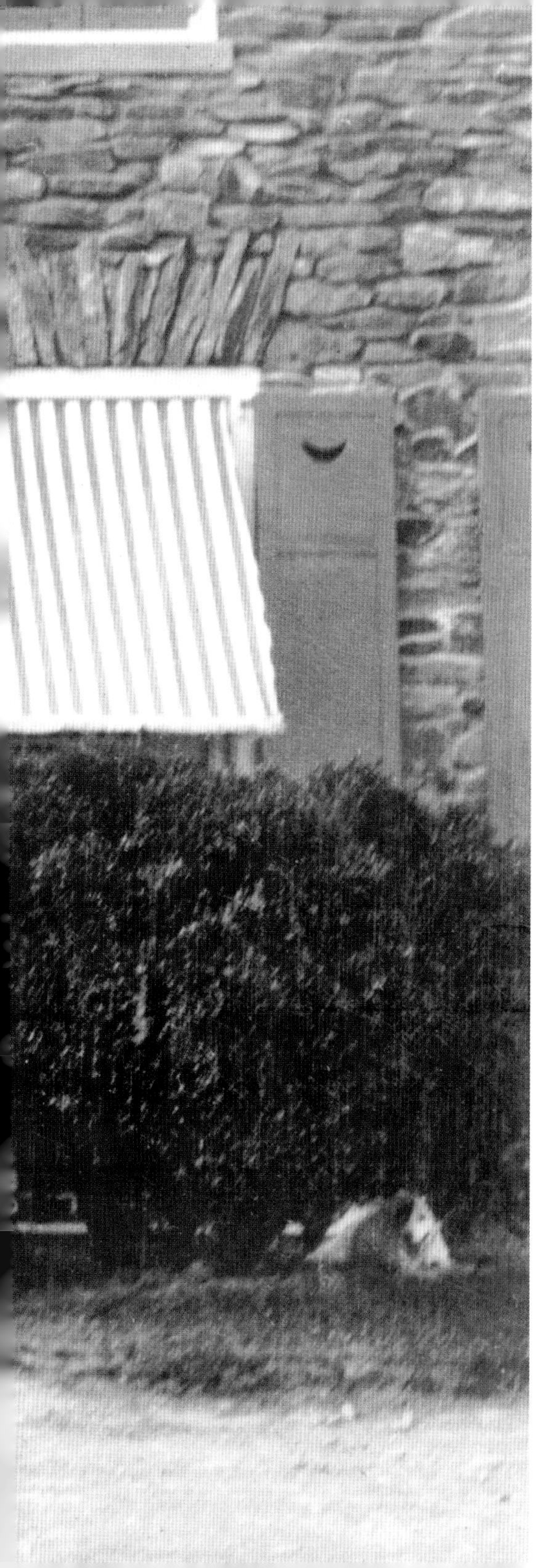

LEFT Harrie Thomas Lindeberg, the architect of Foxhollow Farm, walking down the steps of Stone Cottage, the first new structure built on the estate in 1907. A former assistant to Stanford White, Lindeberg and a fellow draftsman, Lewis Colt Albro, left the firm of McKim, Mead & White after White's death in 1906 and formed their own practice. Together they became one of the most sought-after designers of country houses for wealthy Americans. One of their first jobs was a country estate for the banker James A. Stillman in Pocantico Hills, New York. It was this commission, together with a recommendation from Charles Dana Gibson, that brought Albro & Lindeberg to Tracy Dows's attention.

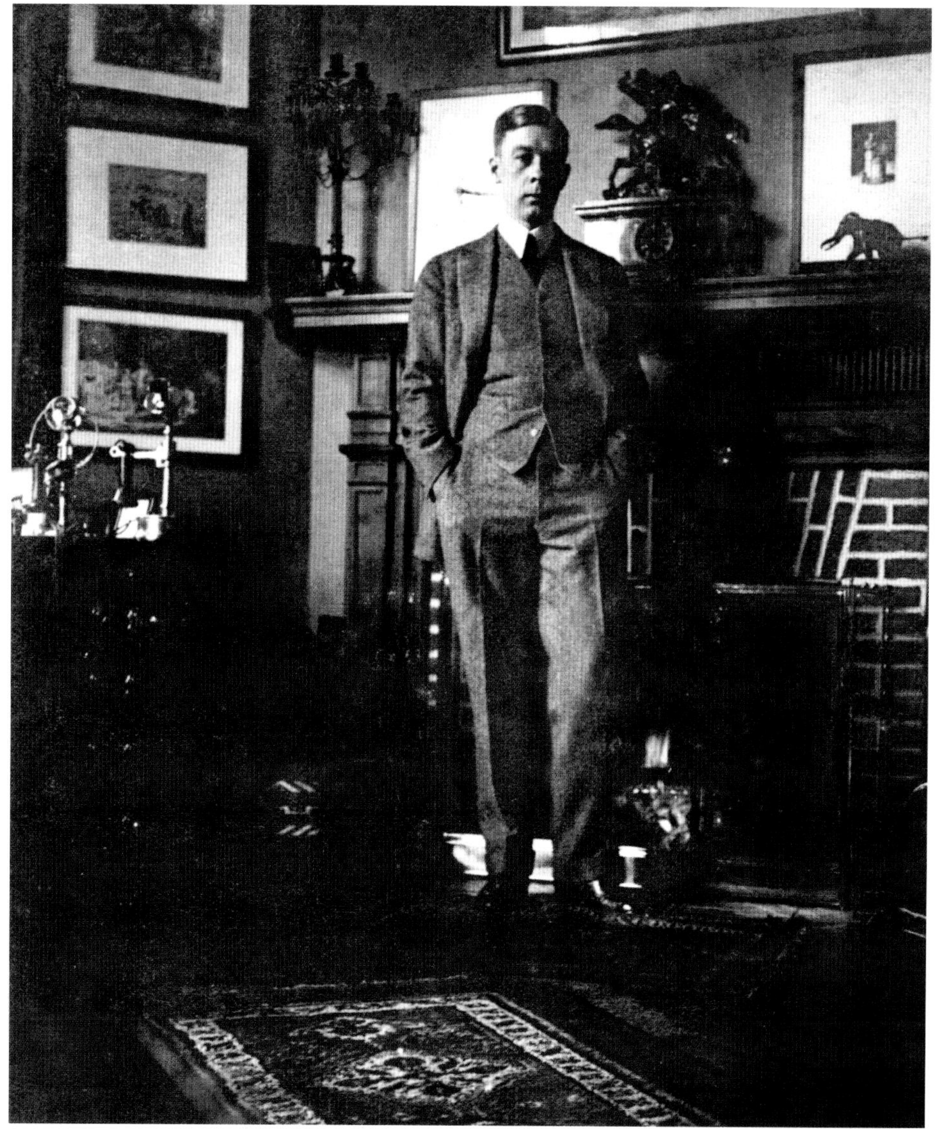

ABOVE Lindeberg in Tracy's office on the first floor of the main house, 1913. He was quoted as saying, "Build simply, whether a cottage or a castle."

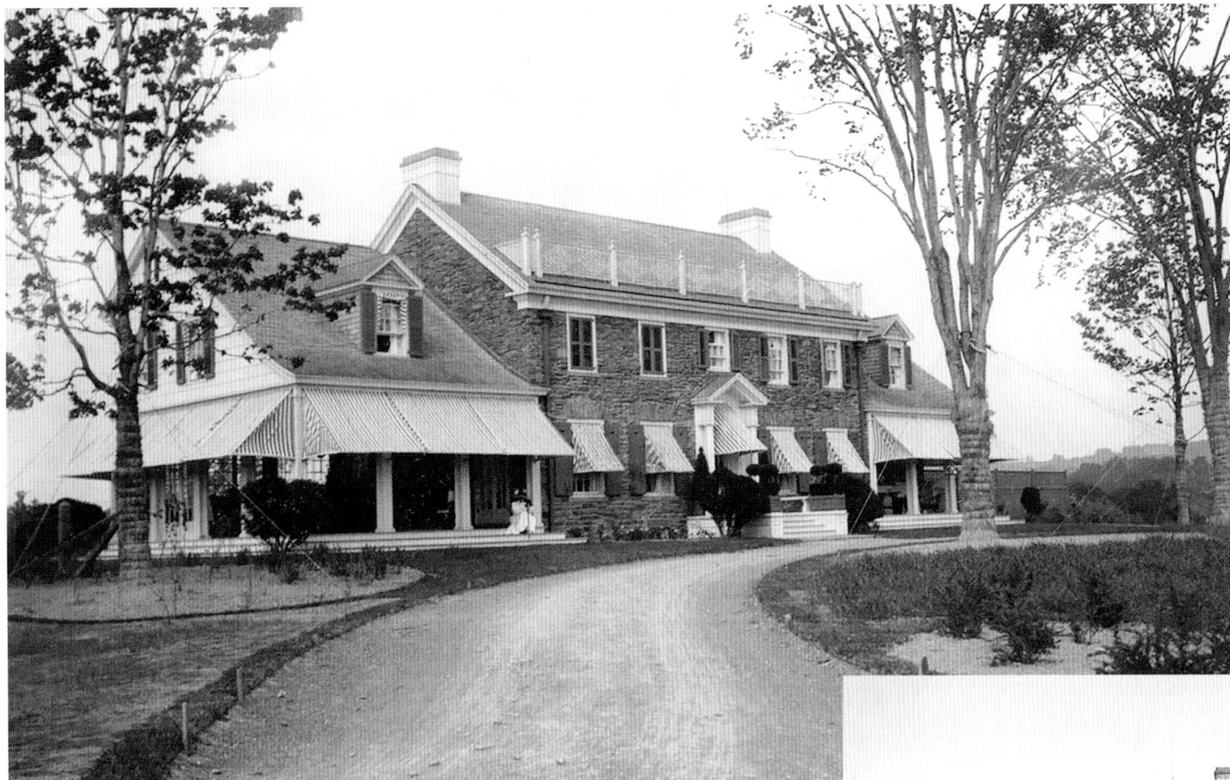

LEFT A view of Stone Cottage shortly after it was completed in 1907. Built of fieldstone with a delightful garden and elliptical fountain, the property was bordered by a white picket fence. Newly planted trees can be seen with cables securing them in place. The Dowses lived here until the main house was completed in 1910.

BELOW LEFT An architectural drawing of the front of Stone Cottage by Albro & Lindeberg. (Courtesy of the National Park Service, Frederick Law Olmsted National Historic Site)

BELOW The cottage, its garden, and fountain seen from the west, 1909.

VIEW FROM SOUTHWEST.

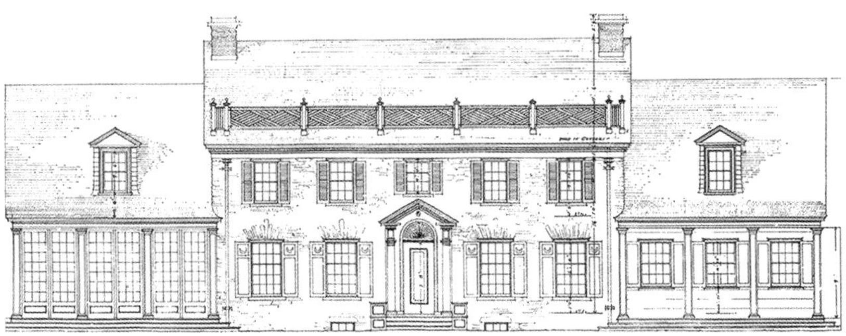

FRONT ELEVATION.

FARM COTTAGE FOR MR. TRACY DOWS, RHINEBECK, N. Y.

Messrs. Albro & Lindeberg, Architects.

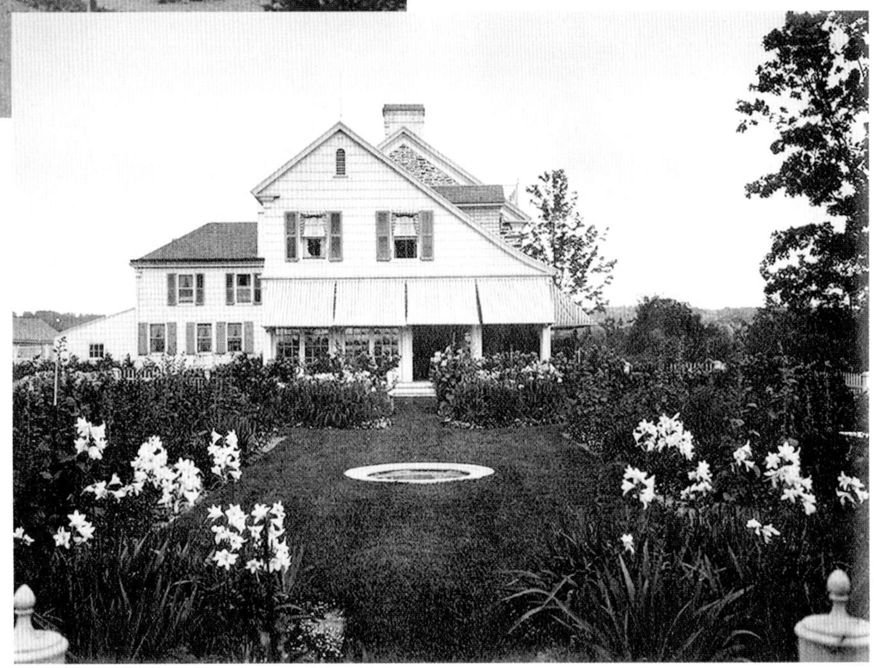

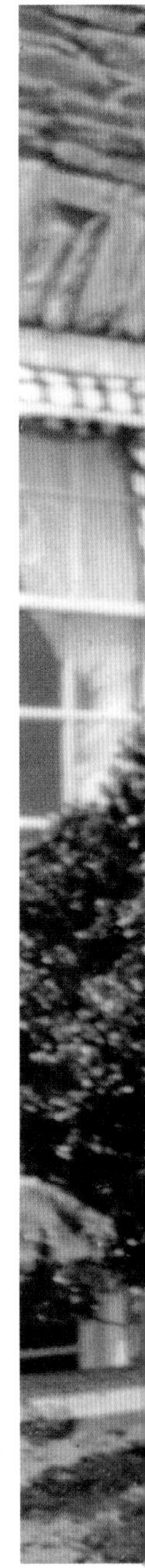

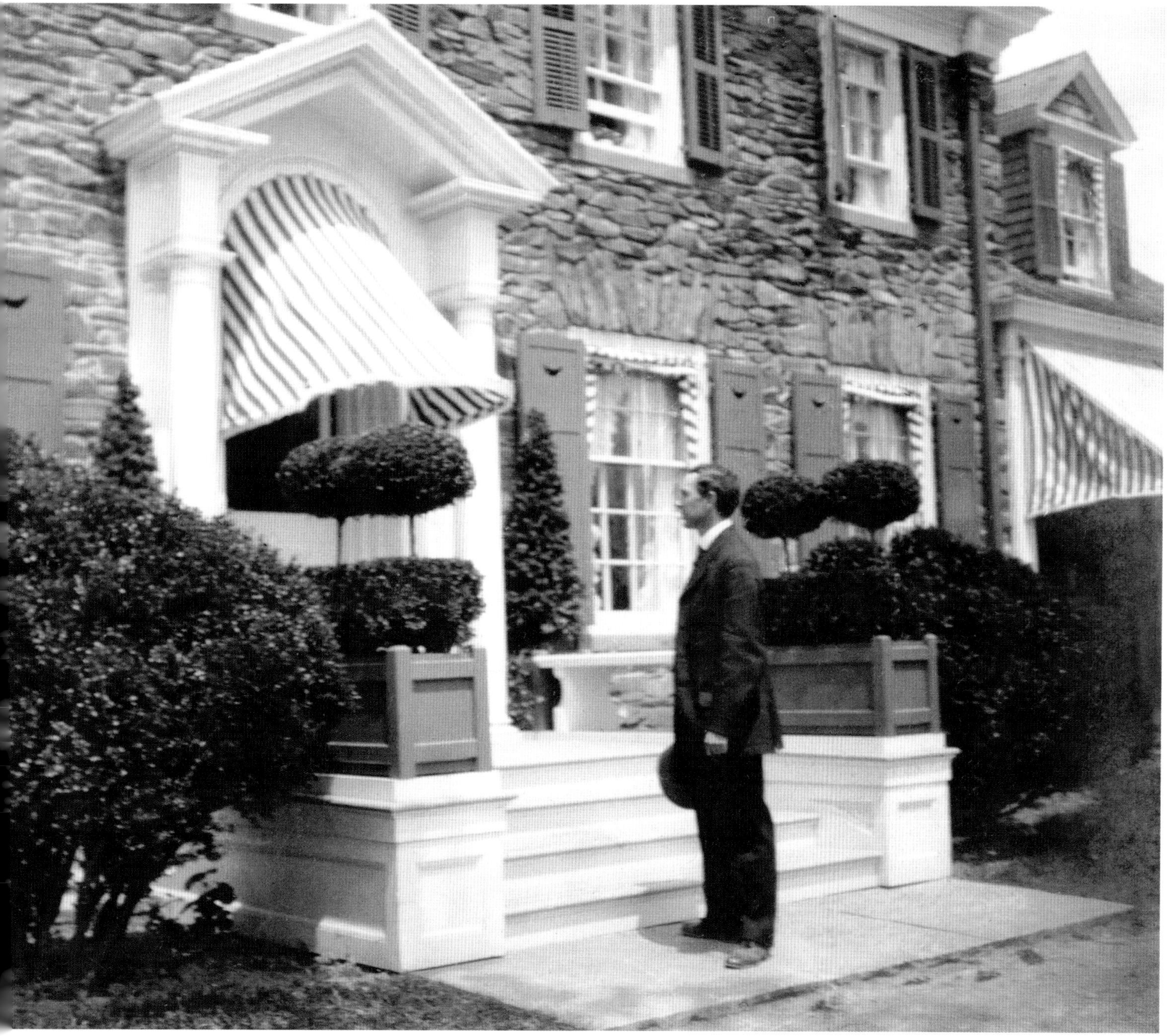

LEFT Frederick Law Olmsted, Jr., in front of Stone Cottage in 1907. His father, Frederick Law Olmsted, co-designed New York City's Central Park and Prospect Park, along with other well-known city parks. Together Frederick Law Olmsted, Jr., and his adopted half-brother, John Charles Olmsted, ran a prestigious company hired by Tracy to landscape his property. The Olmsted Brothers firm chose simple shrubs and topiaries for Stone Cottage and an extensive rural form of landscaping for the rolling hills of the estate. They traveled back and forth from their studio in Brookline, Massachusetts, to supervise the project.

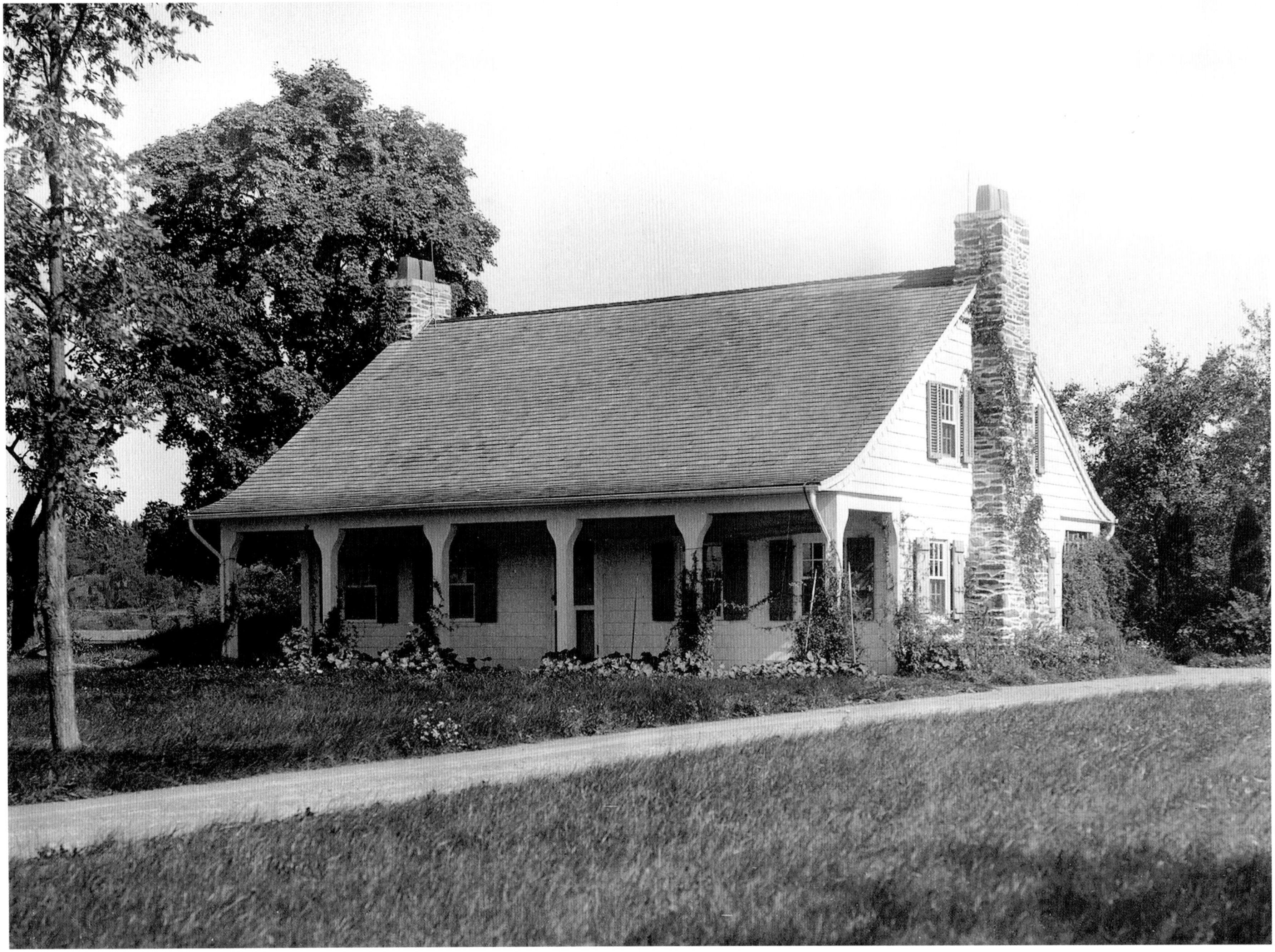

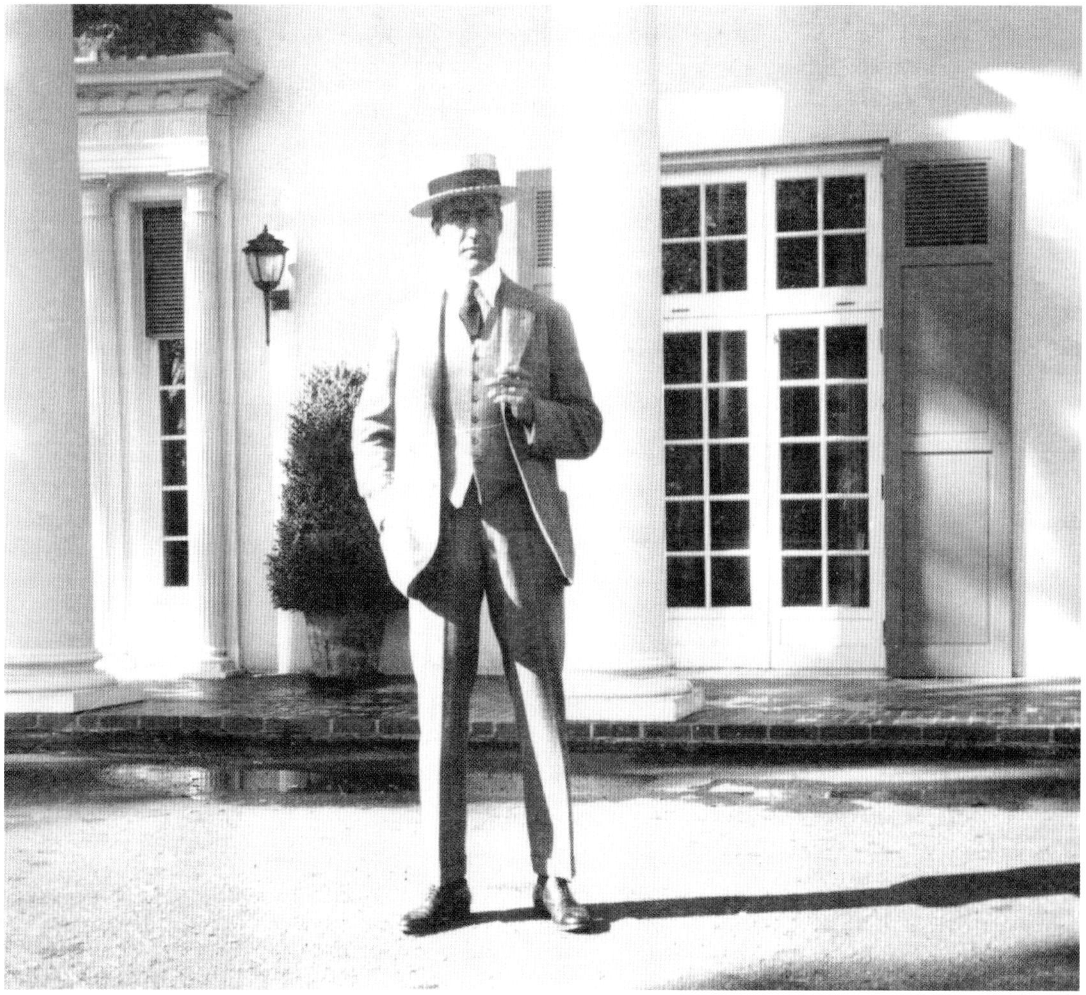

LEFT Clarence Colt Colburn in front of the Foxhollow Farm house in 1919. Tracy hired him to manage the estate in 1907 on the recommendation of the Olmsted Brothers. In 1908, Colburn married Alida Livingston Ehlers, daughter of Louis Augustus Ehlers, the landscape architect for William Backhouse Astor, Jr. Colburn, who would serve in the U.S. Army during World War I, moved into Stone Cottage in 1910 after Tracy and his family moved into the main house.

BELOW John W. Pottenburgh, seen in 1927, succeeded Colburn as superintendent of Foxhollow Farm. He had previously worked in the violet business and had been a well-known baseball player in Rhinebeck in his youth. During an exhibition game with the Kingston Colonials, he had the distinction of striking out Babe Ruth three times.

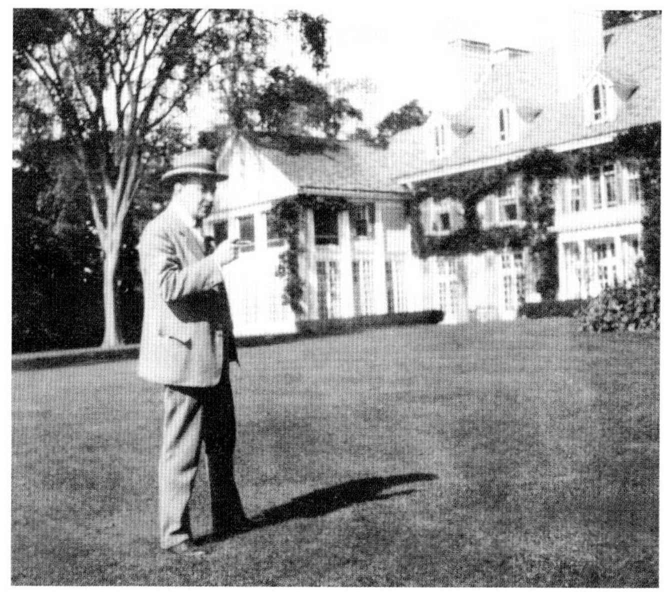

OPPOSITE The Gardener's Cottage in 1917. Lindeberg designed the house as a simple Colonial-style, white-shingled structure with stone chimneys. After it was completed in 1907, it was first used as the home of the estate superintendent, Clarence Colt Colburn, and later became the gardener's house. (Courtesy of the National Park Service, Frederick Law Olmsted National Historic Site)

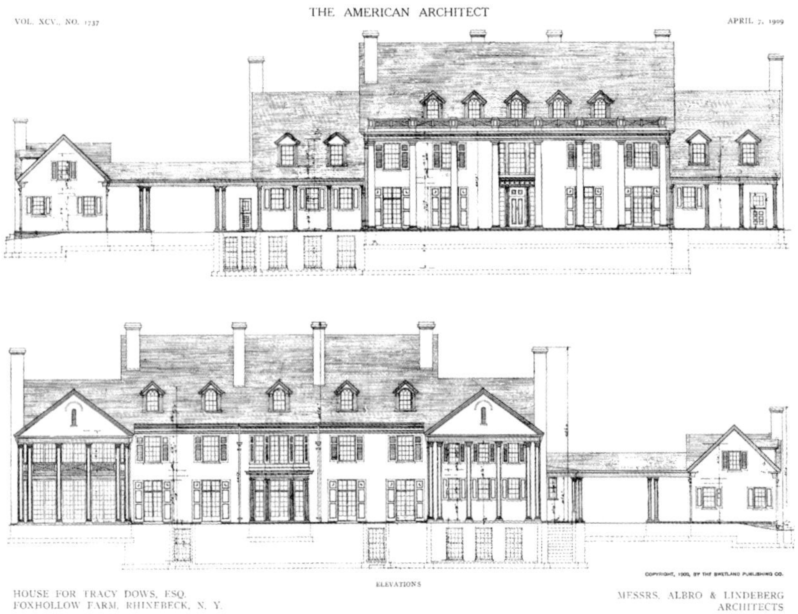

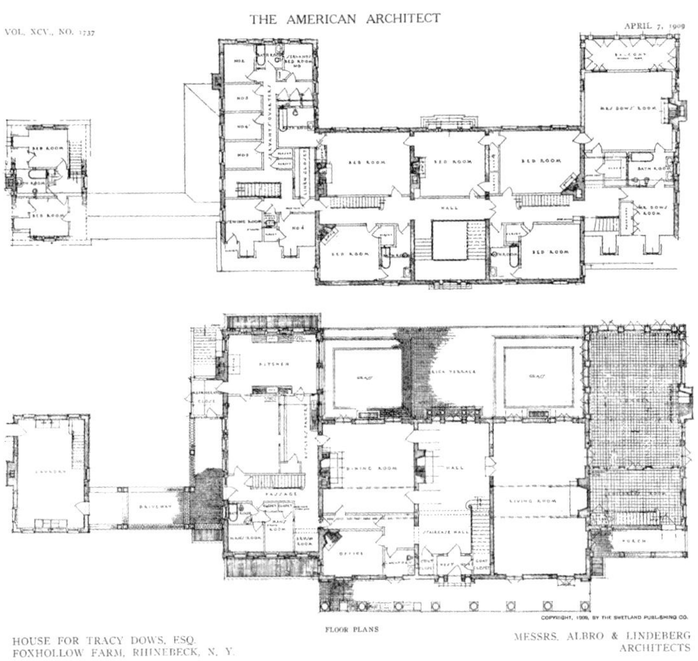

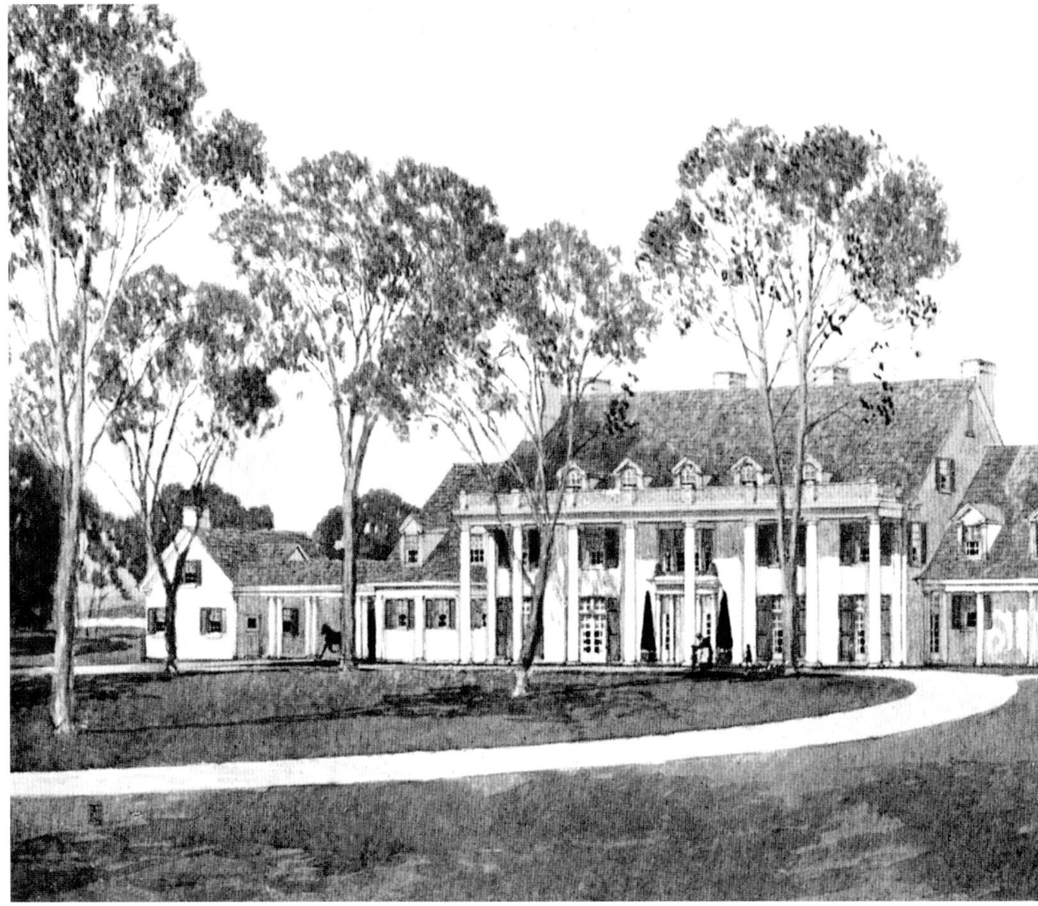

ABOVE AND LEFT The original rendering of the family house by Birch Burdette Long, and drawings by Albro & Lindeberg, both published in the April 1911 edition of *The American Architect*. Foxhollow Farm appeared in several publications during the 1910s. The October 1911 issue of *Architectural Record* noted that "Mr. Dows' residence is situated on eight hundred acres and has, consequently, some right to be considered a manor house. To keep a residence which contains twelve masters' beds and bathrooms and accommodations for fourteen servants subdued to the domestic atmosphere of a farm house was certainly an incredible achievement." (Courtesy of the National Park Service, Frederick Law Olmsted National Historic Site)

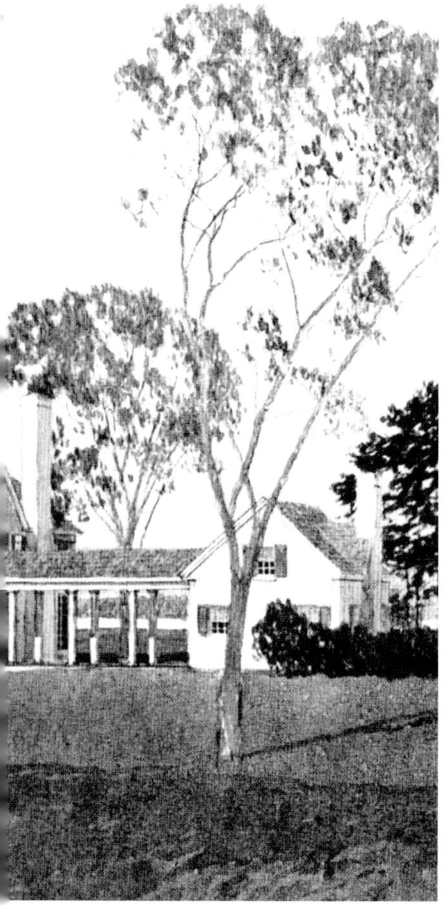

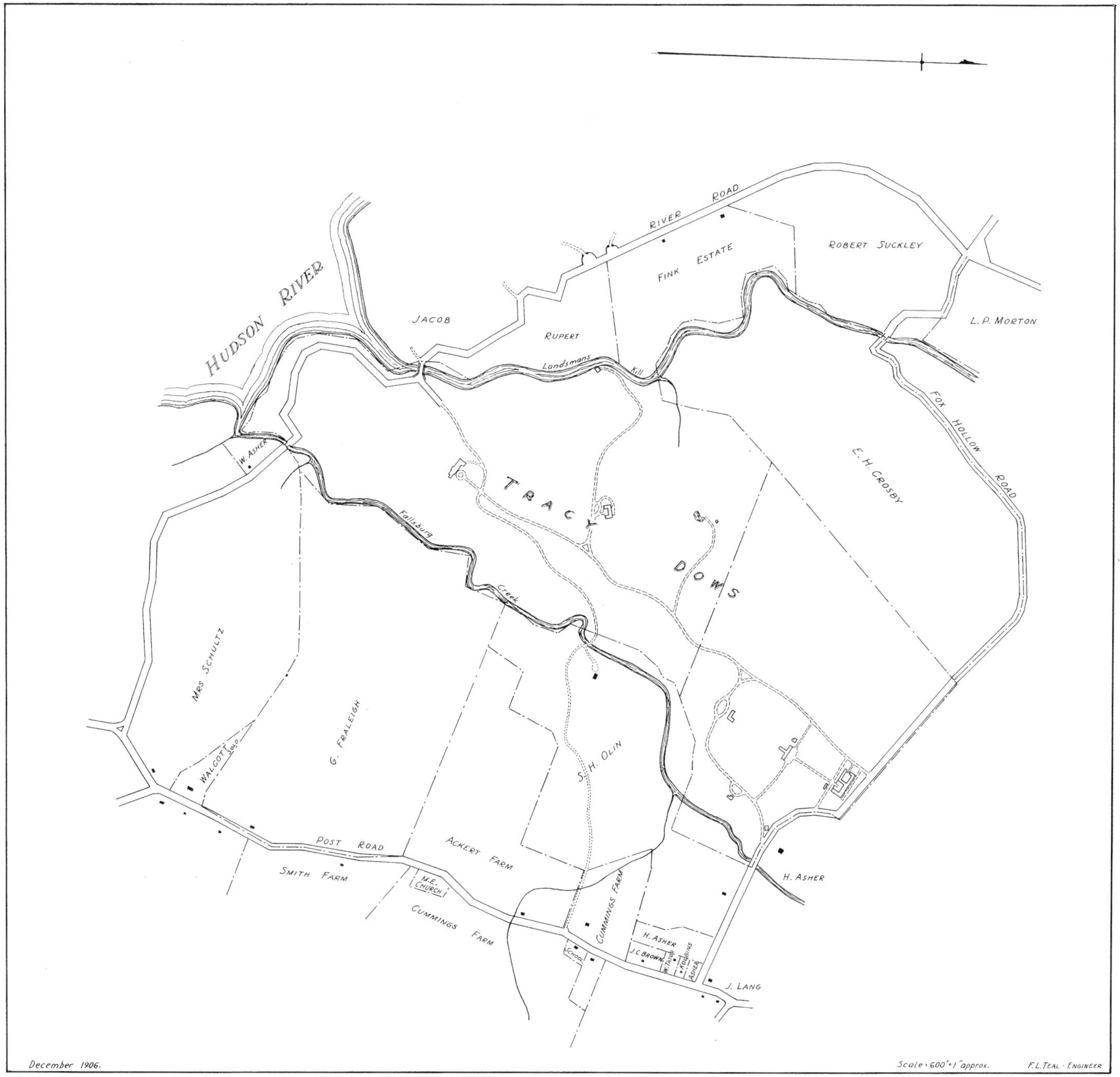

RIGHT A map drawn by local surveyor Frank L. Teal in 1906. He worked alongside the Olmsted Brothers as they mapped the Foxhollow Farm property for Tracy Dows. The drawing shows all the adjoining farms that Tracy purchased to incorporate his estate. Central to the estate is Alice's ancestral home, Glenburn, seen as S. H. Olin on the map. (Courtesy of the National Park Service, Frederick Law Olmsted National Historic Site)

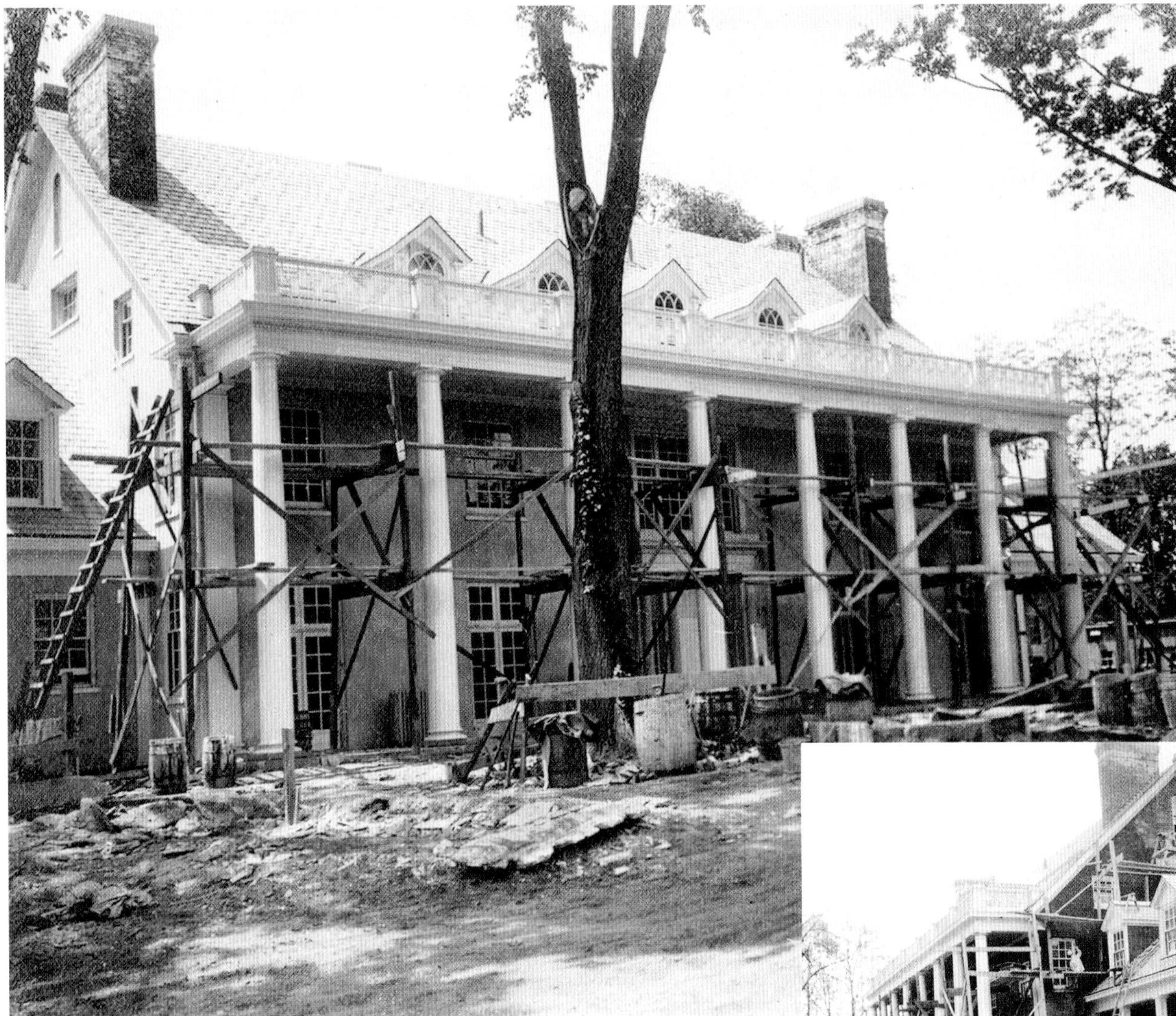

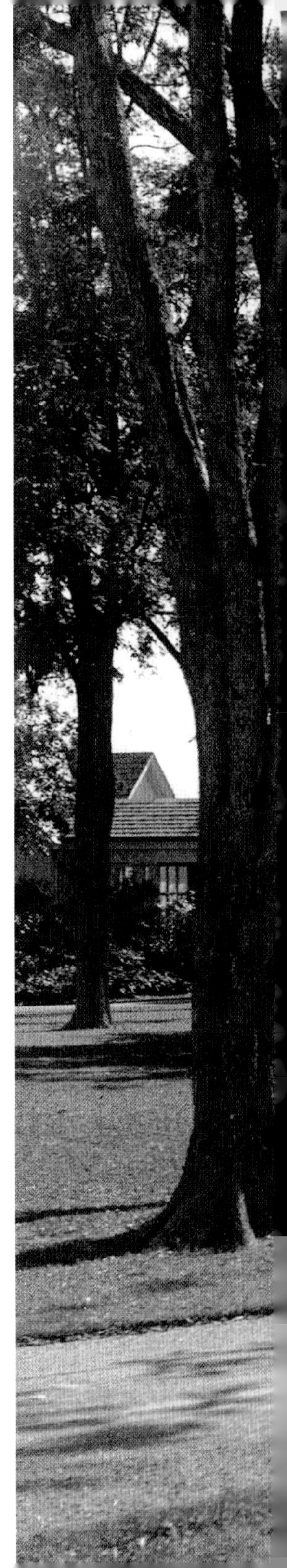

RIGHT A photograph of the house taken in 1917, showing its expansive view of the Hudson River from the back. The Olmsted Brothers had drafted plans for a sunken formal garden behind the left side of the house, and a landscaped path that led to a tennis court with benches and an arbor. These were never built. (Courtesy of the National Park Service, Frederick Law Olmsted National Historic Site)

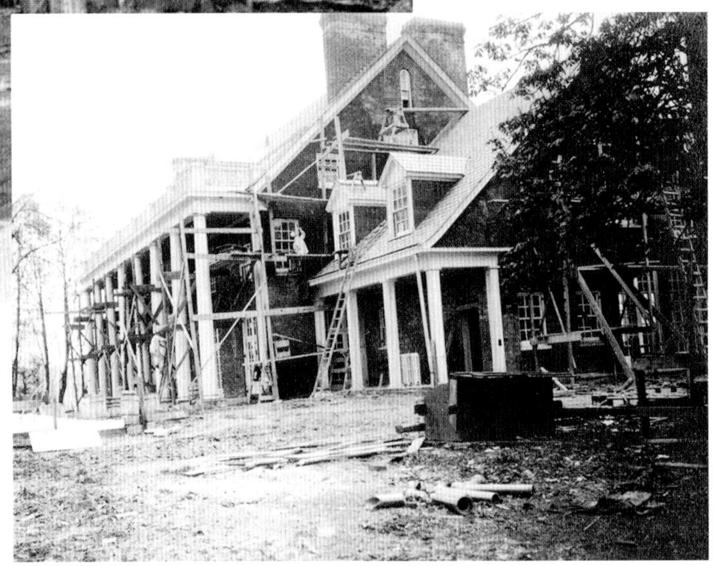

ABOVE AND RIGHT The house in April 1910, during construction. Its white-painted brick exterior and Colonial Revival style was considered modern compared to its nineteenth-century Hudson River neighbors.

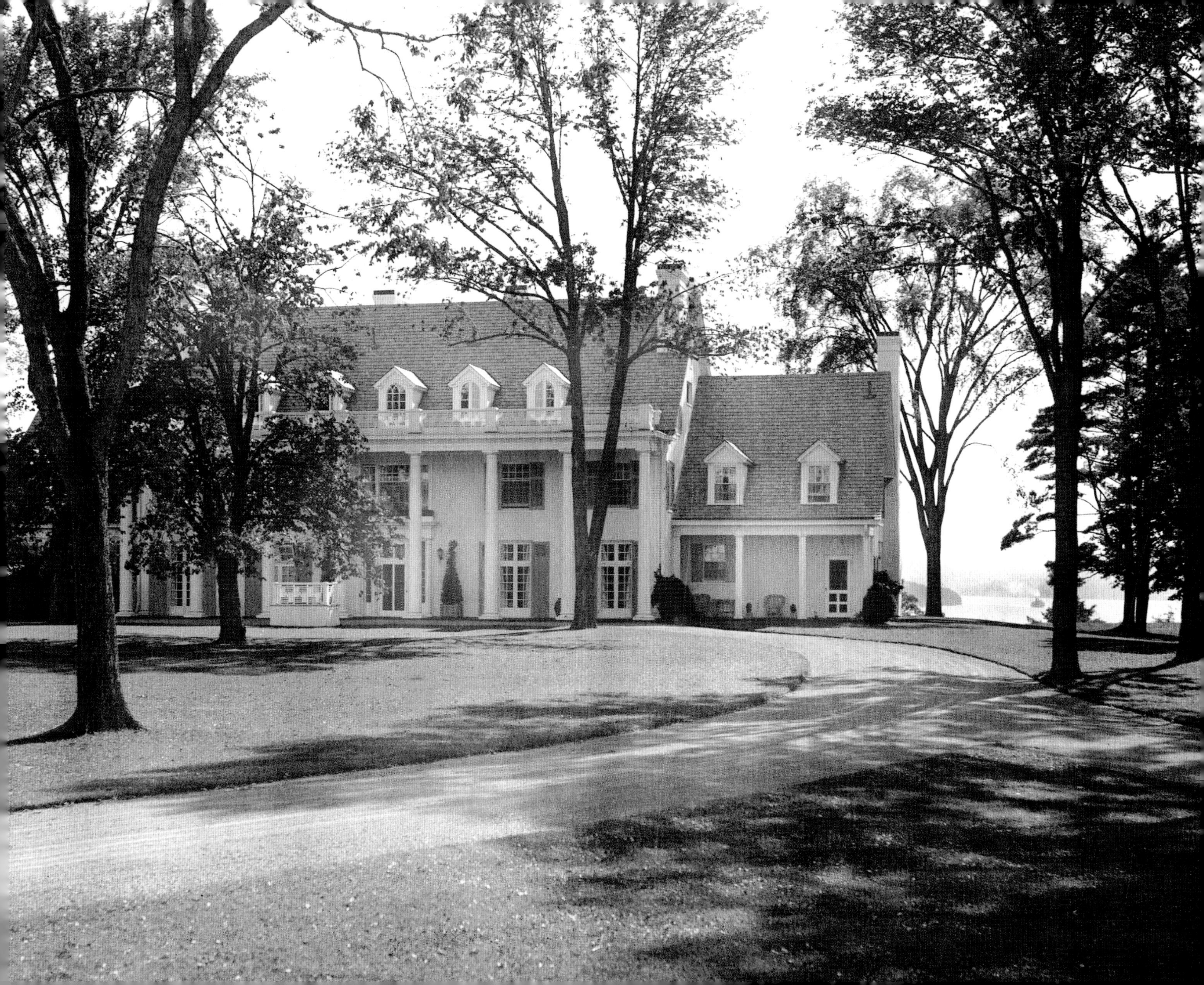

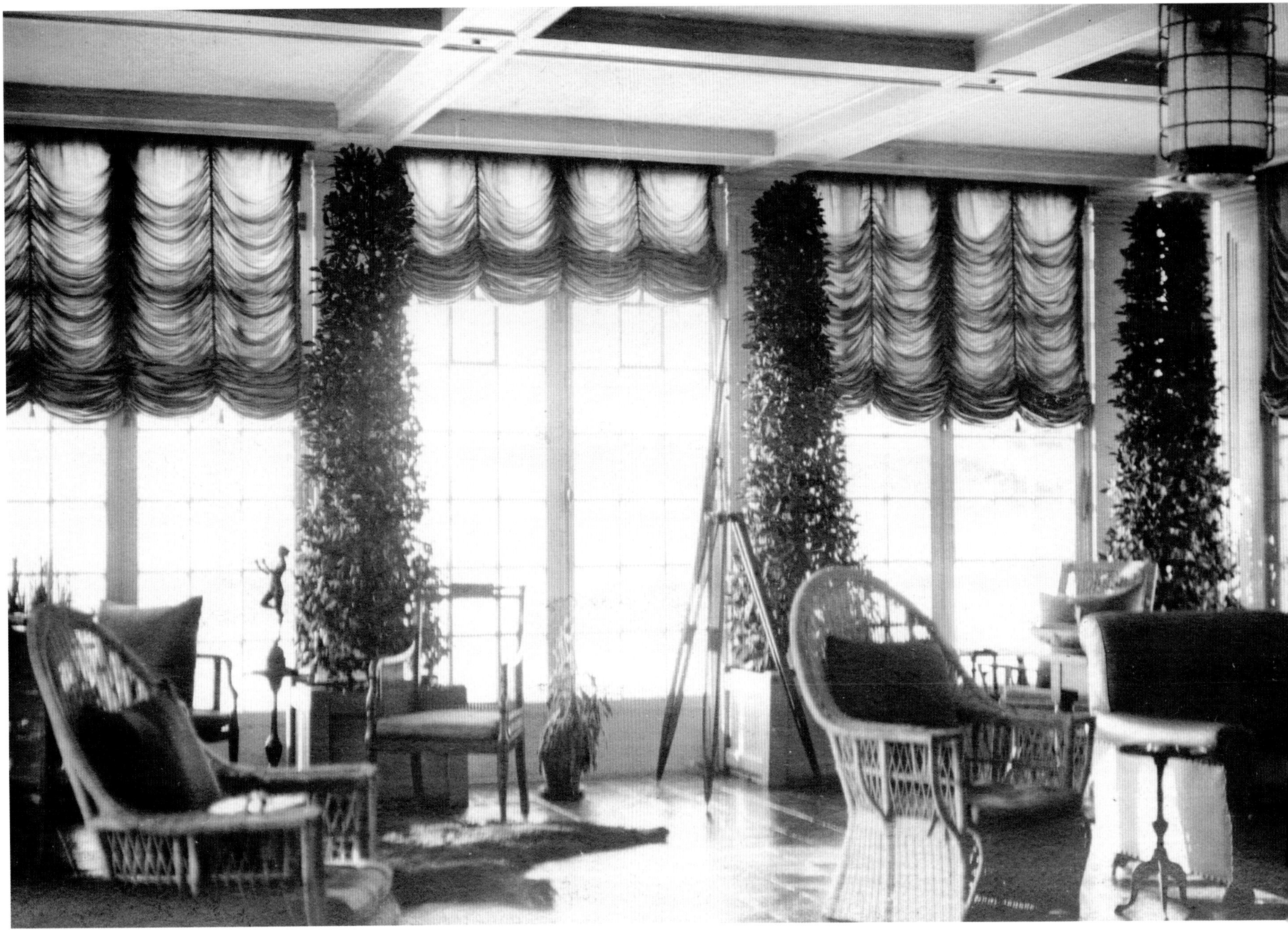

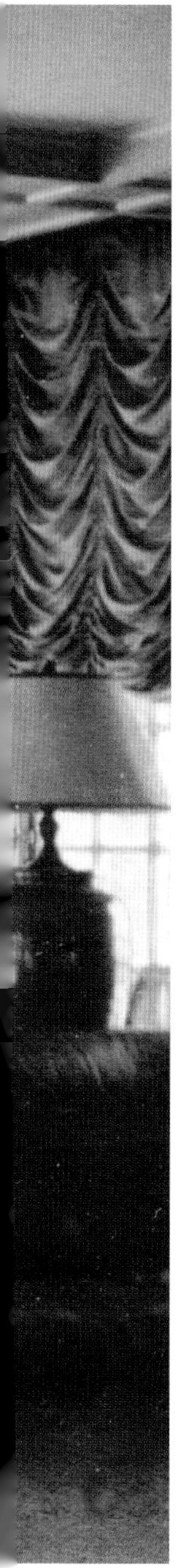

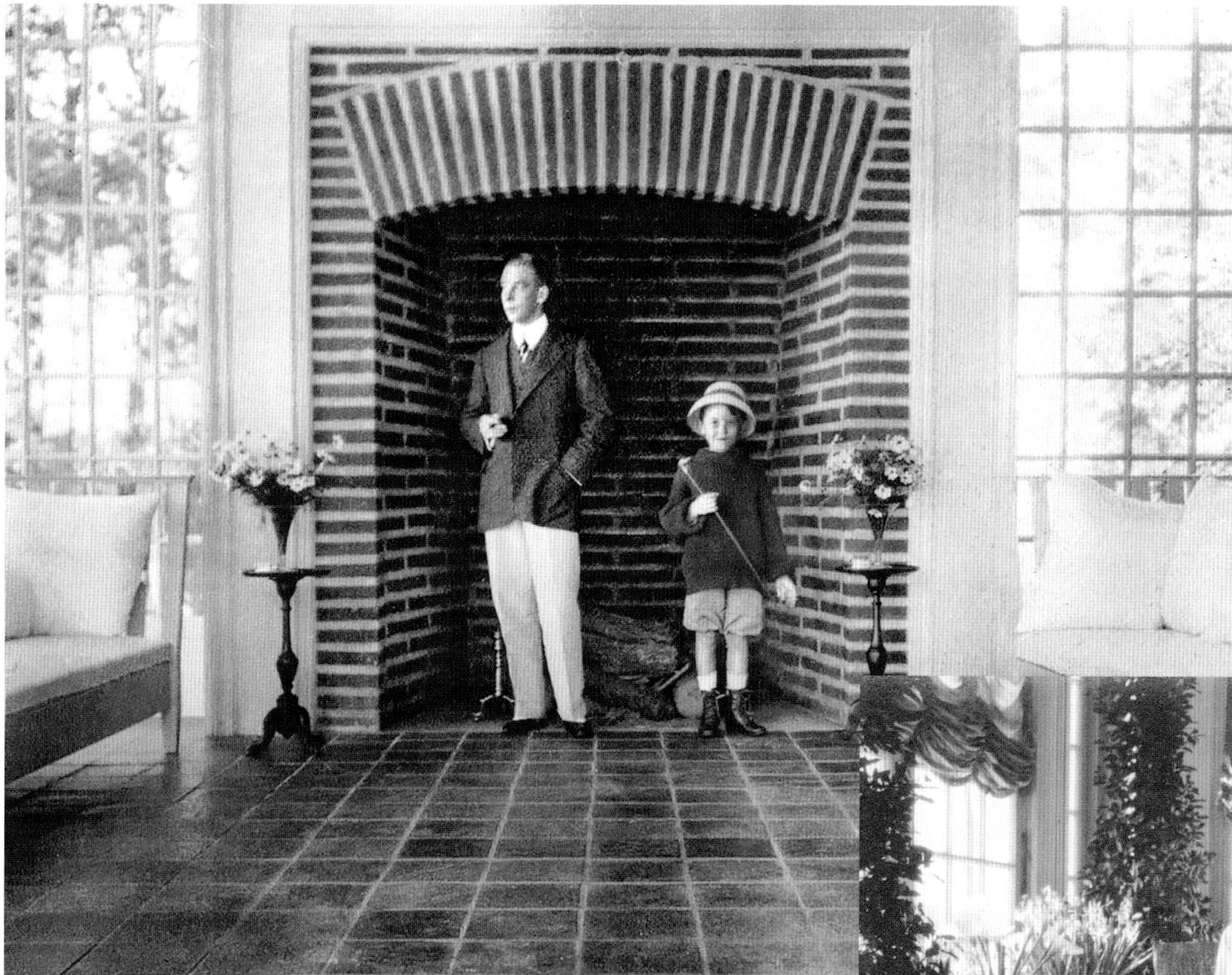

LEFT Harrie T. Lindeberg standing with Olin Dows in the large brick loggia fireplace in 1910.

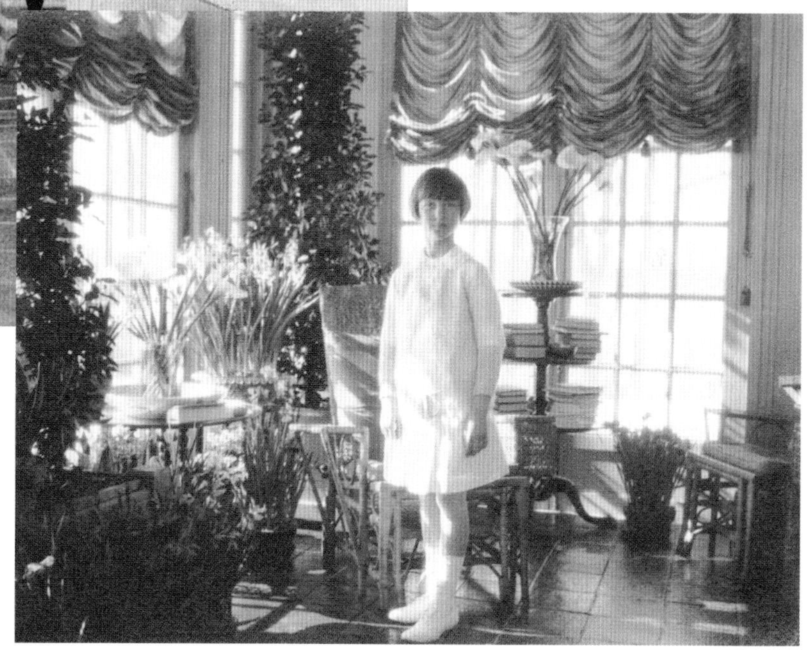

BELOW Margaret Dows among vases of fresh cut flowers and potted plants in 1914. The room maintained a garden-like atmosphere throughout the year.

LEFT The family's favorite room, the loggia, in the winter of 1912. Located in the first-floor wing of the house, in summer its doors opened on to the back terrace, while in winter its potted topiary shrubs and glazed green tiles retained its feeling of lushness.

BELOW A guest mixes a cocktail in Tracy's office on the main floor of the house, 1912. Tracy, in 1929, was elected as a director of the New York division of the Association Against the Prohibition Amendment.

OPPOSITE Tracy in front of the staircase in the entrance hall, 1926. Some of Lindeberg's designs included the nickel sconces and crystal newel post. Tracy's collection of etchings are seen displayed on the walls in both photographs.

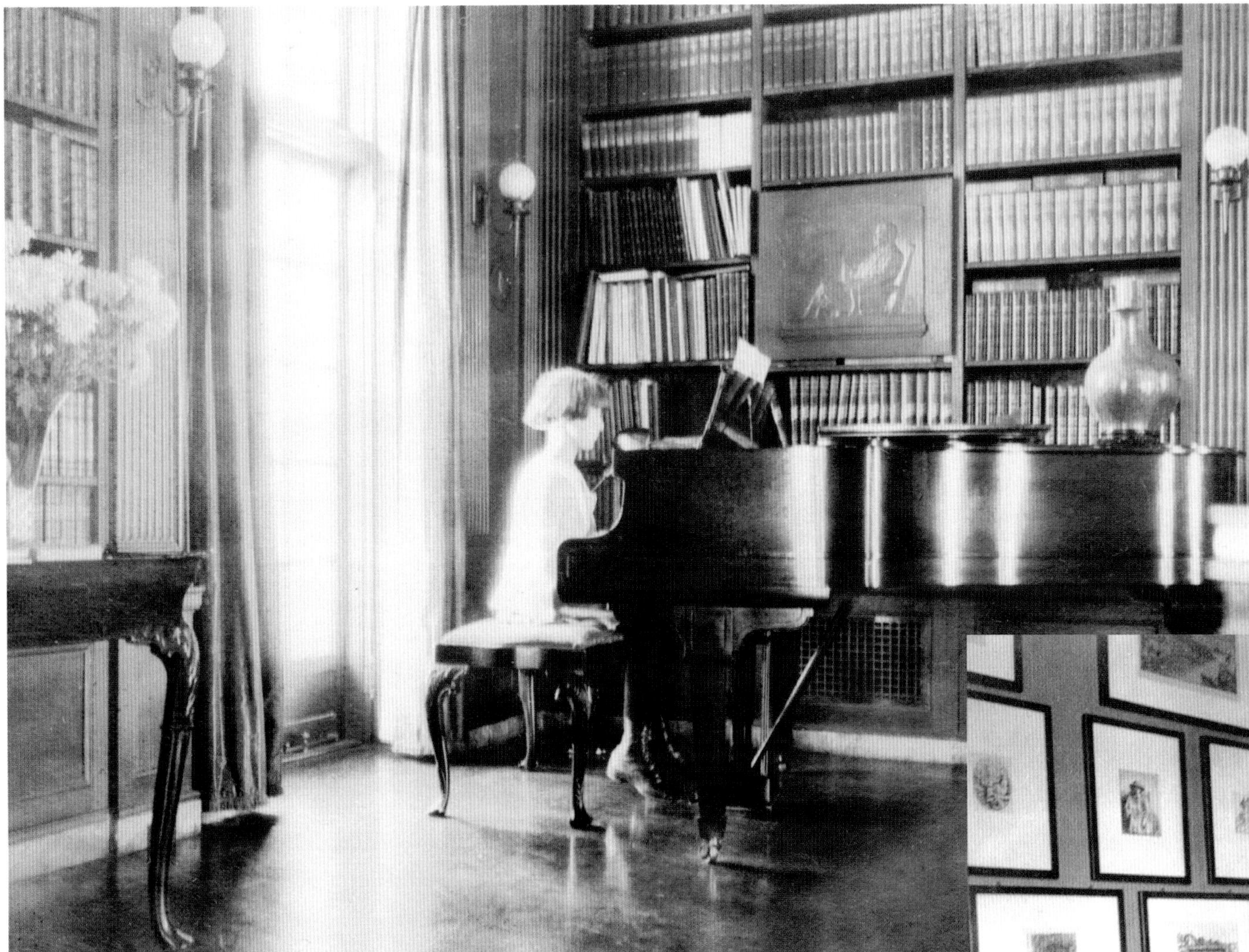

ABOVE Eight-year-old Margaret plays the piano in the living room. The room was paneled in English oak with recessed bookshelves and an intricately molded ceiling. The bronze bas-relief portrait of Stephen Henry Olin hanging on the bookshelves was designed by the noted American sculptor Henry Hering in 1909.

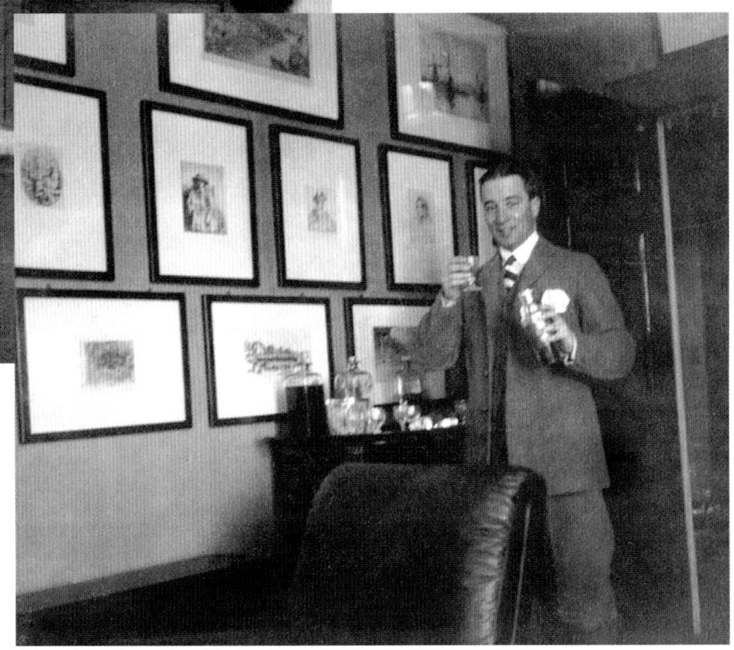

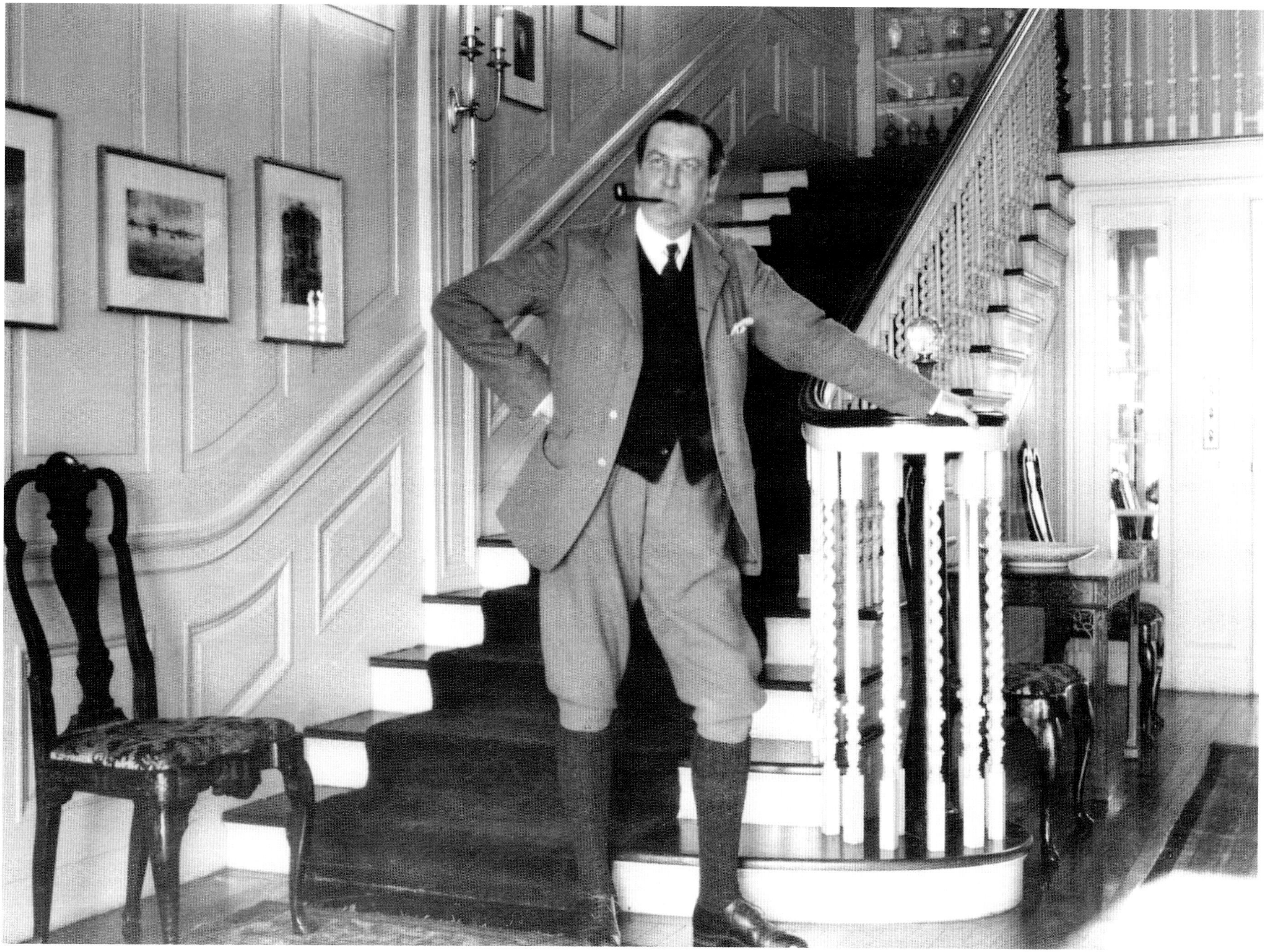

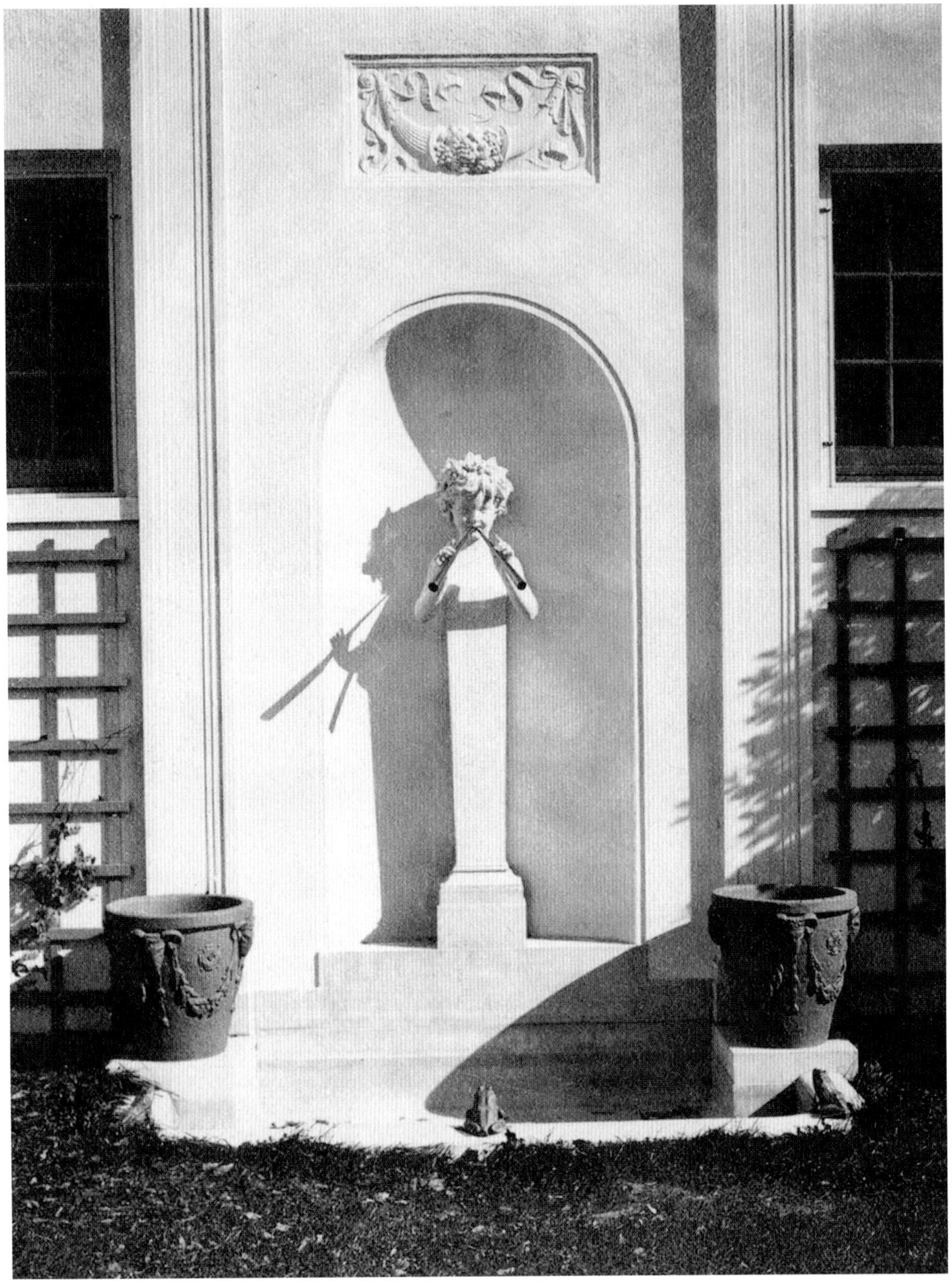

LEFT Tracy hired Henry Hering, best known for his sculptural and architectural work, to design the wall fountain on the back terrace. It featured a Pan-like cherub playing flutes above a basin into which water streamed from the mouths of three bronze frogs. Hering had been a student of Augustus Saint-Gaudens at Cooper Union, whom he also assisted, and studied at the Art Students League of New York and the École des Beaux-Arts in Paris. His studio in New York City was heavily damaged in 1945 after an American B-25 military plane, disoriented by dense fog, crashed into the Empire State Building. One engine, ripped from its wing, landed in Hering's penthouse studio nearby, setting it on fire and destroying much of his important work.

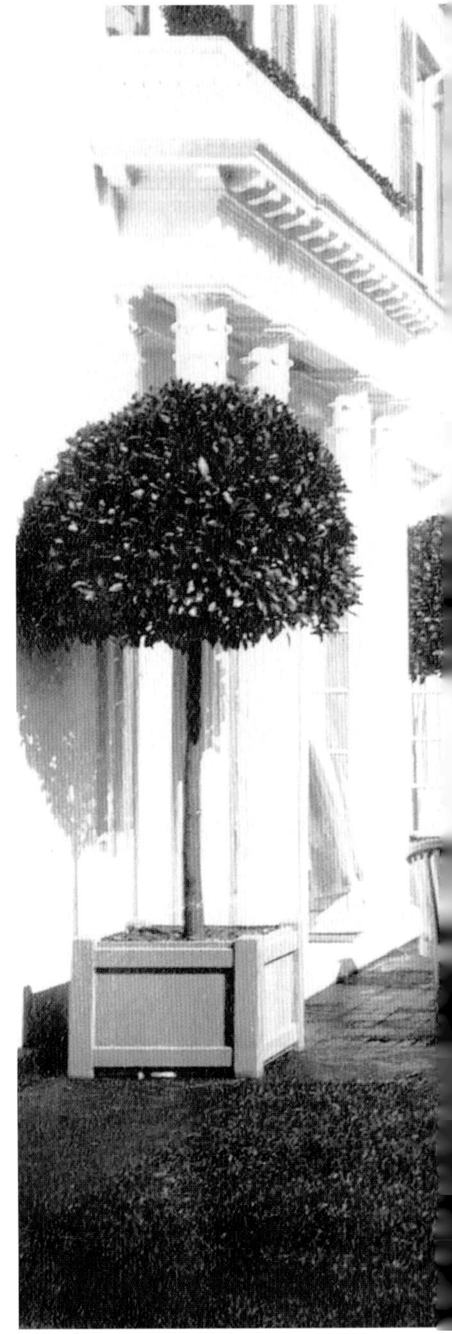

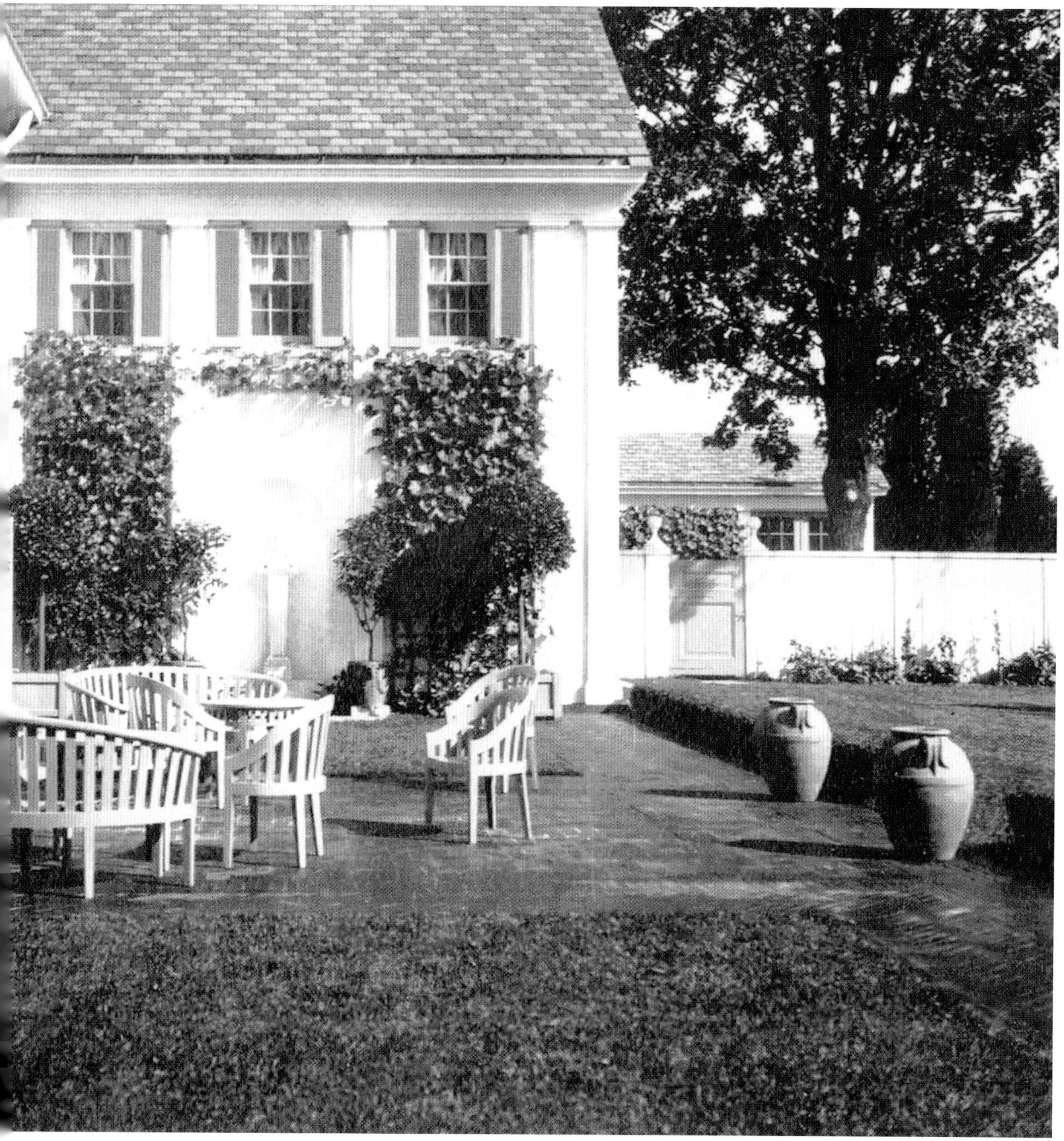

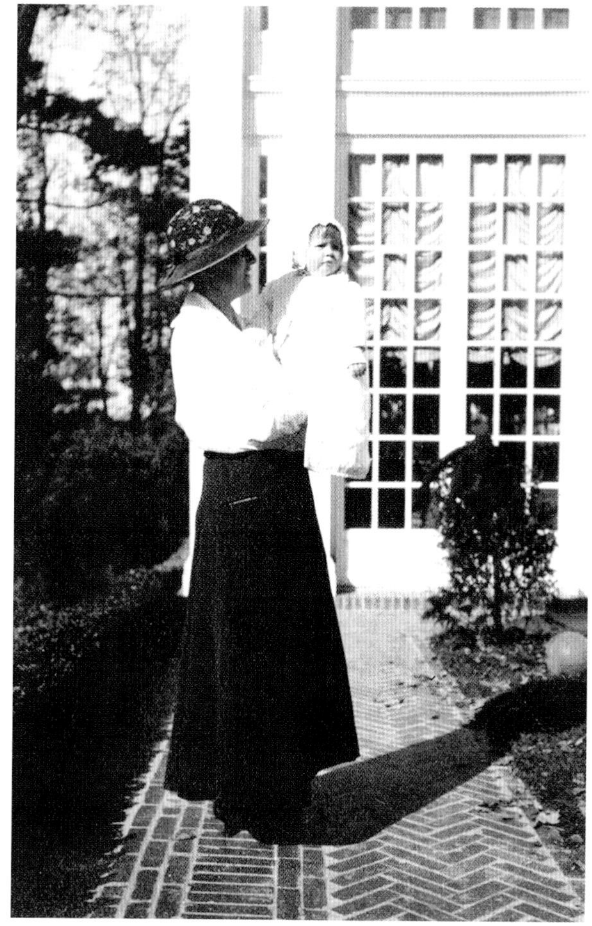

ABOVE Alice holding her third child, one-year-old Deborah (known as Deb), on the terrace's herringbone-patterned brick walkway, 1915.

LEFT The terrace was a pleasant, informal space for entertaining. The urns and exquisite furniture were complemented by the ivy growing up the latticework and the topiary bay trees planted in decorative wooden containers.

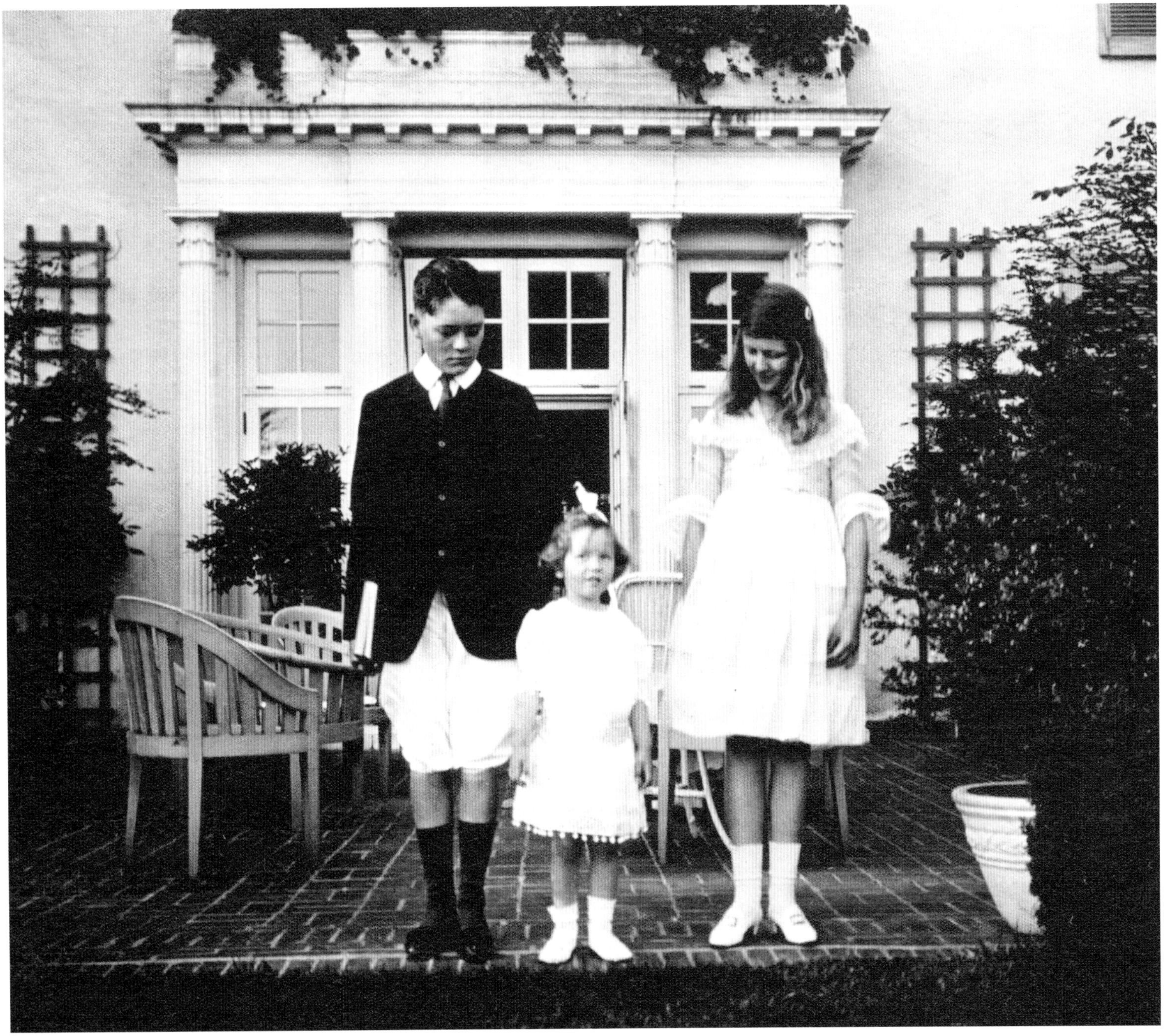

LEFT The Dows children dressed for an occasion in 1917. Olin was thirteen, Margaret eleven, and Deb three.

OPPOSITE The family being served on the terrace in the spring of 1917. Tracy and Alice would often have guests drop by for afternoon tea, a social event popular with the upper class.

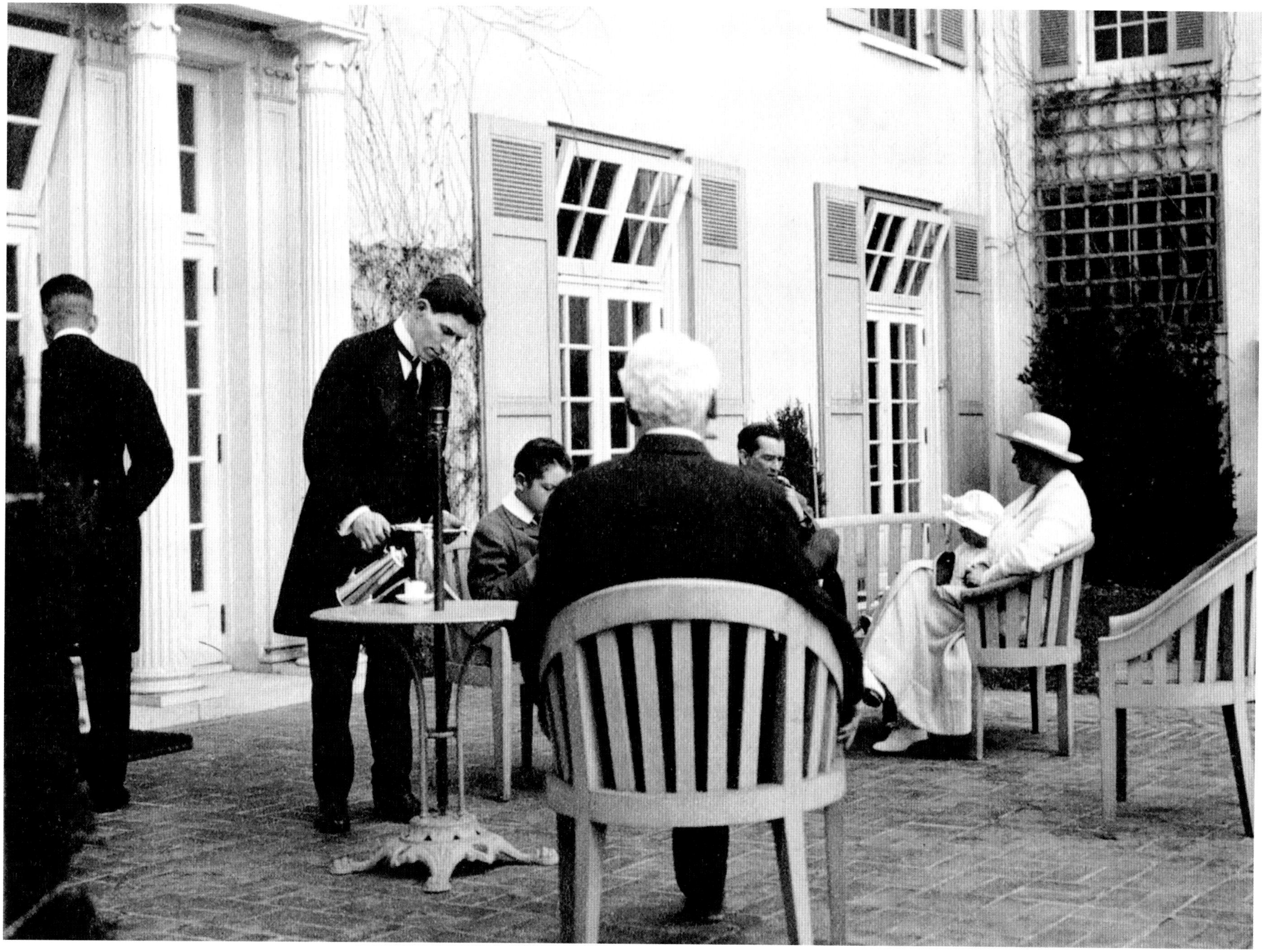

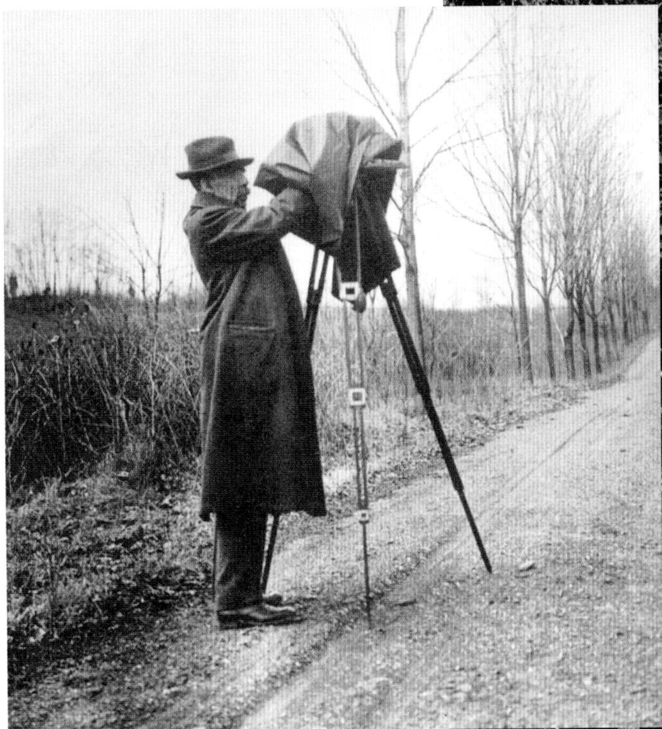

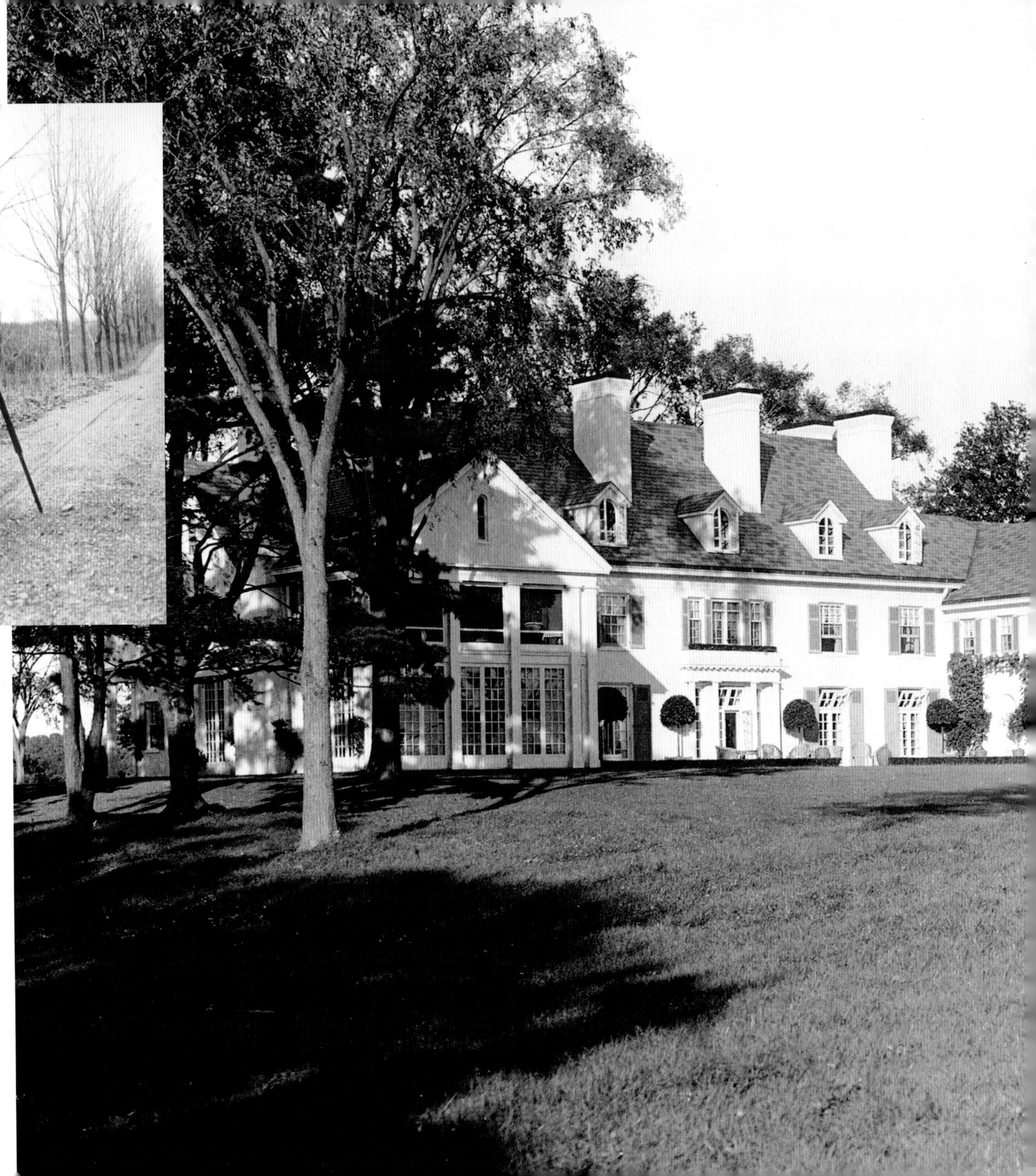

ABOVE Harry Coutant at Foxhollow Farm in 1919. An established photographer who had mastered the technique of chiaroscuro, Coutant was hired to take pictures of the main house and other buildings on the property. His photograph of the Dowses' terrace wall fountain appeared on the cover of the September 1920 issue of *Photo-Era*. A fan of natural light, Coutant had patiently waited for the sunlight to be at just the right angle before taking the shot.

RIGHT A 1916 photograph by Coutant shows the imposing scale and beauty of the house as seen from the back.

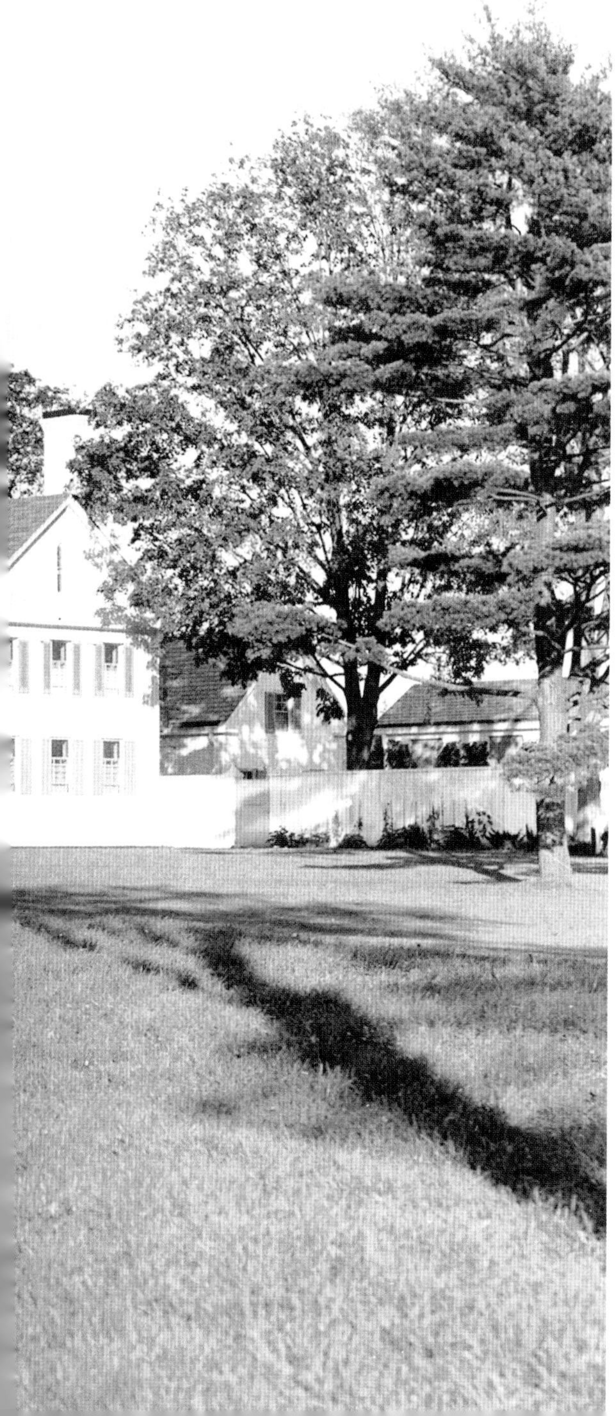

BELOW Margaret sitting on a garden bench next to the walled courtyard of the house, summer 1911.

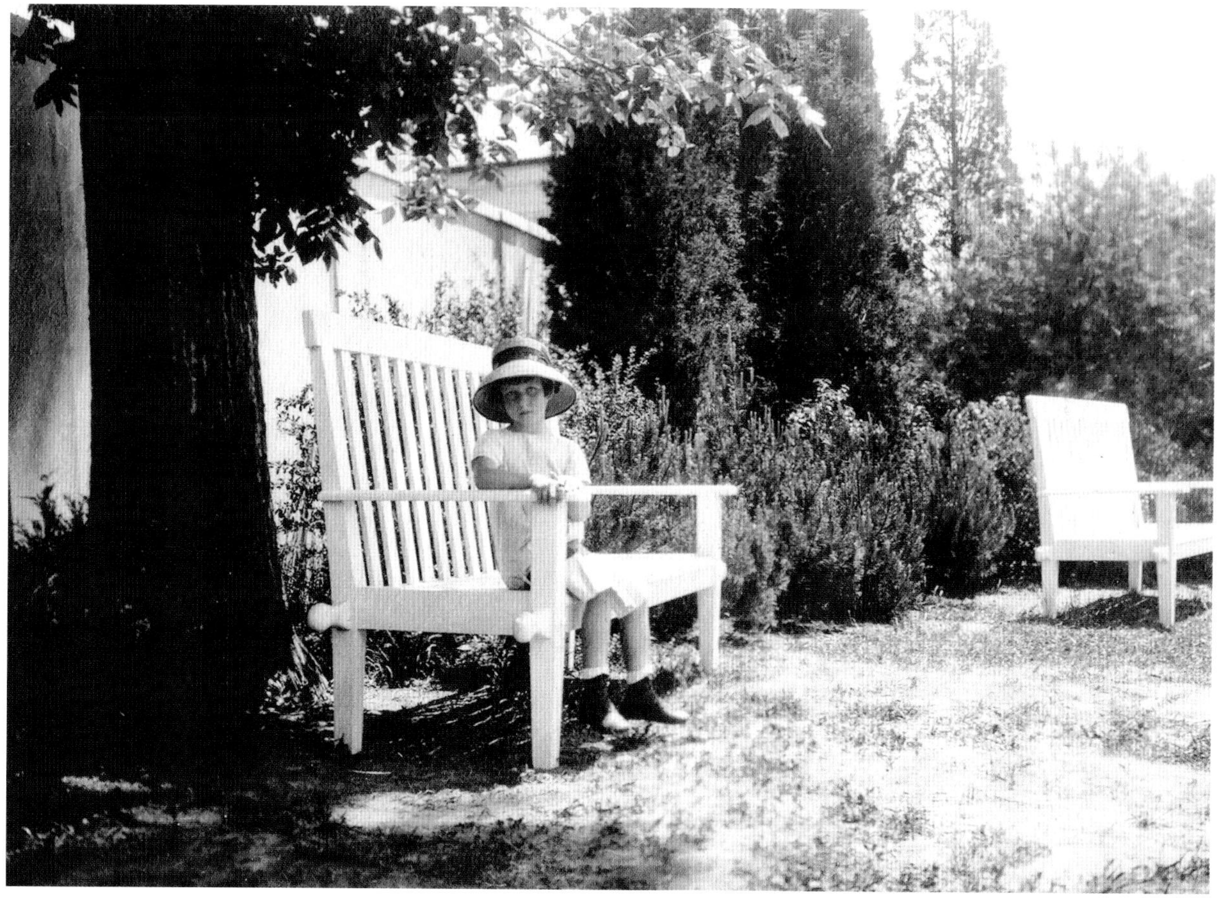

"Foxhollow is a wonderful embodiment of the spirit of our American Renaissance in a country house meeting the more complex needs of the twentieth century."

Country Life in America, February 1916

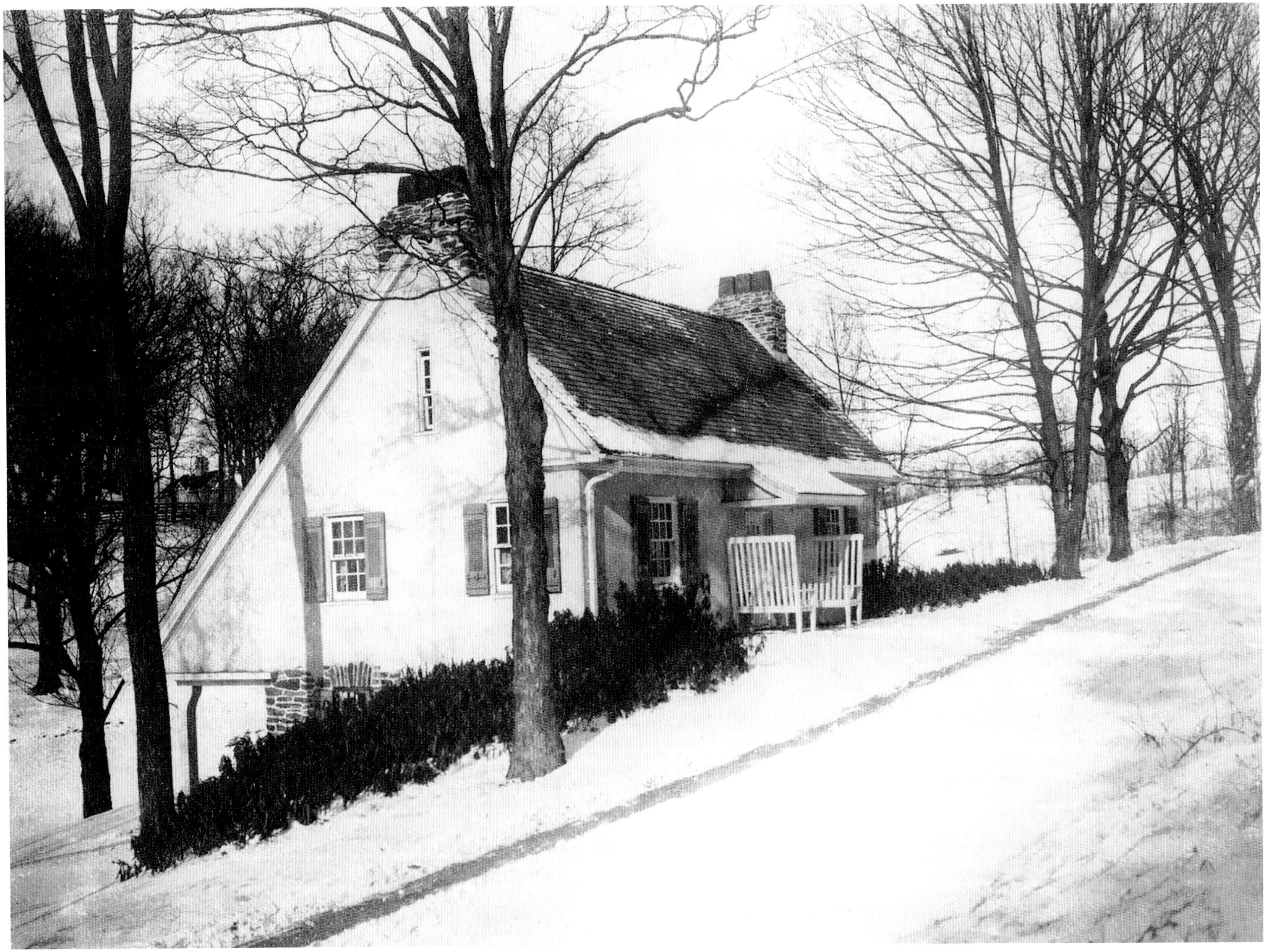

OPPOSITE The Gate Lodge, winter 1912. Designed in the estate's Colonial Revival style in stone and stucco by Lindeberg in 1910, the lodge was sited at the rear entrance of the Foxhollow Farm property at Vanderburgh Cove, where Landsman's Kill meets the Hudson River. In the late 1920s, the American author Thomas Wolfe, a Harvard classmate of Olin Dows, spent several summers at the lodge writing his classic novel, *Look Homeward, Angel.*

BELOW A serene view of the lodge in the summer of 1927 showing the original bridge on South Mill Road at Vanderburgh Cove. It was later replaced by a concrete version in 1939 by the Dutchess County Highway Department.

RIGHT Olin and Margaret, with matching hats, in a canoe on Landsman's Kill near the Gate Lodge in the summer of 1910.

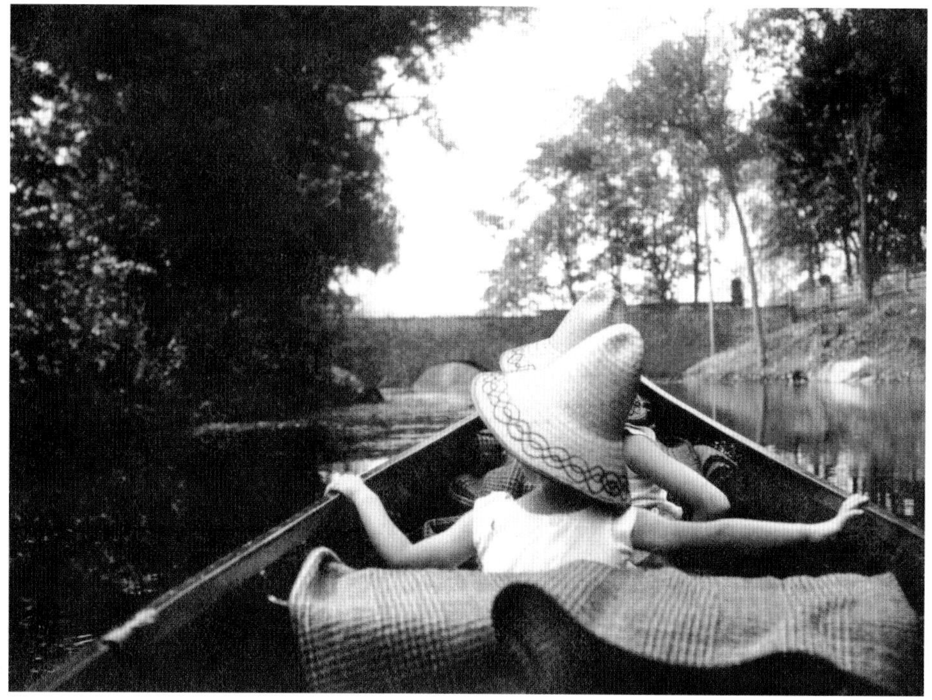

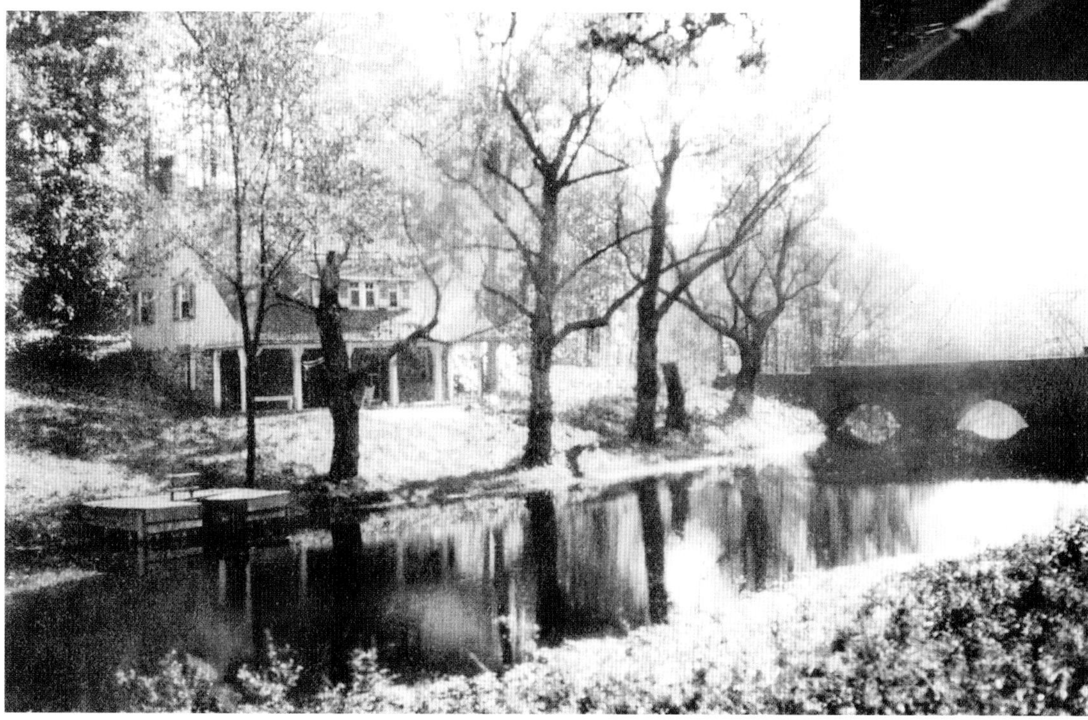

BELOW The waterfall under the South Mill Road bridge where Landsman's Kill flows into the marshes along the Hudson River. A grist mill once occupied this spot in the 1700s.

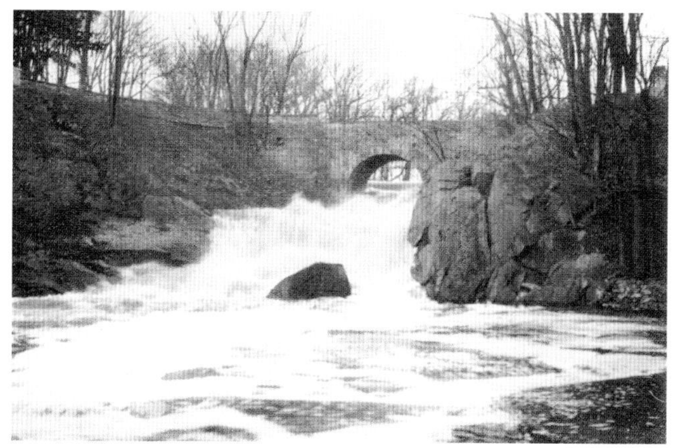

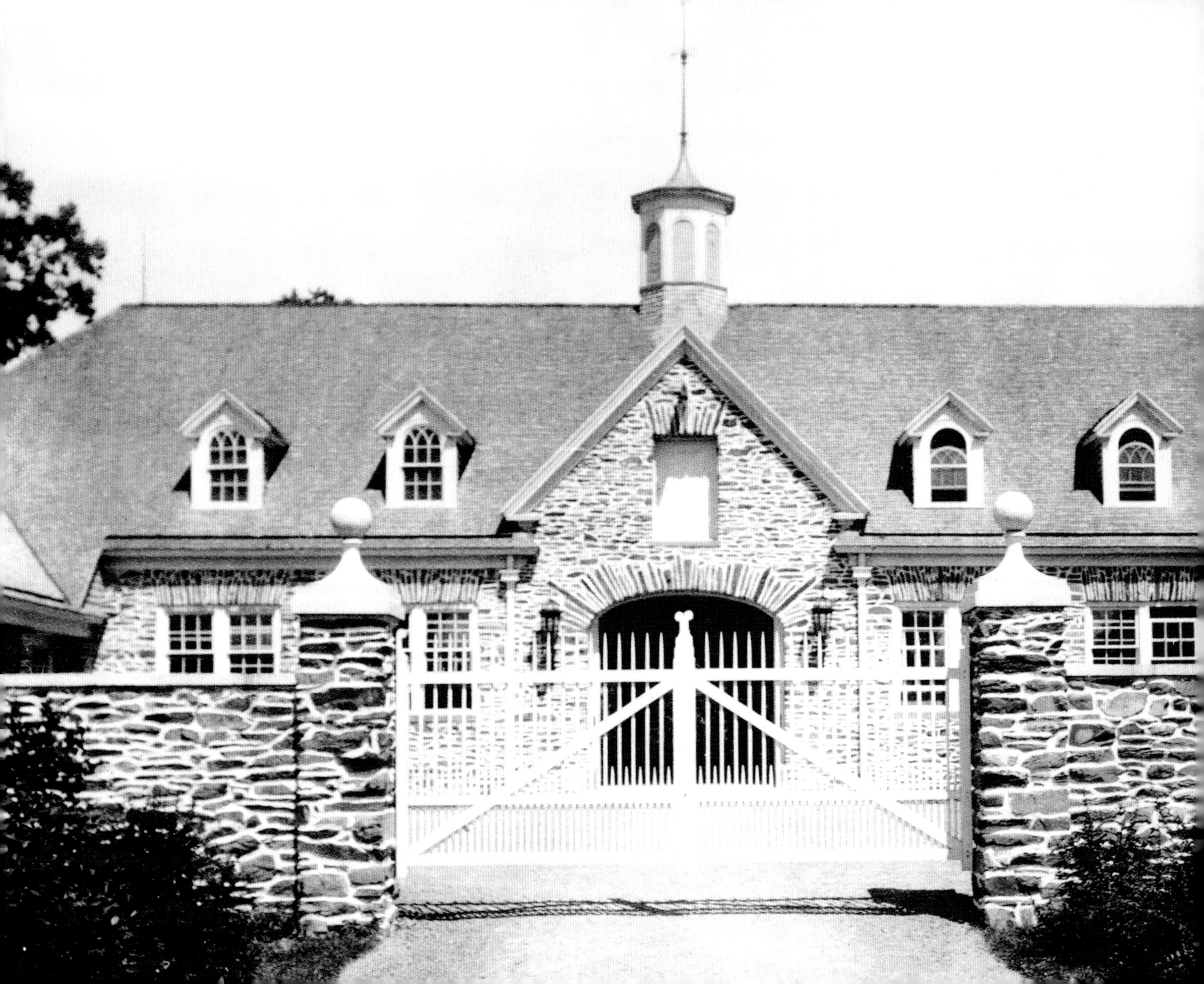

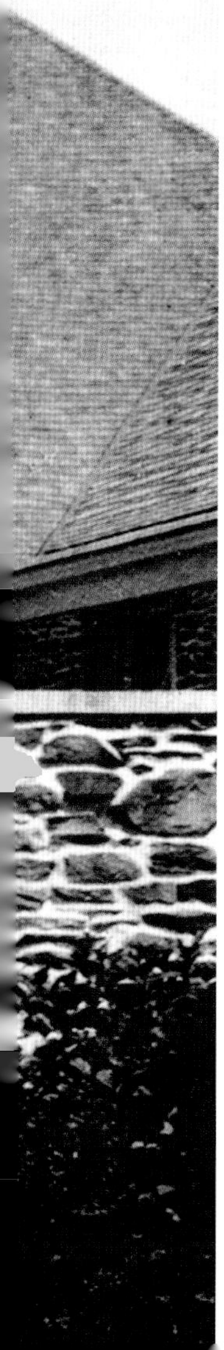

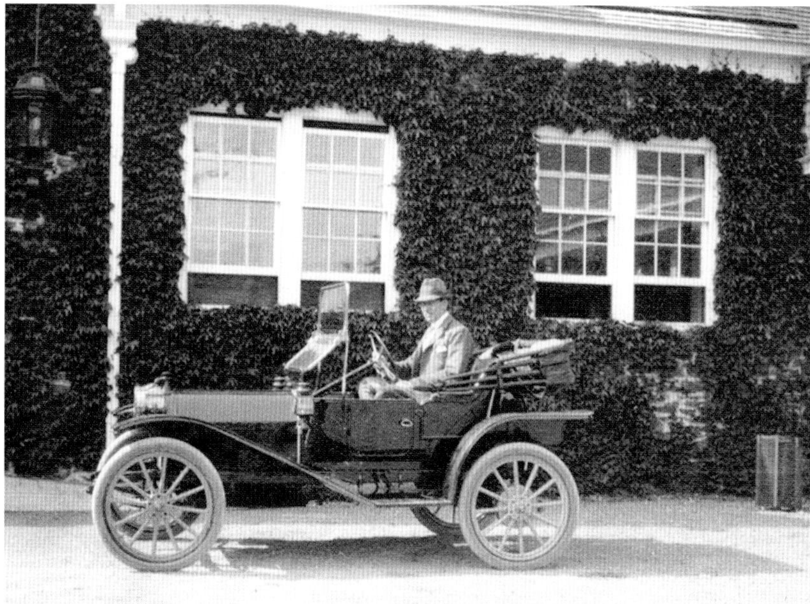

LEFT Tracy in his 1912 Hupmobile parked in front of the carriage house. He referred to it simply as "The Hup." Tracy enjoyed owning a variety of automobiles over the years and would often record the mileage and hours of travel in his diaries after motor trips.

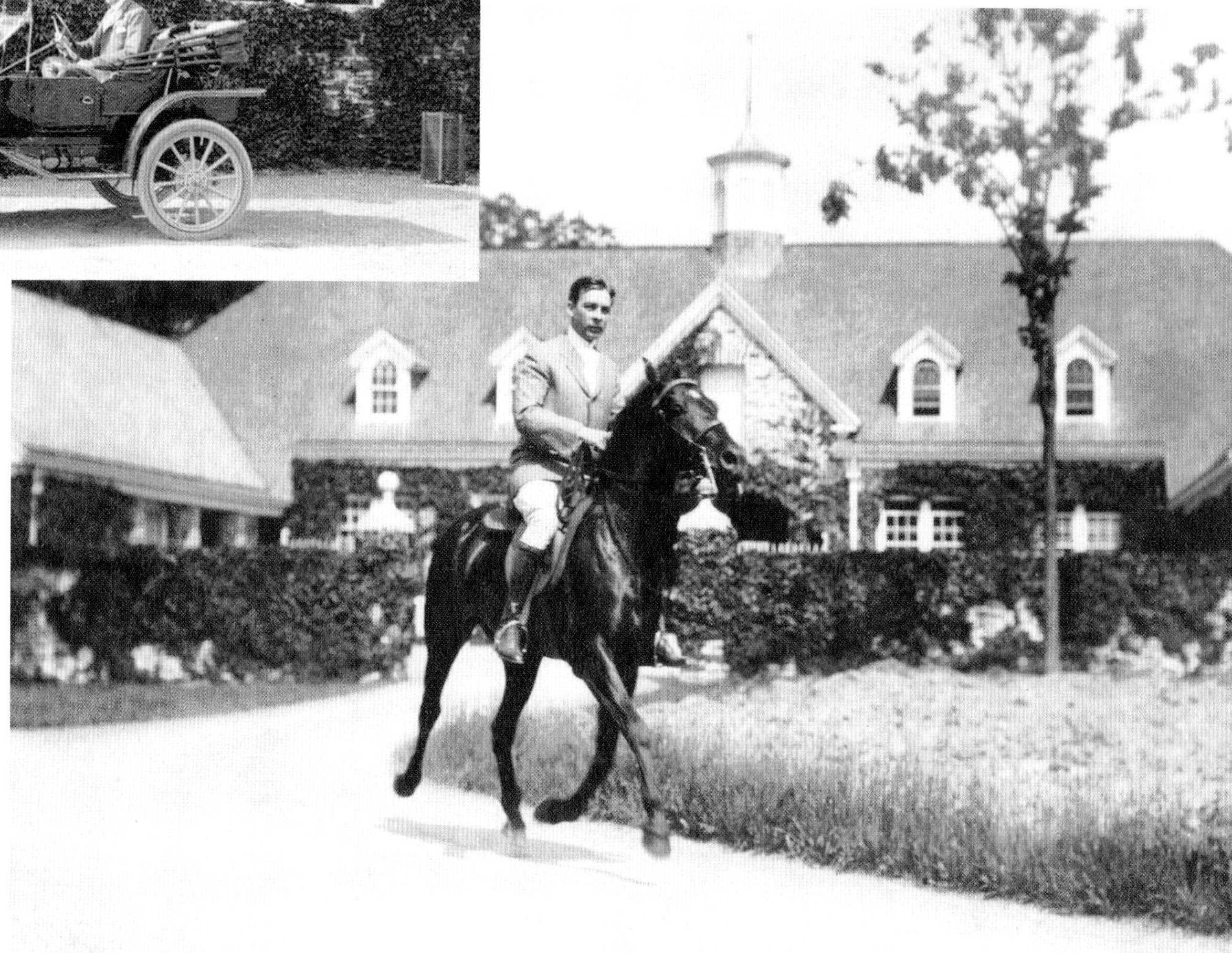

LEFT The carriage house and coachman's quarters were built in 1907. Lindeberg designed the beautiful fieldstone structure to have a walled courtyard with a large entrance at its center. The left side housed automobiles, the right side horses and carriages.

RIGHT The architect out for a ride in the summer of 1912. After the work on the estate was completed, Lindeberg remained a close friend of the Dows family and visited often. Tracy recorded in his 1910 diary that on the evening of May 7, he and Lindeberg stopped along the road from Poughkeepsie to Rhinebeck to witness Halley's Comet in the sky, the phenomenon that only happens every 76 years.

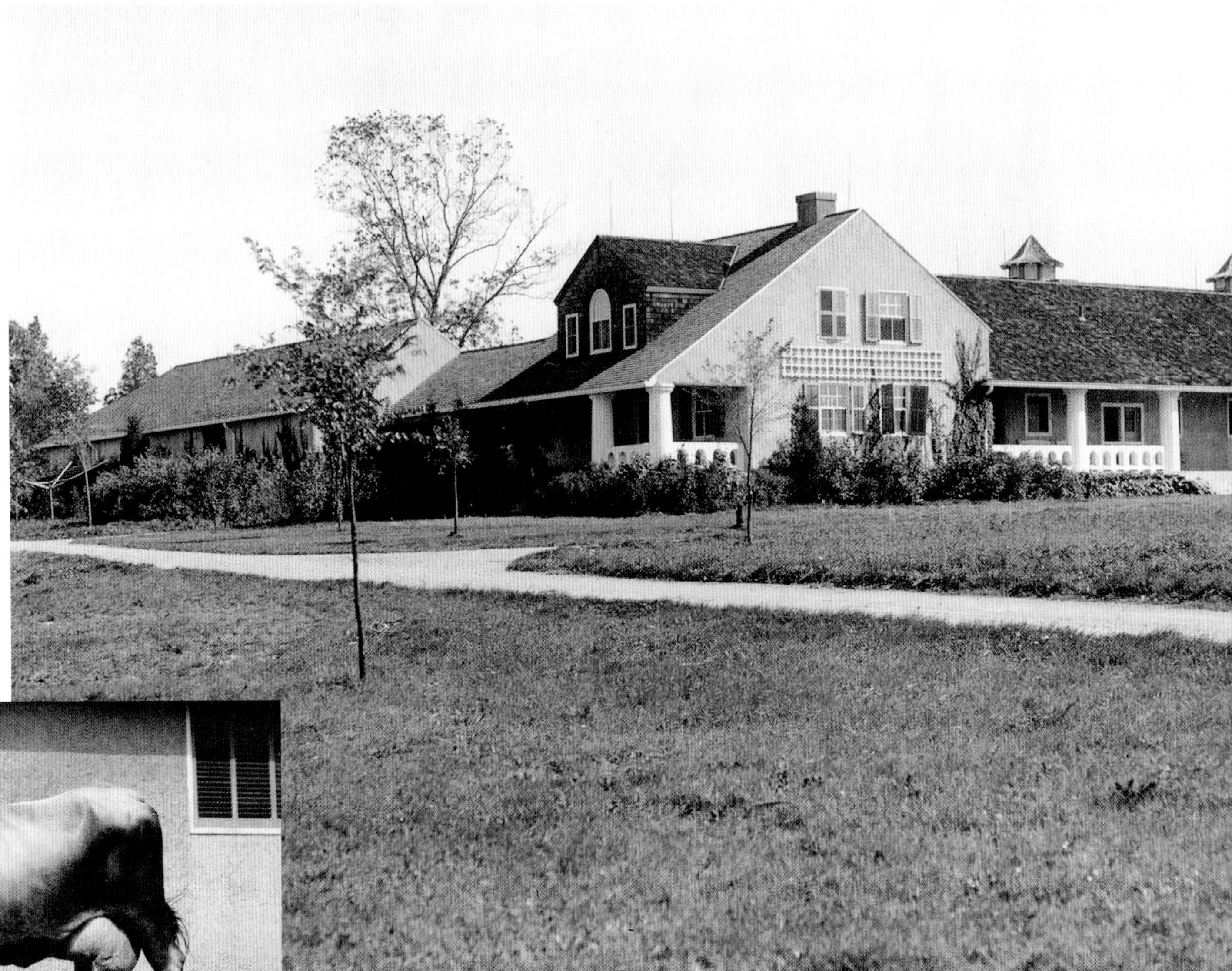

RIGHT A view of the barn complex, photographed by Harry Coutant in 1910. Completed in 1907, the interconnected buildings were designed by farm architects Edward Burnett and Alfred E. Hopkins. Edward was the son of Joseph Burnett, the prominent Massachusetts pharmacist who is credited with creating the first liquid vanilla extract. During the design stages, Burnett worked closely with J. C. Olmsted in the planning of the structure and its relationship with the landscaping. The complex included a residence and office for the farm manager, as well as barns for the animals. The *New York Times* reported that in August 1913 a fire broke out in the hay barn. Seven of the buildings were damaged but all the animals, some of which were well-known blue-ribbon prizewinners, were rescued. The complete structure was never rebuilt.

BELOW One of Tracy's prized Brown Swiss cows outside the dairy area of the complex in 1912. He kept records of their weight as well as the percentages of milk and butter produced by each.

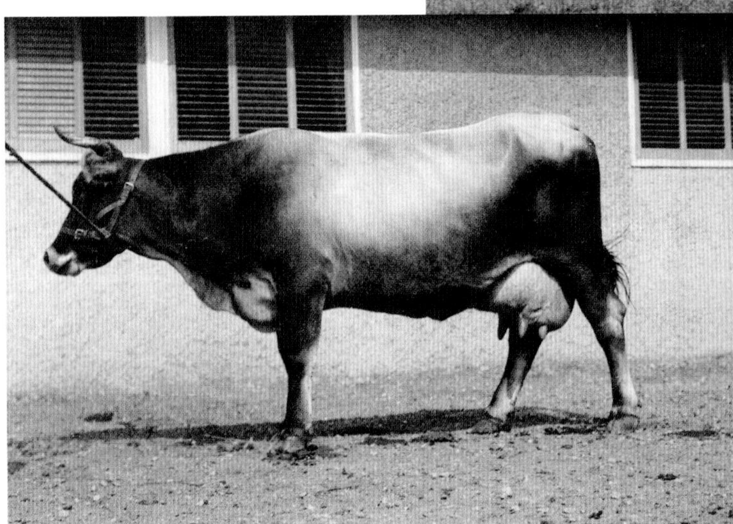

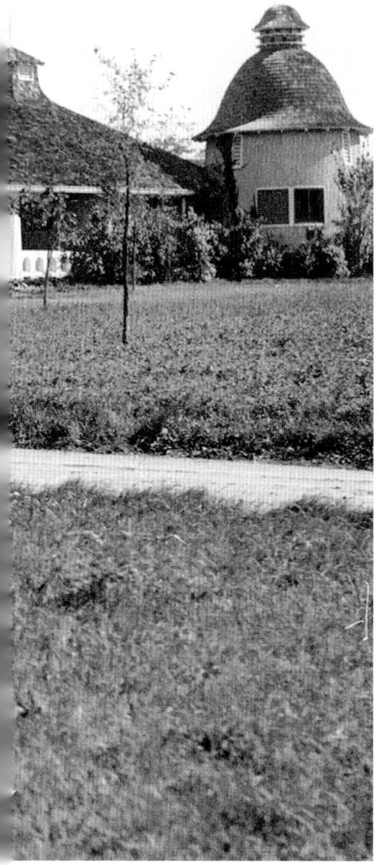

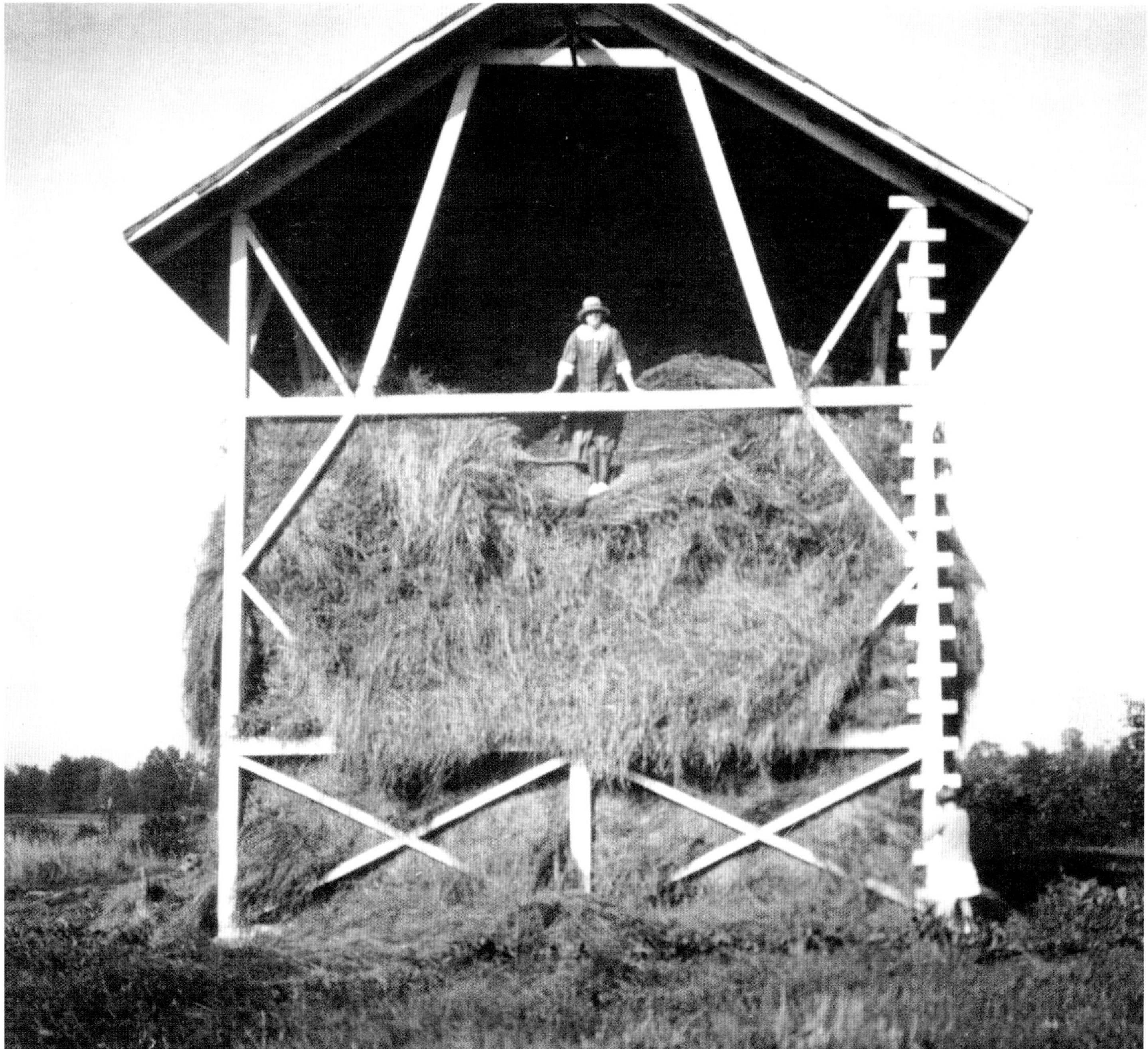

RIGHT Margaret and Deb having fun in the hay storage loft out in the fields, 1920. Even this simple building had a pleasing architectural style.

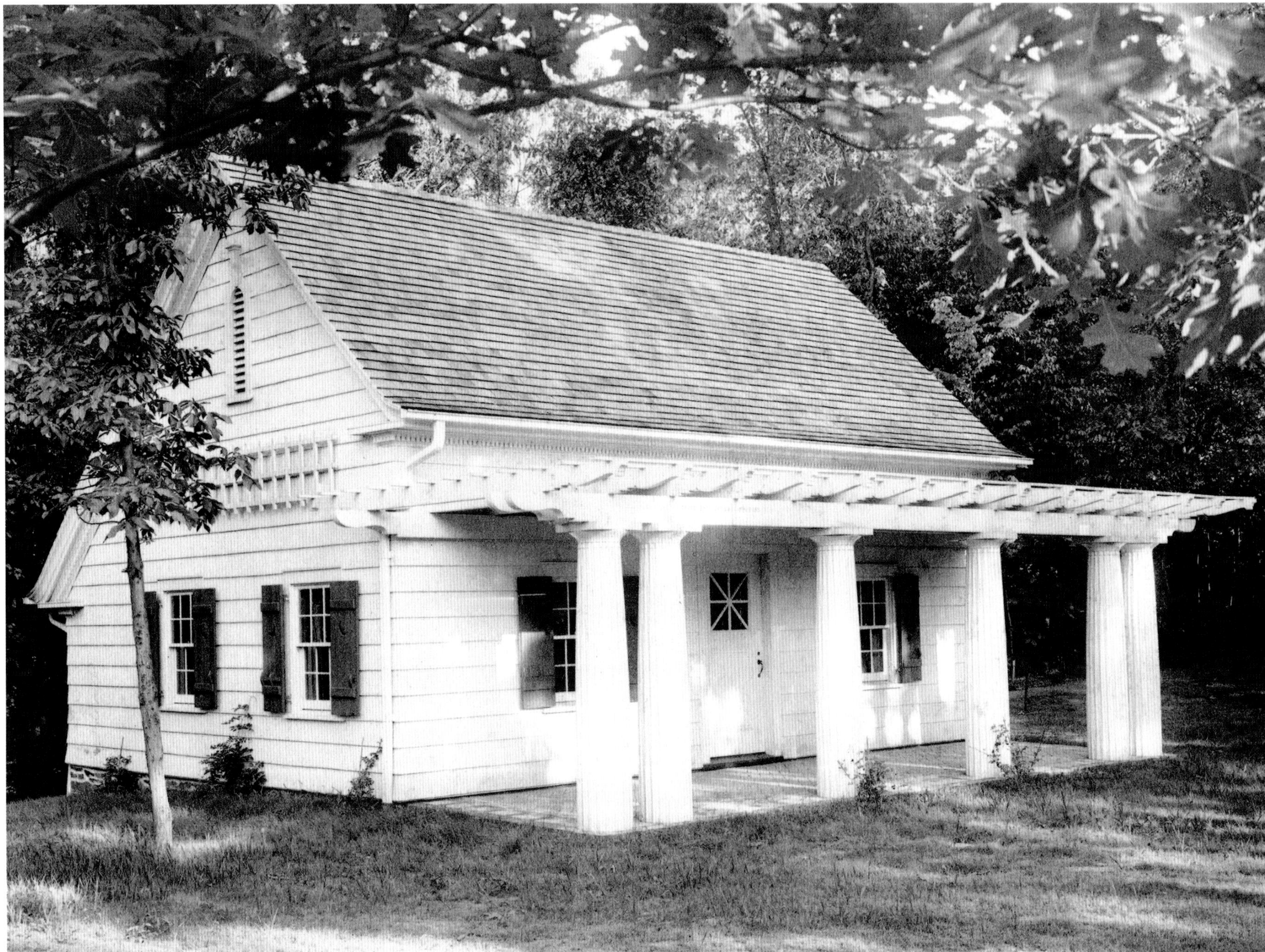

OPPOSITE The children's playhouse captured by New York City photographer De W. C. Ward in 1909. Built the previous year, Lindeberg designed it as a scaled-down version of a country cottage. Tracy and Alice named it Fallsburg, after the beautiful waterfalls spanned by the nearby Fallsburg Bridge.

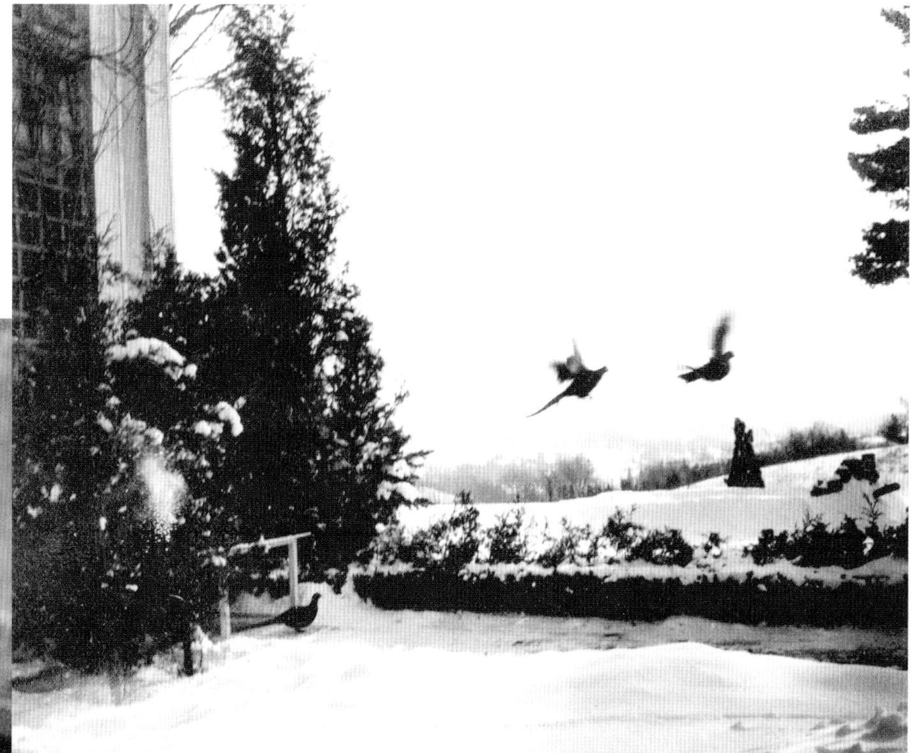

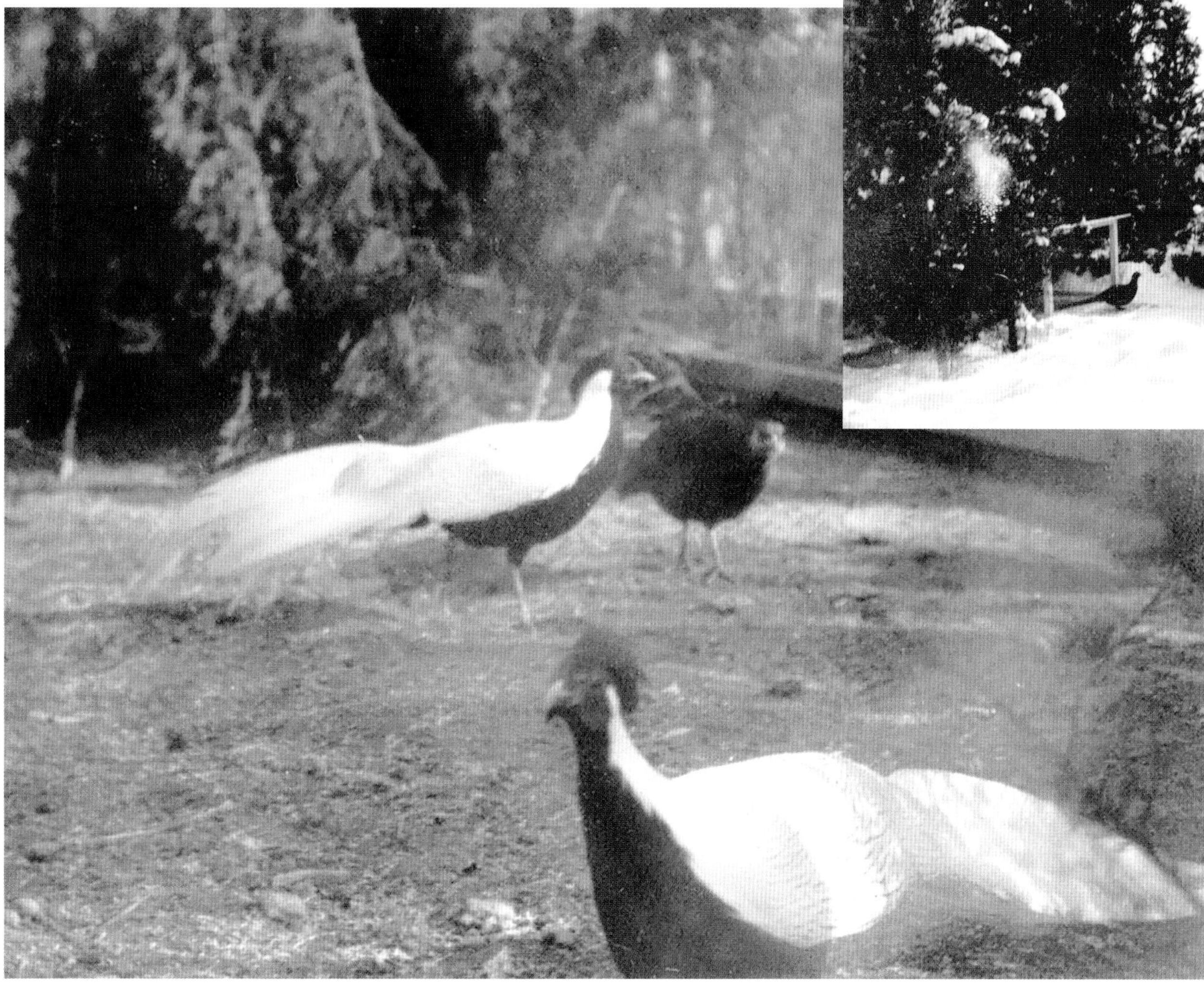

ABOVE Ring-necked Pheasants in flight, seen from the terrace on a snowy December day, 1916. Tracy constructed a pheasantry on the Foxhollow Farm property where he raised them, along with other birds such as Hungarian Partridges and Ruffed Grouse, as a hobby. He was an active member of the Rhinebeck Bird Club, which was founded in 1914 by his good friend, Maunsell Crosby.

LEFT Silver Pheasants in the pheasantry. A breed that originated in China, they were raised in the United States and Europe as ornamental birds.

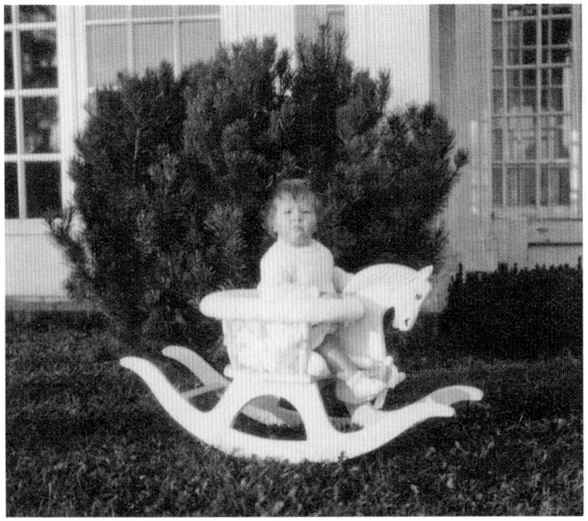

LEFT Deb Dows on a rocking horse on her first birthday, 1915. Horses would become a lifelong passion.

BELOW Five-year-old Deb takes her doll for a ride on a wooden horse, 1919.

RIGHT Deb with her first horse, a Hackney mare, in front of the coachman's quarters, 1926. The horse is wearing a cooler, which is designed to help keep it dry after a workout and prevent chills.

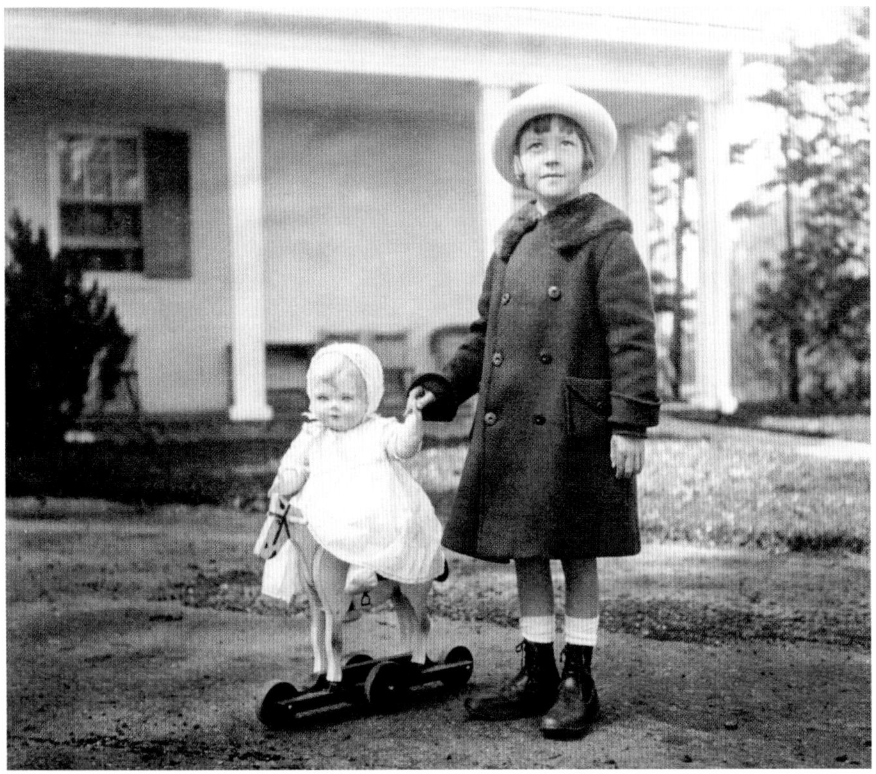

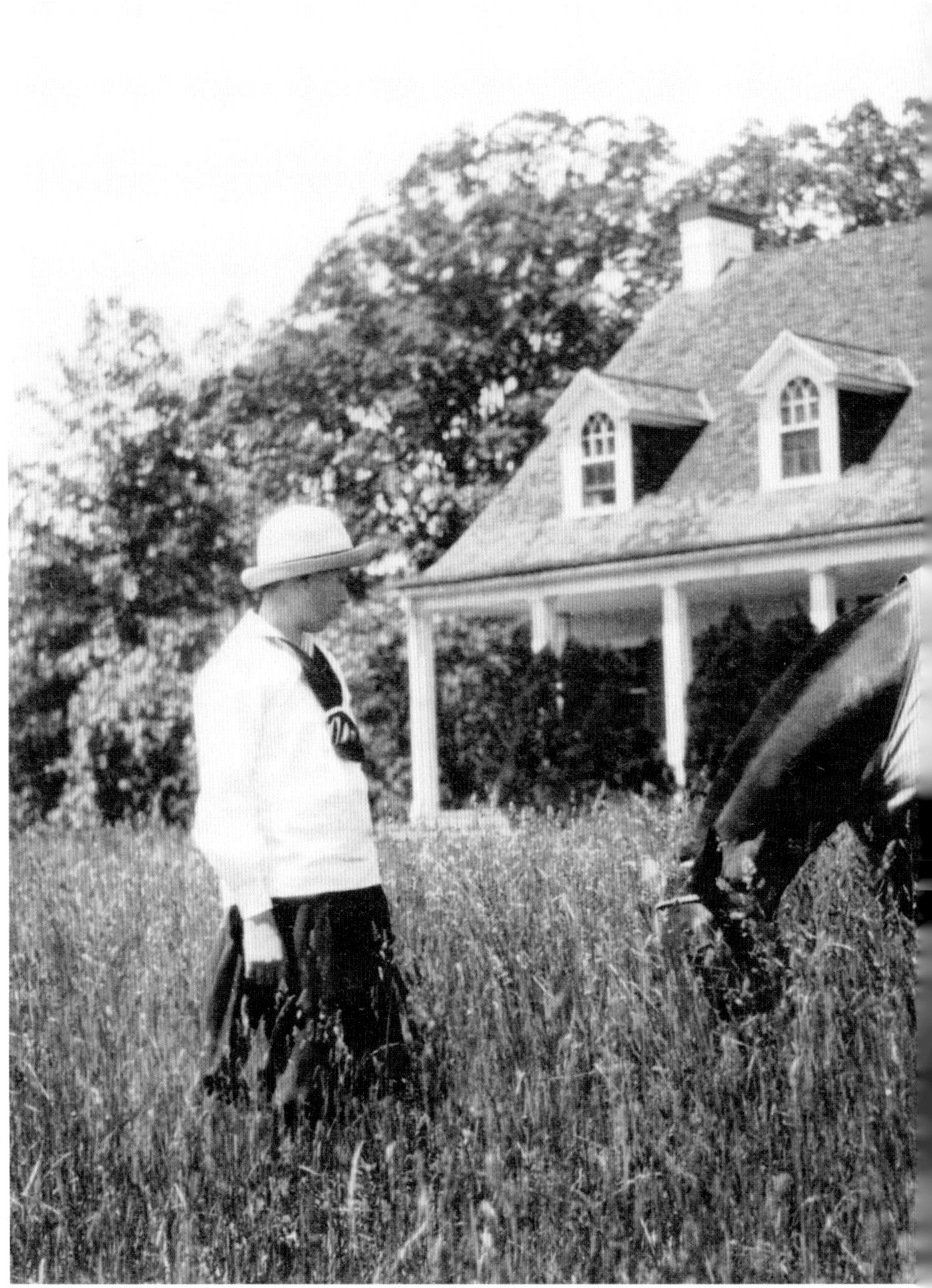

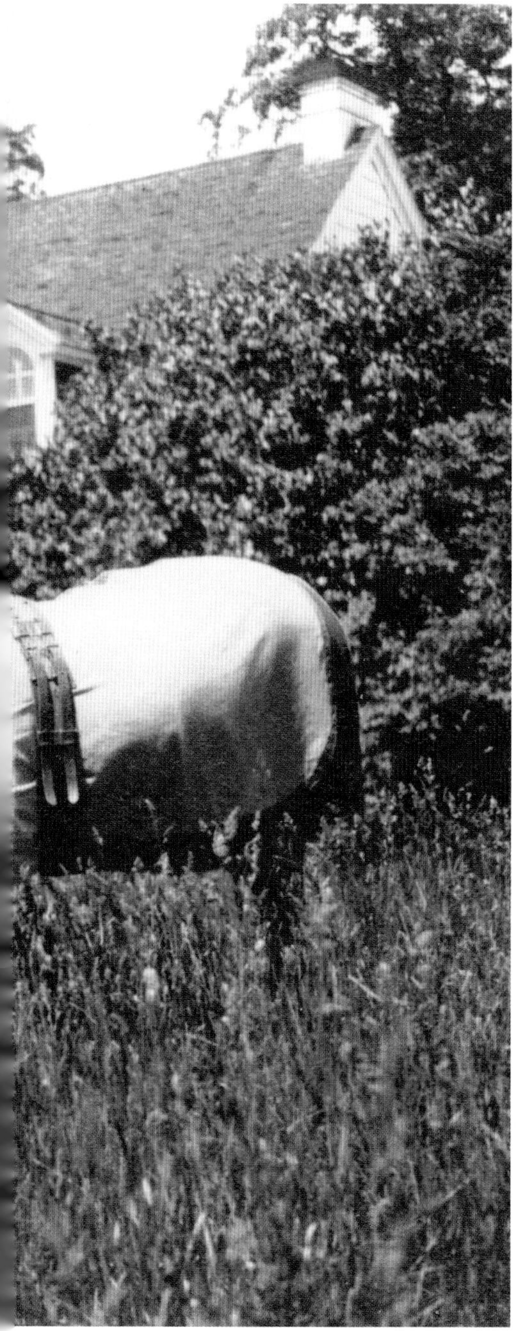

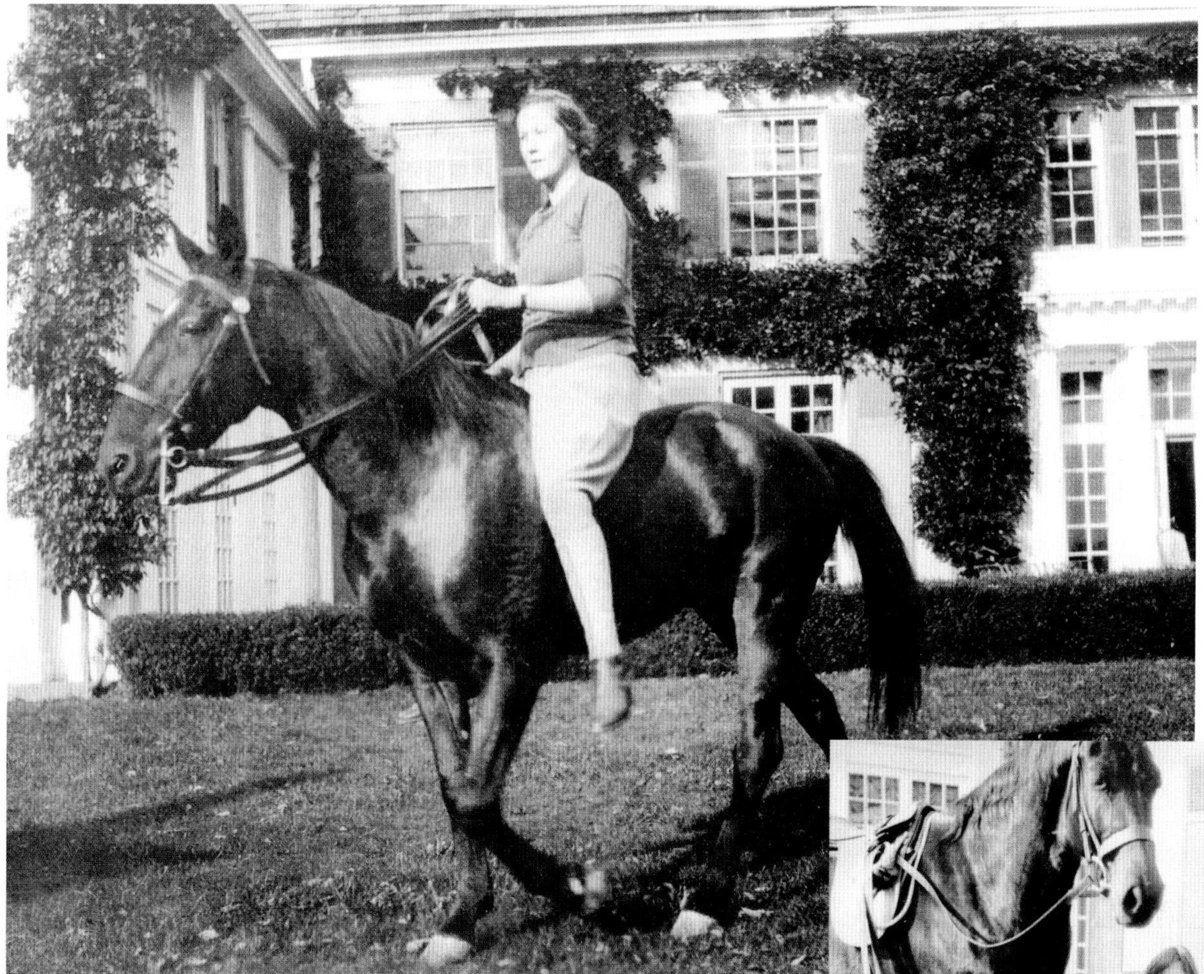

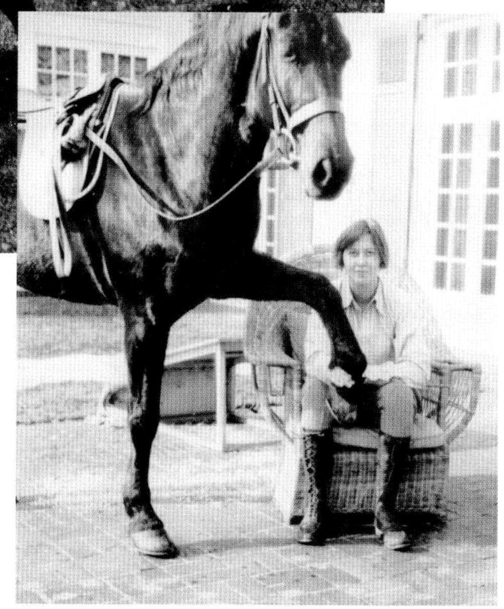

ABOVE Riding along the back lawn on her Standardbred in the fall of 1929. By this time, Deb had become an expert horsewoman.

RIGHT Deb demonstrates training techniques on the terrace, 1930. This was the last year the family lived at Foxhollow Farm.

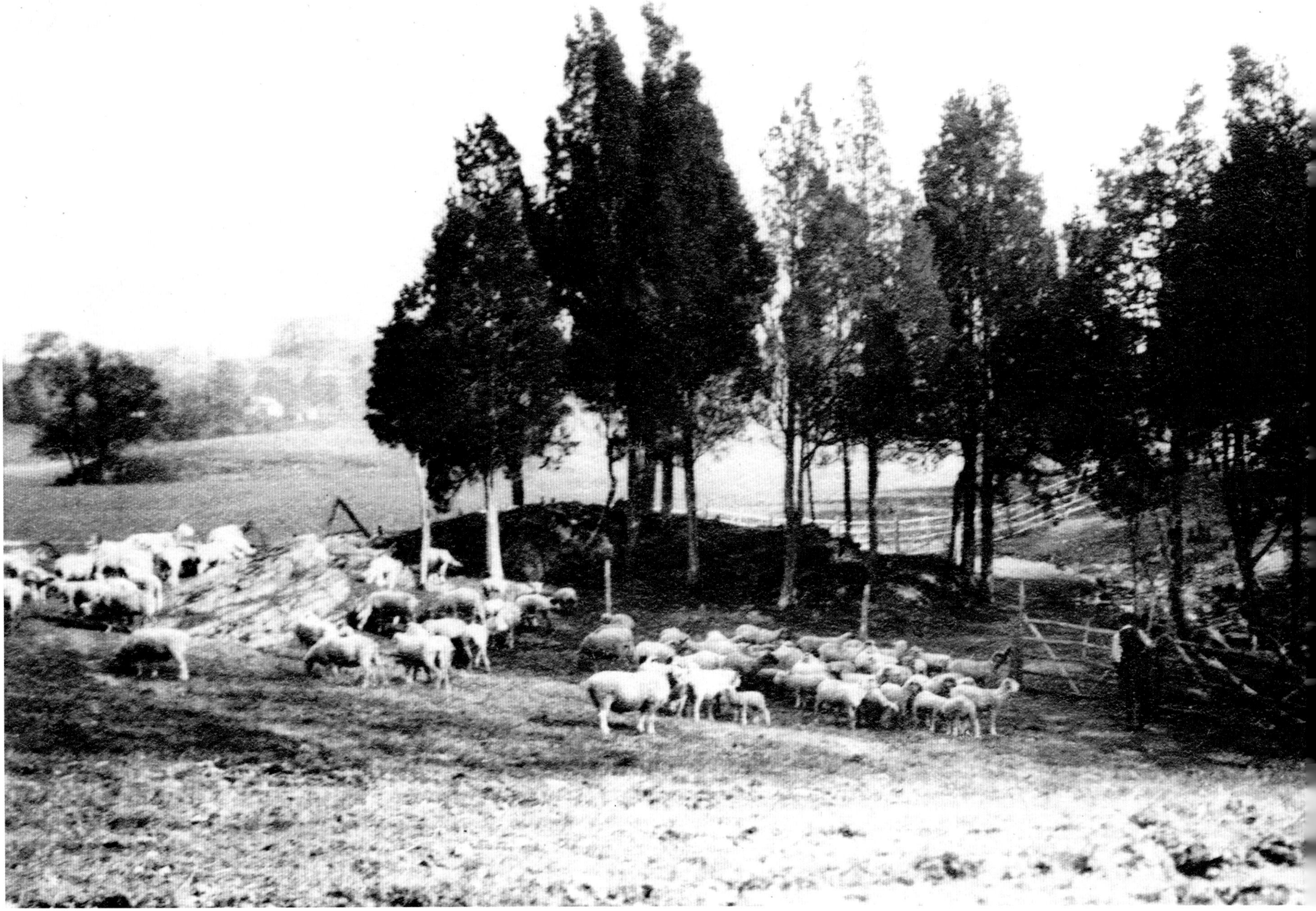

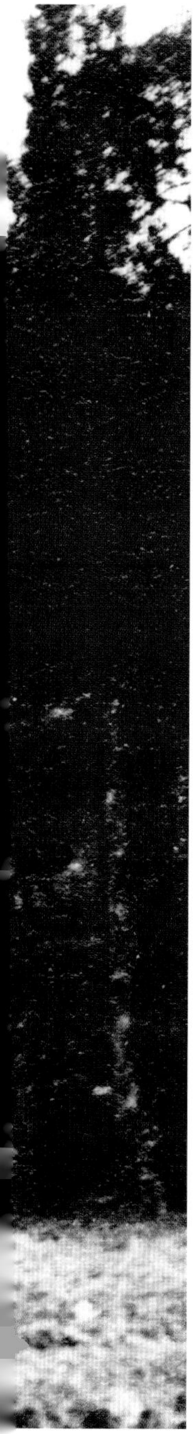

LEFT A flock of sheep in the fields at Southlands, a 200-acre area of the estate designated for riding and as pasture for the animals. Tracy wanted to preserve the beautiful rolling fields, which dated back to Alice's forebears with the original Beekman patent in the late 1600s. The land would remain in the hands of Deb Dows long after the Foxhollow Farm property was no longer owned by the Dows family. She opened a riding academy there in the late 1930s, dedicating her life to the teaching of horsemanship and a respect for the land and animals. Deb turned the Southlands Farm into The Southlands Foundation in 1983, and in 1987 she granted a conservation easement to Scenic Hudson, a non-profit environmental organization, protecting Southlands in perpetuity.

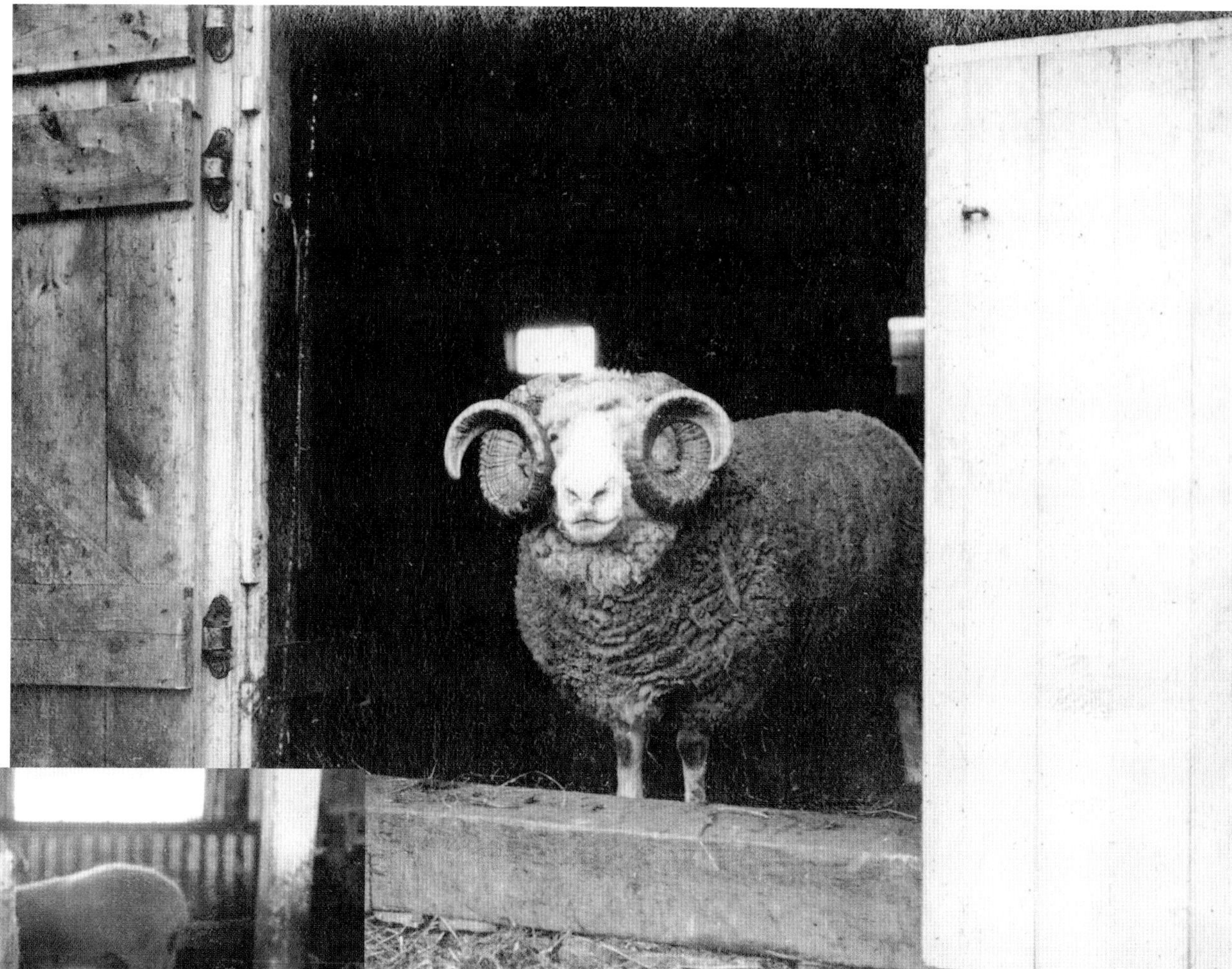

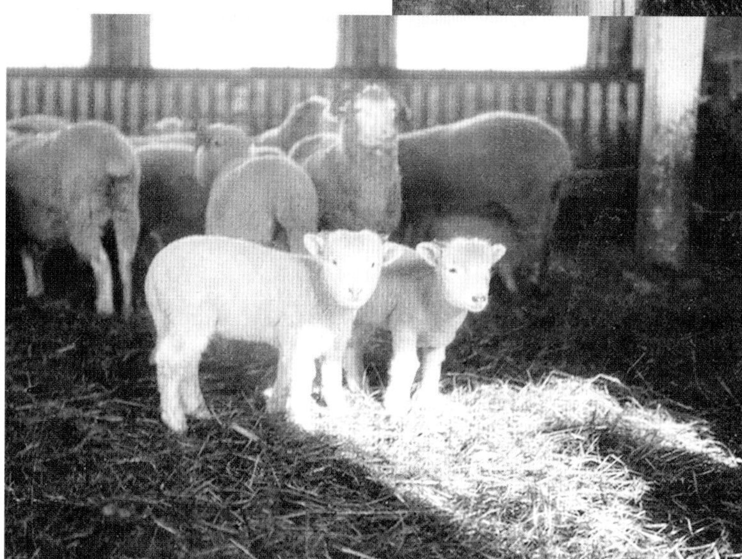

ABOVE A photogenic ram in the sheep barn at Southlands prior to being sheared, 1911. The barn was originally part of the Fraleigh farm, purchased by Tracy when he expanded his property.

LEFT Lambs inside the barn, 1912.

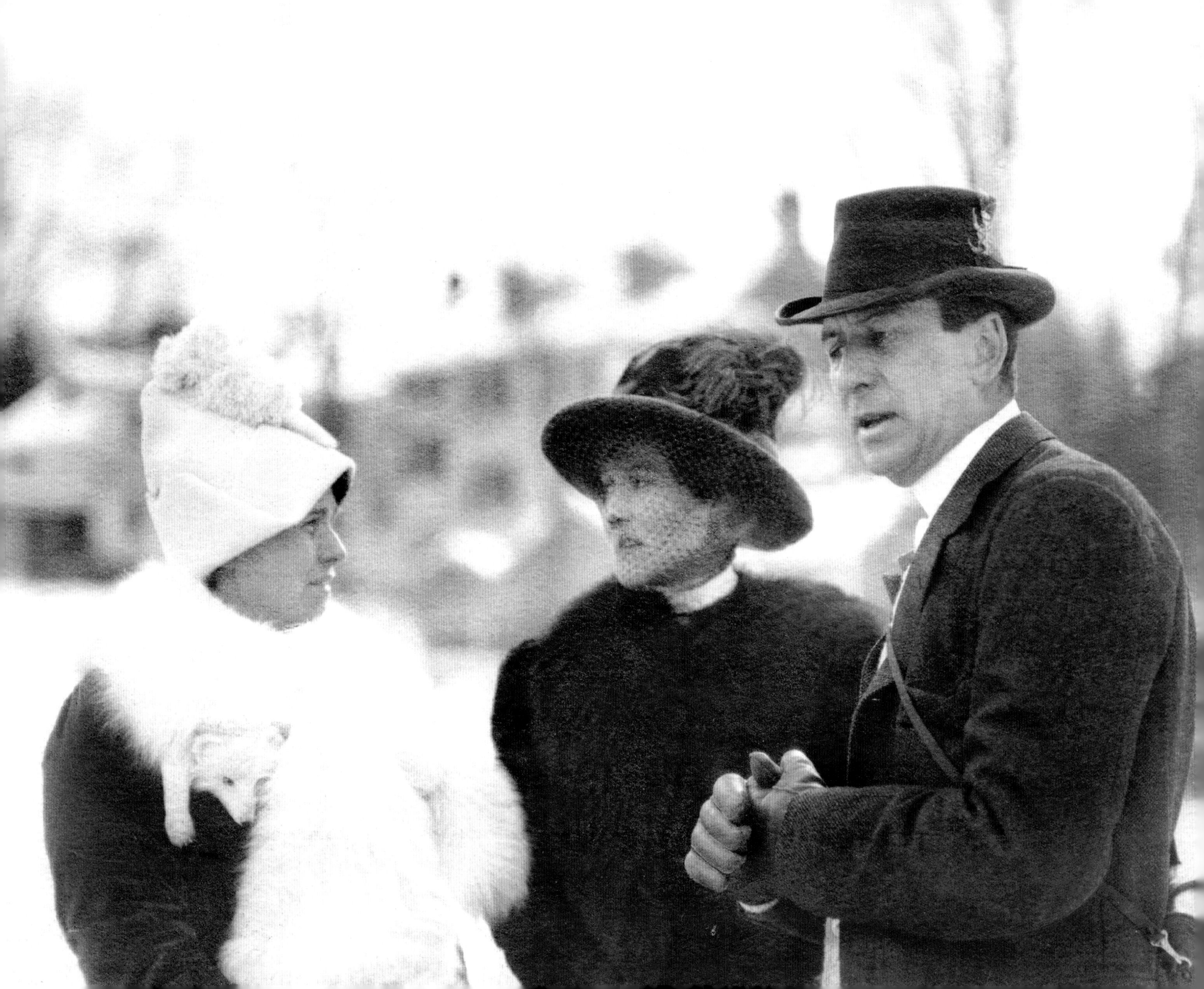

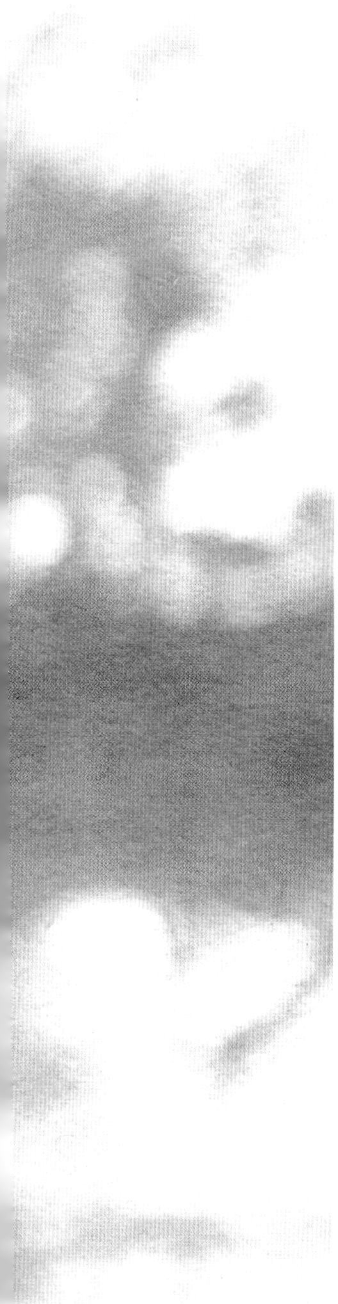

CHAPTER THREE

SOCIAL LIFE

Family and Friends

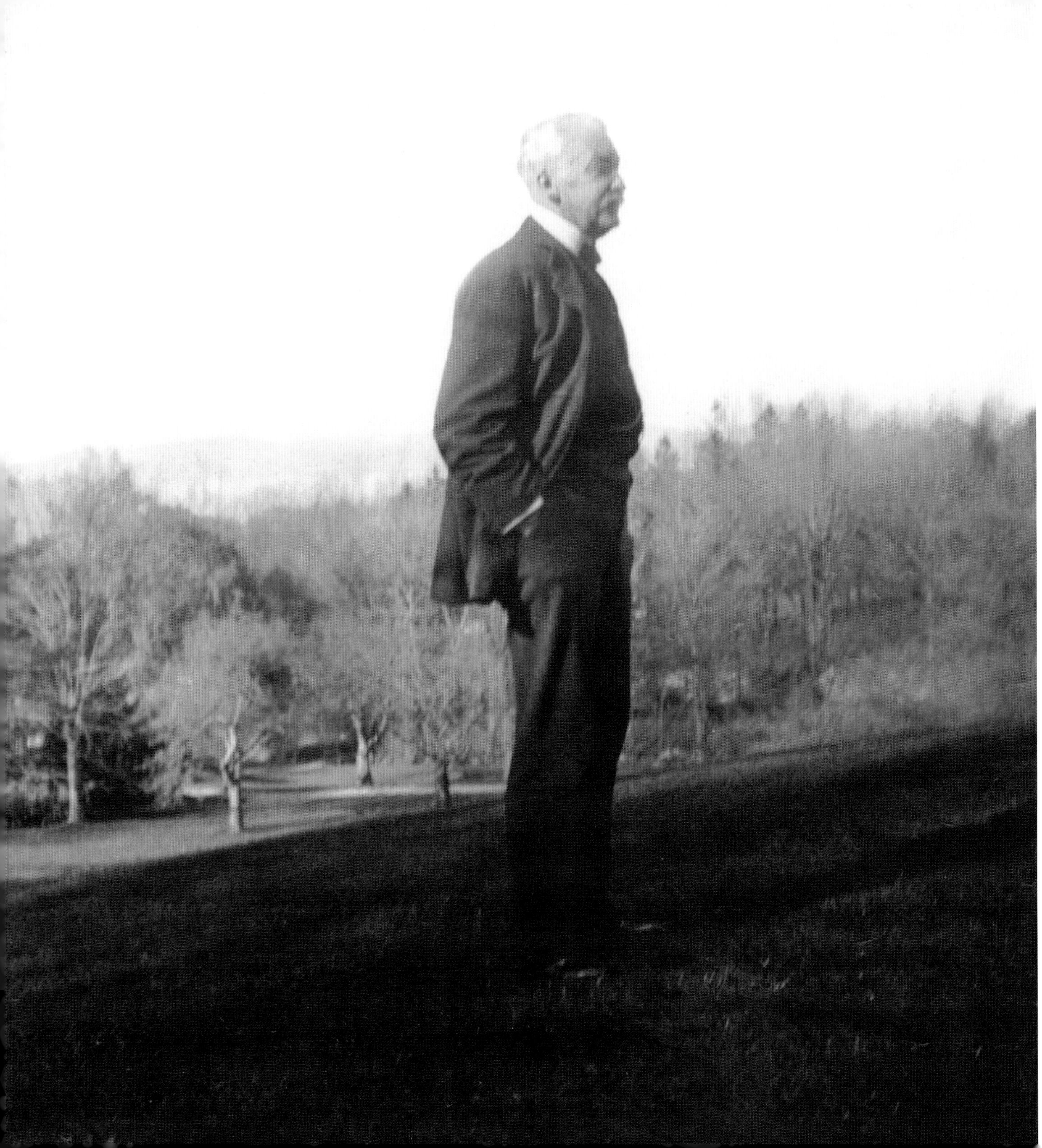

PREVIOUS PAGES Alice, Mrs. Lewis Iselin, and Tracy on Glenburn Pond, winter 1912. Lewis Iselin took the photograph.

LEFT Alice's father, Colonel Stephen Henry Olin, standing on the lawn at Woodland Cottage in Irvington, while visiting his daughter and son-in-law in 1904. The son of Reverend Stephen Olin, travel writer and president of Wesleyan University from 1842 to 1851, Stephen Henry Olin was educated at private schools and graduated from Wesleyan University with a law degree in 1866. He served as a Lieutenant-Colonel in the National Guard and was a member of the 7th Regiment of the New York Militia. He first practiced law with his friend, George Lockhart Rives, and later with the firm of Olin, Clark & Phelps. He married Emeline Harriman Dodge in 1903. His first wife, Elsie Barlow Olin, died while giving birth to Alice's sister, Julia, in 1882. Stephen Henry Olin was a trustee of the New York Public Library and acting president of Wesleyan from 1922 to 1923. He became one of the founders of The Players, the social club on Gramercy Park, in 1888. Other distinguished founders included Mark Twain, Edwin Booth, and William Tecumseh Sherman.

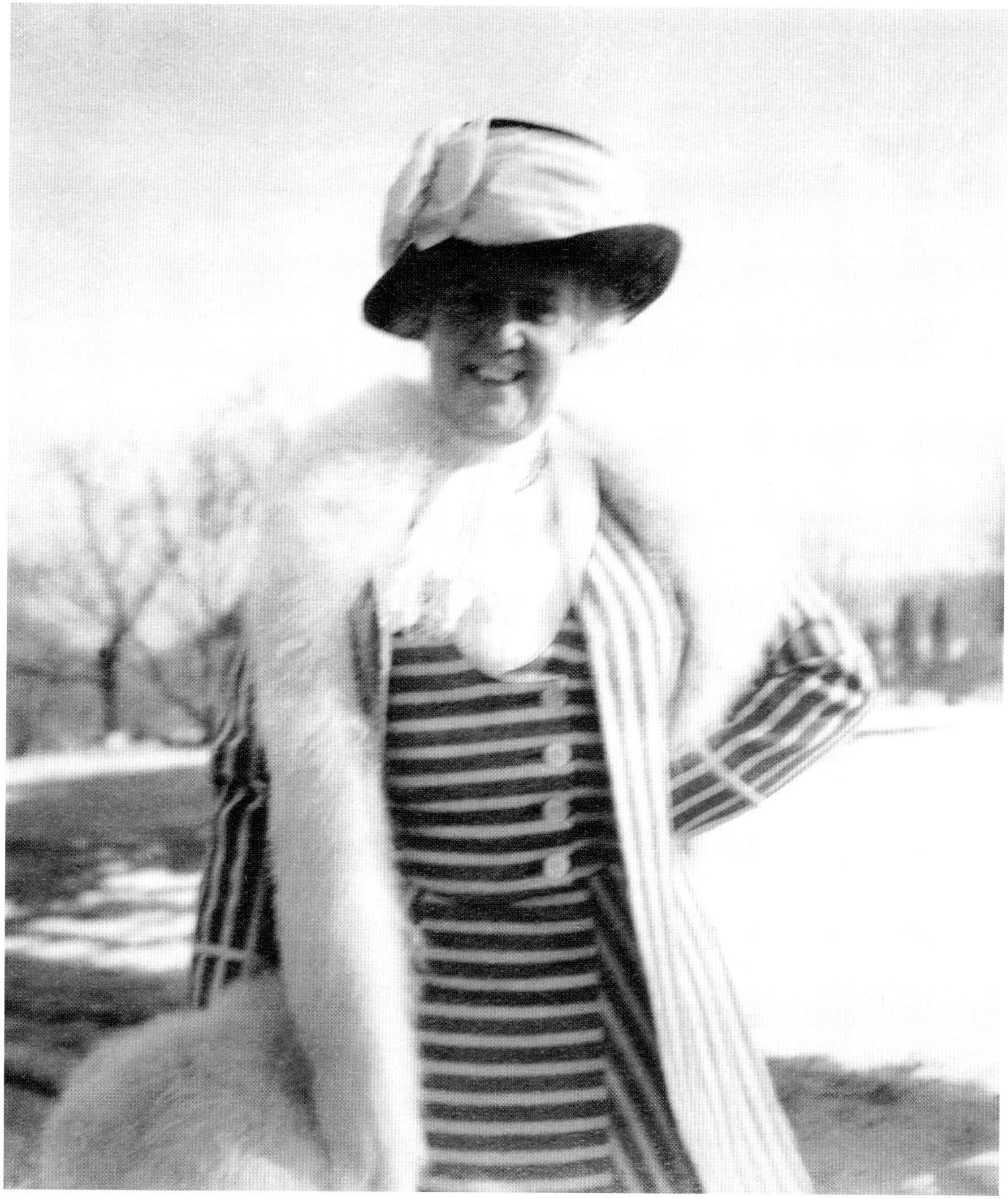

LEFT A fashionably dressed Emeline Harriman Olin in 1909. The daughter of investment banker and dry goods merchant Oliver Harriman, Emeline and her sisters all made illustrious marriages. One was Mrs. William K. Vanderbilt, Sr., another Mrs. Frederick C. Havemeyer, and Emeline was the widow of William Earl Dodge III when she married Stephen Henry Olin. One of her brothers, J. Borden Harriman, married Florence (Daisy) Jaffray Hurst, a national figure in the women's suffrage movement. After her husband's death in 1925, Mrs. Olin donated the funds for the construction of the Olin Memorial Library at Wesleyan University, designed by Henry Bacon, which was dedicated in 1928.

BELOW Mr. and Mrs. Stephen Olin at 1 East 69th Street in Manhattan, the home of Tracy's mother, Mrs. David Dows, in 1903.

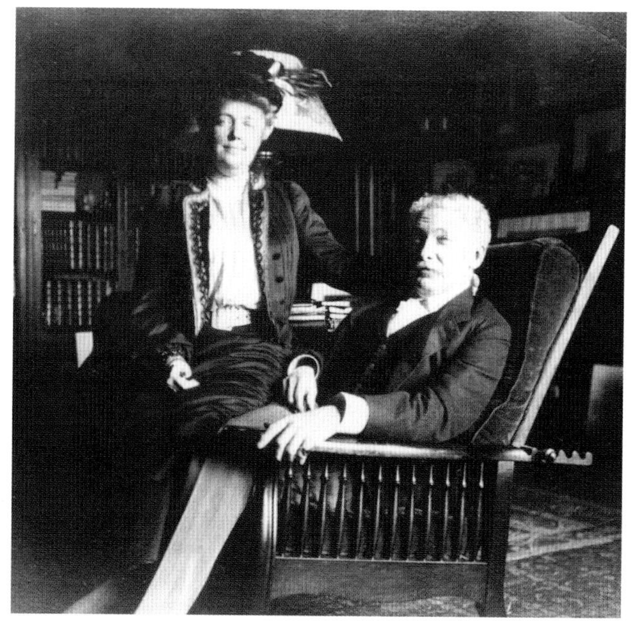

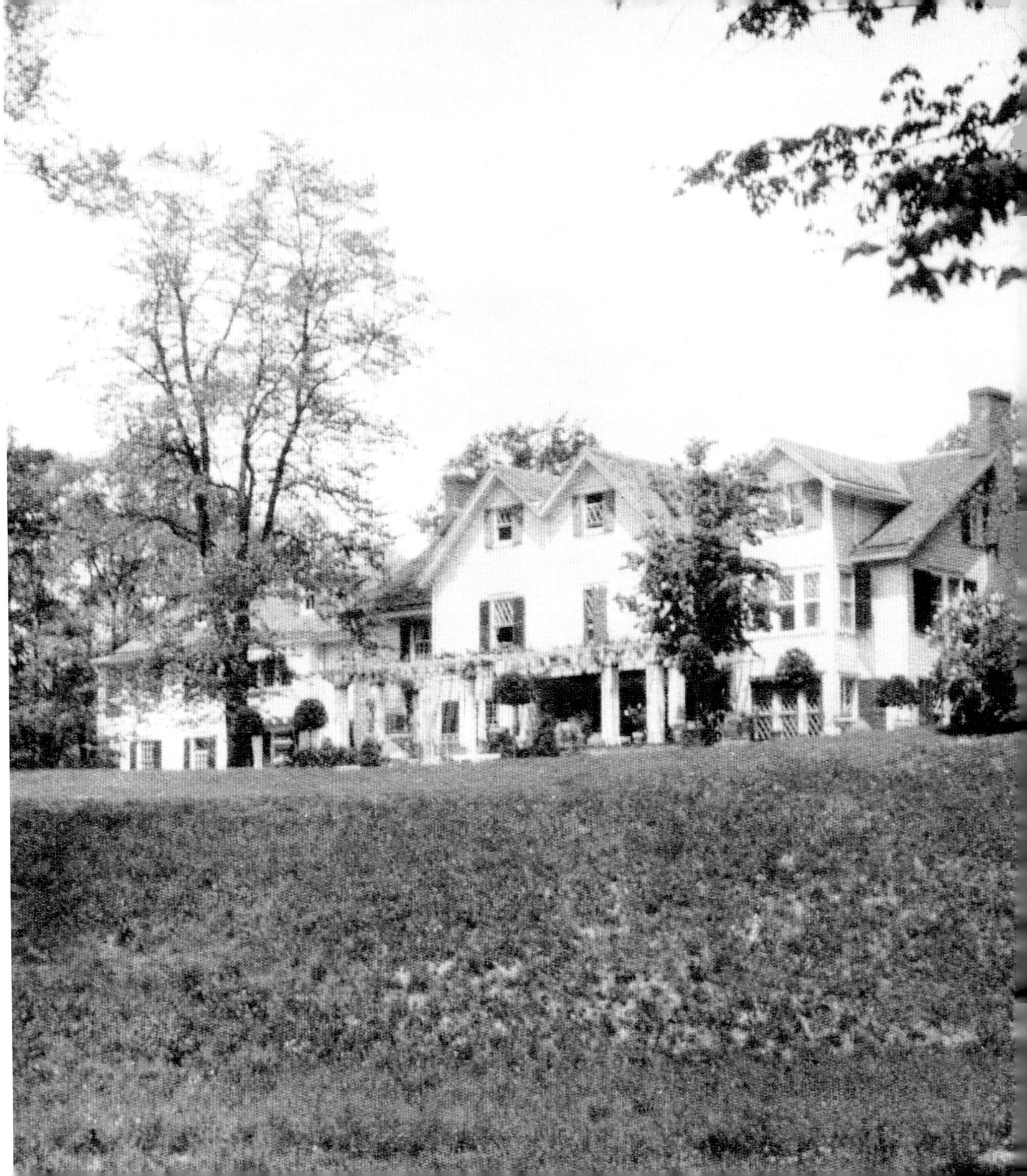

RIGHT A sprawling Glenburn in 1913, nine years after it was transformed into a much larger house by Harrie T. Lindeberg. From the age of eight, Alice had spent summers at Glenburn with her father and sister. The land was part of an original Beekman patent passed on to Margaret Livingston, the daughter of Margaret Beekman and Judge Robert Livingston of Clermont, after her marriage in 1779 to Dr. Thomas Tillotson. In 1830 Dr. Tillotson gave his twelve-year-old granddaughter, Julia M. Lynch, the wooded gorge containing the waterfalls of Fallsburg Creek because she loved playing in the stream. Shortly afterward, Julia's father, James Lynch, built a Victorian cottage for their family as a summer home. In 1843, Julia married Reverend Stephen Olin and the property became theirs. It later passed down to their son, Stephen Henry Olin, who had the house completely remodeled by Harrie T. Lindeberg in 1904, including the addition of a wing to the west. Further renovations were done by Henry Bacon in 1914, which gave the house a more classical look.

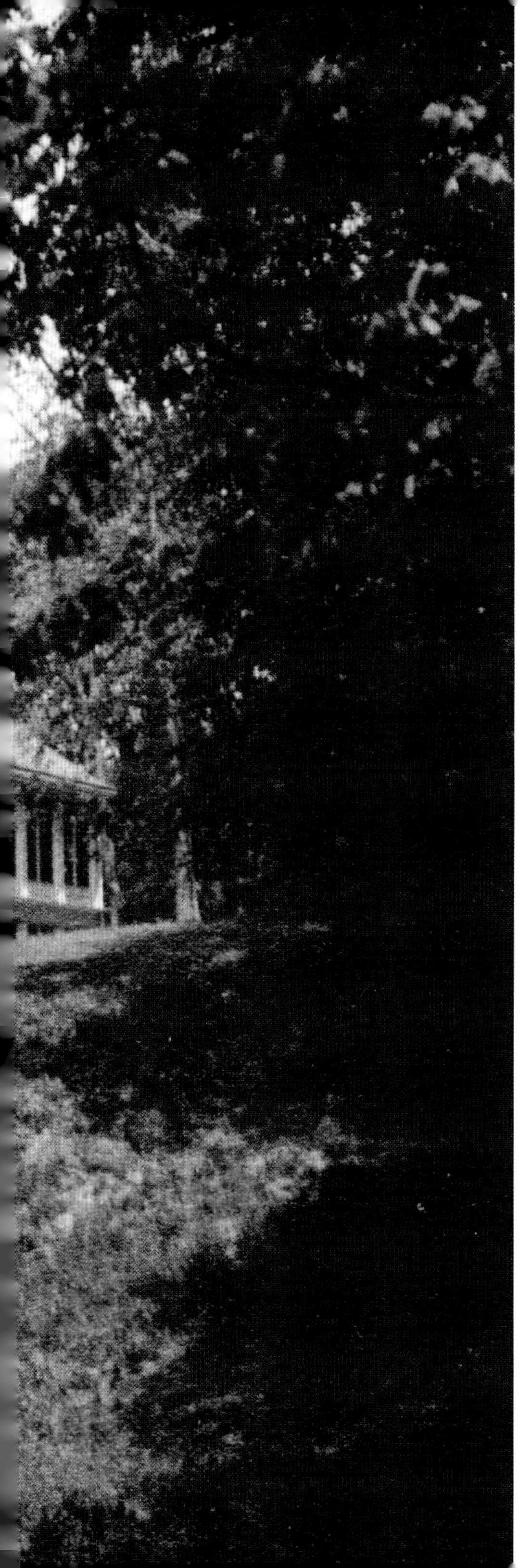

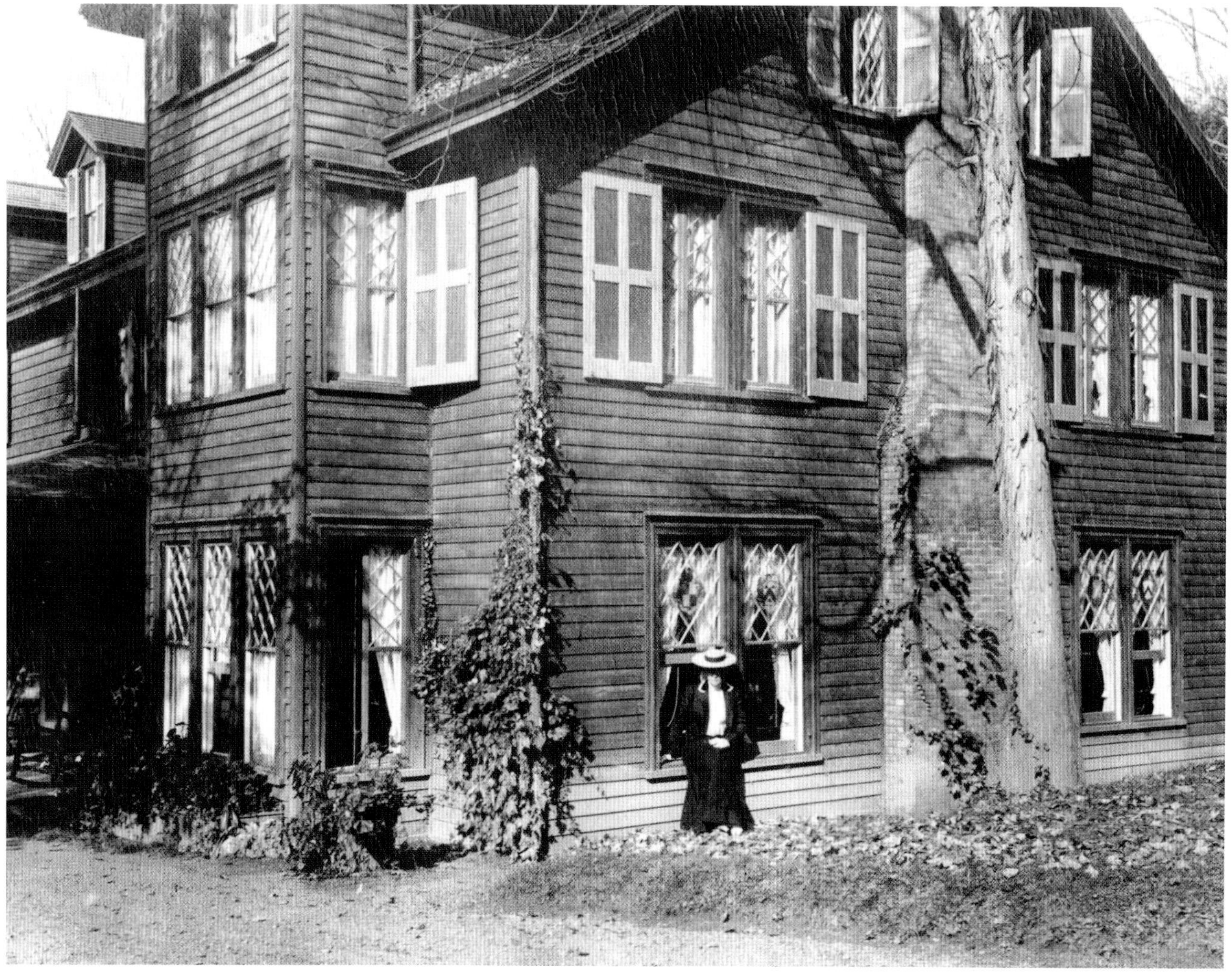

ABOVE Alice sitting on the window sill at Glenburn in 1903, a year before the renovation by Lindeberg. Etched into the upper sashes of these windows are the Livingston, Tillotson, and Lynch coats of arms of her ancestry. The house was painted dark brown with red trim and shutters, in keeping with the Victorian style of cottage architecture.

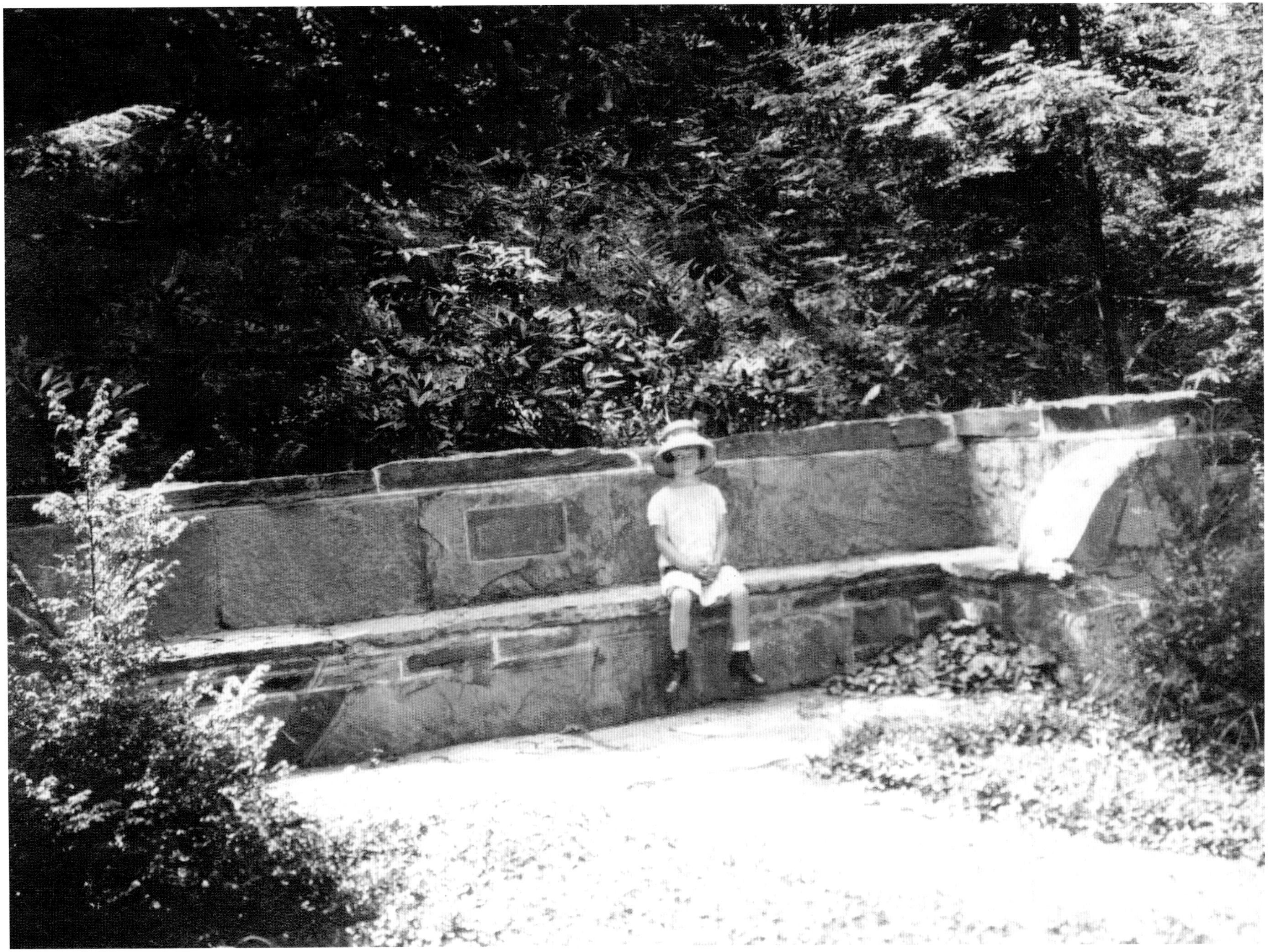

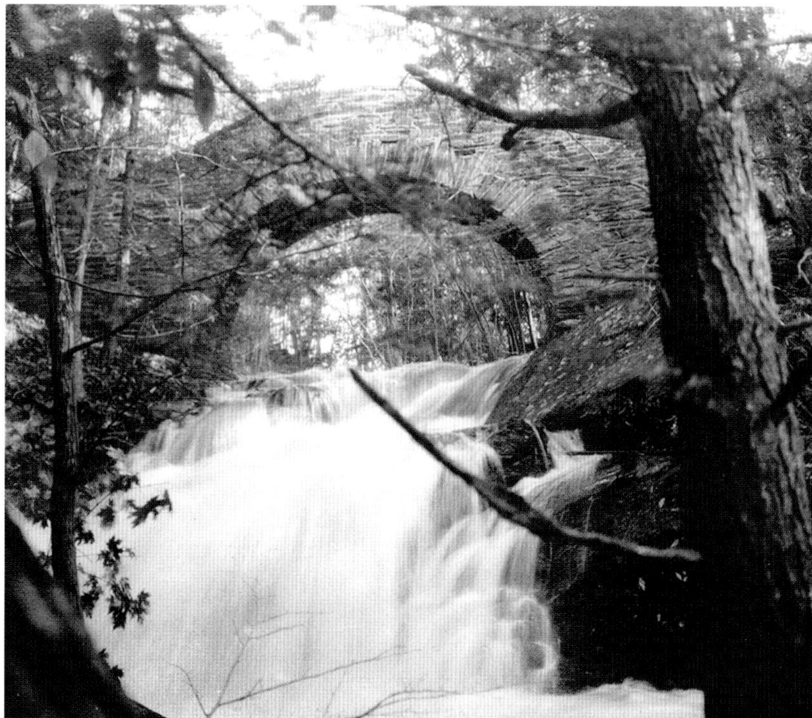

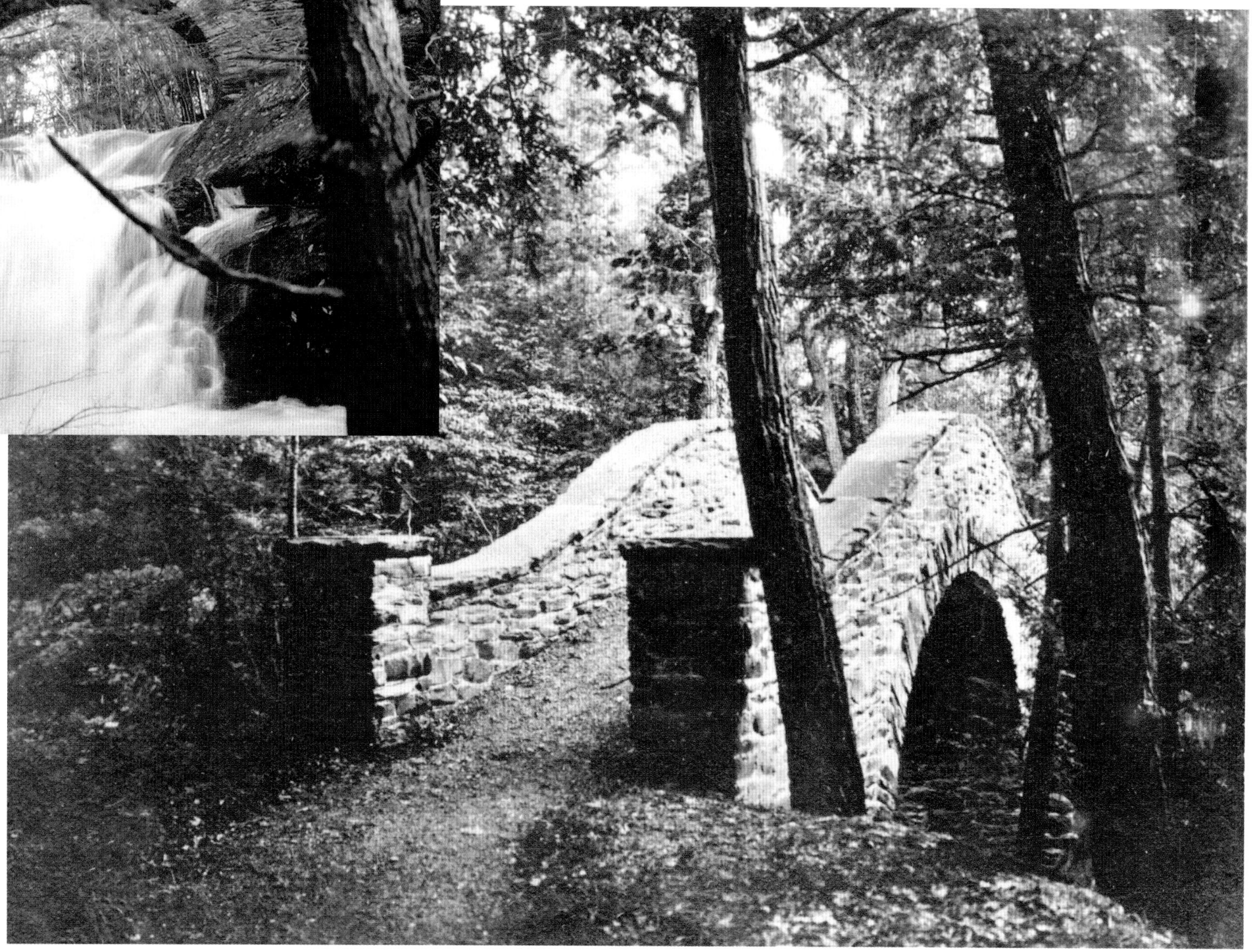

ABOVE AND RIGHT The beautiful Fallsburg Bridge as seen in 1908. Built over a rushing rocky waterfall in Fallsburg Creek, it would become part of a favorite trail for Deb Dows as she rode through the wooded areas of Glenburn.

OPPOSITE Margaret Dows on a stone bench next to Fallsburg Bridge. As commemorated in a plaque, this was where Alice's grandmother, Julia Lynch Olin, taught Sunday School to a gathering of children in the summers of 1840 to 1855.

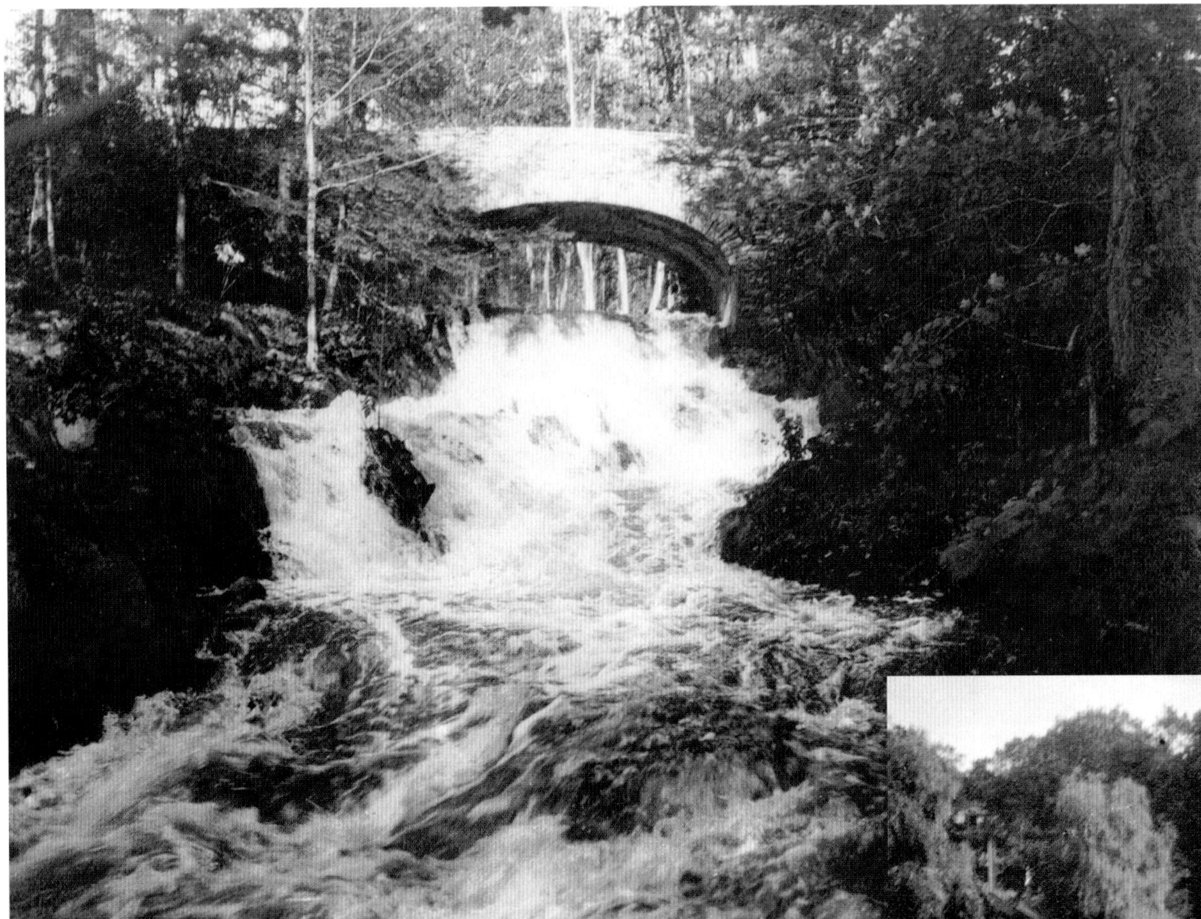

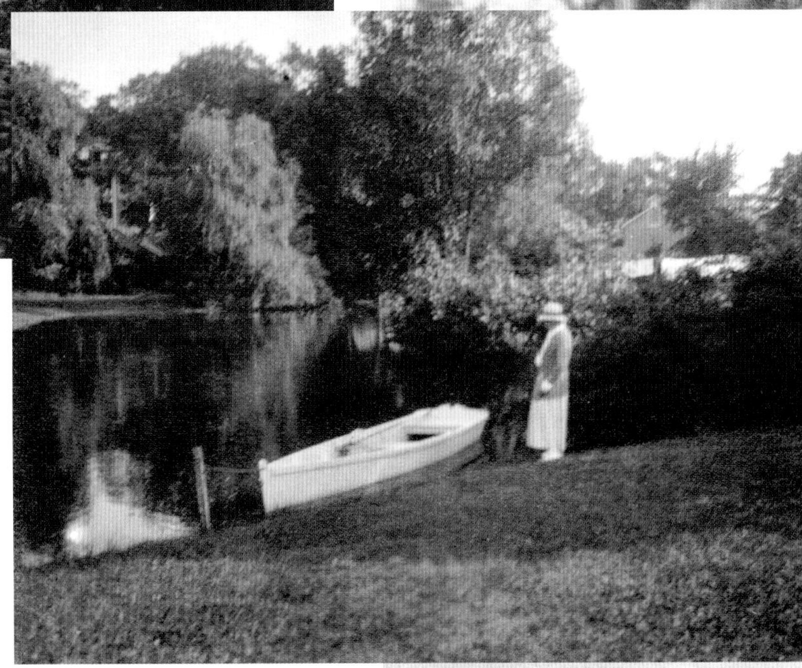

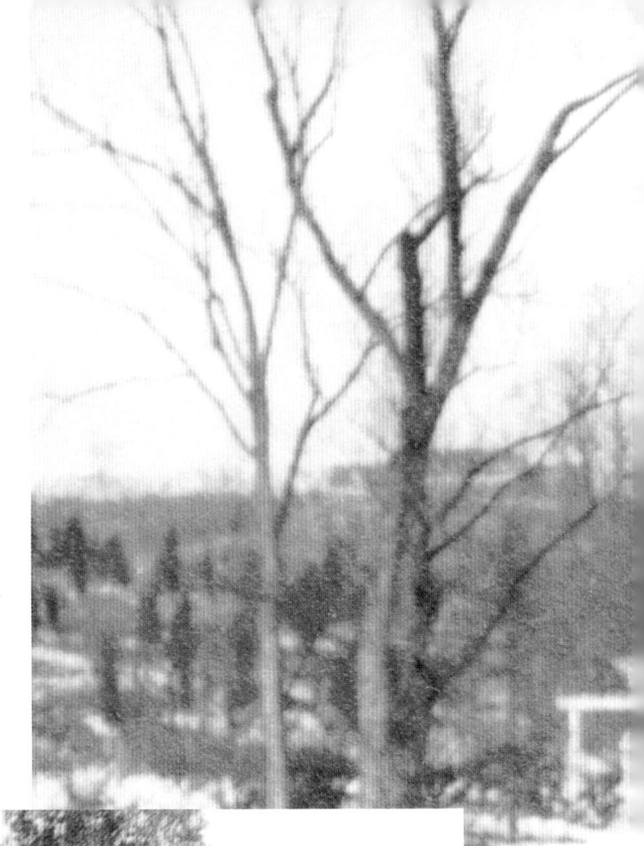

ABOVE Fallsburg Creek also flowed along the back of the property, through Glenburn Pond, and under Olin Bridge, which connected the main drive to the carriage house. From here the stream continued to travel along the property and emptied in the Hudson River.

RIGHT Alice next to the Olins' rowboat on the pond in the summer of 1915. Water flowed into one end of the pond and out of the other, cascading over a stone dam designed by the Olmsted Brothers.

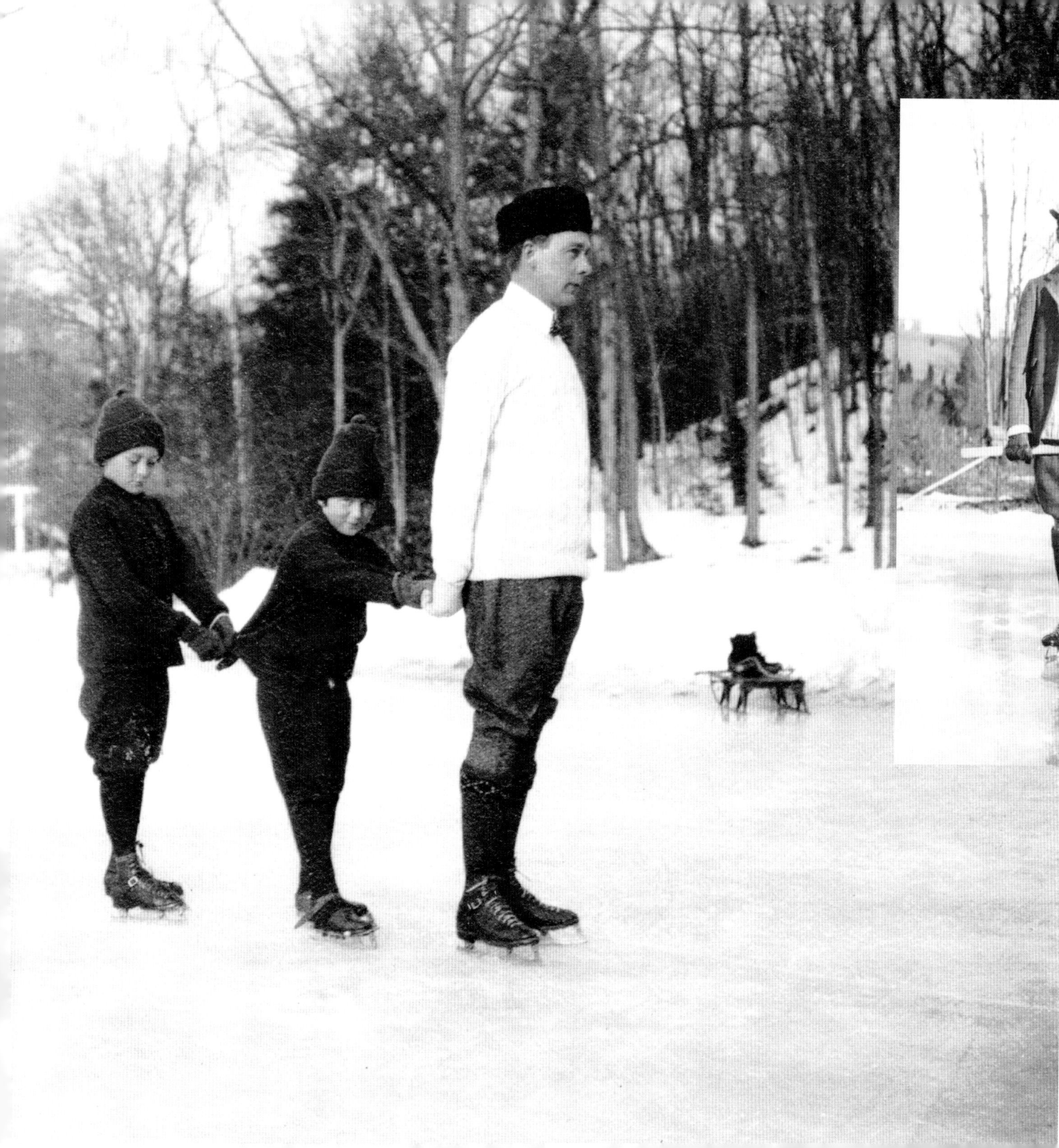

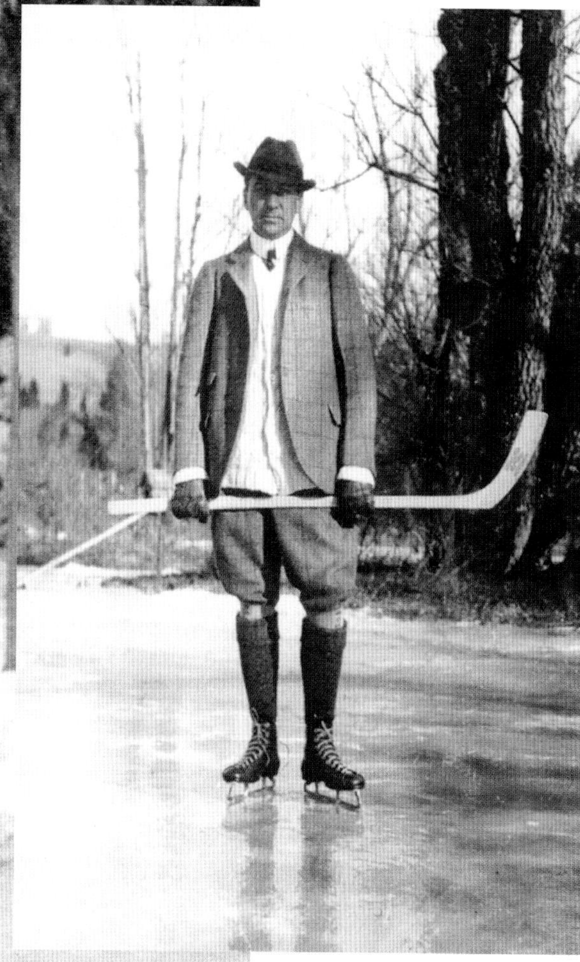

ABOVE Tracy taking advantage of a frozen Glenburn Pond to play hockey in December 1910.

LEFT Harrie T. Lindeberg forms a skating line with Olin and Margaret on the pond in 1912. Visitors to Foxhollow Farm and Glenburn enjoyed skating and playing games on the large pond while it was frozen during the winter months.

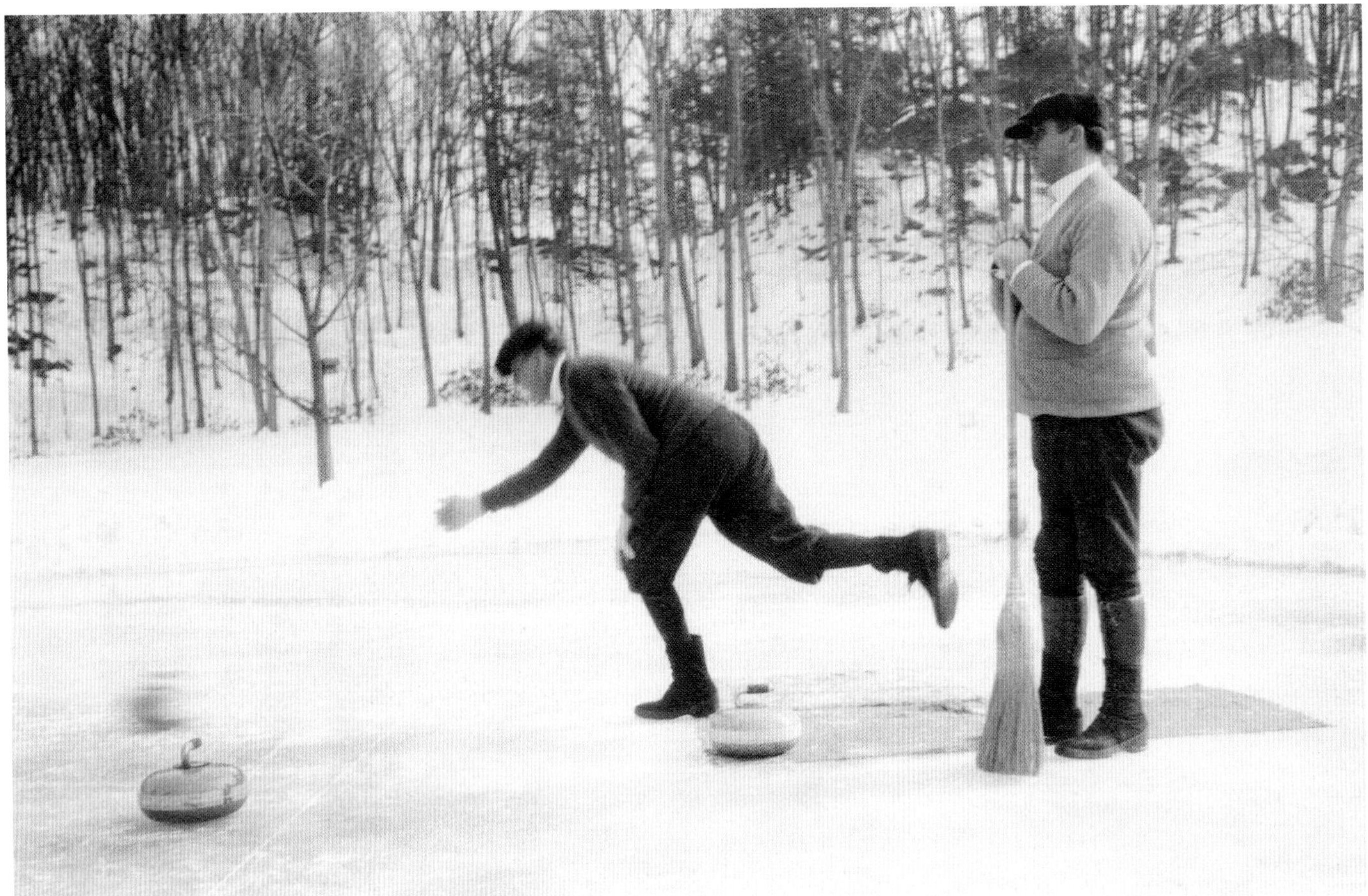

ABOVE A curling competition on Glenburn Pond in January 1912. Tracy organized matches that winter to include workers from both Foxhollow Farm and Glenburn.

RIGHT Tracy, on the far left, posing with the workers in another match held a month later on Landsman's Kill. Clarence Colt Colburn, the superintendent of Foxhollow Farm, is second from the right.

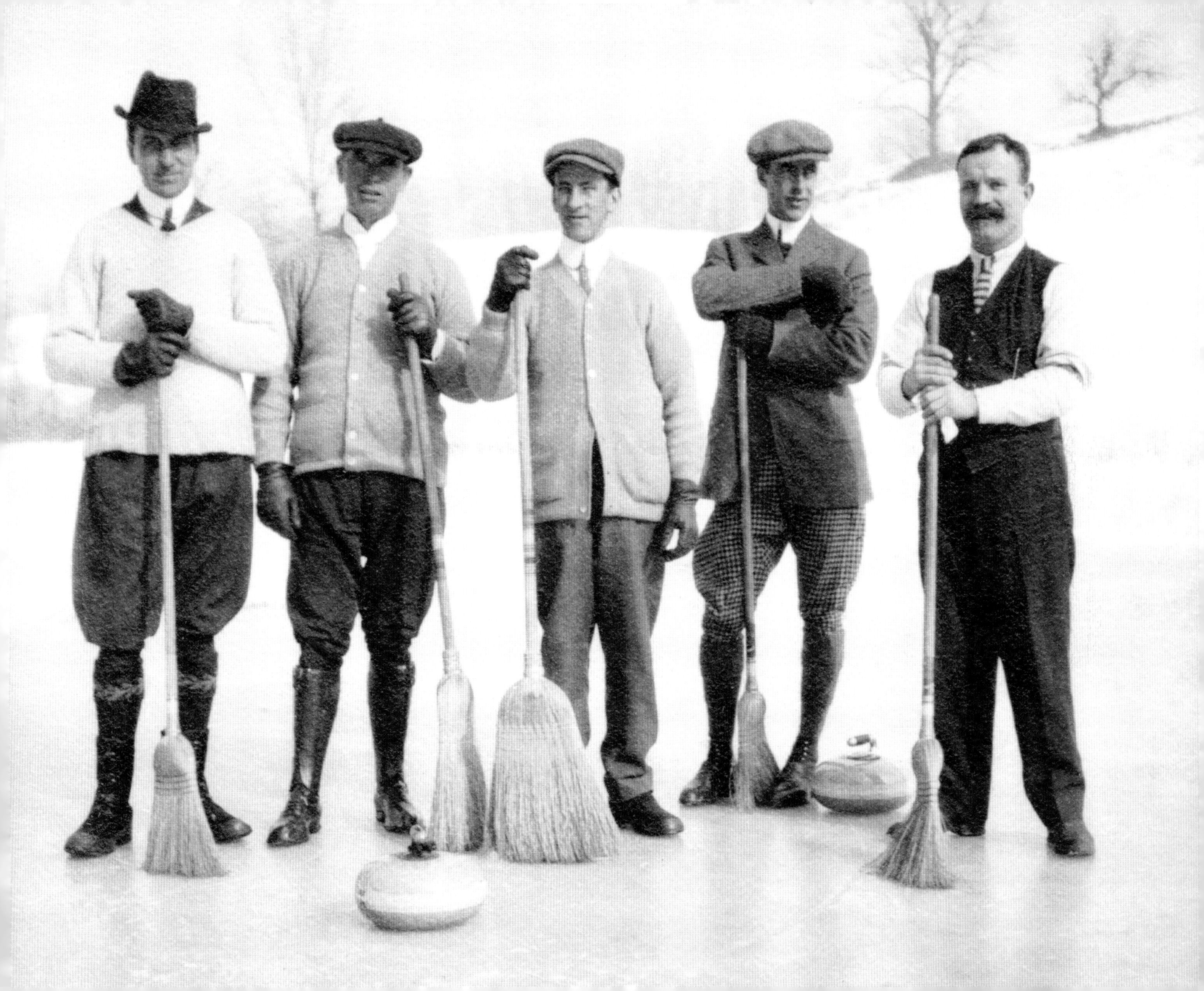

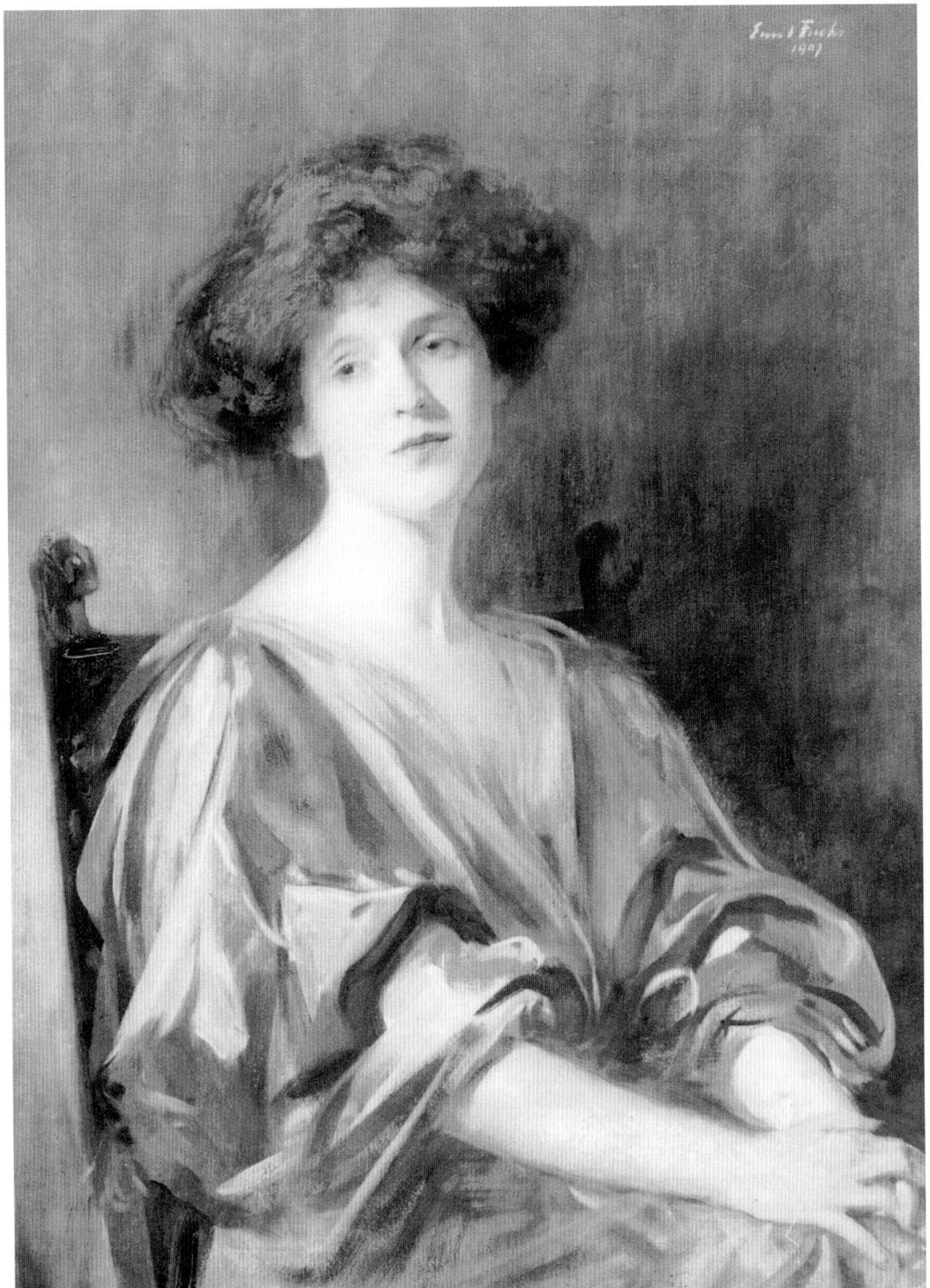

LEFT A 1907 portrait of Alice's sister, Julia Lynch Olin Benkard, painted by Emil Fuchs, the Austrian artist known for his portraits of the British aristocracy and American socialites. Julia married J. Philip Benkard in 1902, a successful New York City businessman who owned a brokerage firm, and had two daughters, Elsie and Phyllis. They divorced in 1920, and the following year Julia married Lewis Stuyvesant Chanler, the ex-lieutenant governor of New York and a former Democratic candidate for governor. He was also one of the eight children, known as the Astor Orphans, whose parents both died within two years of each other while they were all young, leaving them to be raised by an elderly cousin and servants, at their sprawling Hudson River estate, Rokeby. Around 1925, Julia and Lewis began studying the teachings of Mírzá Aḥmad Sohráb and the Bahá'í faith. They established the New History Society in their Manhattan townhouse, which later became Caravan House. In 1956 Julie (as she was then called) published her autobiography, *From Gaslight to Dawn.*

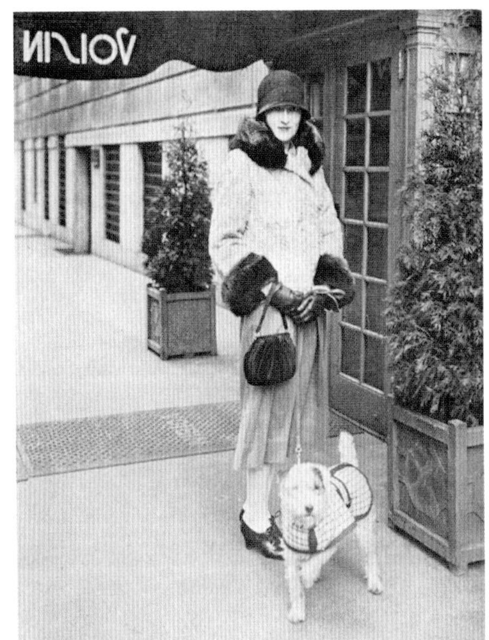

LEFT A photograph of Julia, from her autobiography, while living in Paris during the 1920s. Alice and Julia were close as children, but not as adults.

OPPOSITE A family gathering at Stone Cottage in 1907. Mr. and Mrs. Stephen Olin are flanked by his daughters Julia, left, and Alice, right. Elsie Benkard, Julia's daughter, sits on the steps with Olin and Margaret.

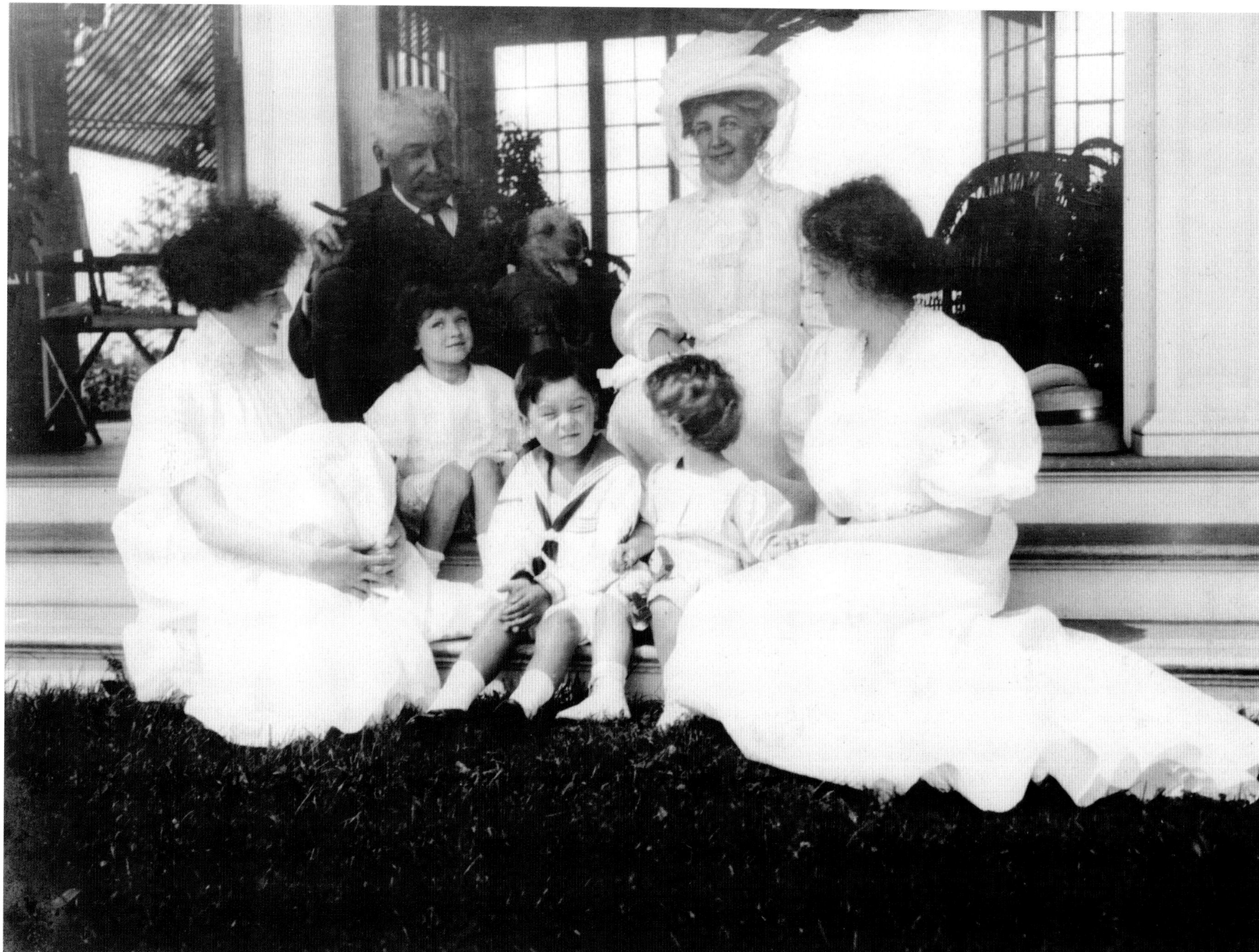

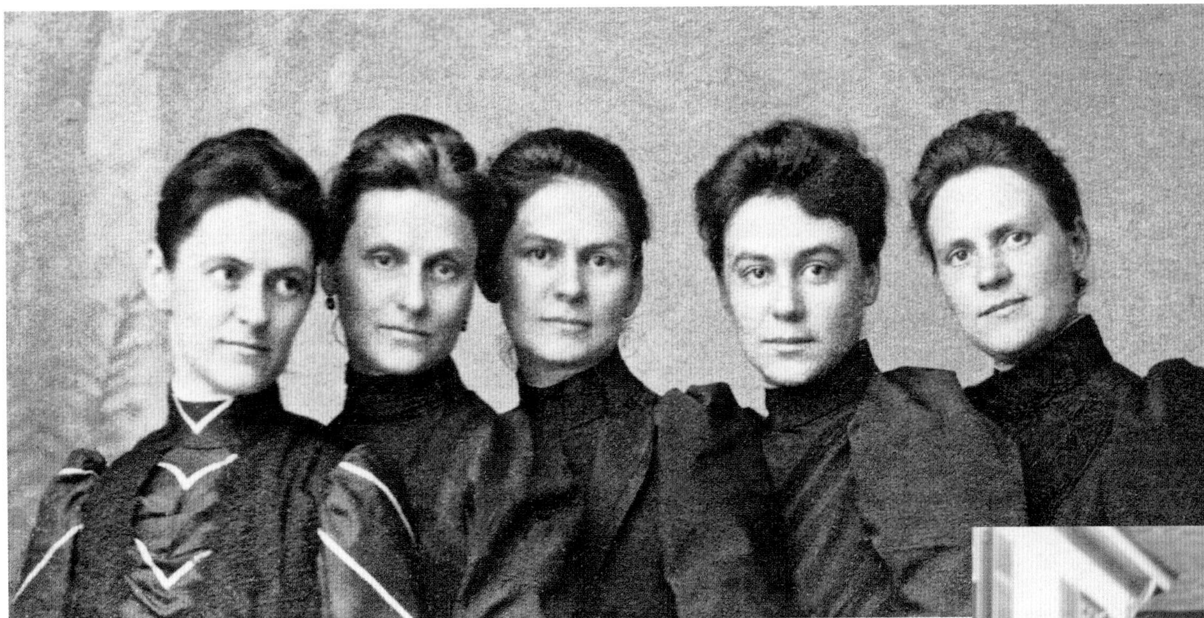

LEFT A photograph of Tracy's sisters taken in the 1880s. From left, Margaret, Annie Louise, Linda, Mary (nicknamed Polly), and Susan. (Courtesy of Collection of Philippa Dunham Shaplin)

BELOW Polly Dows and her husband, Dr. Edward Kellogg Dunham, with Alice at Foxhollow Farm in 1913. Dunham was a respected physician and leader in the medical community, known for the discovery of the cholera-red reaction. Polly had suffered from polio in her childhood but lived life to the fullest and became an avid traveler.

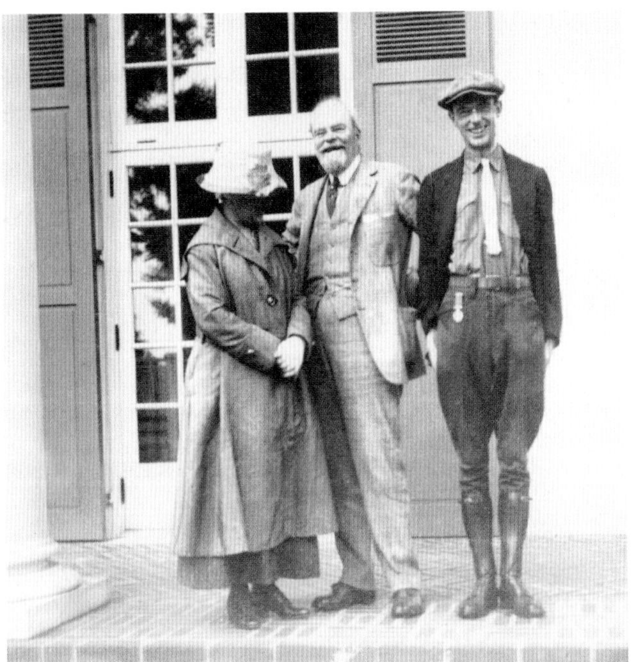

LEFT Like his brother, an accomplished physician and biochemist, Dr. Carroll Dunham, center, also married a Dows sister, Margaret, seen here with their son, Dows Dunham, at Foxhollow Farm, 1919. Dows Dunham became a well-known archaeologist and noted Egyptologist. He was present at the opening of the tomb of Queen Hetepheres in 1927, and for many decades was the curator of the Egyptian collection at the Museum of Fine Arts in Boston.

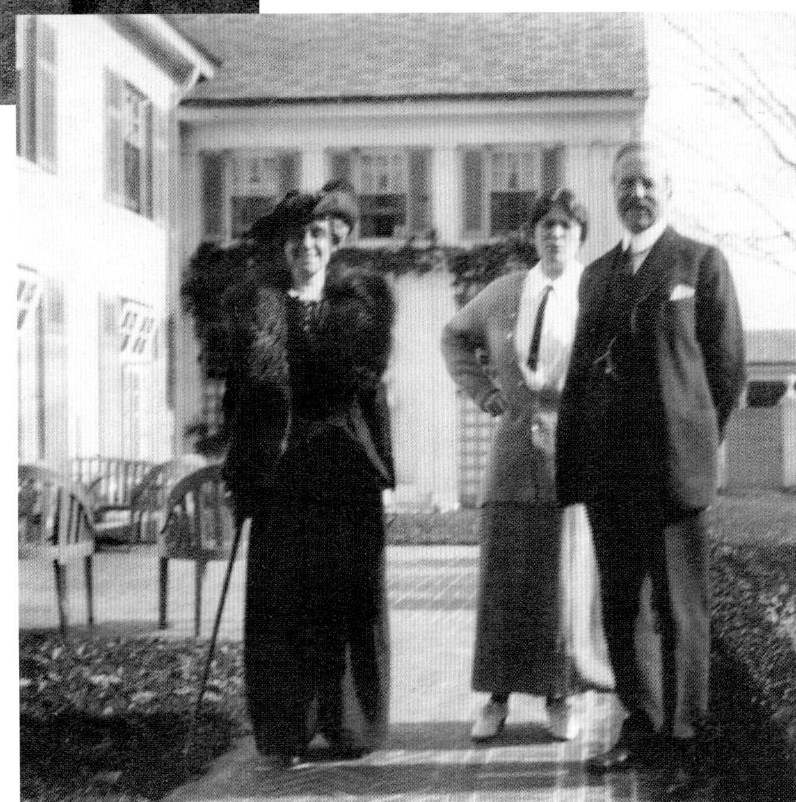

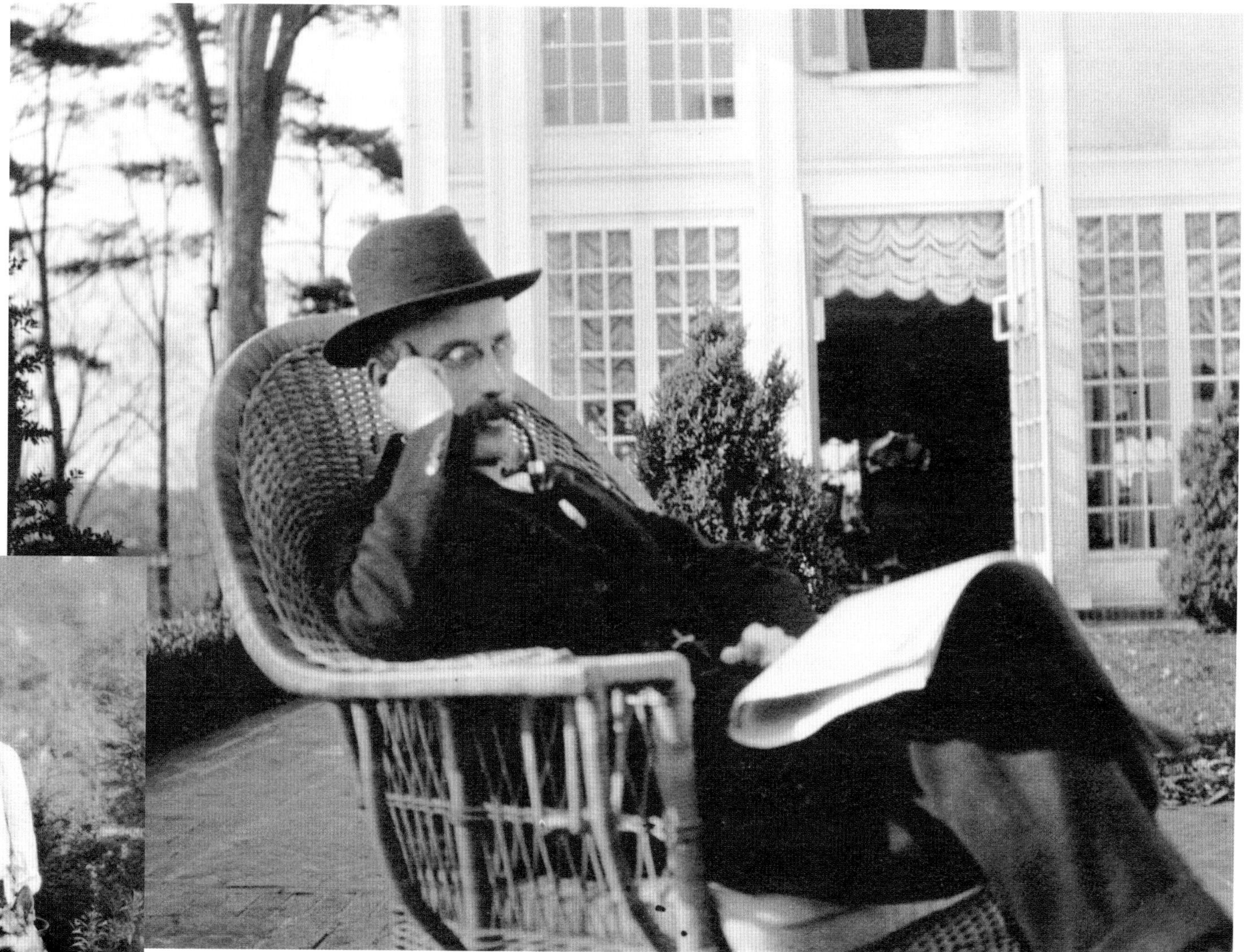

RIGHT Henry Drysdale Dakin on the terrace at Foxhollow Farm, 1917. Born in London, Dakin studied chemistry at the University of Leeds and in 1905 worked in the Columbia University lab of physician and pathologist Christian Archibald Herter. In 1914, Dakin returned to England to help with the war effort, where he and a fellow chemist developed the Carrel-Dakin method of treating wounds, which consisted of irrigating the wound with Dakin's Solution, an antiseptic still available today. Dakin continued to work as the director of Herter's private laboratory after Herter's untimely death in 1910, and in 1916 he married Herter's widow, Susan Dows Herter, another of Tracy's sisters.

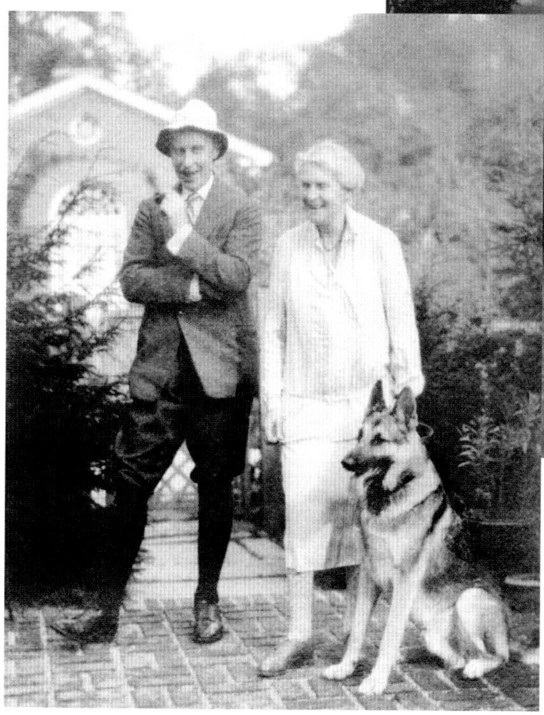

LEFT Henry and Susan Dakin with Rosso, their German Shepherd, at Edgehill, their home in Scarborough, New York, 1927. Dakin built his own laboratory there for further research and was nicknamed "Zyme" because of his extensive work with enzymes.

RIGHT Tracy's nephew, David Dows III, with his fiancée, Gwendolyn Burden, at Foxhollow Farm in 1911. Six feet six inches tall, he was nicknamed "Big Dave." After selling his grandmother's Irvington estate, Charlton Hall, David Dows hired the architect Horace Trumbauer in 1916 to design his Long Island country house, which he also named Charlton Hall. It was modeled after a seventeenth-century English mansion.

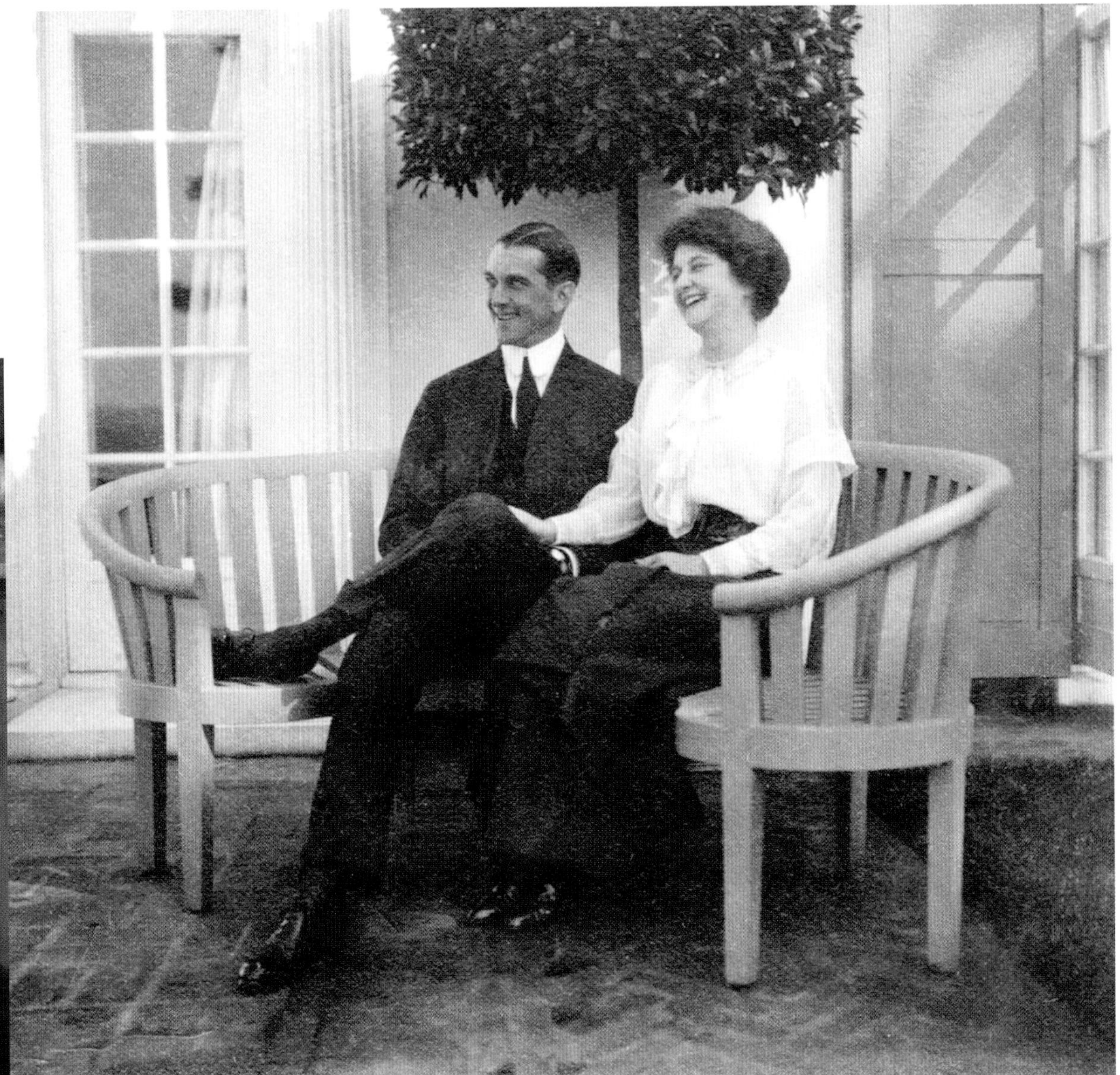

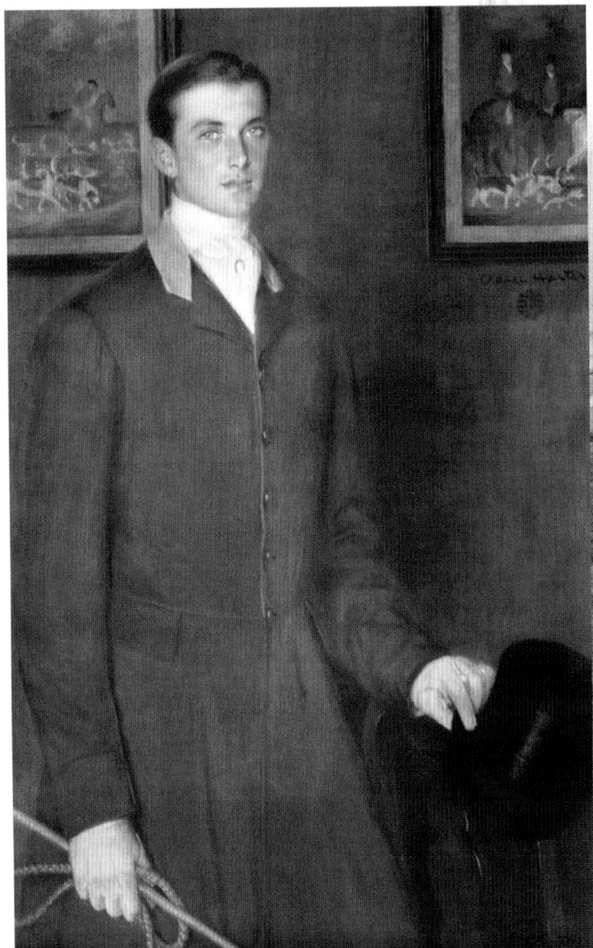

LEFT A painting of David Dows III in fox-hunting attire by Adele McGinnis Herter, who was married to fellow artist, Albert Herter.

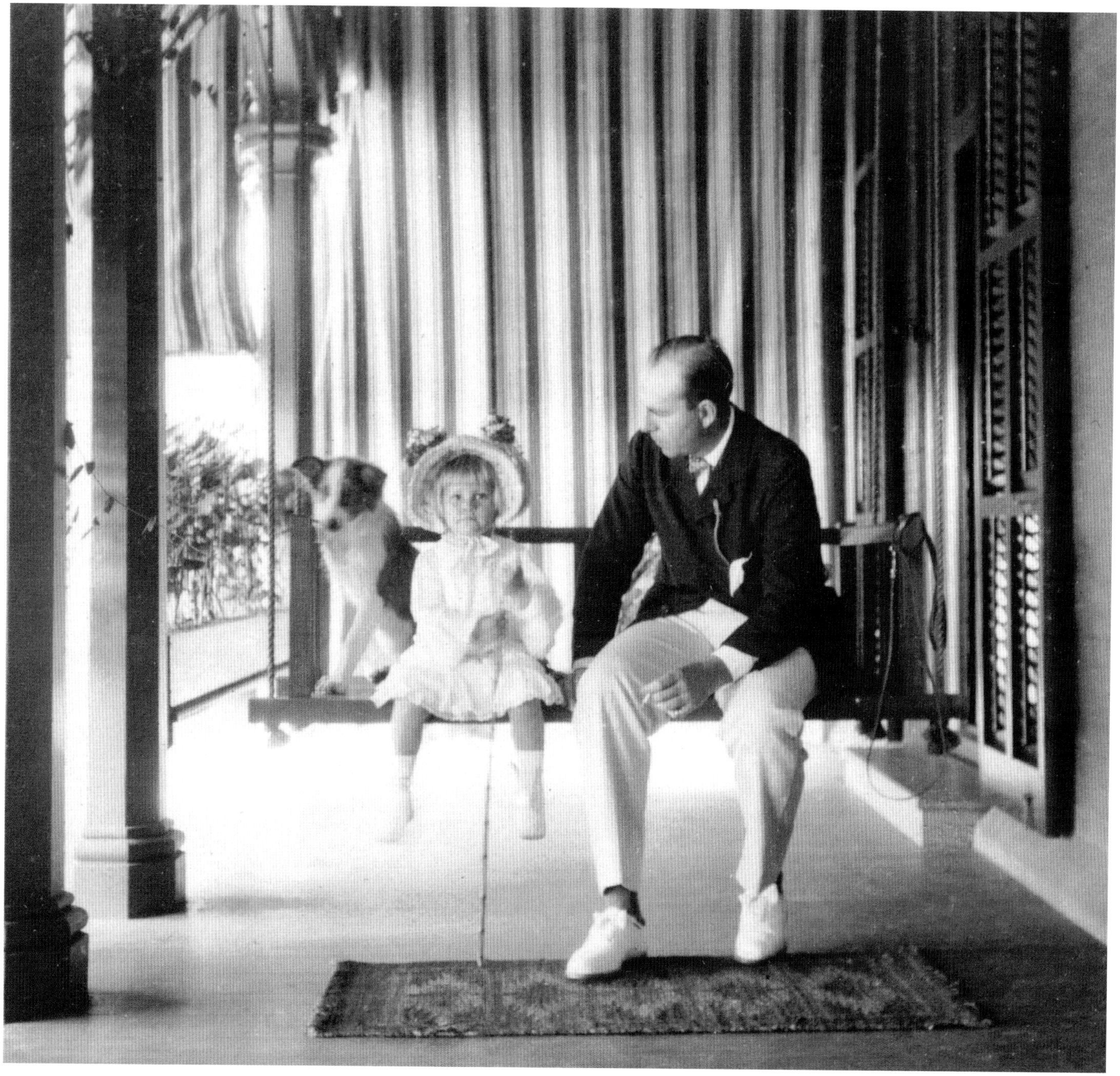

LEFT James Alexander Stillman on the piazza at Woodland Cottage with his daughter, Anne, while visiting Tracy and Alice in 1904. Stillman was the son of the successful businessman and chairman of National City Bank of New York, James Jewett Stillman. He graduated from Harvard College in 1896 and married Anne "Fifi" Urquhart Potter in 1901 at Grace Church in New York. Mondanne, their country estate in Pocantico Hills, New York, built in 1907, was designed by Albro & Lindeberg. Stillman later became president of National City Bank, and he and his wife made headlines while involved in a scandalous divorce trial. The couple, however, remained married and sailed to Europe to receive counseling from Carl Jung. They finally divorced in 1931.

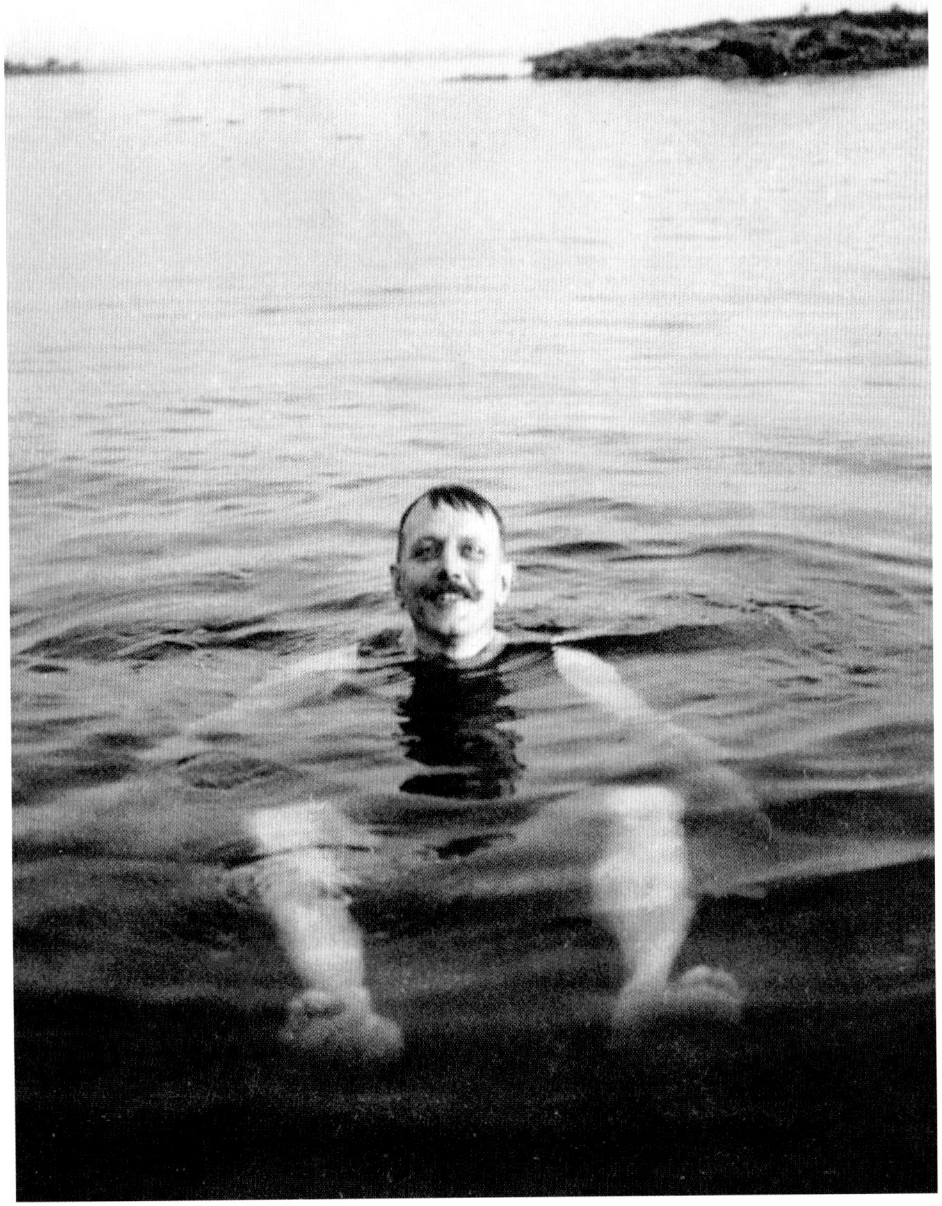

LEFT Lewis Iselin swimming in the Long Island Sound in New Rochelle, New York, in 1920. He and his wife, Marie de Neufville Iselin, were frequent guests at Foxhollow Farm. From an illustrious family that included his grandfather, Adrian Iselin, a banker and philanthropist, and his uncle, C. Oliver Iselin, a prominent yachtsman and three-time defender of the America's Cup, Lewis was a partner in the family banking business.

BELOW Lewis Iselin and his family spent summers in New Rochelle at Breakwater House, built by his grandfather.

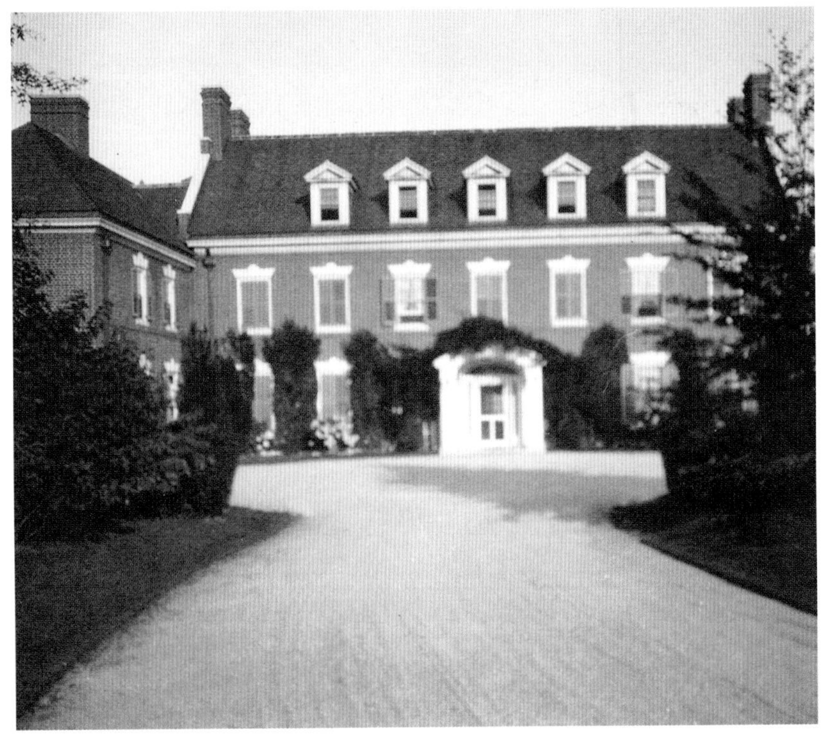

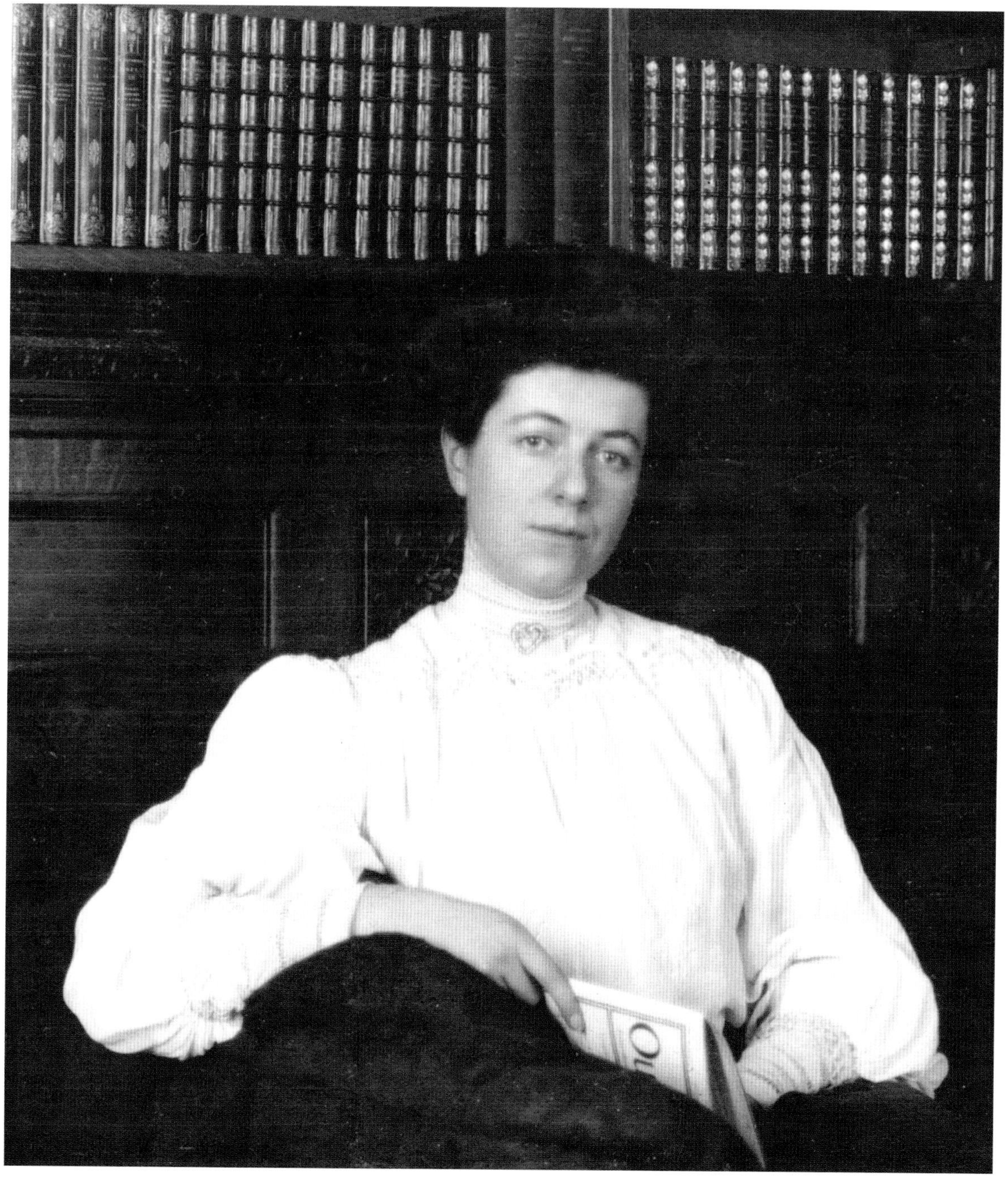

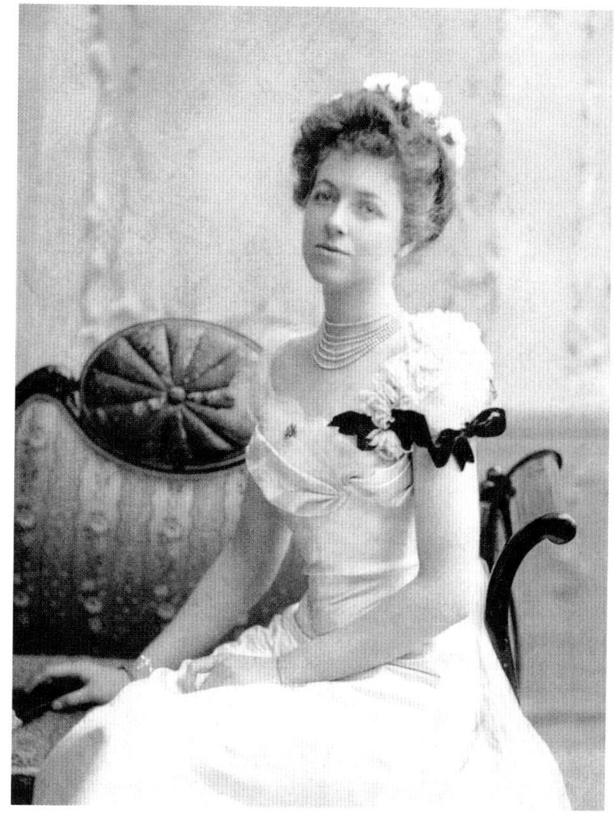

LEFT Lewis's cousin, Eleanora "Nora" Iselin, visiting Alice and Tracy in 1904 at Woodland Cottage. Nora and Alice were close friends and, as a young girl, Alice would often visit the Iselins at their New Rochelle summer home, All View, which was designed by Stanford White in 1890.

ABOVE A society portrait of Nora taken around the time she married the Austrian diplomat Count Ferdinand Colloredo-Mansfeld in 1909.

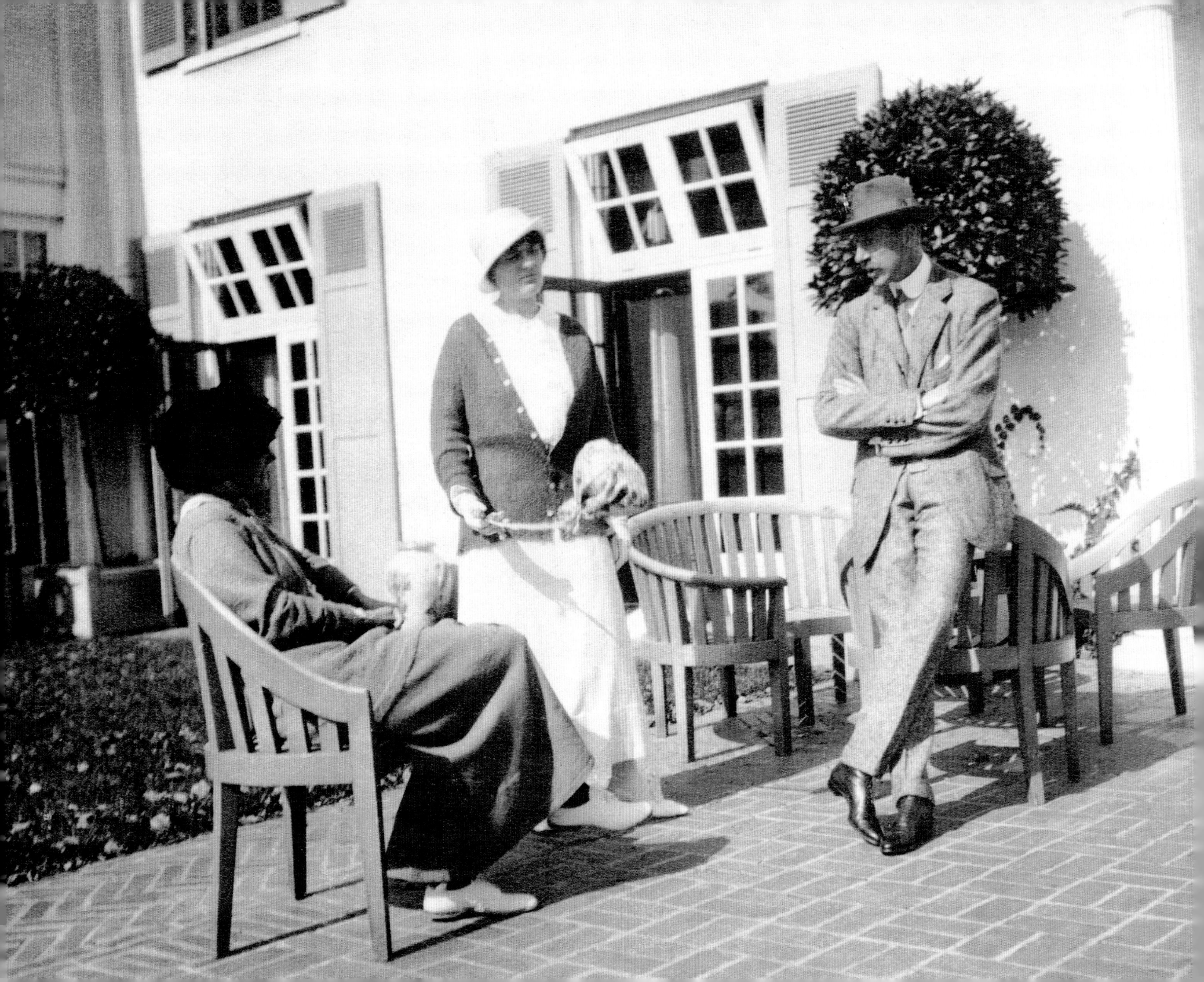

OPPOSITE Alice playfully swinging a bag on the back terrace with the very dapper Francis "Frank" Stanton Blake, and his wife, Eugenie, in the fall of 1913. Frank and his brother, George Baty Blake, Jr., were senior members of the Boston stock brokerage firm, Blake Brothers & Company. Both were Harvard classmates of Tracy Dows, graduating in 1893. After their marriage in 1902, Frank and Eugenie Blake moved to Roquebrune-Cap-Martin in France, where they built an exquisite villa in 1905. They visited Foxhollow Farm on their annual trips to America.

RIGHT Tracy and Alice's good friend Morton Jackson Henry with Olin and Margaret, visiting Foxhollow Farm in the summer of 1915. Raised in Philadelphia and educated at Harvard, Henry married Rebecca Anjelica Morrison in 1902, who belonged to one of the oldest colonial lines in Maryland. Henry was a lieutenant colonel in the U.S. Army during World War I. His nephew, Barklie McKee Henry, married Barbara Whitney, the daughter of Harry Payne Whitney and Gertrude Vanderbilt Whitney.

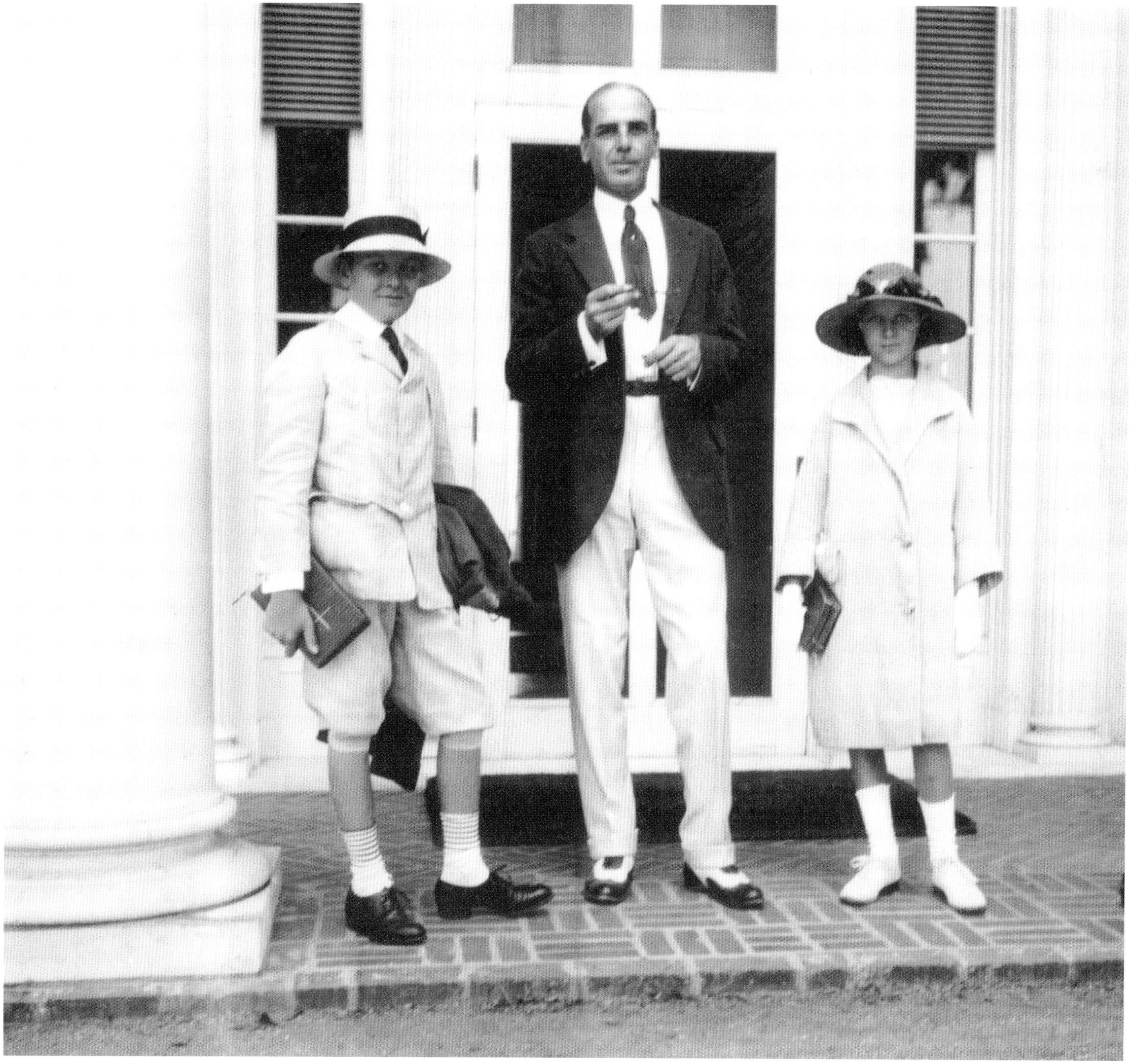

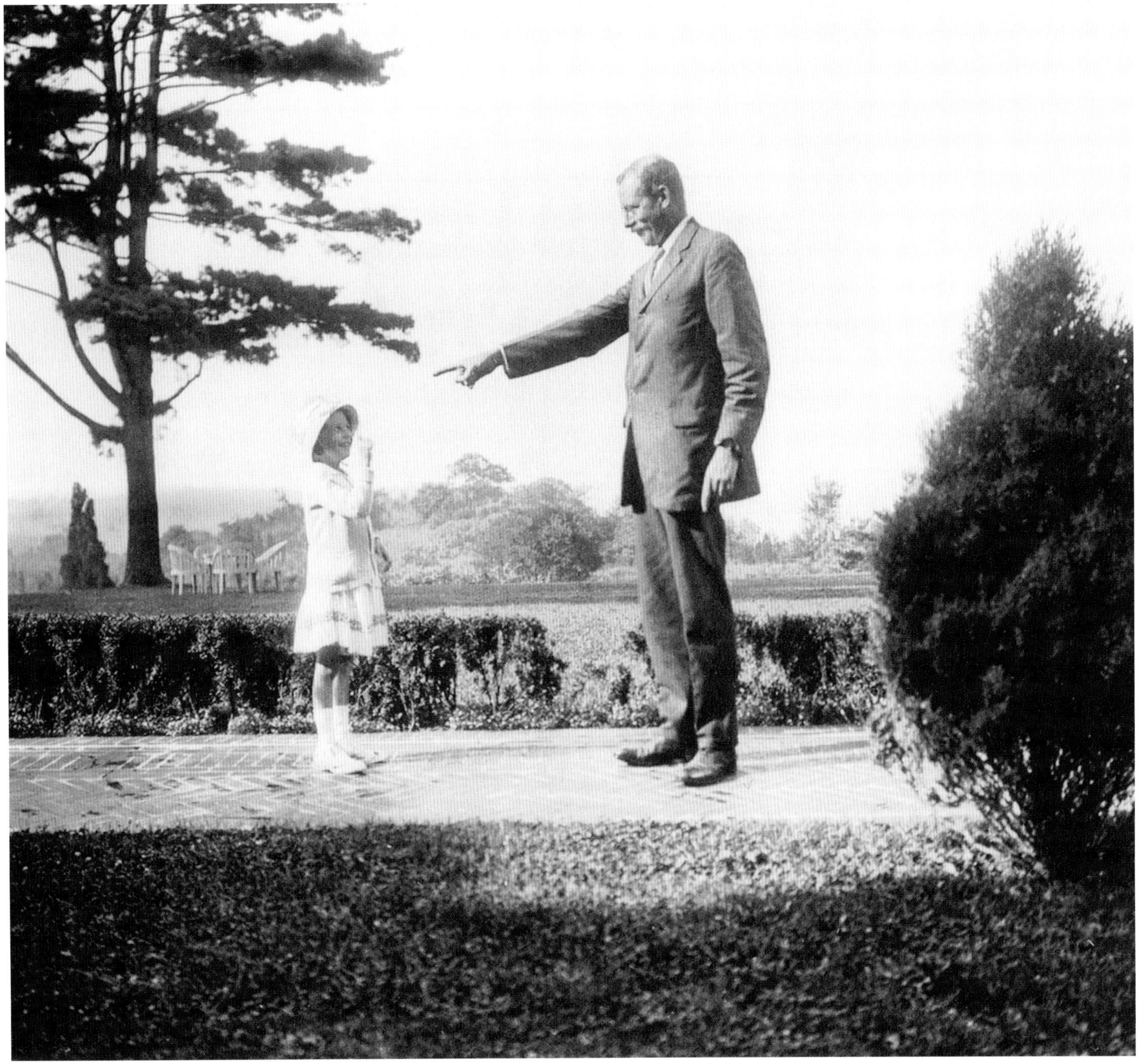

LEFT A very tall Henry G. Barbey, towering over Deb Dows at Foxhollow Farm in 1919. He was a close friend of Tracy's and the best man at his wedding. With his business partner, Cary Smith, Barbey designed some of the finest pleasure boats owned by American yachtsmen. Eva, his youngest sister, had one of the largest weddings of the season in 1903 when she became the bride of Baron André de Neuflize of Paris. Barbey was the nephew of Pierre Lorillard IV, who developed Tuxedo Park.

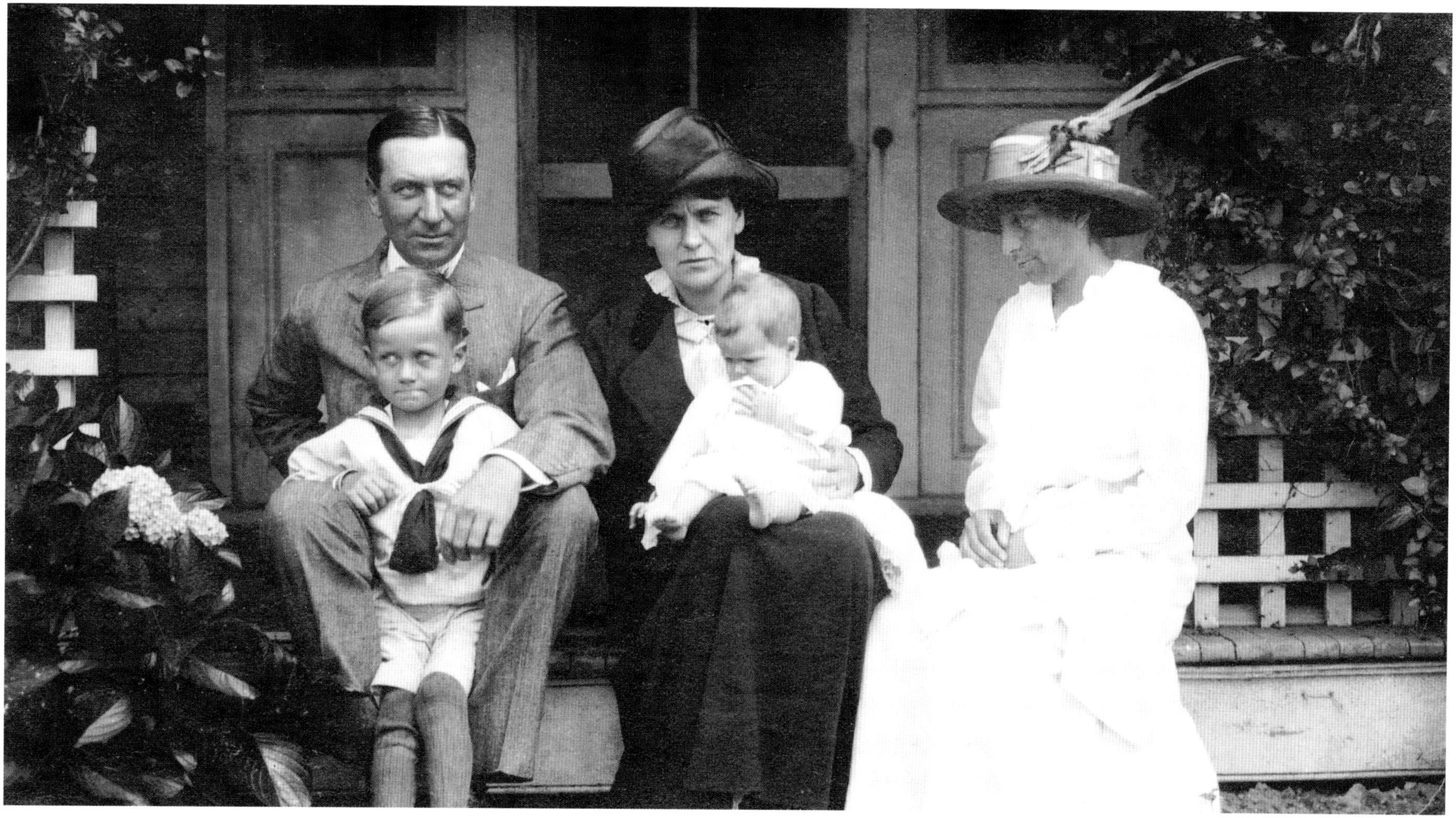

ABOVE Tracy and Alice with Mrs. Alonzo Potter and her children at the Potters' Southampton residence in 1912. Alonzo Potter was the son of Henry Codman Potter, the noted bishop of the Episcopal Diocese of New York City. The young boy standing with Tracy is Henry Codman Potter, named after his grandfather. He became a successful film director of such movies as *Hellzapoppin'*, *The Farmer's Daughter*, and *Mr. Blandings Builds His Dream House*.

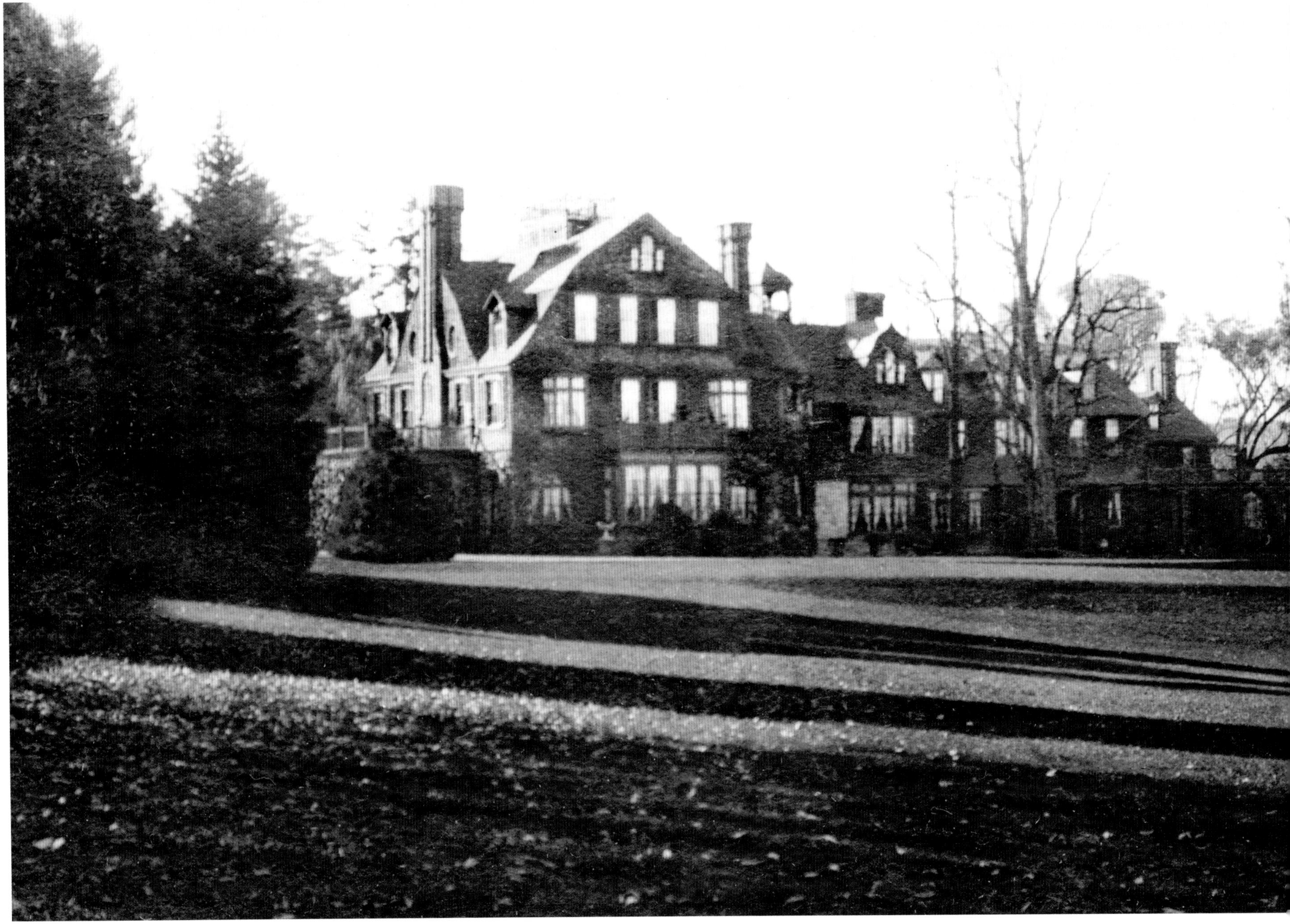

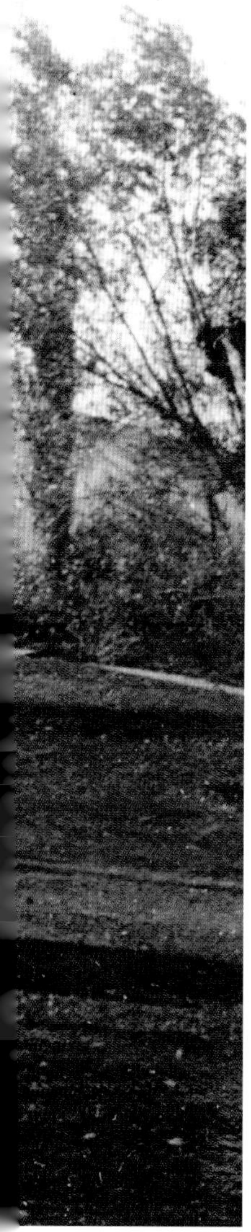

LEFT Tranquility Farms, the expansive estate of Rutherfurd Stuyvesant, in the Allamuchy area of New Jersey, November 1906. Known for introducing the English pheasant to America, Stuyvesant held a popular pheasant shoot that Tracy and Alice attended. He was the son of astronomer Lewis Morris Rutherfurd and a descendant of Peter Stuyvesant, the Dutch governor of New York in the late 1600s. In order to receive the Stuyvesant family inheritance, he legally changed his name from Stuyvesant Rutherfurd to Rutherfurd Stuyvesant. Tranquility Farms' large Shingle-style mansion mysteriously burned down in 1959.

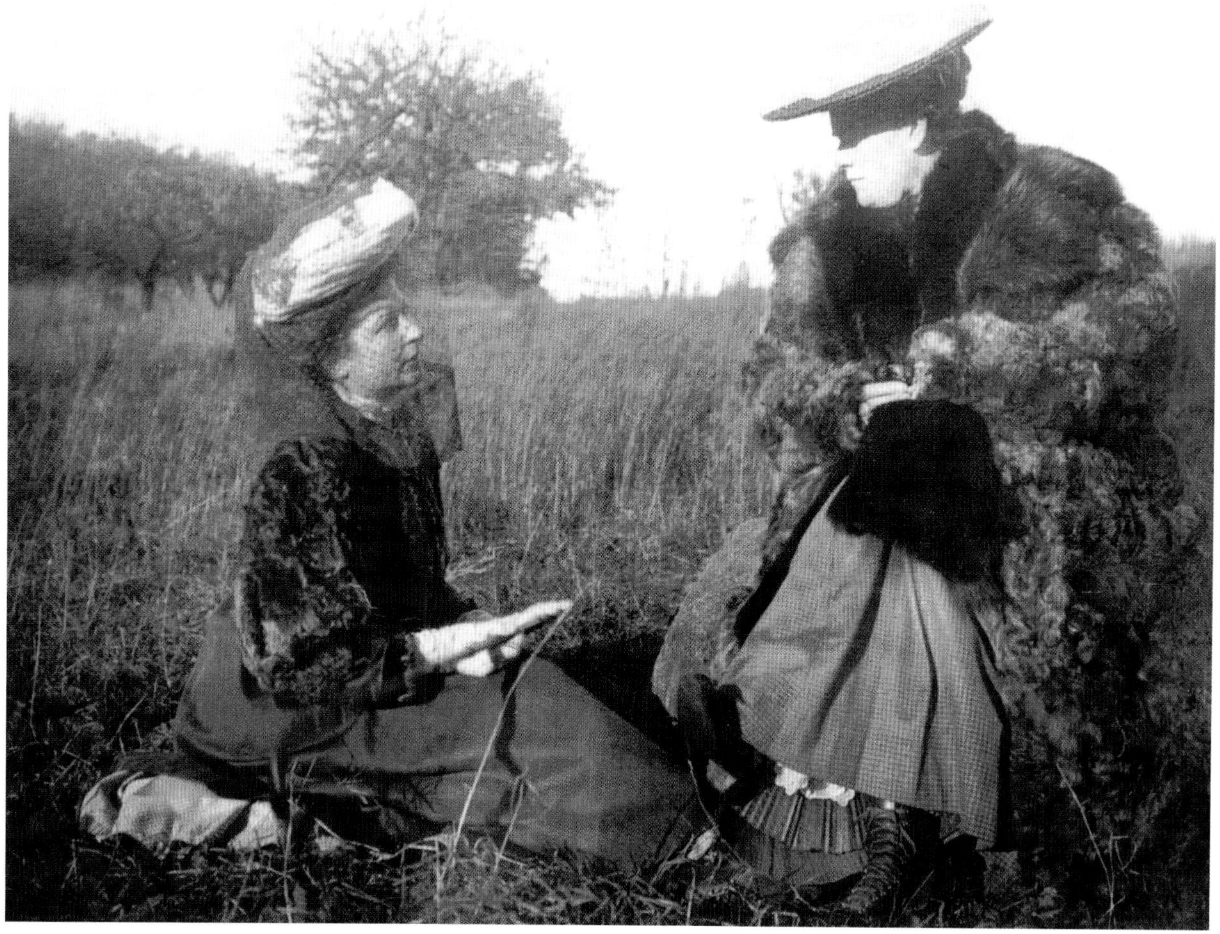

ABOVE Mrs. Rutherfurd Stuyvesant (formerly Mathilde de Wassanaer, the widow of a Dutch count), with Alice, right, in the fields at Tranquility Farms during the pheasant shoot.

RIGHT The terrace façade view of Avalon, the Mount Kisco, New York, estate of Robert Stanton Brewster, in 1917 when the Dowses were guests there. The house was designed by Delano & Aldrich and built in 1910. Brewster and Delano were Yale classmates. In the 1920s, the landscape architect Ellen Biddle Shipman was hired to enrich the plantings. Mrs. Brewster was a knowledgeable horticulturist and carefully maintained the gardens throughout her life. The estate was sold in 1948 to the Yeshiva of Nitra Rabbinical College.

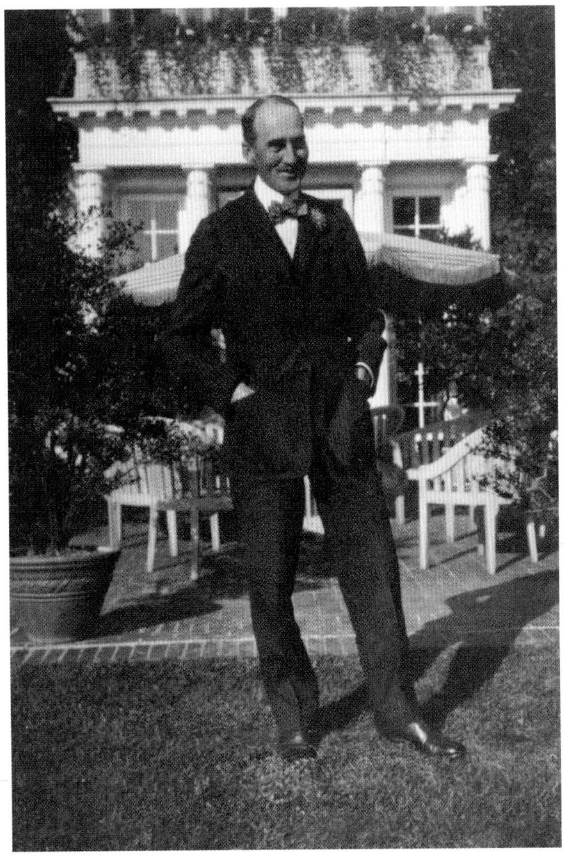

LEFT Robert S. Brewster at Foxhollow Farm in 1920. His father, Benjamin Brewster, was a founding trustee of Standard Oil and a board member of David Dows & Company, and his mother, Elmina Hersey Dows, was Tracy's cousin.

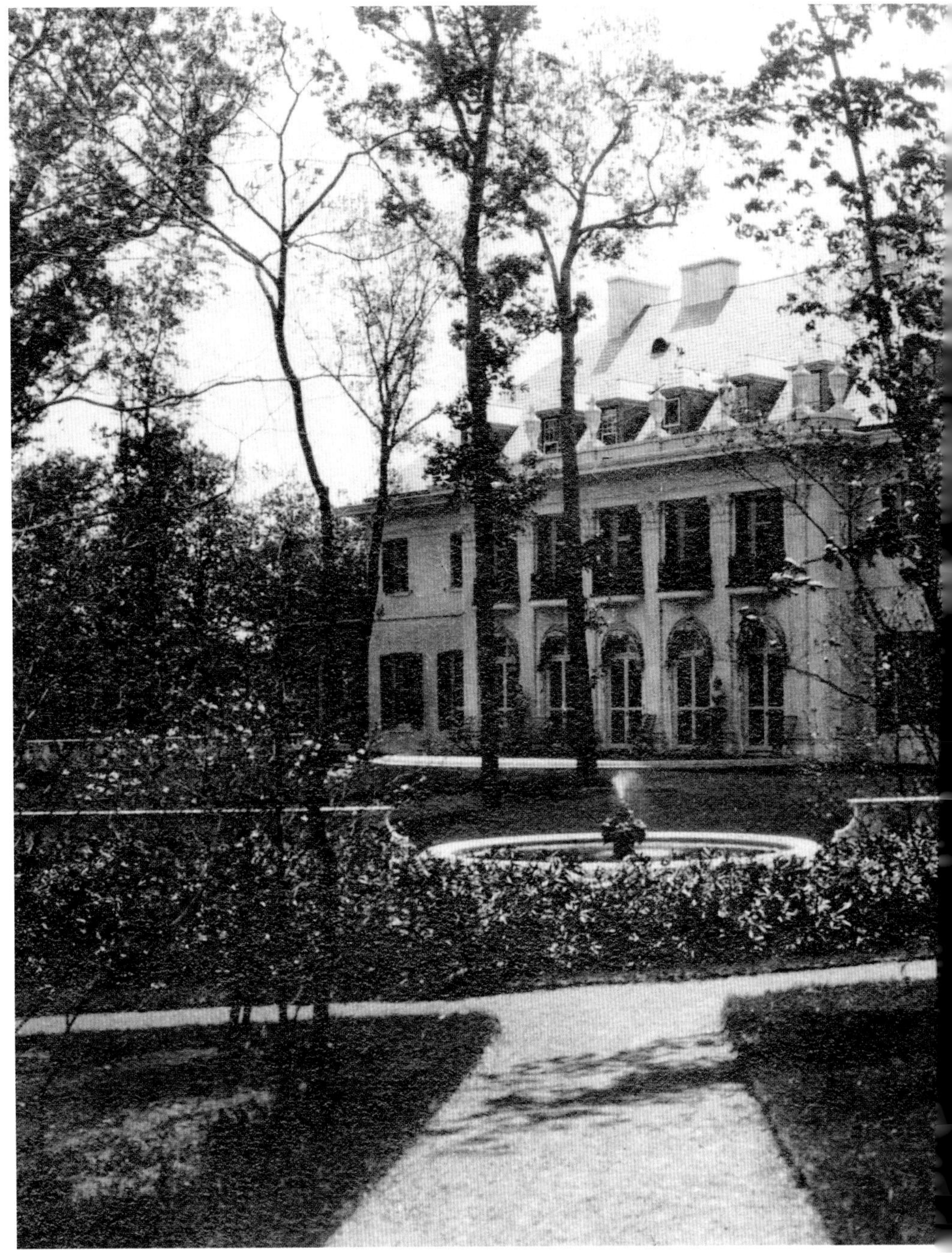

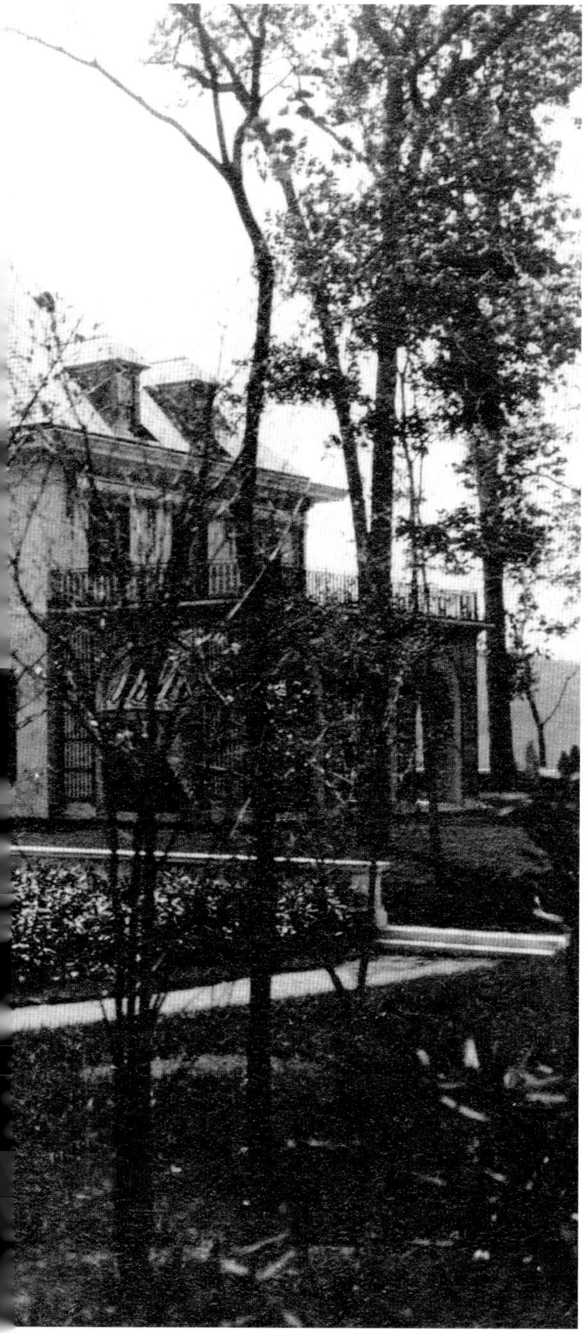

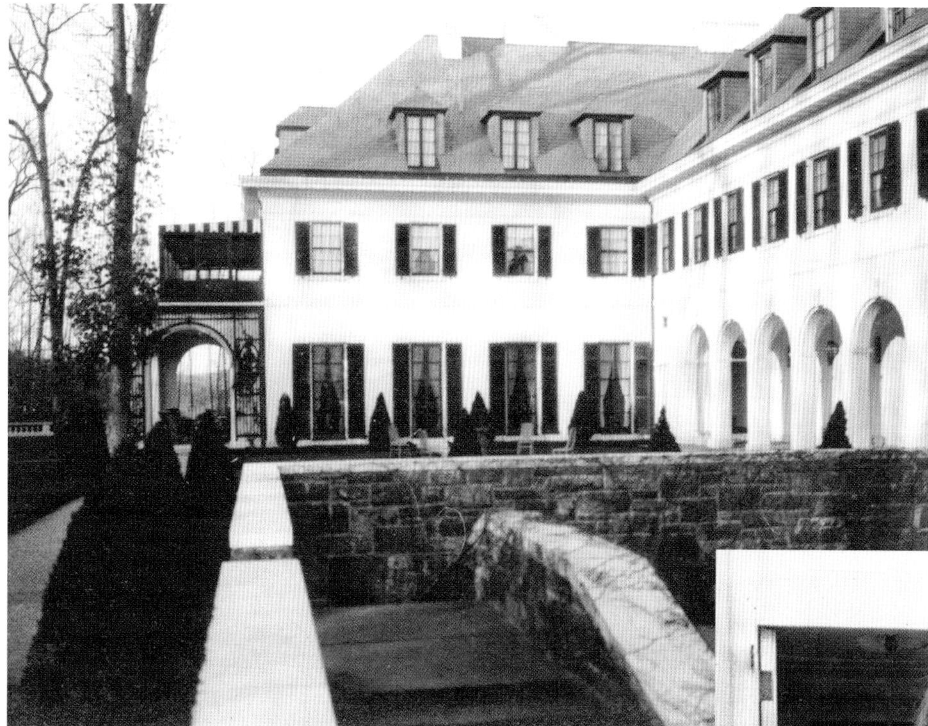

ABOVE A view of the courtyard of the French Renaissance–style house. The beautifully landscaped hilly estate included a grass terrace with four circular fountains, a Palladian-inspired pool house, a round pergola at the entrance to a large sunken elliptical garden, and a woodland path that led to a folly. After a devastating fire burned the house to the ground, Brewster had Delano & Aldrich build a fireproof replica to reproduce the original in every detail.

BELOW The Brewsters' oldest daughter, Sylvia, left, with Margaret Dows at Foxhollow Farm in 1919. Margaret was two years older than Sylvia and they became close friends. In 1929, Sylvia married Lieutenant Colonel Edward Frederick Maude, a descendant of Henry VIII.

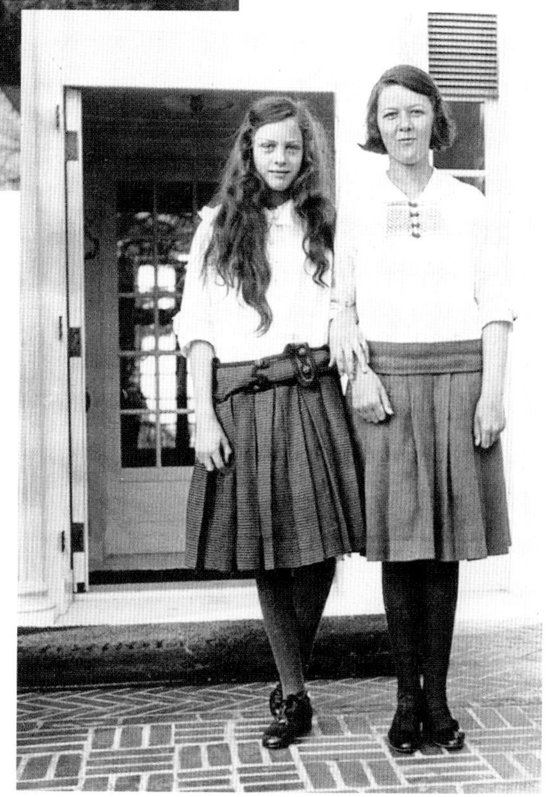

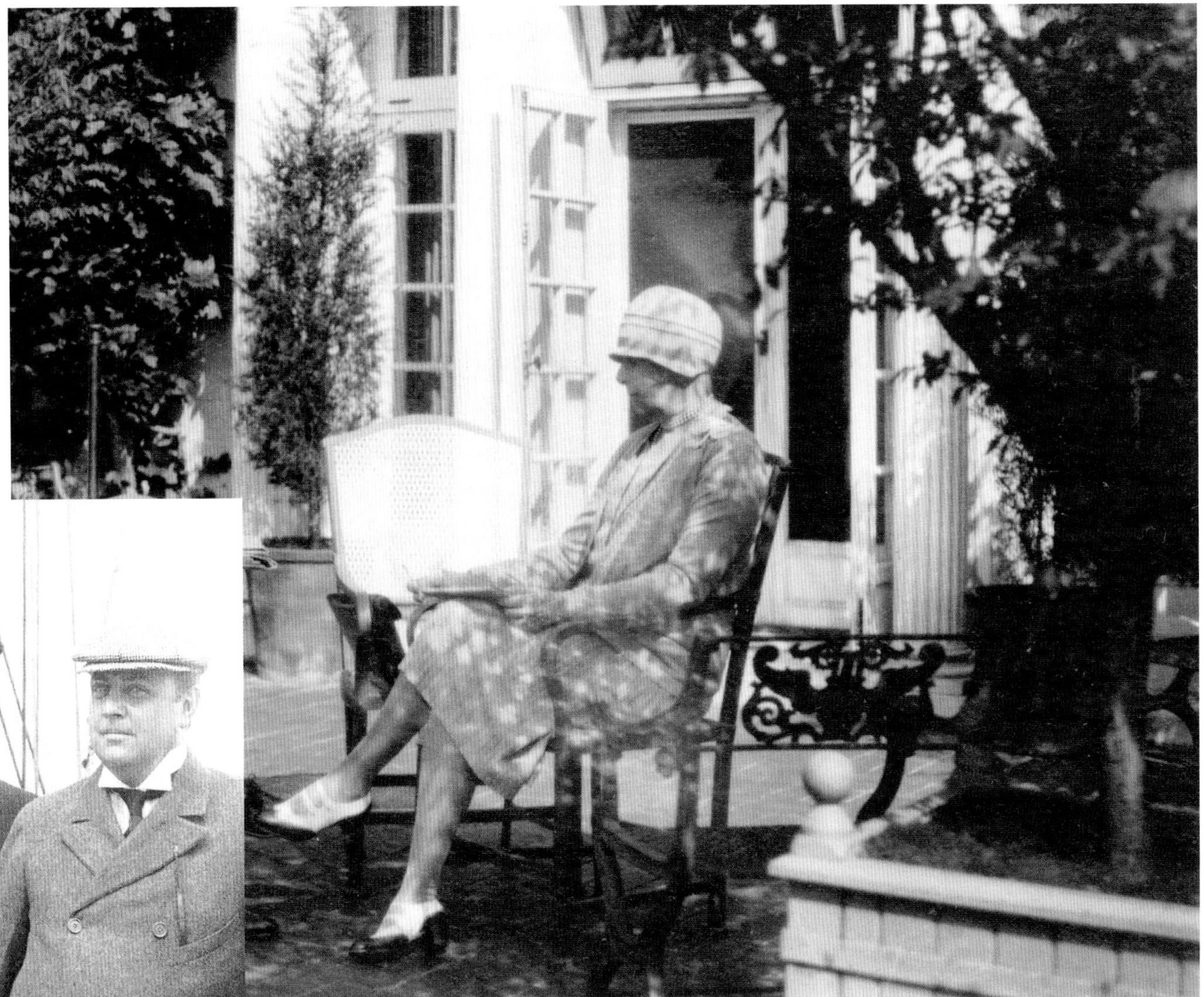

RIGHT Florence "Daisy" Hurst Harriman on the terrace at Foxhollow Farm in 1927. Daisy, the daughter of shipping magnate Francis William Jones Hurst, married J. Borden Harriman in 1889, a New York City financier and member of the Gilded Age's hunting set and a brother of Mrs. Stephen Henry Olin. In 1903, Daisy cofounded the Colony Club, along with Mrs. John Jacob Astor IV and Mrs. Payne Whitney. She was involved in the women's suffrage movement, and, in 1912, took an active role in the election of Woodrow Wilson while living in Washington, D.C. She was widowed two years later. In 1937, President Franklin D. Roosevelt appointed her as the U.S. Minister to Norway. At age 92, she received a Citation of Merit for Distinguished Service from President John F. Kennedy.

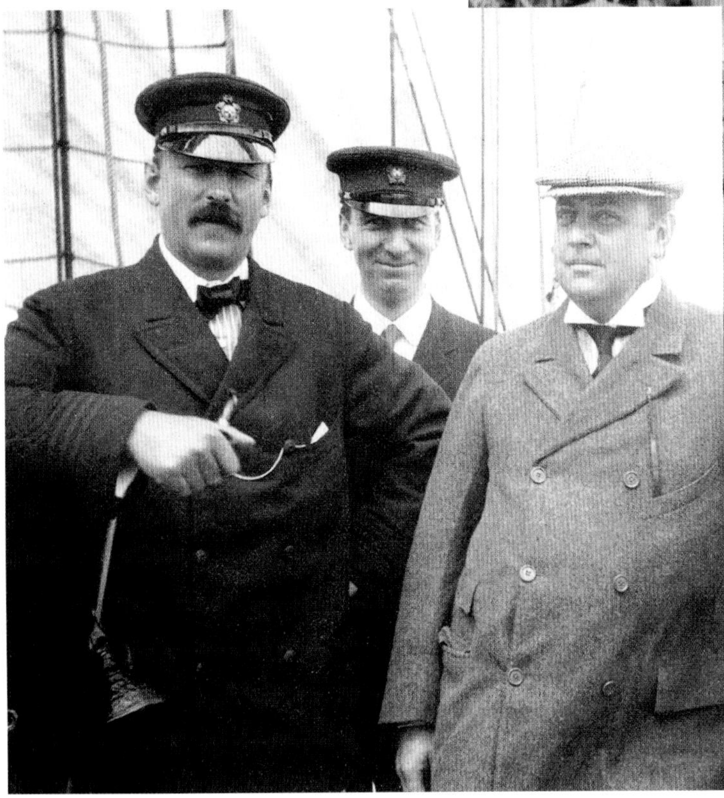

LEFT J. Borden Harriman, right, and Tracy Dows, center, with the *Mohican*'s captain, Rochester Cuming, aboard the yacht on a sailing excursion to Newport around 1903. Tracy sold the *Mohican* to Harriman in 1905.

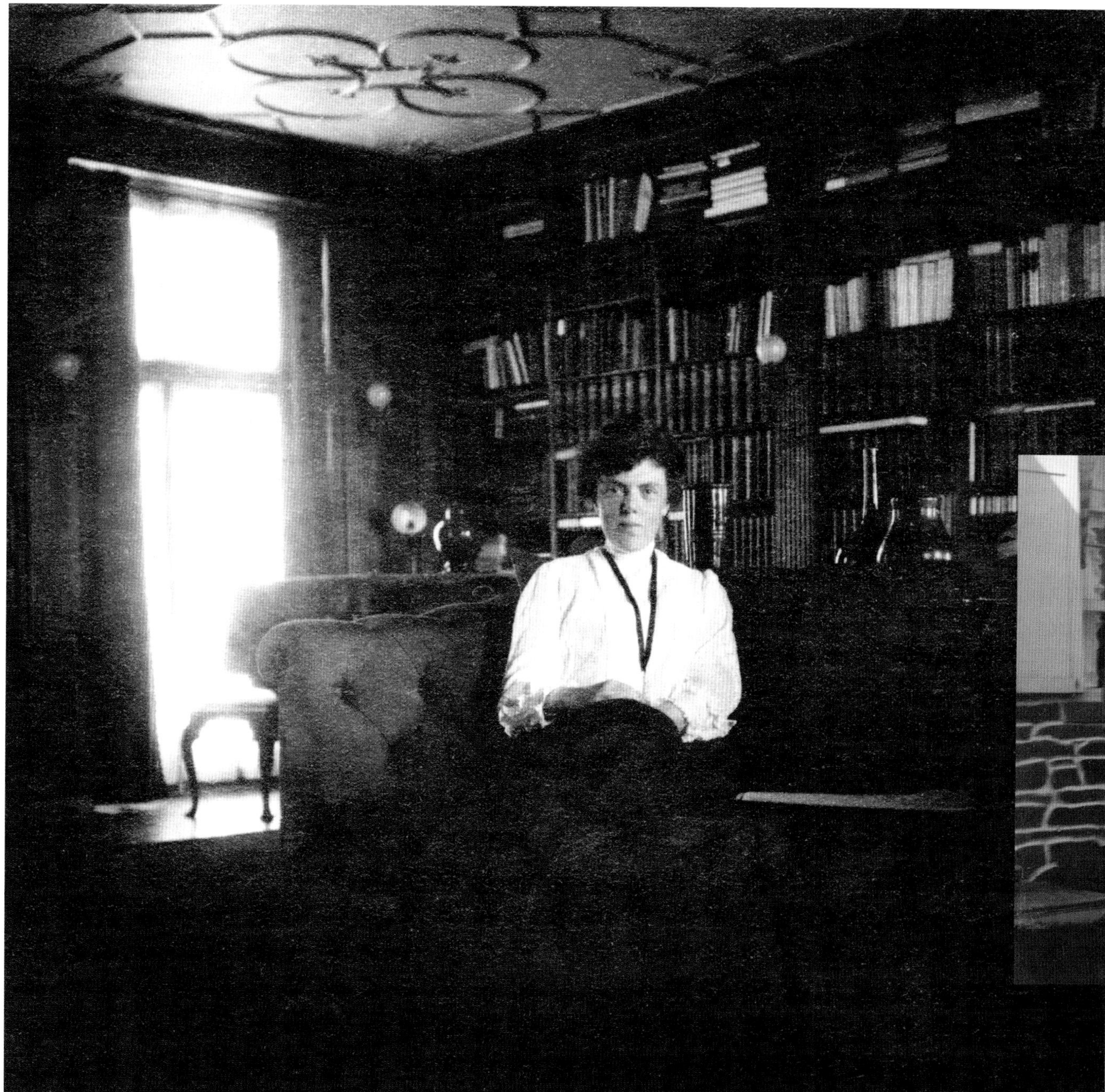

LEFT Lillie Harriman Havemeyer in the living room at Foxhollow Farm, 1910. Mrs. Havemeyer was the younger sister of Mrs. Stephen Henry Olin and J. Borden Harriman. She was married to Frederick Christian Havemeyer, the son of Theodore A. Havemeyer, whose family owned the prosperous Sugar Refineries Company, later reorganized as the American Sugar Refining Company. Frederick's great-grandfather and great-uncle came to New York from Germany in 1802 and established their sugar refining business. Soon the sons of the two brothers joined the business, followed by their own sons, including Frederick's father, Theodore. The American Sugar Refining Company became Domino Sugar in the early 1900s.

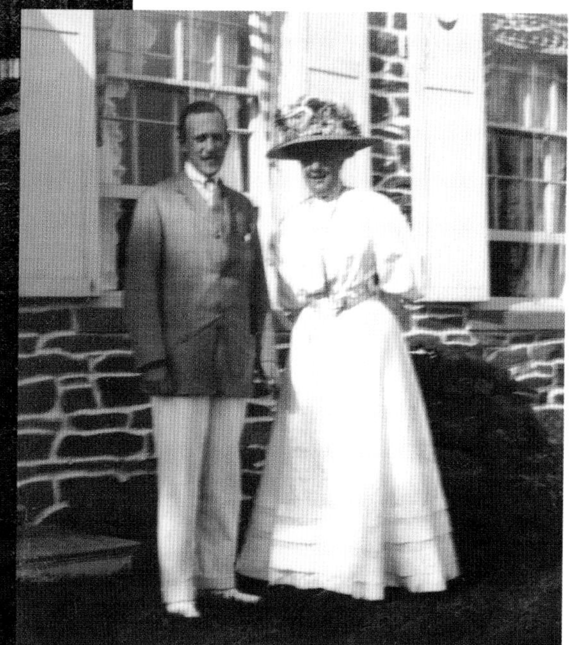

ABOVE Frederick Christian Havemeyer with Mrs. Stephen Henry Olin at Stone Cottage, 1908.

RIGHT A view of Hopeland House, the Staatsburg, New York, country estate of Mr. and Mrs. Robert Palmer Huntington, in 1914, a few years after it was completed. A direct descendant of Samuel Huntington, a signer of the Declaration of Independence, Robert married Helen Gray Dinsmore, the Adams Express Company heiress, in 1892. An avid yachtsman and champion tennis player, Huntington joined the architectural firm of Hoppin & Koen in 1904. Hopeland House was his own design, and the estate, with its series of rolling hills and valleys, was considered one of the most beautiful properties on the Hudson River. A magnificent driveway wound its way through valleys and woods. The stately thirty-room Tudor-style mansion was built with gray-red brick and limestone terra-cotta trim. The estate eventually passed down to the Huntington children, who, in the 1950s, had the house demolished.

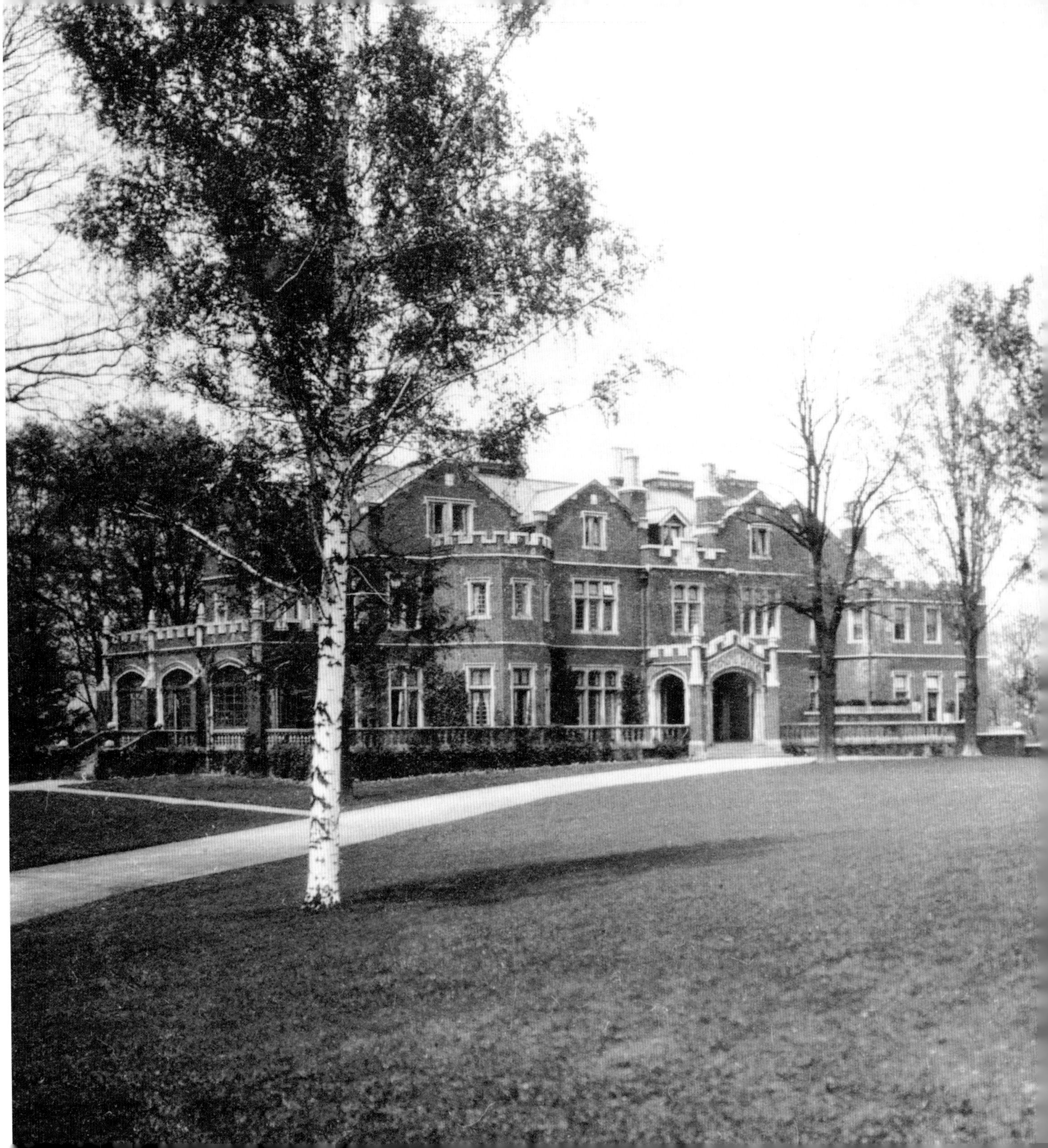

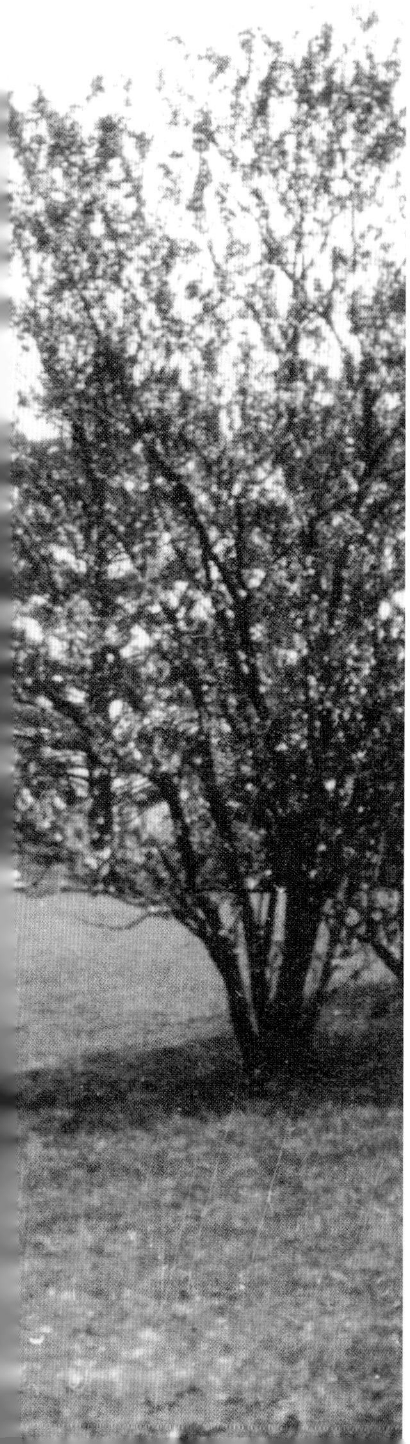

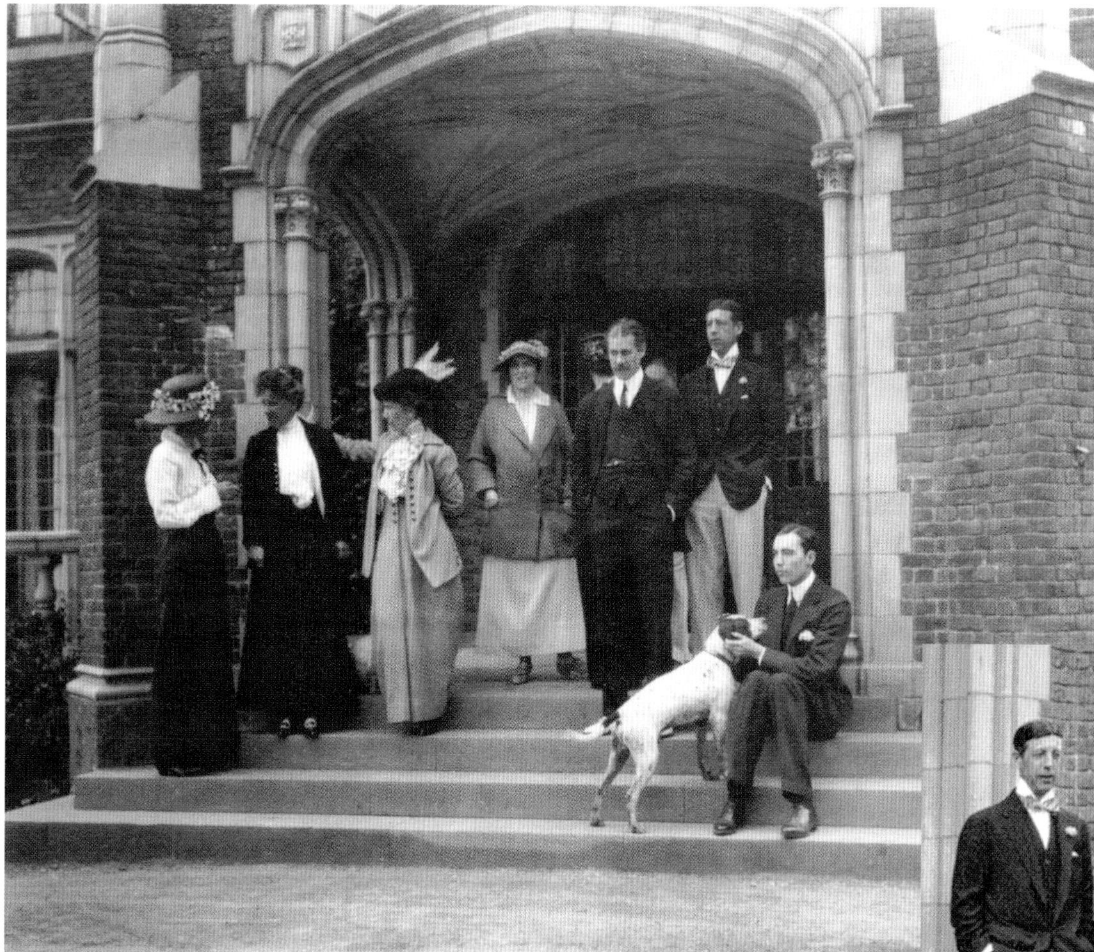

ABOVE A gathering at Hopeland House in May 1912. The party includes, from left, Helen Huntington Astor, Mrs. Robert Palmer Huntington (Helen's mother), Madeline Ingraham Dinsmore, Alice Dows, Robert Palmer Huntington (Helen's father), Oliver Samuel Campbell, and Vincent Astor. The Astors had married a month earlier.

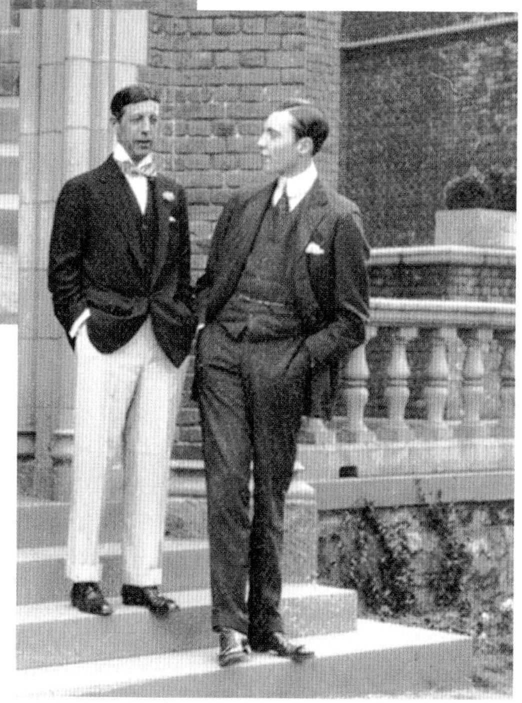

BELOW Oliver Samuel Campbell, left, and Vincent Astor having a conversation. Campbell was considered the golden boy of tennis in his day and often won doubles titles with Robert Huntington. In 1890, at age 19, he became the youngest male player in history of tennis to win the U.S. singles championship and held that honor for over a century, until Pete Sampras, a few months younger, took the title in 1990. Campbell chose to retire from professional tennis in 1892, at just twenty-two years old.

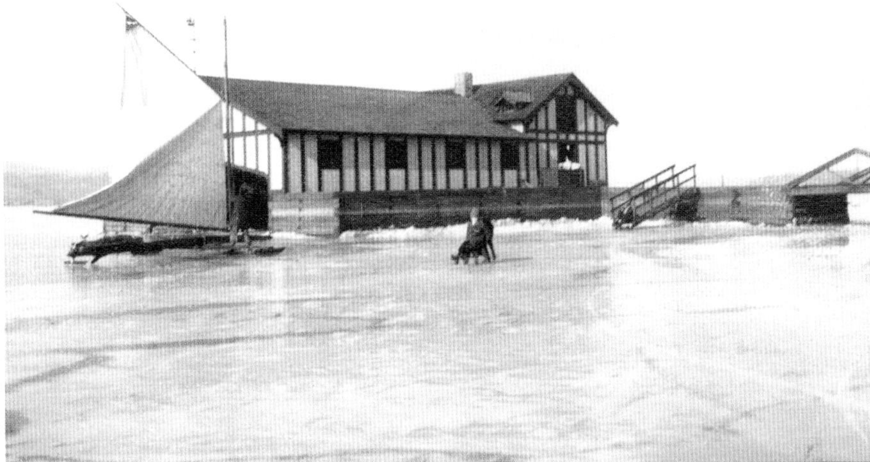

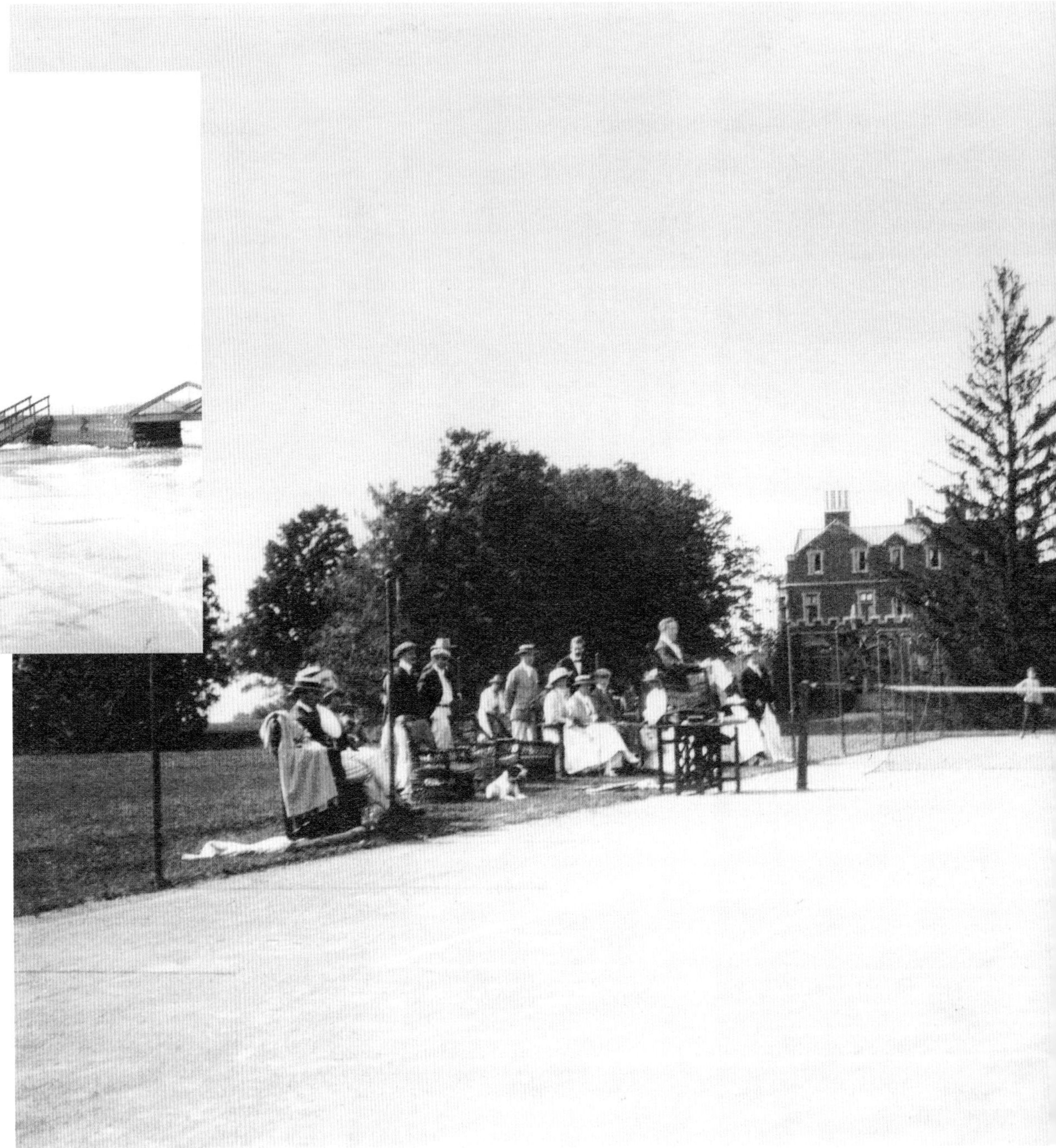

ABOVE Olin and Margaret playing on the frozen Hudson River in front of Robert Huntington's boat house in 1915. Huntington's ice boat, the *Pathfinder*, is about to venture out. Ford Huntington, Robert's brother, gave the *Pathfinder* to Richard Aldrich, of Rokeby, in the 1930s, where it remains today.

RIGHT A tennis match at Hopeland House on May 31, 1913. The game was part of a two-day tournament played on the courts of Foxhollow Farm, Ferncliff, and Hopeland House. Spectators from neighboring estates came to watch the matches. On the last day of the tournament, Tracy and Alice hosted a dinner and dance at Foxhollow Farm, catered by Sherry's of New York City.

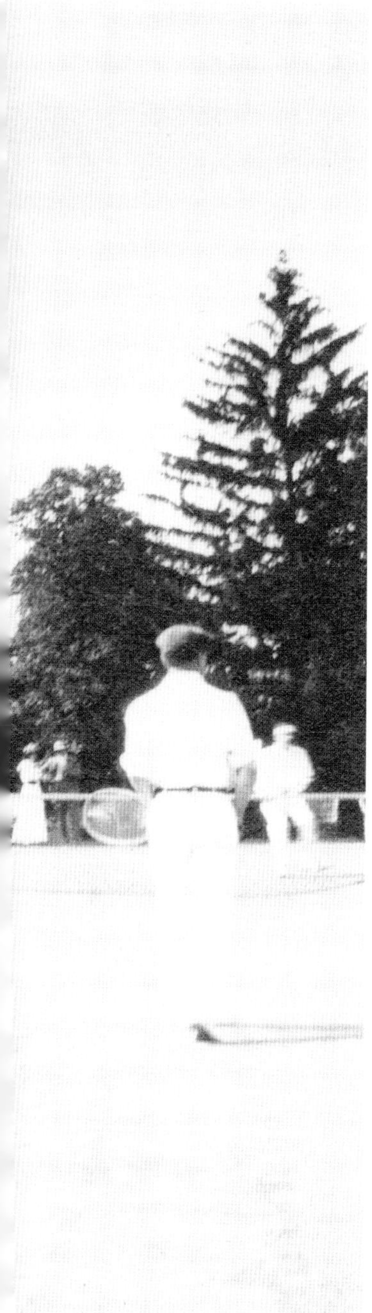

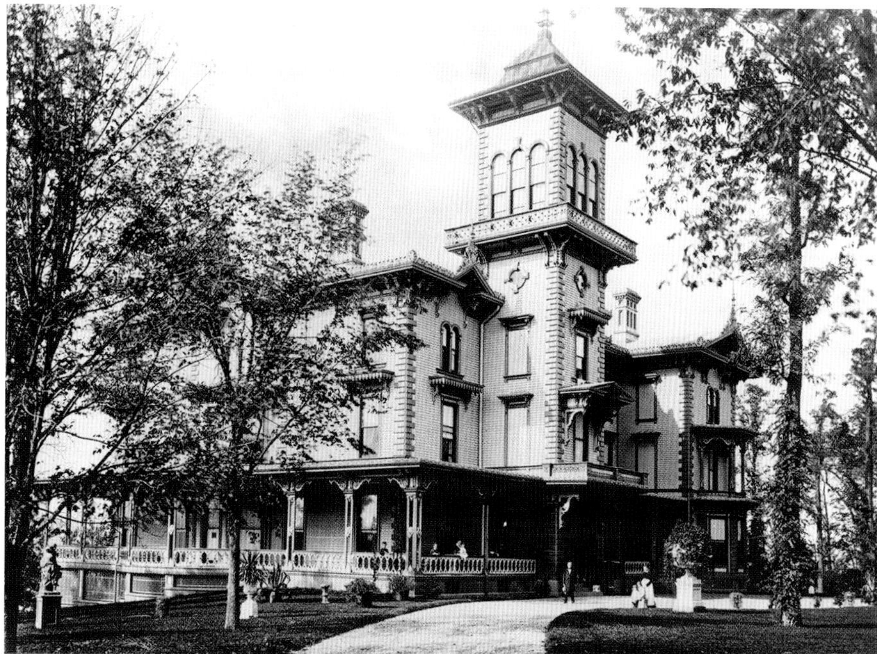

LEFT The Locusts, the country home of the Dinsmore family, in the early 1900s. The property was originally developed in the 1780s by Henry Brockholst Livingston, a great-grandson of Robert Livingston, First Lord of the Manor. In later years it was purchased by William B. Dinsmore, president of the Adams Express Company, who greatly expanded the property. He demolished the existing house around 1871 and built an ornamental ninety-room Italianate mansion on its site overlooking the Hudson River. He became an expert in horticulture and laid out extensive drives and walkways with greenhouses, gardens, and statuary. The estate later passed on to his son, William B. Dinsmore II, the father of Helen Gray Dinsmore Huntington. (Courtesy of Dinsmore & Huntington Family Archives)

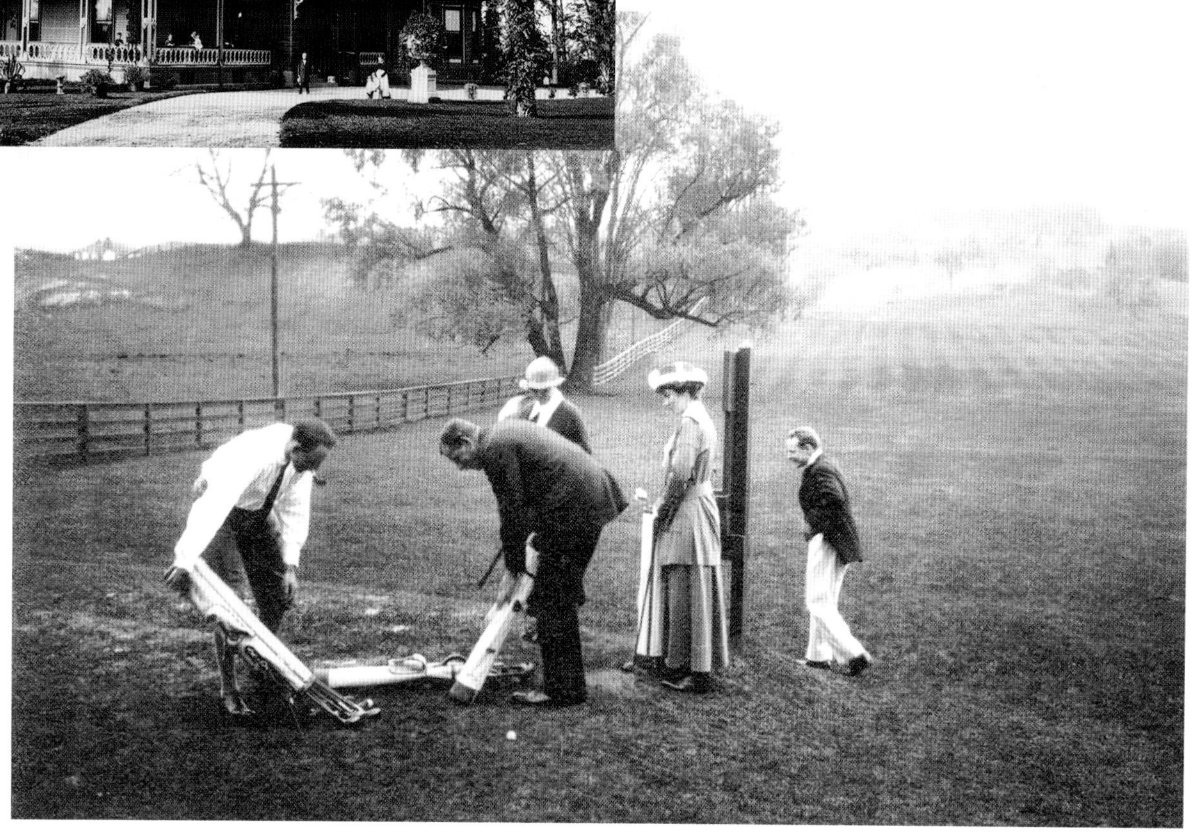

RIGHT Alice and visiting friends play golf in Staatsburg on the Dinsmores' course, 1915. The land was established as a private nine-hole golf course for the Huntington, Dinsmore, Hoyt, and Mills families in the 1890s. Now public, it is one of the oldest golf courses in the United States.

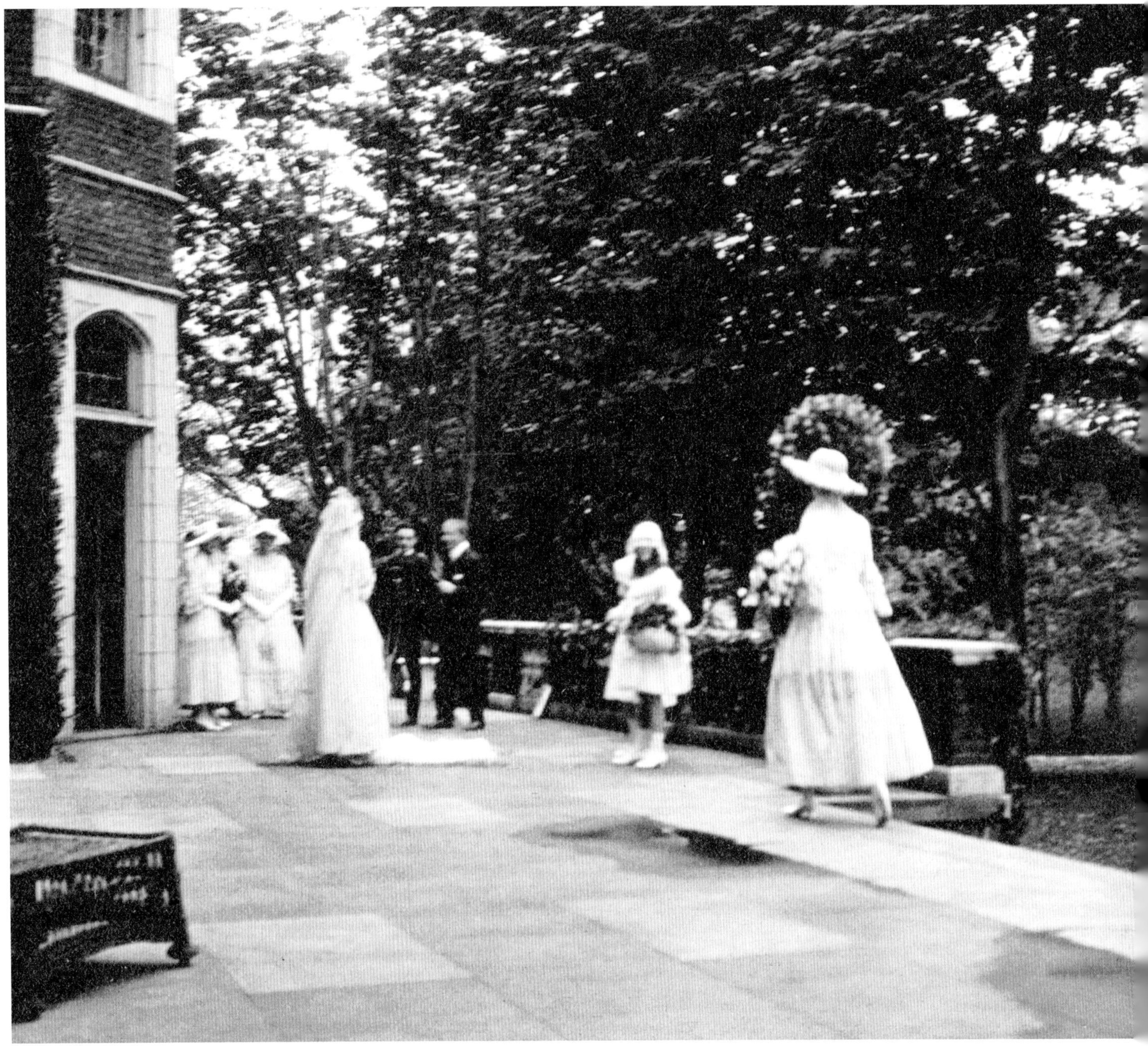

RIGHT Helen Huntington Astor walking toward her newly married sister, Alice, on the terrace at Hopeland House. The young flower girl is Margaret Dows. Alice Ford Huntington married Charles Henry "Buddy" Marshall, Jr., on June 3, 1917, reported by the *New York Times* as one of the most important weddings of the year. The ceremony took place at St. Margaret's Church in Staatsburg, and the reception was held at Hopeland House, where, after threatening weather, the skies cleared in time for the celebration. Guests from New York City traveled on a special rail car attached to an express train. The matrons of honor were Helen and Mrs. Marshall Field, and the best man was Marshall Field III. Cole Porter and W. Averell Harriman were two of the ushers. When Alice and Buddy divorced in 1932, he became the second husband to Brooke Russell Kuser, who later became Vincent Astor's third wife.

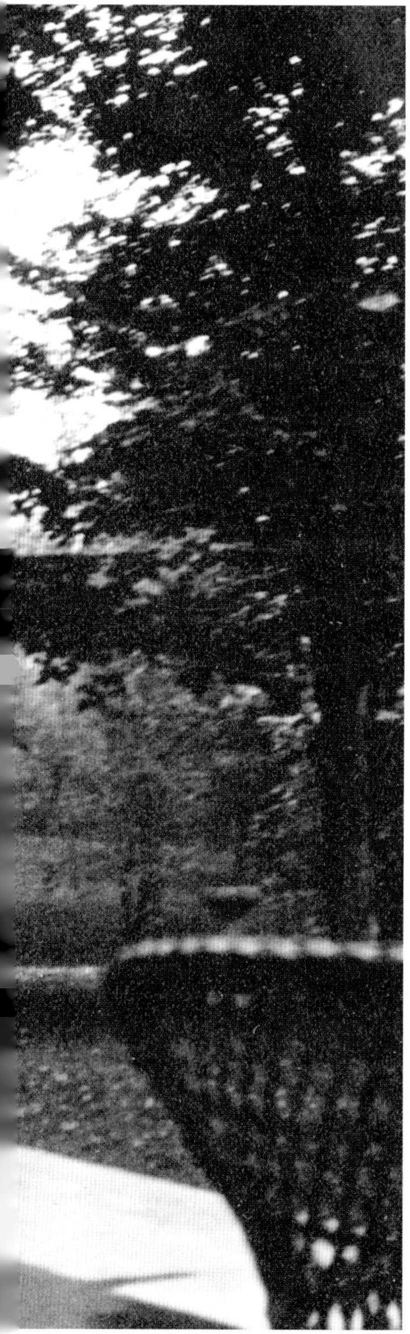

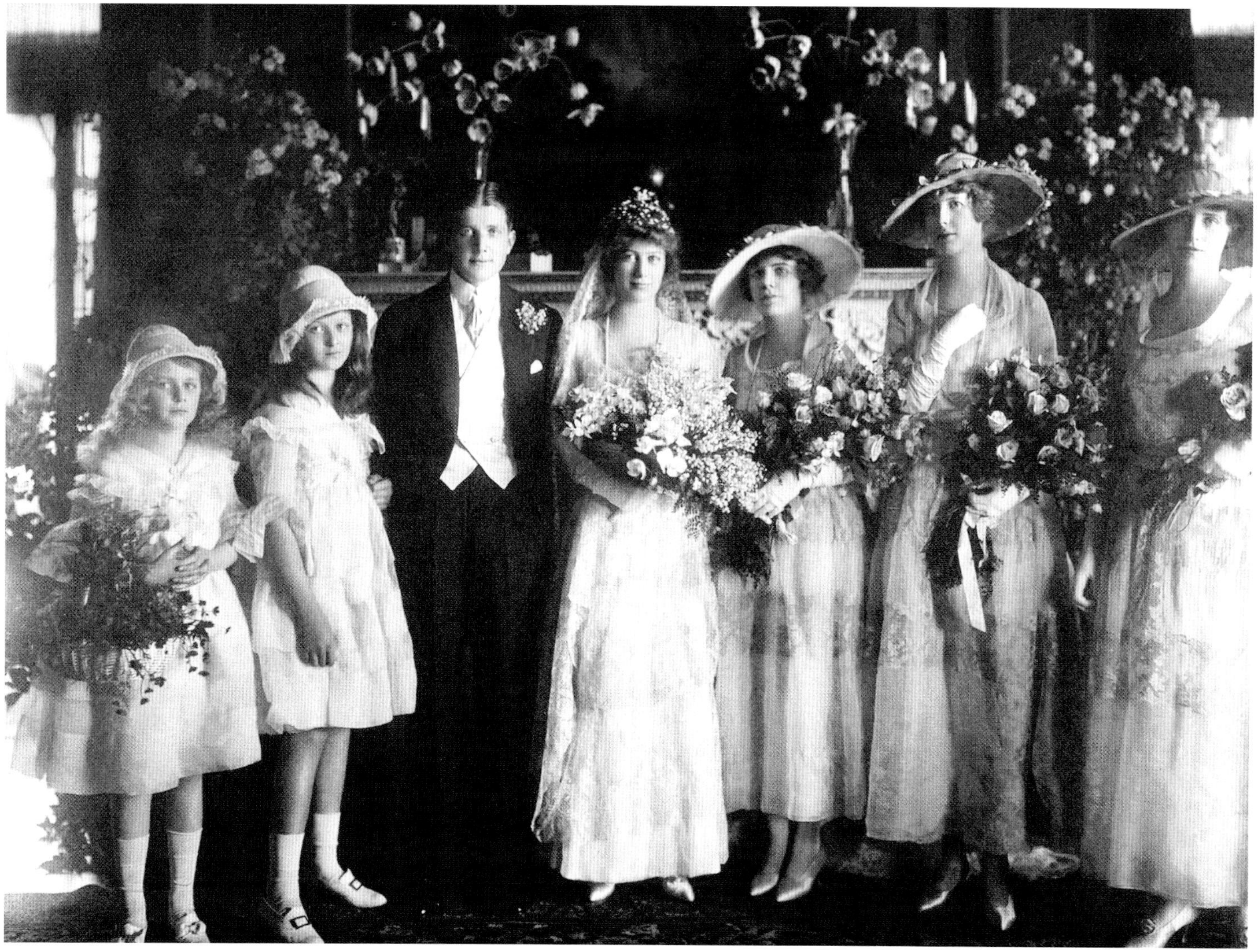

ABOVE A photograph of the wedding party. From left are Clare Dinsmore, Margaret Dows, Buddy Marshall, Alice Huntington Marshall, Marion Carey Dinsmore, Helen Huntington Astor, and Mrs. Marshall Field. (Courtesy of Dinsmore & Huntington Family Archives)

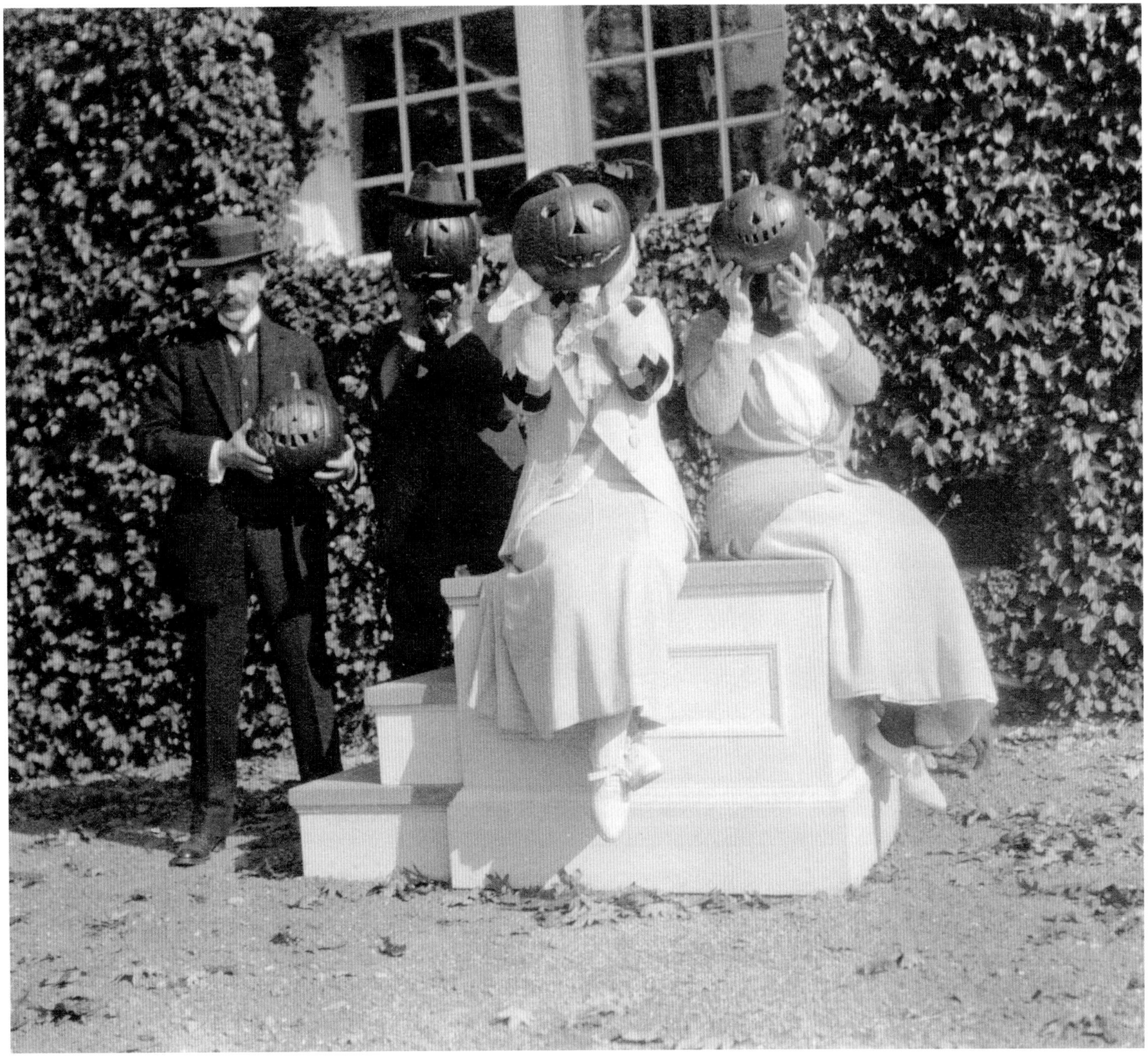

LEFT Having fun with pumpkins on Halloween 1911. Visiting the Dowses were Victor Morawetz, a successful New York City lawyer, and his wife Violet, who was a cousin of Tracy's. The Morawetz's Long Island country house, Three Ponds, was designed by Delano & Aldrich in 1912.

OPPOSITE Harrie T. Lindeberg with Alice, Margaret, and Olin on the front steps of Stone Cottage in February 1910 after cross-country skiing on the hills of the property.

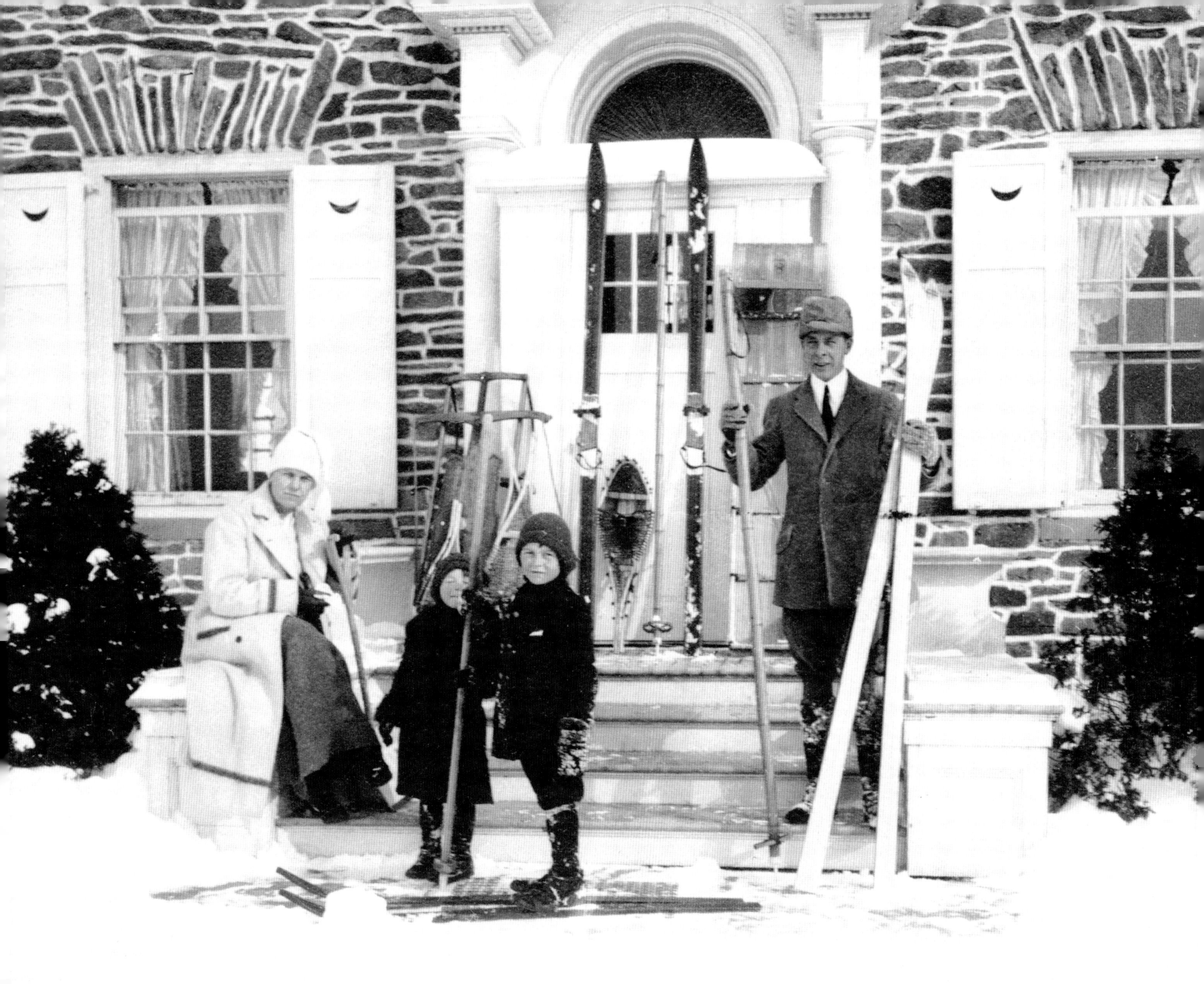

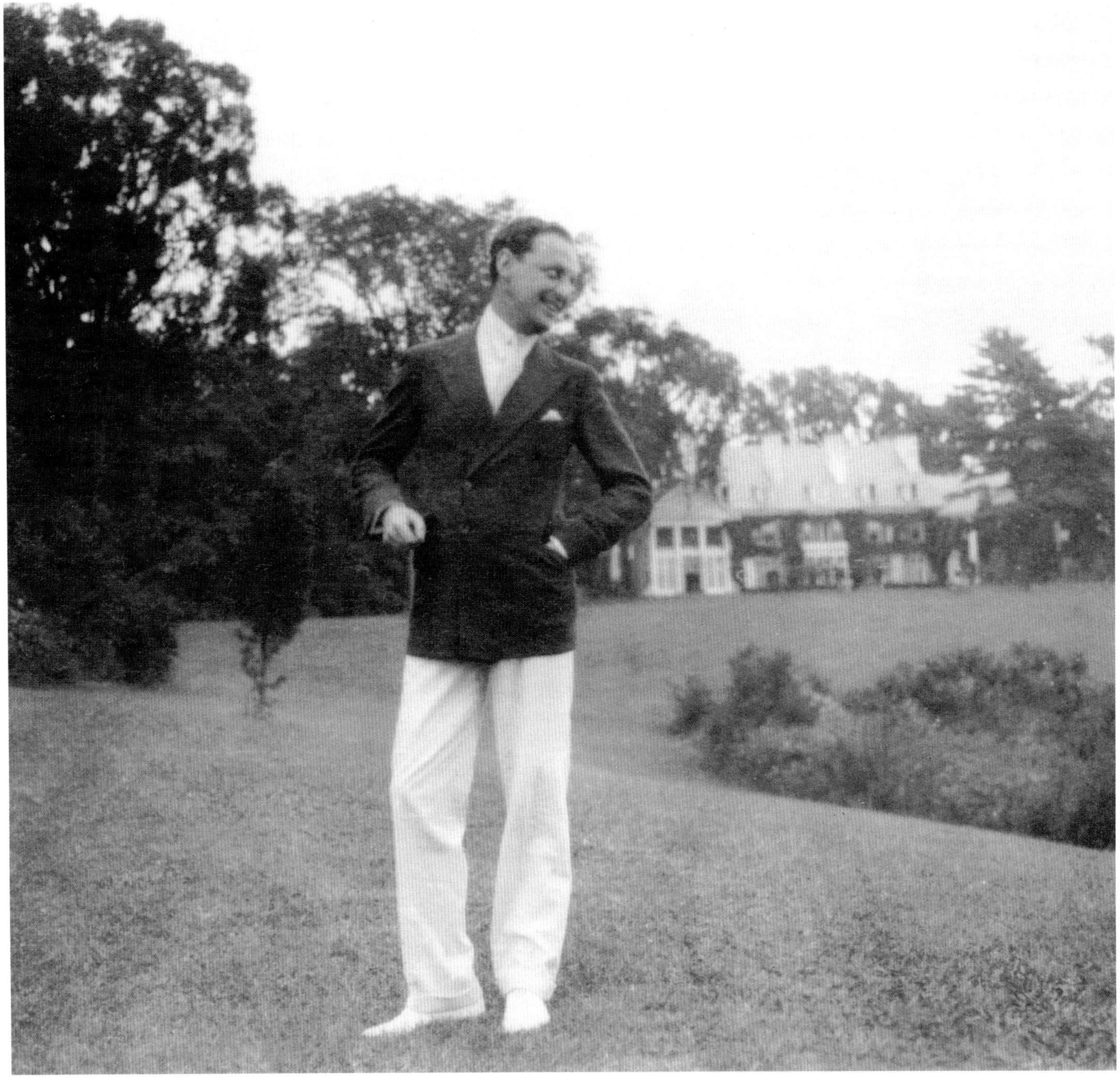

LEFT Jan Carel Juta standing on the back lawn at Foxhollow Farm in the summer of 1927. Born in Cape Town, South Africa, Juta was the son of Sir Henry and Lady Juta, who were prominent members of the Cape Colony. He became an established painter, designer, author, and lecturer, illustrating books for his close friend, the writer D. H. Lawrence, and creating murals for the Cunard liners *Queen Mary* and *Queen Elizabeth*. Juta spent much of the 1920s on the French Riviera. In Èze he painted extensive murals for a chateau owned by the American composer Samuel Latham Mitchill Barlow, Jr., who was Alice Dows's first cousin. Juta married Alice Huntington Marshall after her divorce from Buddy Marshall in 1932.

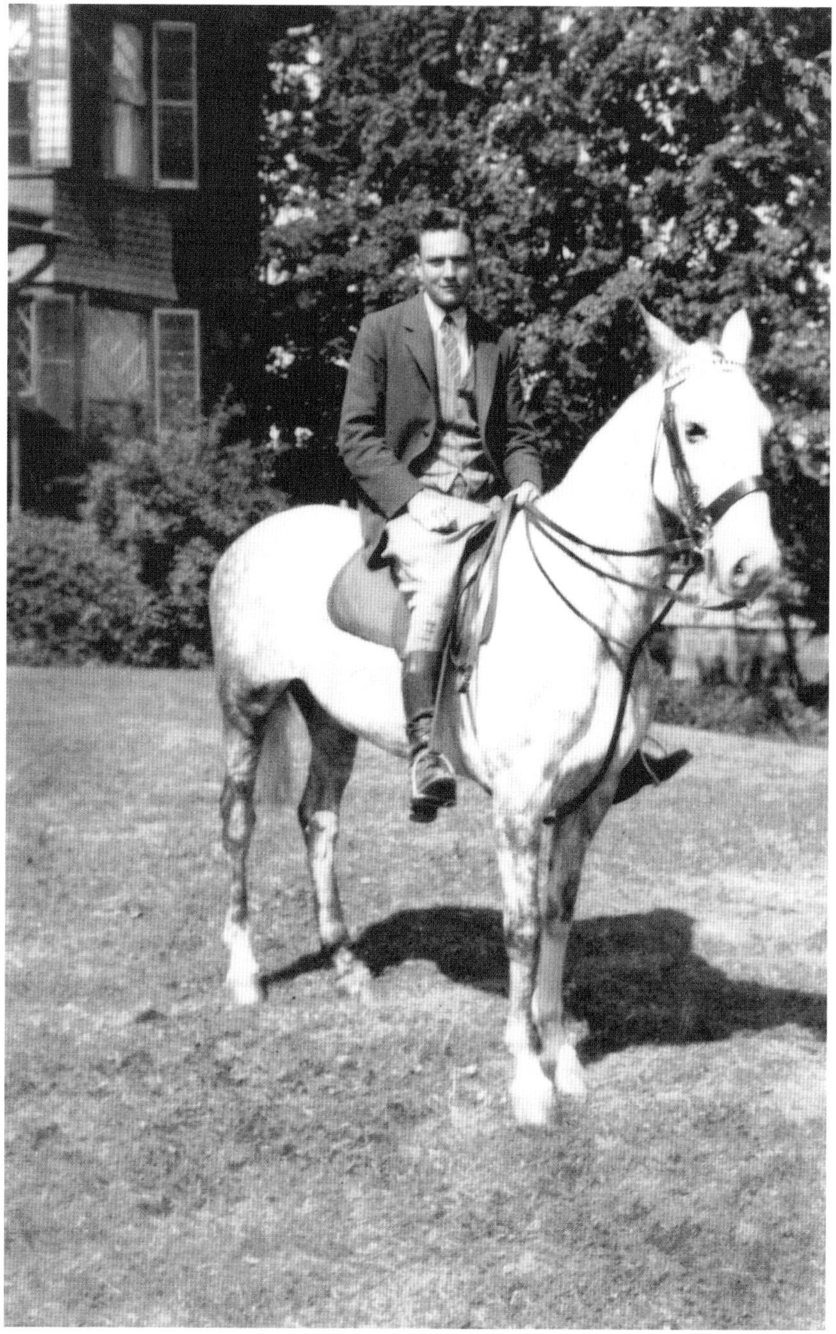

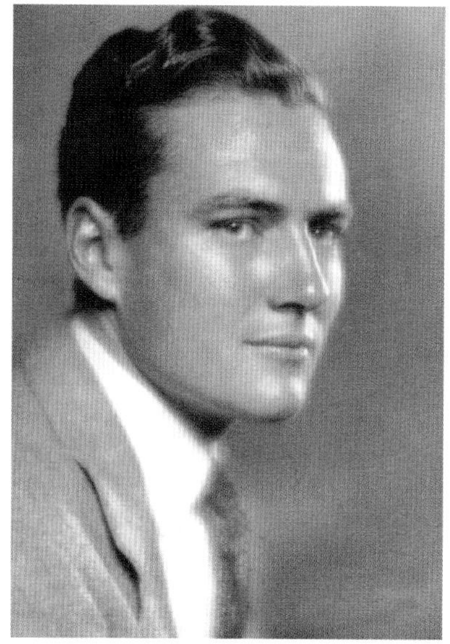

BELOW A signed photograph of Langdon in Kashmir that he sent to Margaret and Knut in 1925, referring to them by their nicknames, "Bargy" and "Knutsky." Langdon enjoyed traveling to exotic places. Sadly, during this trip, he mysteriously disappeared and never returned. The *New York Times* reported that he was found drowned in a river in northern India. Some said that the identification was inconclusive and his fate was unknown.

ABOVE A photograph of John Langdon taken by Pirie MacDonald, a New York City photographer known for his portraits of international heads of state, religious leaders, and American presidents. It was Langdon who introduced Margaret Dows to his friend, the Swedish diplomat Knut Richard Thyberg, whom she later married.

LEFT Langdon on his horse at his Rhinebeck estate, Mansakenning. Alice Dows described him as a rare and handsome creature.

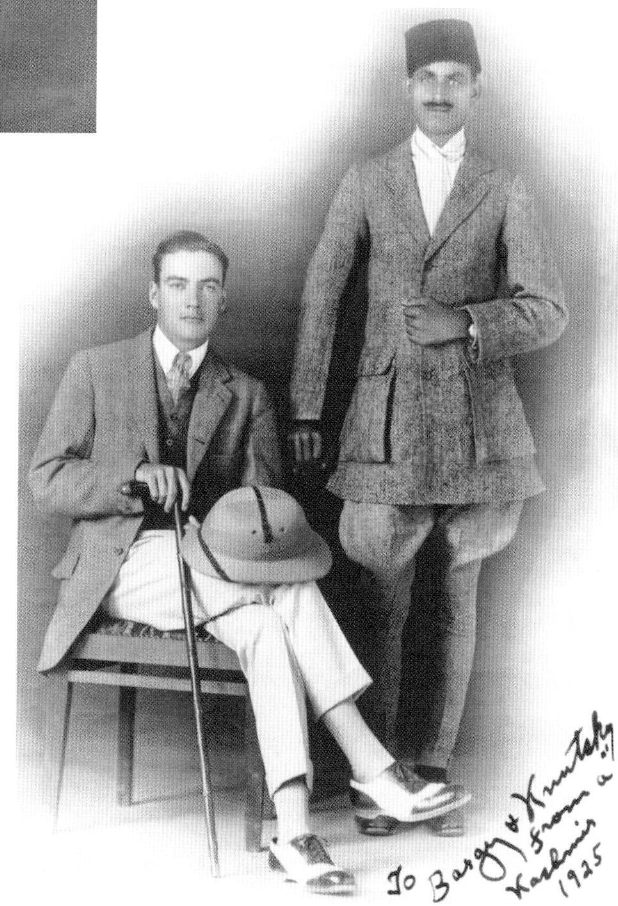

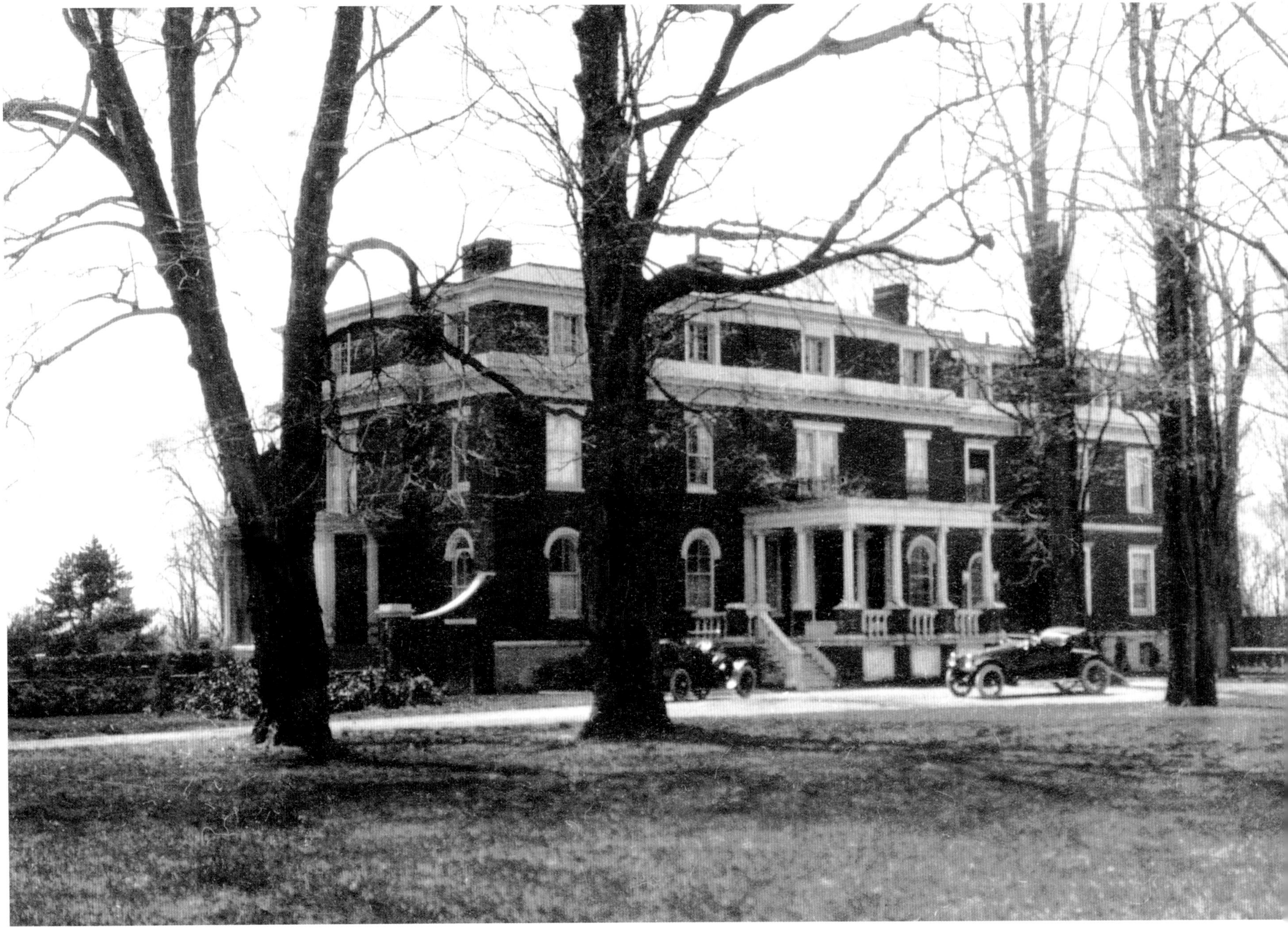

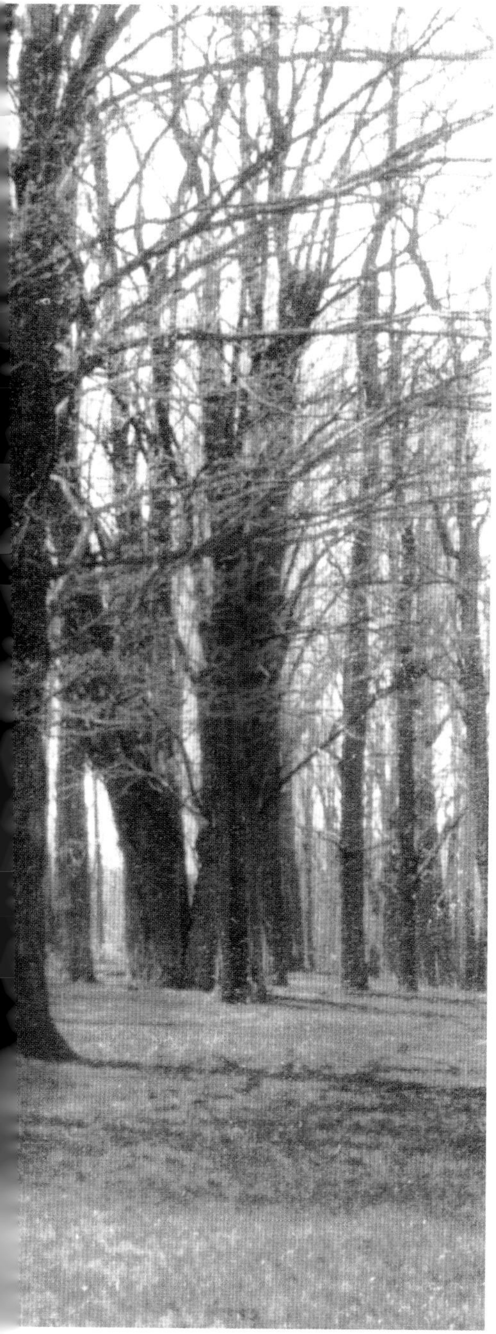

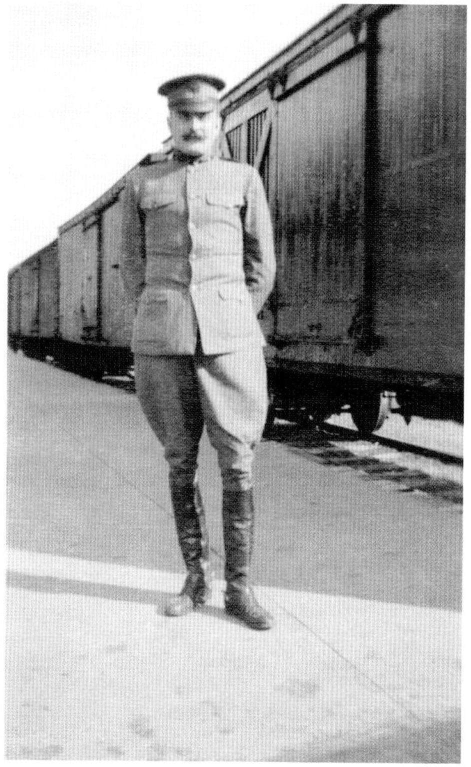

LEFT A photograph of Captain Maunsell Crosby sent to Tracy during World War I. After graduating from Harvard College in 1908, Crosby spent time traveling overseas and later served as captain in the U.S. Army Quartermasters Corp during the war.

BELOW Crosby greeting a two-year-old Deb, sitting in the lap of Helen Huntington Astor, at Foxhollow Farm, summer, 1916. Alice is knitting for World War I soldiers.

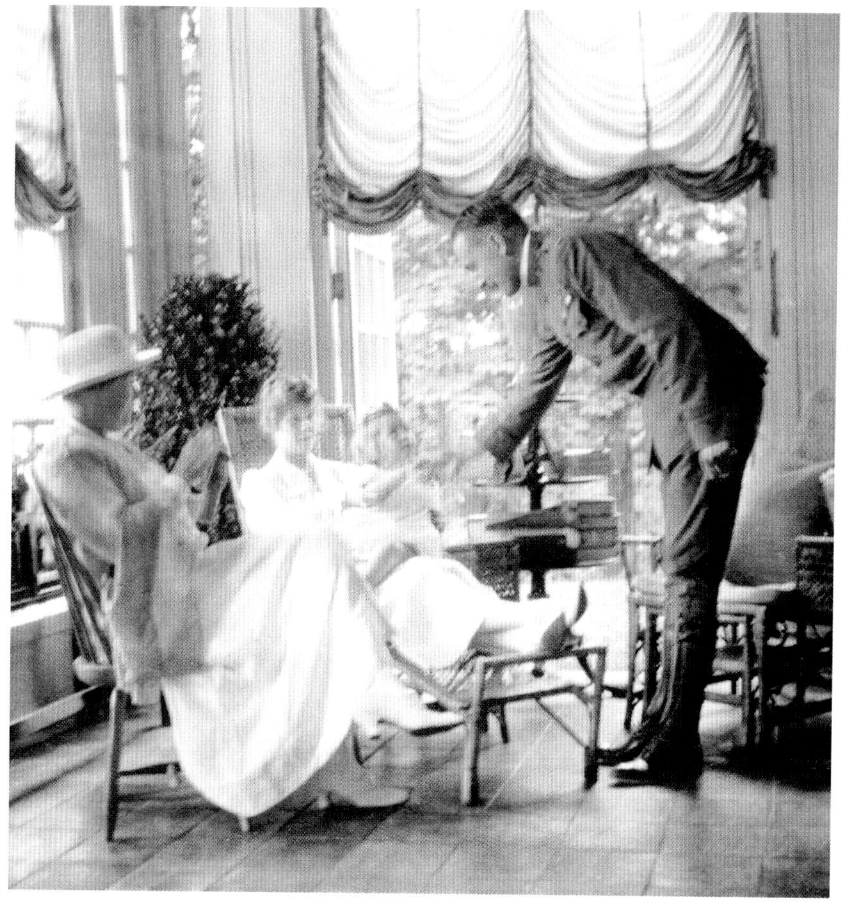

LEFT Maunsell Crosby's estate, Grasmere, in 1914. Adjacent to Foxhollow Farm, the land dates back to the 1770s, when General Richard Montgomery and his wife Janet Livingston Montgomery built the first house on the property. Grasmere passed on to several Livingston family members, and the house was rebuilt after it burned in 1820s. In 1893 it was purchased by Ernest Crosby, a member of the New York State Assembly who worked under President Benjamin Harrison. Ernest added many architectural embellishments, including formal gardens and stone walls and barns. The estate was inherited by his son, Maunsell, who became a noted ornithologist. Tracy Dows and Maunsell Crosby were members of the Rhinebeck Bird Club.

RIGHT Albert Sterner on the terrace at Glenburn, while visiting Mr. and Mrs. Stephen Henry Olin in 1915. In 1885 Sterner established a studio in New York City and began illustrating for such magazines as *Harper's*, *Scribner's*, *Century*, *Vogue*, and *Collier's*. His work was exhibited at the Metropolitan Museum of Art, the Pennsylvania Academy of the Fine Arts, the Carnegie Museum, and the Art Institute of Chicago. In 1909, Tracy Dows commissioned Sterner to copy a portrait of Alice's great-great grandfather, Dr. Thomas Tillotson, from the original painted by Gilbert Stuart around 1794. Tillotson was the surgeon general under George Washington.

BELOW The Tillotson portrait painted by Sterner on the wall in the dining room, 1914. The cake was to celebrate the birthdays of Margaret Dows, age 8; Helen Dinsmore Huntington, age 21; Alice Olin Dows, age 33; and Harrie T. Lindeberg, age 34, during the Easter holiday.

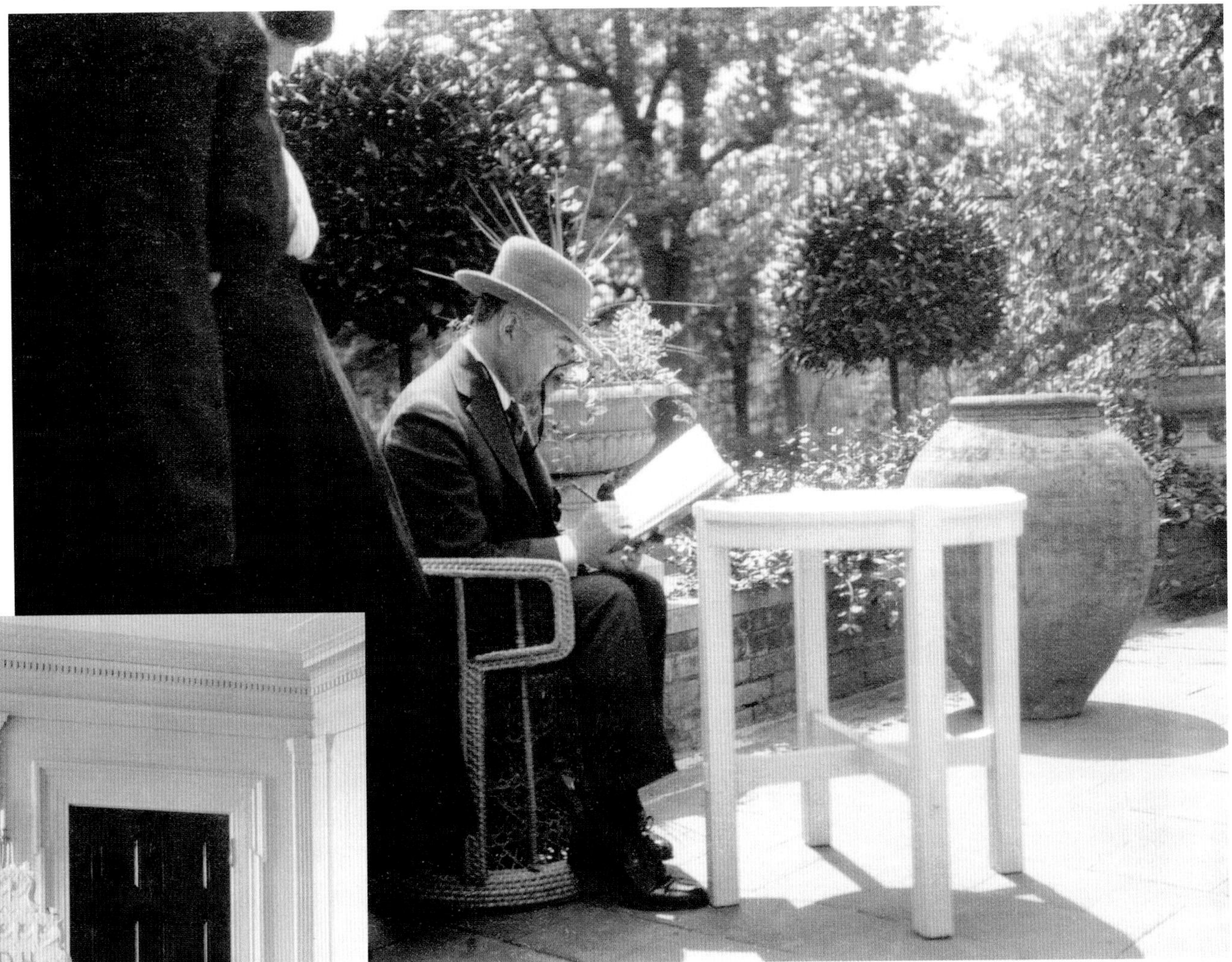

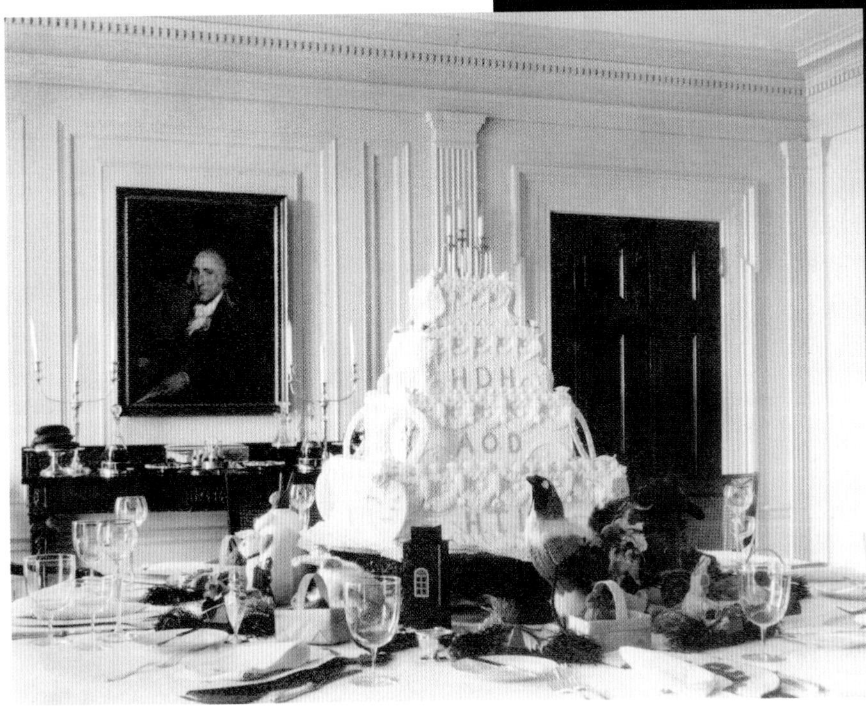

OPPOSITE Standing on the back lawn at Foxhollow Farm in 1924 are Elsie Benkard, Olin, Margaret, Alice, and Thomas Clayton Wolfe. Considered an important American writer of the early twentieth century, Wolfe became friends with Olin in 1922 when he was earning his master's degree at Harvard, and Olin was studying art. Wolfe was a frequent summer guest of the Dowses and stayed in the Gate Lodge while writing his great novel, *Look Homeward, Angel*. Many of the characters in *Of Time and the River*, published in 1935, were based on the Dows family and places of the Rhinebeck area.

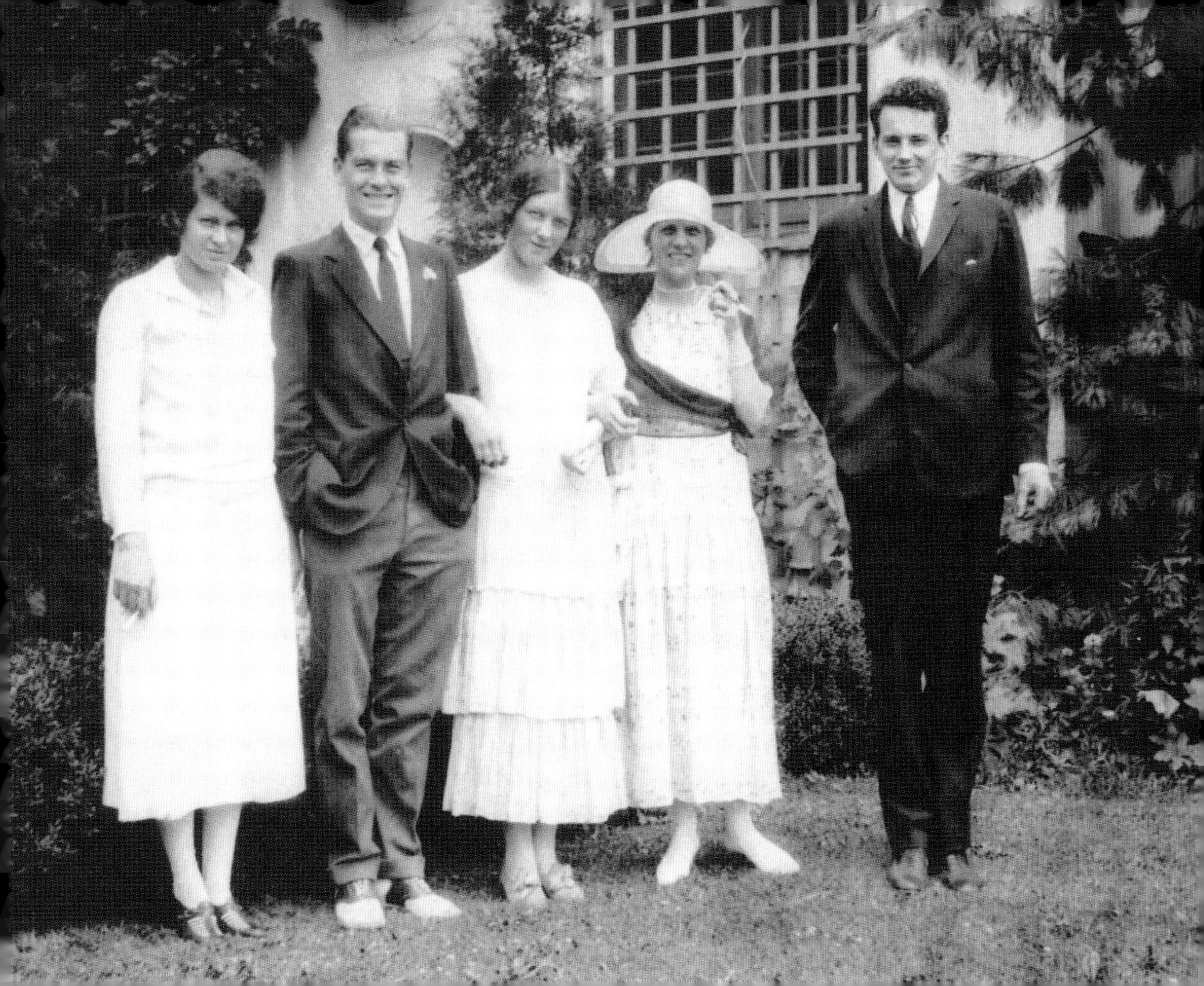

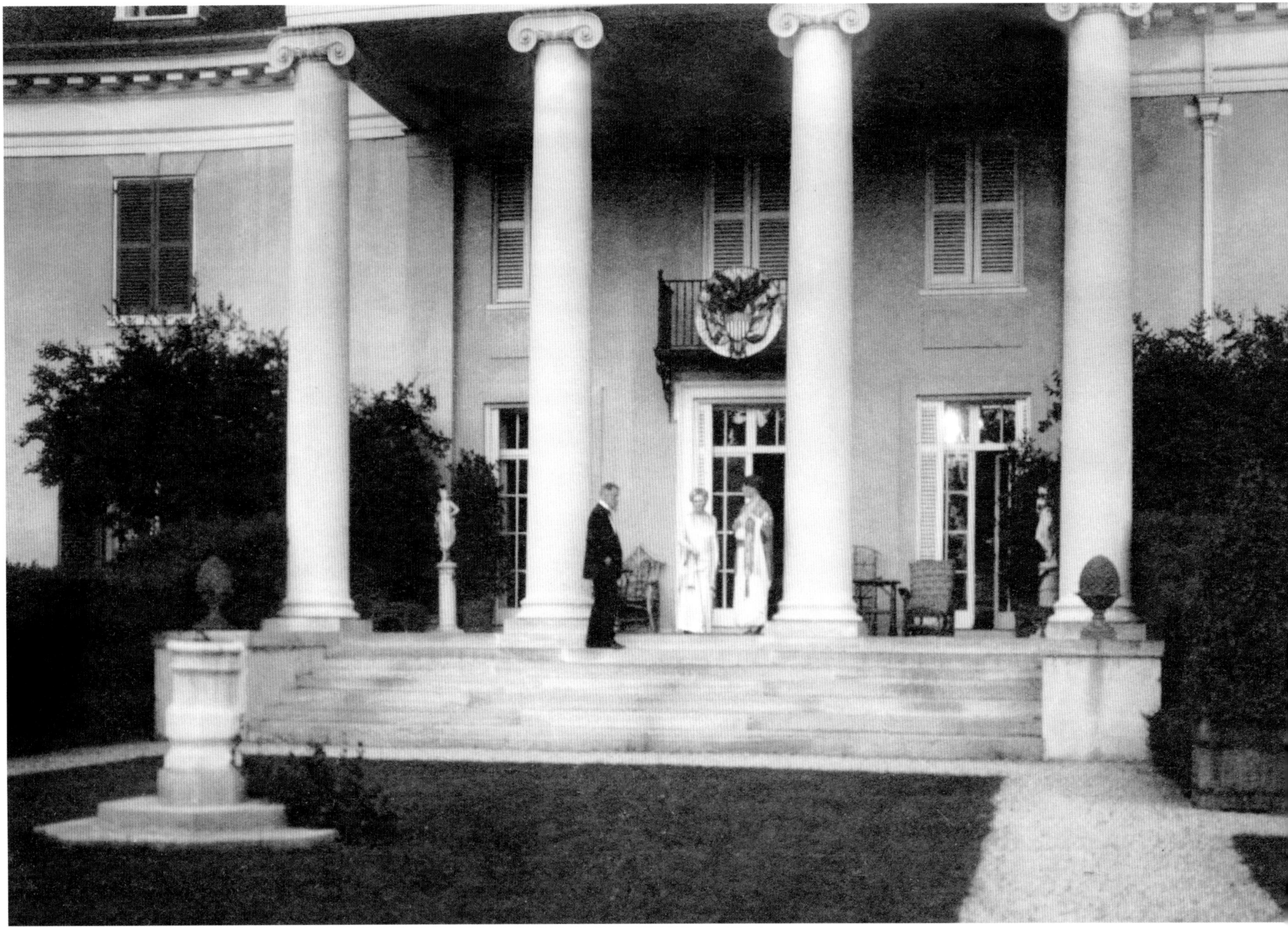

LEFT Alice with Mr. and Mrs. John Jay Chapman on the steps of Sylvania, their country estate in Barrytown, New York, 1922. A memorial shield had been placed above the door by the Chapmans to mourn the death of their son, Victor, who was shot down in 1916 while flying with the Lafayette Escadrille after joining the French Air Service. He was the first American pilot to die in World War I. A novelist and playwright, John Jay Chapman was also involved in politics and supported the campaign of Theodore Roosevelt. His wife, Elizabeth Chanler Chapman, one of the Astor Orphans, grew up at Rokeby, close to Sylvania.

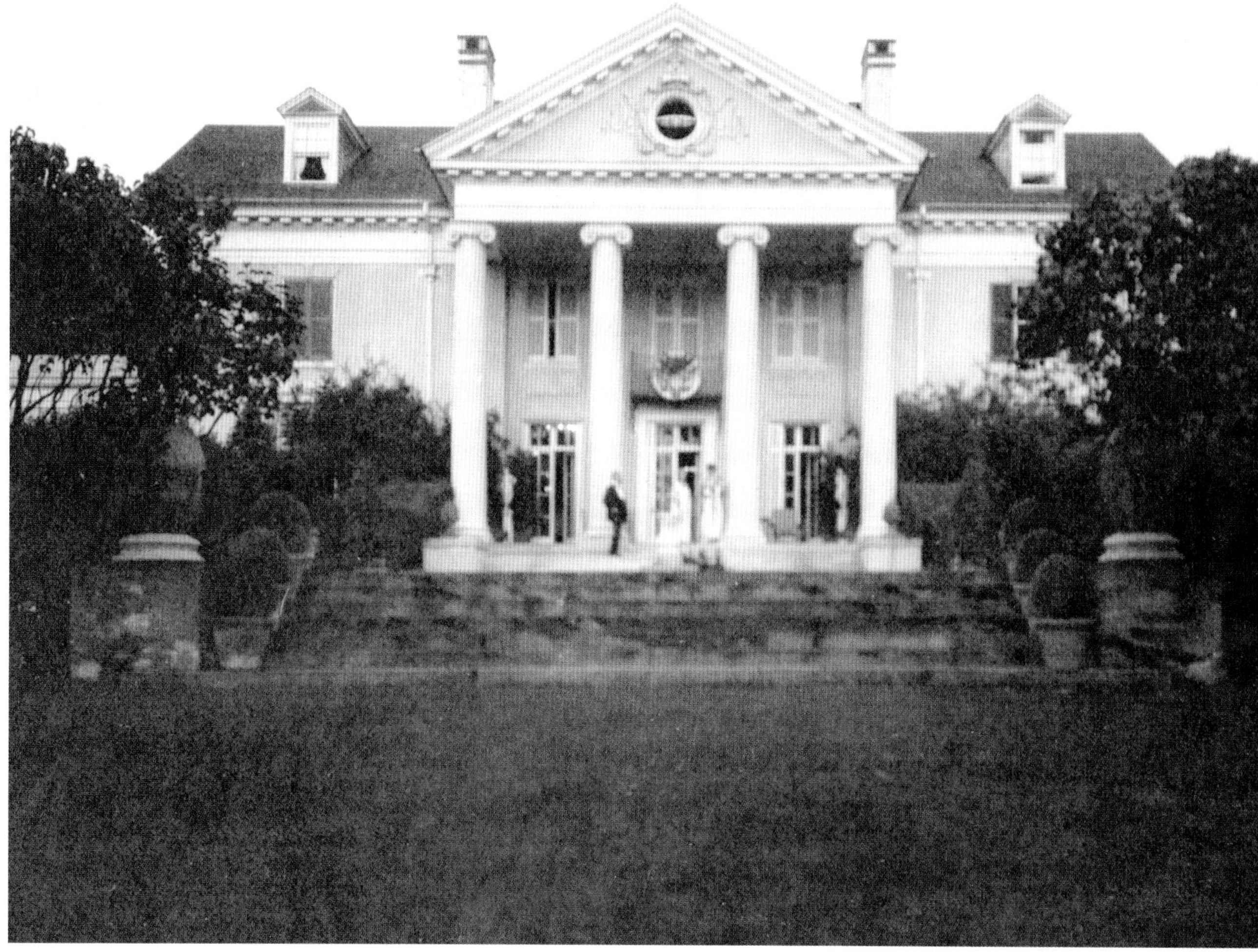

ABOVE A view of the elegant façade of Sylvania. The Georgian-style house and Italian gardens were designed by Charles A. Platt in 1905. With its symmetry and classical details, it is one of the most attractive country houses on the Hudson River.

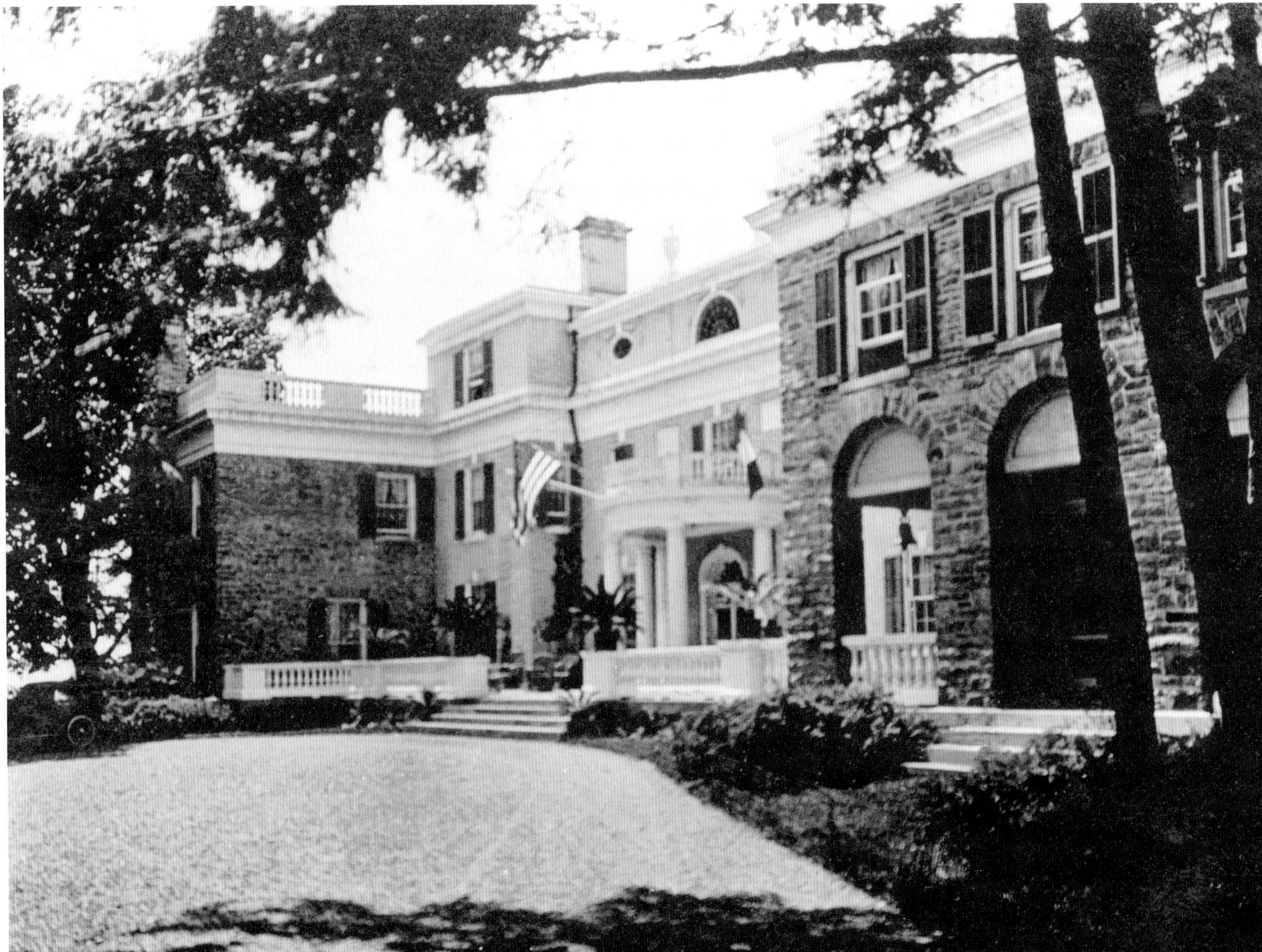

OPPOSITE Springwood as seen when Tracy and Alice were visiting Eleanor and Franklin Roosevelt in 1917. Franklin's father, James Roosevelt, purchased the Springwood property in 1867. Shortly after they were married in 1905, Eleanor and Franklin moved there. In 1915, Franklin and his mother, Sara Roosevelt, then a widow of fifteen years, hired the architecture firm of Hoppin & Koen to transform the seventeen-room villa into a Georgian Revival mansion of thirty-five rooms. The estate remained the center of President Roosevelt's life in all stages of his career, and was where he famously entertained European royalty. Alice Dows had known Franklin as a child, and in later years she remained friendly with the Roosevelts during his presidency.

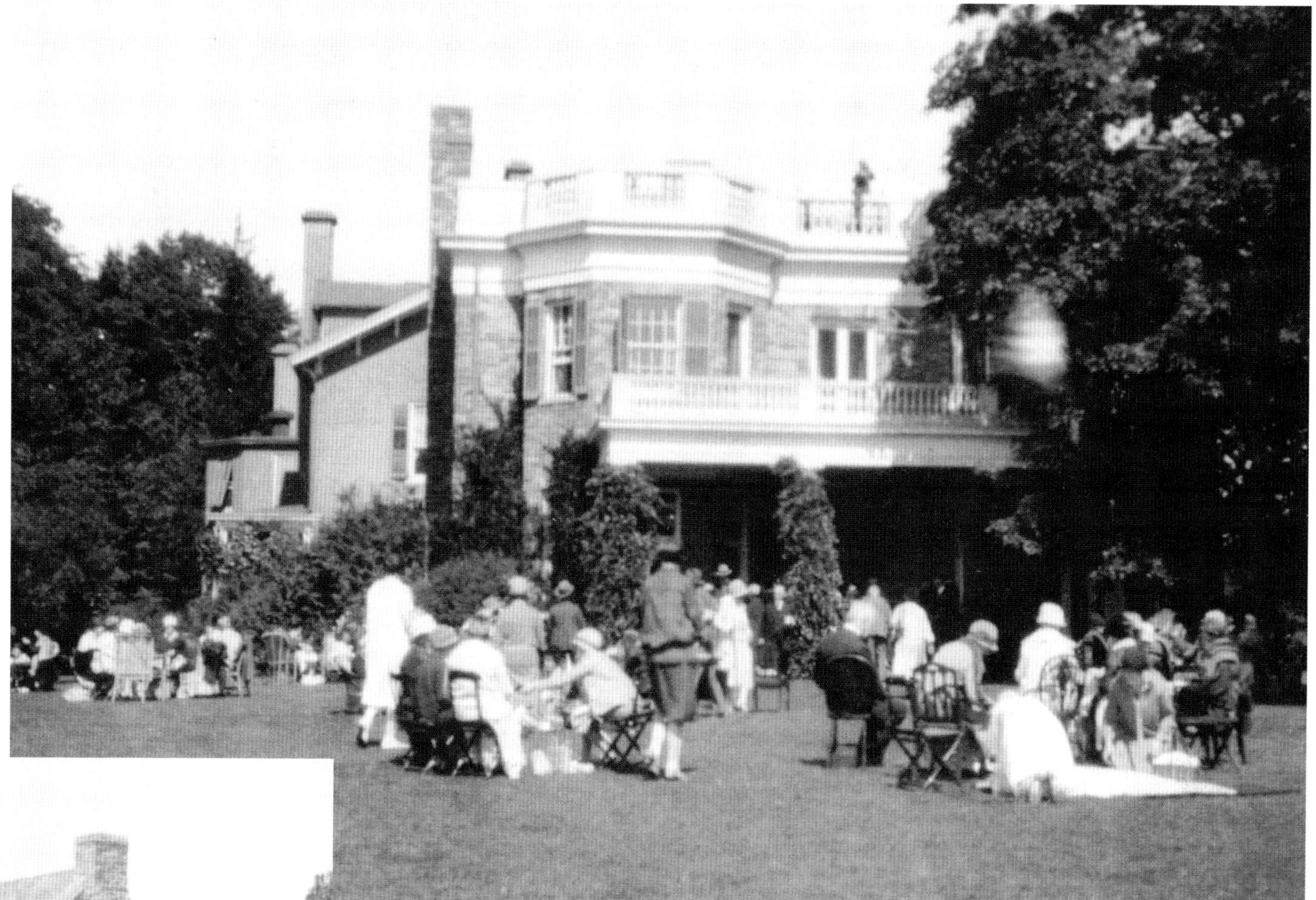

ABOVE A gathering on the grounds of Springwood at the annual pilgrimage of the Dutchess County Historical Society, September 16, 1927. Franklin D. Roosevelt joined the organization when it was founded by Miss Helen Wilkinson Reynolds in 1914. During that time, Roosevelt and Miss Reynolds drove all over the county examining cemetery headstones and records, and locating historic sites.

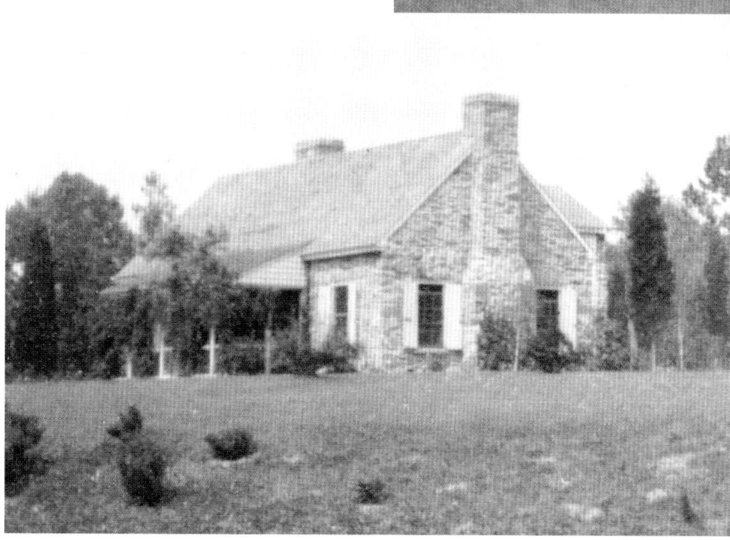

BELOW Stone Cottage at Val-Kill in 1927. At the urging of her husband, Eleanor Roosevelt developed Val-Kill as a place for employment for rural workers and women.

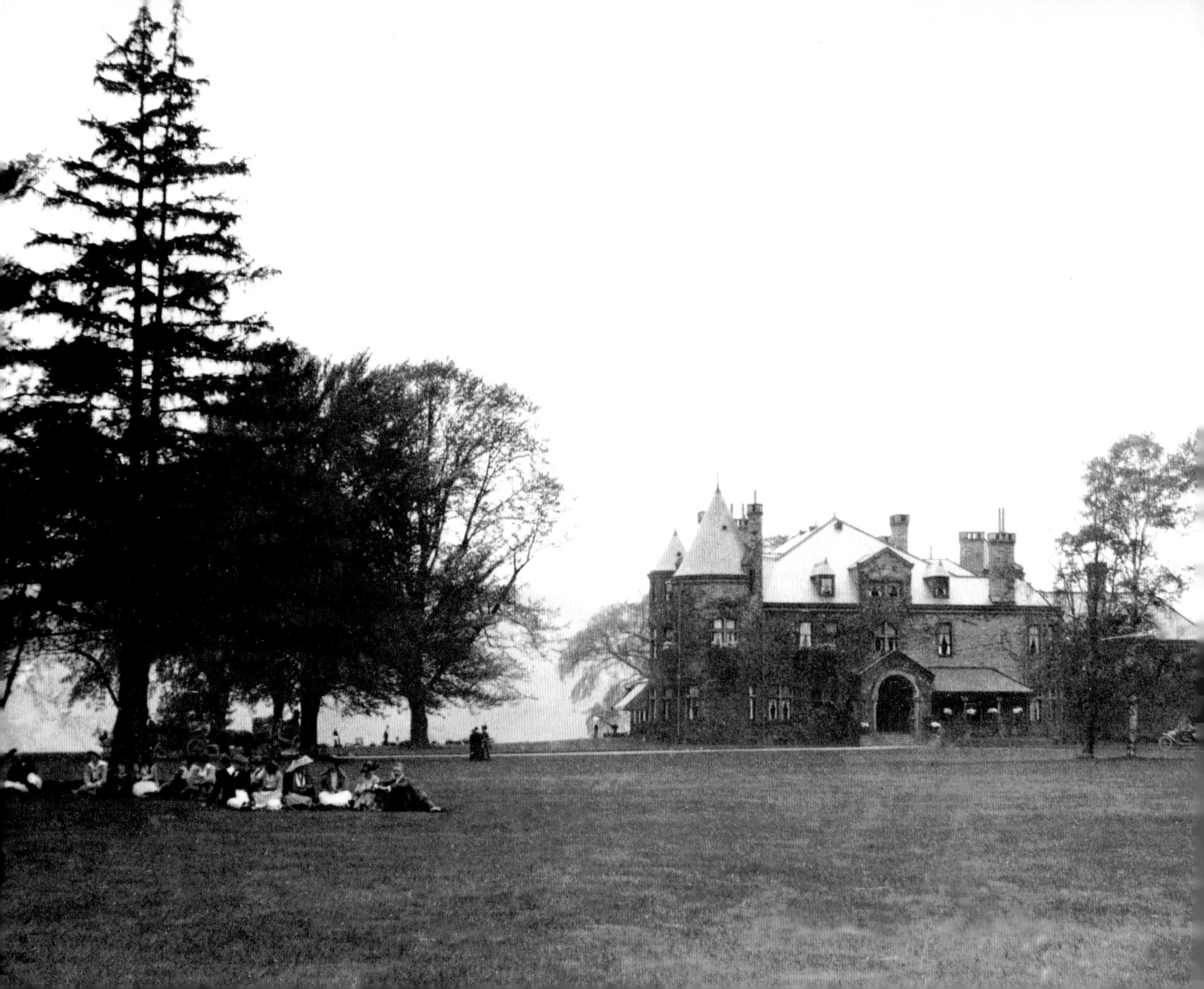

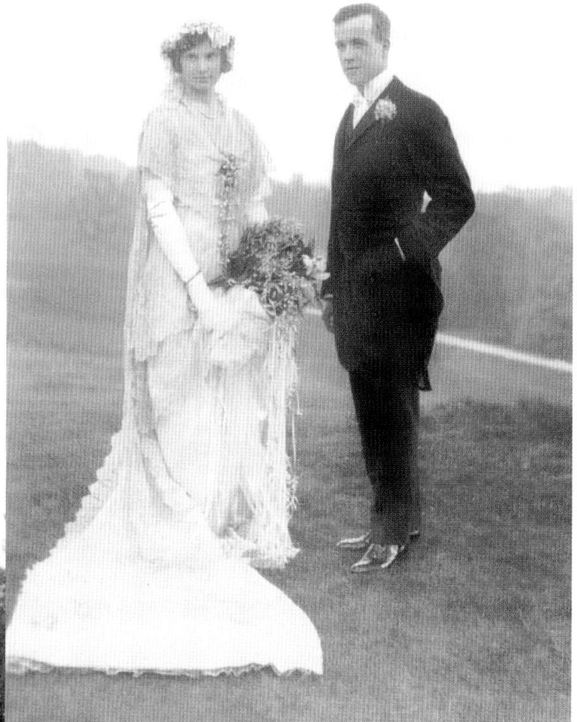

LEFT Anne Pendleton Rogers and John Griswold Webb on their wedding day, May 16, 1914. She was the daughter of Colonel and Mrs. Archibald Rogers, and he was the son of Henry Walter Webb, vice president of the New York Central Railroad. The marriage was held at St. James Church in Hyde Park, New York, with a reception on the grounds of Crumwold Hall, her family's Hyde Park estate.

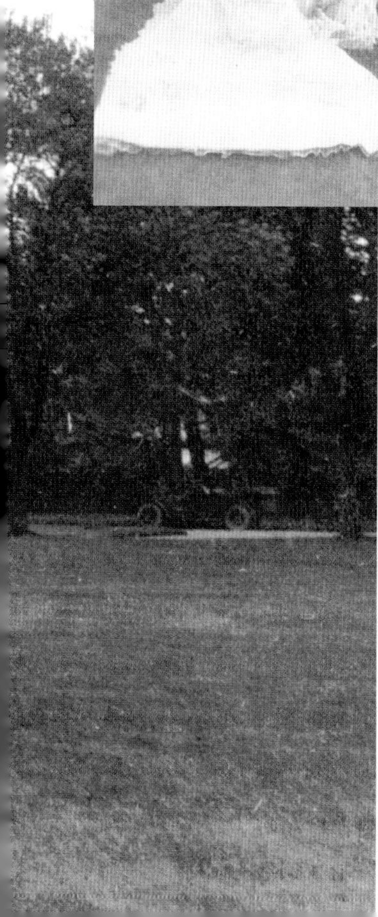

LEFT Wedding guests relaxing on the vast lawn of Crumwold Hall. The house was designed by noted architect Richard Morris Hunt between 1886 and 1889.

RIGHT The Webbs leaving in their automobile after the ceremony among a very festive crowd. Frederick W. Vanderbilt (with white moustache and hat), whose estate was nearby, is seen in the bottom right corner of the photograph.

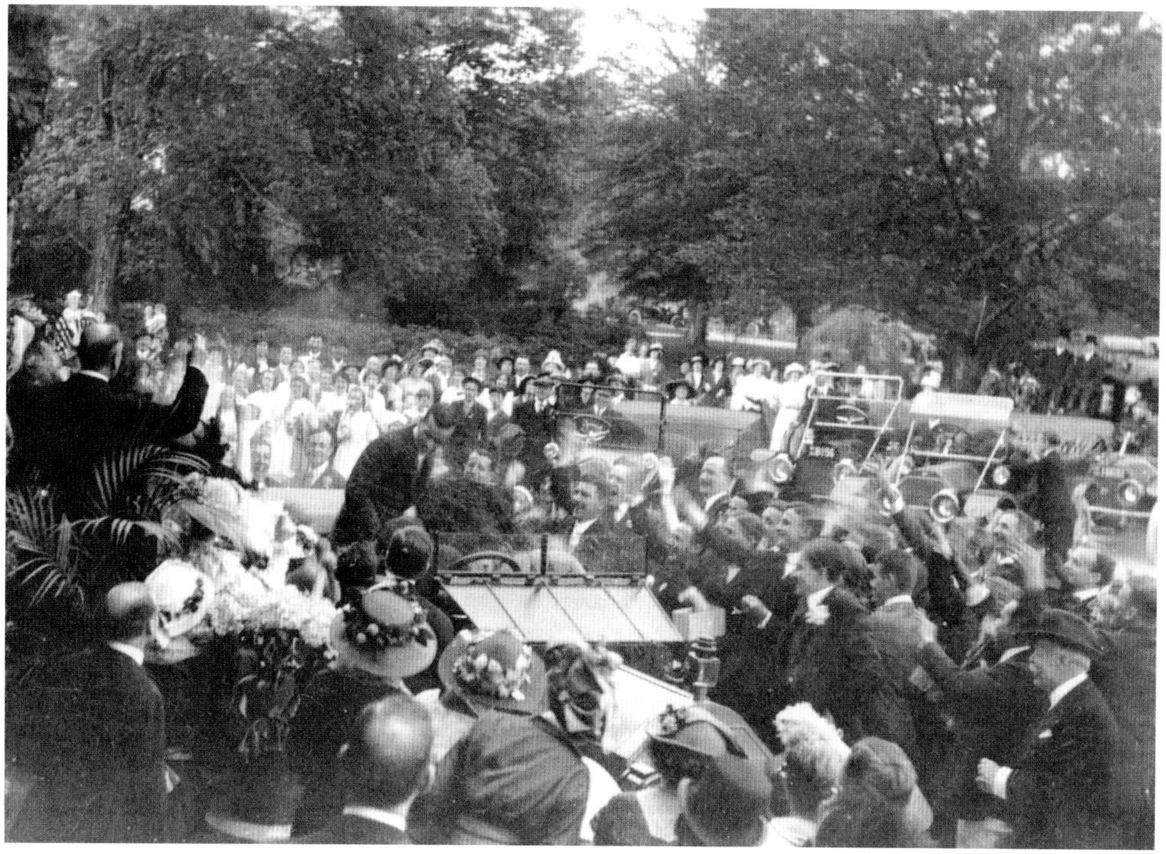

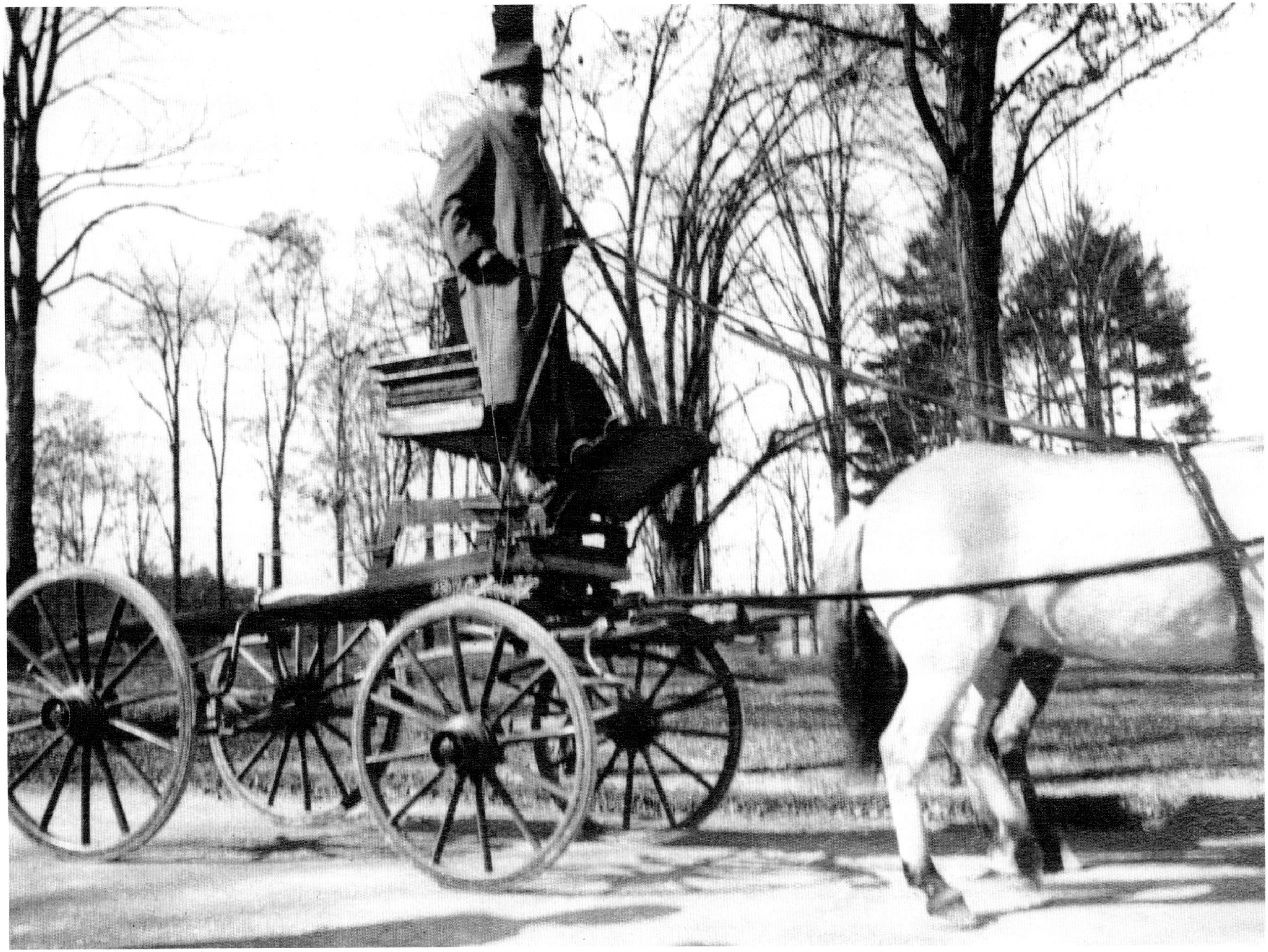

OPPOSITE Warren Delano III driving with four-in-hand, 1910. Delano, who was married to Jennie Walters of the prosperous Baltimore family, inherited his uncle's large Hudson Valley estate, Steen Valetje, in 1894. At one time, Warren had sixty-five horses in his stable, many of them fine breeds.

RIGHT Laura Delano with one of her beloved Irish Setters in 1923, during the time she was renting Stone Cottage from Tracy Dows. Laura (known as Polly) was the daughter of Warren Delano III. She had a commanding and vibrant personality. In later life she developed a particular style of dressing, including blue-dyed hair with a sharply accented, painted-in widow's peak. Laura traveled with her cousin, President Franklin D. Roosevelt, on his tours during World War II.

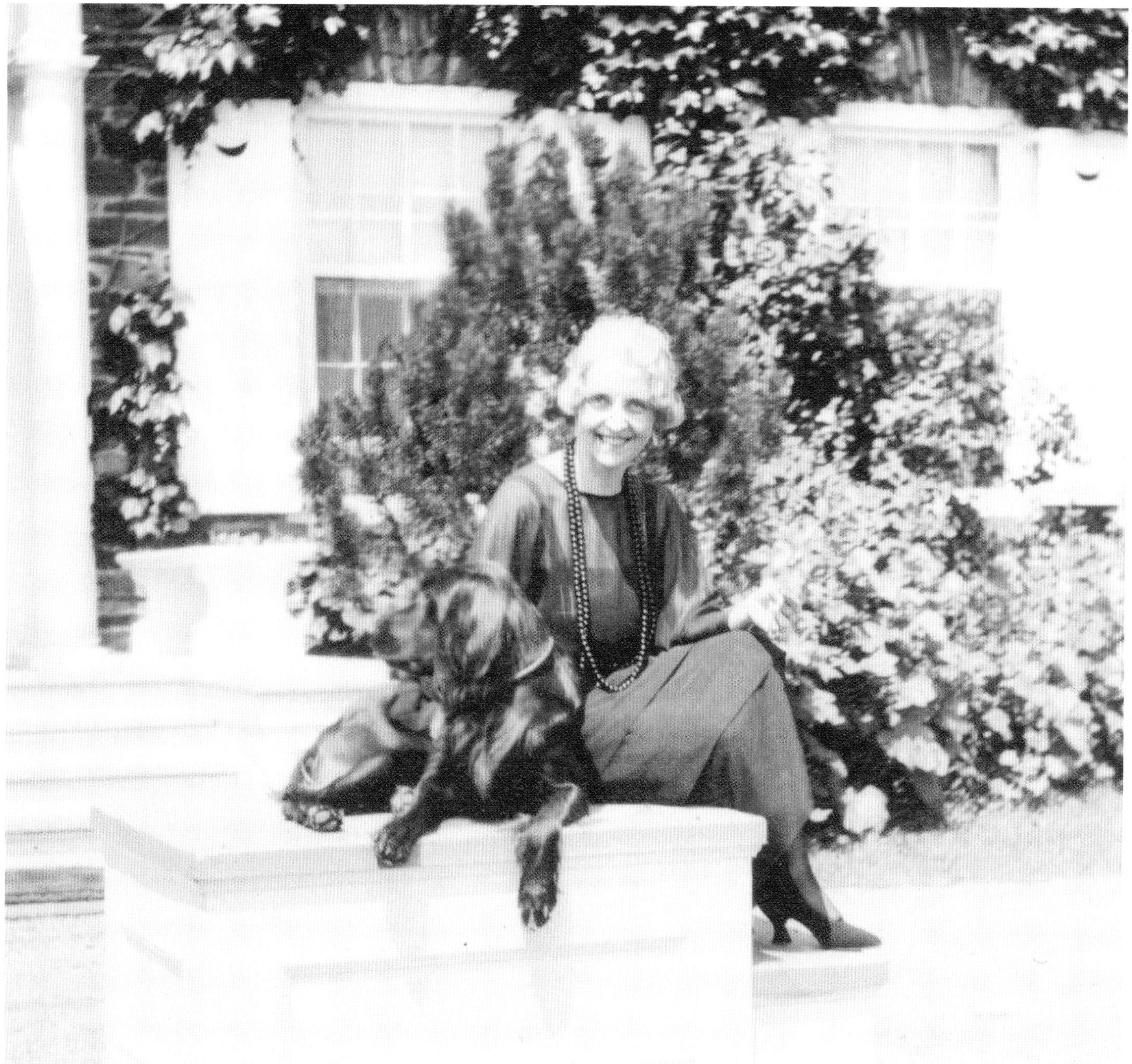

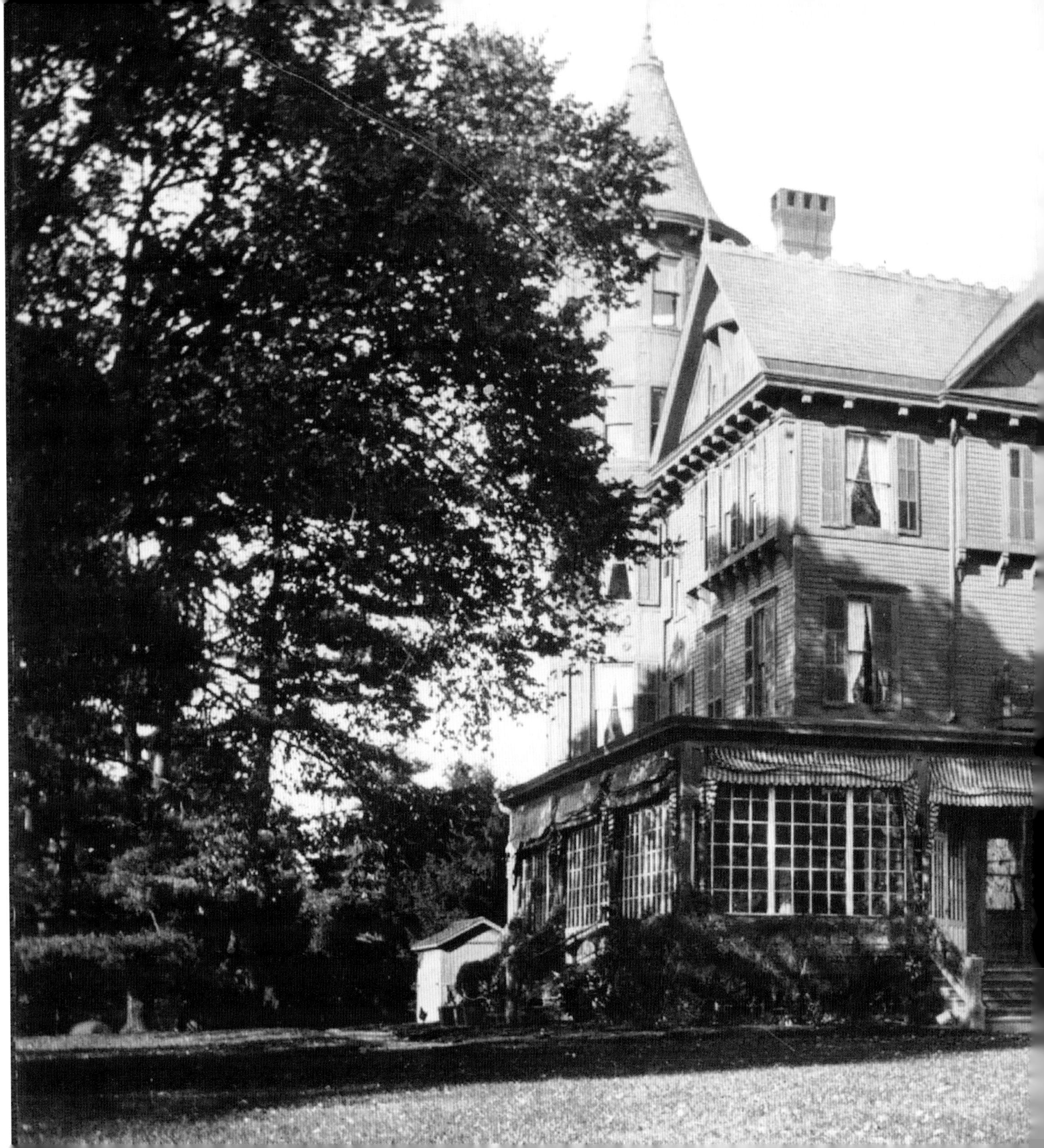

RIGHT Wilderstein, with its distinctive five-story circular tower, in 1917. The original house was built for Thomas Holy Suckley in 1852, whose father had made a fortune investing in Manhattan real estate. In 1888, Thomas's son, Robert Bowne Suckley, hired Arnout Cannon, Jr., a Poughkeepsie architect, to enlarge the house and completely transform it into a Queen Anne castle. The grounds were designed by Calvert Vaux and the interior by Joseph Burr Tiffany, a cousin of Louis Comfort Tiffany. Robert Bowne Suckley's seven children were raised at Wilderstein, the most noted being Margaret Lynch Suckley, (known as Daisy), who never married and lived in the house her entire life, well into her hundredth year. (Courtesy of Wilderstein Archives)

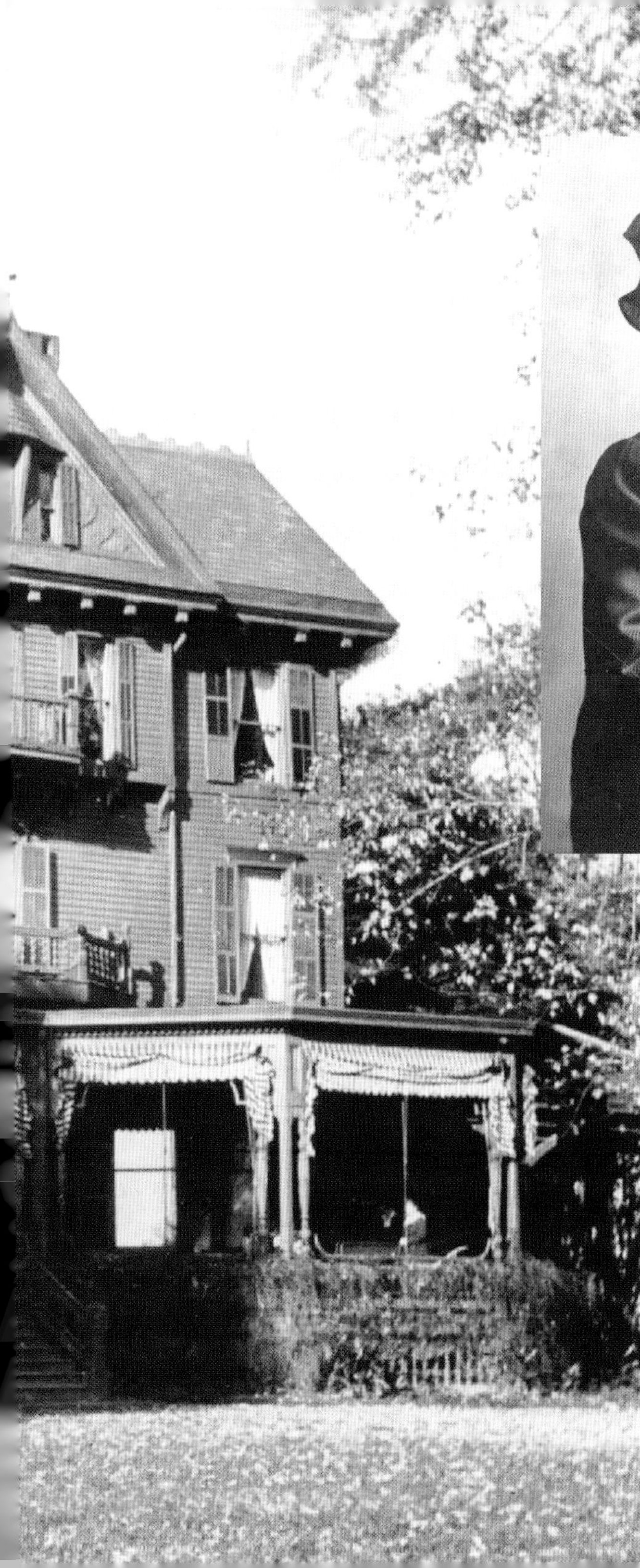

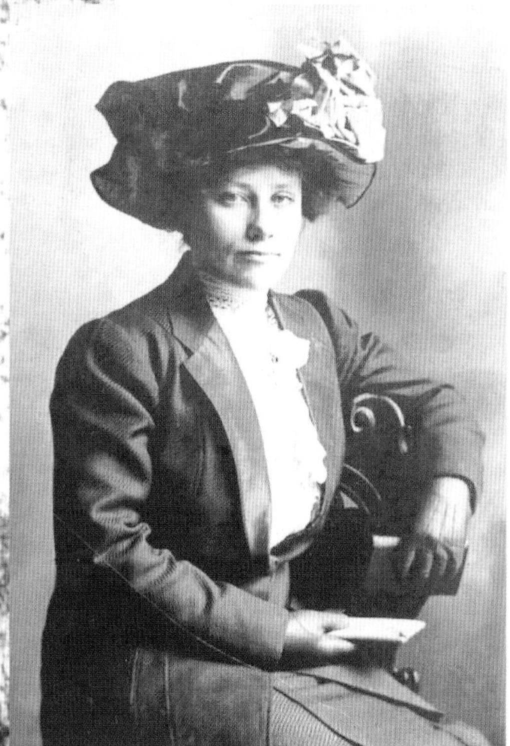

LEFT Daisy Suckley in 1910. She was a close companion to President Franklin D. Roosevelt, who was her sixth cousin. Daisy and Laura Delano were with him when he died in Warm Springs, Georgia, in 1945. (Courtesy of Wilderstein Archives)

BELOW Alice Dows at Foxhollow Farm, talking to Daisy's brother, Henry Suckley, and a fellow passenger, 1913. Alice was Daisy's godmother, as well as her distant cousin. (Courtesy of Wilderstein Archives)

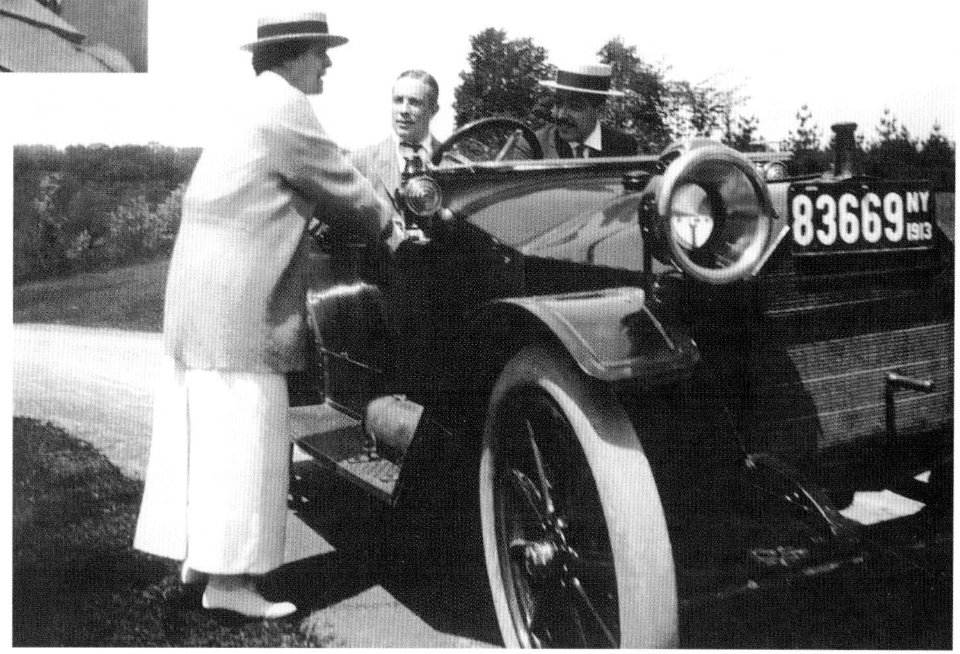

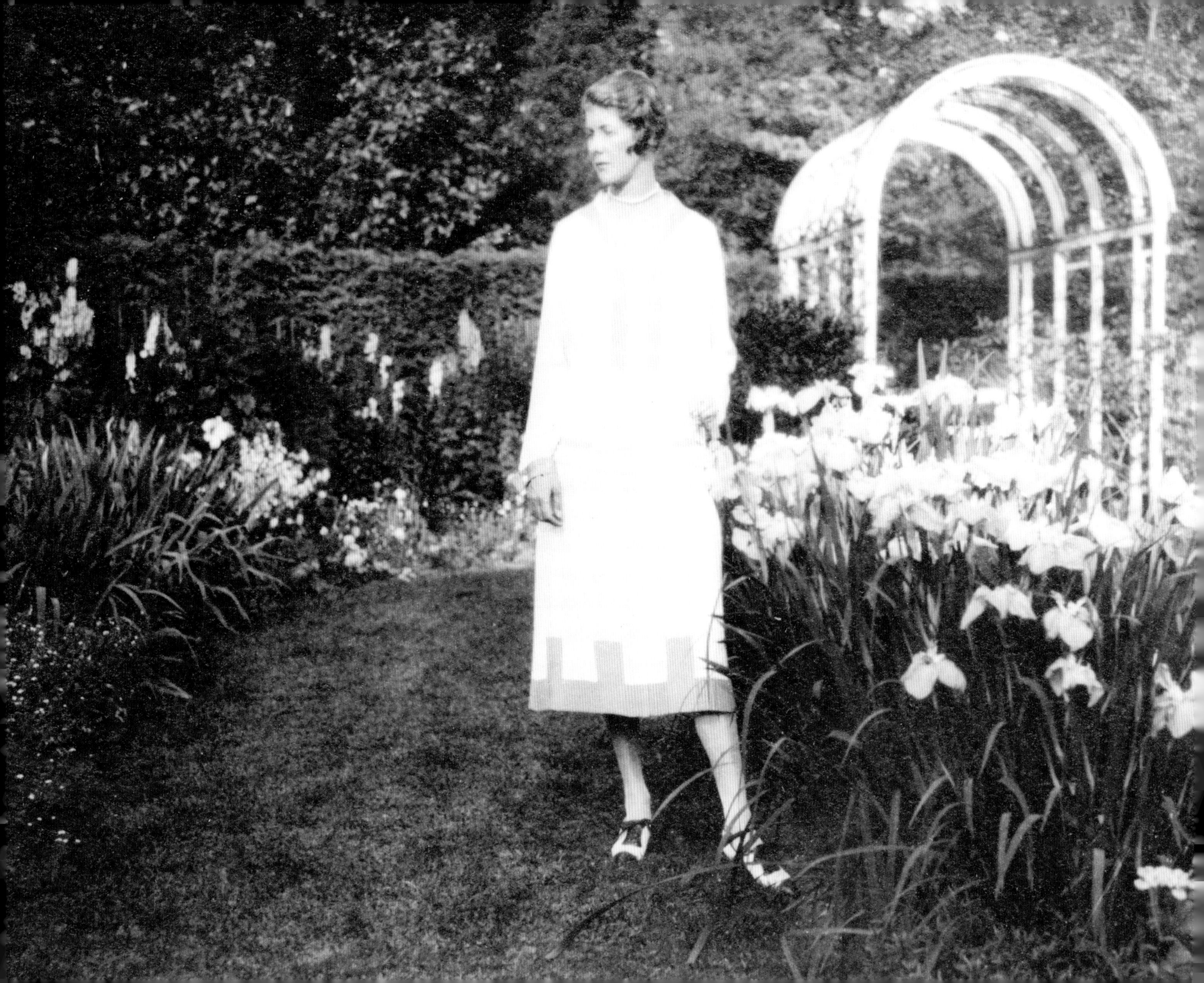

CHAPTER FOUR

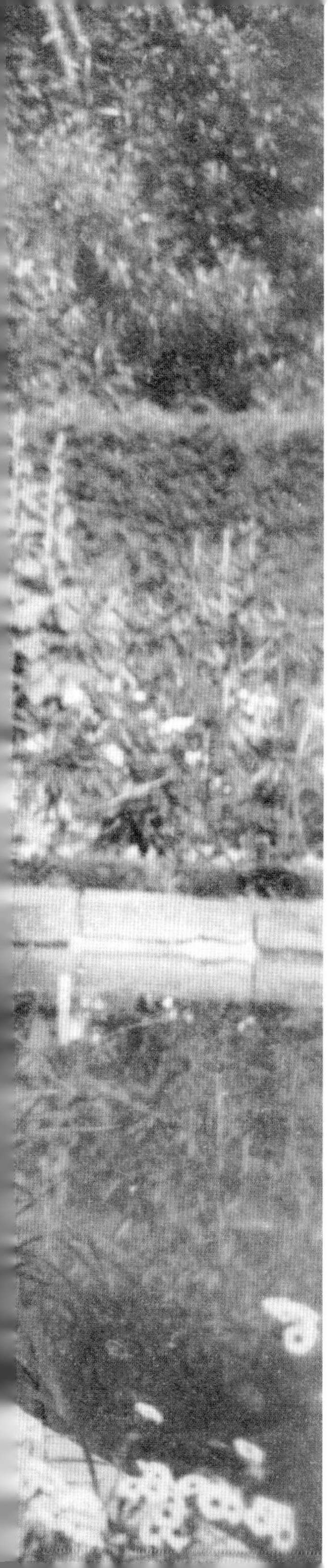

The ASTORS and FERNCLIFF

PREVIOUS PAGES Helen Huntington Astor in the gardens at Ferncliff, 1927.

RIGHT Helen at Seal Harbor, Maine, in August 1913, eight months before her wedding to Vincent Astor. The daughter of Robert Palmer Huntington and Helen Gray Dinsmore Huntington, Helen grew up spending her summers at The Locusts, her great-grandfather's estate in Staastburg, and later at her family's Hopeland House, adjacent to The Locusts. She made her debut into New York City society in 1912 and often appeared on the pages of *Vogue*. Helen married William Vincent Astor on April 30, 1914, at Hopeland House. She and Vincent became Tracy and Alice's best friends. During World War I, she set up a convalescent home near Paris to care for wounded American soldiers. Guided by a devotion to music that began in childhood, in later life Helen would become the leading music patron of New York City, helping to start the Musicians Emergency Fund in 1931. Helen and Vincent divorced in 1940.

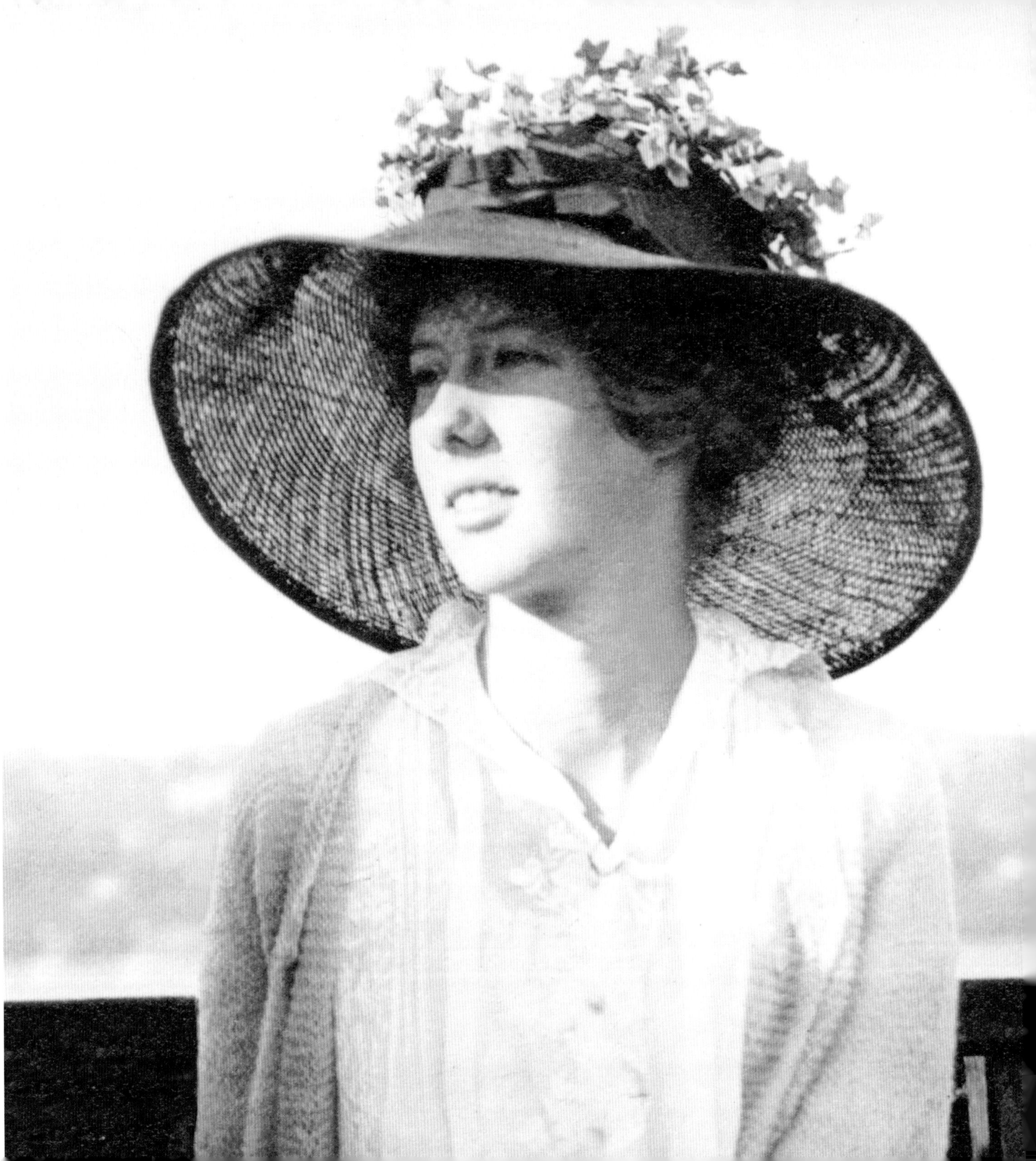

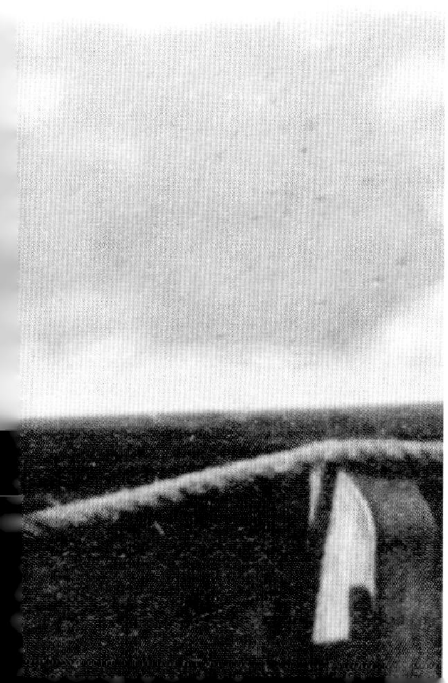

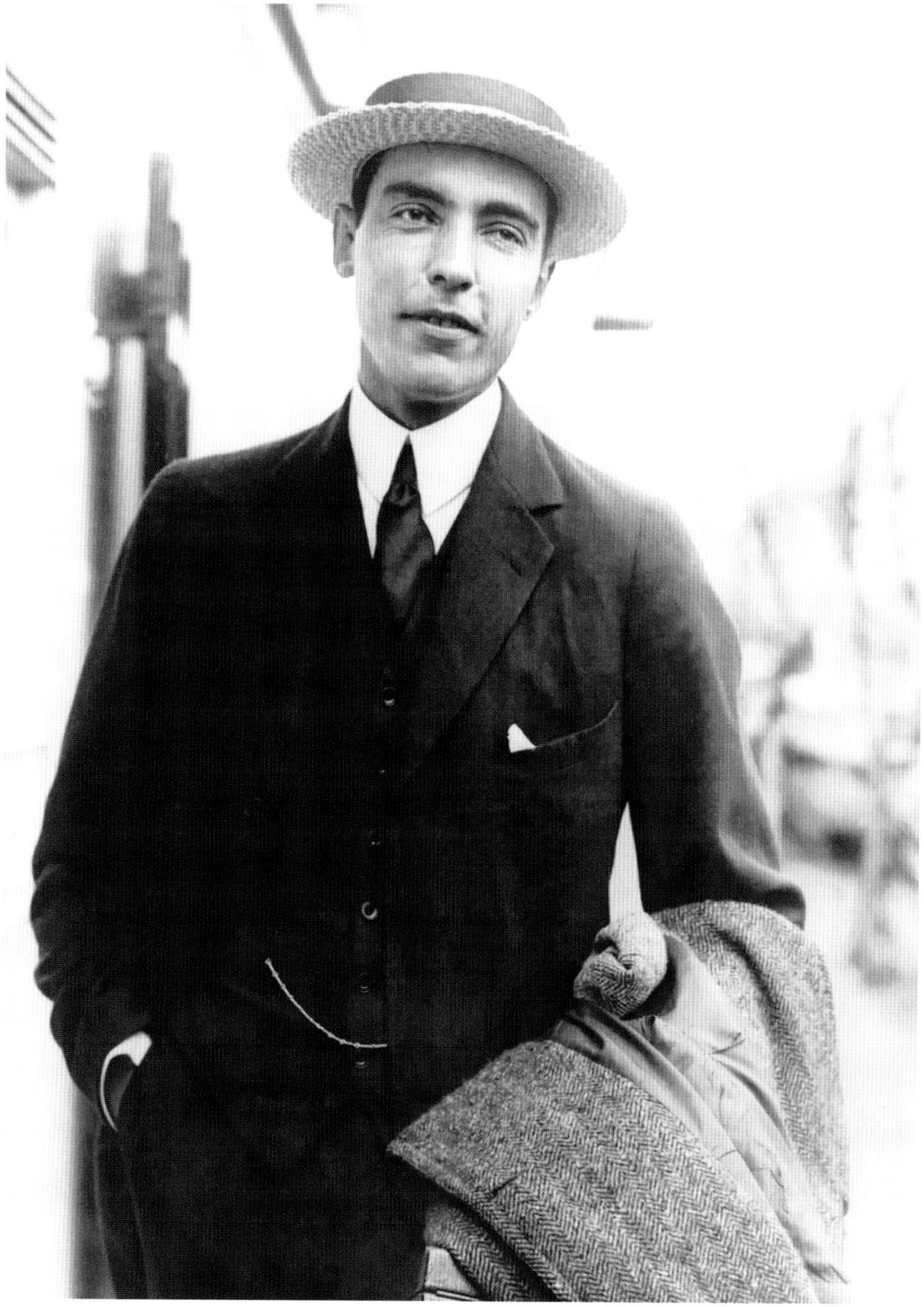

LEFT Vincent Astor, returning from a trip to Europe in 1922, in a photograph by Underwood & Underwood. Vincent Astor was the son of the millionaire and inventor John Jacob Astor IV and his first wife, Ava Lowle Willing Astor, an heiress from Philadelphia. His great-great-grandfather, John Jacob Astor, who came to New York around 1784 from Germany, made a fortune in fur trading and real estate investment. In 1911, a year after his divorce from his wife, John Jacob Astor IV married Madeleine Talmadge Force, who was twenty-nine years his junior. The newlyweds set off on an extended honeymoon and sailed on the *Titanic*. At age 20, Vincent inherited an estimated $87 million after his father perished on that ship's ill-fated voyage in 1912. He attended Harvard College from 1911 to 1912 but dropped out after his father's death. He spent time in the Naval Reserve during World War I. As a businessman, Vincent was involved in New York City real estate and chairman of the board of *Newsweek* between 1937 and 1959.

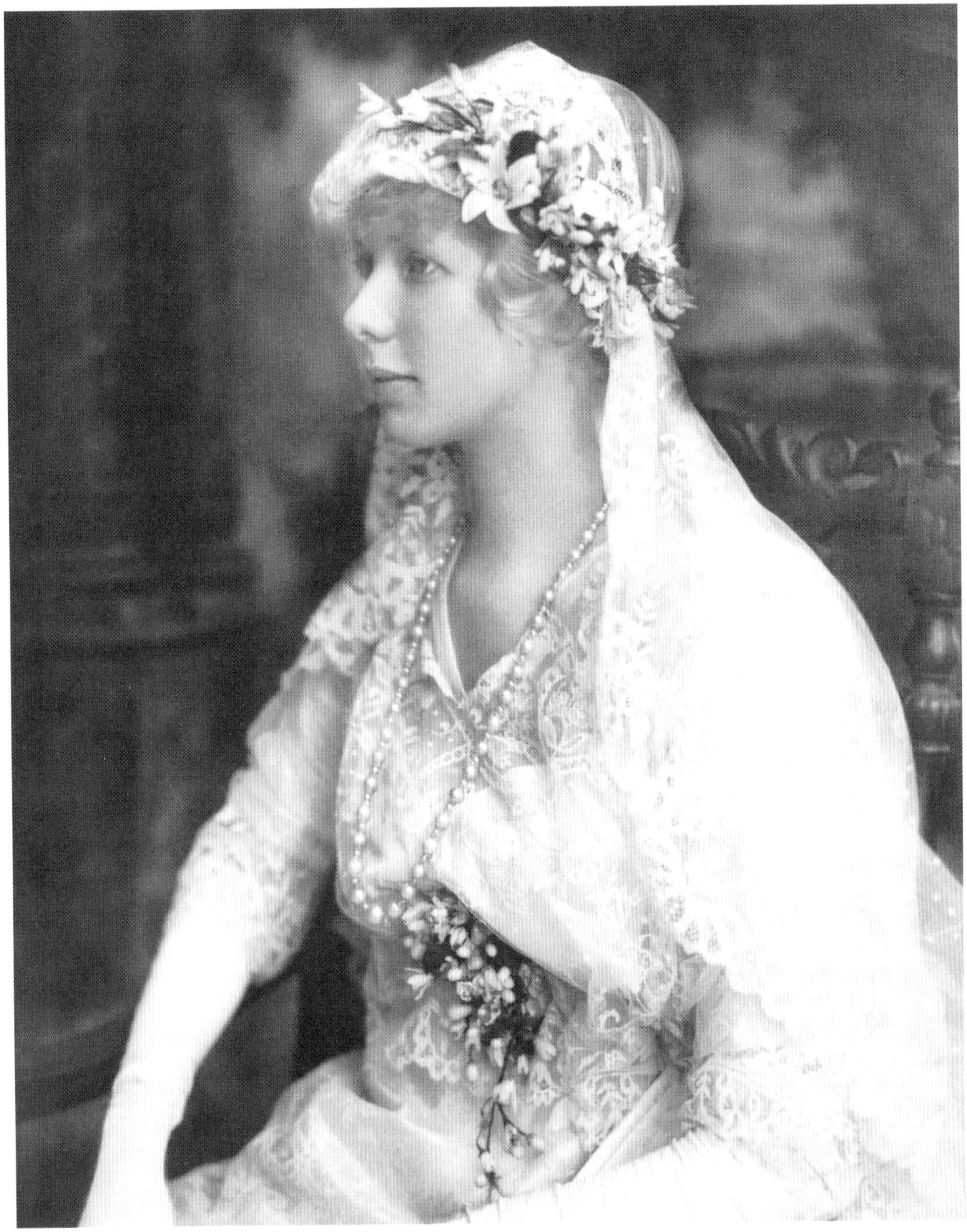

LEFT A society portrait taken of the bride-to-be, Helen Dinsmore Huntington, in her wedding dress. Helen's sister, Alice Huntington, was maid of honor. Margaret Dows and Vincent's sister, Alice Astor, were flower girls. The *New York Times* reported that the wedding was of the utmost simplicity and informality, and the guests included only immediate relatives and a few intimate friends, numbering around fifty. The Huntington dogs wore white satin ribbons.

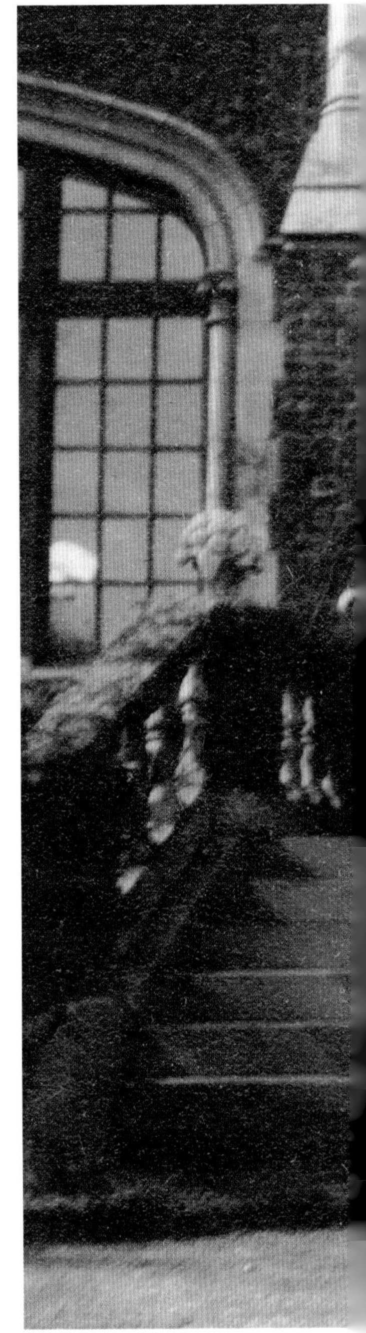

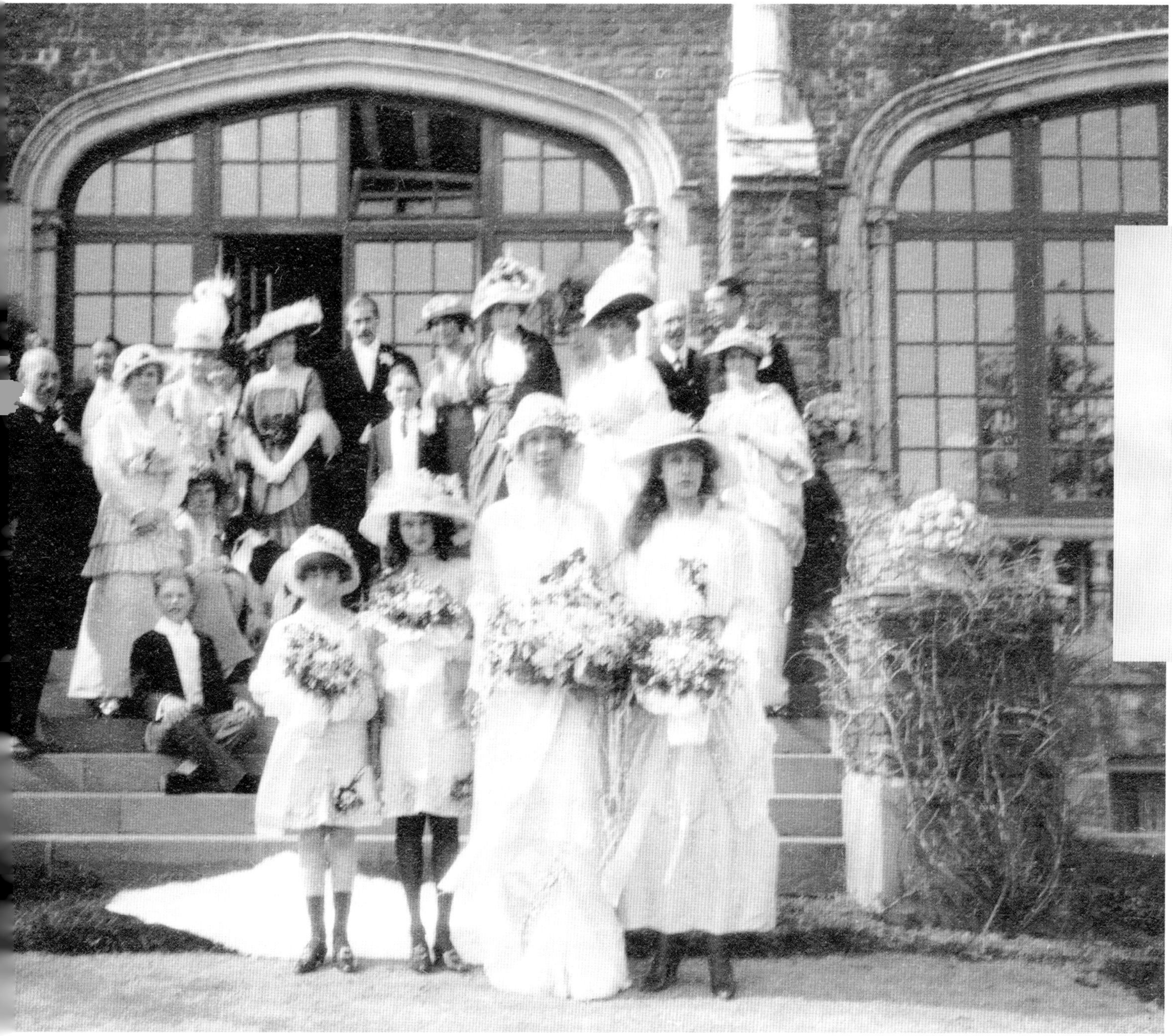

LEFT Guests gathered on the steps of Hopeland House at the wedding in 1914. Seen at the center of the photograph (in white gloves) is Vincent's mother, the former Mrs. John Jacob Astor IV, who had traveled from England with her daughter to attend her son's wedding.

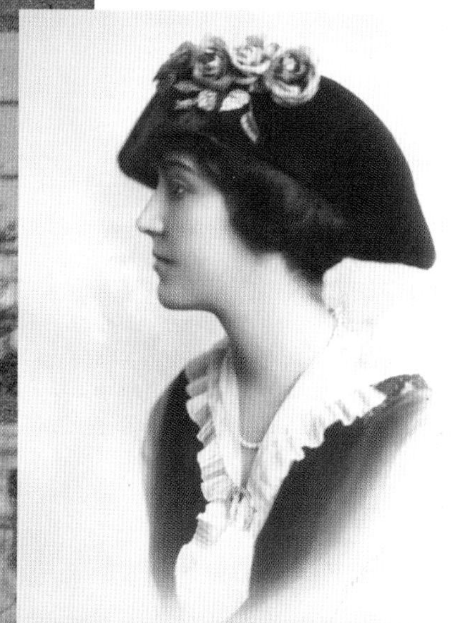

ABOVE A portrait of Ava Lowle Willing Astor in the early 1900s by Davis & Sanford, the Fifth Avenue studio known for their photographs of New York society. Ava married John Jacob Astor IV in 1891. The marriage was tumultuous, and they were divorced in 1910. Ava moved to London and married Thomas Lister, fourth Baron Ribblesdale, in 1919, where she became known as Lady Ribblesdale. After his death in 1925, she eventually returned to live the rest of her life in New York City. (Courtesy of Emily Harding)

RIGHT Tracy's photograph of Ferncliff on a bleak winter day in 1922 resembles a painting. The estate was purchased in 1858 by William Backhouse Astor, Jr., whose wife, Caroline, reigned over American society during the Gilded Age as "the" Mrs. Astor. Ferncliff was a lavish estate with sweeping lawns, pleasure grounds, numerous driveways and paths, parklike scenery, gardens, parterres, conservatories, and an extensive system of barns and stables. The house was built of brick in the Italianate style, with a front portico supported by Corinthian columns. The estate passed on to William and Caroline's only son, John Jacob Astor IV, in 1892. He purchased more property to the west and built a grand carriage road, naming it Astor Drive, which extended nearly a mile in length from its gates in the village of Rhinebeck. Vincent inherited Ferncliff after his father's death in 1912. He and Helen continued to use the house as their country home. It was demolished in the 1940s, while Vincent was married to his second wife, Mary Benedict "Minnie" Cushing.

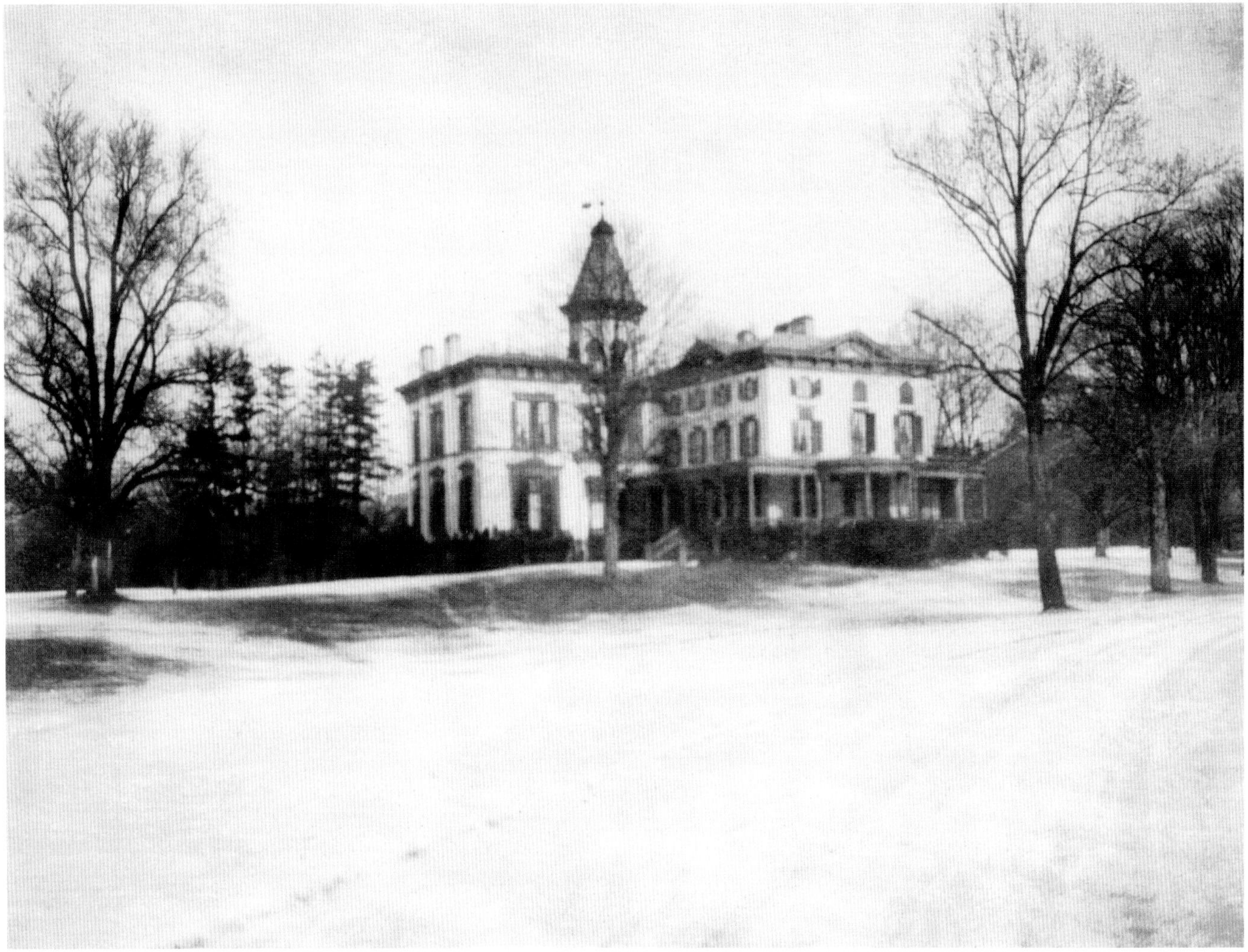

OPPOSITE The Ferncliff coachman assisting Helen as she leaves to visit her sister-in-law, Alice Astor Obolensky, at her house, Marienruh, in early March 1929. The sleigh was a practical form of local travel in the Hudson Valley during snowy months.

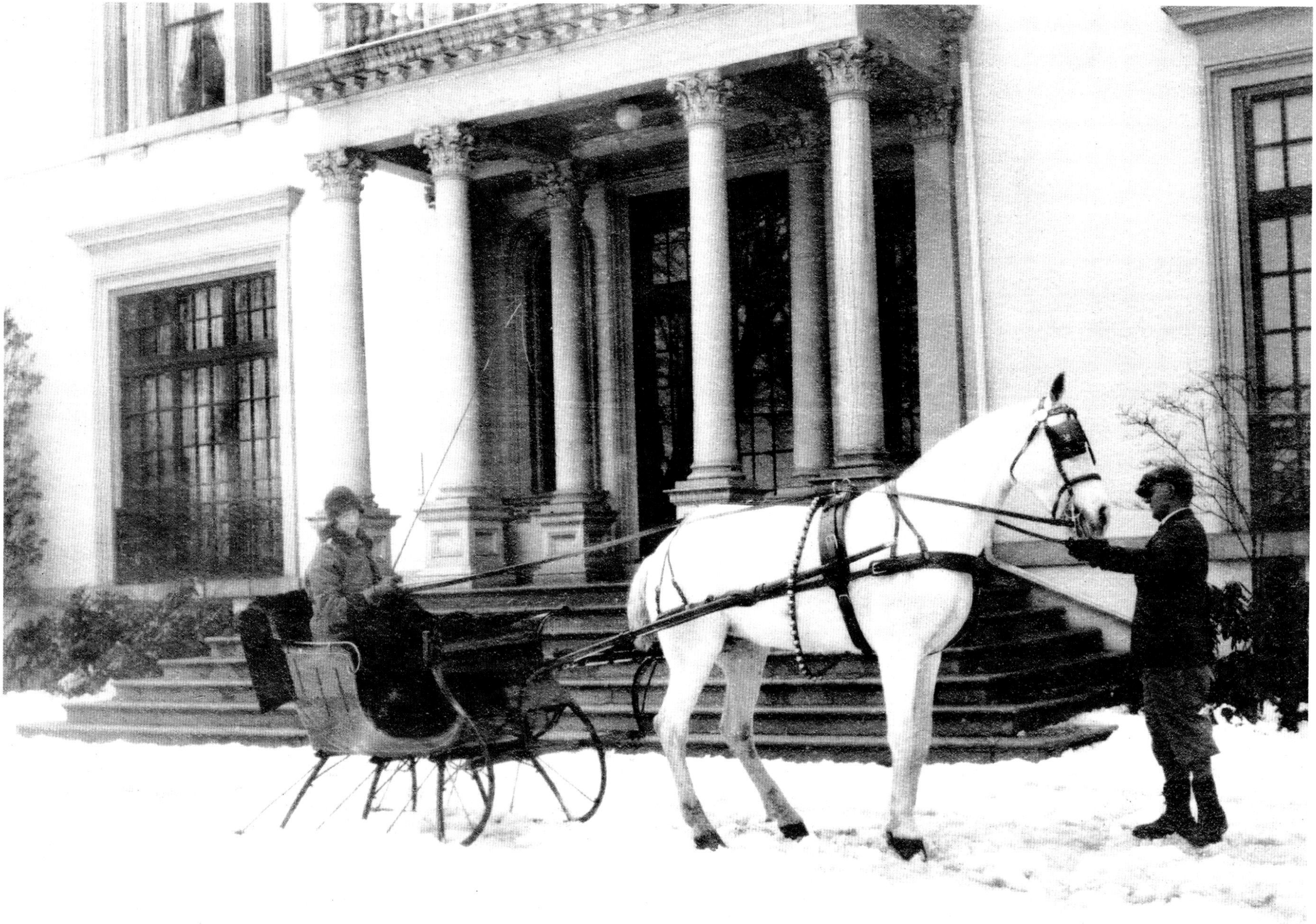

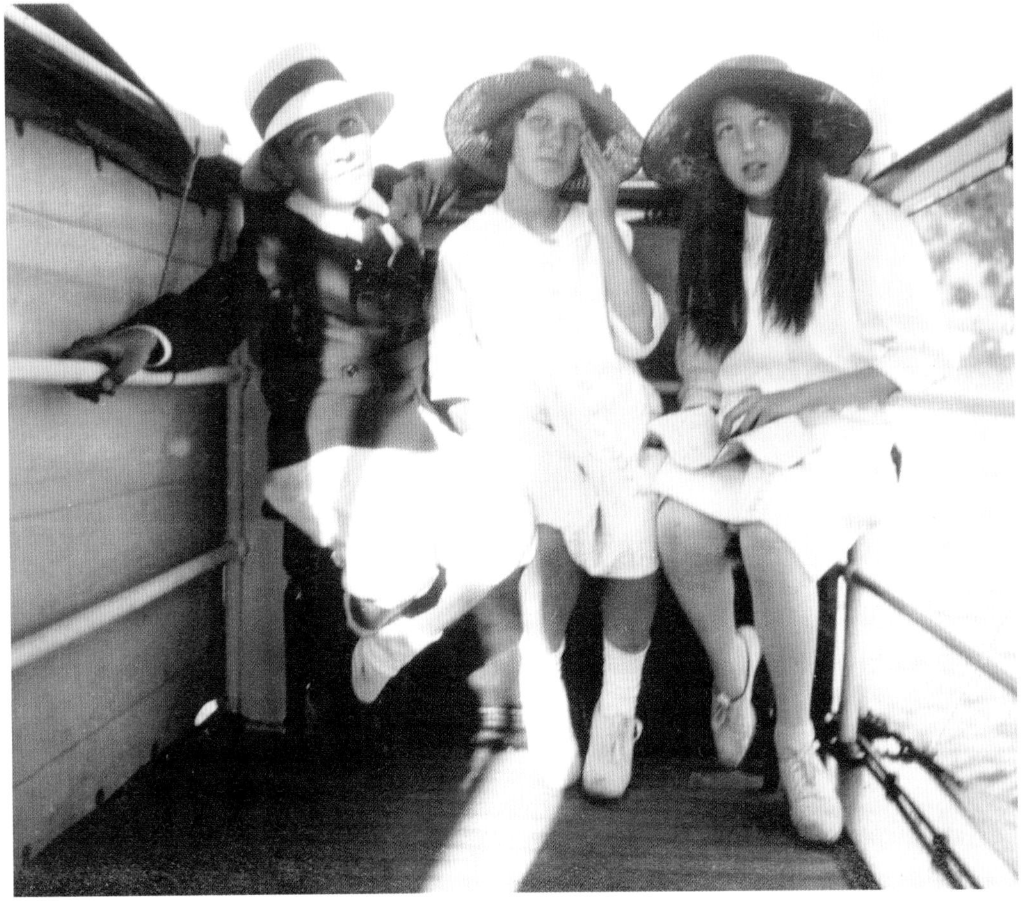

ABOVE Olin and Margaret Dows with Vincent's sister, Alice Astor, far right, on Vincent's yacht, the *Noma*, at a regatta in Poughkeepsie in 1915. Close in age, the three enjoyed spending time together as children. Born Alice Ava Muriel Astor in 1902, Alice spent her childhood years in New York City and summers at Ferncliff. After her parents divorced in 1910, she moved to England with her mother. Alice was ten years old in 1912 when her father died on the *Titanic*.

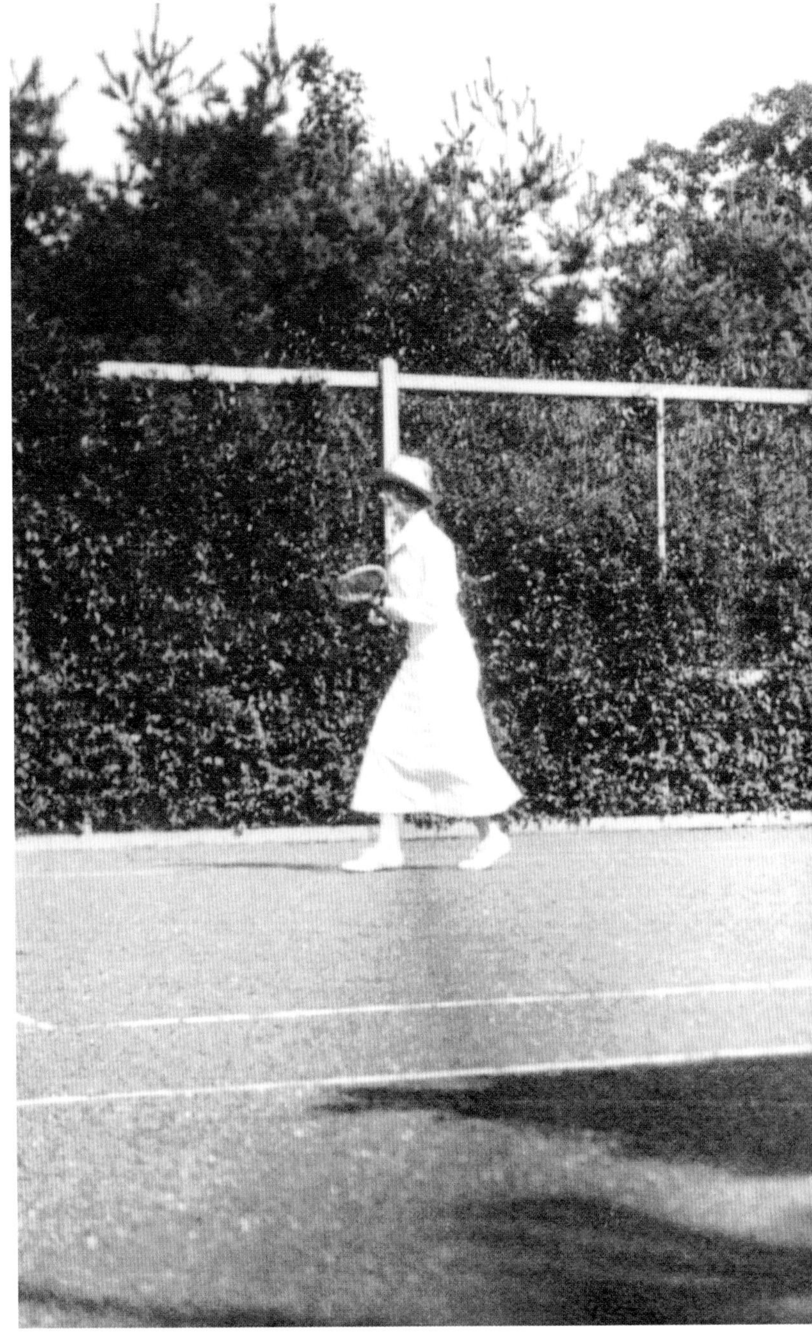

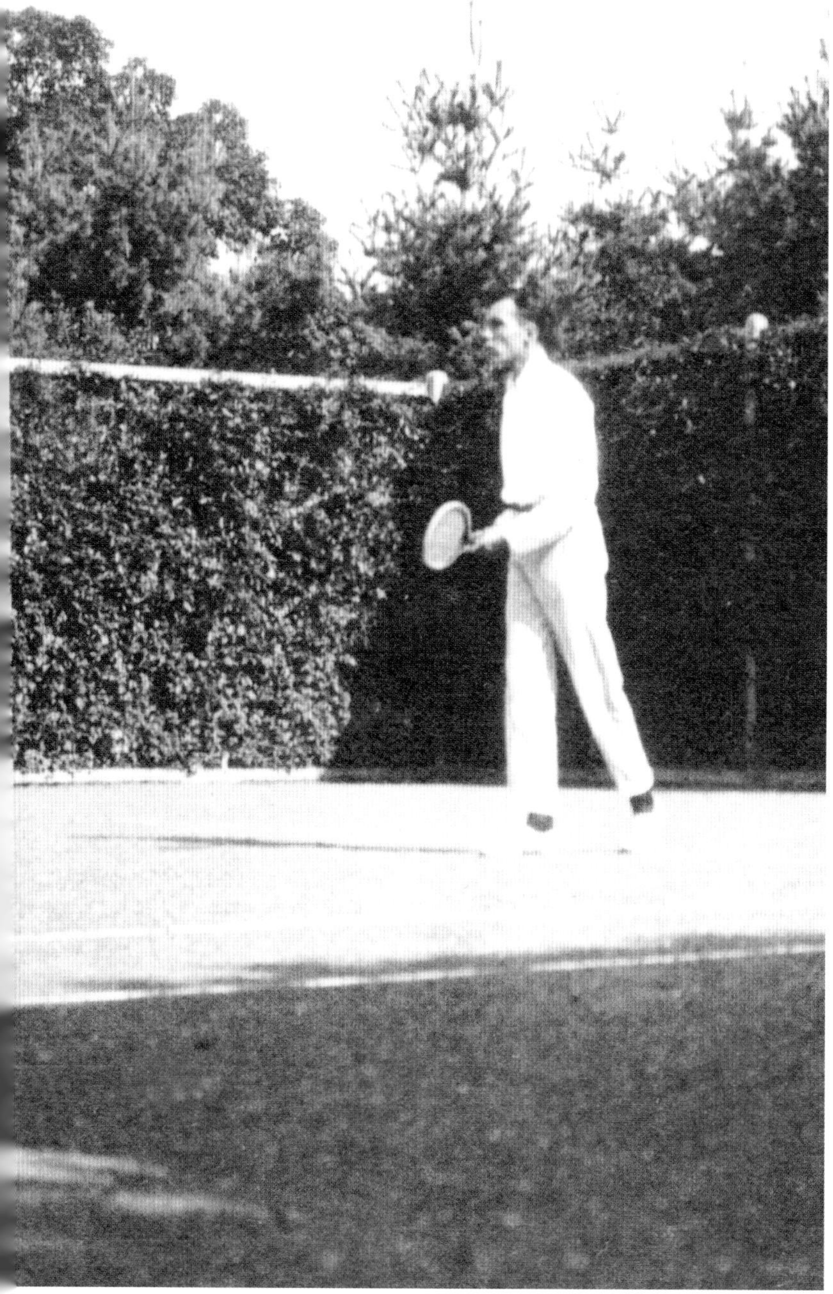

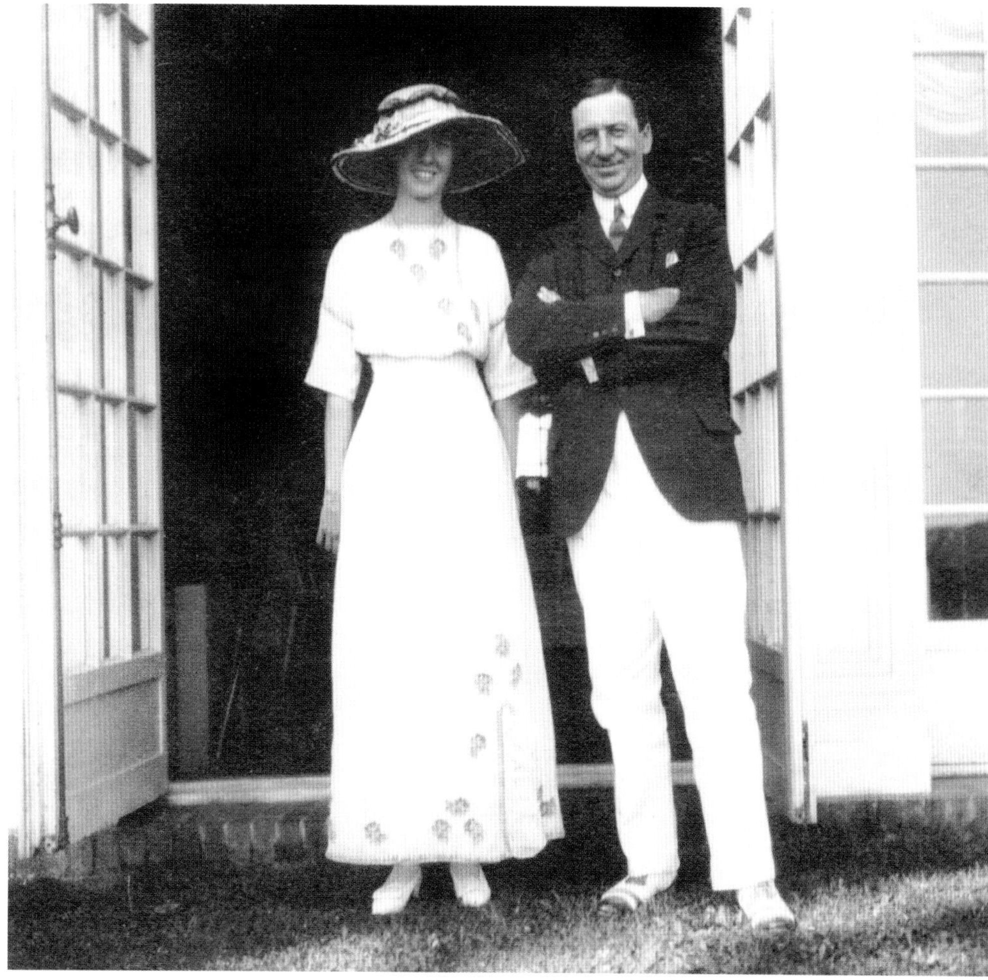

ABOVE Helen and Tracy at Foxhollow Farm, 1913. Summer was a particularly social season with outdoor activities enjoyed by the Dowses and Astors.

LEFT Vincent, playing partners with Helen, during a round of tennis on the court at Foxhollow Farm, 1919.

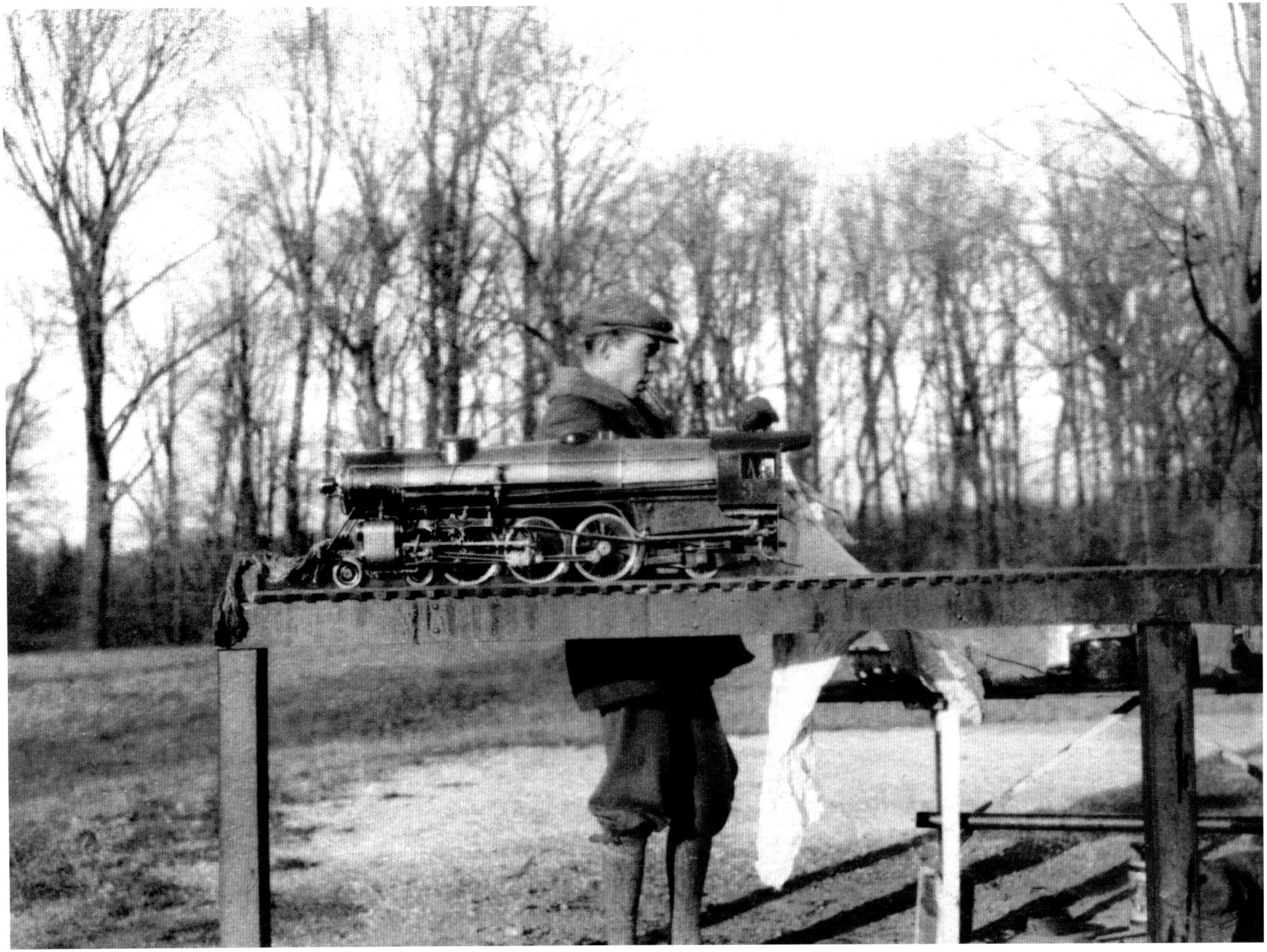

OPPOSITE Fascinated by trains, Vincent had a small-scale model version built with tracks that ran along the grounds of Ferncliff, seen here in 1925. The locomotive was built by Pete Snyder, the skilled machinist at Rhinebeck's Hub Garage. Vincent rode behind the engine in an attached car equipped with a seat and would place his feet on poles that extended on each side of the engine. Extra cars with seats could be attached for passengers. Olin Knut Thyberg, Tracy's grandson, remembers riding on the train with Serge Obolensky's son, Ivan, as children in 1940. Hunter Paston, the character based on Vincent Astor in Thomas Wolfe's novel, *Of Time and the River*, also was depicted as having a miniature locomotive on his property.

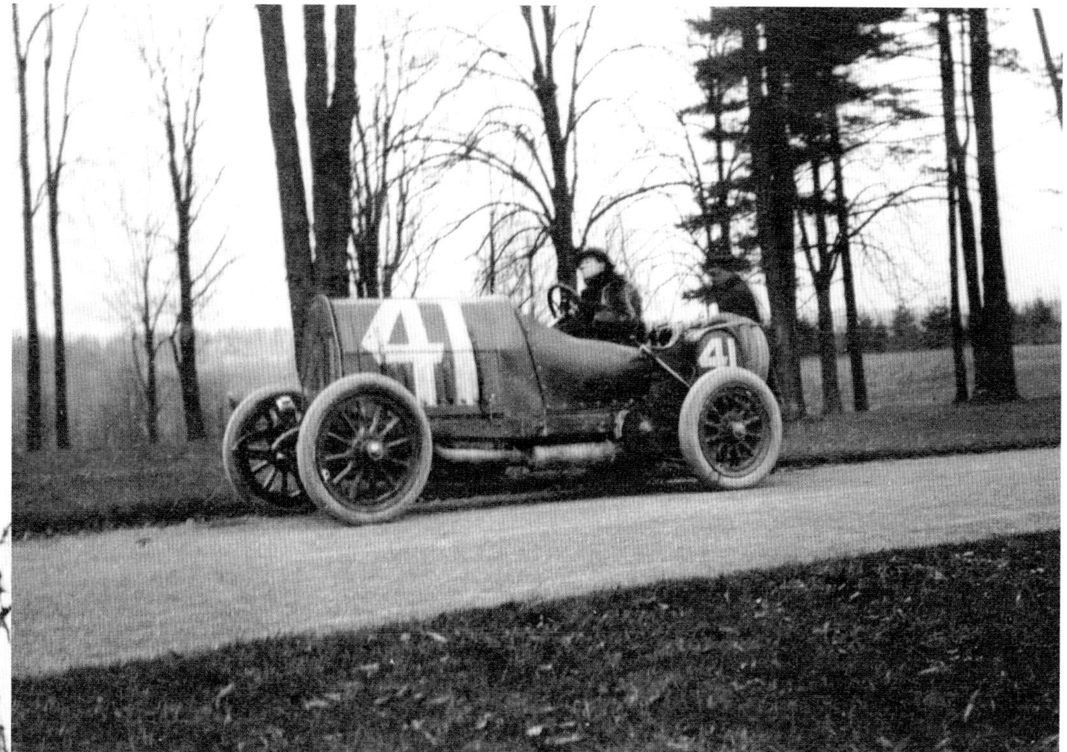

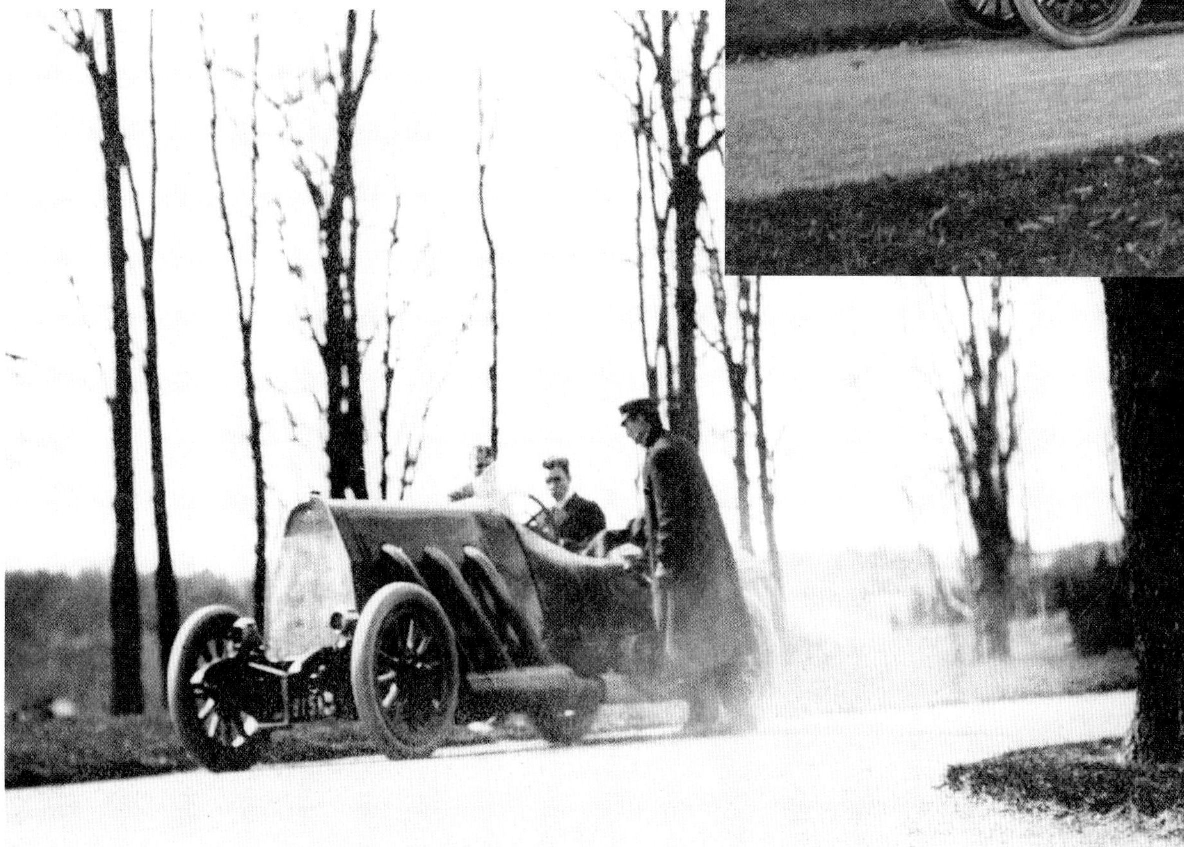

ABOVE Vincent in a Fiat S74 at Ferncliff in 1912. French Grand Prix driver, Louis Wagner, drove the car in the 1911 American Grand Prize race in Savannah, Georgia. Vincent had inherited an interest in automobiles and machinery from his father, whose passion led to road improvements in the Rhinebeck area.

LEFT At the wheel of a customized version of the Fiat S74, Vincent prepares for an outing in 1913. He was known to race his cars along the roads near Ferncliff and in Rhinebeck. Extra tires were strapped to the back as punctures were a common problem.

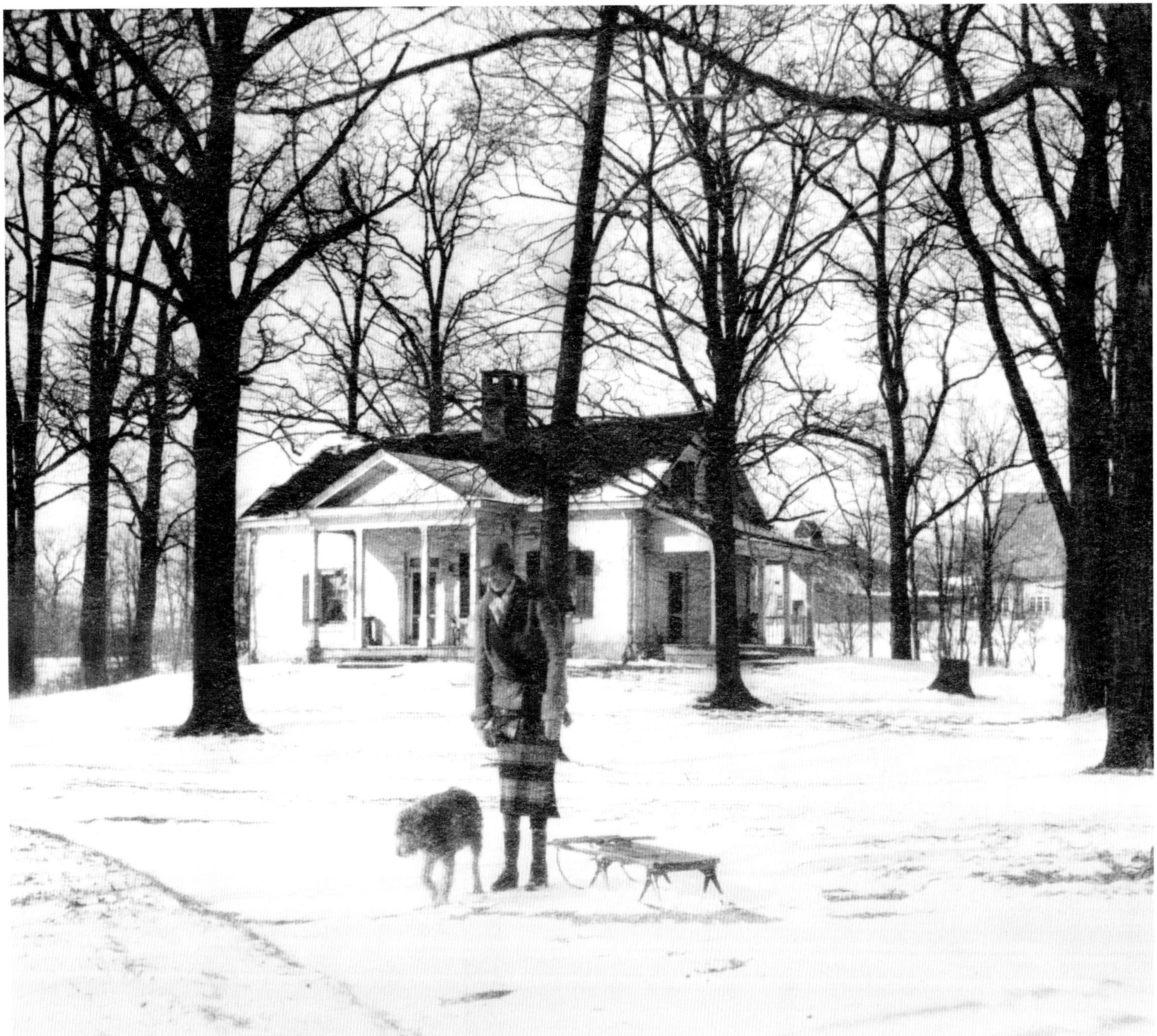

LEFT Helen with her dog, Tatters, at Pond Cottage in 1926. The house dates from the eighteenth century, and is the oldest structure on the Ferncliff estate.

OPPOSITE Tatters walking on the frozen pond next to the cottage. Tracy's shadow is reflected on the pond as he takes the photograph. In the background are the Normandy-style dairy barns built by Charles A. Platt for Vincent Astor in 1918. Harrie T. Lindeberg began the original design, but left to serve time overseas during World War I. Platt took over the drawings and completed the project.

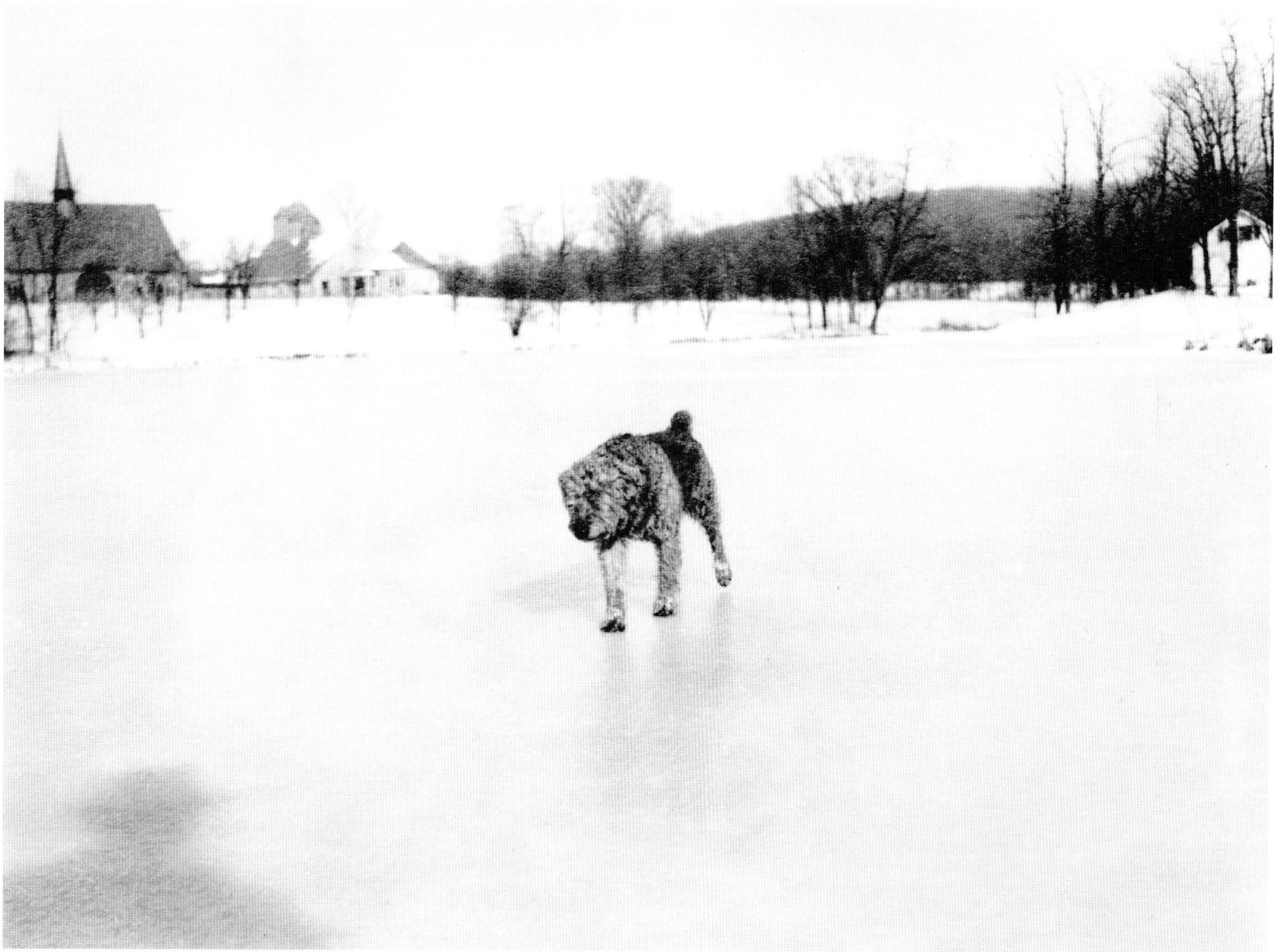

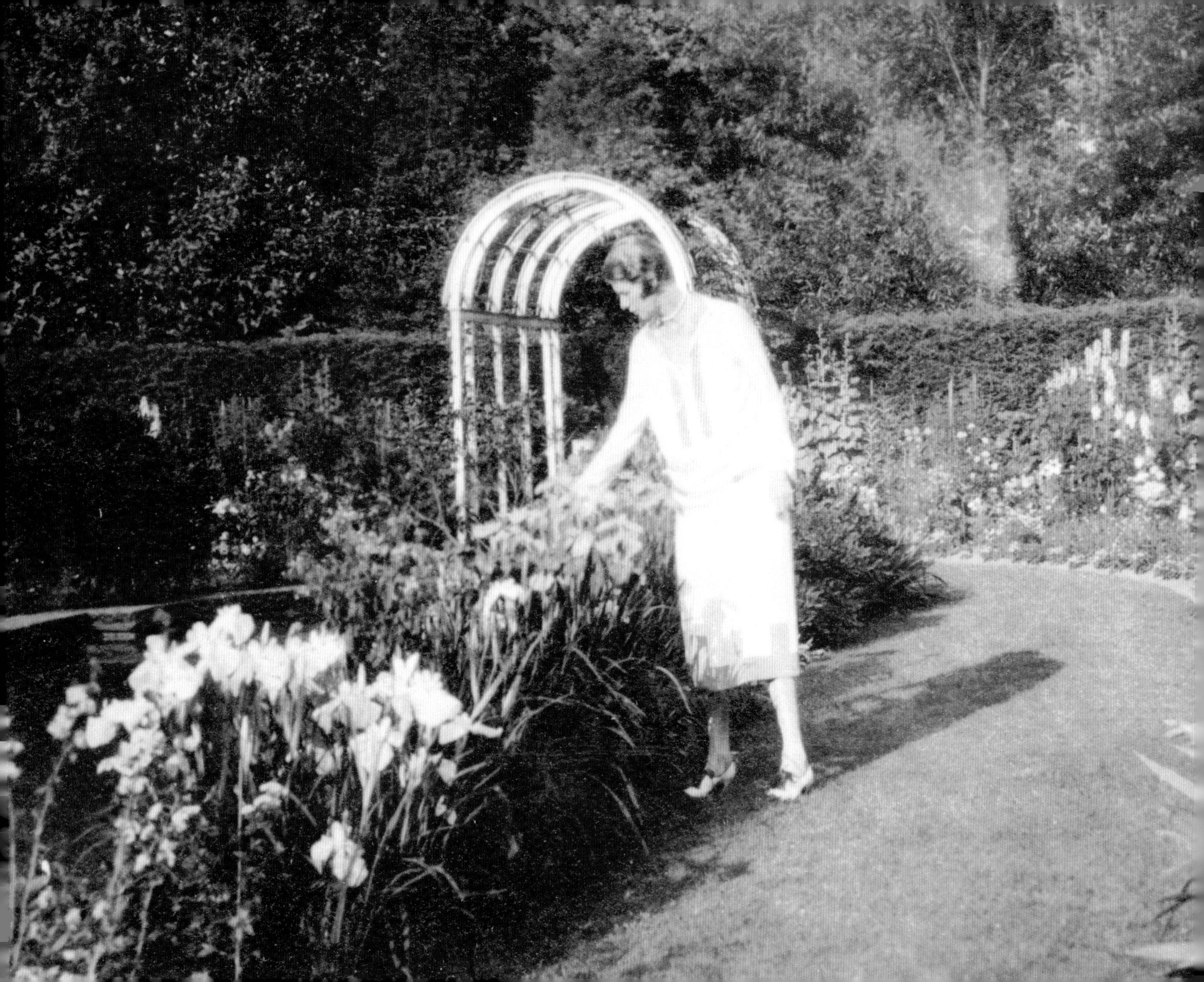

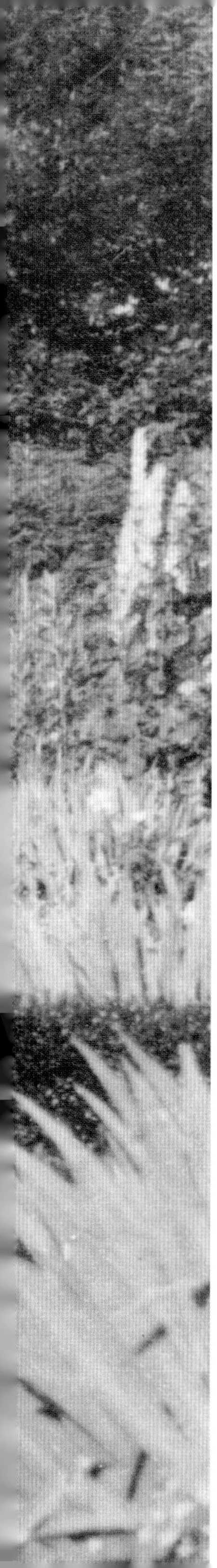

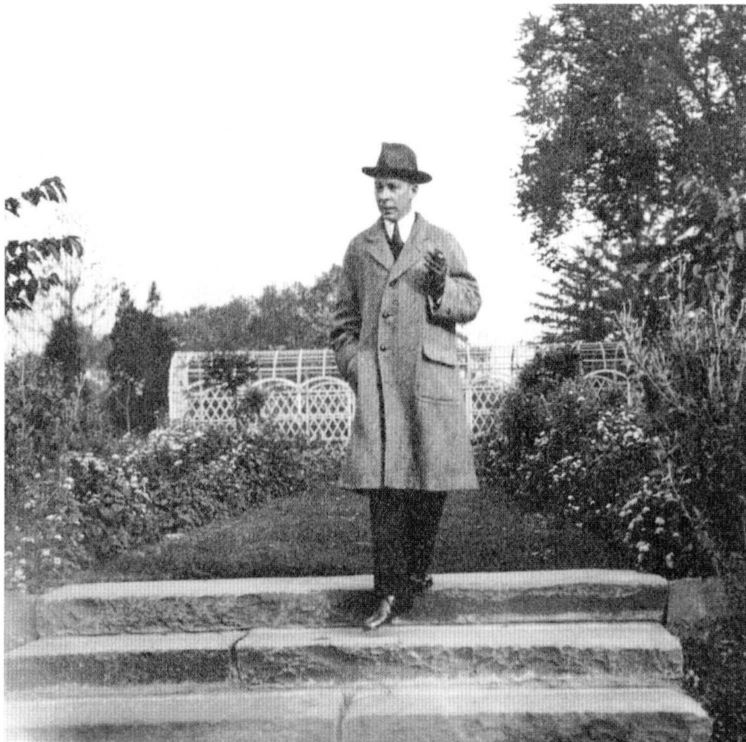

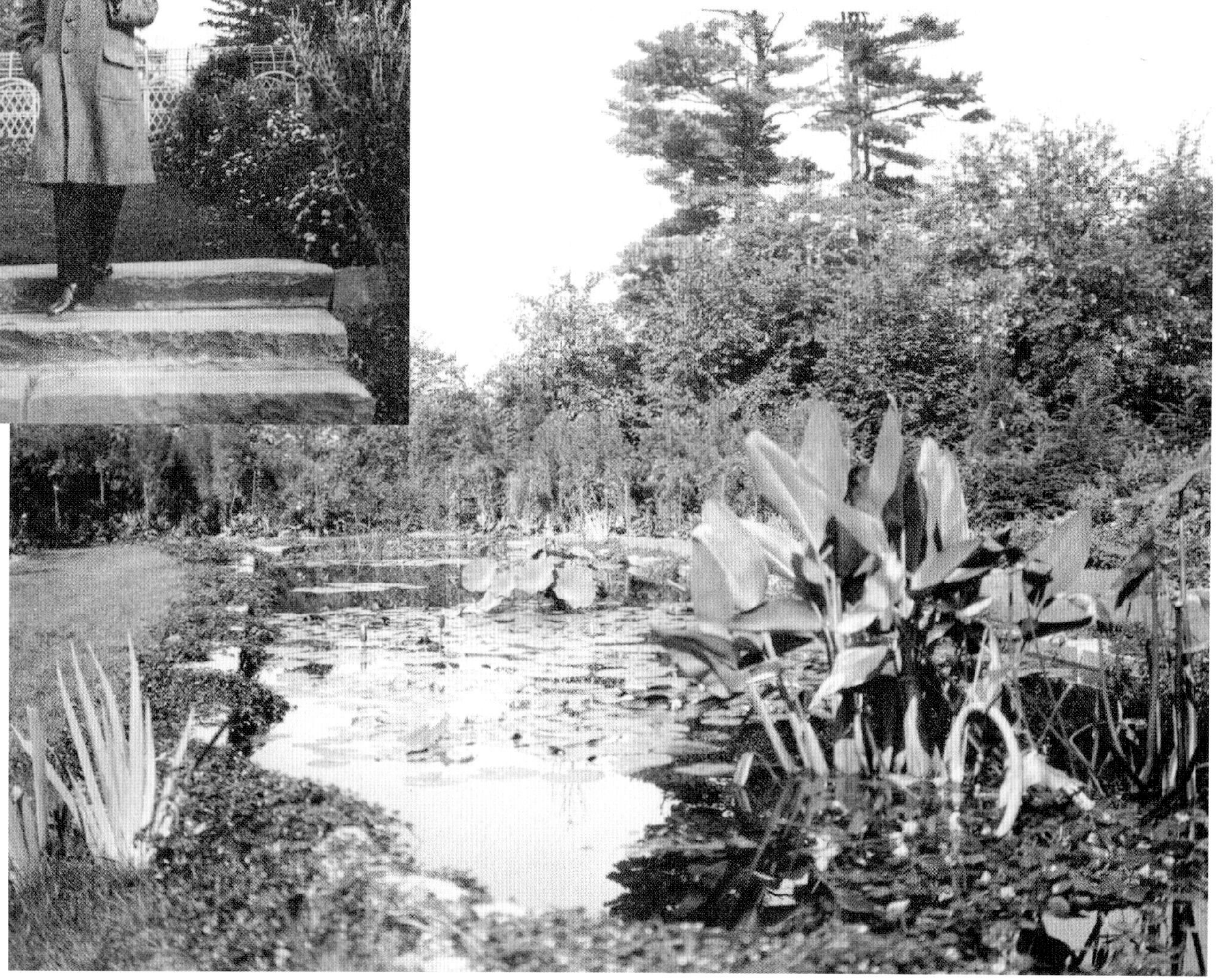

ABOVE Harrie T. Lindeberg, in 1917, taking a stroll through the Italian gardens at Ferncliff. In 1912, Lindeberg had married his second wife, Lucia Hull, a friend of Helen and Vincent's and sister to Lytle Hull, who later married Helen after her divorce from Vincent.

LEFT Helen admiring the irises and other lush plantings in the gardens of Ferncliff, summer 1927.

RIGHT The lagoon filled with exotic plants during the summer.

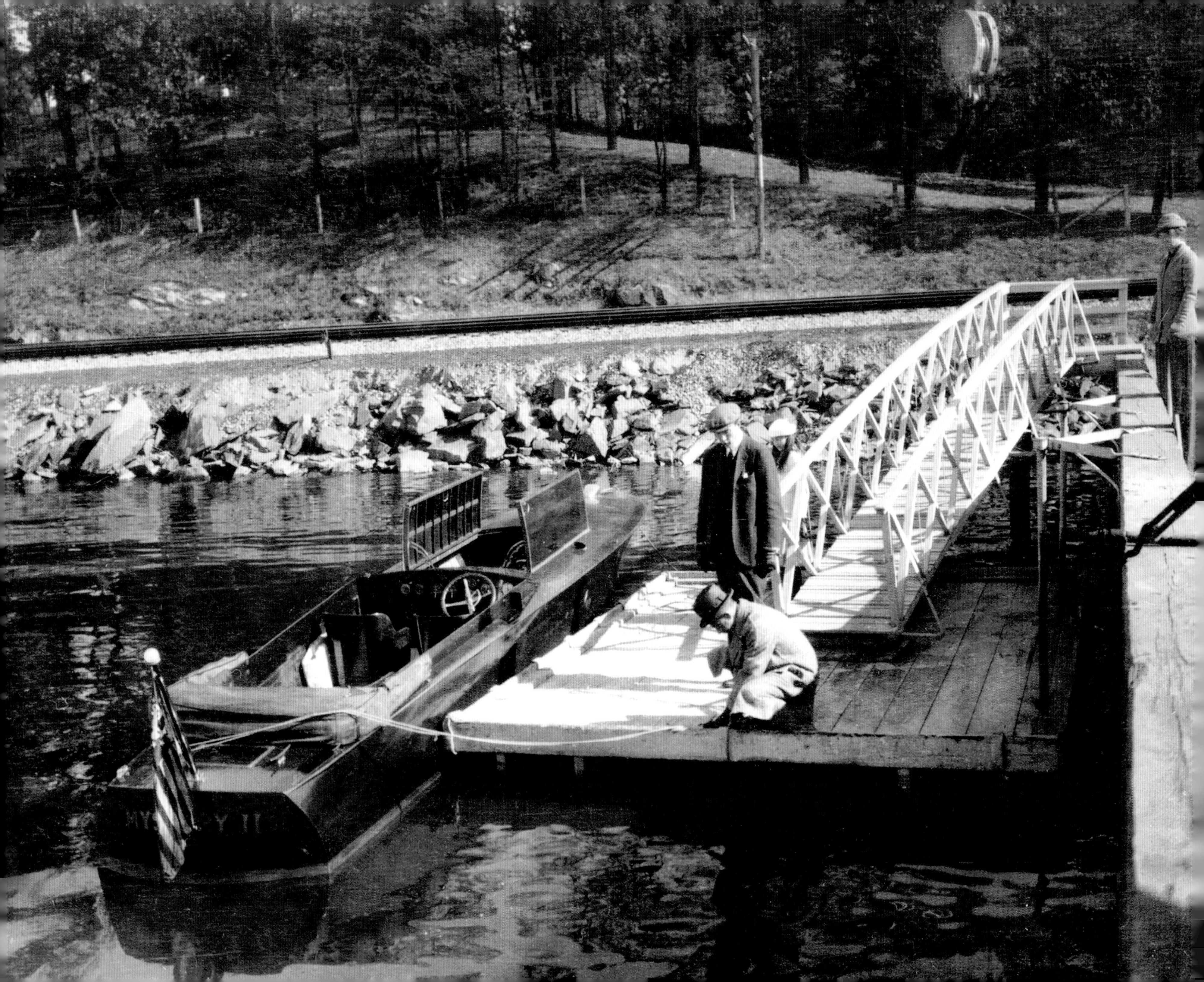

LEFT Vincent and his sister, Alice, at the Ferncliff dock on the Hudson River after a ride in his speedboat, the *Mystery II*, in the fall of 1915. Helen observes from the pier. The *Mystery II* was a swift little runabout built by the Albany Boat Corporation. Visible beside the river are the tracks of the New York Central Railroad. The dock featured a boon crane with a pulley attachment for unloading cargo.

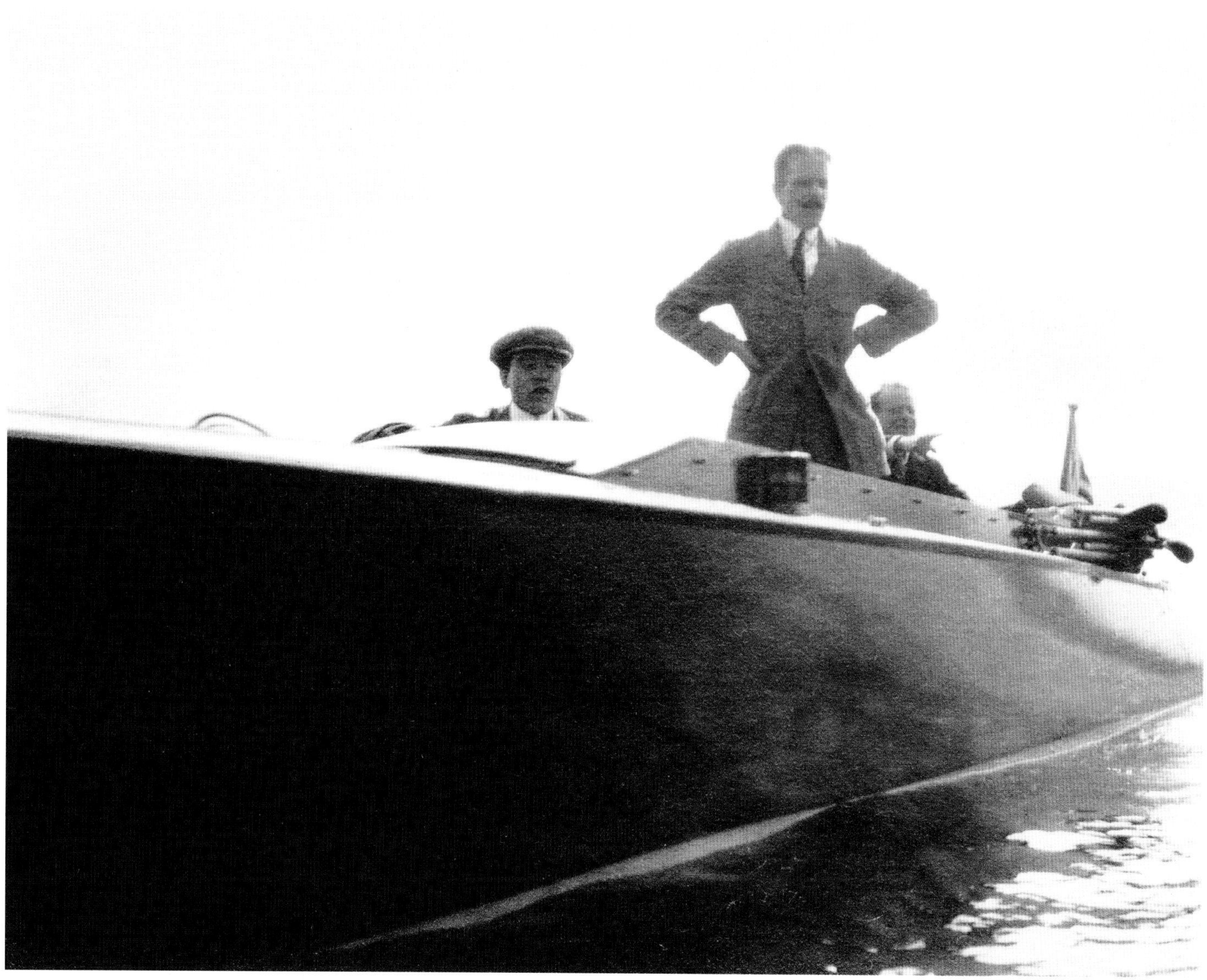

ABOVE Vincent with Henry G. Barbey (standing) and another friend leaving for an outing on the Hudson River aboard the *Mystery II* earlier that summer, 1915.

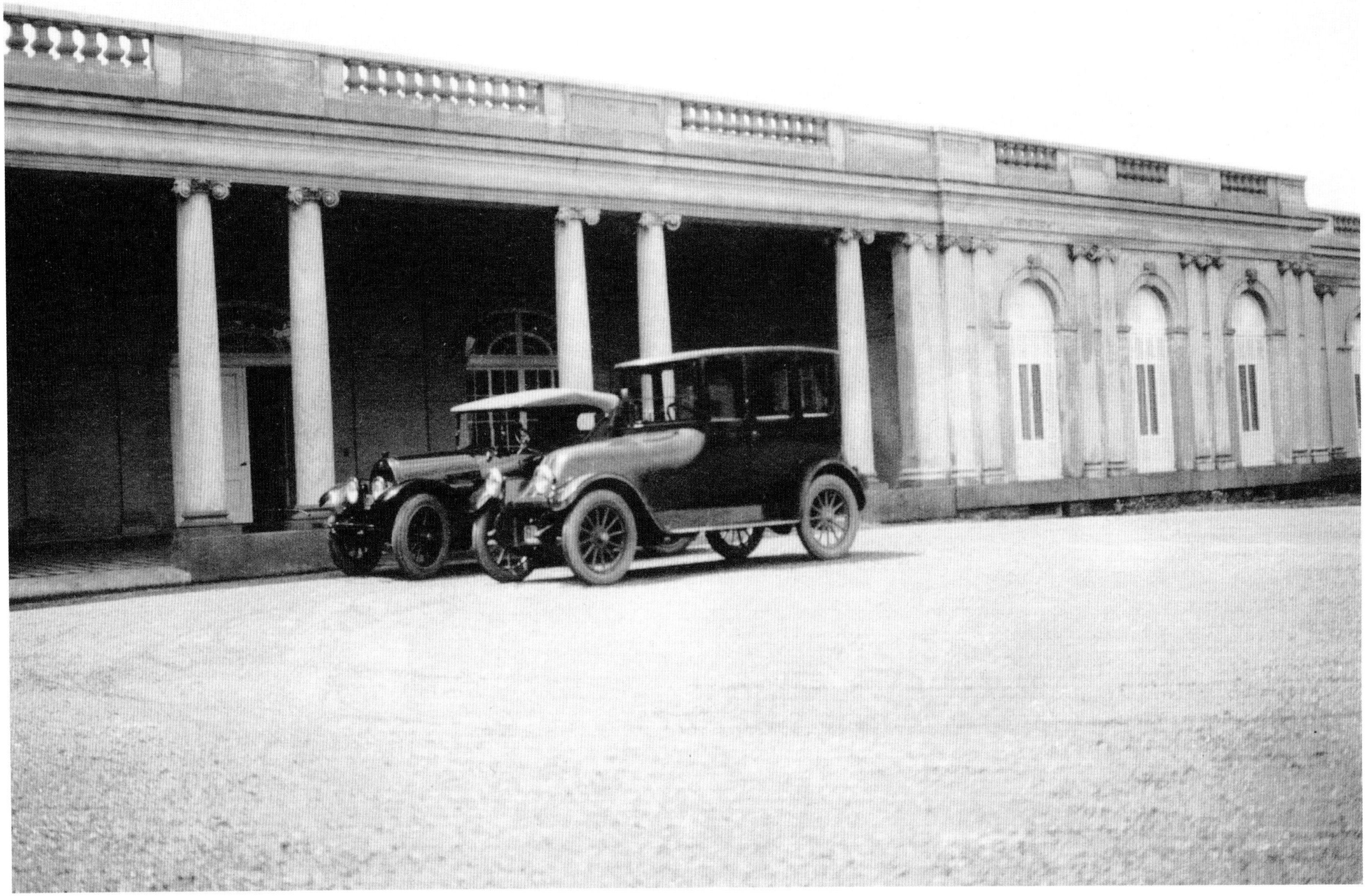

OPPOSITE The front of Ferncliff Casino in 1920. The 40,000-square-foot Beaux-Arts sporting pavilion, inspired by the Grand Trianon at Versailles, was designed by Stanford White in 1902. The building was completed in 1904, just two years before Stanford White was fatally shot at Madison Square Garden in New York City. The casino had an indoor clay tennis court, an indoor heated swimming pool (reported to be the first in America), a bowling alley, an outdoor grass tennis court, two squash courts, and guests bedrooms. After the main house at Ferncliff was razed in the 1940s, Vincent used the casino as his country home. His third wife, Brooke Russell Marshall Astor, whom he married in 1954, donated the estate to the Archdiocese of New York after Vincent's death in 1959. The building, now privately owned, is called Astor Courts.

RIGHT The Astors' Christmas tree in 1920 under the beautiful round skylight designed by Stanford White.

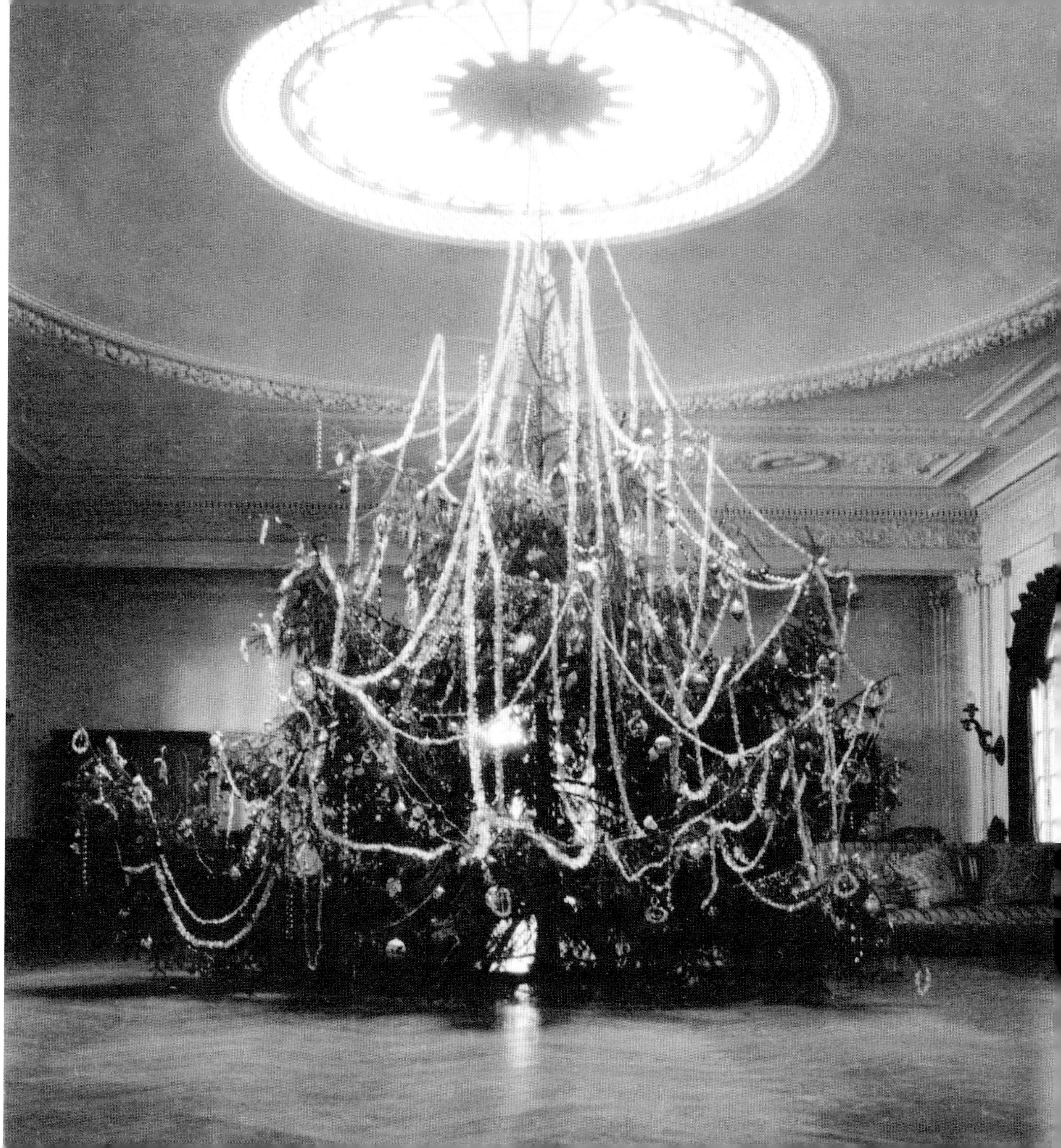

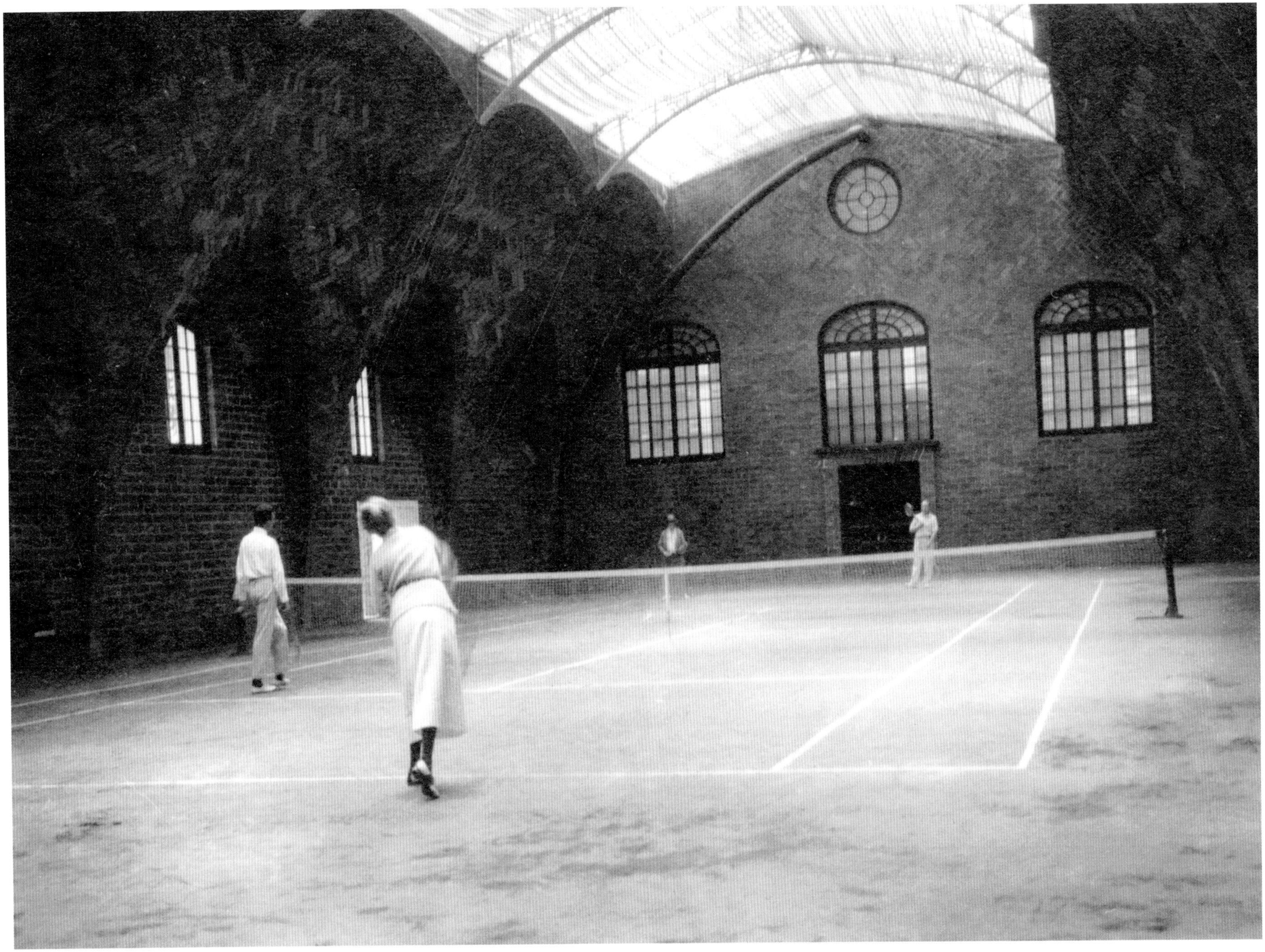

OPPOSITE Vincent and Helen playing against Alice and a friend in the indoor tennis court of the casino, 1915. The tile work was by Rafael Guastavino.

RIGHT Olin and Margaret on a raft in the indoor pool, 1915. The sparkling vaulted ceiling supported by Corinthian columns was painted turquoise and embedded with mica chips.

BELOW Helen in a diving suit in the summer of 1917, about to practice her diving skills in the pool, perhaps for an upcoming trip to the Caribbean or the island of Bermuda. In the 1930s, Vincent built a twenty-two-acre estate in St. George's Ferry Reach on Bermuda.

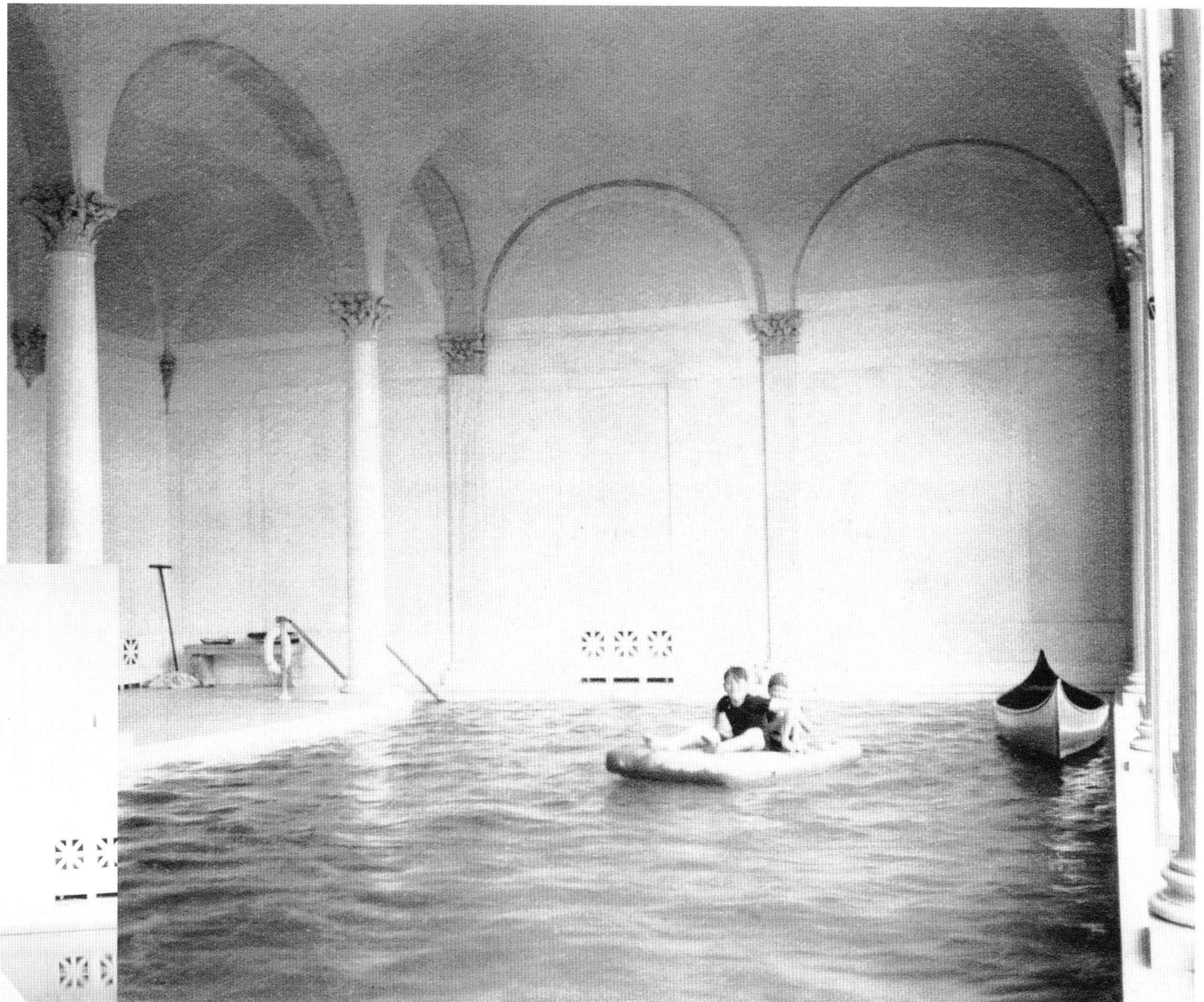

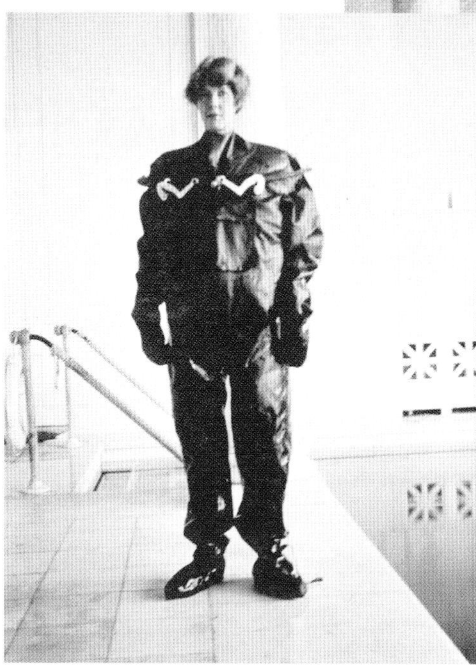

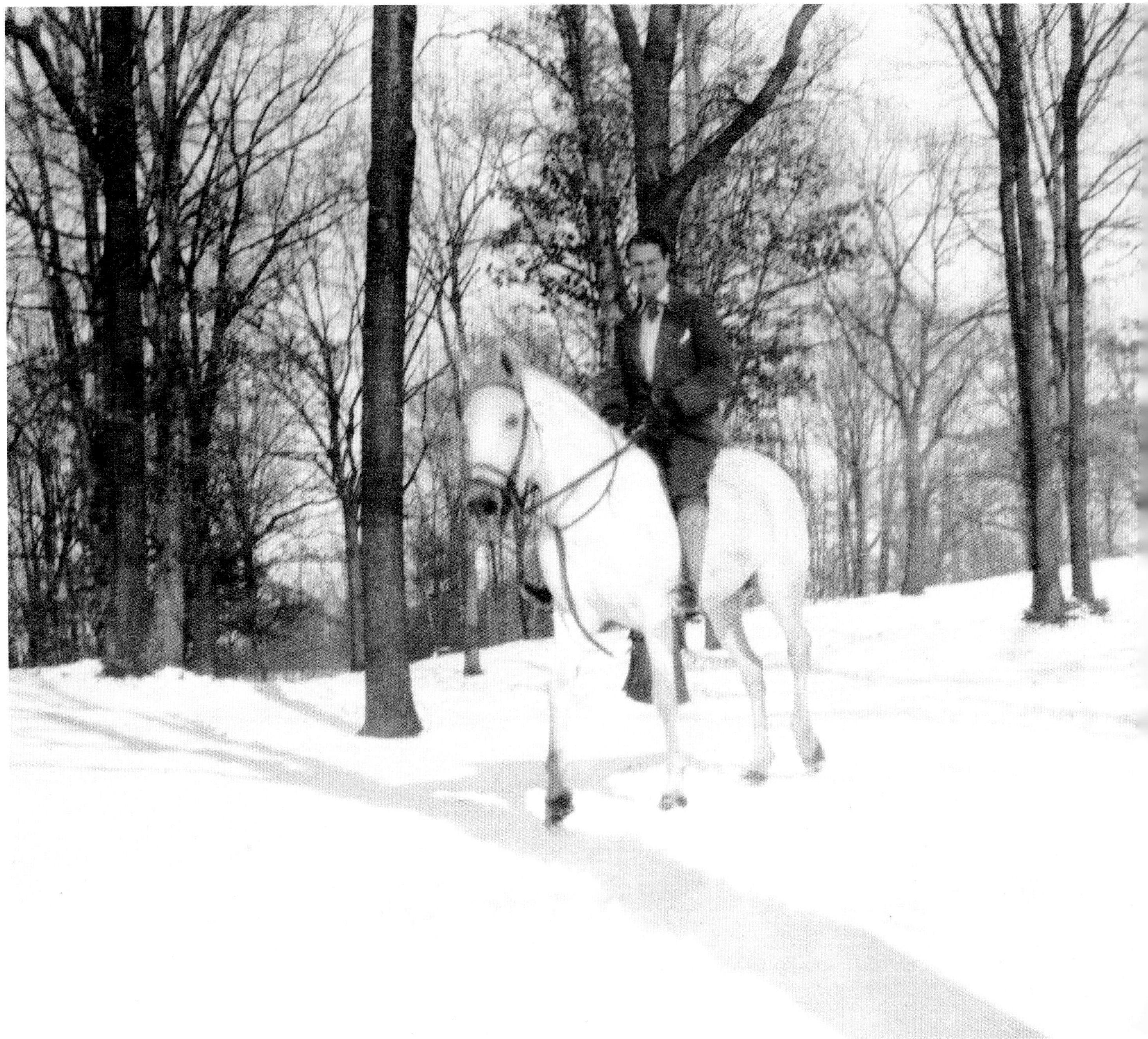

RIGHT The prince on a white horse out for a ride on the Ferncliff property, 1926. Prince Sergei Platonovich Obolensky Neledinsky-Meletzky, the son of Russian aristocracy, was born in Saint Petersburg and served as an officer in the Chevalier Guards during World War I. He was first married to a Russian princess but divorced her in 1924 and married Alice Astor the same year. Their wedding in London was considered the event of the season. They divorced in 1932. For many years Serge was the director of the St. Regis Hotel in New York City for Vincent Astor, who had inherited it from his father. Describing his life with Alice during their marriage, he wrote in his 1958 autobiography, *One Man in His Time: The Memoirs of Serge Obolensky*, "We lived like this: in midsummer we visited the United States, first at Newport, then to Rhinebeck for the fall, returning to London for Christmas, and leaving in January for St. Moritz to ski, then stopping off awhile in Paris before going to the south of France for the spring and returning to London as the new season began."

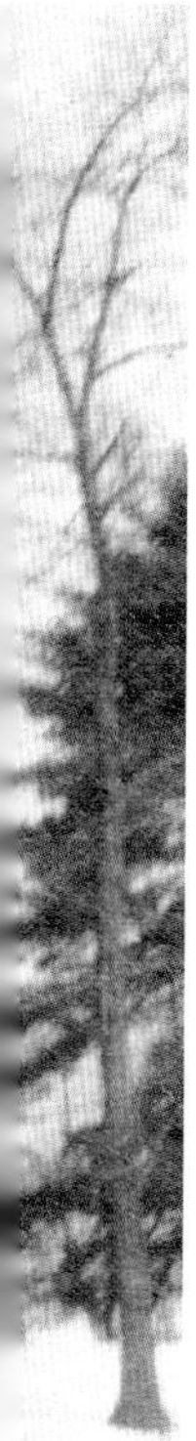

BELOW Marienruh, the Obolensky's Rhinebeck country house, under construction in 1927. Alice received the northern part of the Ferncliff estate from Vincent as a wedding present. The land and original Marienruh house had been purchased by John Jacob Astor IV in the early 1900s from Louis Augustus Ehlers, the landscape architect of Ferncliff. The Obolenskys hired the architect Mott B. Schmidt to design a new stone Georgian house, keeping the name Marienruh. Schmidt was also the architect of Vincent Astor's townhouse in New York City.

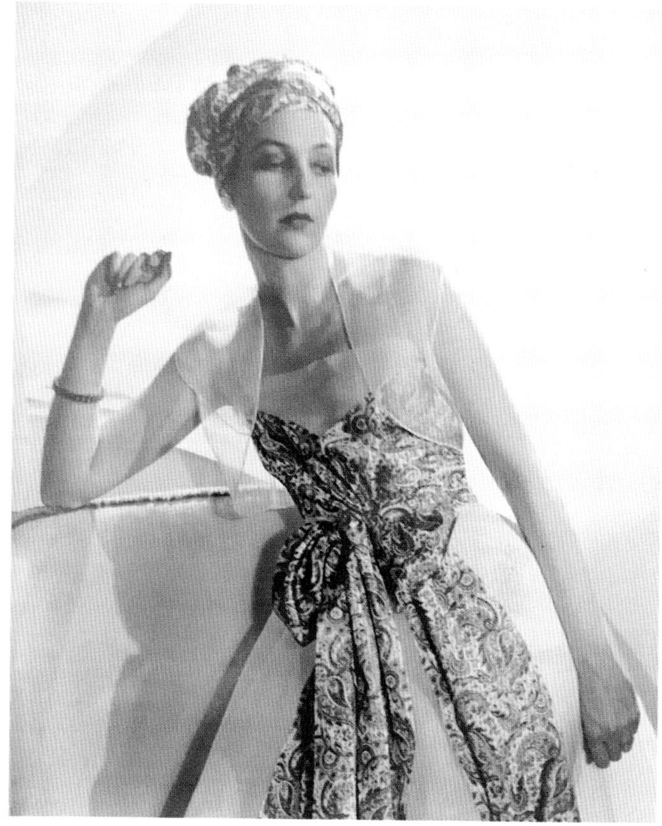

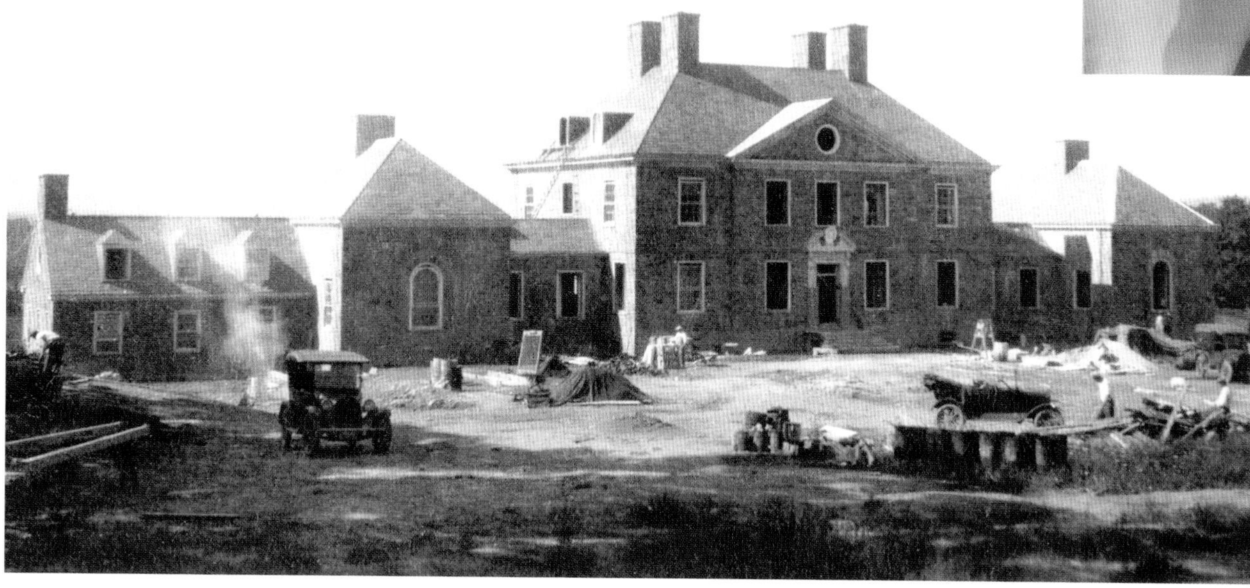

ABOVE As a young woman Alice was known for her exotic beauty, as captured in this portrait by her friend, the celebrated photographer, Cecil Beaton, in 1936. She led an active social life and was married four times. Alice gave birth to her first two children, Ivan and Sylvia, while married to Serge. After their divorce, she married Raimund von Hofmannsthal, the son of the Austrian poet and librettist Hugo von Hofmannsthal, in 1933. They had one daughter, Romana, and divorced in 1939. Her third husband was the British journalist Philip Harding, with whom she had her last child, Emily. After divorcing him she married the British architect David Pleydell-Bouverie in 1946 and divorced him in 1952. (Courtesy of Emily Harding)

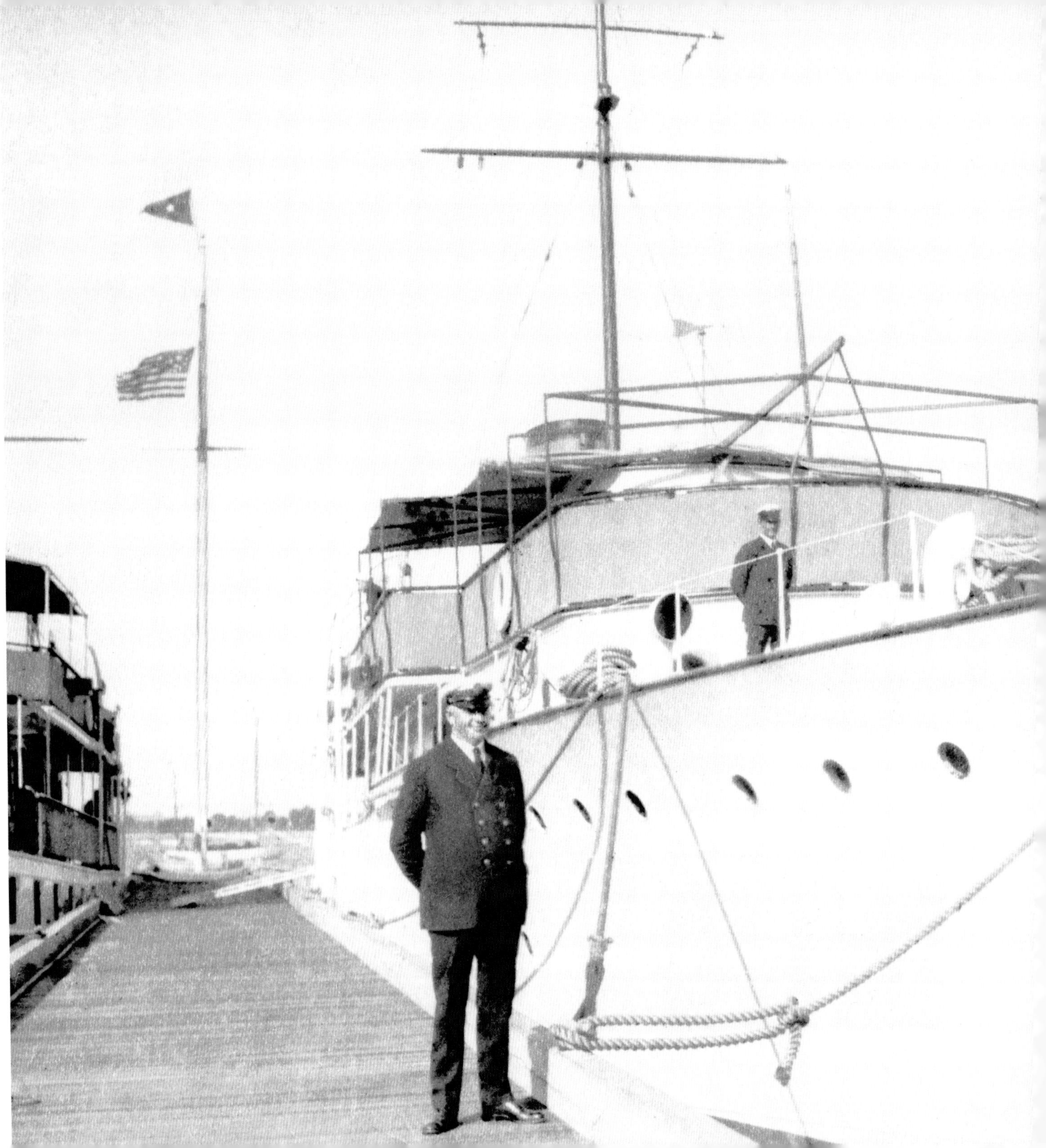

RIGHT The *Nourmahal*, Vincent's second yacht, docked in Newport, 1925. Tracy Dows had been invited to join the Astors, the Obolenskys, and other friends on a trip to Seal Harbor, stopping in Newport along the way. Vincent, who took the name from a steam yacht his father had owned in the early 1900s, had the 160-foot pleasure yacht built in 1921 to replace the *Noma*, which he loaned to the U.S. Navy in 1917 for use during World War I. Vincent's *Nourmahal* was designed to provide maximum comfort on long deep-sea cruises, with diesel engines, electric hoists, and other devices that eliminated the need for a large crew. In 1928, Vincent commissioned the Krupp Iron Works in Kiel, Germany, to build a third *Nourmahal* that was larger, faster, and even more luxurious.

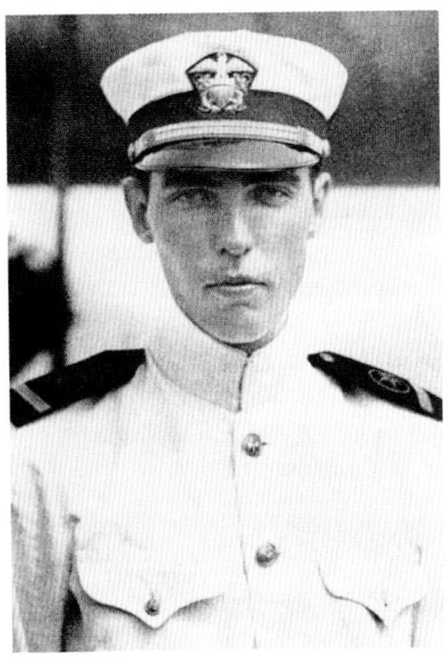

ABOVE A 1926 International Newsreel photograph of Vincent Astor after his promotion to Lieutenant Commander in the U.S. Naval Reserve.

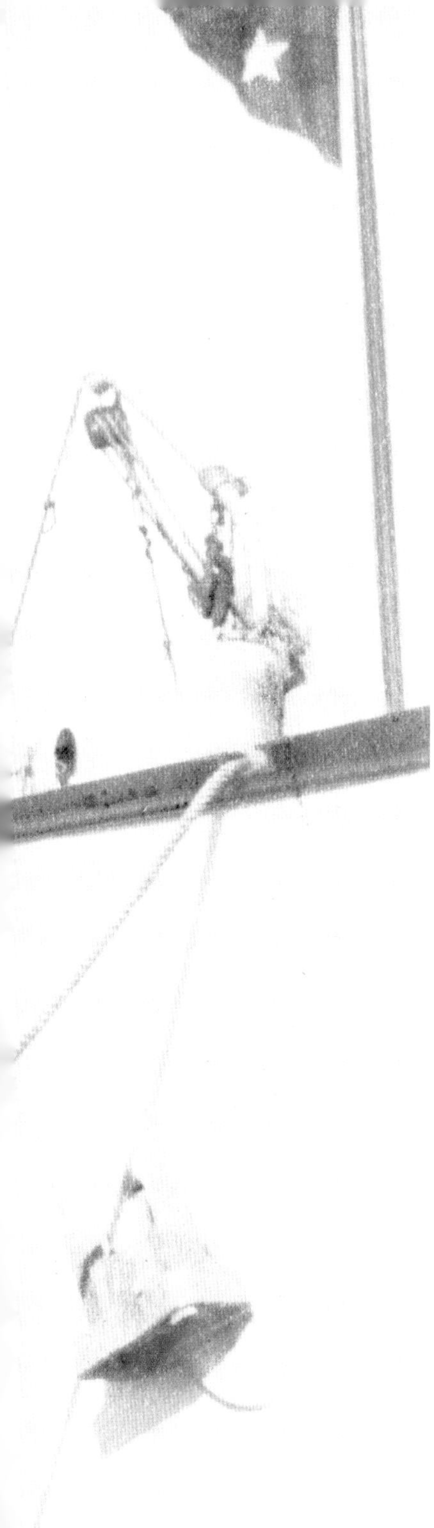

BELOW Relaxing aboard the *Nourmahal* on their return from Seal Harbor are Tracy Dows, John Hays Hammond, Jr., Helen Huntington Astor, Alice Astor Obolensky, and an unidentified friend. John Hays Hammond, Jr., was an inventor and the son of a successful mining engineer. At the age of twelve, Hammond had accompanied his father on a business trip to Thomas Edison's laboratory in West Orange, New Jersey. Years later, Edison became Hammond's mentor. He worked at the U.S. Patent Office and is credited with many foreign and domestic patents, mostly in radio control. Aside from his inherited wealth, Hammond's inventions earned him a considerable fortune.

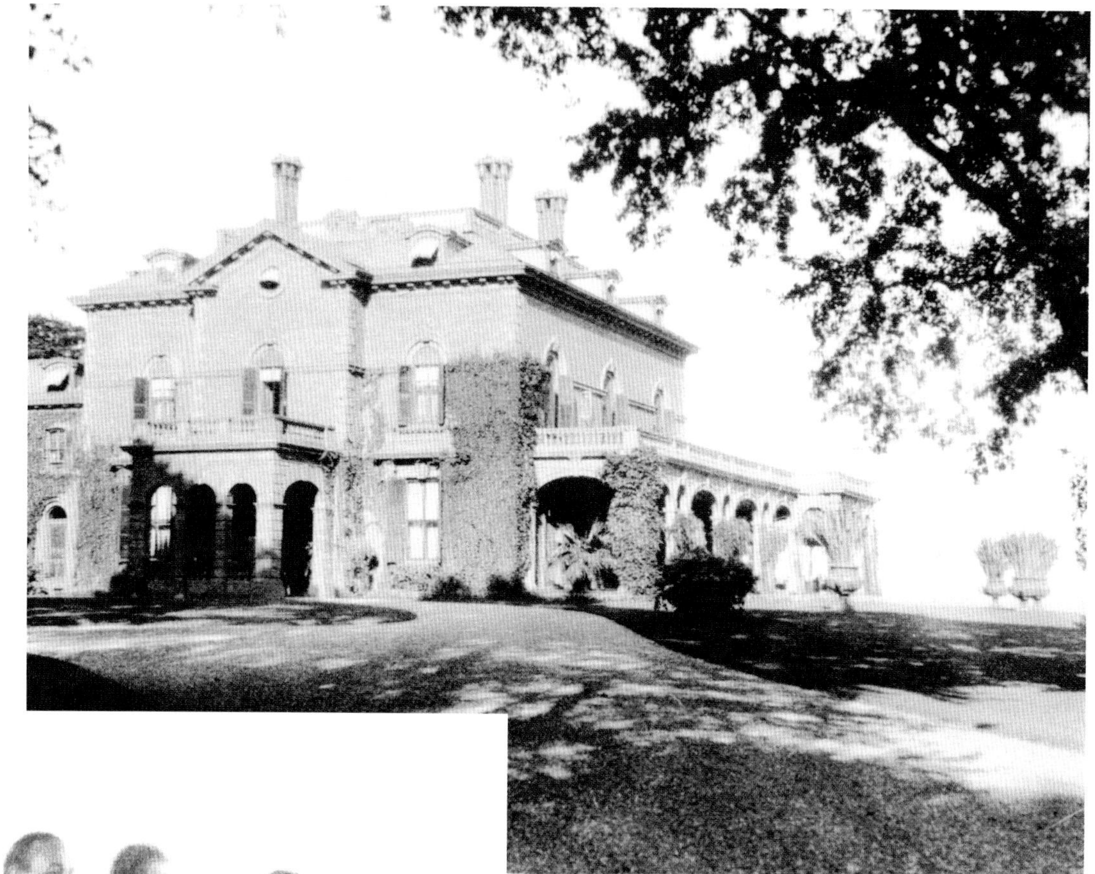

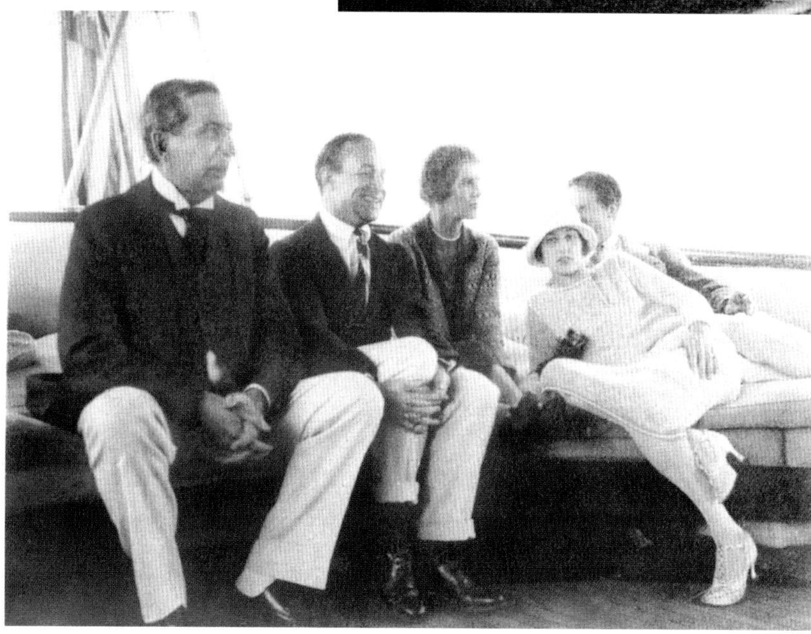

ABOVE While in Newport, the Astors and their guests visited Beechwood, the cottage that had belonged to Vincent and Alice's late grandmother, Caroline Schermerhorn Astor. Built in 1851 for New York merchant Daniel Parish by Andrew Jackson Downing and Calvert Vaux, it later became the summer home of the Astor family. Caroline Astor hired the architect Richard Morris Hunt to make further renovations, including the addition of a ballroom to fit the famous "Four Hundred."

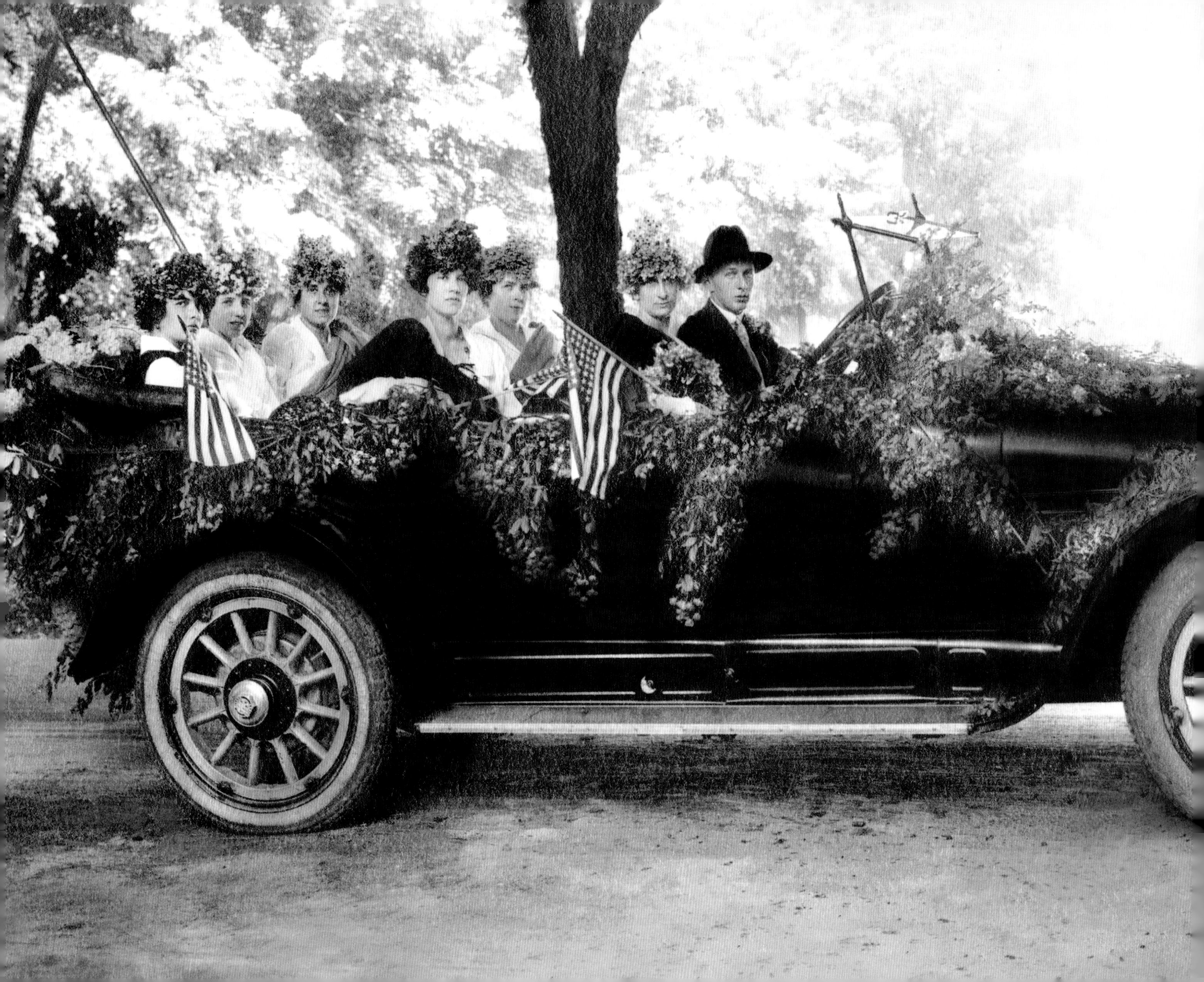

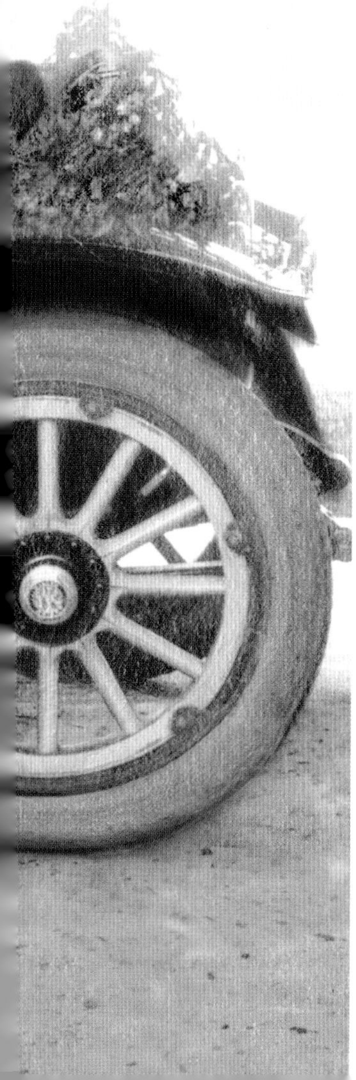

CHAPTER FIVE

TOWN and COUNTRY

In and around Rhinebeck

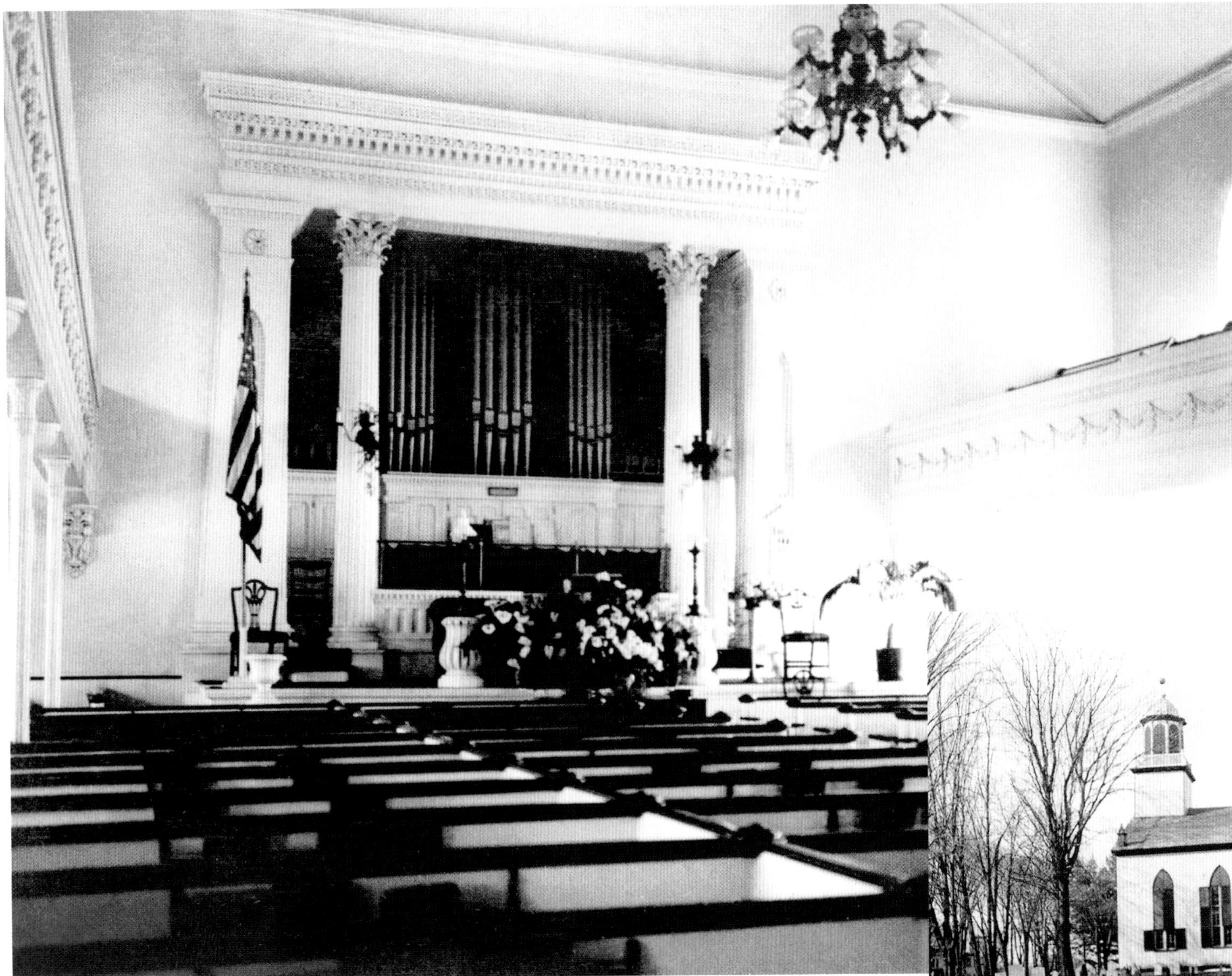

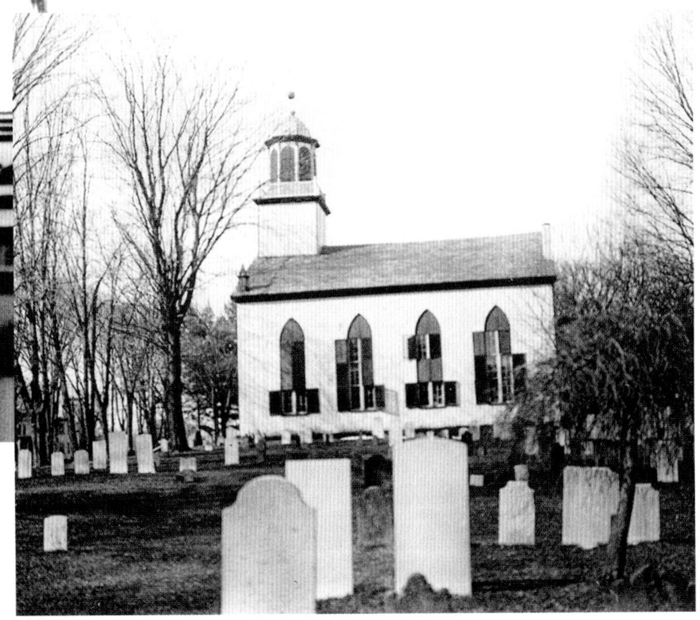

PREVIOUS PAGES The patriotic local women of the Girls' Friendly Society preparing for the Rhinebeck Independence Day parade on July 4, 1919. The July 12, 1919 edition of the *Rhinebeck Gazette* reported that the car was "a dream in flowers and beauty. Blooms of red, white and blue were employed in the decorations and the effect was charming."

OPPOSITE Olin on a pony in front of Hillside Chapel, 1913. Alice Dows's grandmother, Julia Lynch Olin, had the chapel built in 1855 on the Albany Post Road opposite the Glenburn property as a memorial to her late husband, Reverend Stephen Olin.

ABOVE AND RIGHT Views of the inside and outside of the Rhinebeck Reformed Church, 1919. The structure was built in 1808.

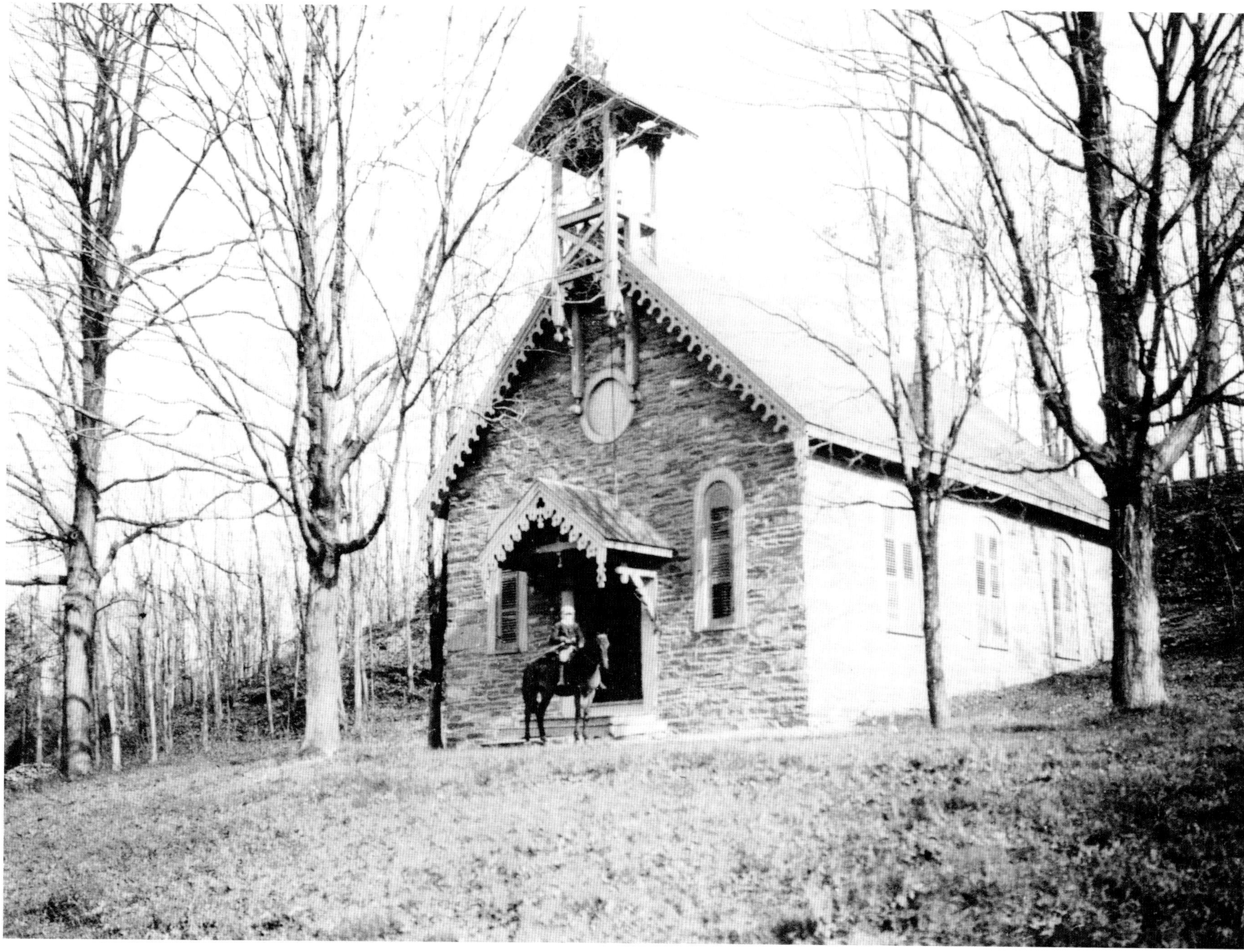

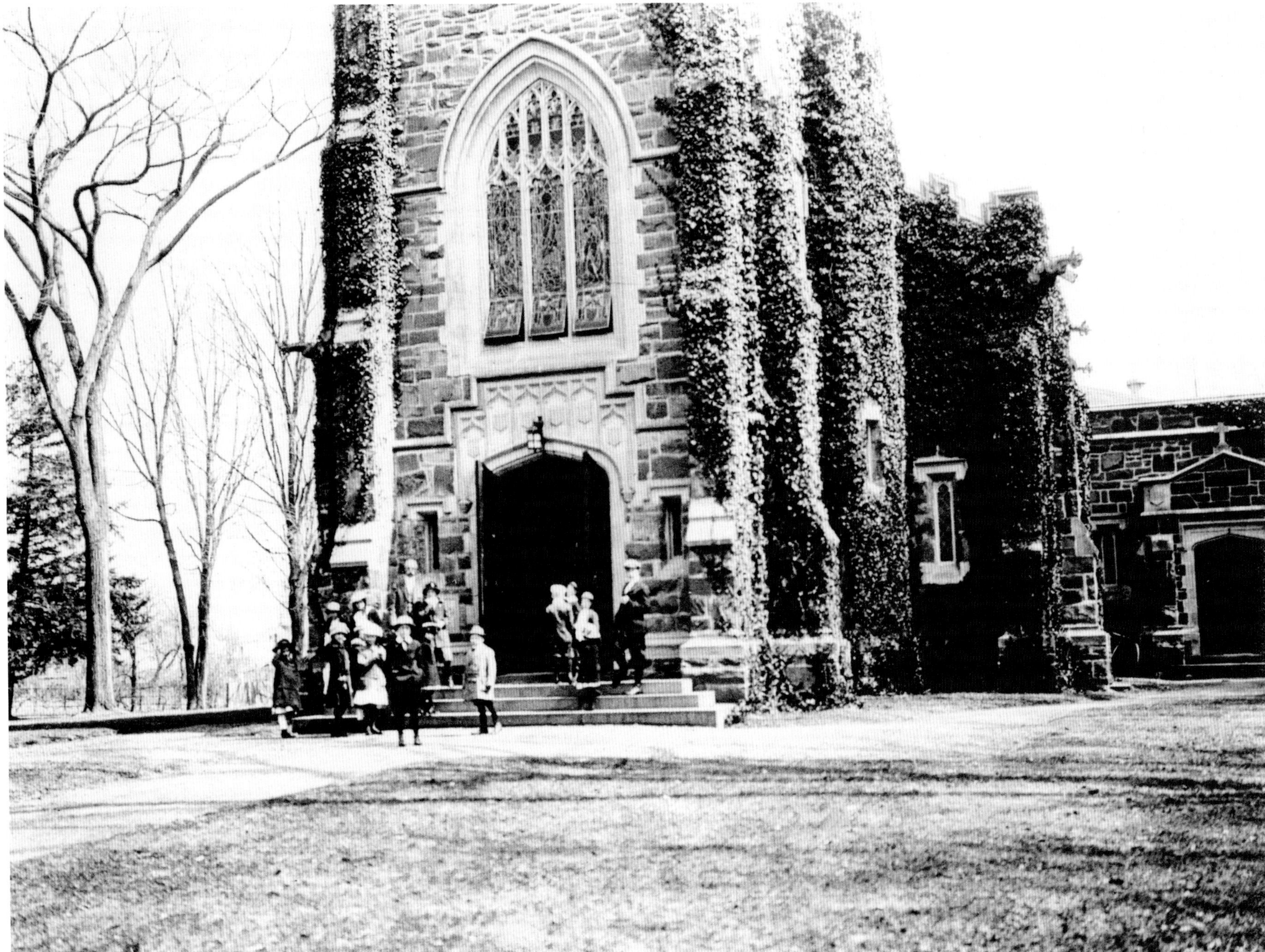

OPPOSITE Children in front of the Church of the Messiah after attending a service in 1917. Built on land donated by Dr. George N. Miller and Robert B. Suckley, the building of the church was financed with real estate proceeds donated by John Jacob Astor IV. Designed in the Gothic Revival style by Hoppin & Koen, the church had its cornerstone laid in 1897 and was consecrated in 1899. Several of the beautiful stained-glass windows, designed by Louis Comfort Tiffany and John La Farge, were installed as memorials. On May 4, 1912, a funeral was held here for John Jacob Astor IV, who had perished on the *Titanic* a month before. On December 27, 1913, a memorial window was installed in his memory and dedicated by his widow, Madeline Force Astor.

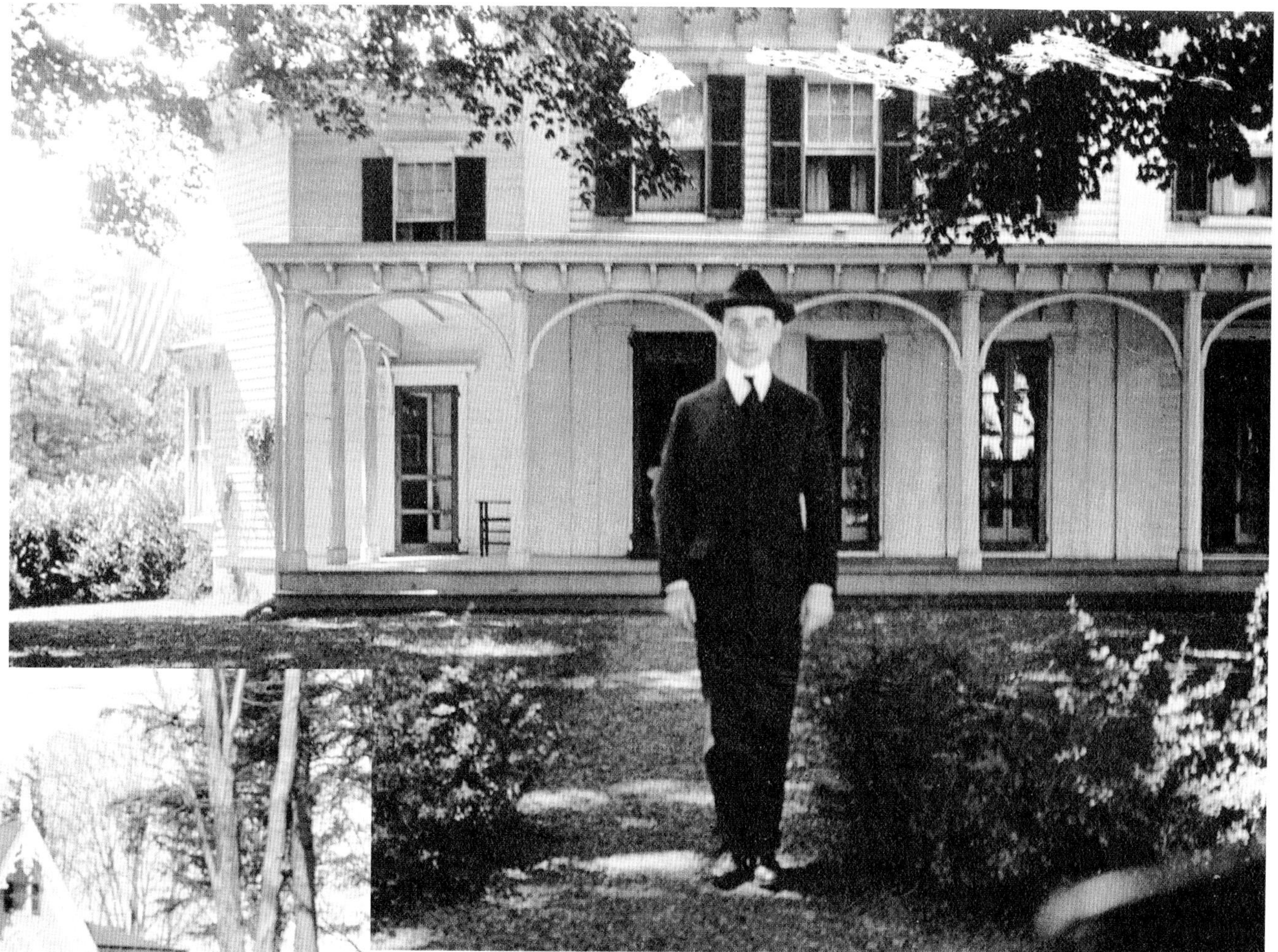

RIGHT Reverend Francis K. Little at the Church of the Messiah rectory on Montgomery Street, 1917. During World War I, he served as an Army chaplain.

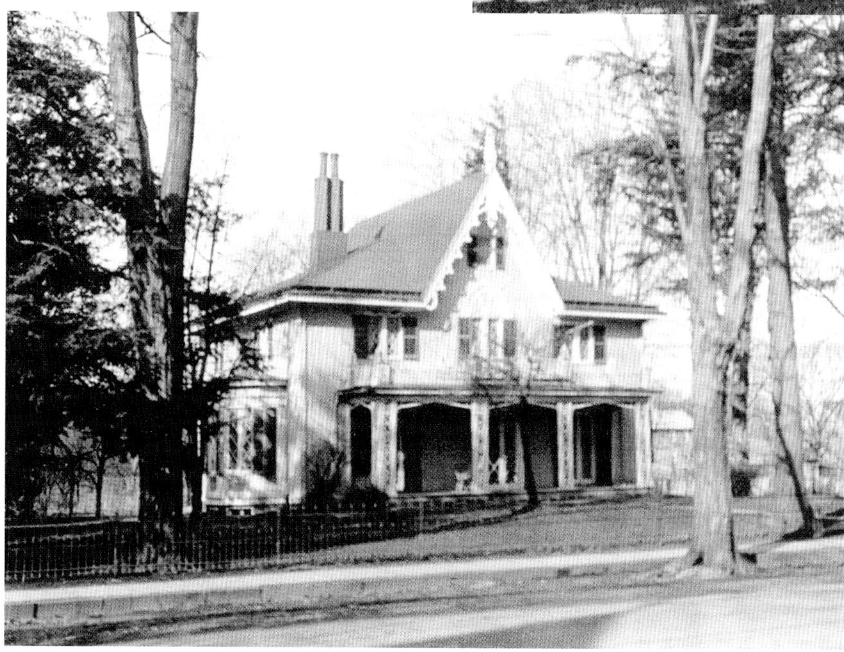

LEFT The Delamater House in 1919. Located across the street from the Church of the Messiah, the Gothic Revival cottage was designed by Alexander Jackson Davis in 1844 for Henry Delamater, founder and president of the First National Bank of Rhinebeck.

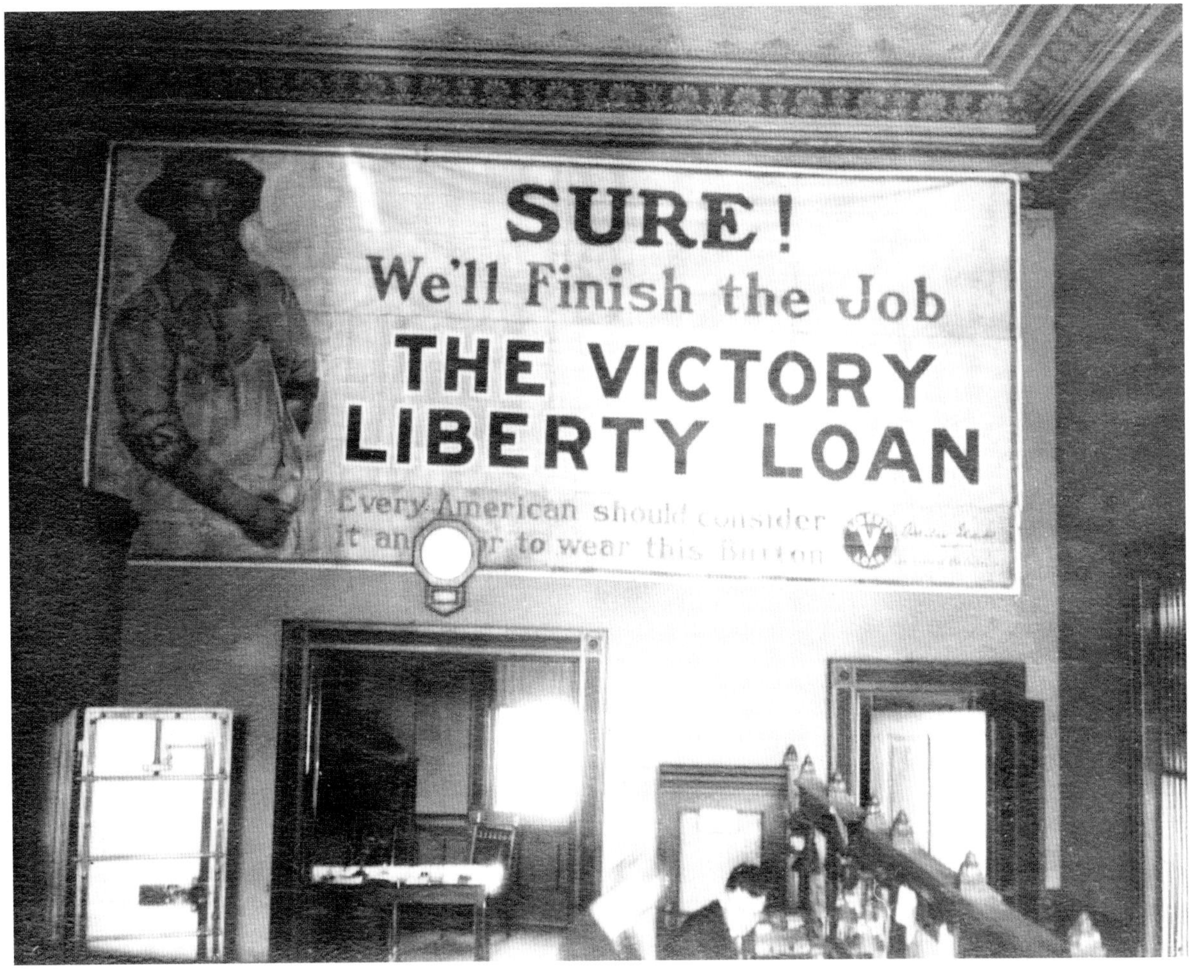

ABOVE The Victory Liberty Loan banner placed inside Town Hall. On April 21, 1919, the final war bond was issued for the relief of World War I. The U.S. Department of the Treasury commissioned the artist Gerrit A. Beneker to design posters and banners using the phrase, "Sure! We'll Finish the Job." When the Victory Liberty Loan first opened, the war had actually been over for five months. However, American soldiers remained overseas and depended on continued support from the United States until it was safe to return home.

RIGHT Arthur Gerald Haen with his plane at Springbrook Park, 1918. He was making exhibition flights over the village of Rhinebeck. He had enlisted with the Army Air Service, which served as the military air service for the United States from 1918 to 1926.

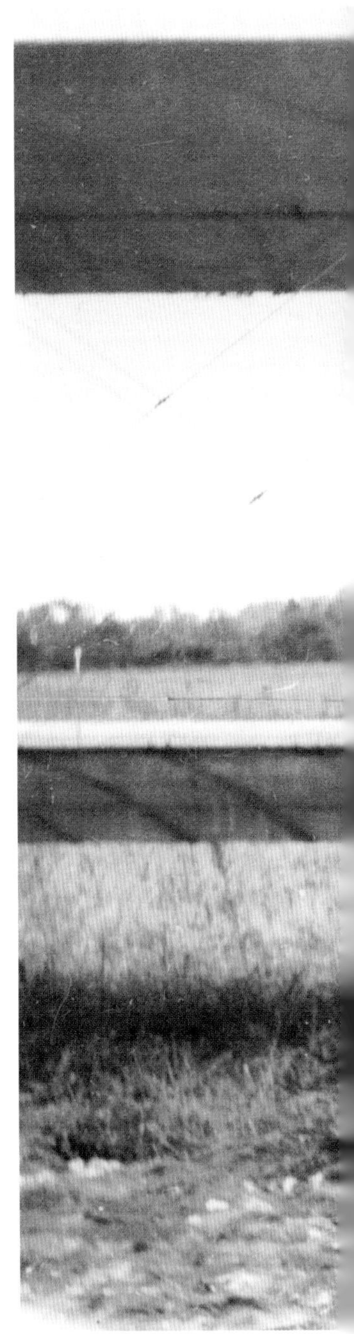

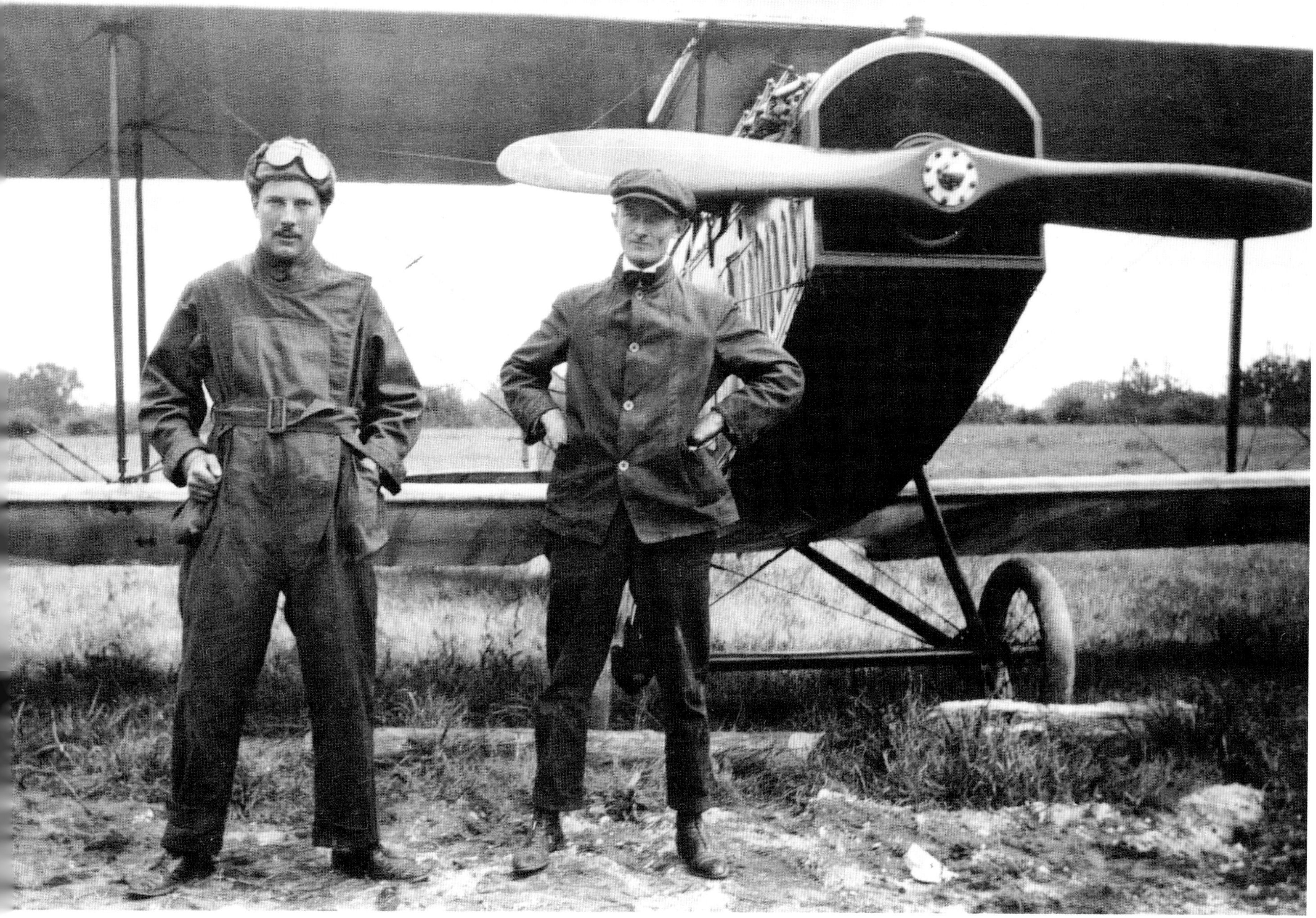

RIGHT A view of Holiday Farm in the winter of 1919. The institution was founded in 1904 in nearby Rhinecliff by Mary Morton, daughter of former New York governor Levi P. Morton. In 1913, Vincent Astor commissioned Harrie T. Lindeberg to design a convalescent home for Holiday Farm as a memorial to his father in the village of Rhinebeck. It opened its doors in 1914, providing care for children too weak to return home after leaving the hospital. It later became the Astor Home for Children and is now Astor Services for Children & Families.

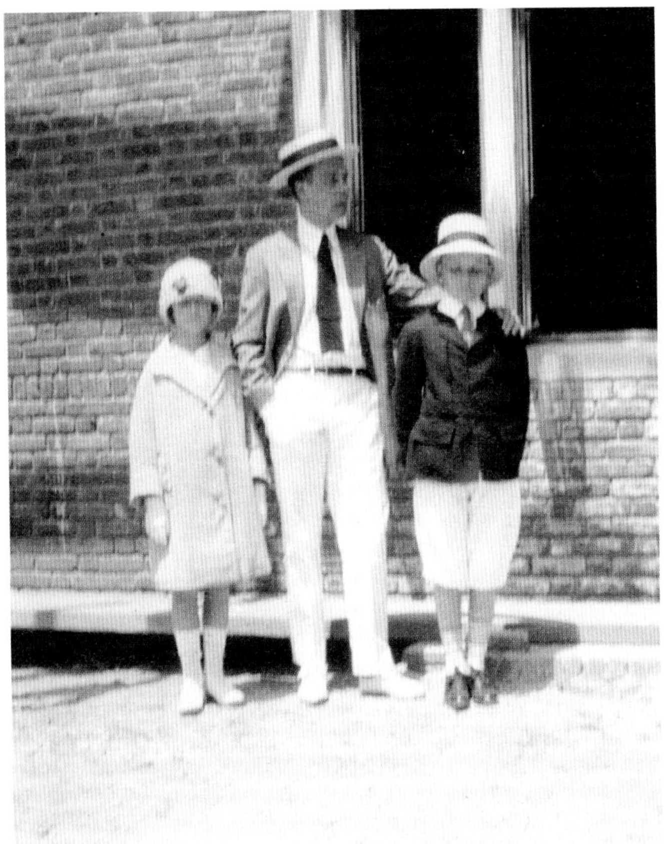

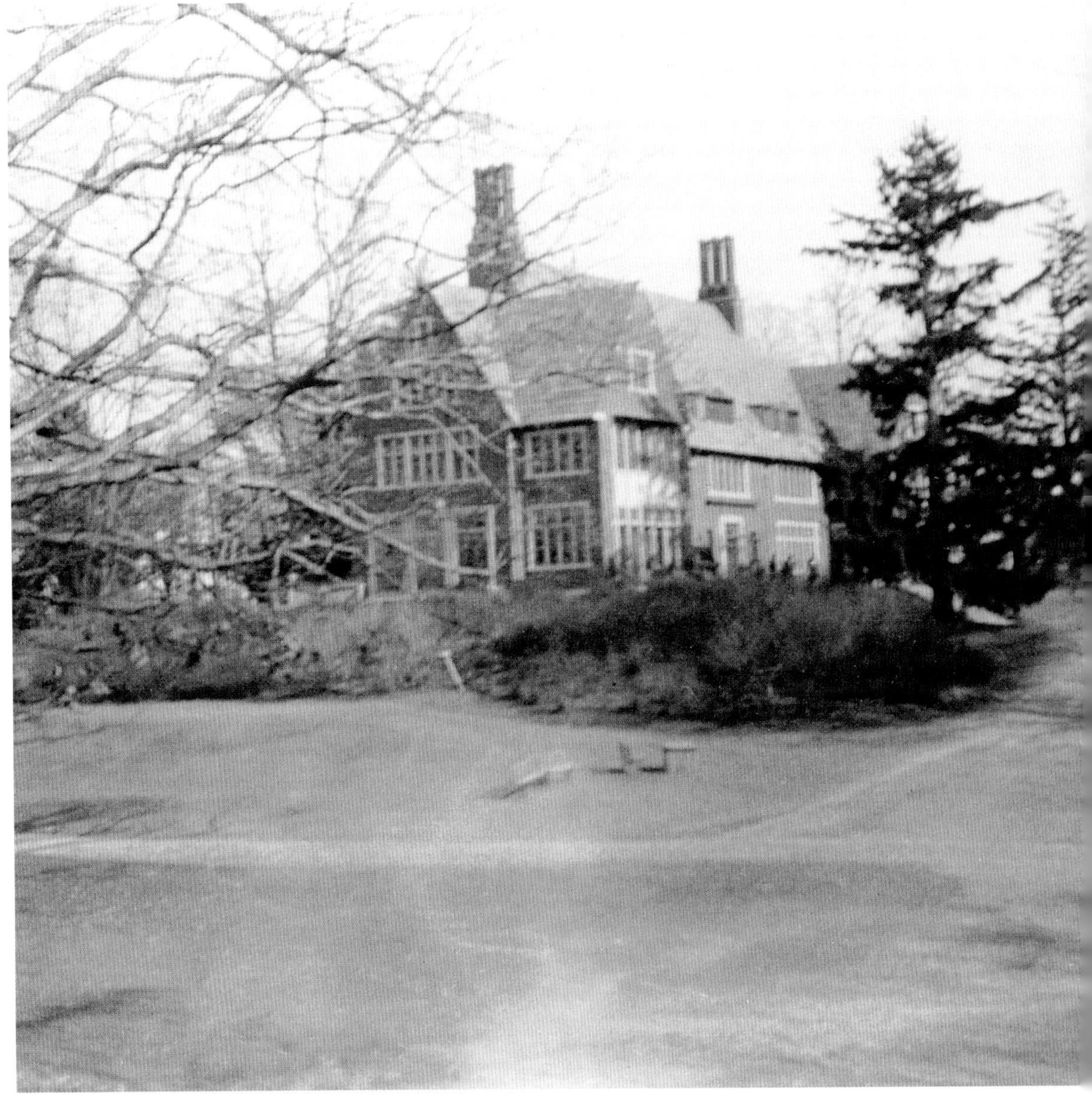

LEFT Margaret and Olin with Lindeberg visiting Holiday Farm during construction, 1914.

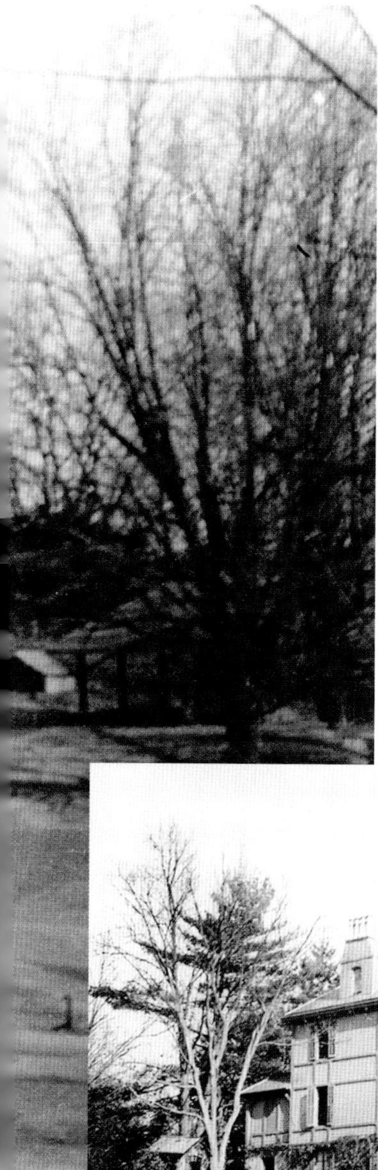

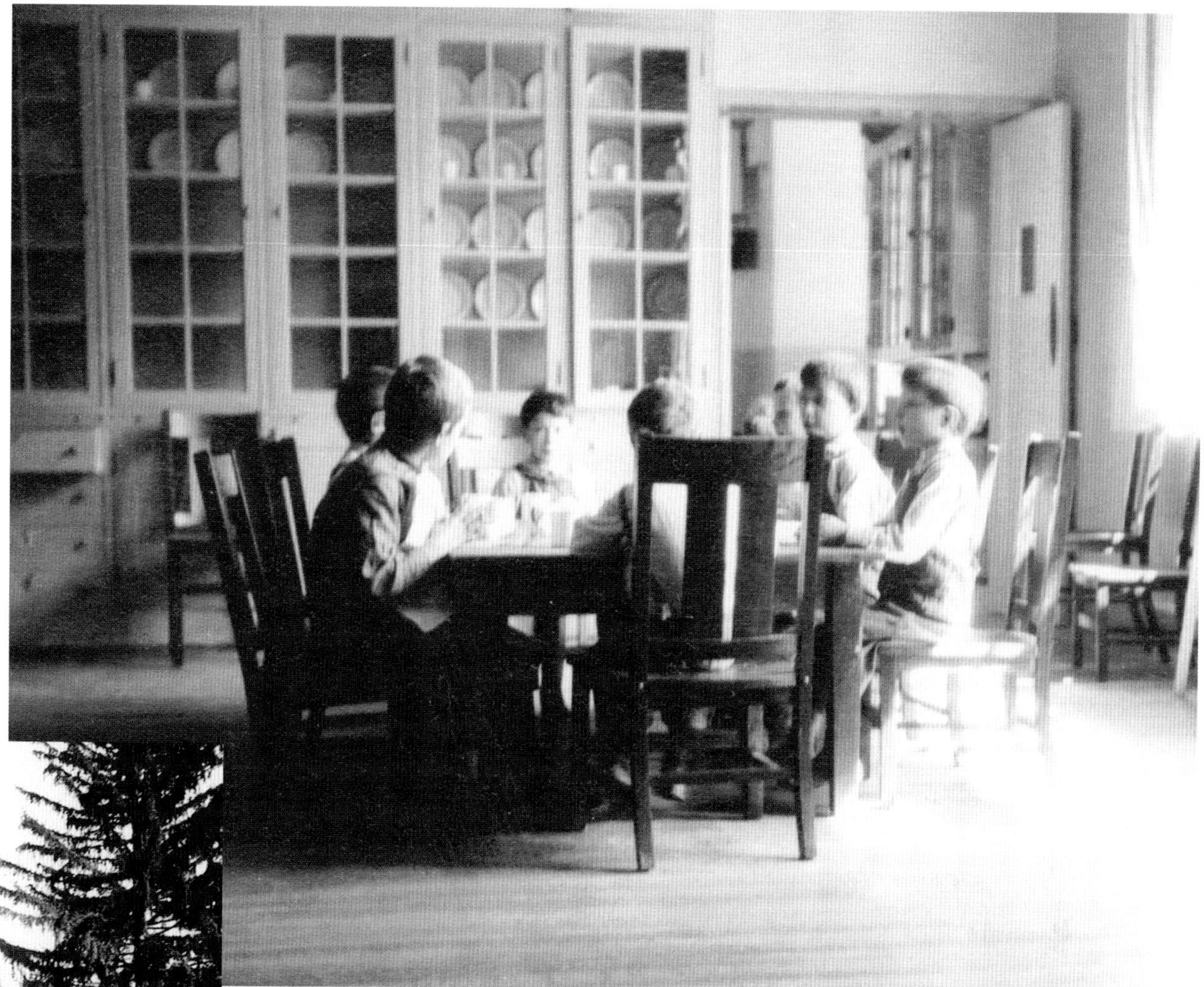

RIGHT The dining room at Holiday Farm, 1914, with its first patients.

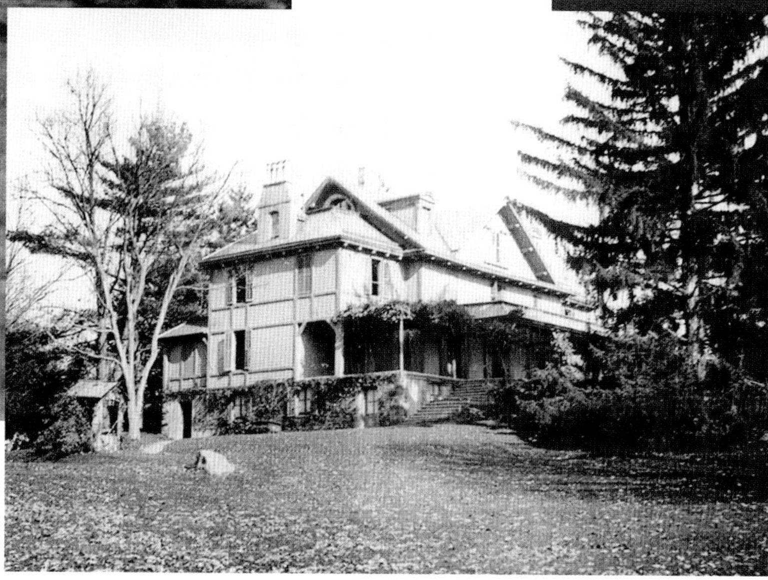

LEFT Bois Doré, the country estate of Robert Palmer Huntington, Helen Huntington Astor's grandfather, in 1903. An illustration of the same view appears in James H. Smith's 1882 book, *History of Dutchess County*. Bois Doré burned in the early 1900s, and Holiday Farm was built on its site.

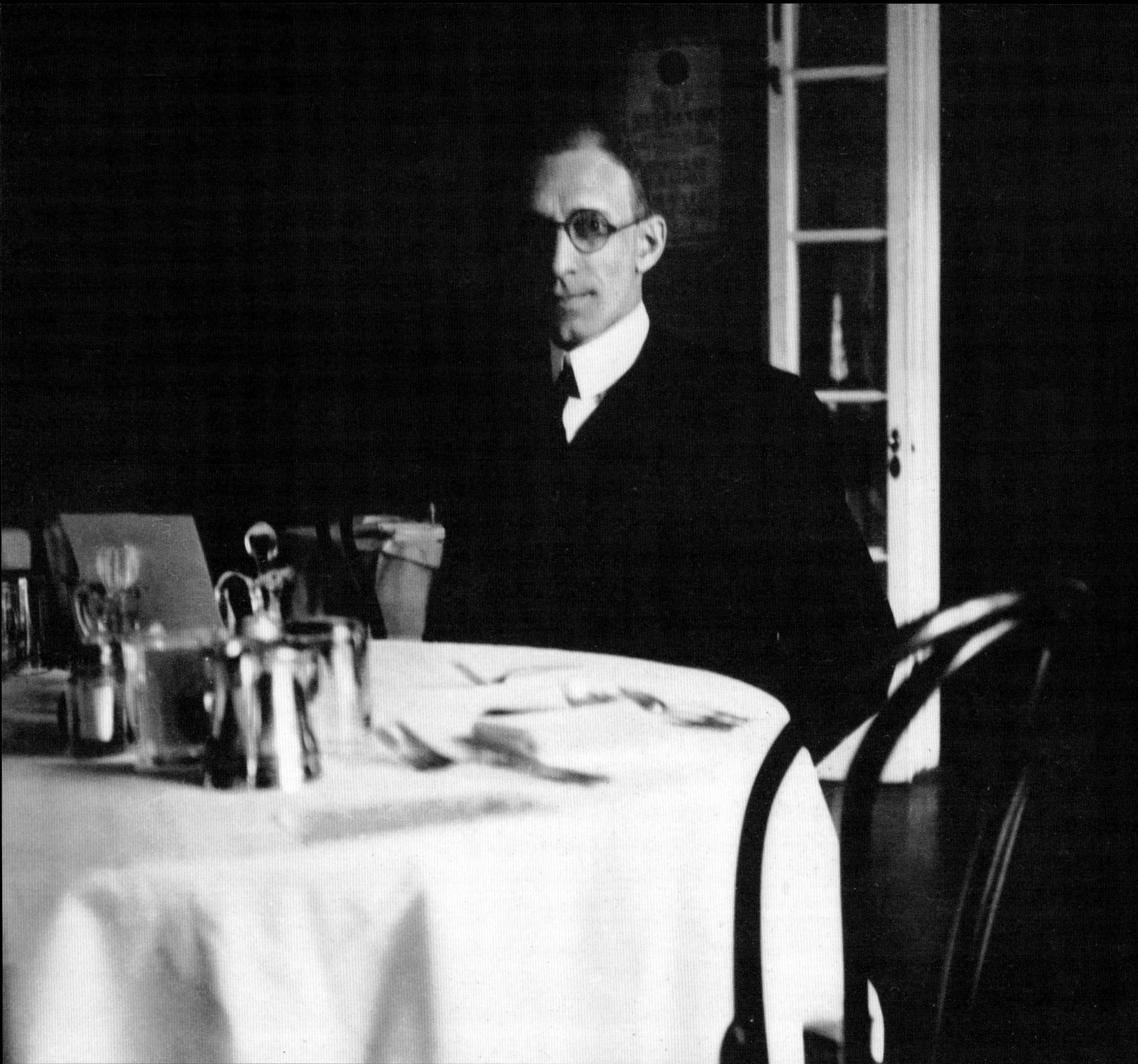

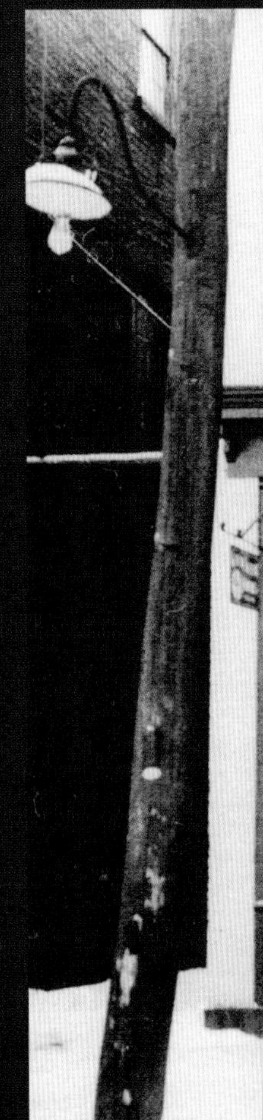

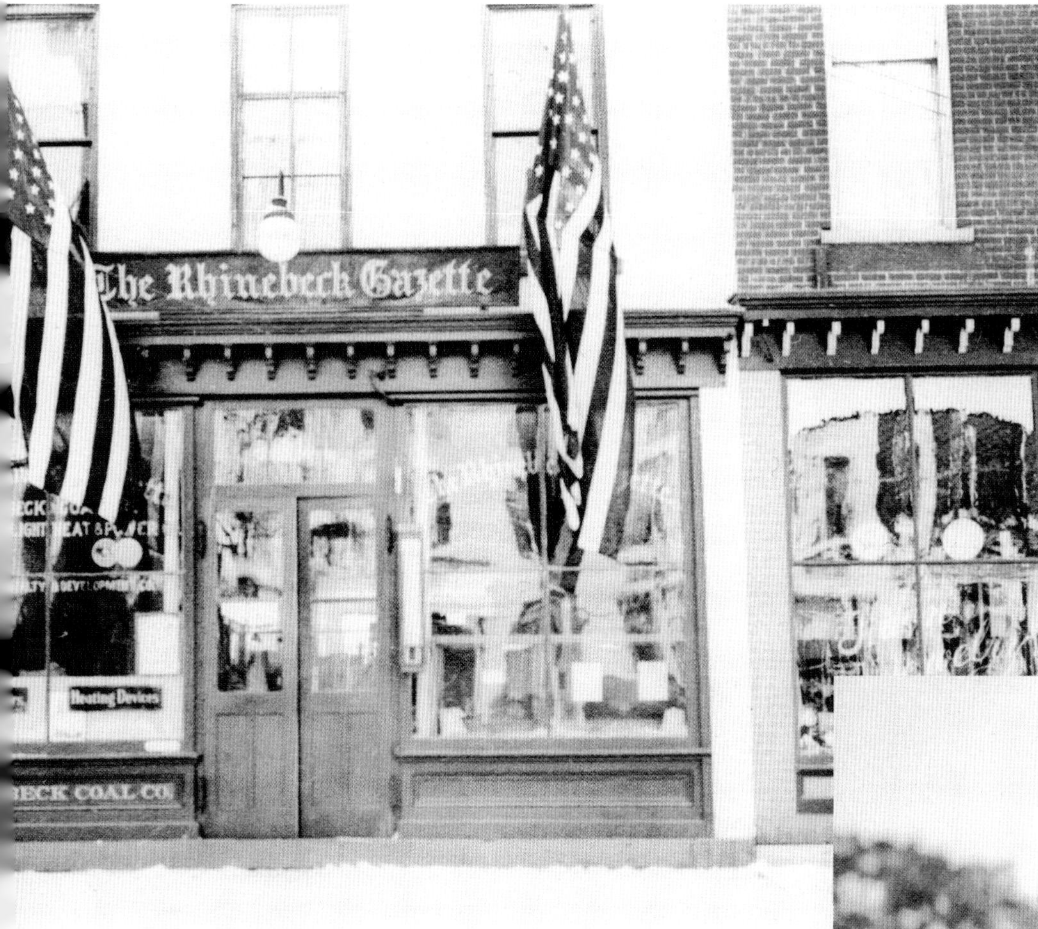

ABOVE The *Rhinebeck Gazette* office on Market Street, 1917. Jacob Hill Strong was owner and editor of the newspaper from 1907 to 1938.

OPPOSITE Strong at the Beekman Arms, 1918. He became a close friend of Tracy's, and together they became active leaders in the Rhinebeck community.

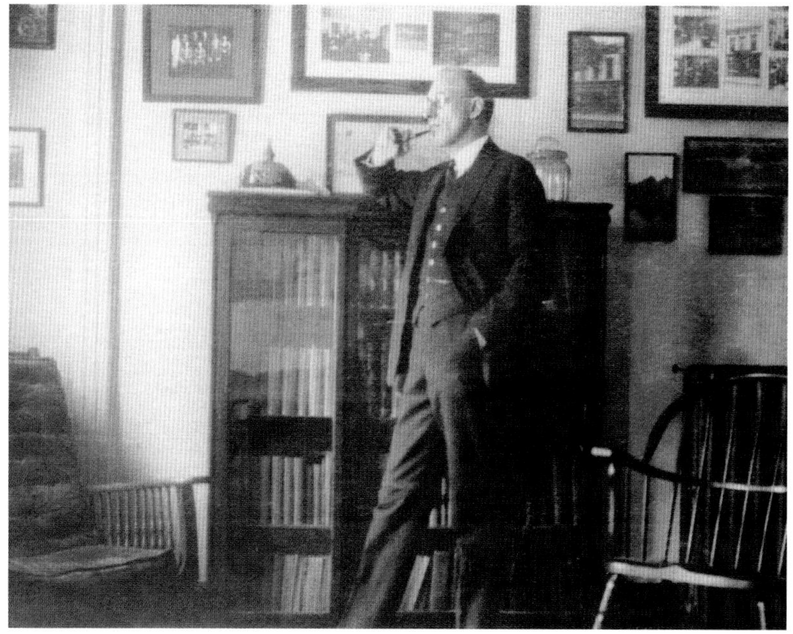

ABOVE Strong in his office at the *Rhinebeck Gazette*, 1925. His son, Jacob "Jakey" Hill Strong, Jr., took over ownership in 1938.

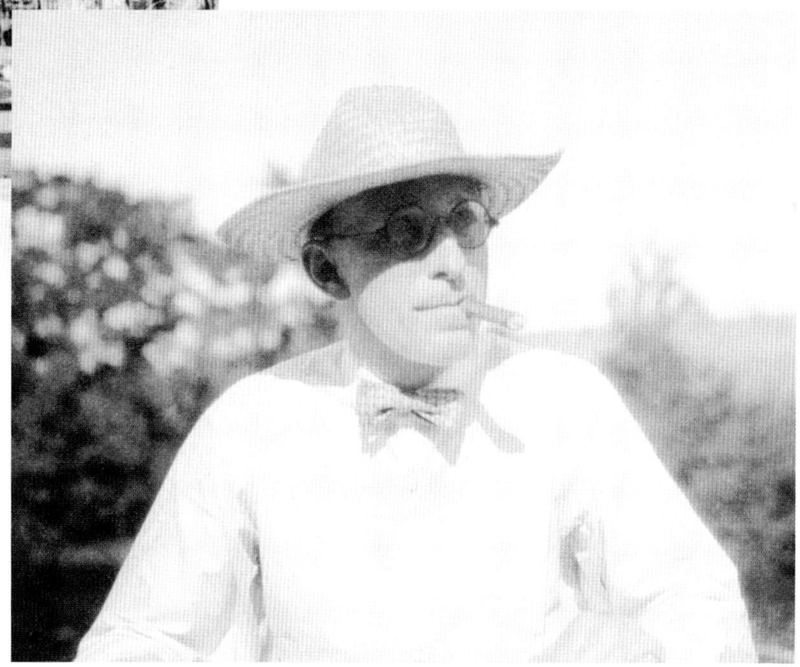

LEFT At an outing on Upton Lake near Clinton Corners, New York, in the summer of 1925.

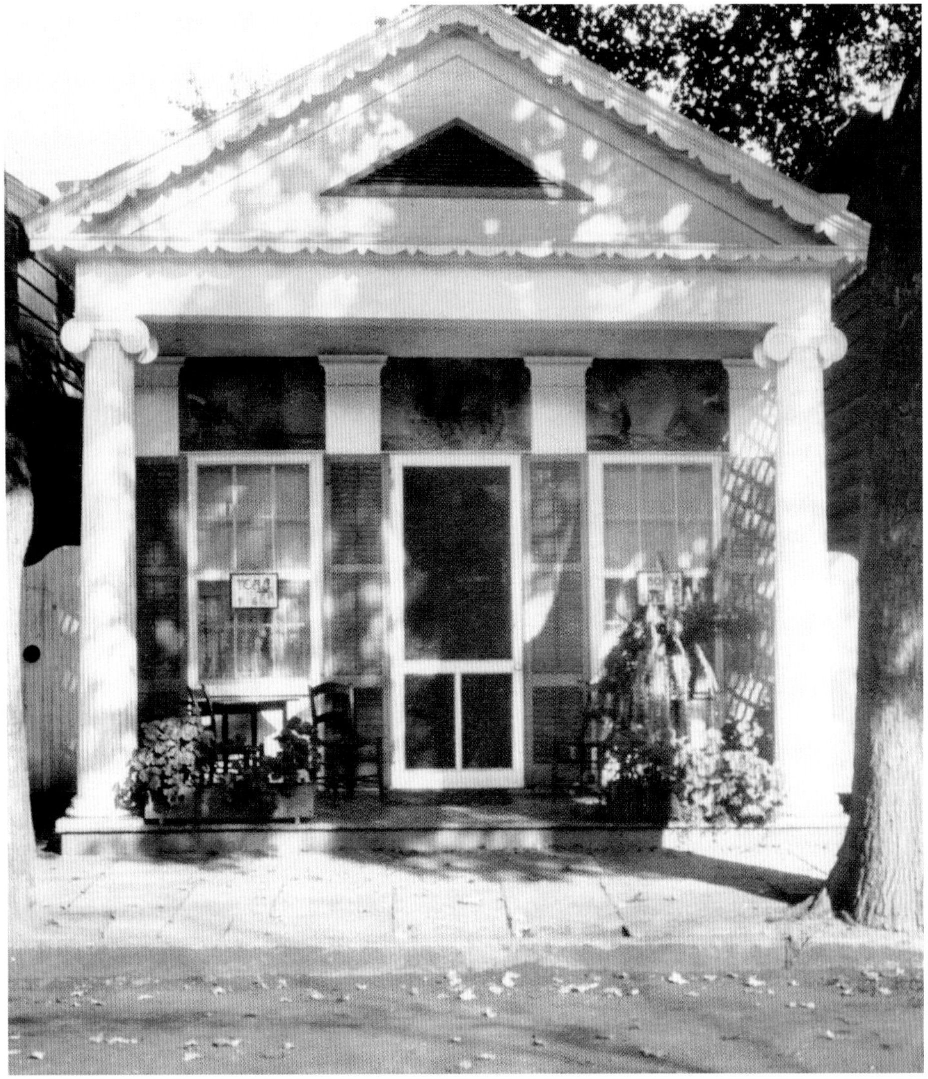

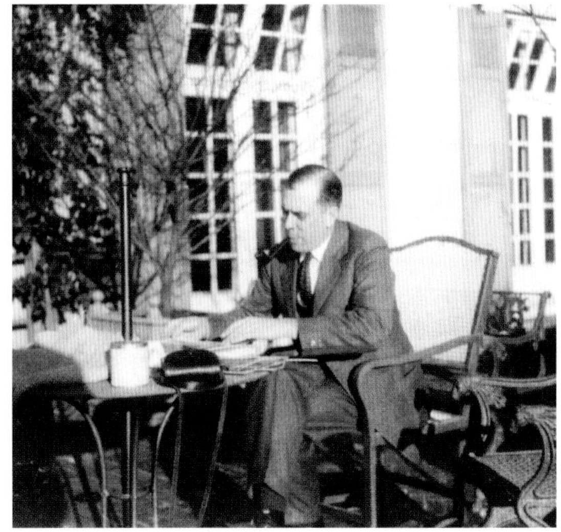

RIGHT Rhinebeck attorney Benson R. Frost on the back terrace at Foxhollow Farm, 1927. A respected businessman who, along with Jacob Hill Strong and Tracy Dows, was instrumental in the progress of the Rhinebeck community.

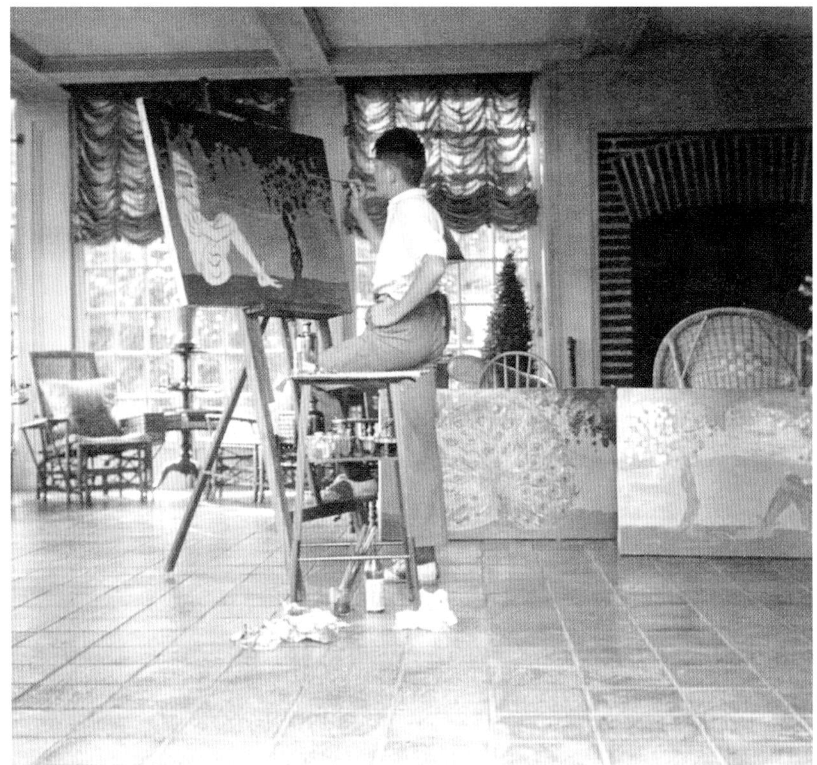

ABOVE AND RIGHT The Exchange for Women's Work Thrift Shop on Montgomery Street, 1919. Alice Dows was involved in the activities of the shop. Olin Dows, seen painting three panels in the loggia at Foxhollow Farm that were installed above the shop's entrance.

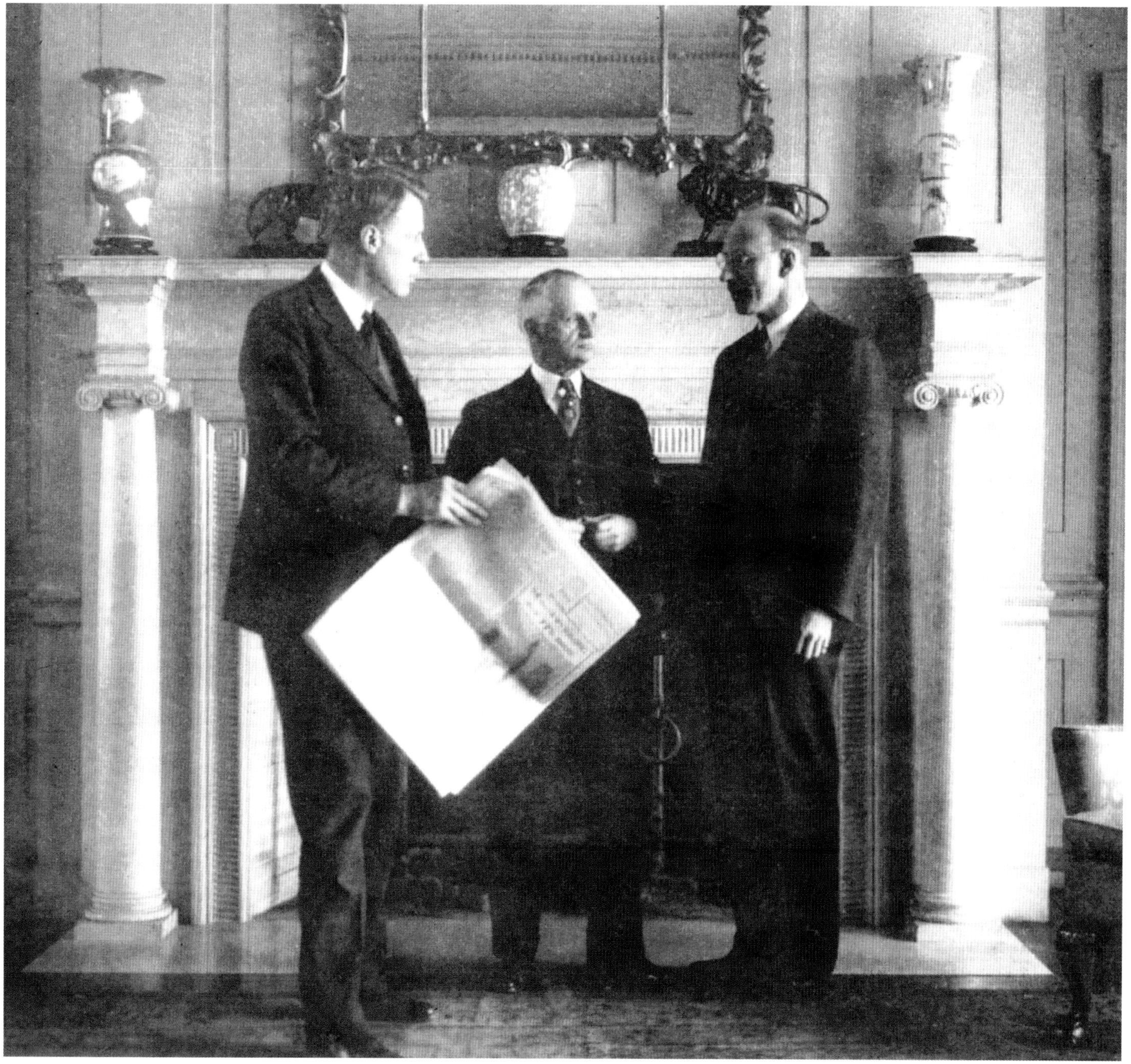

LEFT A meeting of the Foxhollow Development Corporation on January 19, 1927. Attorney Paul G. Gravenhorst (holding newspaper), Ferdinand C. Townsend, and Jacob Hill Strong, were members of the newly formed organization, as well as Tracy Dows. Townsend was a New York City accountant who, in his early years, represented the estate of Edward Mott Robinson, the father of the famous miser Hetty Green (who at one point became America's richest woman), which was in litigation for many years. His firm, Townsend & Dix, audited many large corporations throughout the United States. In 1925, Tracy and Alice transferred Foxhollow Farm over to the corporation to manage the estate.

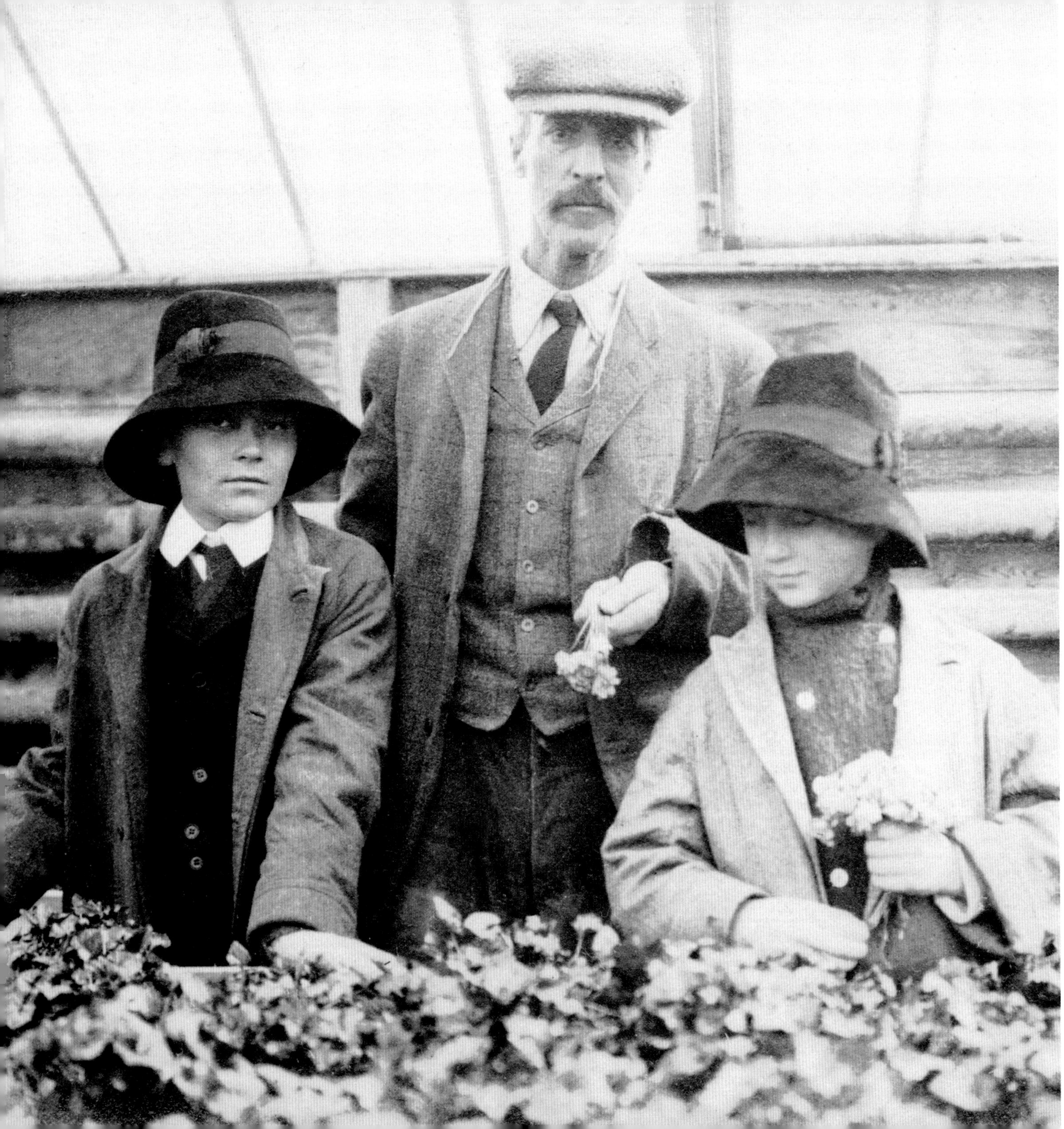

LEFT Olin and Margaret with Herman A. Asher picking violets in 1914. Asher lived on a farm adjacent to Foxhollow Farm and worked as the head gardener at The Grove, the estate of Dr. George Miller, in Rhinebeck. Asher won several awards for his violets in the late 1890s. By that time, Rhinebeck had became the violet capital of the world. Numerous greenhouses were constructed around the village, and in 1908 the violet trade brought in an annual income of over a million dollars. It began to fade in the 1920s, and by the 1960s anemones had replaced violets in popularity. Local growers switched from the purple flowers once sported on the lapel of Eleanor Roosevelt to the multicolored anemones popularized as the favorite flower of Jacqueline Kennedy.

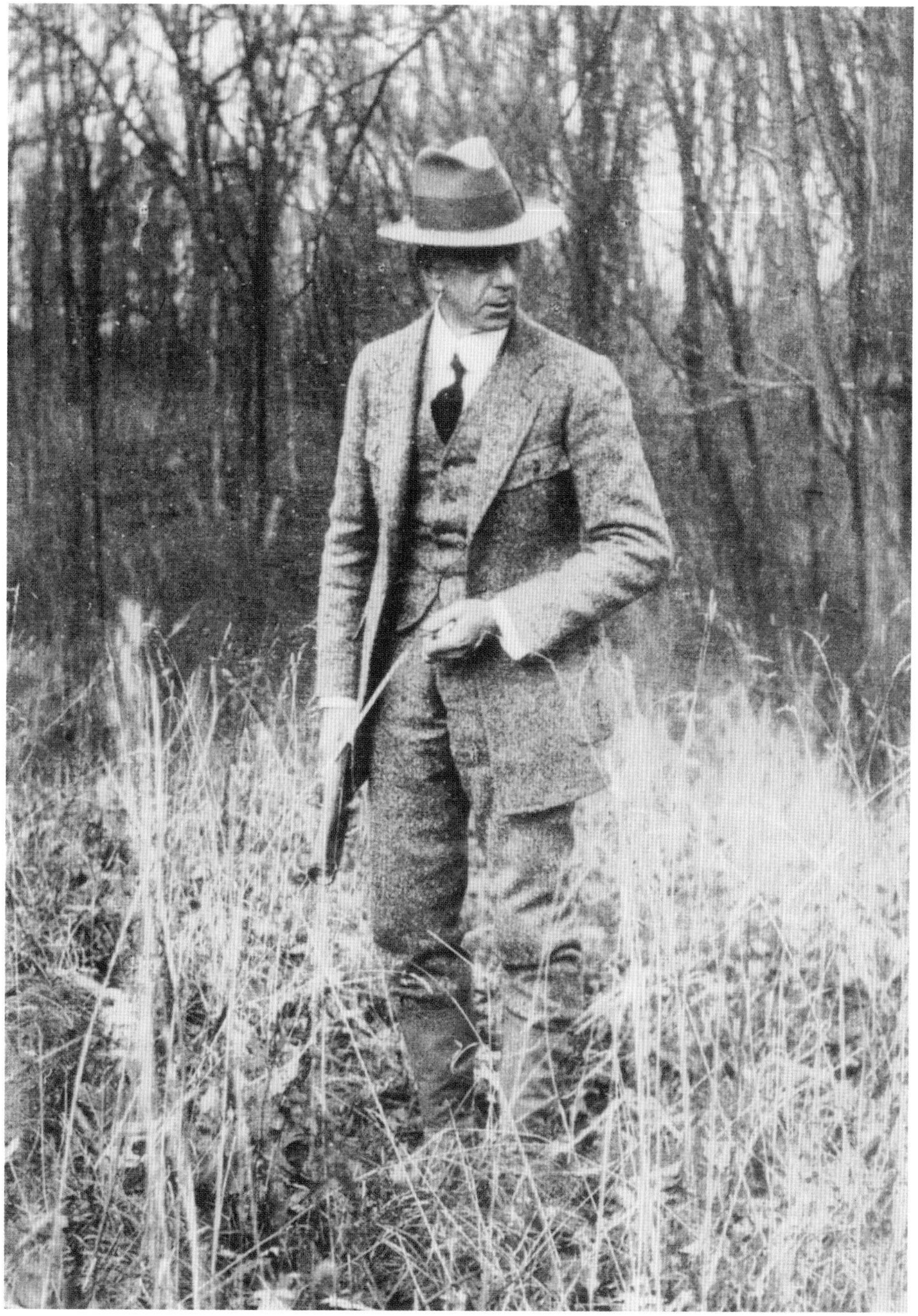

LEFT Frank L. Teal surveying the property line at Glenburn, 1927. Teal had worked alongside the Olmsted Brothers as they mapped the Foxhollow property for Tracy Dows in 1906. A civil engineer and popular surveyor who created many maps for the Rhinebeck area, Teal was a talented researcher who studied property ownership history. Something of a hermit in his social life, he lived his entire life in small house that did not have electricity or running water.

BELOW Jacob Hill Strong, president of the Rhinebeck Cemetery Association in 1918, pointing to a monument at his ancestral family plot where members of the Fultons, Van Ettens, Hills, and Strongs are buried. The cemetery was deeded by Catherine Livingston Garrettson in 1835.

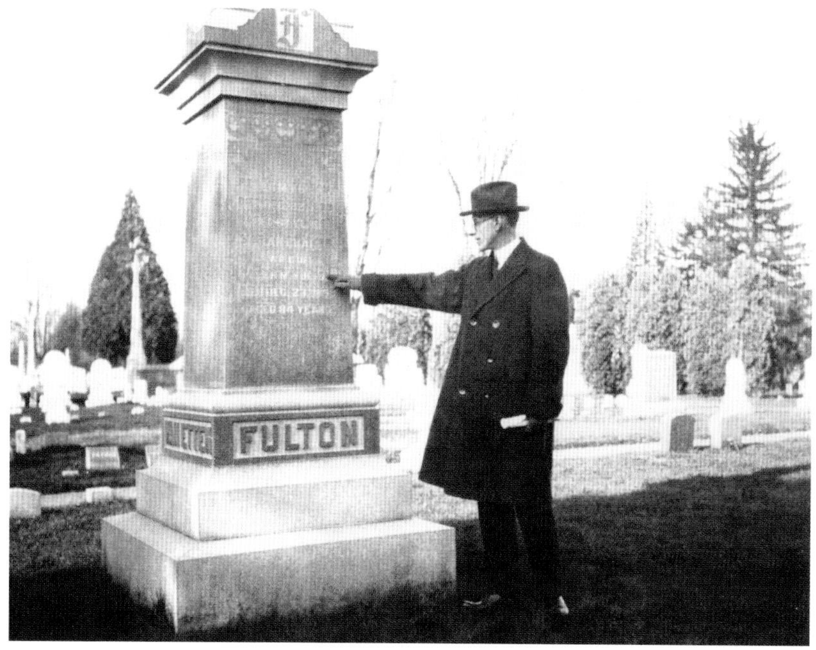

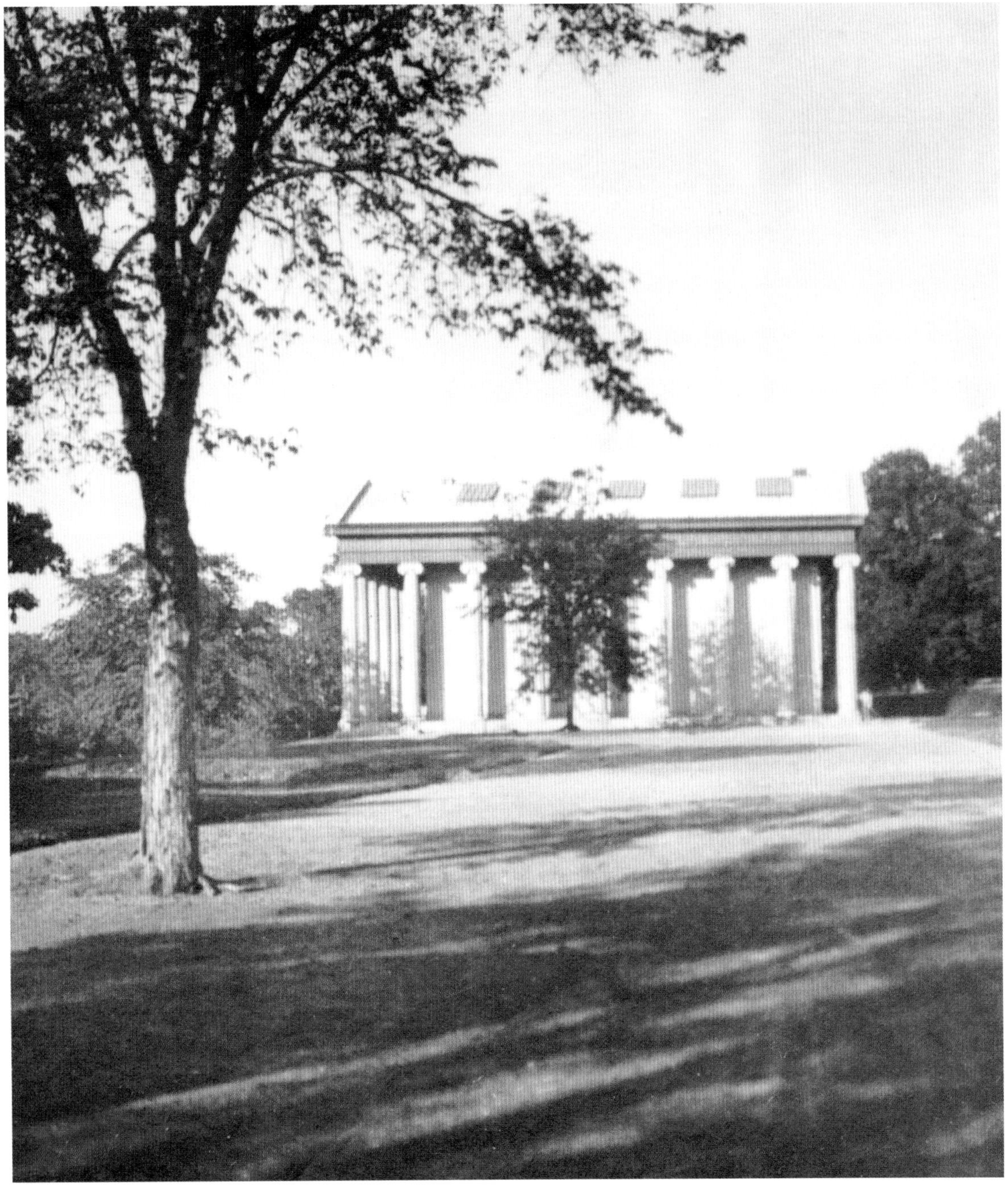

LEFT The Hoffman Memorial Library at Bard College, 1920. Built in 1893 when the campus was still St. Stephens College, the library is a classically designed structure based on an Ionic temple with pediments facing east and west.

RIGHT A local Red Cross truck in front of the Starr Institute, 1919. In 1862, Mrs. William Starr Miller had the building built as a memorial to her late husband, a New York congressman. She deeded the building, its grounds, and furnishings to the Board of Trustees of the Starr Institute. It served as Rhinebeck's library for over a hundred years, as well as a community center. During World War I, the Red Cross met there to make bandages and gather care packages for the men in service.

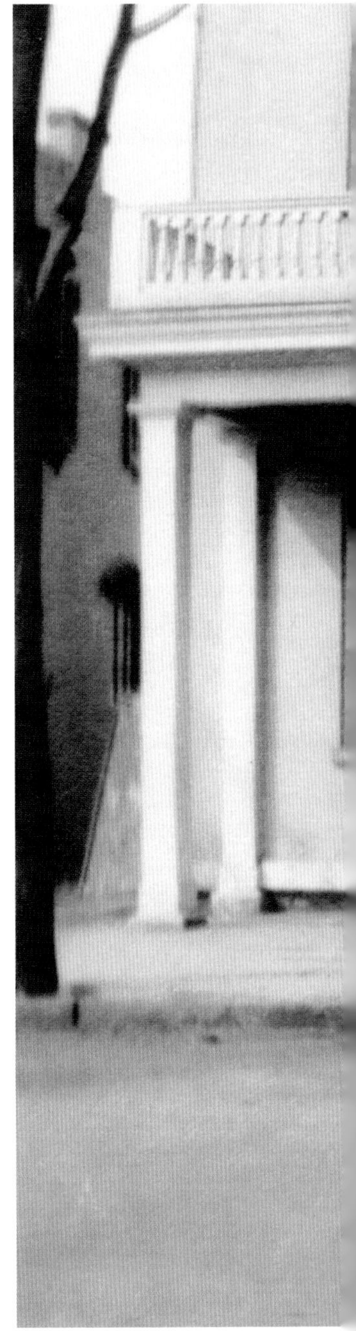

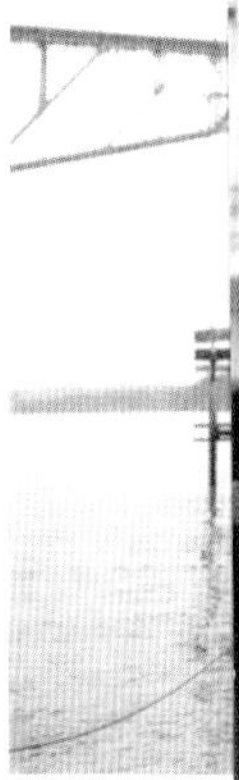

ABOVE AND B
joined the *N*
The *Norwich*
steamship at
Bridge, comp
background.
pedestrian w
elevated foot

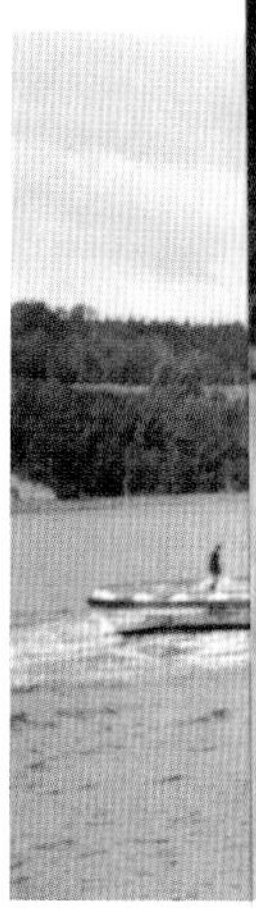

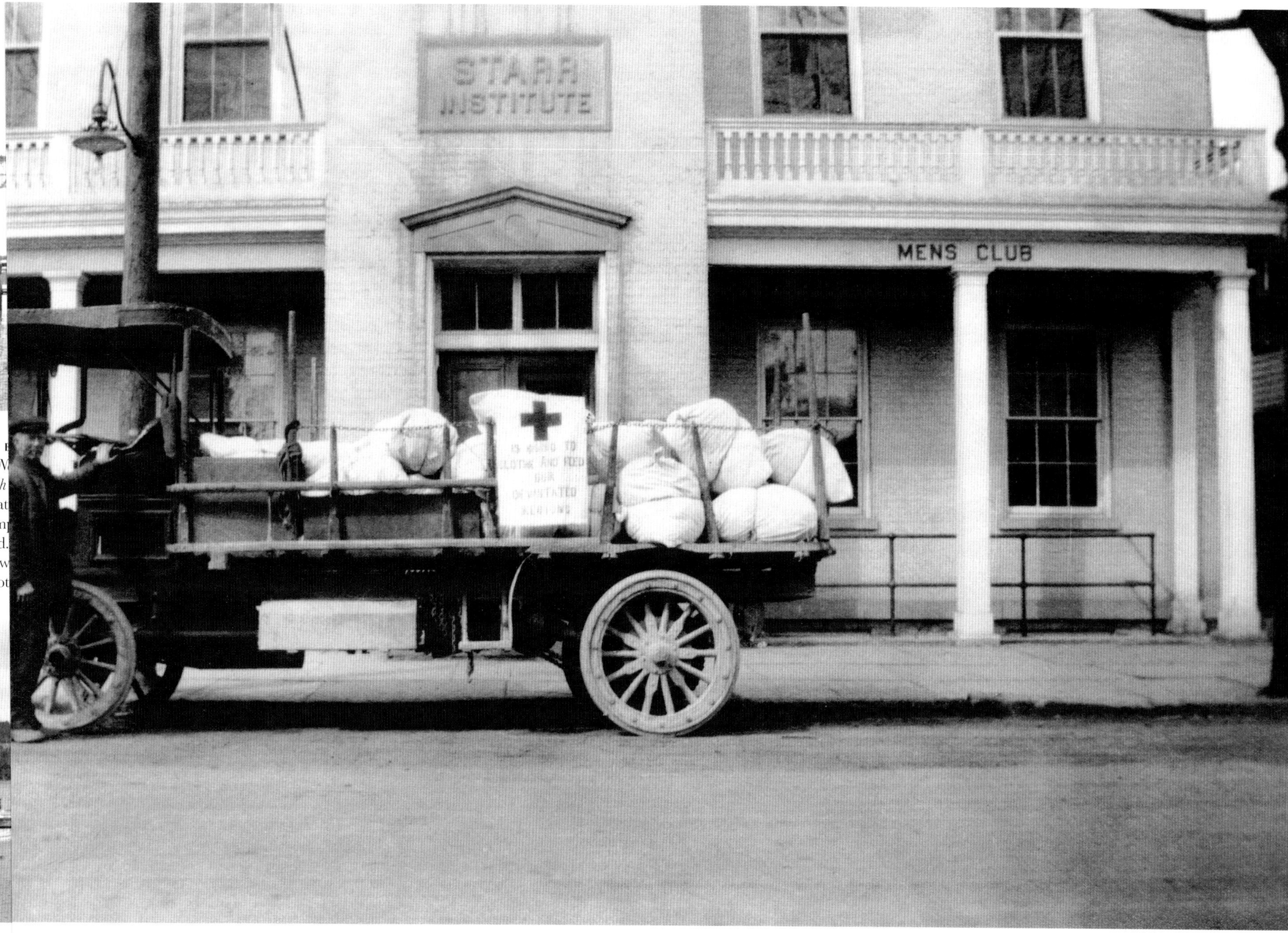

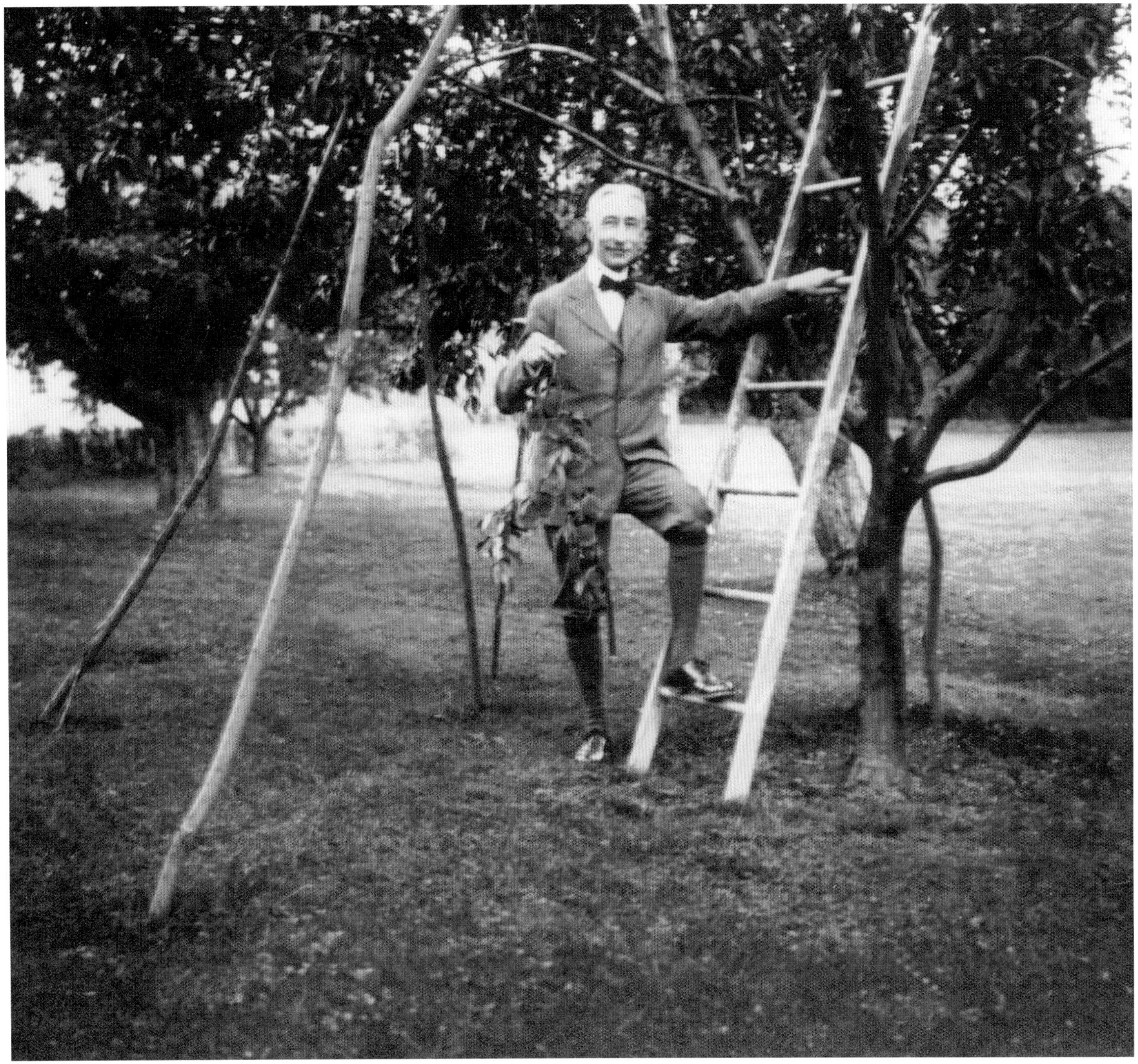

LEFT Peter H. Troy pruning trees at Birchwood, his country house in Barrytown, New York, 1921. Troy lived in Poughkeepsie, where he owned an investment securities company. He was also the founder and president of the Red Hook Telephone Company. Troy and Tracy Dows were good friends and were involved in local business organizations together. Troy was the first person Tracy contacted when the stock market crashed in October 1929.

OPPOSITE The dedication of the Rhinebeck Cemetery Gates on July 5, 1926. The ceremony was held by the Chancellor Livingston chapter of the Daughters of the American Revolution, and children dressed in period costumes. The design of the gates by Delano & Aldrich included bronze swords and the engraved names of local soldiers from past wars.

BELOW Alice holding Olin's hand while mingling with other visitors aboard the *Clermont*.

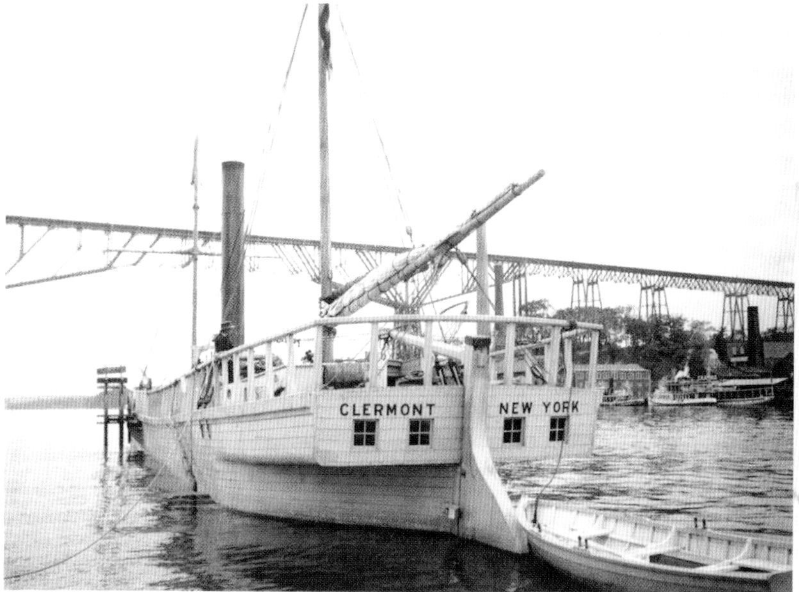

ABOVE AND BELOW A replica of the *Clermont* joined the *Norwich* as part of the festivities. The *Norwich* was the world's oldest operating steamship at the time. The Poughkeepsie Bridge, completed in 1888, is seen in the background. In 2009, it was converted to a pedestrian walkway, making it the longest elevated footbridge in the world.

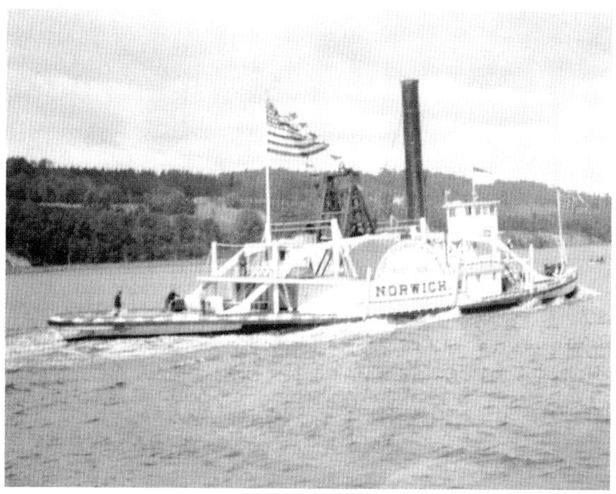

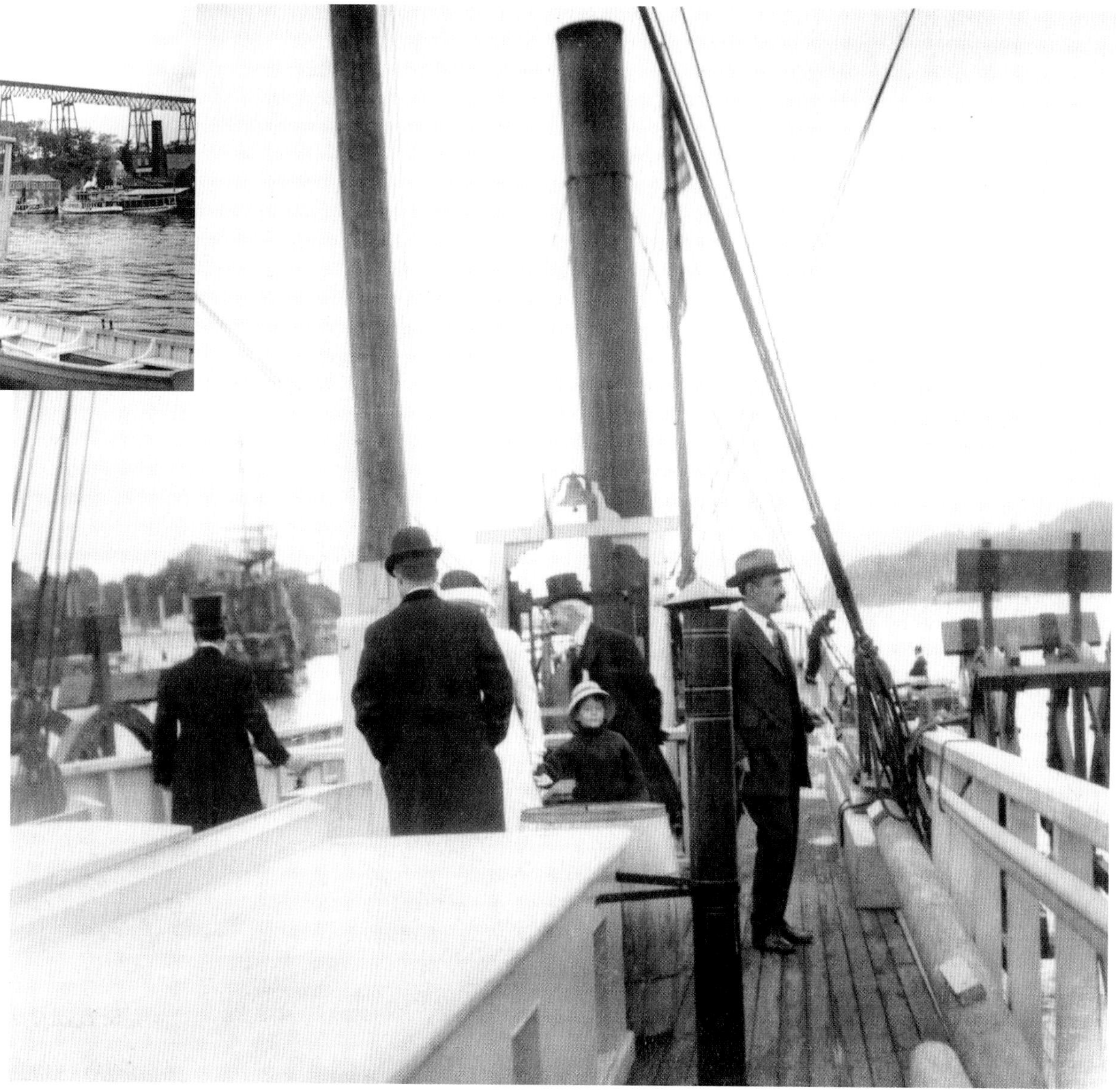

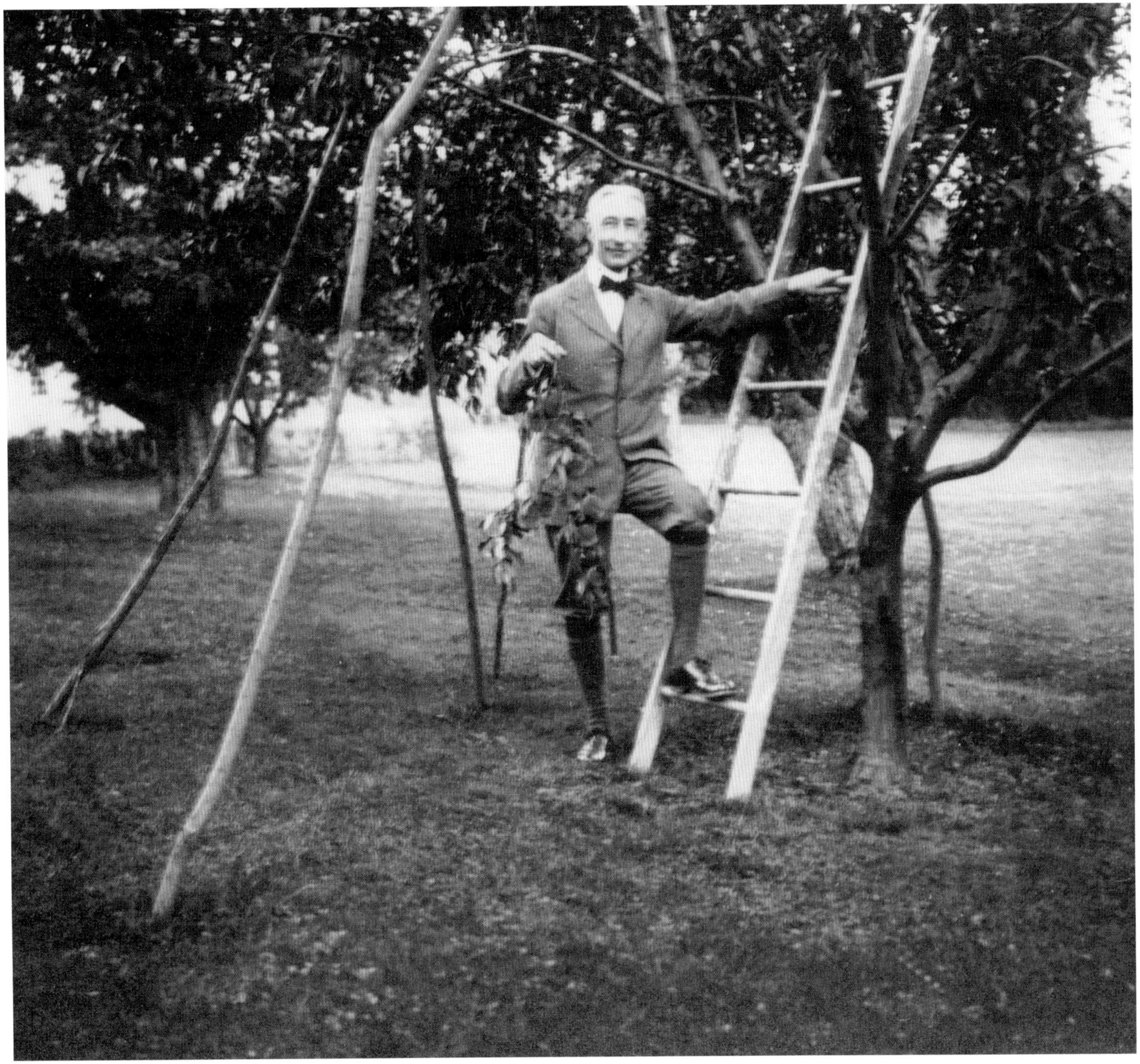

LEFT Peter H. Troy pruning trees at Birchwood, his country house in Barrytown, New York, 1921. Troy lived in Poughkeepsie, where he owned an investment securities company. He was also the founder and president of the Red Hook Telephone Company. Troy and Tracy Dows were good friends and were involved in local business organizations together. Troy was the first person Tracy contacted when the stock market crashed in October 1929.

OPPOSITE The dedication of the Rhinebeck Cemetery Gates on July 5, 1926. The ceremony was held by the Chancellor Livingston chapter of the Daughters of the American Revolution, and children dressed in period costumes. The design of the gates by Delano & Aldrich included bronze swords and the engraved names of local soldiers from past wars.

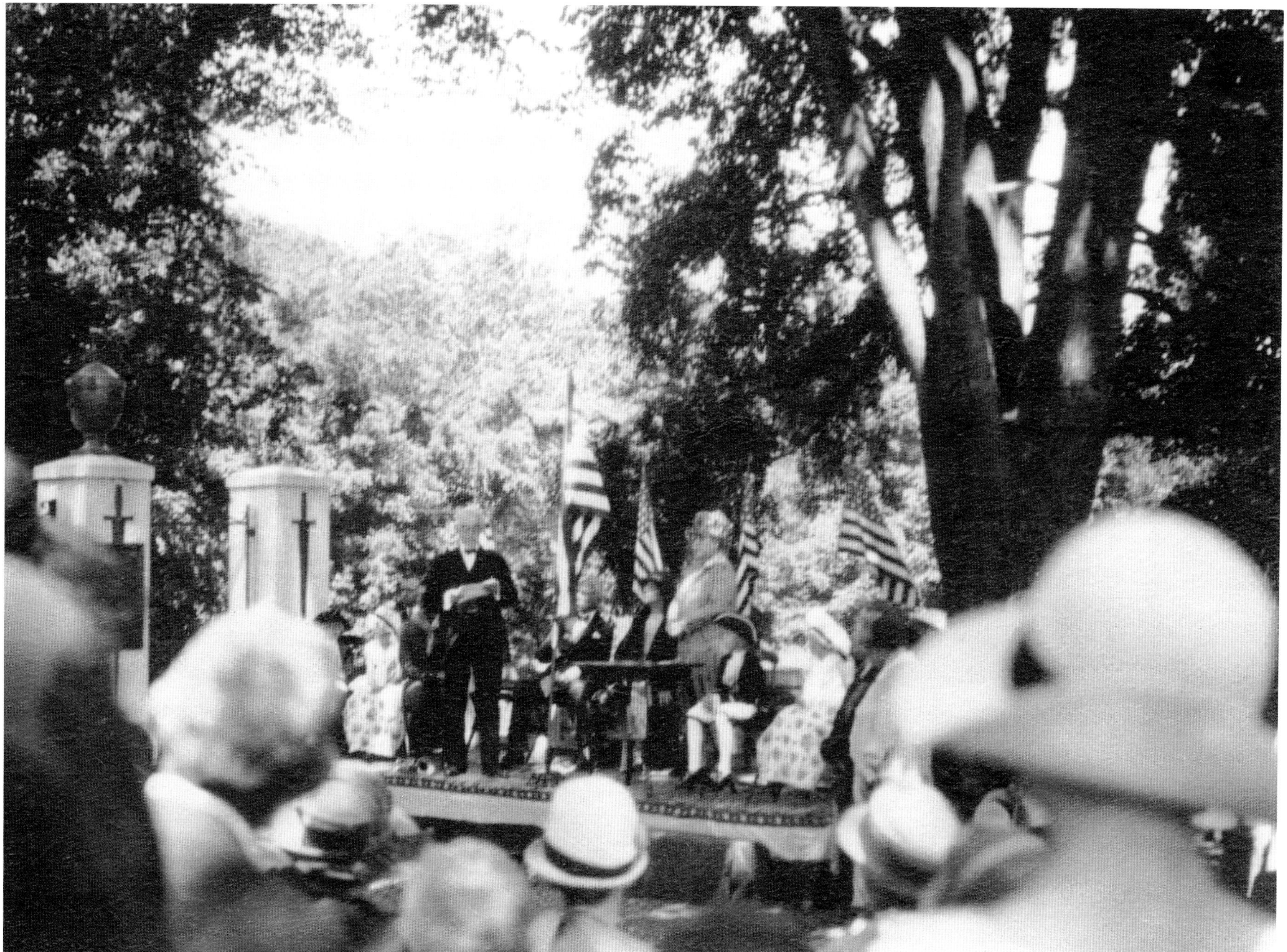

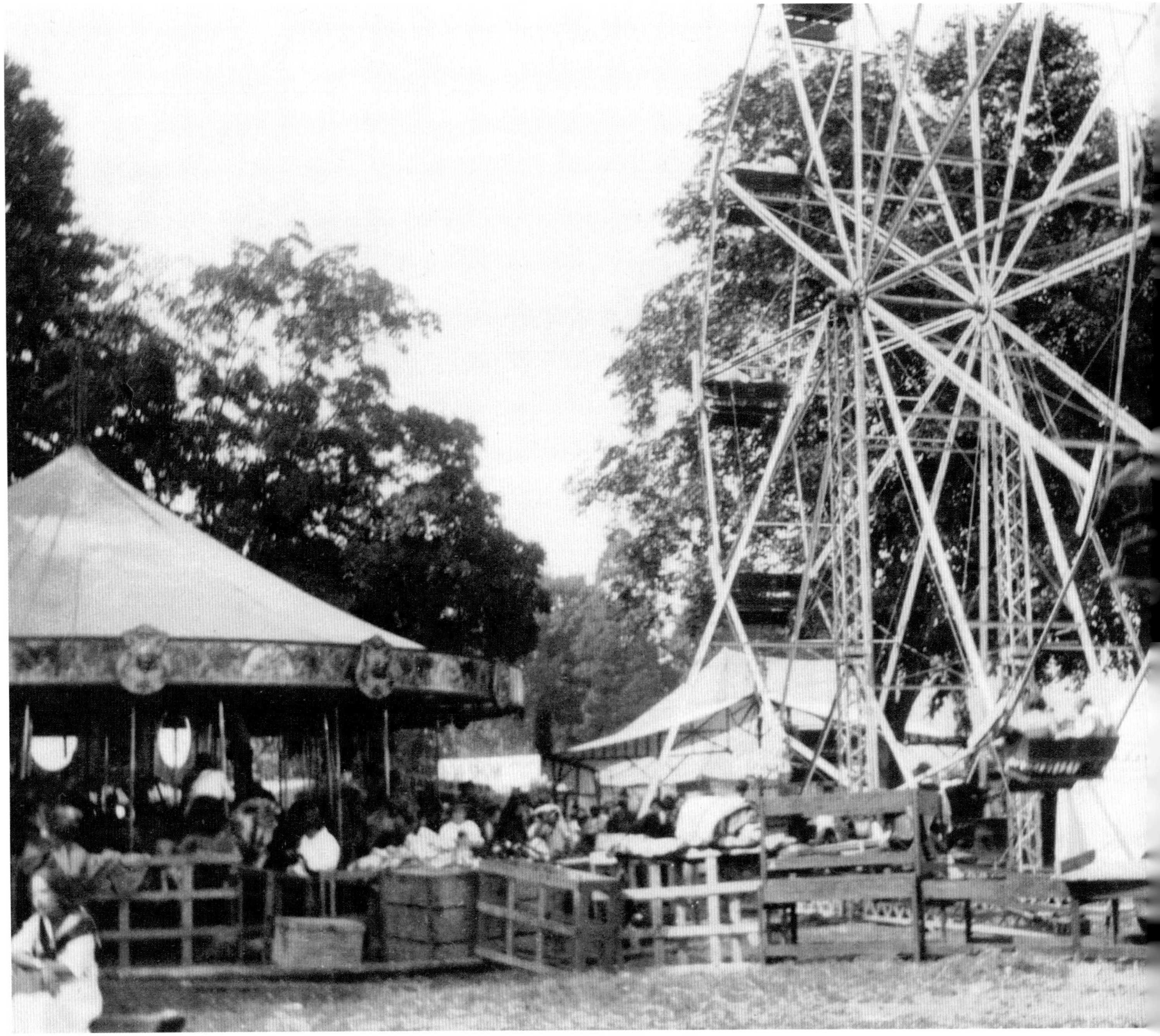

RIGHT A scene from the 1921 Dutchess County Fair in Rhinebeck. The first official fair was held in Washington Hollow by the Dutchess County Agricultural Society in 1842, dedicated to exhibiting livestock and crops produced by local farmers. As its popularity grew, the event moved to Poughkeepsie. World War I brought considerable challenges, and the future of the fair was uncertain. In 1919, with the help of Tracy Dows, it was relocated to Springwood Park in Rhinebeck, where it has continued ever since. In 1950, the Dutchess County Agricultural Society, Inc., purchased Springwood Park and renamed it the Dutchess County Fairgrounds.

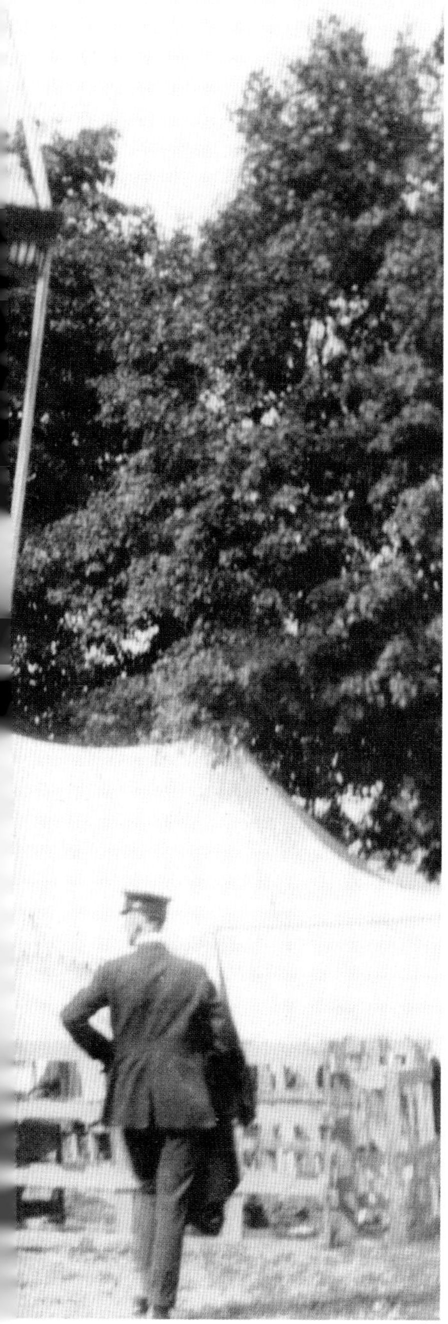

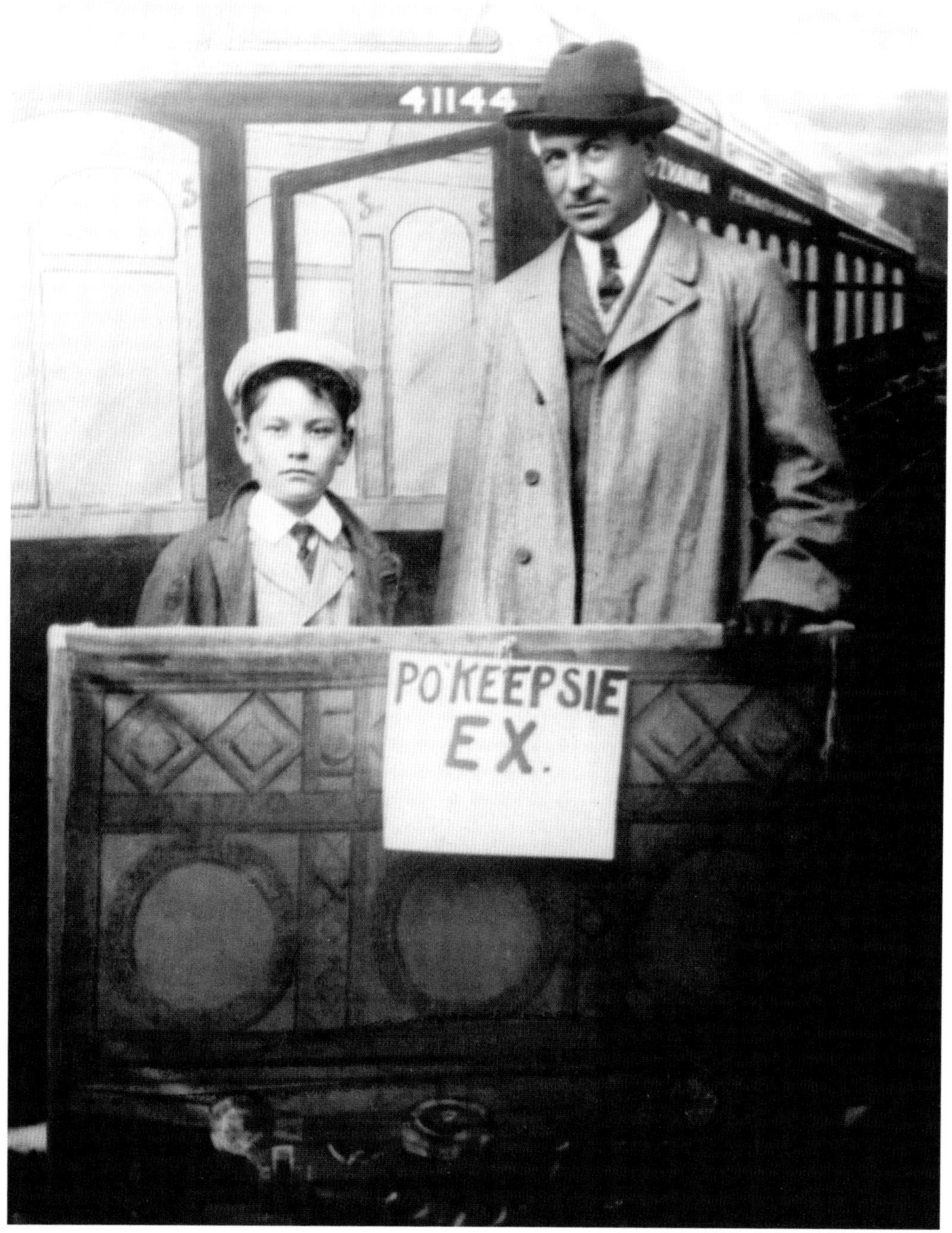

RIGHT Tracy and Olin posing in a New York Central Railroad replica photo booth at the County Fair in Poughkeepsie on October 3, 1913. Two days before, the fair had experienced a record downpour of rain. The *Poughkeepsie Daily Eagle* reported that even though outside it was very wet, the suffrage tent was dry, and so many came to its comfortable shelter that the supply of buttons ran out and many who braved the elements were turned away disappointed.

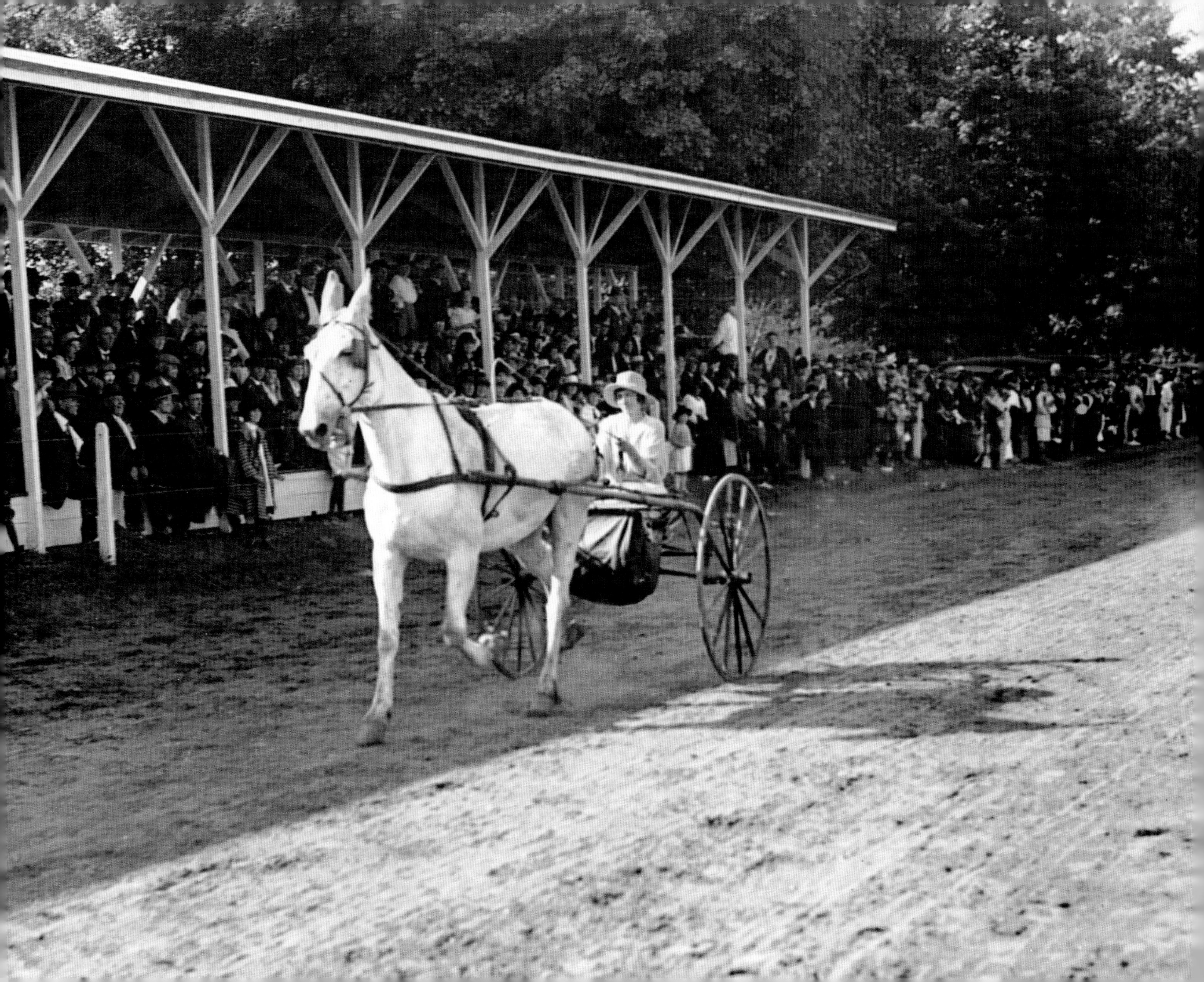

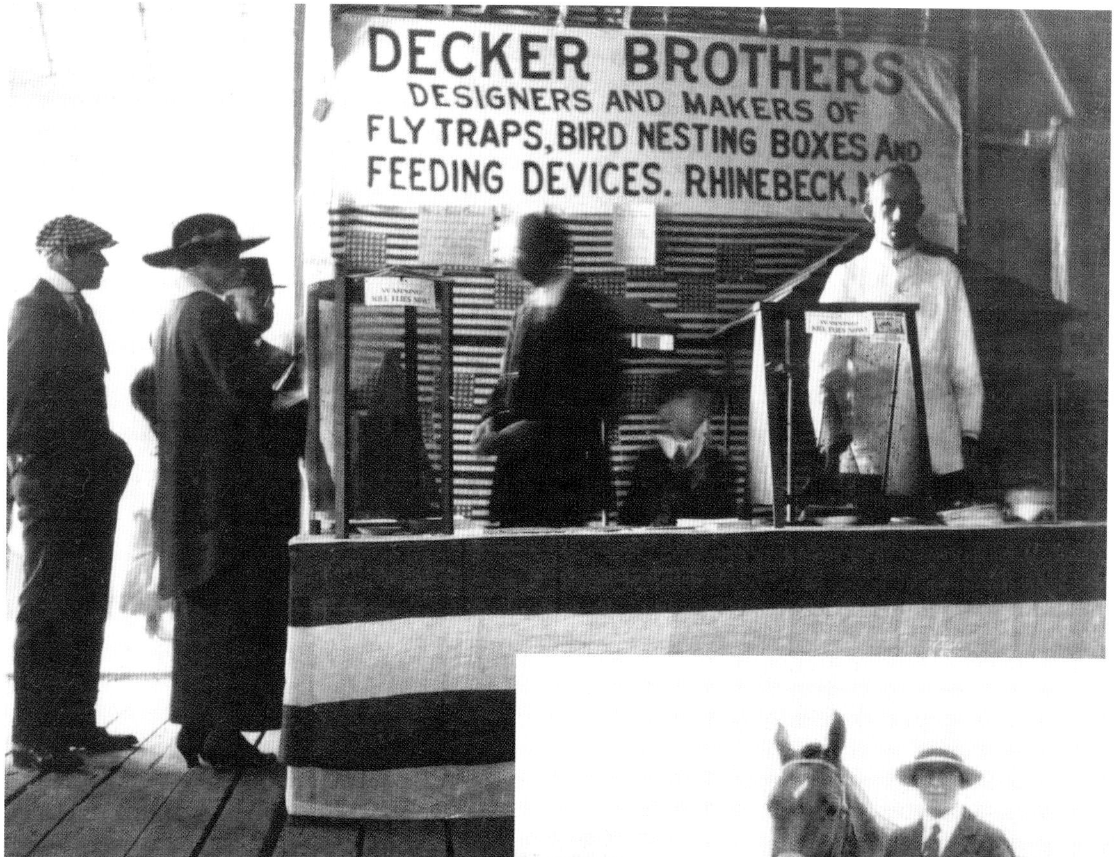

ABOVE A Decker Brothers exhibit at the 1915 fair in Poughkeepsie. Manufacturers of bird houses, the Decker Brothers built the pheasantry and other bird-keeping structures for Tracy at Foxhollow Farm.

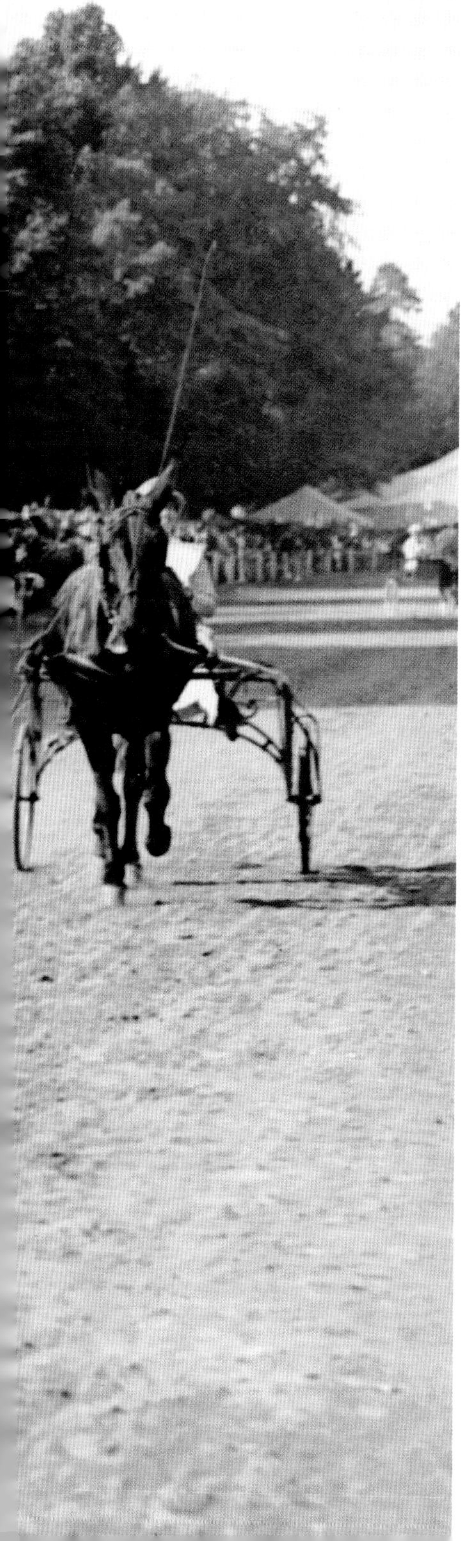

LEFT Mule races were very popular among the affluent women of the Hudson Valley. Mrs. J. Griswold Webb is seen here winning a race at the 1919 fair in Rhinebeck.

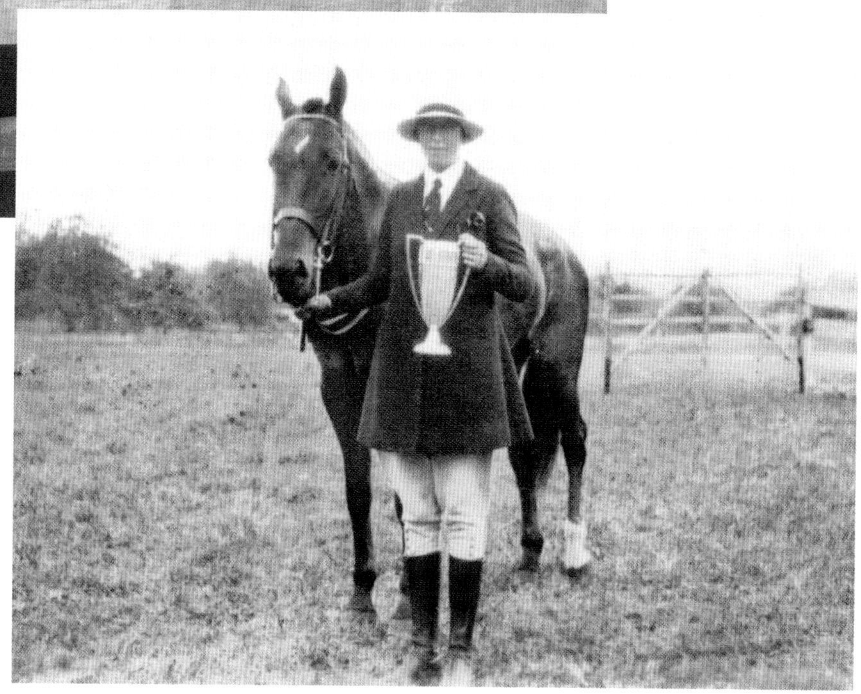

BELOW The 1927 fair included stunt riding, baseball games, and dog competitions. Deb Dows, age 13, proudly shows off her cup after winning Best Rider.

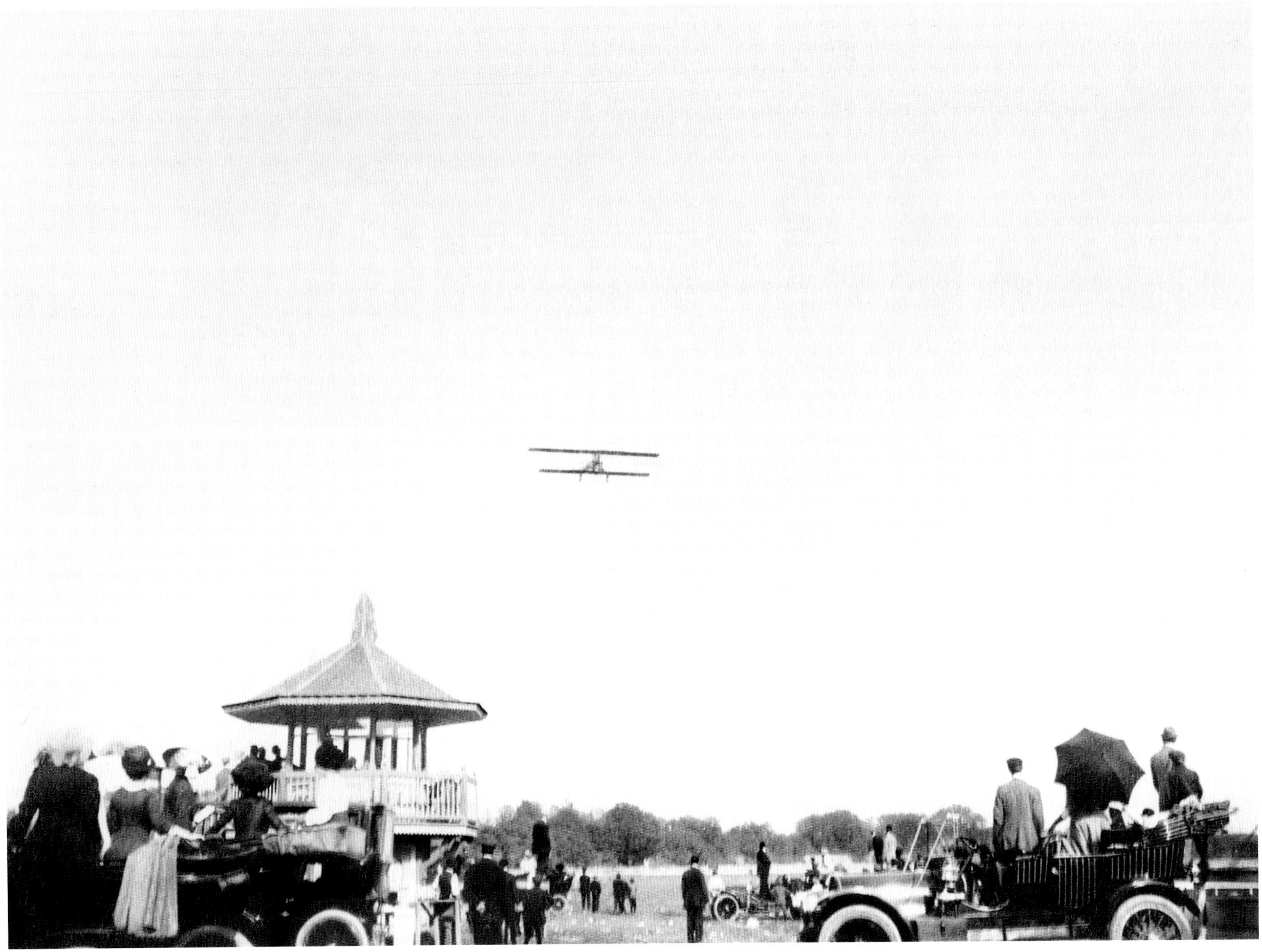

OPPOSITE Spectators watching Eugene Ely, an aviation pioneer, performing in a Curtiss biplane over the Poughkeepsie fairgrounds, 1910.

RIGHT Watching the flight as balloons float past them are Harrie T. Lindeberg, Helen Dinsmore Huntington, center, Alice Dows, and an unidentified friend.

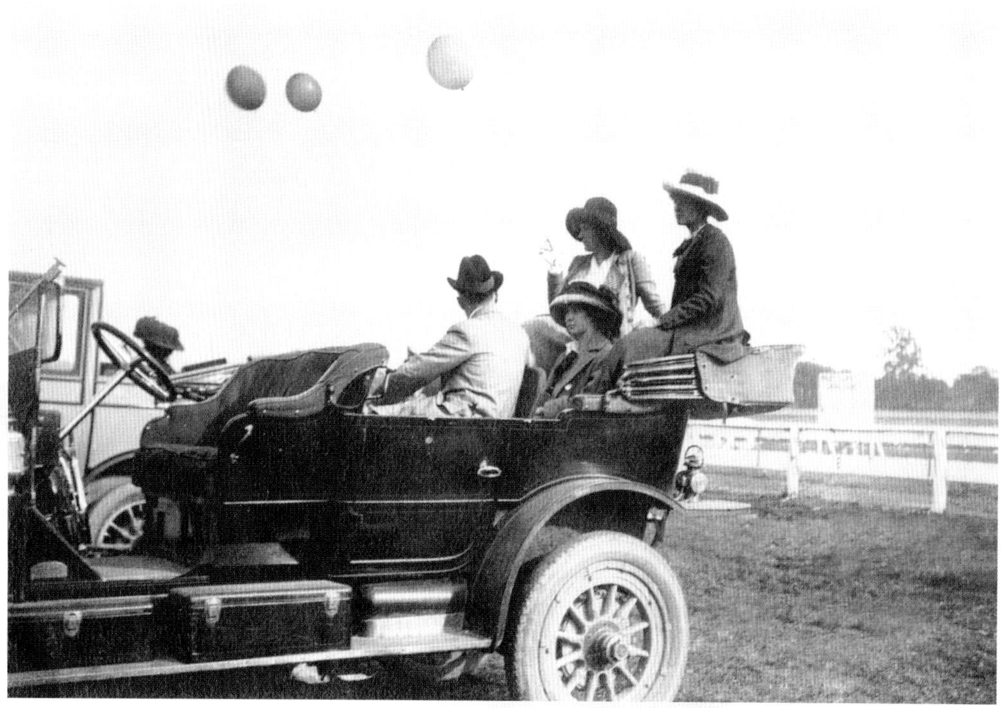

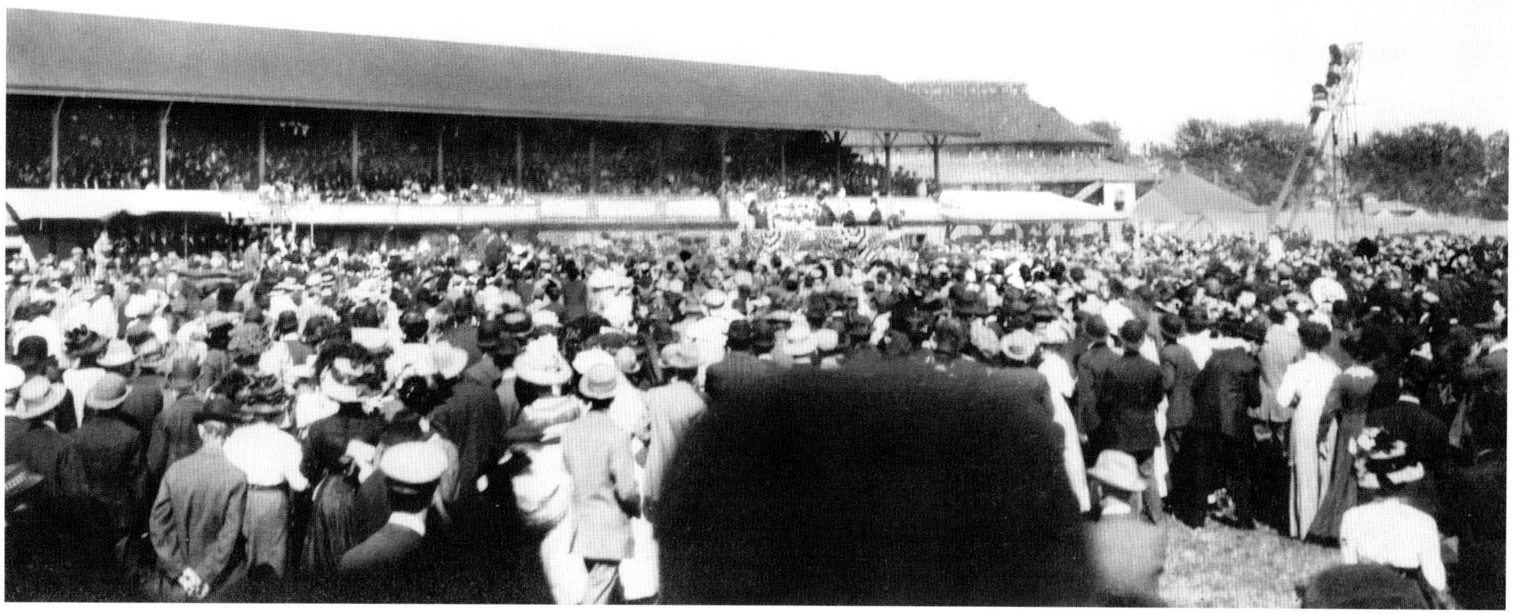

LEFT A huge crowd gathered to hear former president Theodore Roosevelt's speech at the same Poughkeepsie fair in 1910.

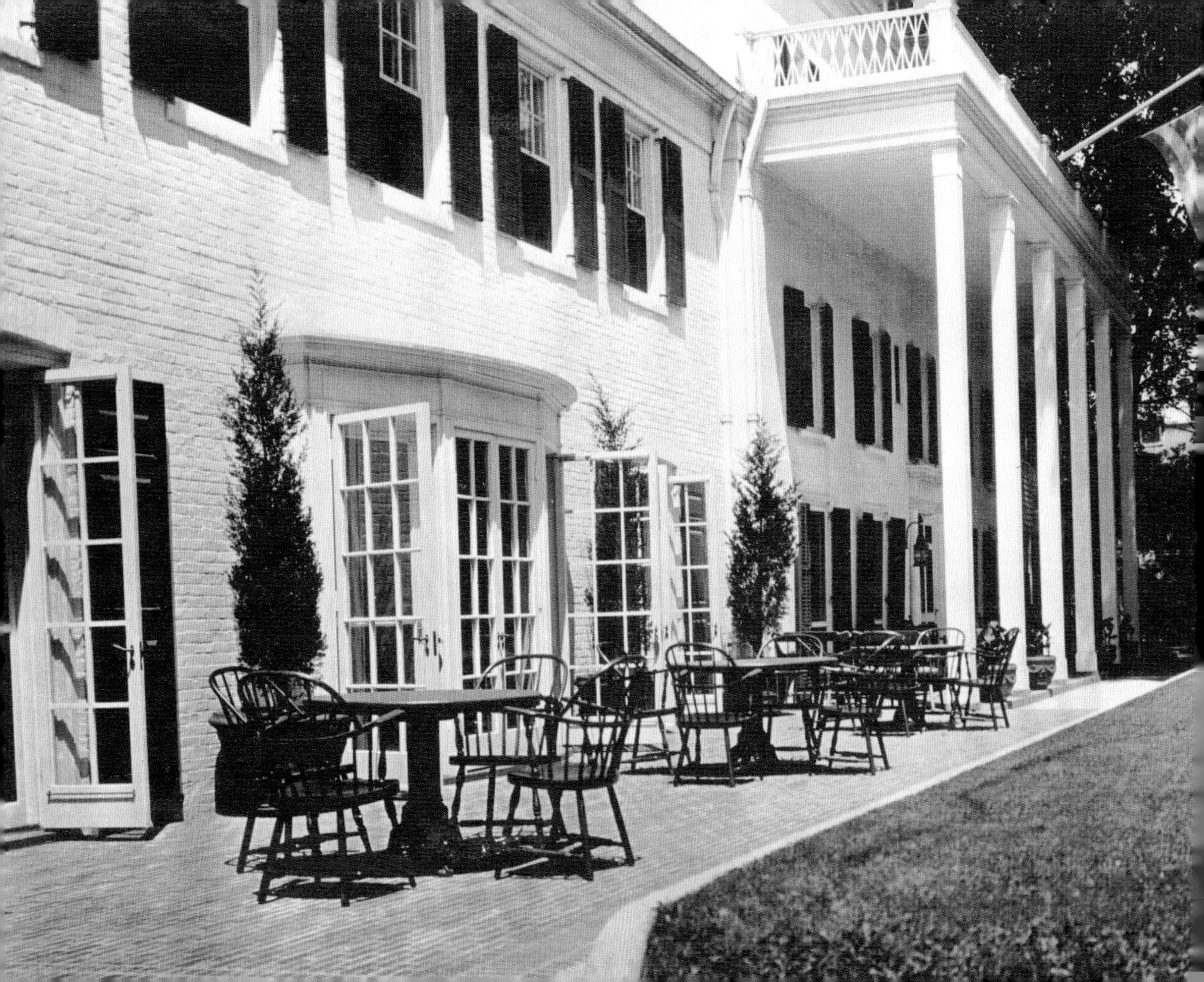

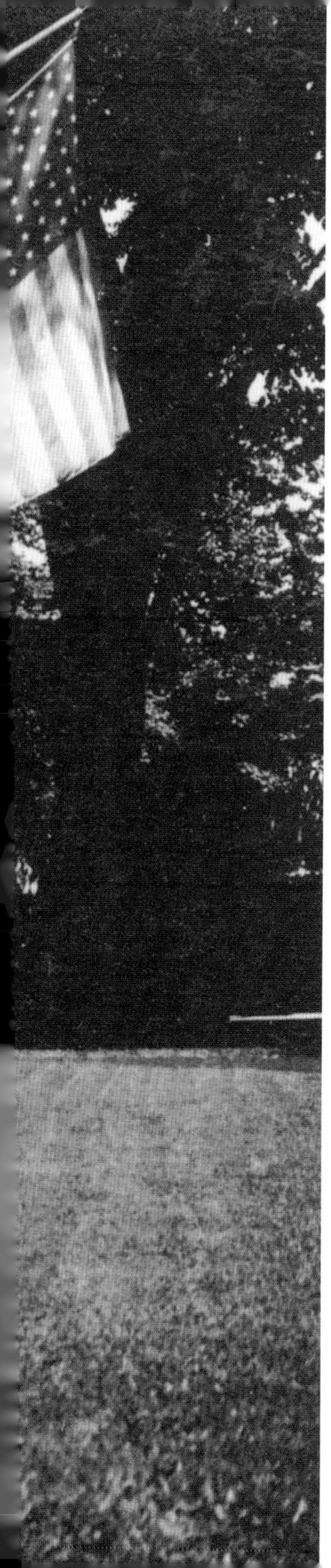

CHAPTER SIX

The BEEKMAN ARMS

PREVIOUS PAGES The Beekman Arms on a summer day, 1918. It is known as the oldest continually operated inn in the United States.

RIGHT The hotel in 1917 after a full renovation. Originally a tavern built on land sold by Henry Beekman to William Traphagen in 1705, many years later the property became the Rhinebeck Hotel. In 1914, it was purchased by Wallace W. Foster of Kingston, with Tracy Dows as an investor. They hired Tracy's good friend, Harrie T. Lindeberg, to transform the existing saloon-like hotel into a modern and attractive inn named the Beekman Arms. Further renovations were made in 1927 to update the rooms with private telephones and bathtubs. By 1930, the inn was managed by Beekman Arms, Inc., with Tracy as president of the board. Over the years, it has passed through several owners and remains a Rhinebeck institution.

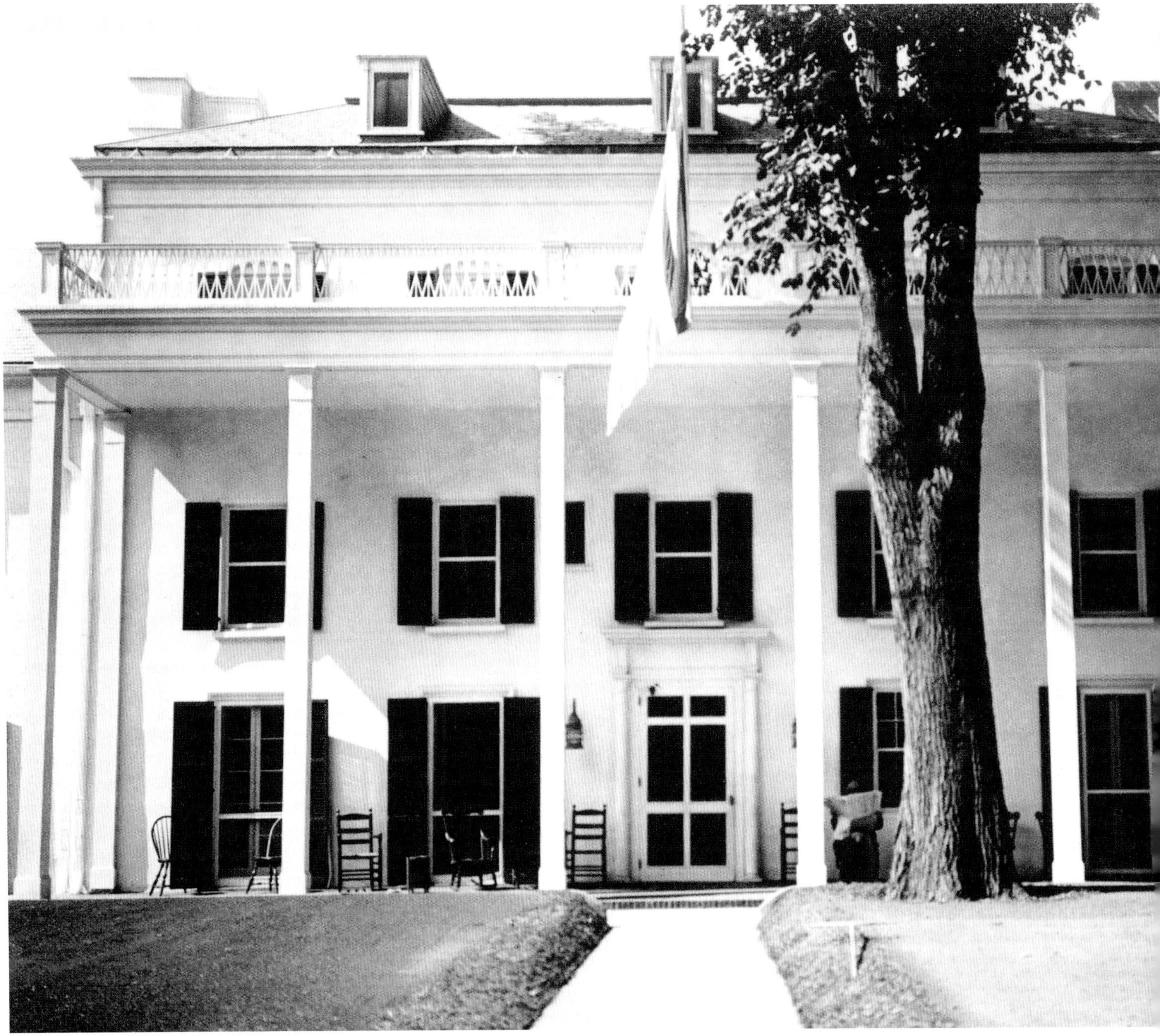

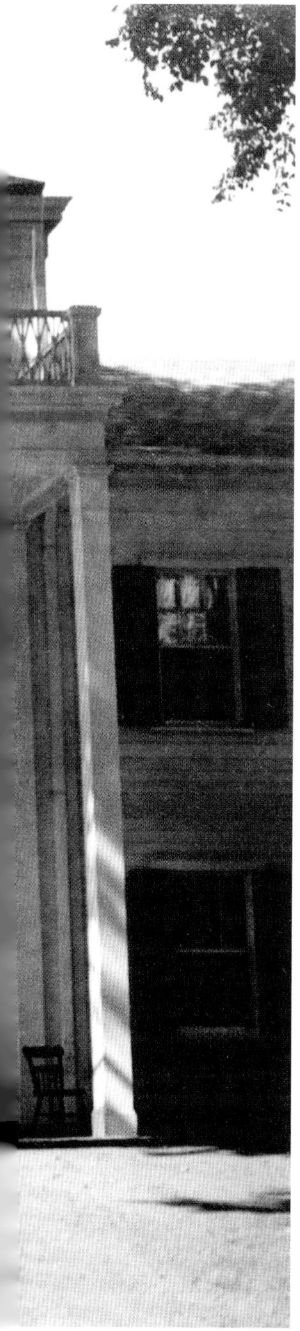

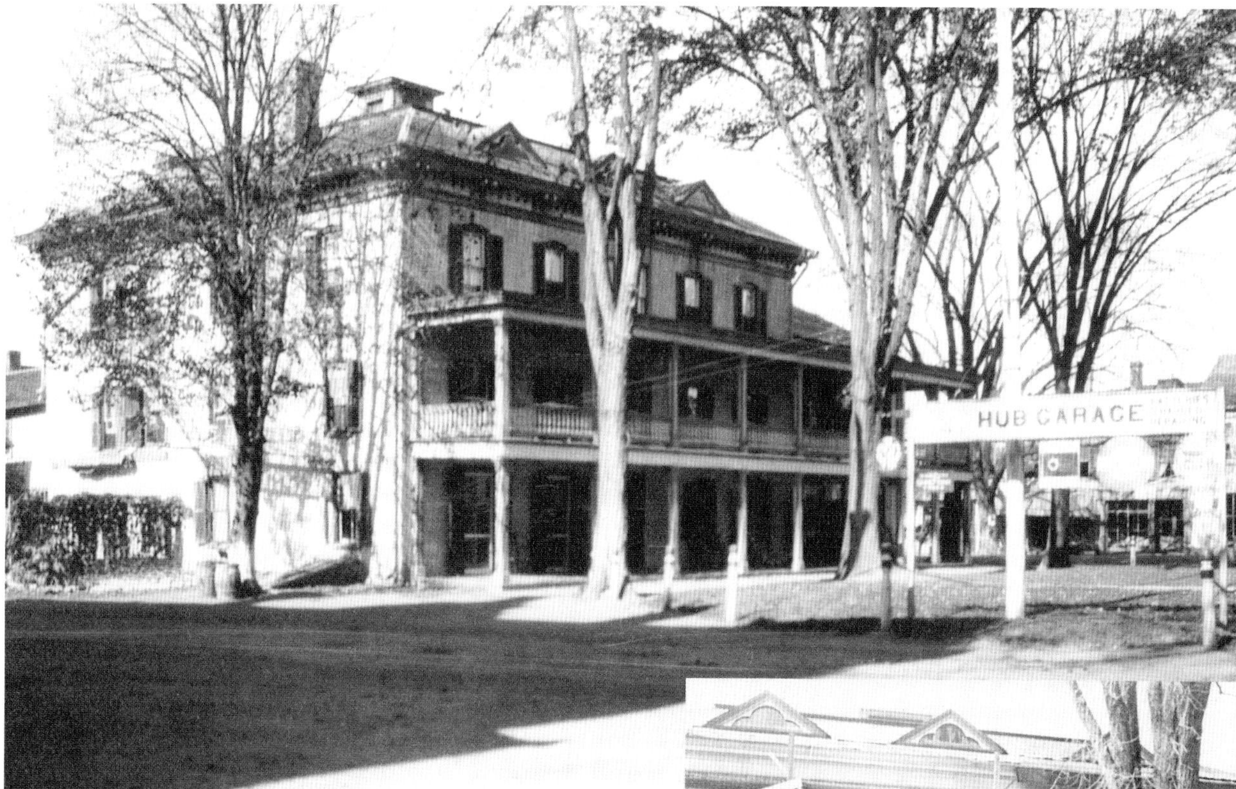

LEFT The Rhinebeck Hotel in 1915 during its last years before becoming the Beekman Arms.

BELOW A view of the front of the hotel during its renovation. The owner, Wally Foster, held an open house on the afternoon of September 12, 1917, for the townspeople to tour the new Beekman Arms. It's record attendance was reported three days later in the *Rhinebeck Gazette*.

"The Beekman Arms, the pride of the Hudson Valley when hotels are mentioned, threw open its doors Wednesday afternoon and welcomed the people of the vicinity to inspect its charms and to enjoy its hospitality. Landlord Foster believes that nearly three hundred people visited the hotel in response to the invitation."

The Rhinebeck Gazette,
September 15, 1917

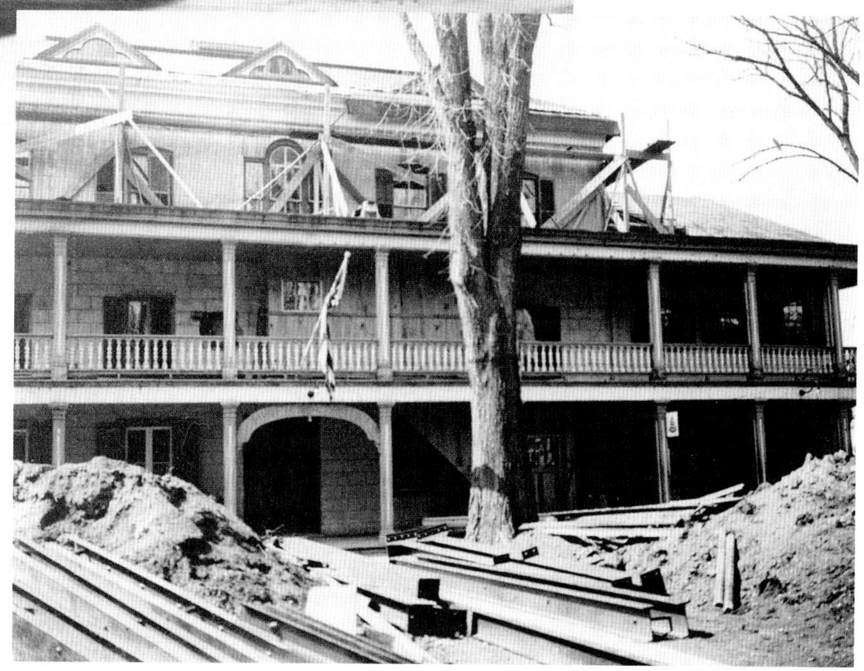

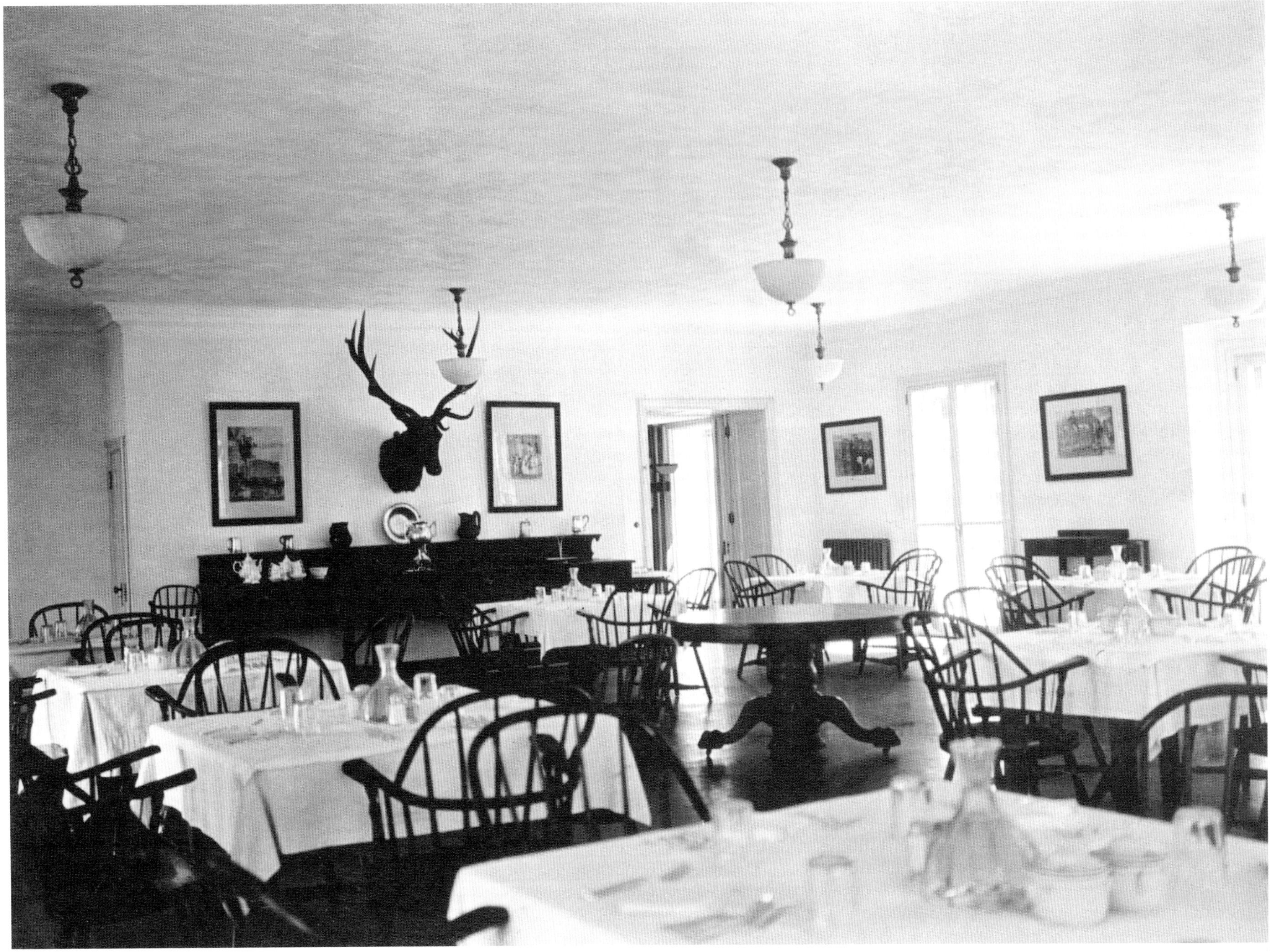

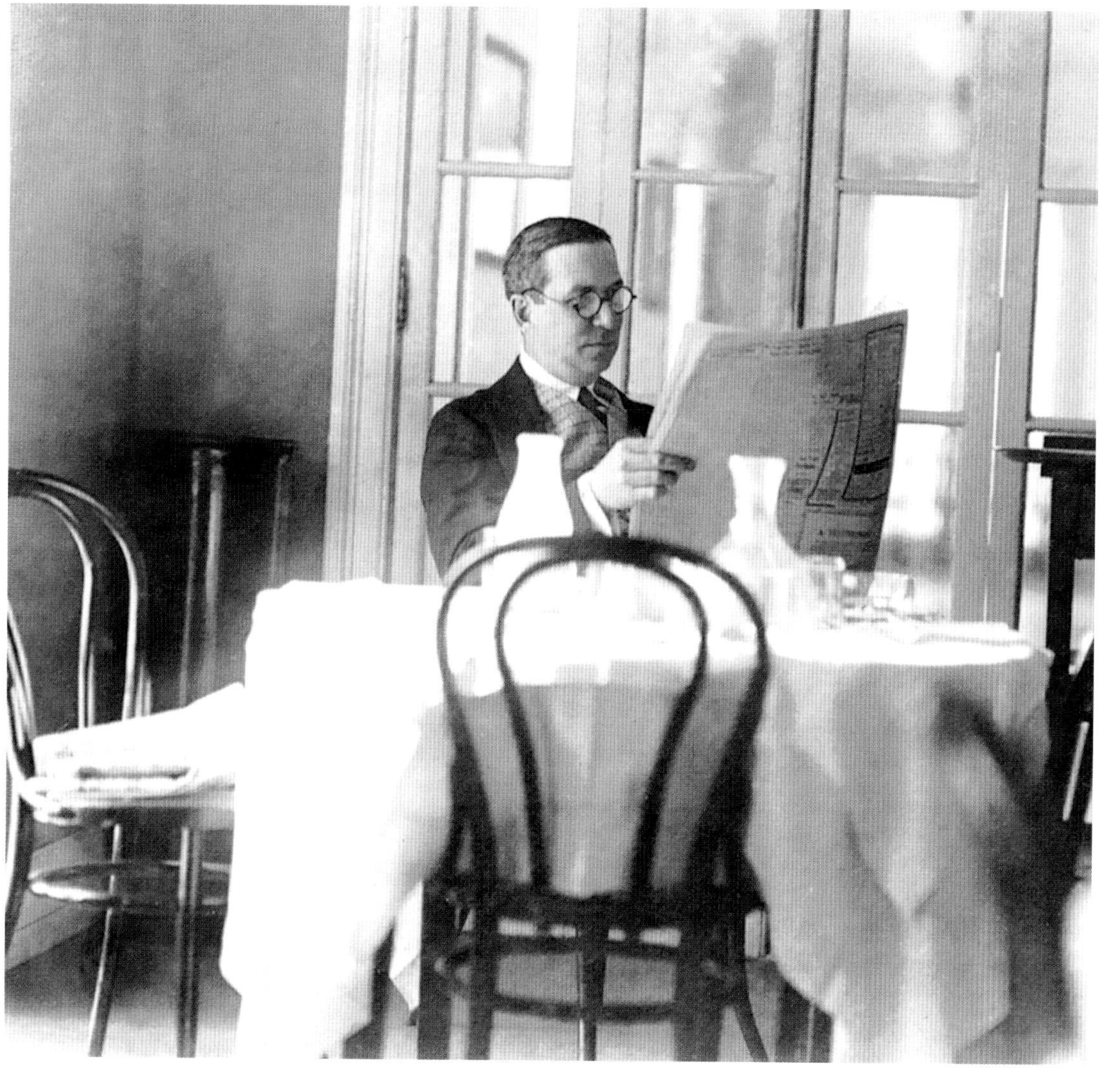

ABOVE Harry Coutant took this photograph of Tracy having breakfast in a side dining room, 1919.

OPPOSITE The pristine, newly refurbished main dining room in 1918.

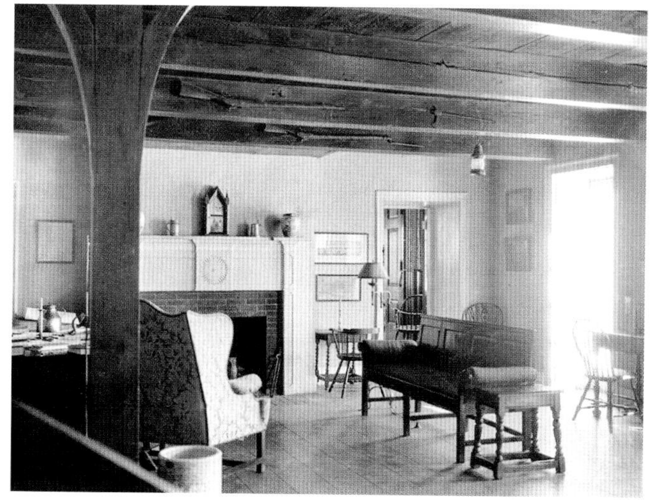

ABOVE AND BELOW Views of the sitting area and north reception room after the renovation. Cigars, seen in the glass case, could be purchased at the counter in the reception room.

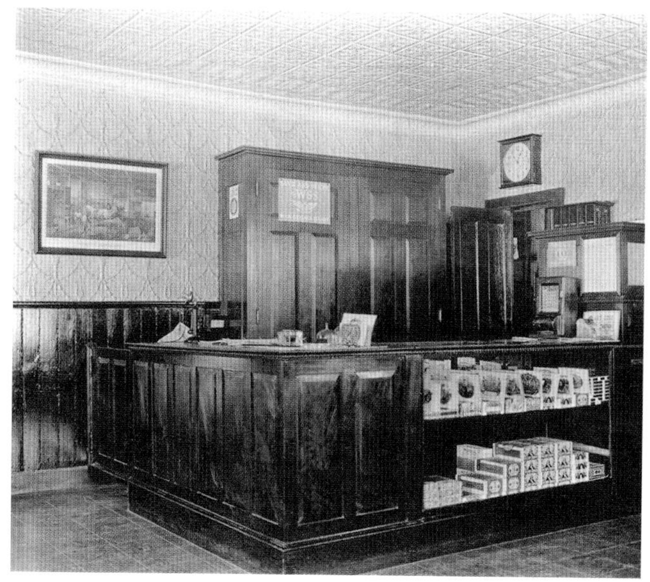

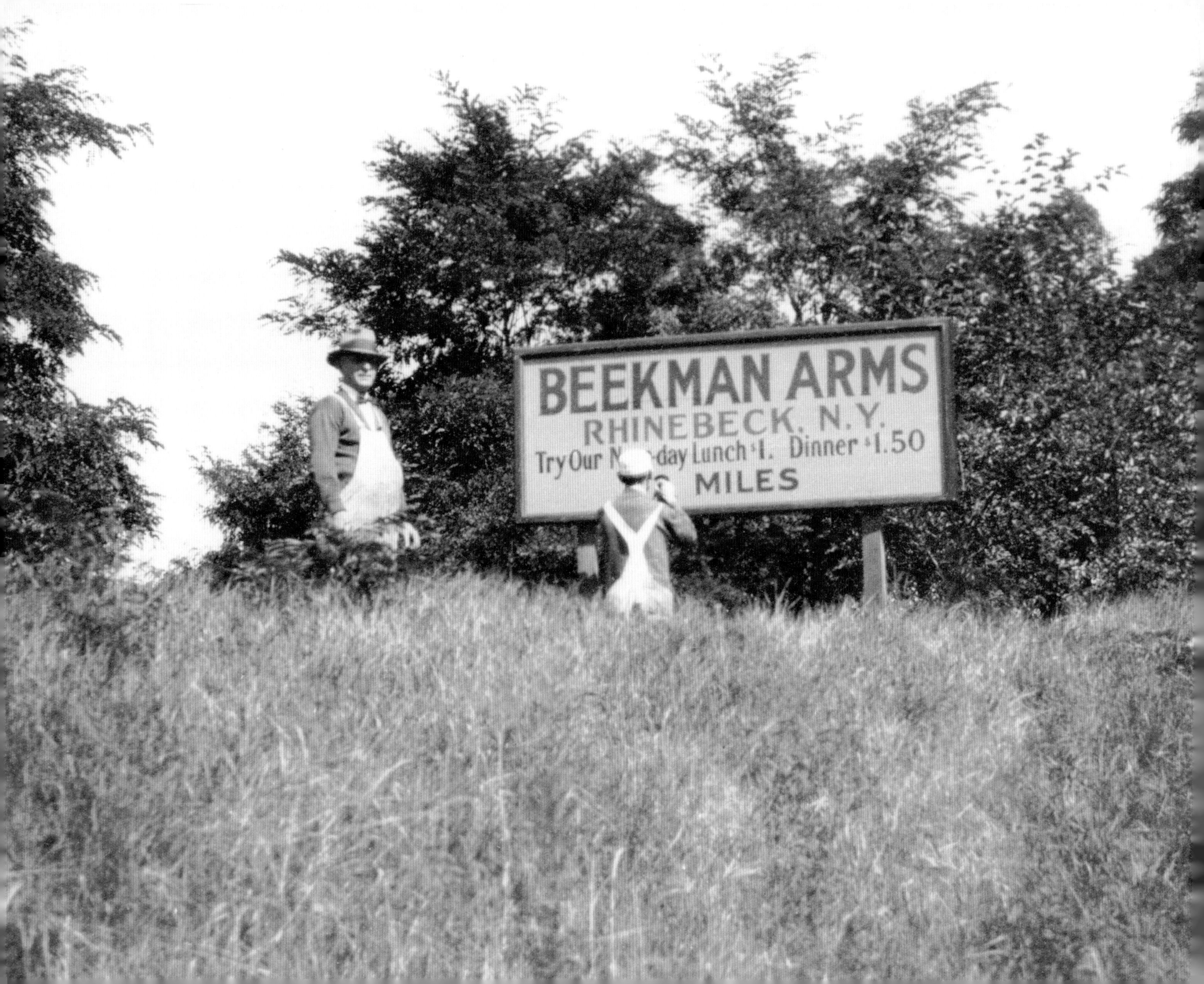
BEEKMAN ARMS
RHINEBECK, N.Y.
MILES

OPPOSITE Workers in 1927 painting a billboard posted outside the village advertising lunch and dinner at the Beekman Arms.

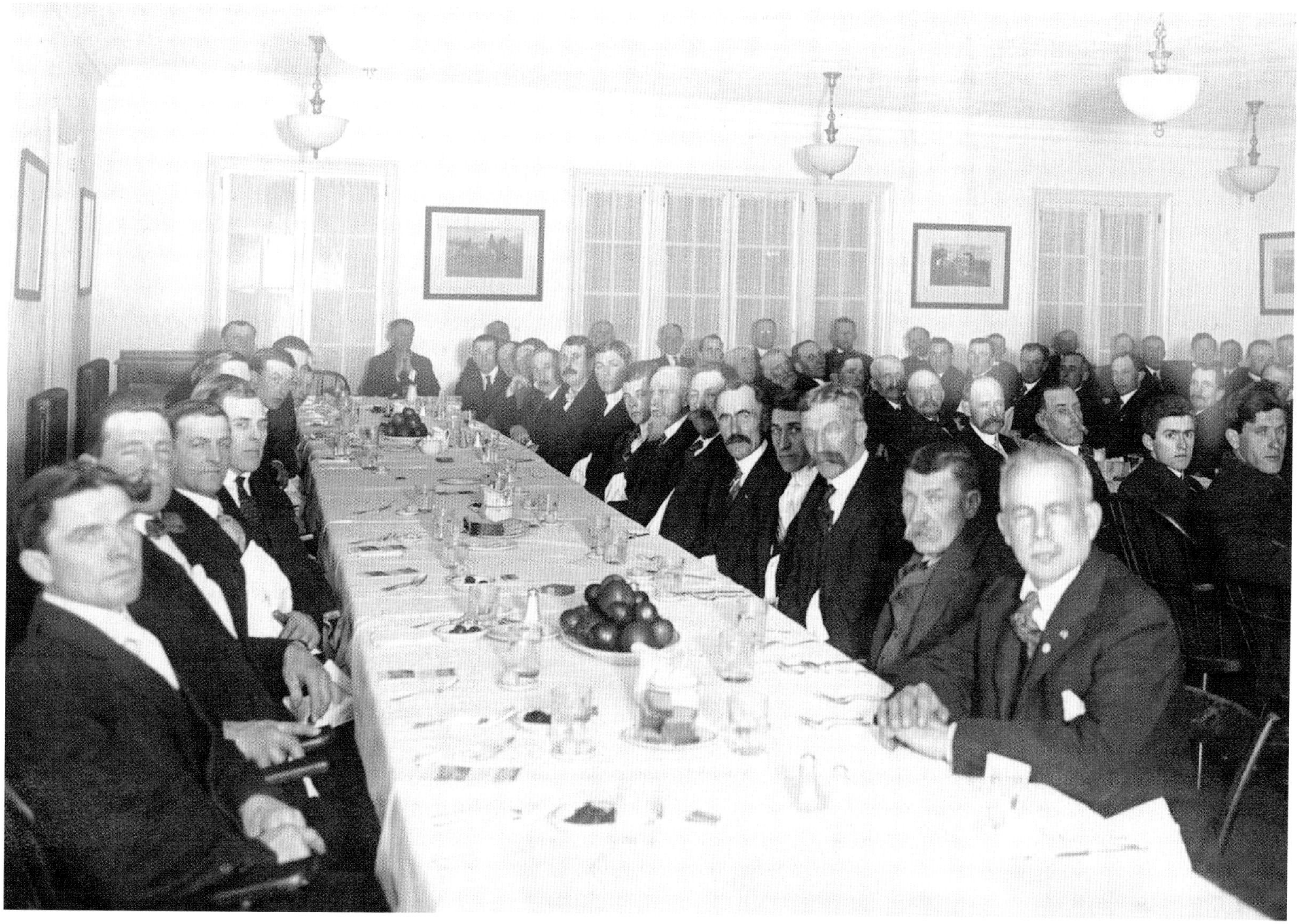

ABOVE A large crowd at the Farmers Supper in the dining room, January 15, 1919. The annual event gave local businessmen and farmers the opportunity to discuss agricultural issues and was always well attended.

OPPOSITE The gentlemen of Rhinebeck, with Jacob Hill Strong at their center, waiting for the arrival of the Liberty Coach. In the background is the original Town Hall, which was demolished and replaced by the Rhinebeck Post Office in 1939.

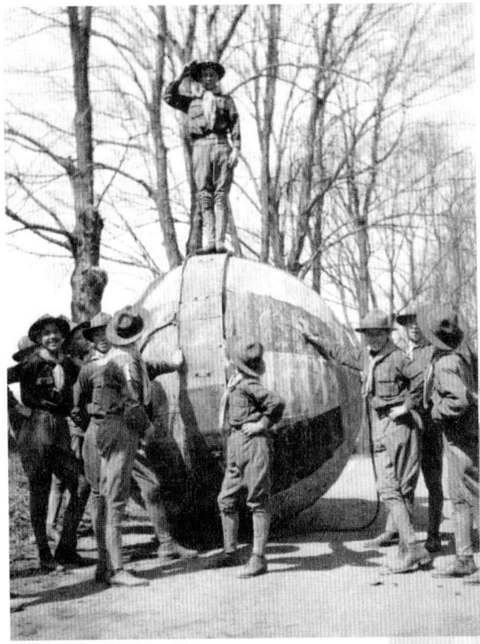

ABOVE The Liberty Ball being rolled by Boy Scouts on April 27, 1918, as it passed through Rhinebeck on its way from Buffalo to New York City. The giant red, white, and blue sphere was seven feet in diameter. It was met at the Rhinecliff ferry and accompanied through the village of Rhinebeck by the scouts. The Liberty Ball and Liberty Coach were part of the efforts of the Third Liberty Loan to encourage people to buy war bonds during World War I.

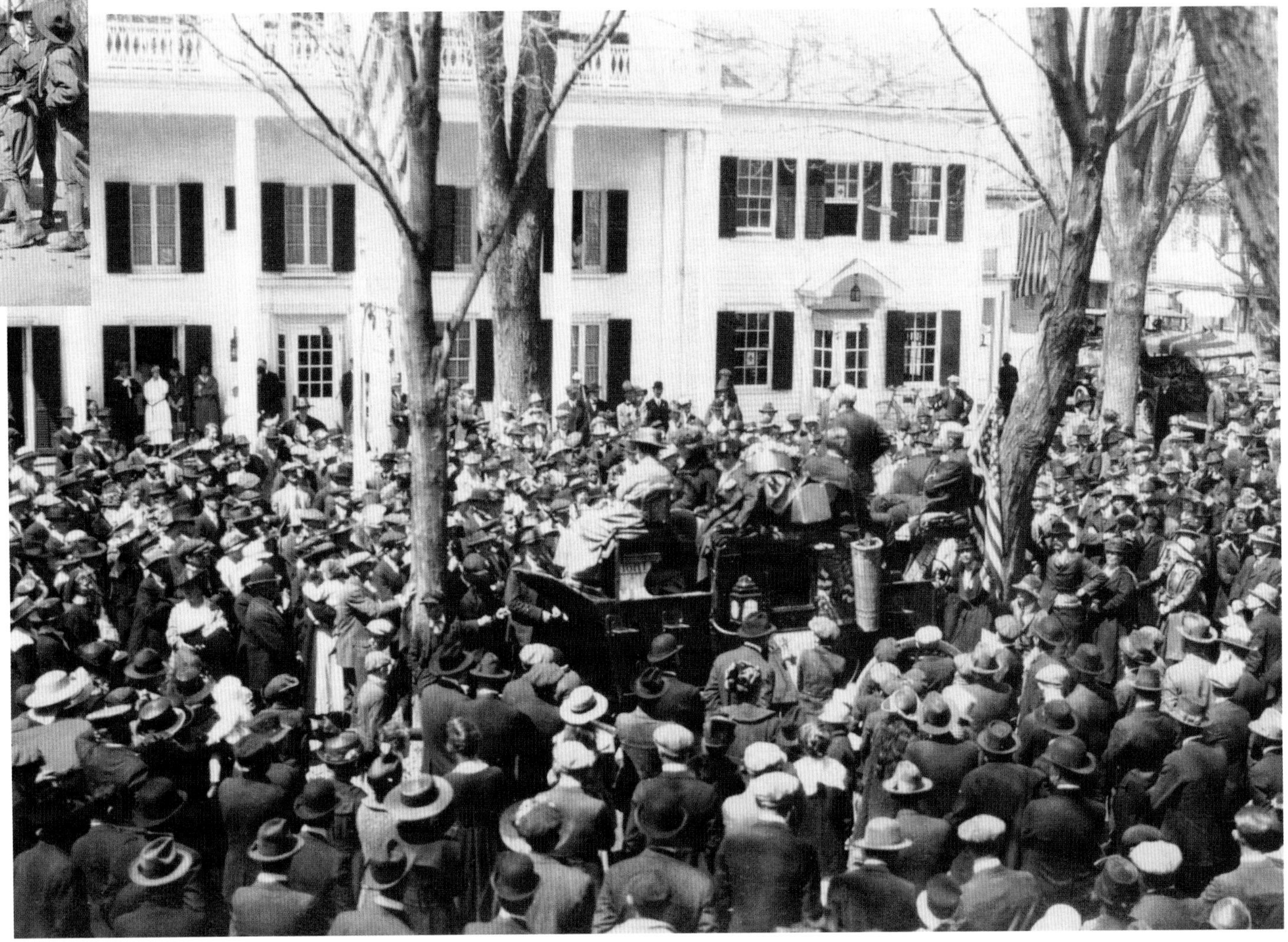

RIGHT A massive crowd assembled in front of the Beekman Arms the next day as the Liberty Coach passed through Rhinebeck. The coach was driven by Morris E. Howlett, a professional English whip. Jacob Hill Strong and Mrs. Stephen Olin joined the ride from Rhinebeck to Hyde Park.

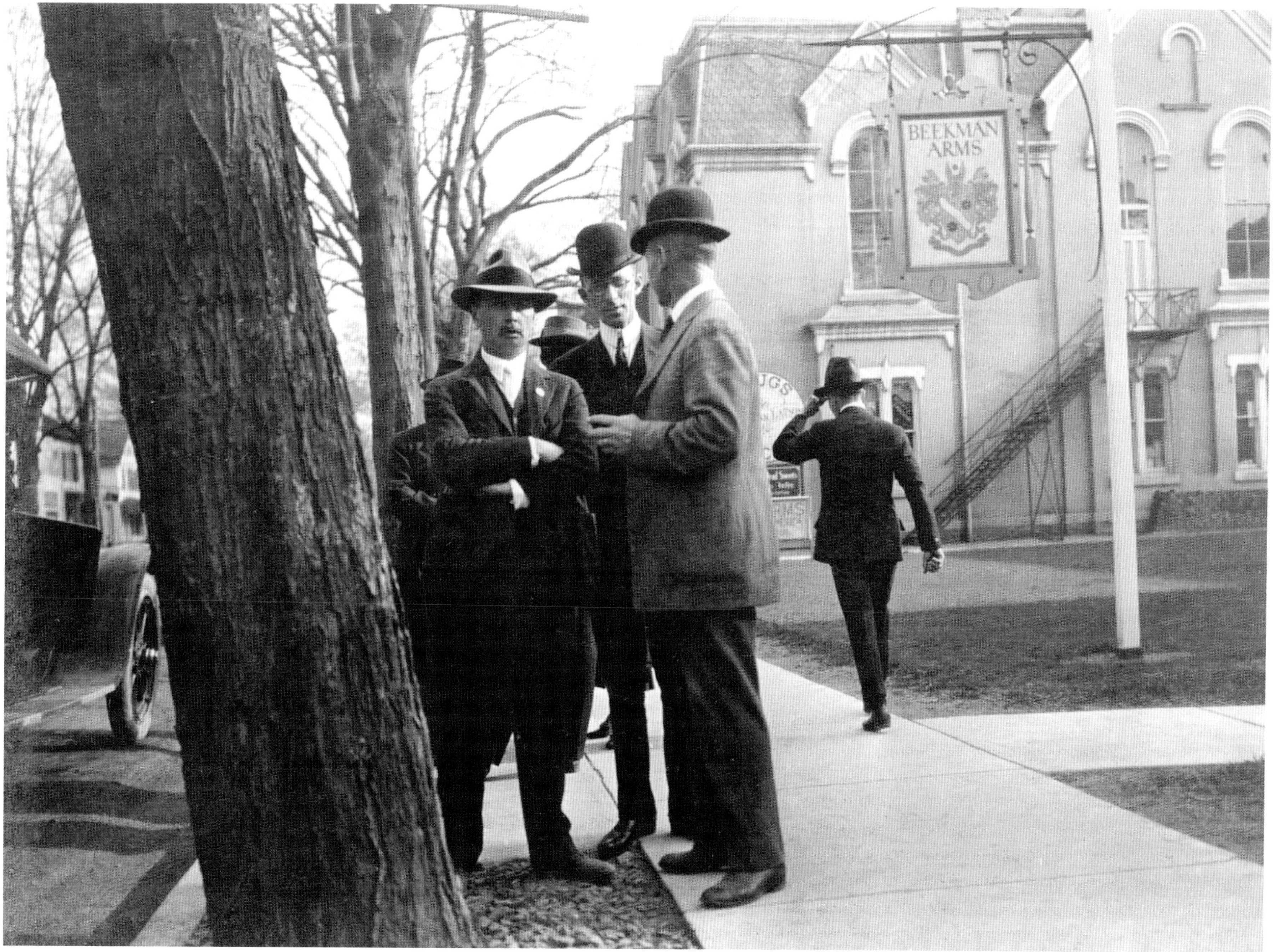
BEEKMAN
ARMS

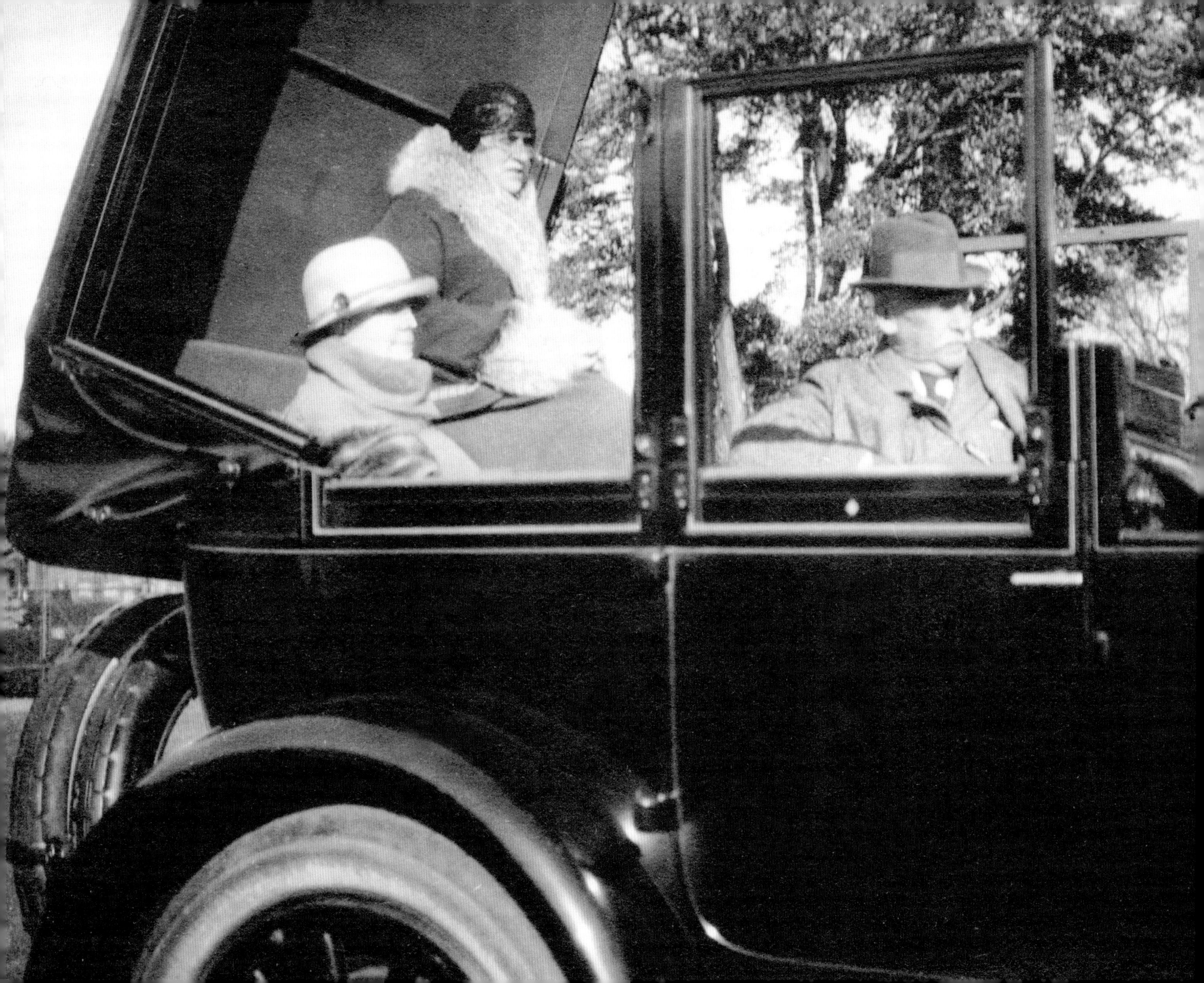

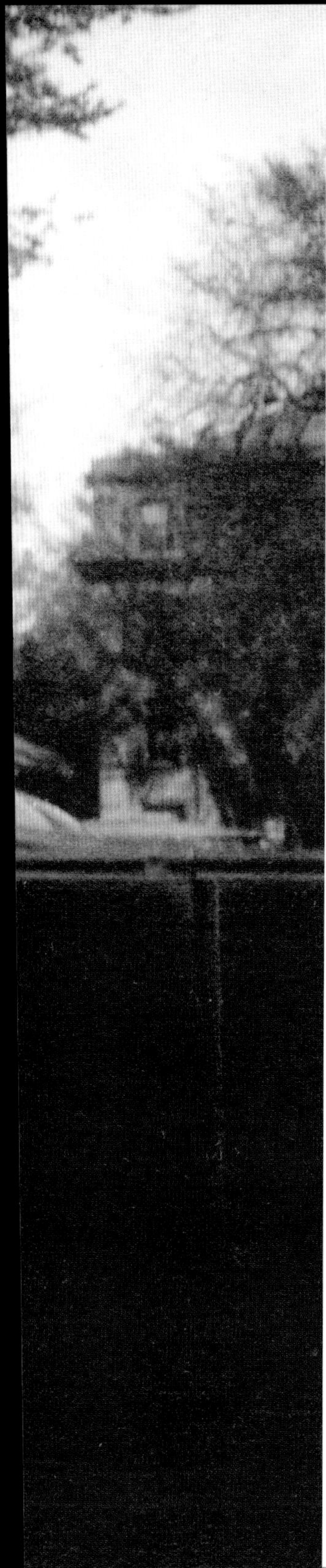

CHAPTER SEVEN

MOTOR TRIPS and AMERICAN TRAVEL

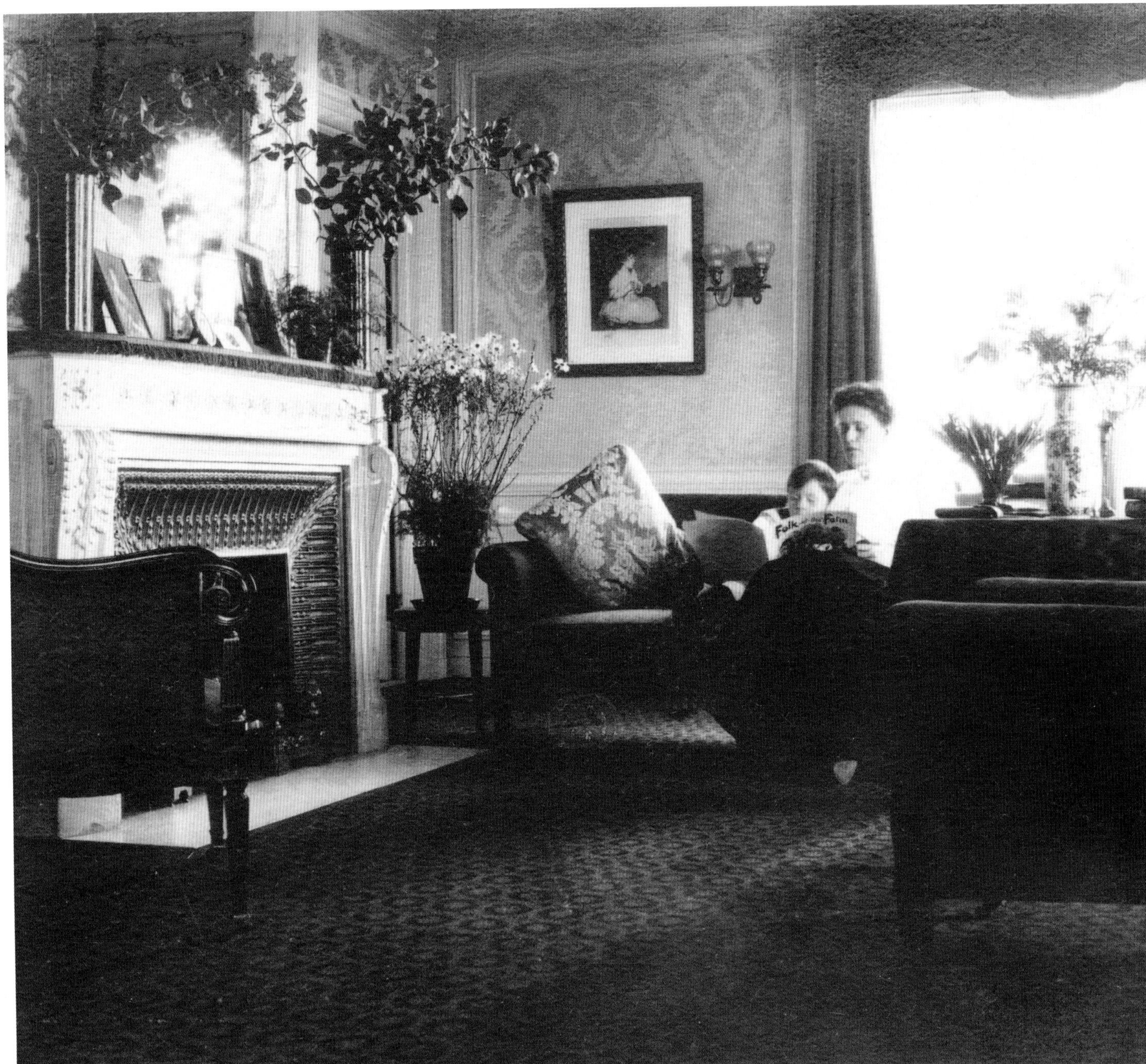

PREVIOUS PAGES Alice Dows with Mr. and Mrs. Stephen Olin on a motor trip to Wesleyan University in Middletown, Connecticut, 1922.

LEFT Alice and Olin in 1908 at the Gotham Hotel, which later became the Peninsula Hotel. For the first few years after the family moved to Rhinebeck, they would travel to Manhattan and spend a few months during the winter and early spring at hotels, where they socialized with friends and attended performances at the theater and opera.

OPPOSITE The family's suite at The Plaza, 1909. To personalize the rooms they would bring framed family photographs and other items to place on tables and mantles.

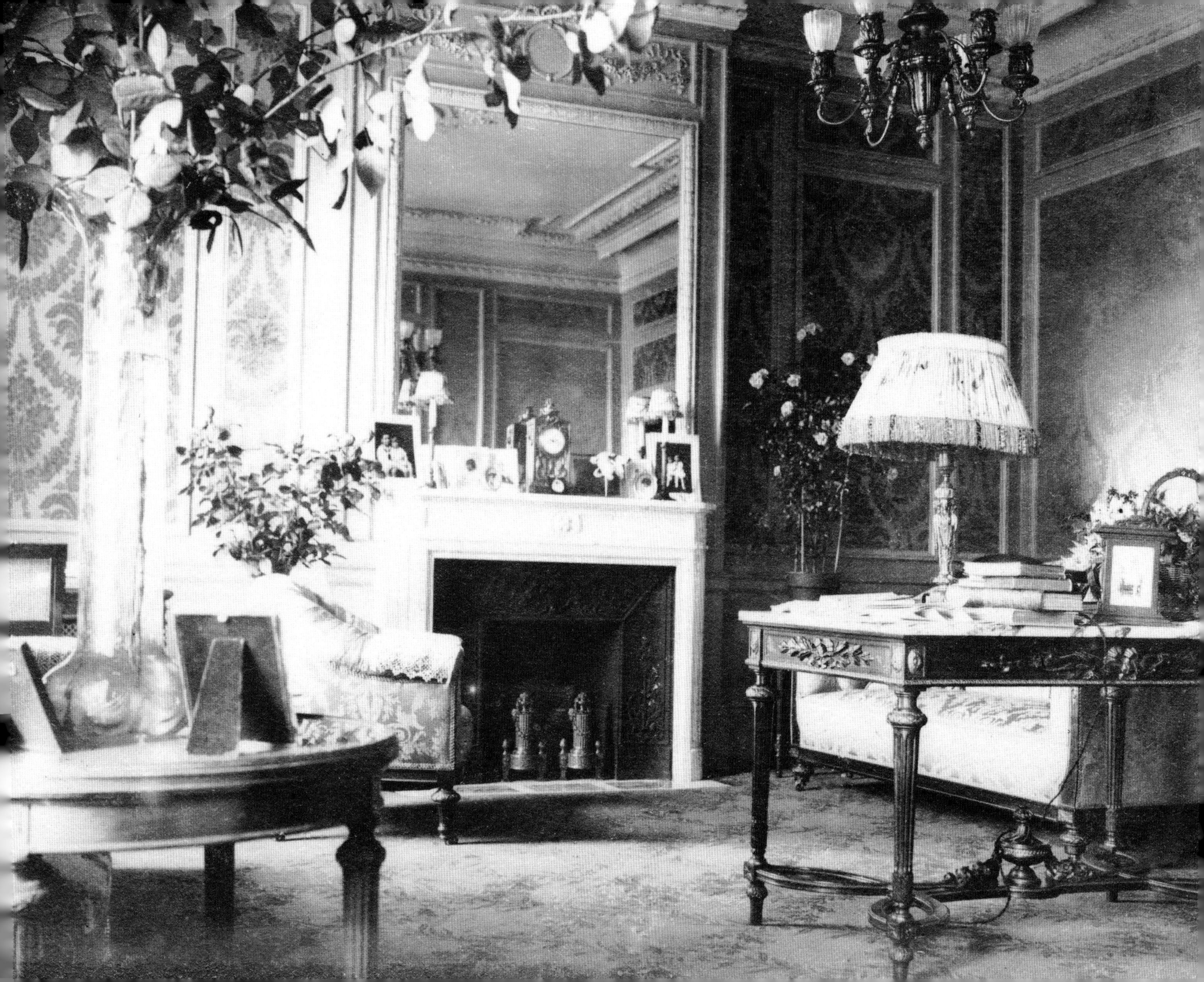

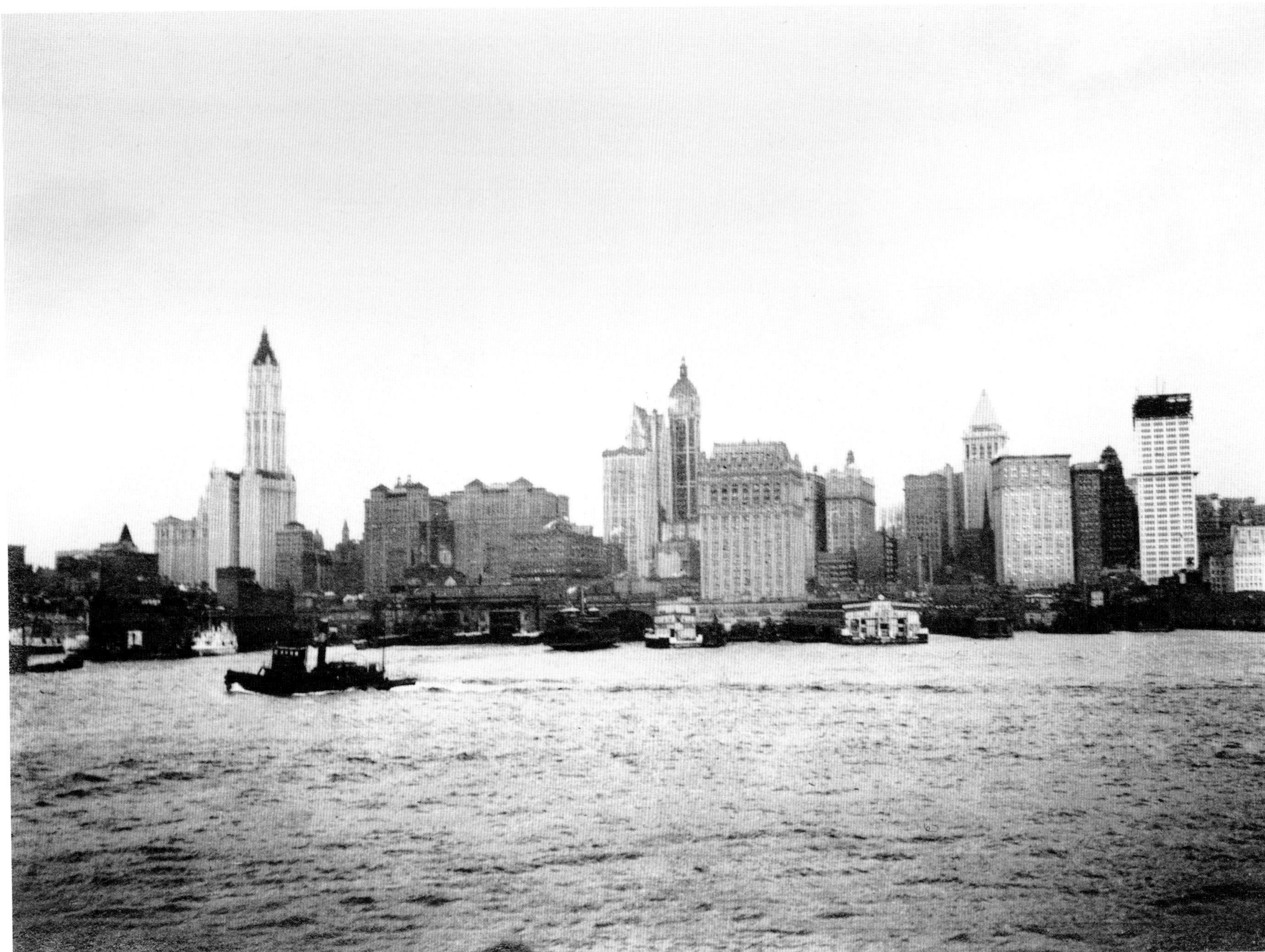

OPPOSITE A view of downtown Manhattan in 1913. The family was en route from the city to Seal Harbor in Maine aboard the passenger steamship *Bunker Hill*. The Woolworth Building (seen on the left) had just been completed, becoming the world's tallest structure.

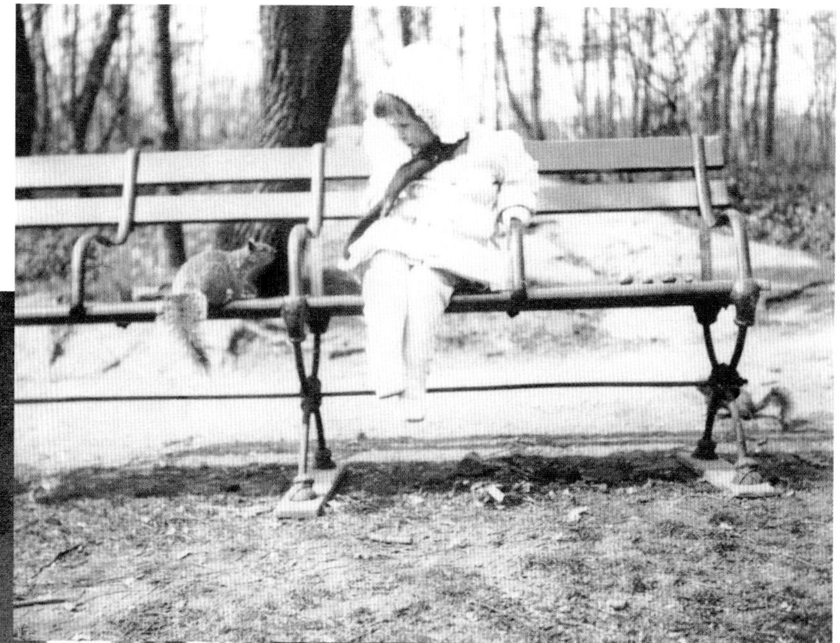

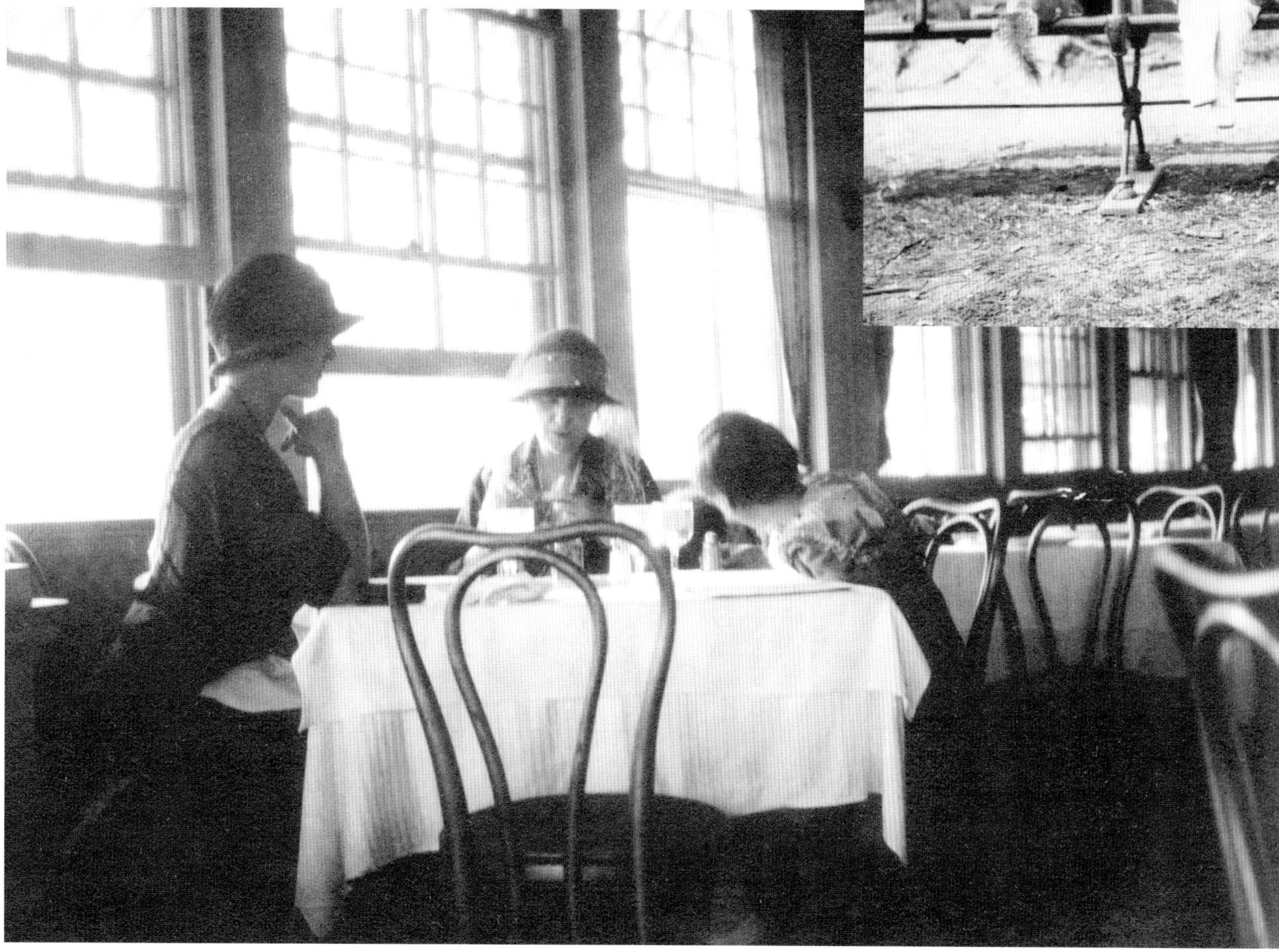

ABOVE Three-year-old Margaret feeding squirrels in Central Park, April 1909, while the family was staying at The Plaza.

LEFT Alice, Margaret, and Deb at Shanley's in New York City, 1922. The Dowses were on their way to visit Mr. and Mrs. Lewis Iselin in New Rochelle. Shanley's was an elegant Manhattan restaurant started by the seven Shanley brothers from Ireland. It became a favorite spot for Ethel and John Barrymore, Theodore Roosevelt, Harry Houdini, and other well-known guests.

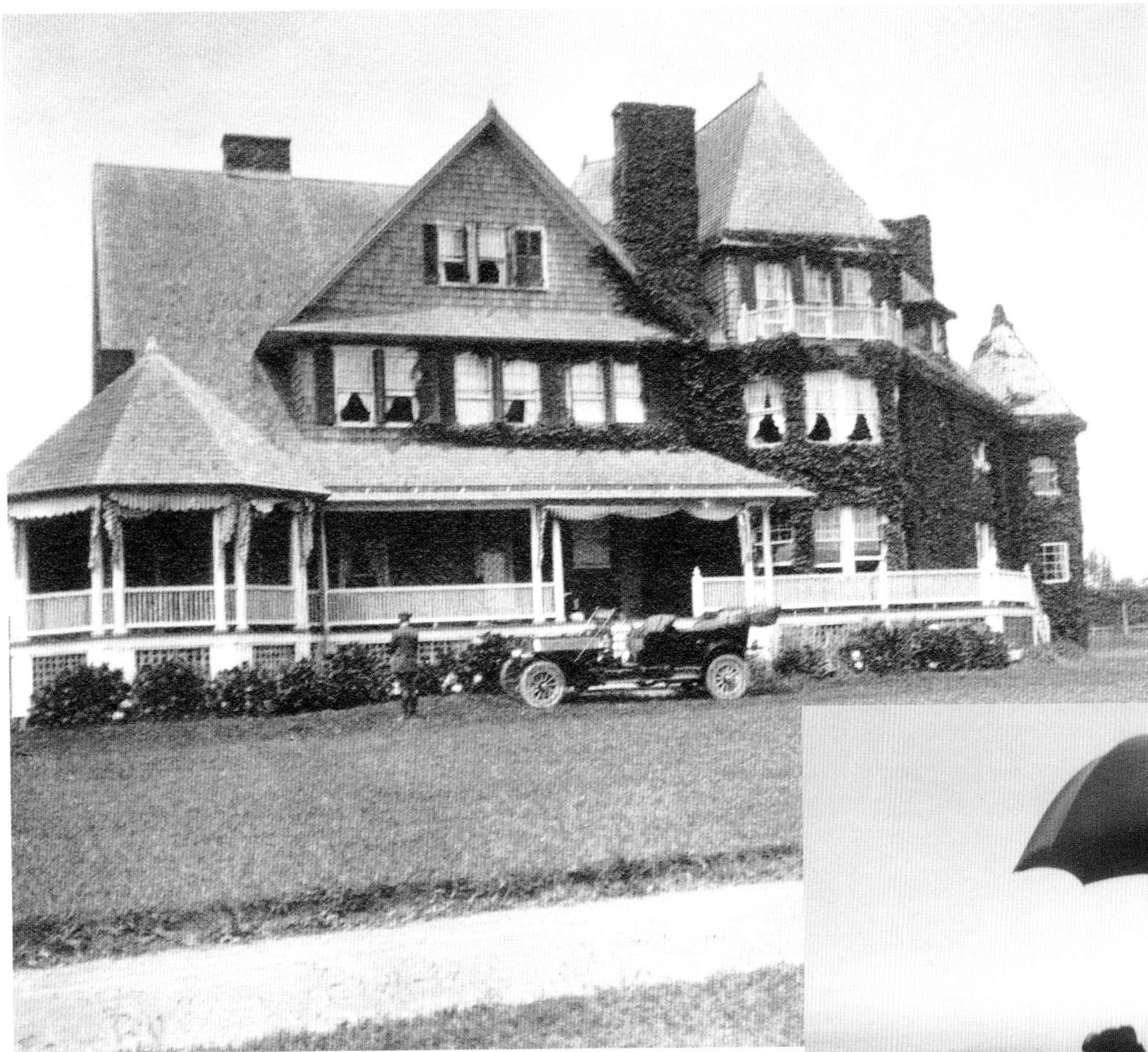

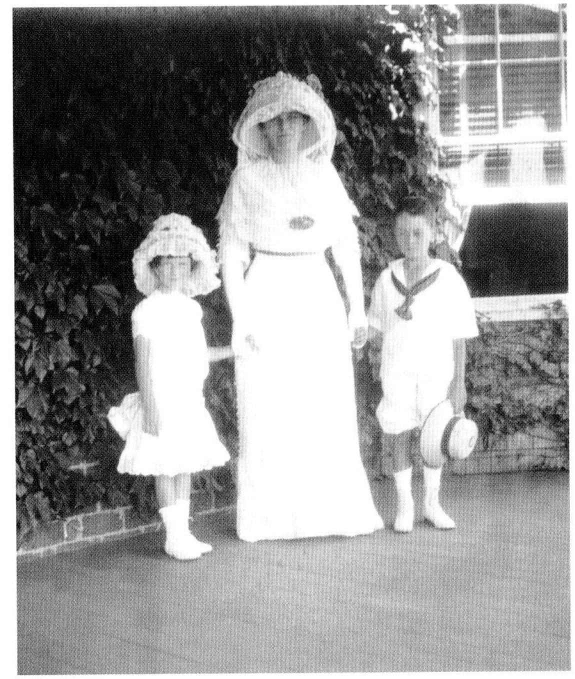

ABOVE Alice with Margaret and Olin, dressed for a social event.

LEFT Alice and Olin sharing a peaceful moment on the beach.

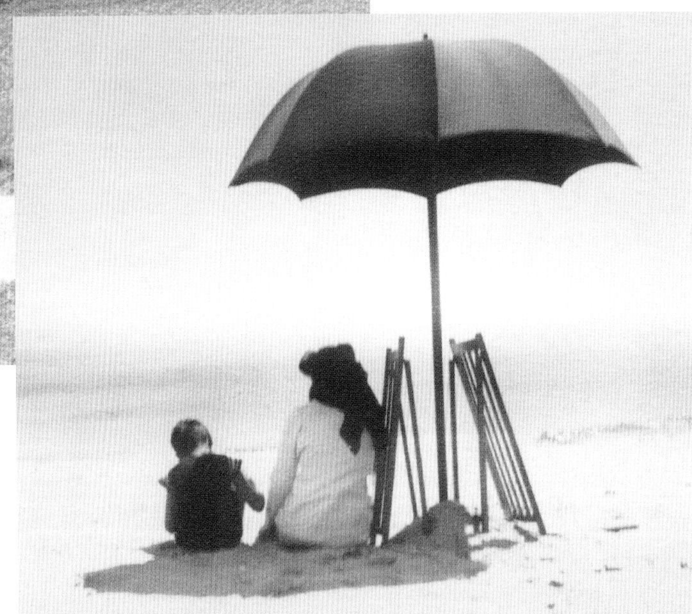

ABOVE In the summer of 1911 the Dowses rented this cottage on the dunes of Southampton for three months. Alice remembered it being a hectic time, crowded with too many people and too much activity.

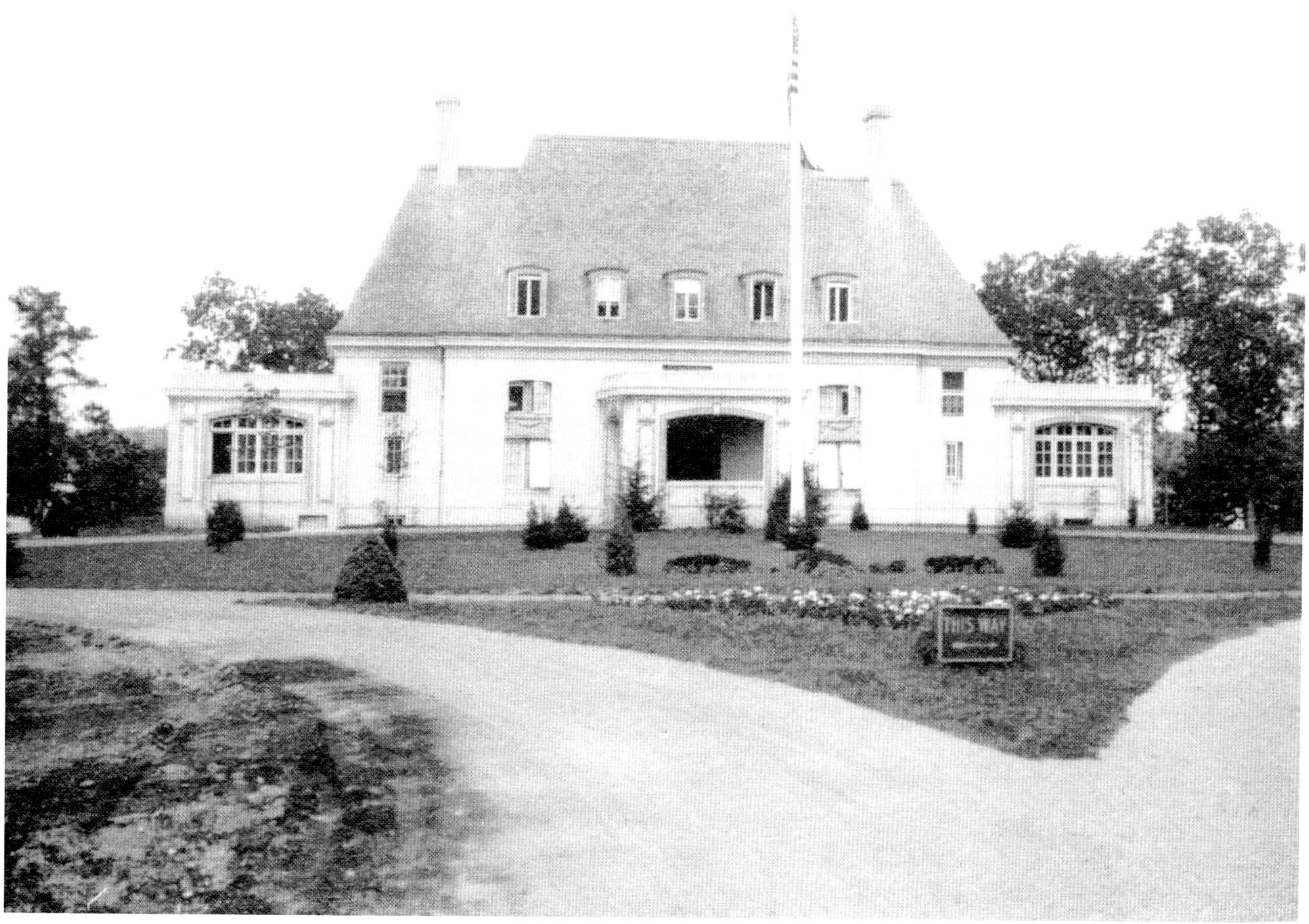

LEFT The Petit Trianon, an inn and restaurant named after the Versailles original, on the Long Island Motor Parkway, 1912. William K. Vanderbilt II built the parkway in 1908 as a paved road on which his friends could drive their expensive automobiles and racing cars. It was over forty miles long, with many bridges and several toll lodges, all designed in the French Provincial style by architect John Russell Pope. The inn at its terminus was also designed by Pope, on the shore of Lake Ronkonkoma. The Depression, along with aggressive building projects by urban planner Robert Moses, caused the demise of the parkway. Only remnants of the road and a few bridges still exist today.

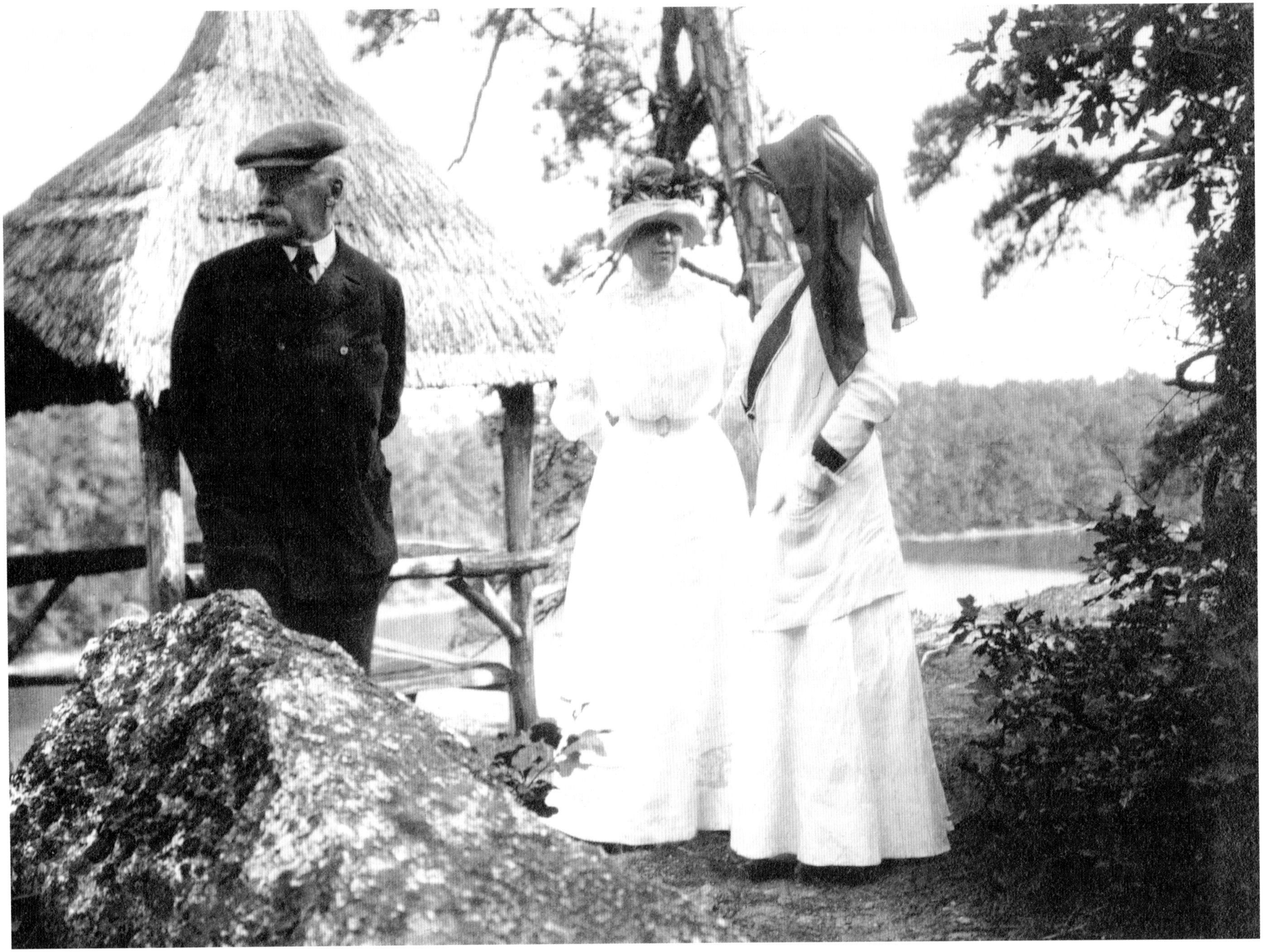

OPPOSITE Mr. and Mrs. Stephen Henry Olin with Alice on one of the walks at the Mohonk Mountain House in the summer of 1910. The resort, located along the Shawangunk Ridge near New Paltz, New York, was built by twin brothers, Albert and Alfred Smiley, between 1869 and 1910. A popular year-round destination, the resort hosted such famous visitors as John D. Rockefeller, John Burroughs, Andrew Carnegie, Theodore Roosevelt, and Rutherford B. Hayes. The property has been owned and operated by descendants of the Smiley Brothers since 1869.

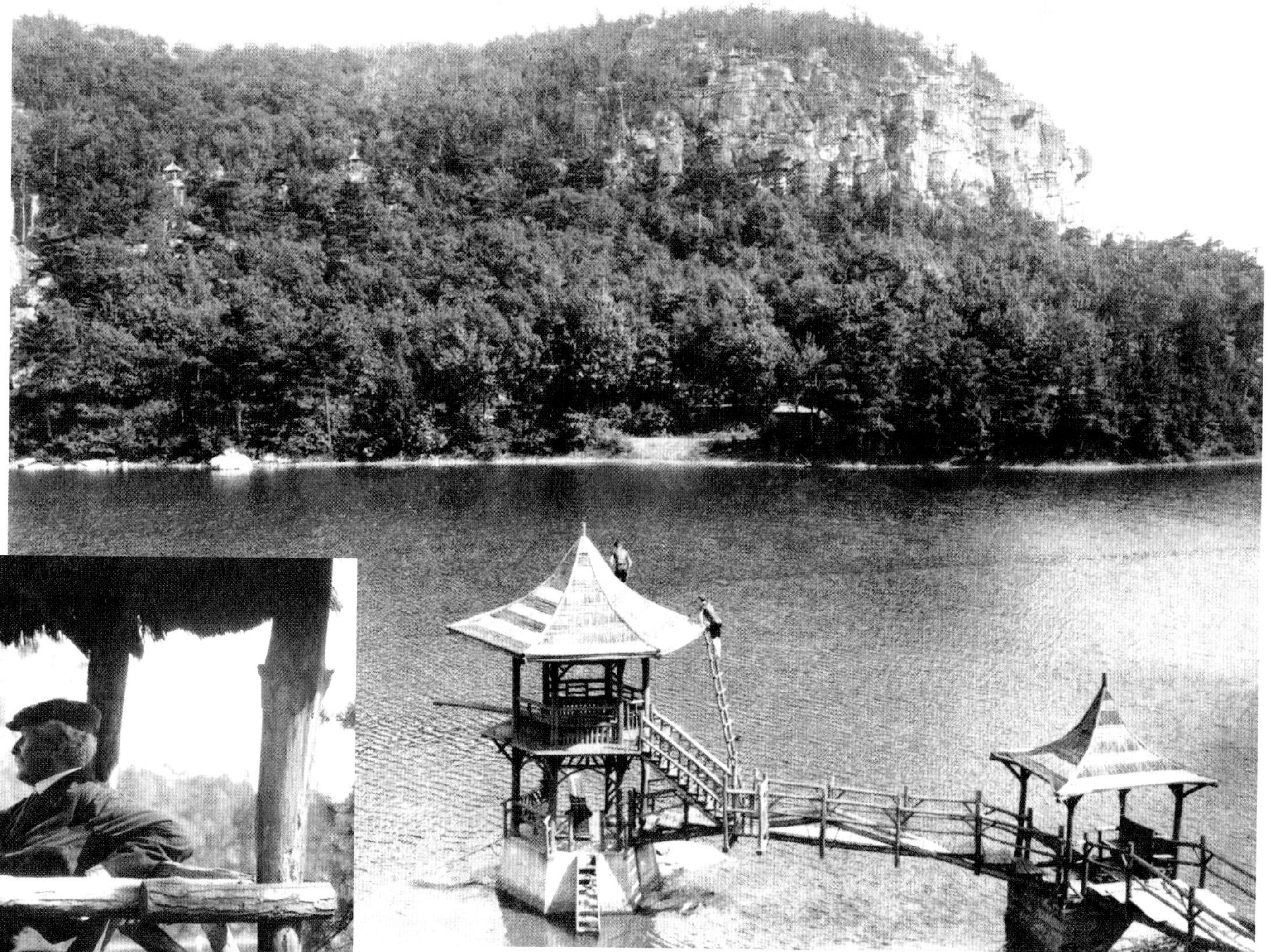

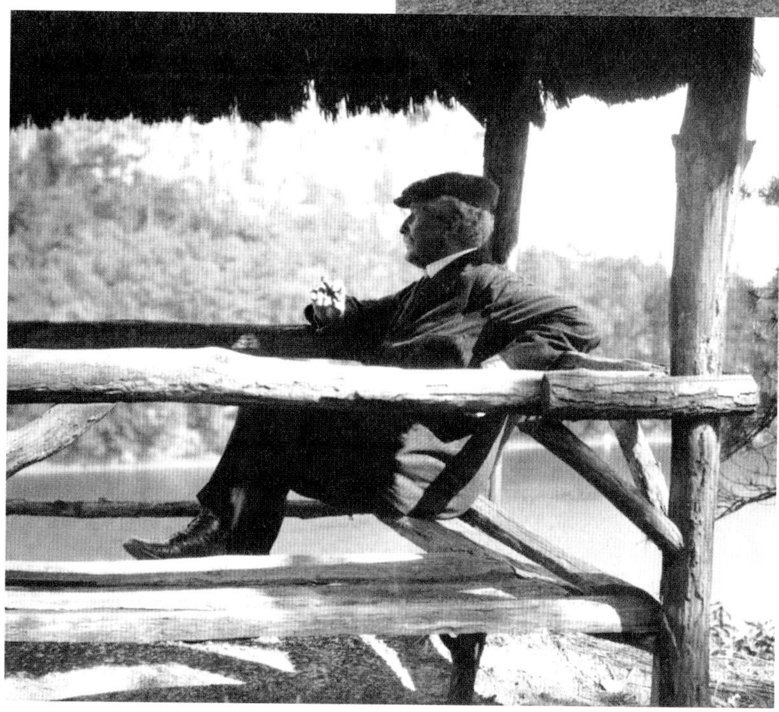

ABOVE Swimmers climbing onto the tower and diving into Lake Mohonk.

LEFT Stephen Henry Olin relaxing in a thatched gazebo.

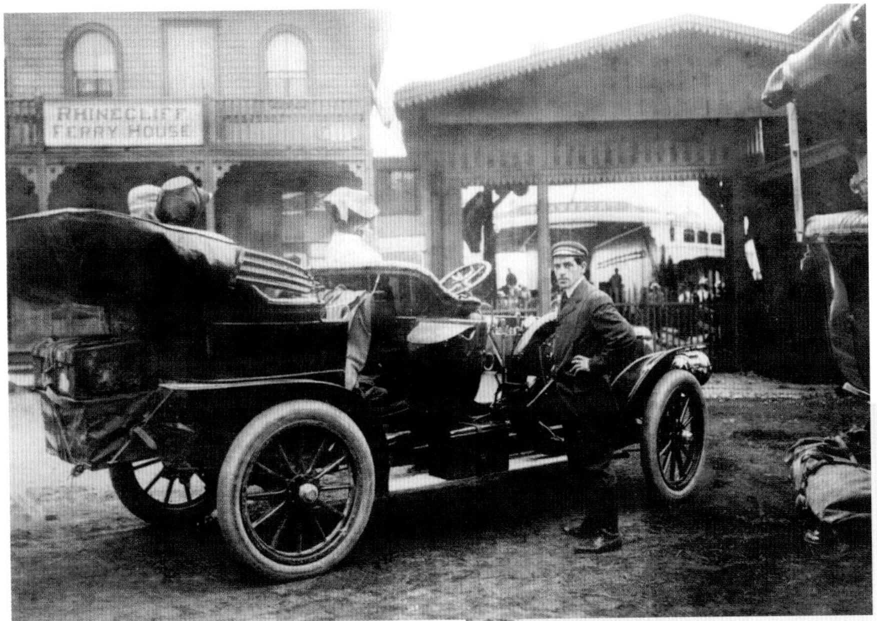

ABOVE The chauffeur with the Dowses and Olins at the Rhinecliff Ferry House, 1915, as they prepared to travel by ferry across the Hudson River to Kingston to begin a motor trip to the Catskill Mountain House. They drove to the Otis Elevating Railway in Palenville, where a funicular car transported them up a steep incline to the resort. In earlier days, before the railway was built, it could take visitors up to six hours to travel there by stagecoach on treacherous roads.

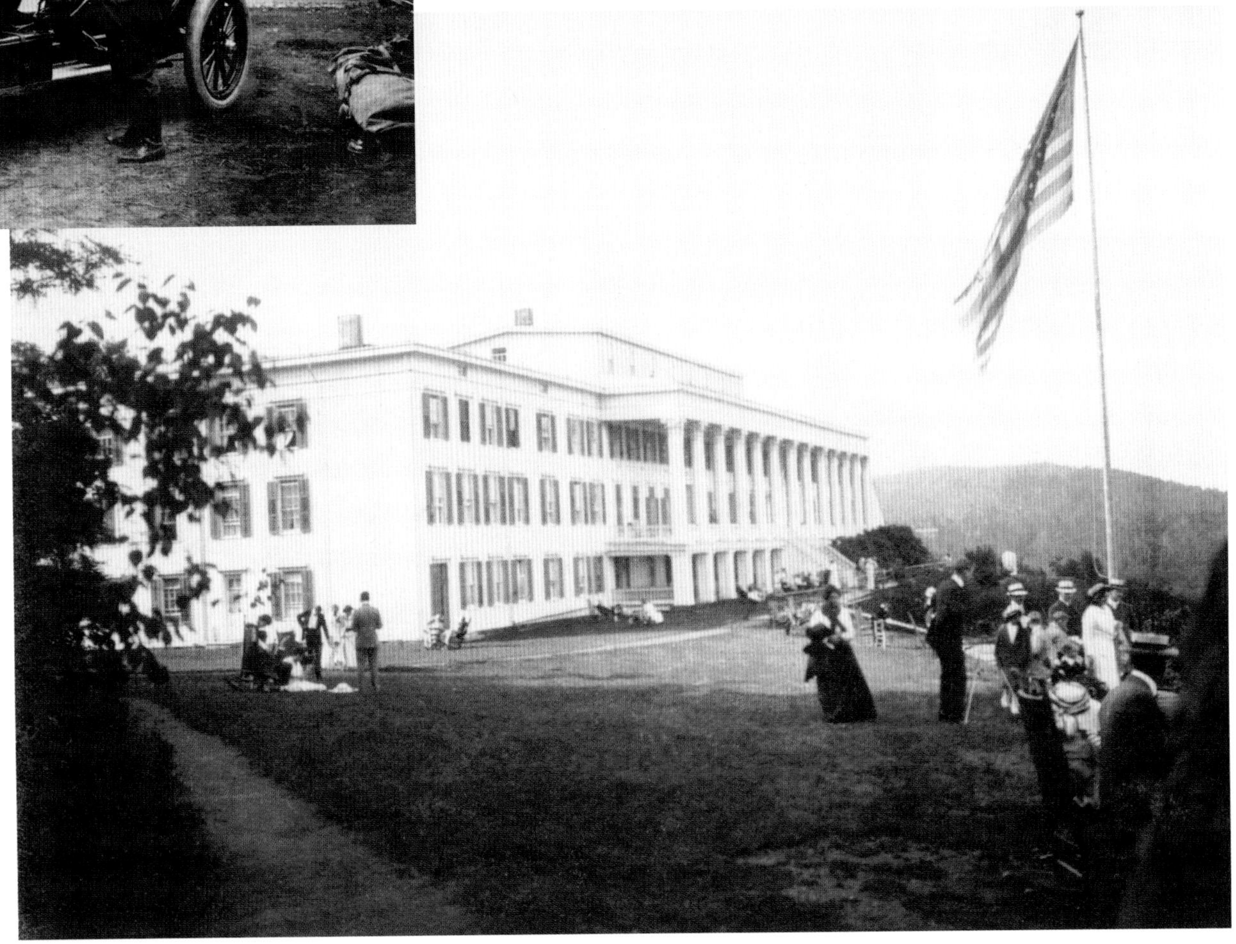

RIGHT The Catskill Mountain House in 1915. Opening in 1824, it became America's first mountain resort. In 1839, it was rebuilt in the Neoclassical style with a columned façade. Known for its dramatic views of the river and surrounding valleys, it was a popular destination for cultivated travelers. After many years the resort faded in popularity and was purchased by the State of New York in 1962. Due to its dilapidated condition, it was burned to the ground by the Conservation Department in 1963.

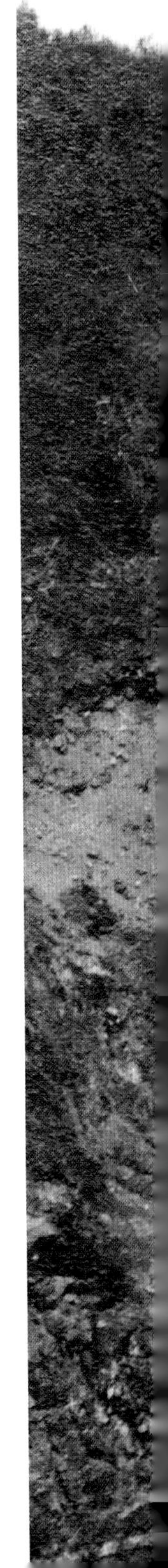

RIGHT The New Croton Dam in 1912. The dam, part of the New York City water supply system, stretches across the Croton River near Croton-on-Hudson, about twenty-two miles north of New York City. Construction began in 1892 and was completed in 1906. At the time of its completion it was the tallest dam in the world and much admired for its scale and elegant design.

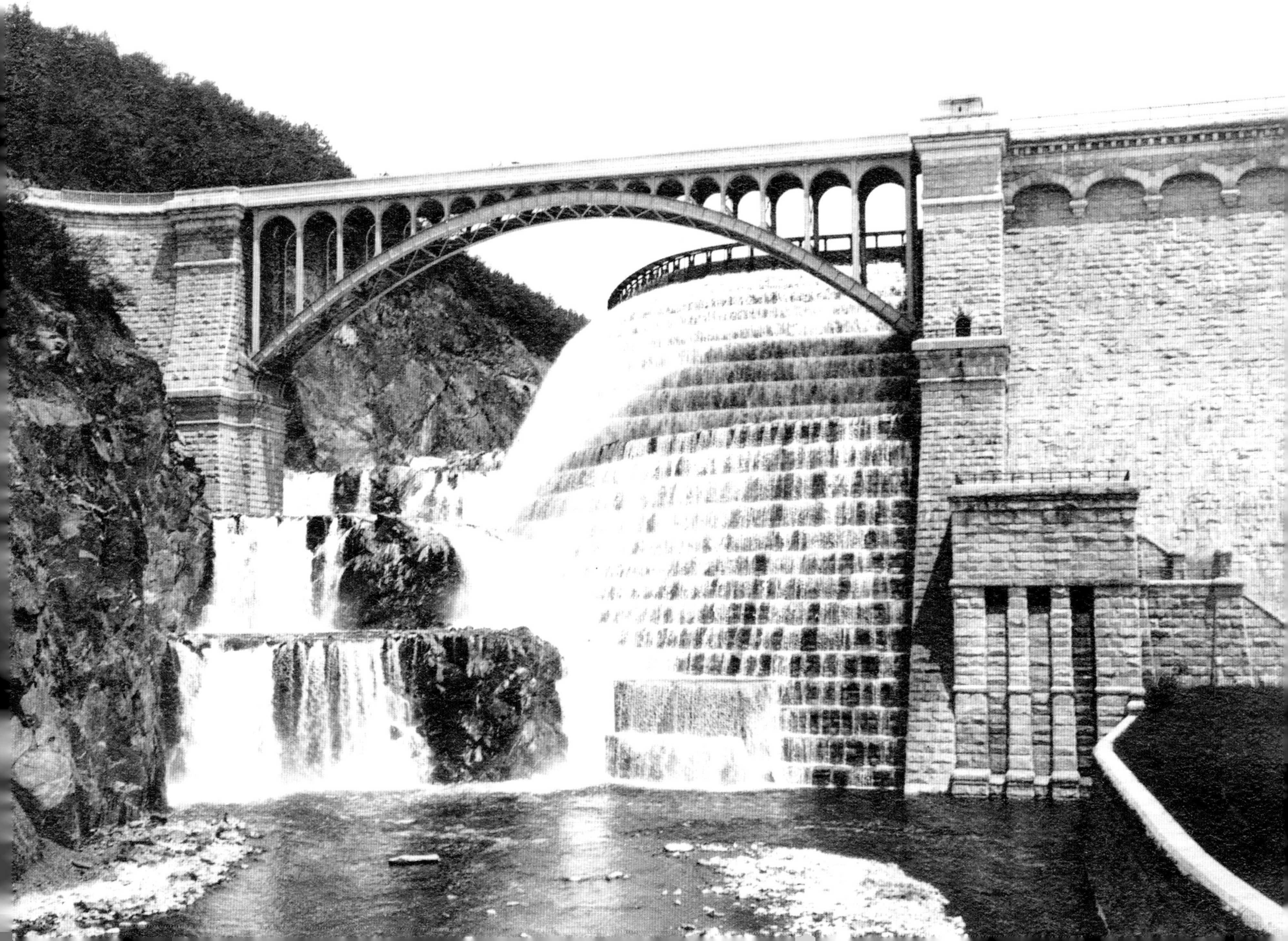

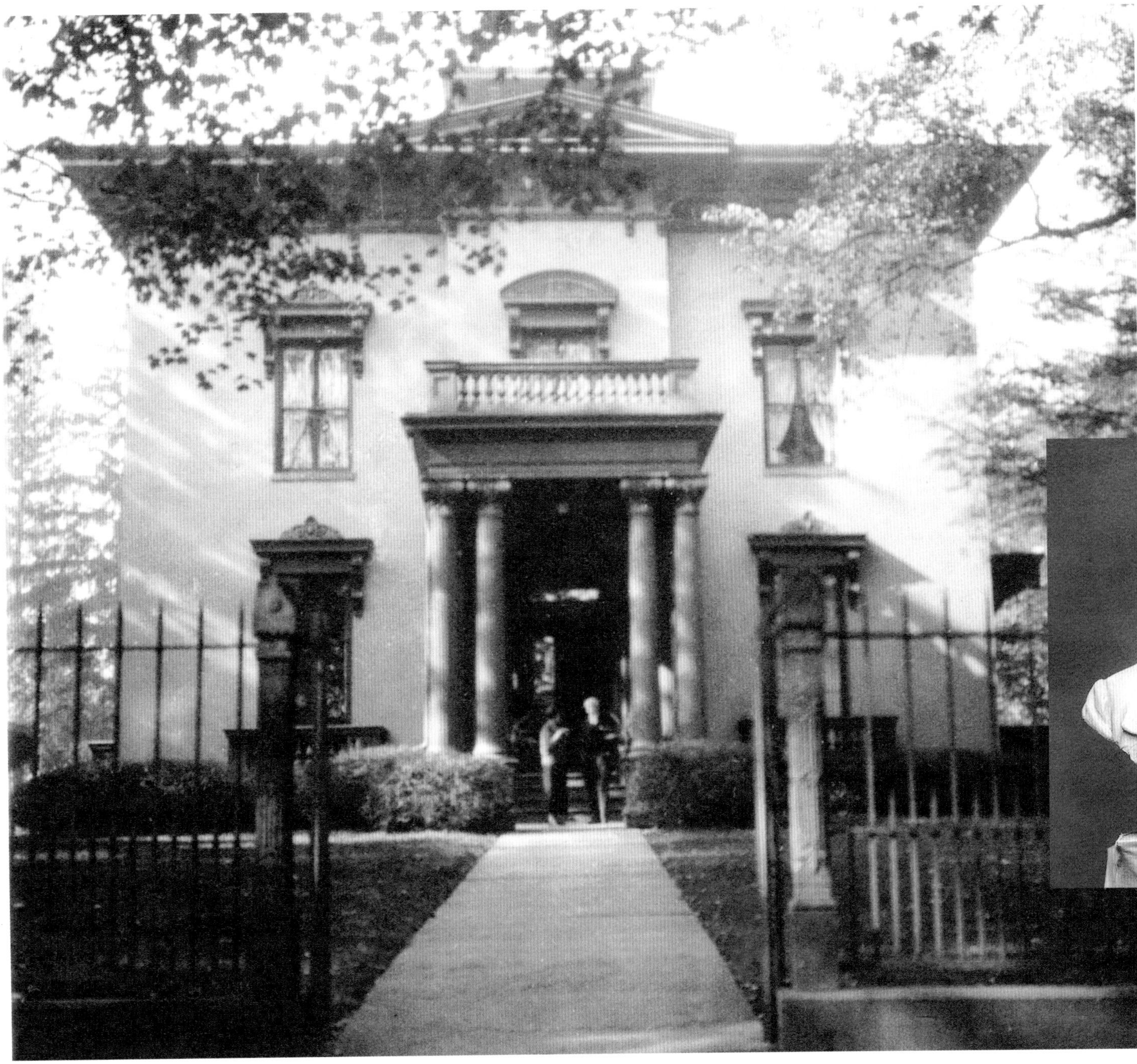

LEFT The president's house on the campus of Wesleyan University in Middletown, Connecticut, 1922. Tracy, Alice, and the Olins took a motor trip to visit the college, from which Stephen Henry Olin had graduated in 1866. Mr. Olin's father, Reverend Stephen Olin, was president of the college from 1842 to 1851.

BELOW The plaster model Henry Hering used to design the bronze bust of Reverend Stephen Olin in 1925, which is installed in the Olin Memorial Library.

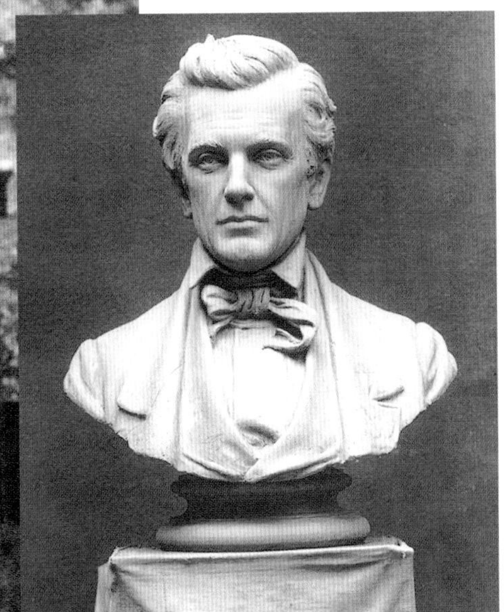

OPPOSITE Alice with her father on the steps of the president's house. He was acting president from 1922 to 1923 and used the house as his residence when visiting the university.

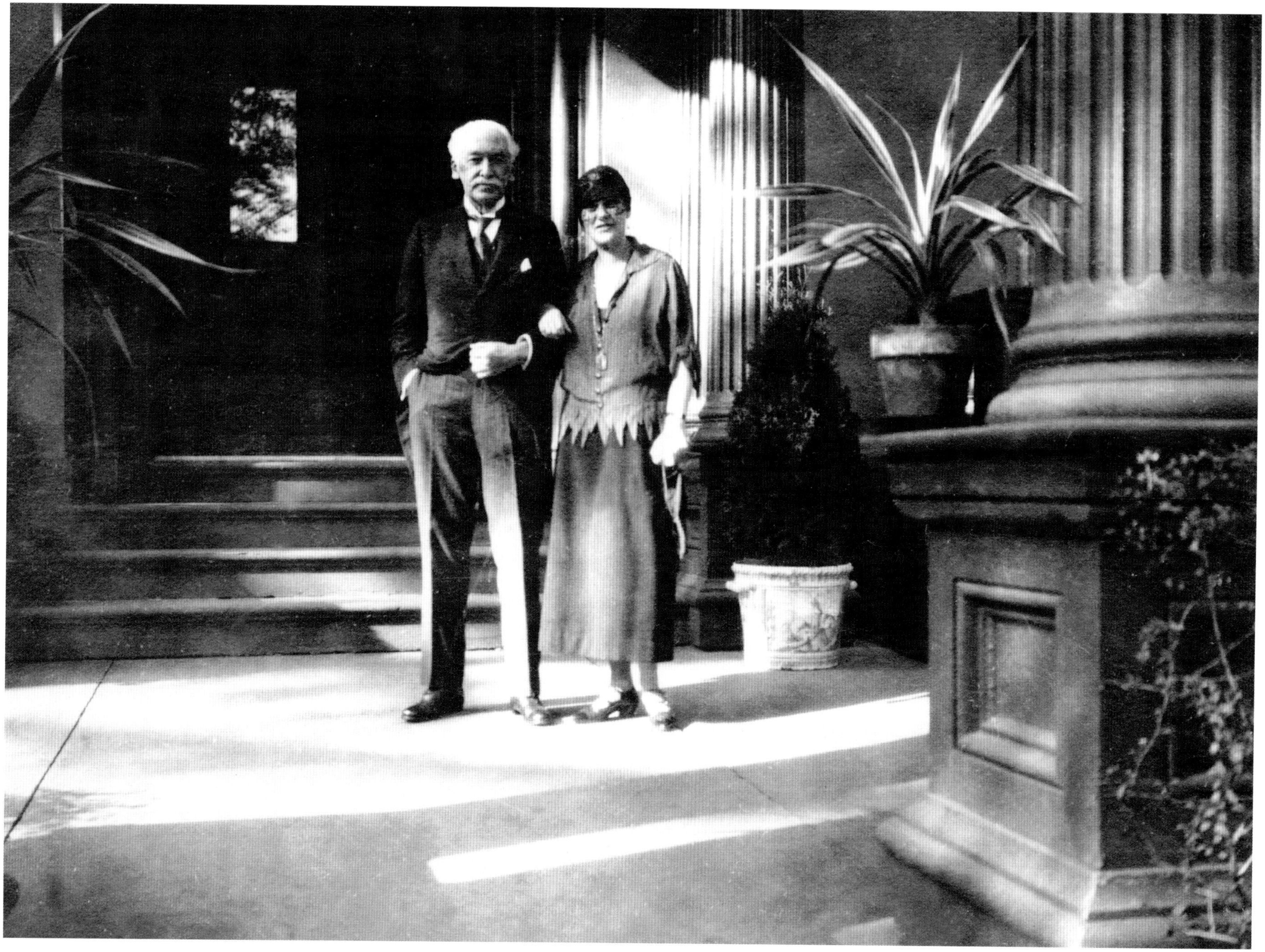

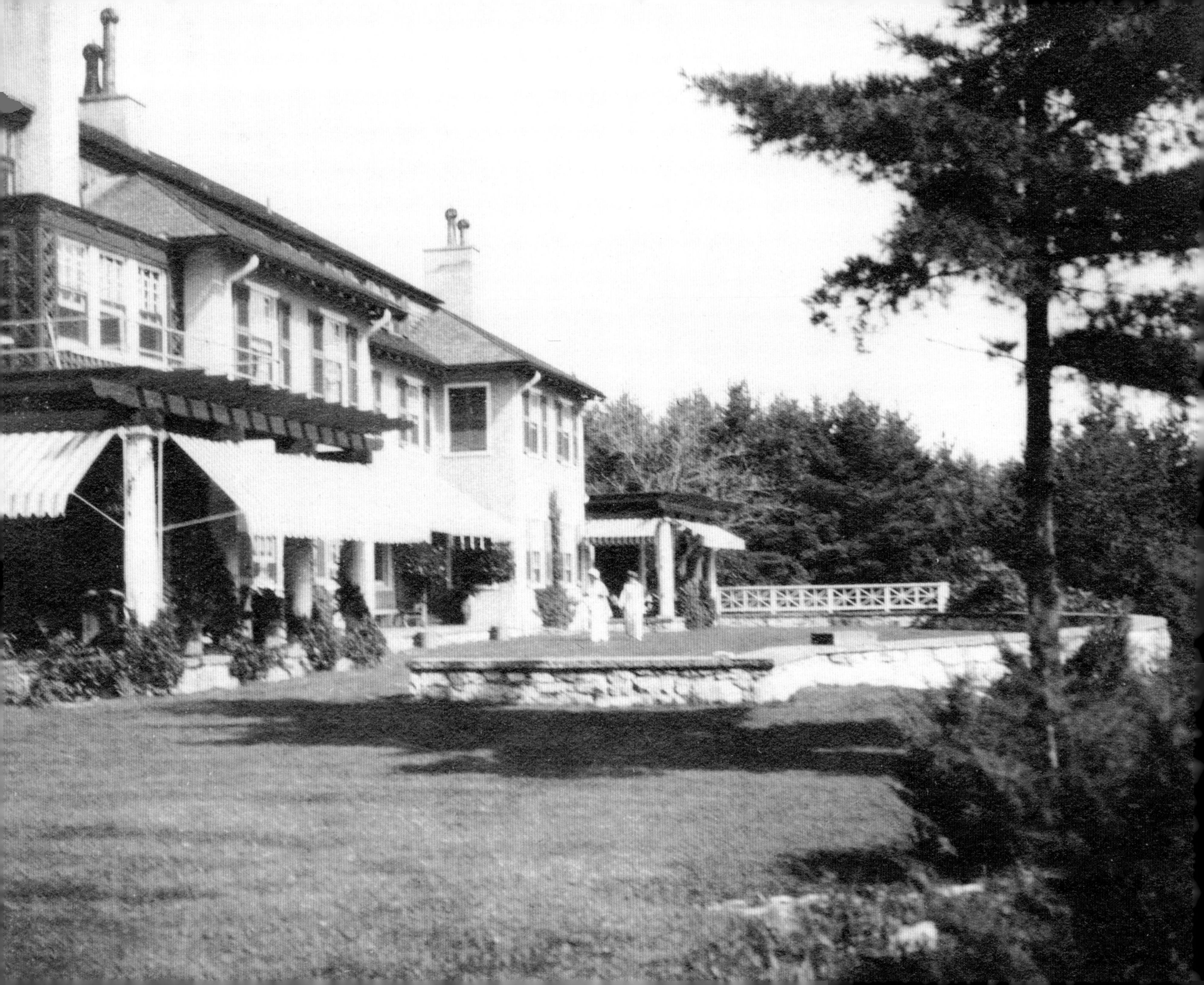

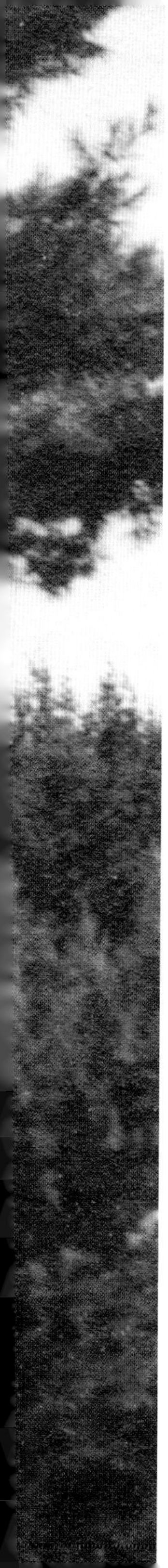

LEFT Pine Needles, the Berkshire cottage of George Baty Blake, in 1912, when the Dowses were visiting. The house was designed by Henry Forbes Bigelow in 1903. Built deep into a forest of pines and hemlock, it had a hillside swimming pool known for its frigid water. George's brothers were Frank Blake (Tracy's good friend) and John Avery Lowell Blake. The Blake brothers were from a prominent Boston family.

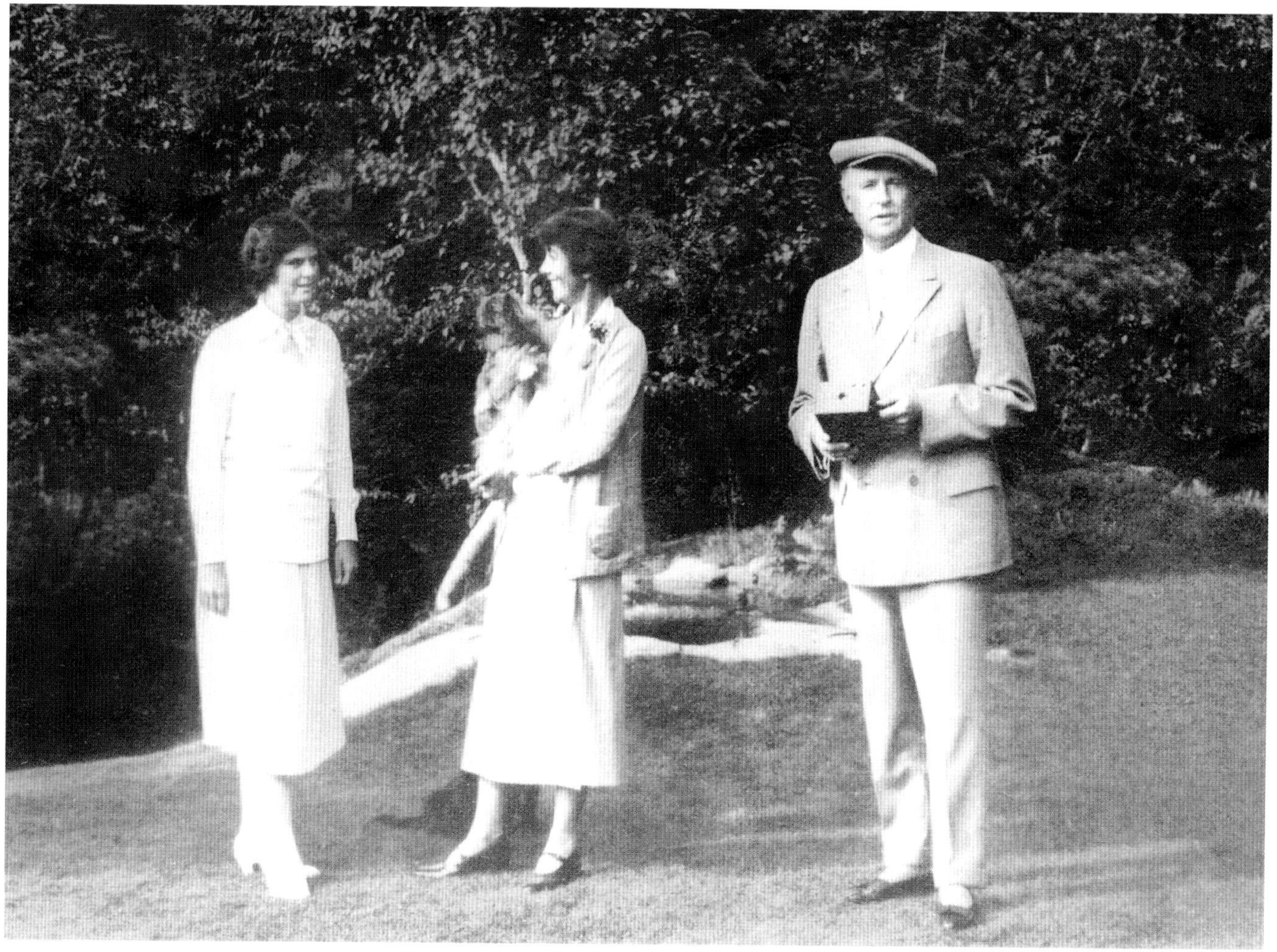

ABOVE Mr. and Mrs. George Baty Blake, with their daughter Margaret, in 1925. Since George suffered from tuberculosis, the Blakes lived at Pine Needles year round so that he could benefit from the mountain air. Margaret became a professional tennis player in the late 1920s. George died in 1928, and his wife, also named Margaret, continued to spend summers at Pine Needles until the late 1960s.

BELOW In 1911, Tracy and Alice were guests at Allanbank, the country home of Bryce J. Allan, in Beverly, Massachusetts. It was designed in 1905 by Guy Lowell, architect of the Boston Museum of Fine Arts. Today the estate functions as Tupper Manor, part of Endicott College.

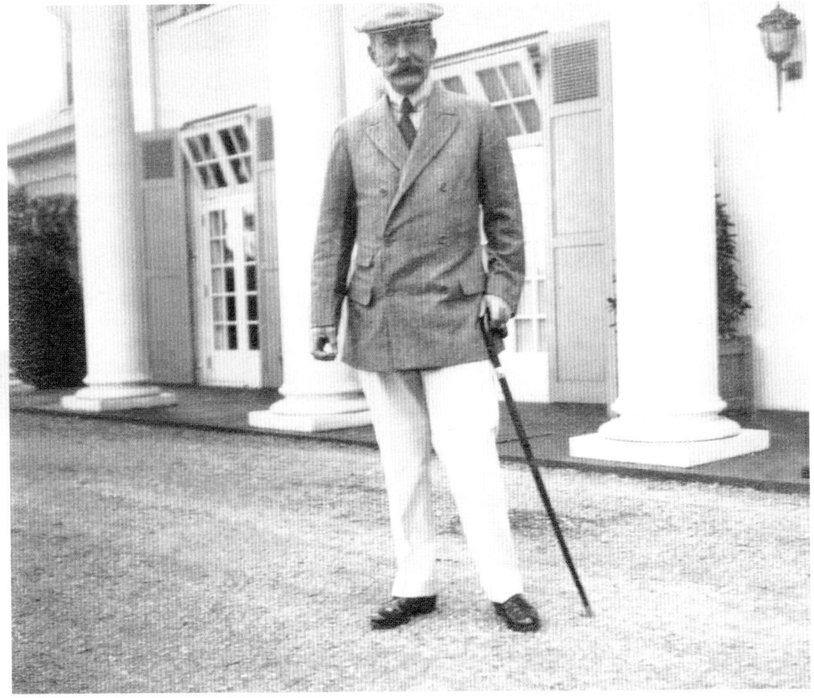

ABOVE Bryce J. Allan at Foxhollow Farm, 1911. He was the son of Sir Hugh Allan, founder and president of the Montreal Ocean Steamship Company (known as the Allan Line) and at one time the wealthiest man in Canada. Allan represented his father's business in Boston.

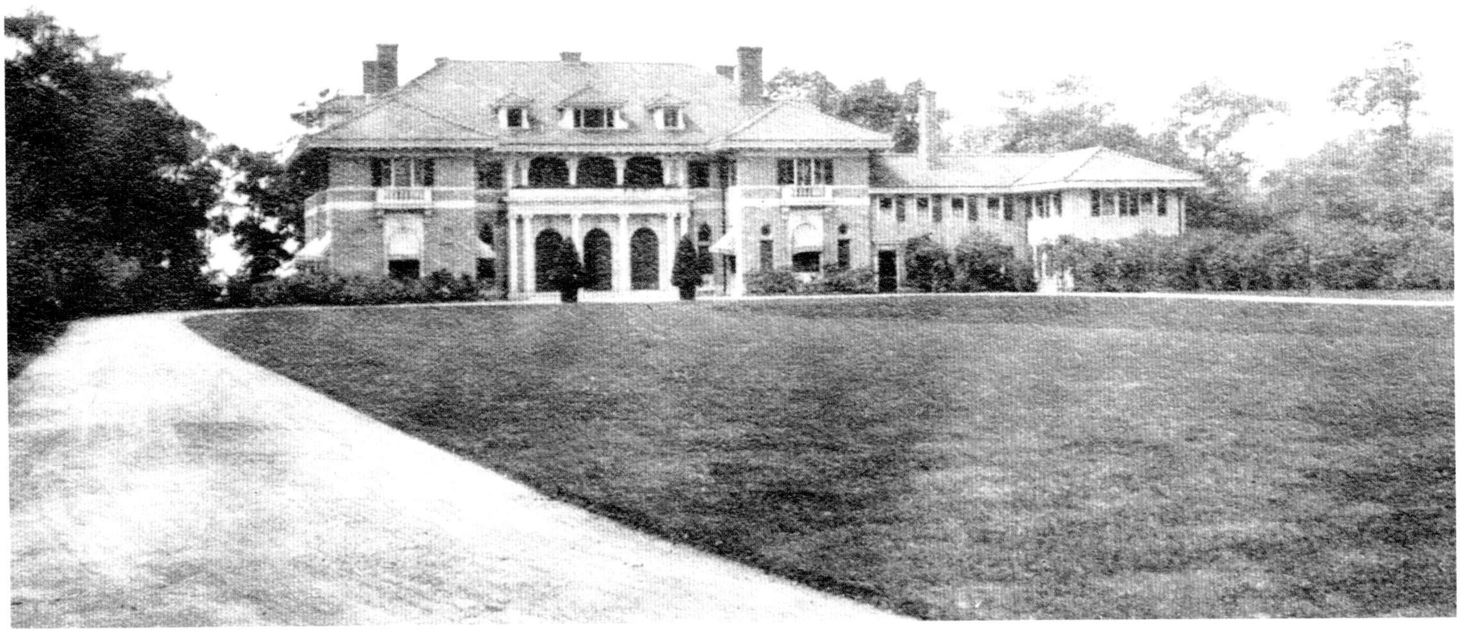

OPPOSITE A 1922 photograph of Margaret Dows at the Henry Wadsworth Longfellow Memorial in Cambridge, Massachusetts. The monument was designed by Daniel Chester French in 1913. The family was visiting Olin, who was attending Harvard College.

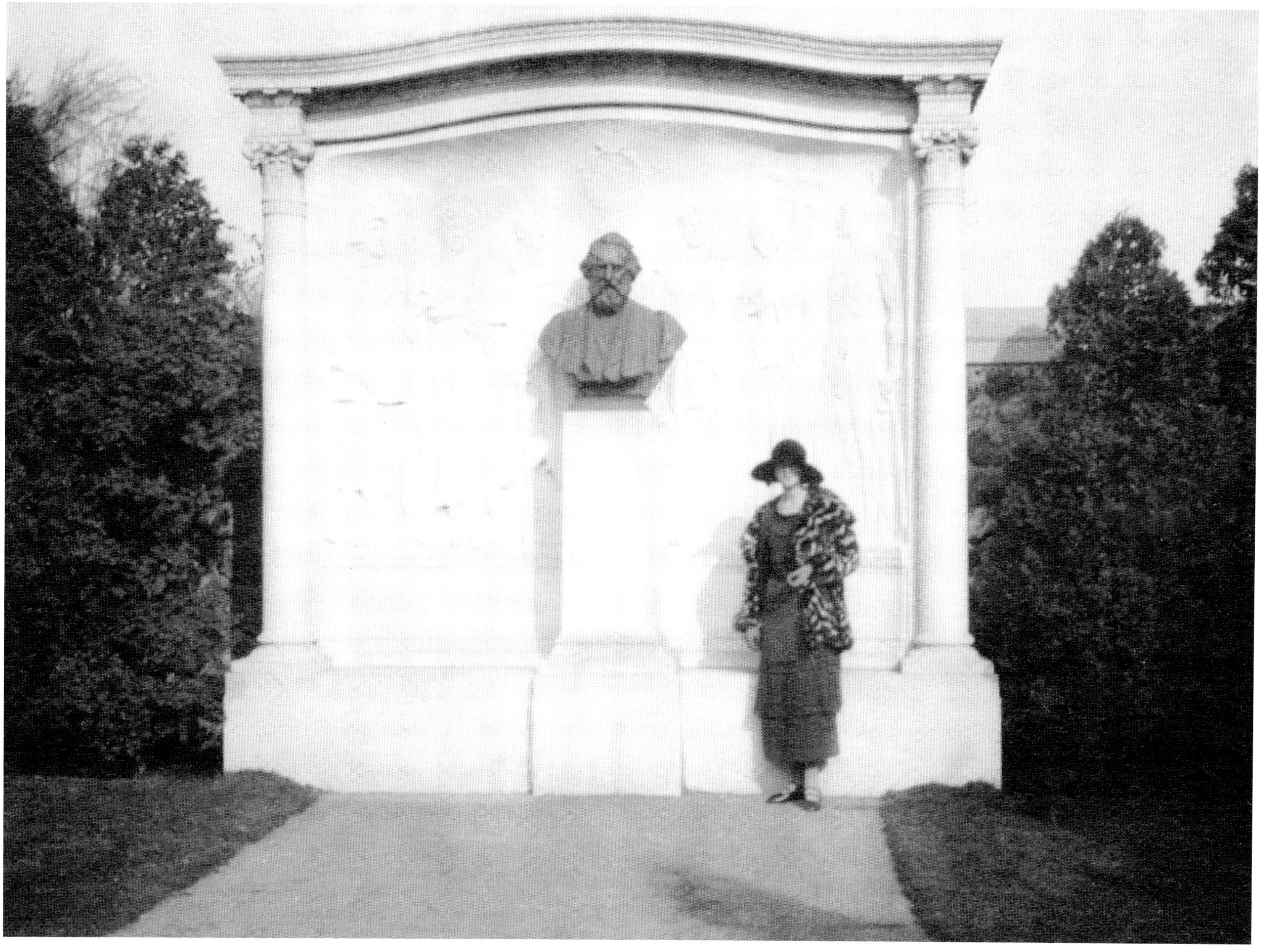

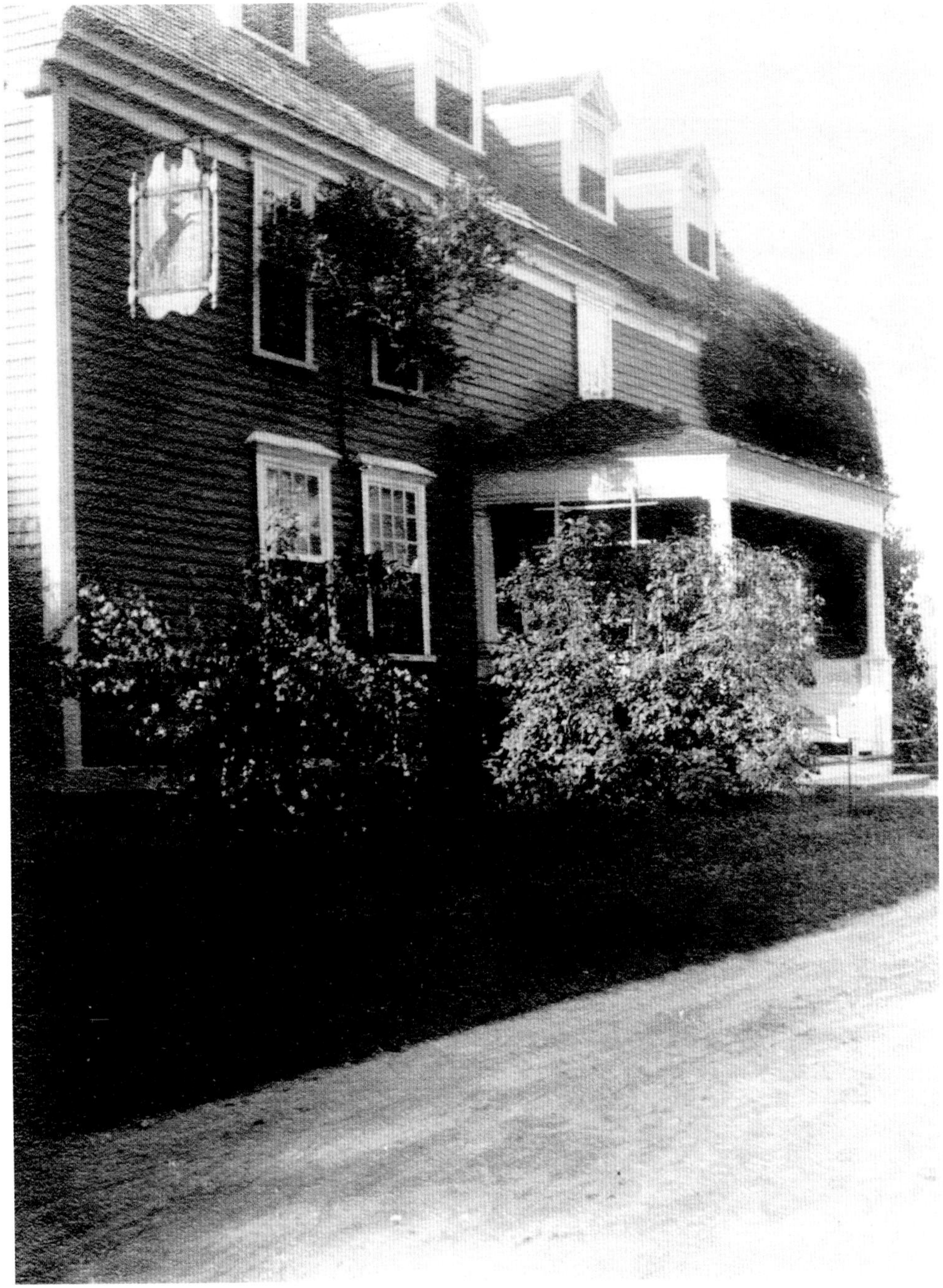

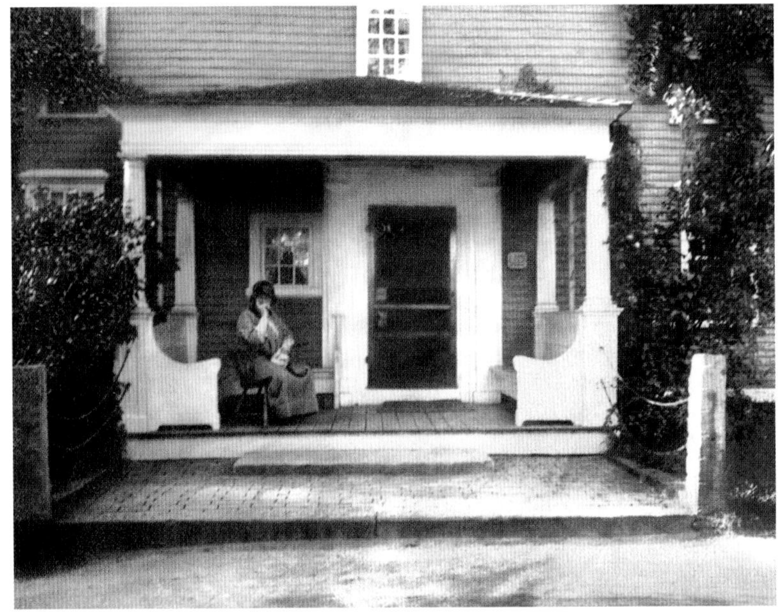

ABOVE AND LEFT Alice on the porch of the historic Wayside Inn in Sudbury, Massachusetts. The family stopped for lunch at the inn while on a motor trip to Boston in 1911. Twelve years later the inn was purchased by Henry Ford, who transformed it into a living museum of American history.

OPPOSITE In 1912 the Dowses and the Olins traveled to Vermont and stayed at the Equinox Hotel, which dates back to the late 1700s, in Manchester Village. During its long history, the Equinox hosted an array of notable guests, including presidents William Howard Taft, Ulysses S. Grant, Theodore Roosevelt (who gave a campaign speech there), and Benjamin Harrison. Mary Todd Lincoln was also a frequent guest with her sons.

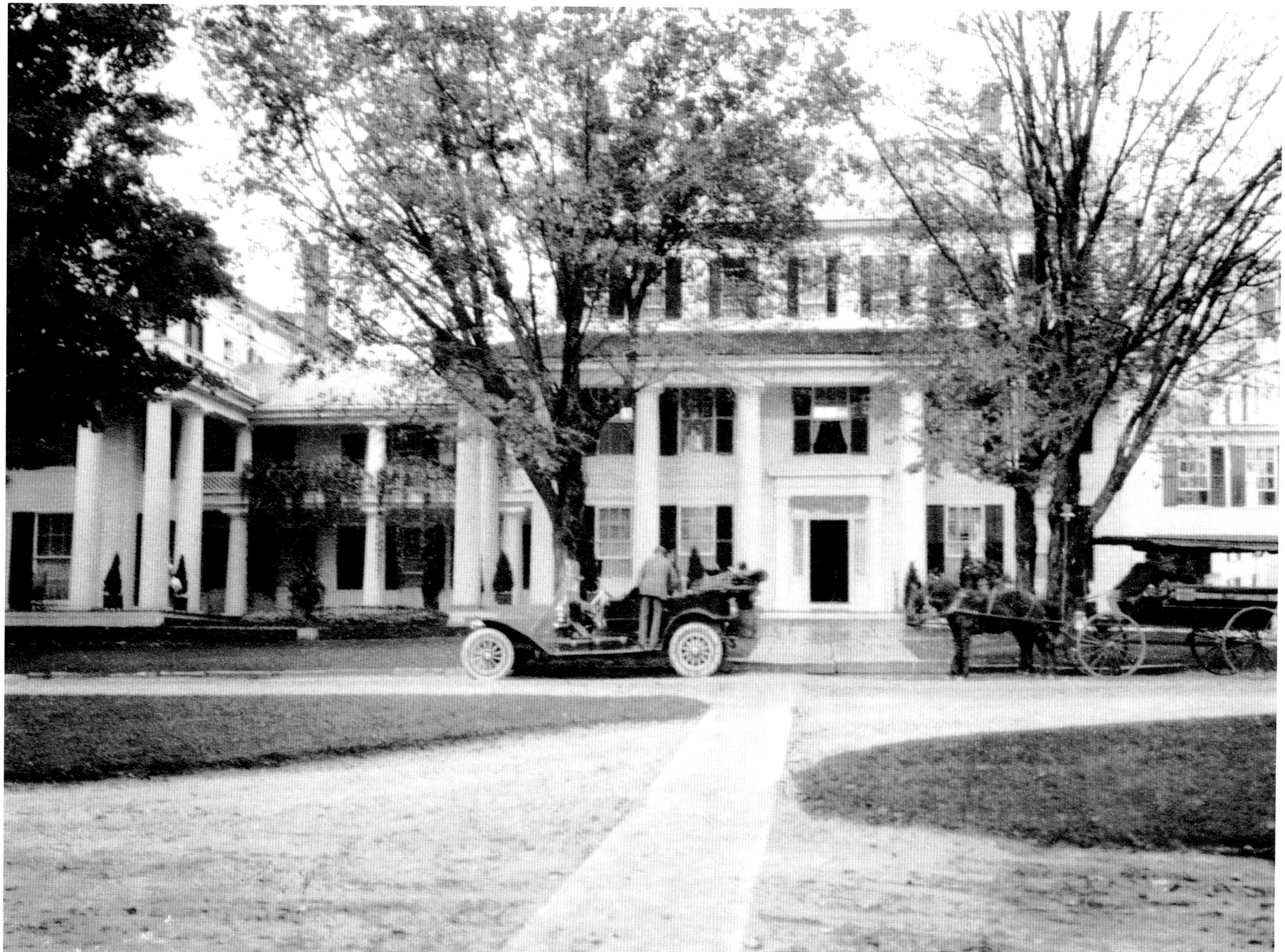

RIGHT The Homestead, in Hot Springs, Virginia, where the family spent a few months in the spring of 1908. The Dowses visited several times during the early years of living at Foxhollow Farm. The resort began as a eighteen-room wooden hotel built in 1766. In 1832 Dr. Thomas Goode purchased the hotel and developed what was then known as "The Cure," which consisted of a salt scrub and shower. In the 1880s, a group of prominent businessmen, including J. P. Morgan, bought the hotel, investing more than $1 million in improvements. More renovation occurred after a devastating fire in 1901. The resort was a popular destination for prominent Americans seeking to rejuvenate themselves.

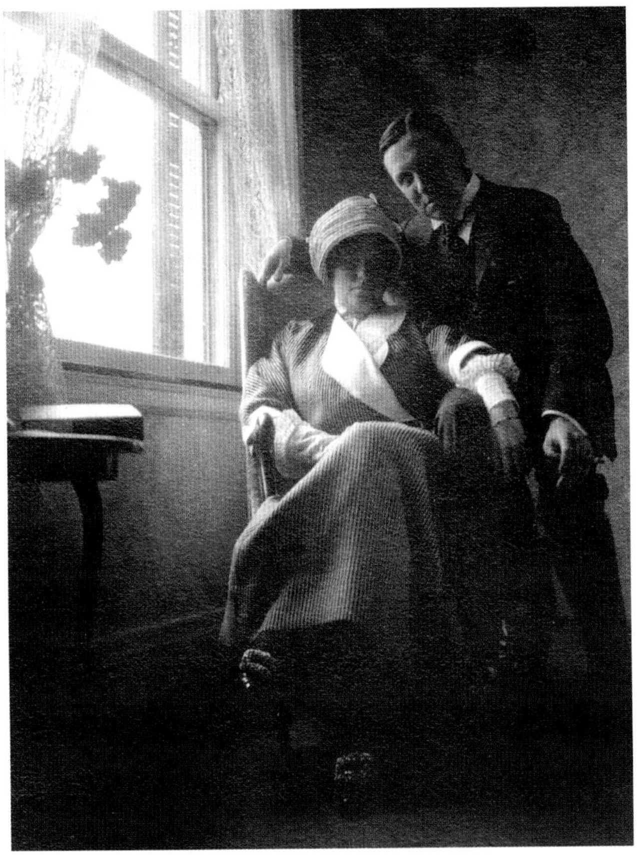

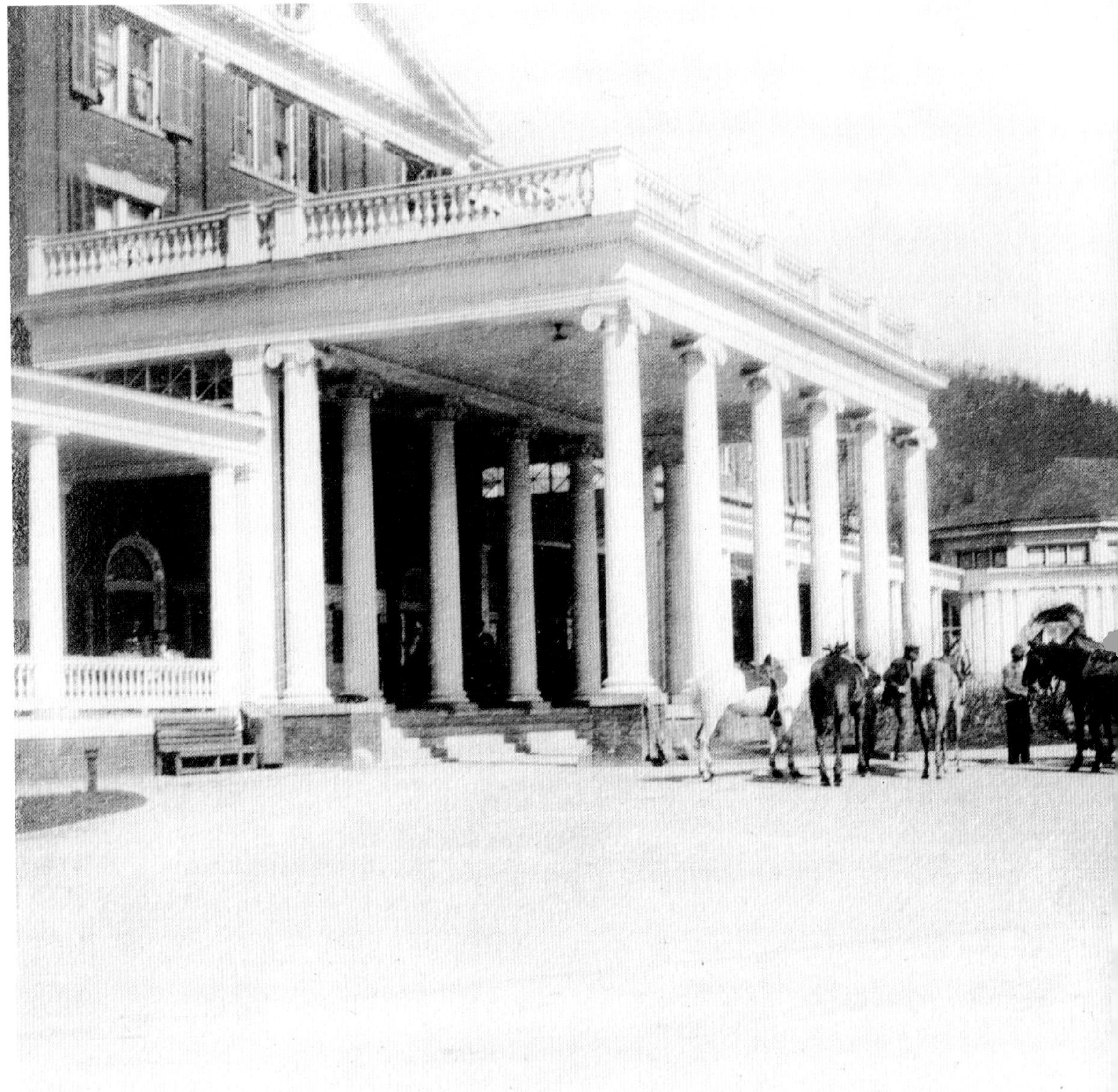

LEFT Alice and Tracy at The Homestead, March 1911. Harrie T. Lindeberg joined them on the trip.

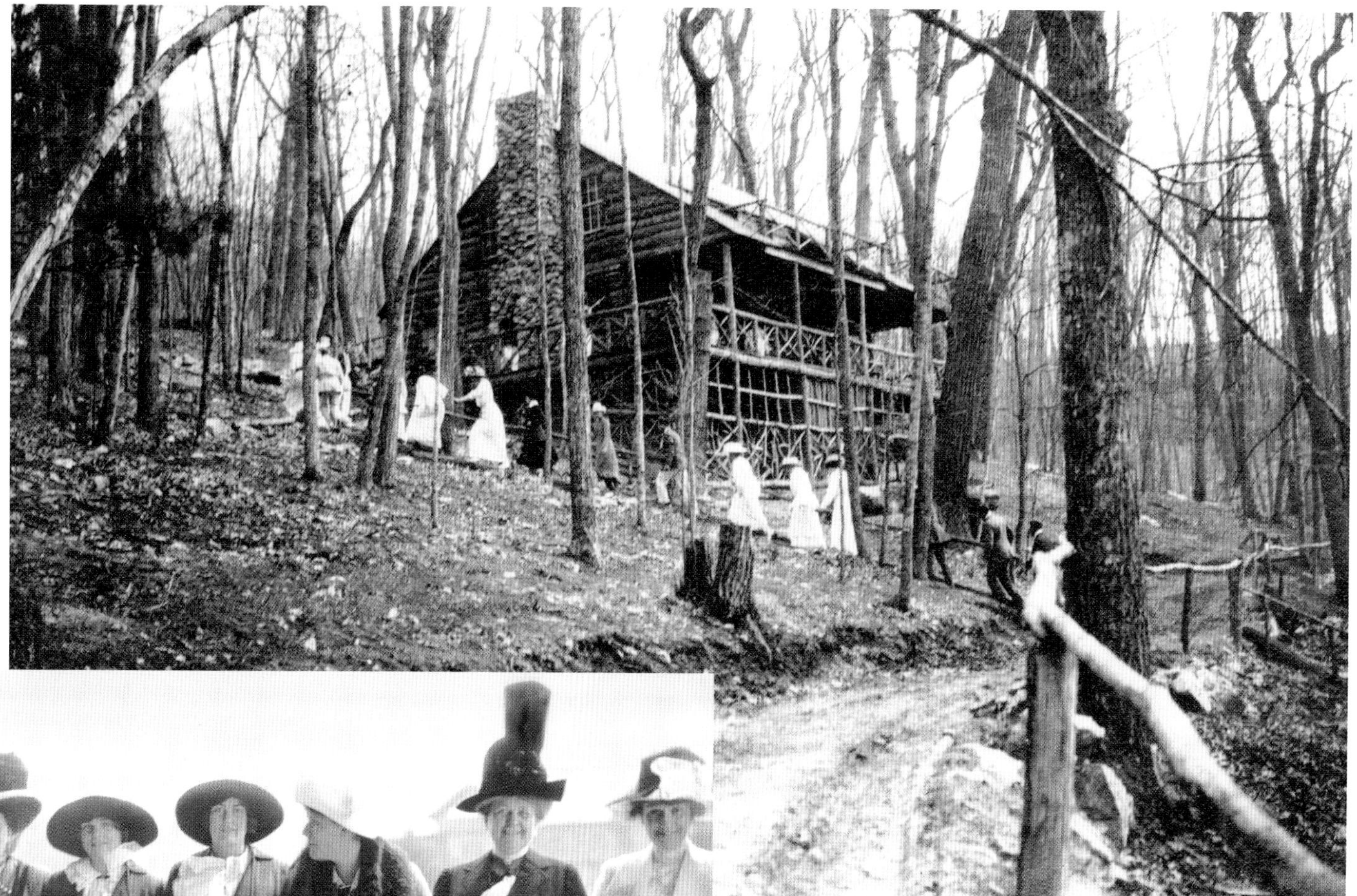

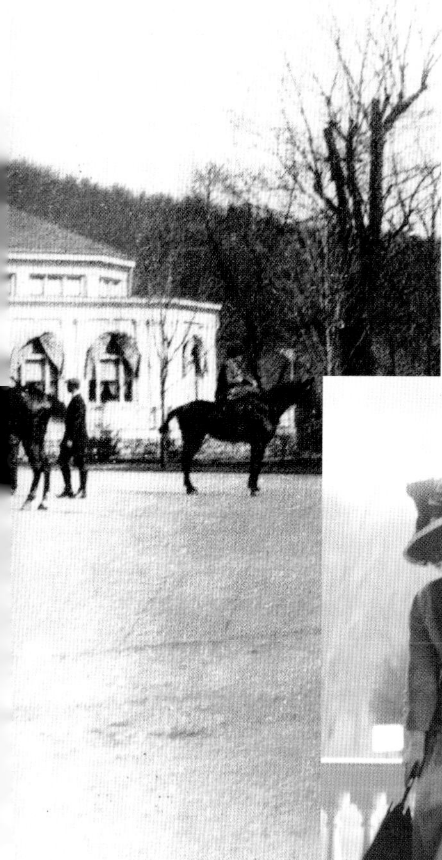

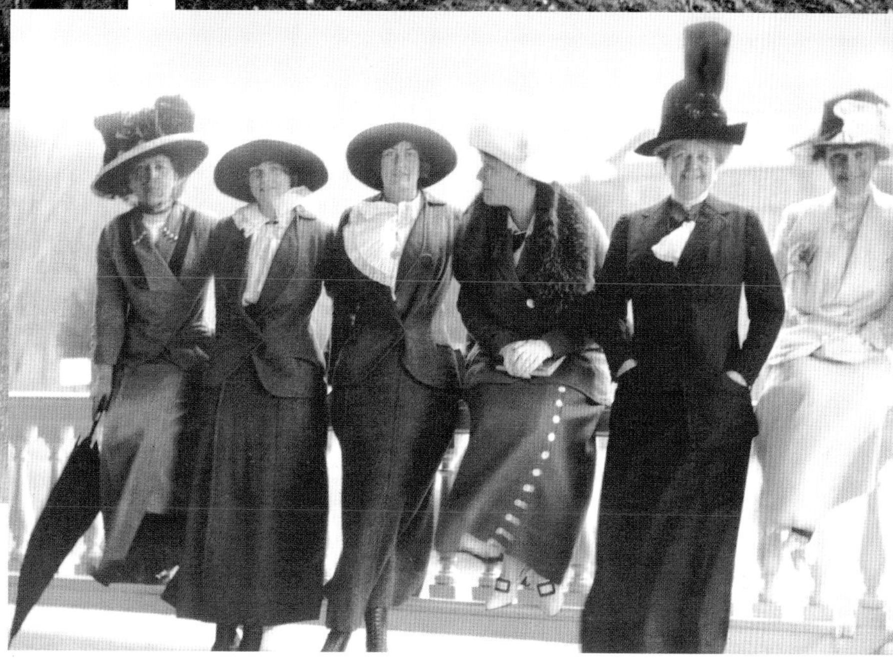

ABOVE While staying at The Homestead in 1912, Tracy and Alice joined a group of friends who toured a historic cabin in Virginia.

LEFT The fashionable women of New York society posing for a photograph at the resort that same year. Mrs. Stephen Olin is second from the right, next to Alice, third from the right.

BELOW In October 1919, Tracy took the family on a one-month motor trip, hiring a chauffeur to drive them from Colorado to California. They stayed at the Broadmoor Hotel in Colorado Springs, built by the entrepreneur and venture capitalist Spencer Penrose, which had been open for only a year. Master golf-course architect Donald Ross designed the resort's first course, and the hotel's indoor swimming pool was the largest in the West when it opened. The Dowses visited Lookout Mountain in Denver, designed by the Olmsted Brothers, and Garden of the Gods in Colorado Springs, the ancient sedimentary rock formations that were discovered around 1859 by land surveyors.

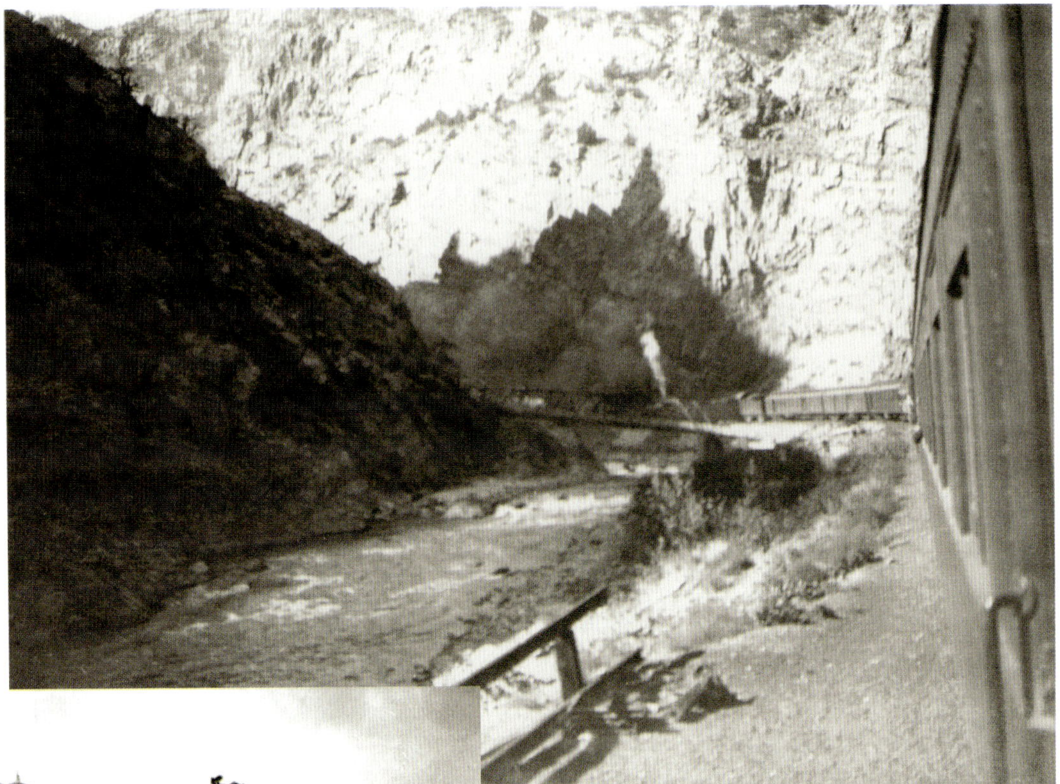

LEFT Tracy leaned out of the window to take this photograph while aboard the Denver & Rio Grande Western Railroad. The family took the scenic train ride with its breathtaking views and narrow passageways as it traveled along the Arkansas River while passing through the famous Royal Gorge.

OPPOSITE On their journey from San Francisco to Los Angeles, the Dowses stayed at El Mirasol in Santa Barbara. The house was designed in 1905 by Delano & Aldrich for Mary Miles Herter, the widow of Christian Augustus Ludwig Herter, of the famous Herter Brothers design company. Frank Lloyd Wright proclaimed that its Cactus Room had the most beautiful wall covering in the world. In 1913 it passed on to Mary Miles' son, Albert Herter and his wife, Adele, both artists, who turned the residence into a hotel. Tracy's sister, Susan, was once married to Christian Archibald Herter, Albert's brother.

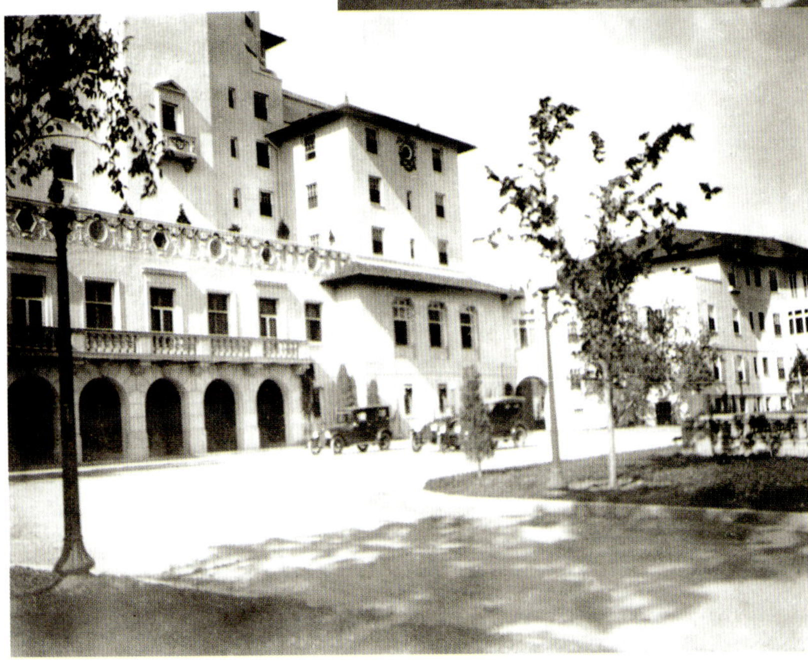

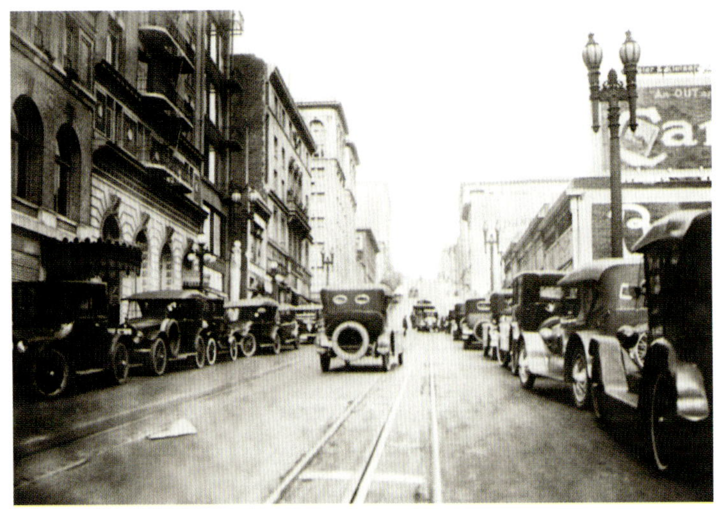

LEFT A view of busy Powell Street in San Francisco.

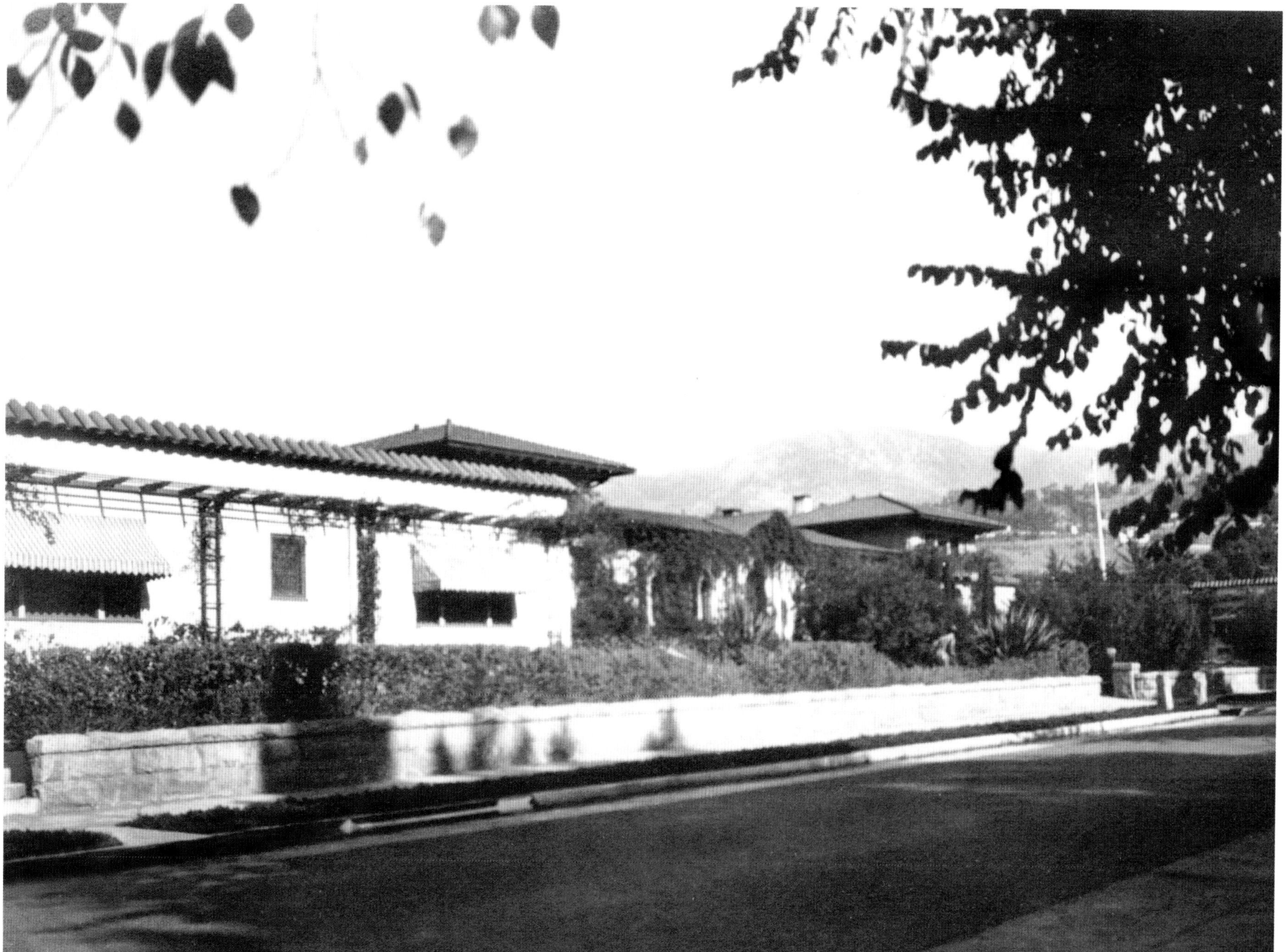

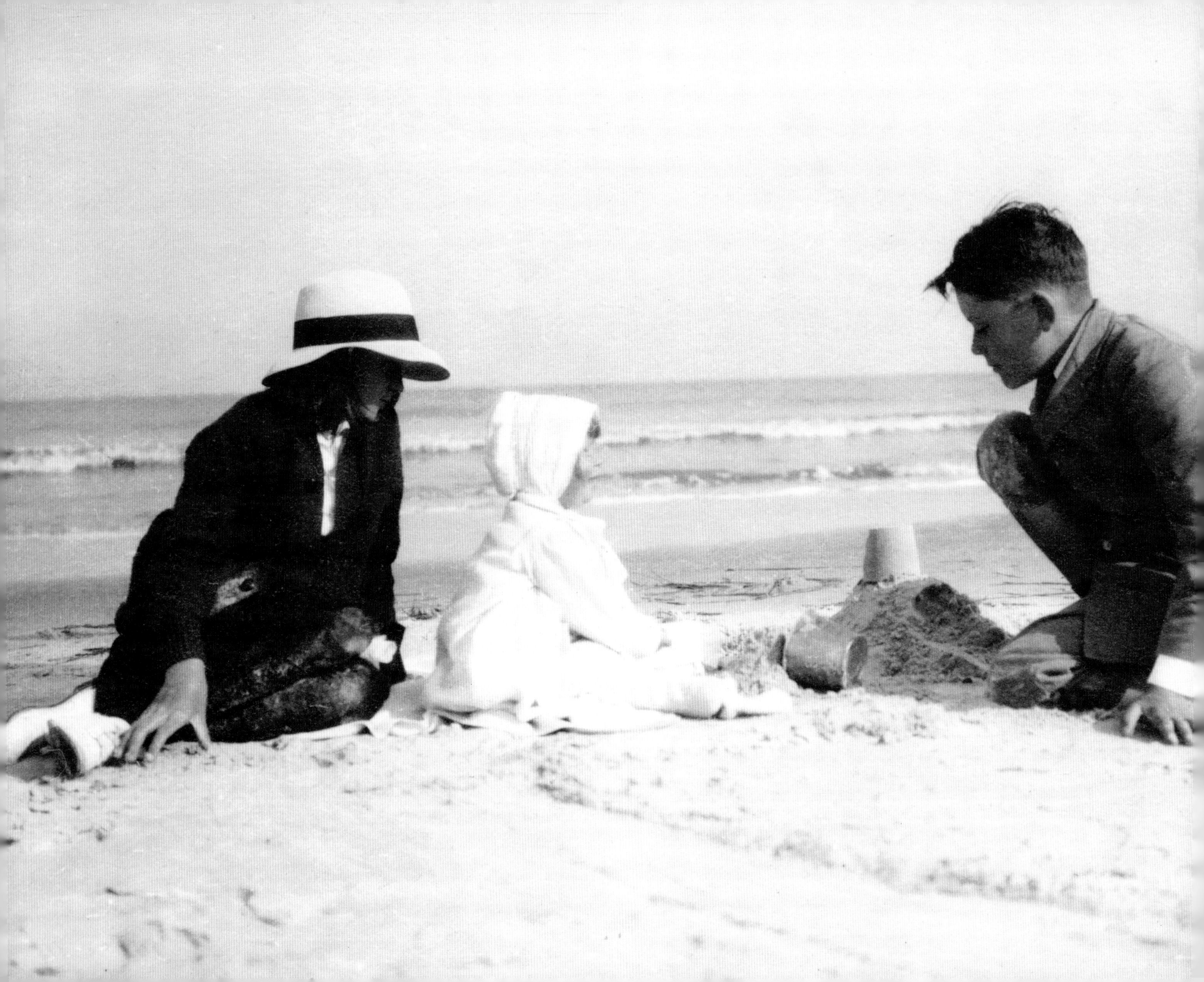

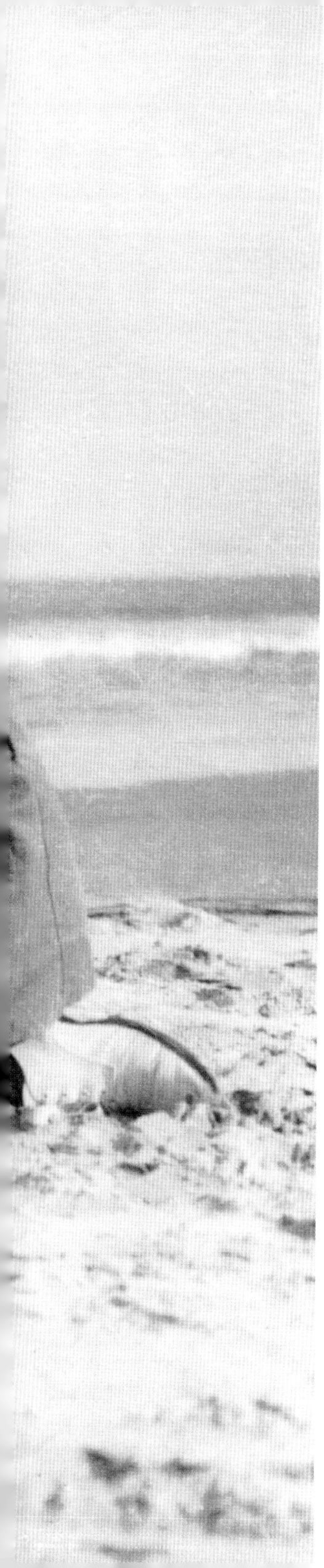

CHAPTER EIGHT

JEKYLL ISLAND and SEAL HARBOR

PREVIOUS PAGES A well-dressed Margaret, Deb, and Olin building a sand castle on the beach at Jekyll Island in 1916.

RIGHT The Jekyll Island Club as seen in 1916 when the Dowses were staying from January to March. Located off the coast of Brunswick, Georgia, it was once called the Island of 100 Millionaires, as its club was limited to just one hundred members. Tracy Dows was one of those members. By 1904, it was considered the most exclusive and inaccessible club in the world. The island was named after Sir Joseph Jekyll soon after the founding of Georgia in the 1730s. It was spelled "Jekyl" until 1929 when the Georgia State Legislature corrected the spelling to "Jekyll." The club first opened on January 1, 1888. The club house was designed by architect Charles A. Alexander and the grounds by Frederick Law Olmsted. The property remains a popular resort today, and some of its historic cottages are part of the hotel.

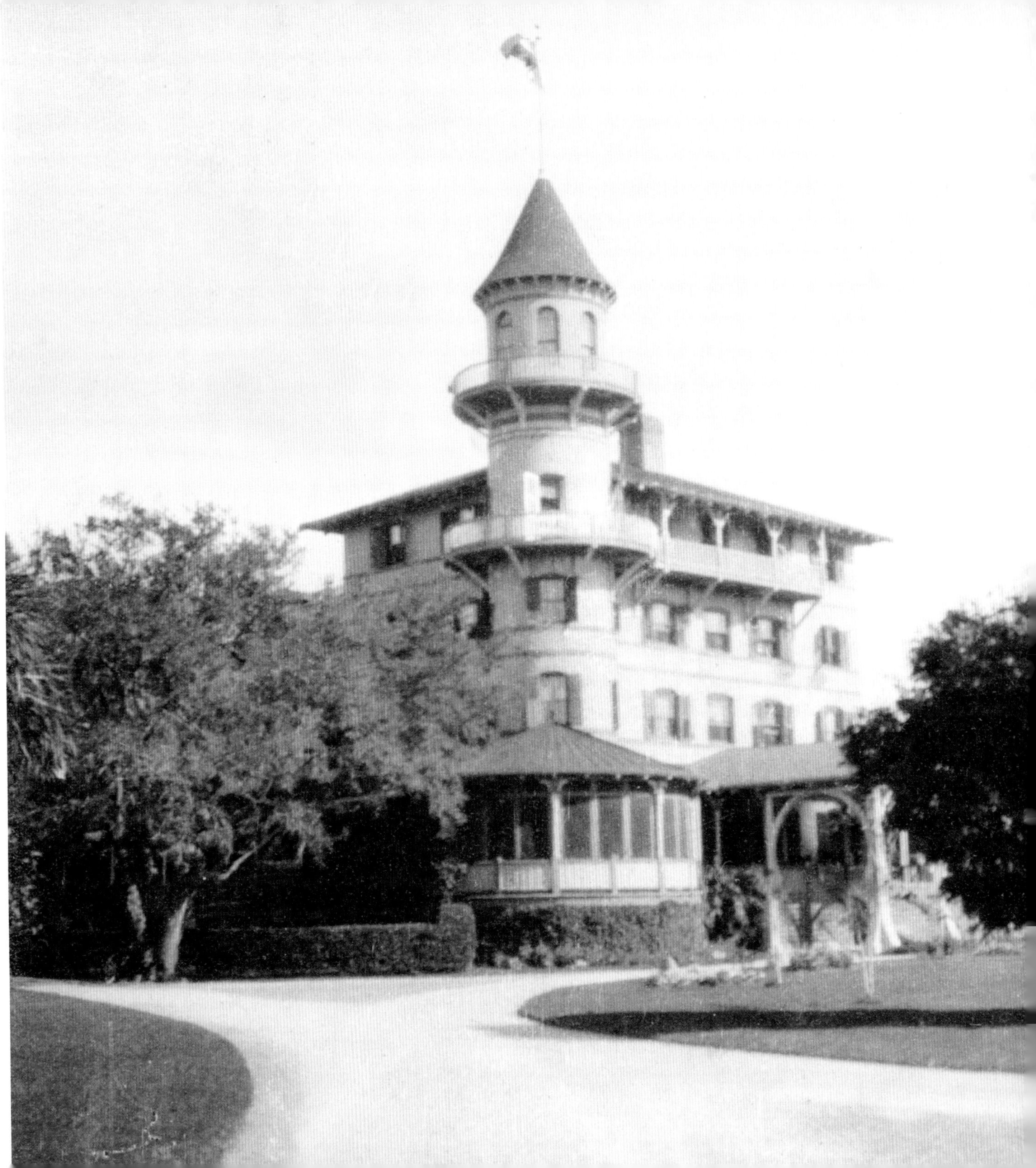

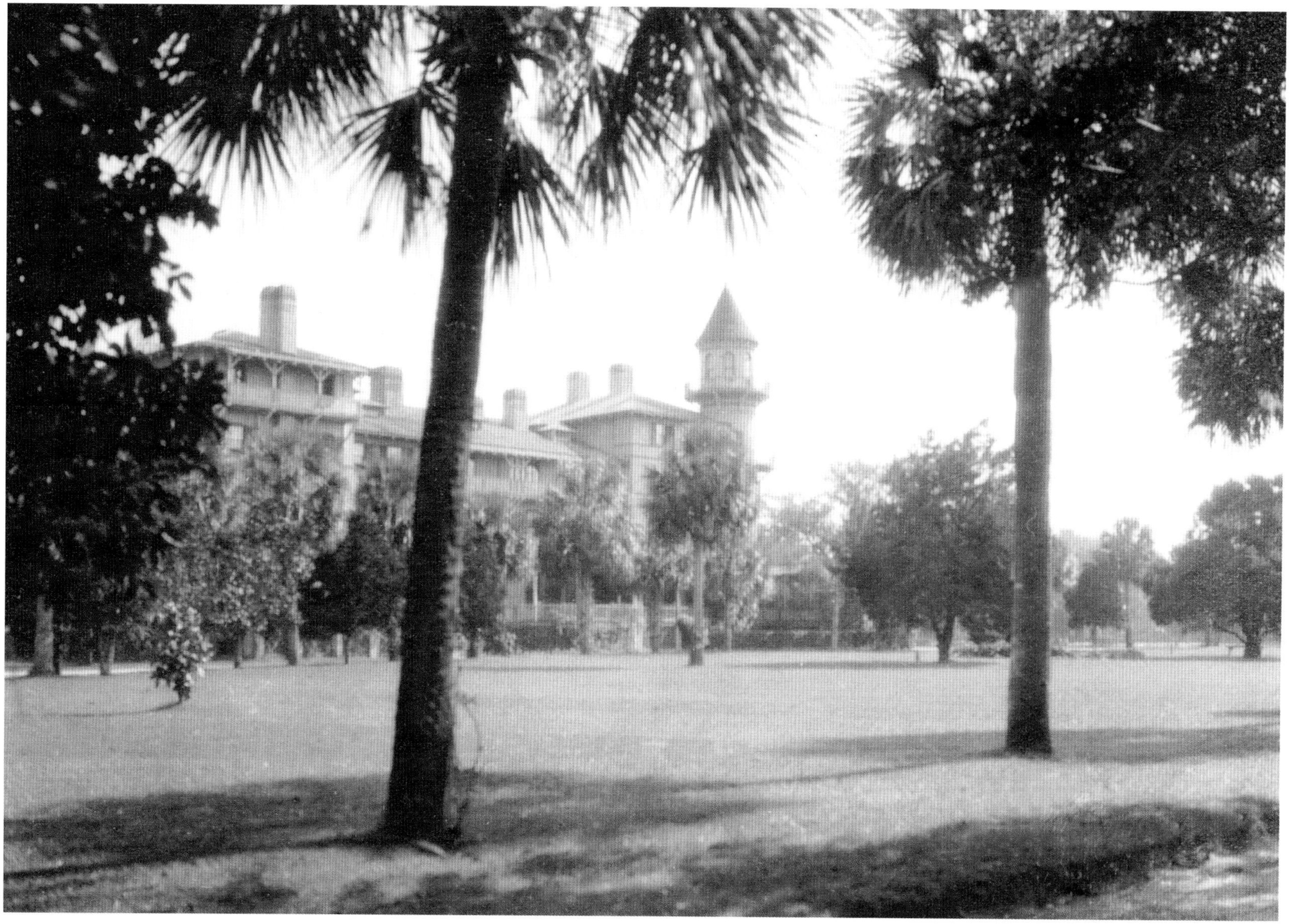

ABOVE The hotel structure was designed in the Queen Anne style. The tower was the distinctive feature of the club house.

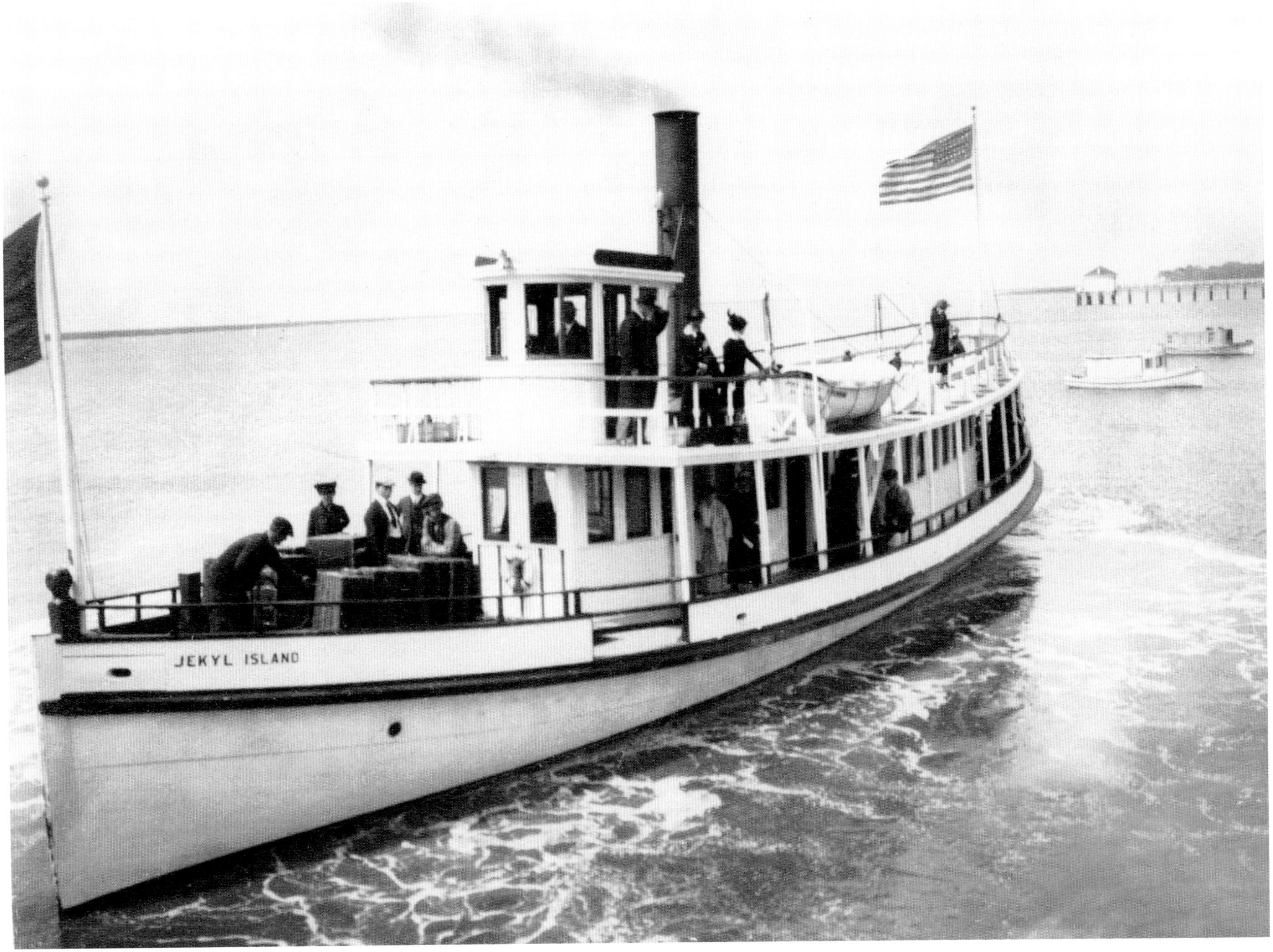
JEKYL ISLAND

OPPOSITE The *Jekyl Island* steamer that took visitors back and forth to the island during the club season.

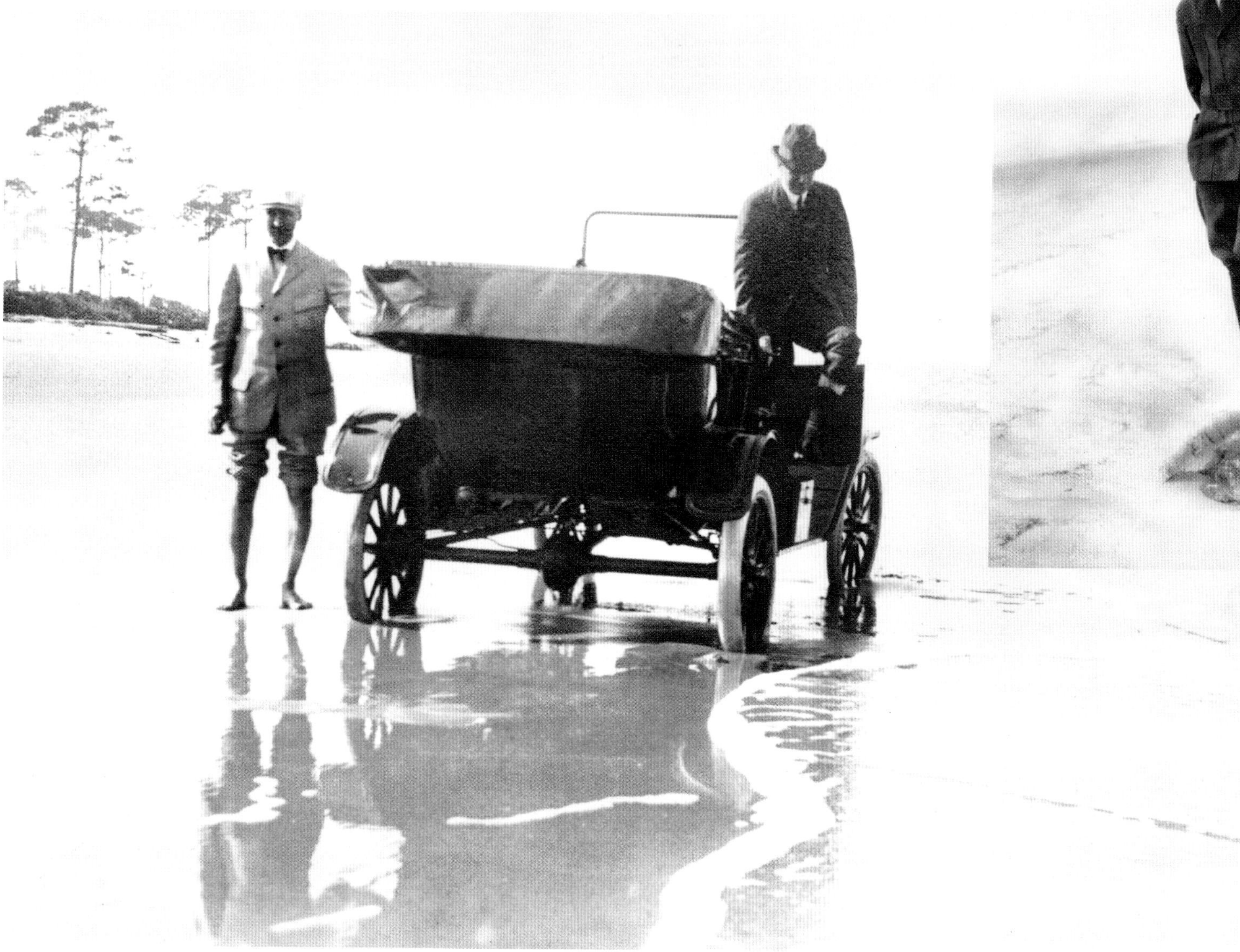

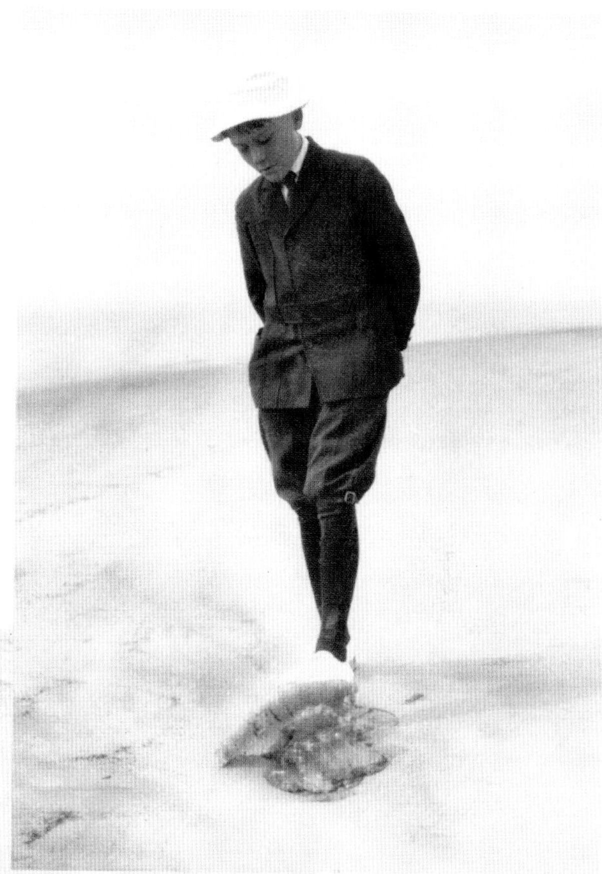

ABOVE Olin studying the jellyfish that had washed up on the beach.

LEFT Tracy in his automobile contemplating the situation as he and Robert Stanton Brewster are stuck in the sand while driving along the beach. Perhaps the chauffeur took the photograph. Brewster was also one of the millionaires that belonged to the club.

BELOW Edwin Gould and Margaret Dows at Chichota, the Gould's cottage on Jekyll Island, in 1916. Edwin Gould was the son of financier Jay Gould, who made his fortune through the ownership of several railroads. After college, Edwin set himself up as an independent broker on Wall Street and within six months made more than a million dollars by speculating in railroads. In 1892, Edwin married Sarah Shrady, and, that same year, his father died. At age 27, with his inheritance from his father's estate and the fortune he made for himself, it was reported that he was worth twenty million dollars.

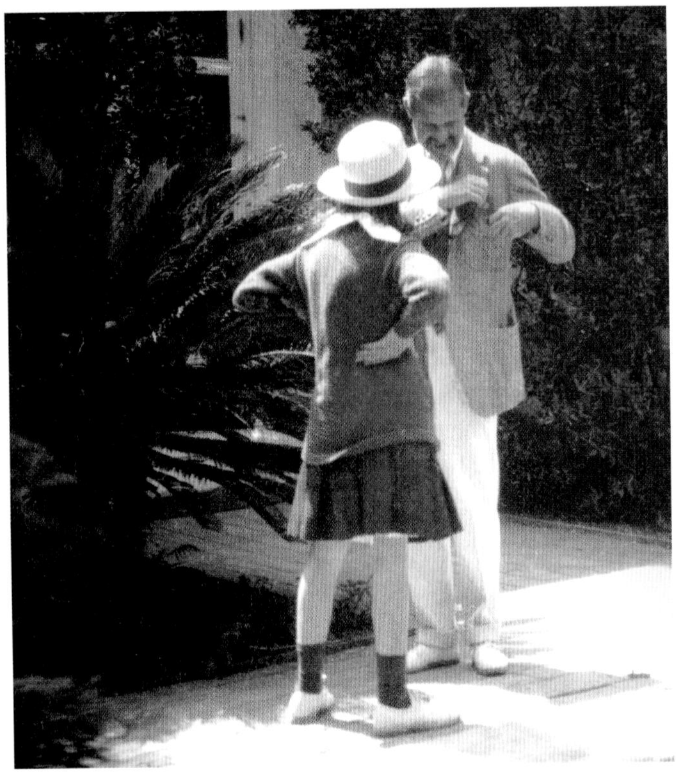

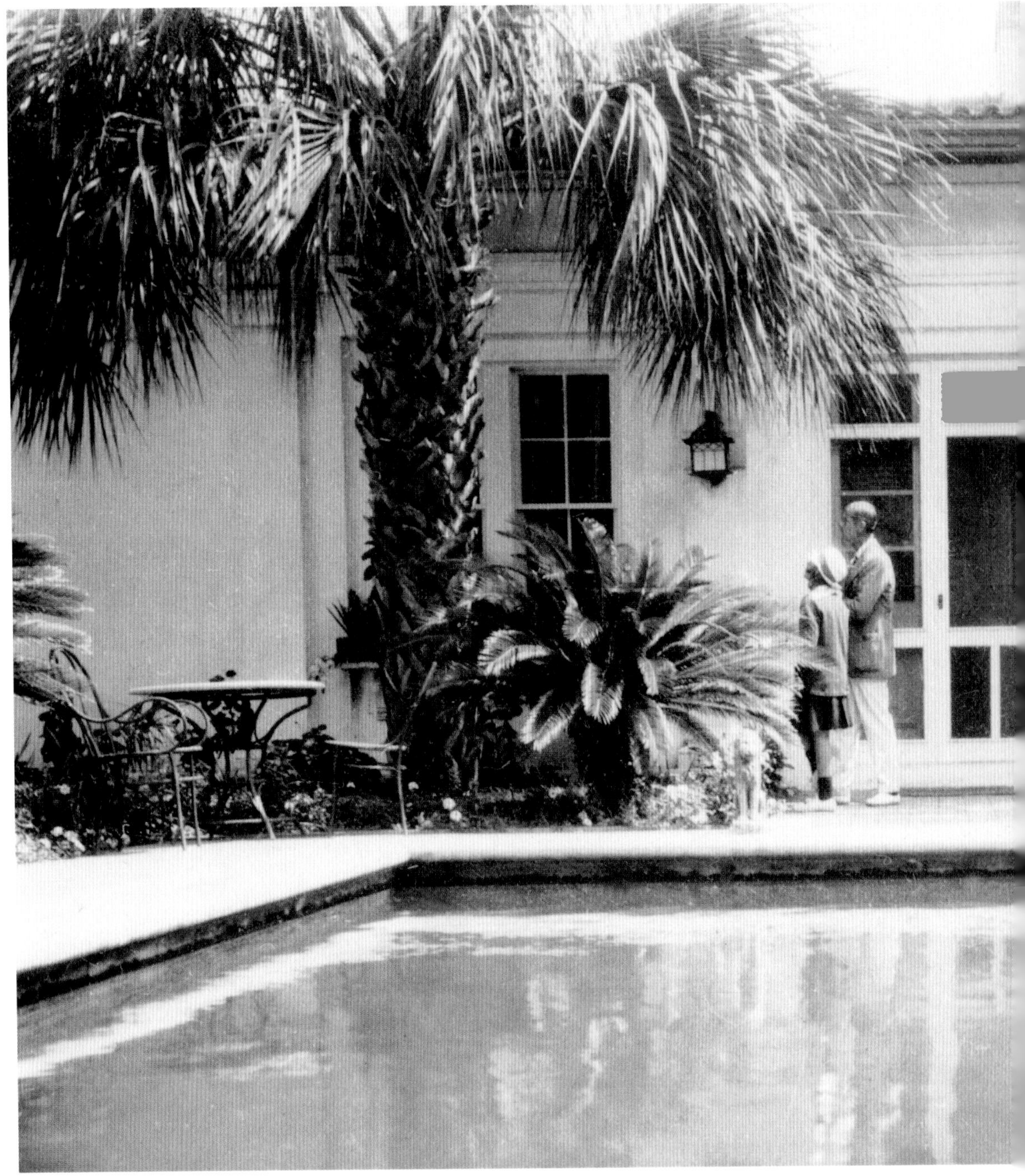

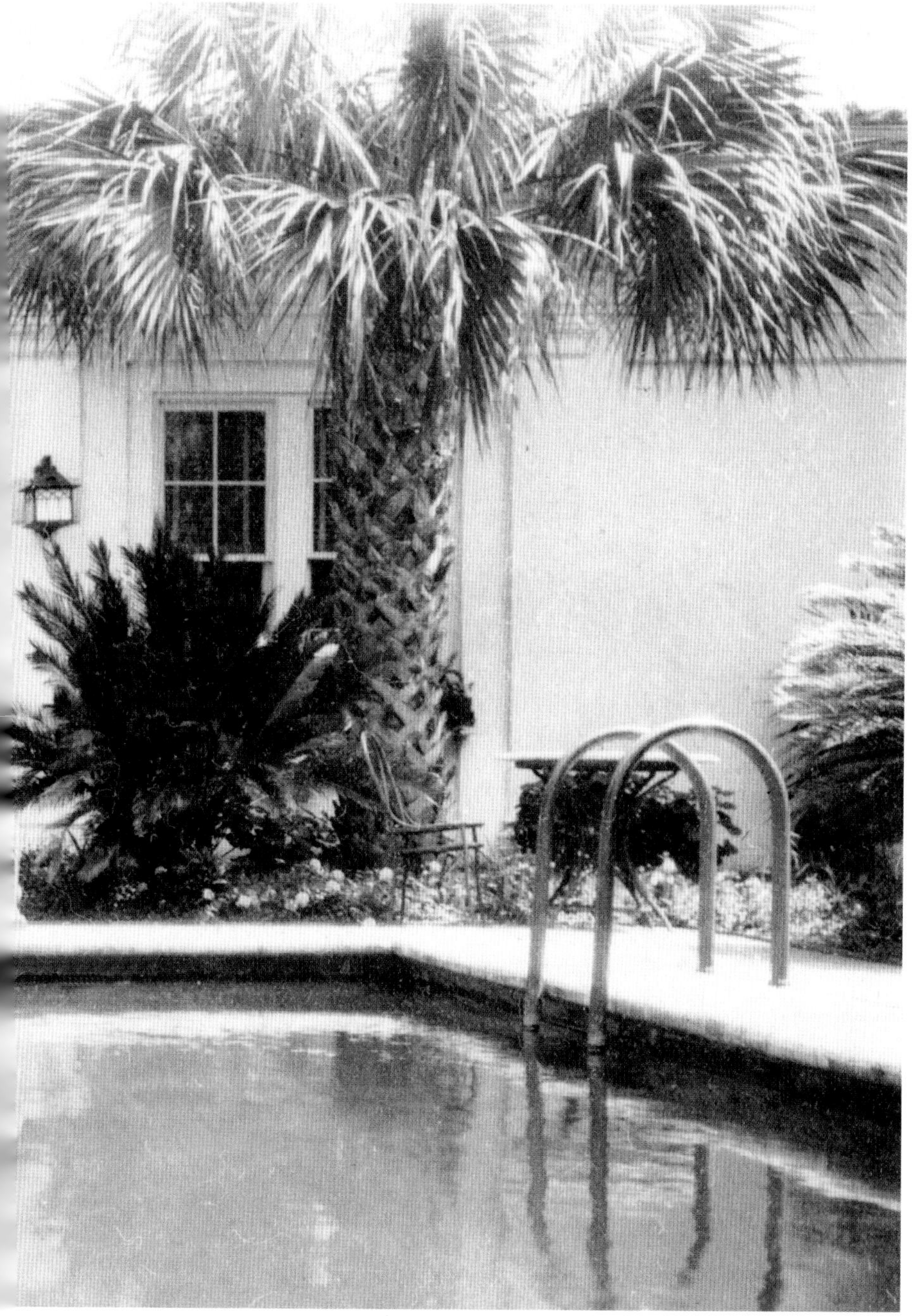

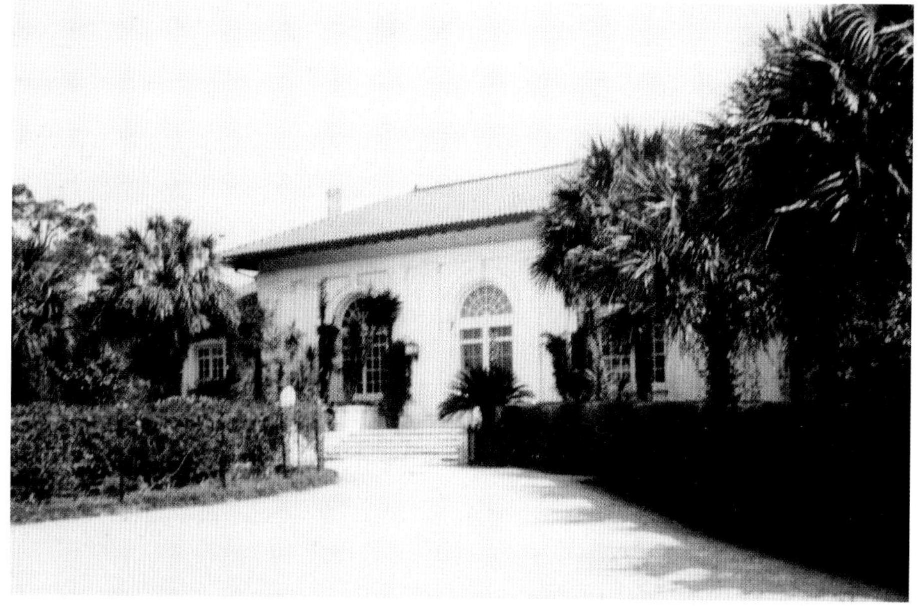

ABOVE The front of Chichota. In 1900, Edwin Gould bought the house from David H. King, Jr., the noted contractor from New York City whose projects included the construction of the base of the Statue of Liberty, Madison Square Garden, and the Washington Square Arch. Gould spared no expense renovating it with modern-day conveniences, as well as adding a boathouse, greenhouse, bowling alley, private stable, private wharf, and covered tennis court.

LEFT Chichota had one of the first outdoor swimming pools in America.

RIGHT The Gould's private pier extended a long distance into the water. Olin standing on the dock proudly holding a crab.

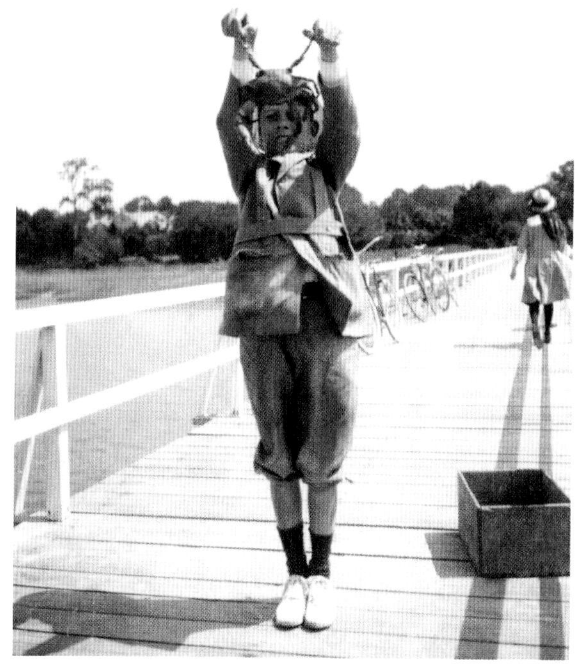

BELOW Olin standing among the palmettos and Spanish moss near the beach.

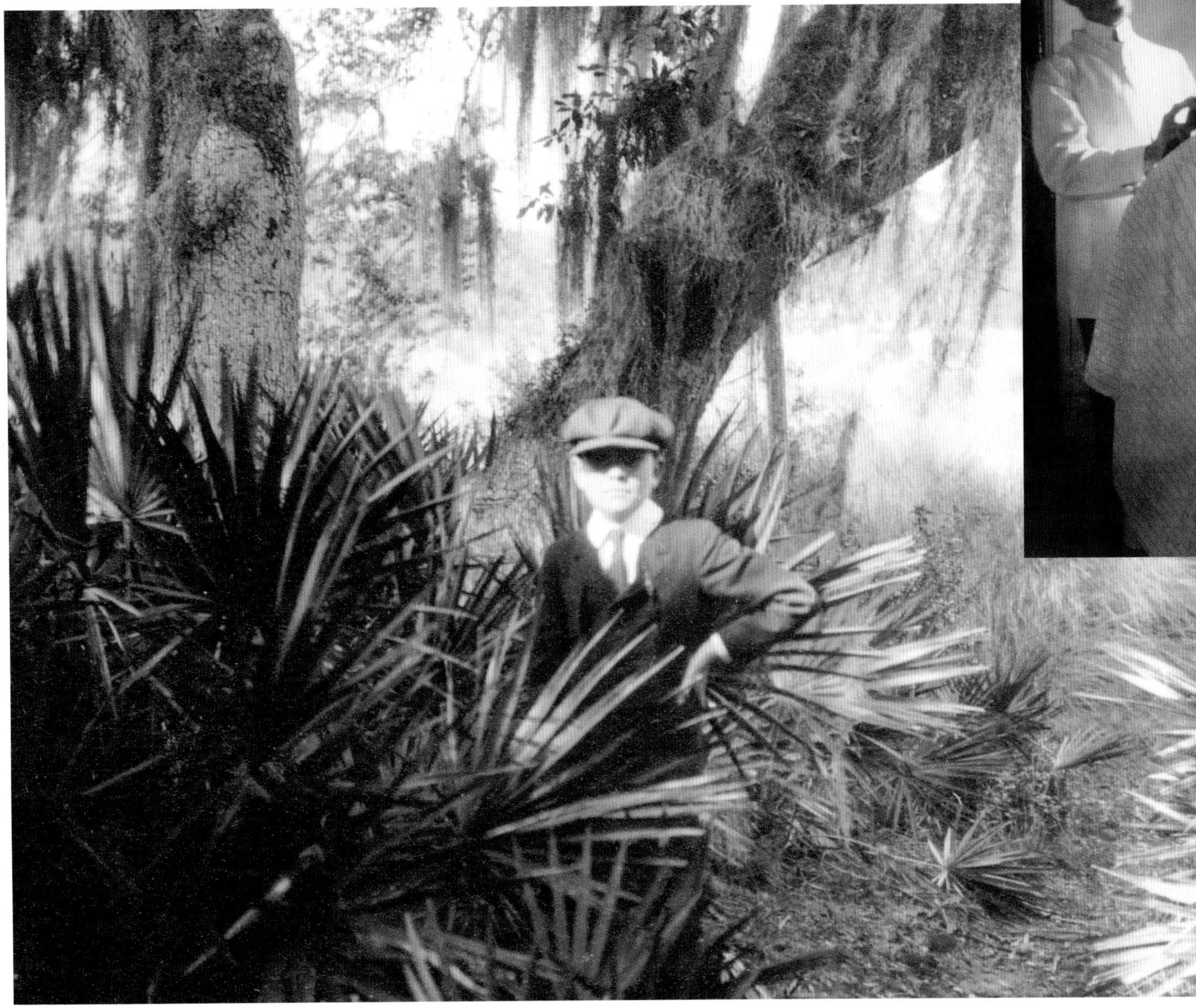

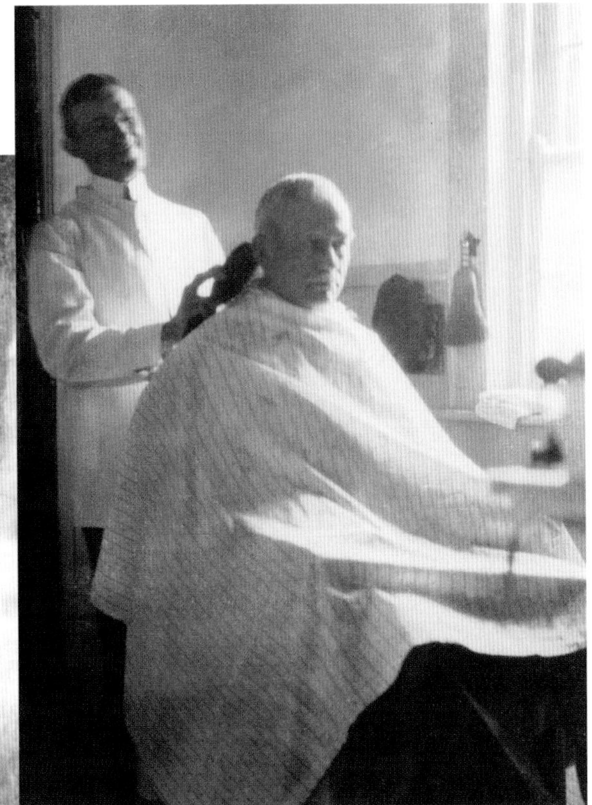

ABOVE Tracy's friend Richard Aldrich at a barbershop on Jekyll Island while they both were visiting the resort in 1916. Aldrich was best known as the music critic for the *New York Times* from 1902 to 1923 and was married to Margaret Chanler Aldrich. They lived at Rokeby on the Hudson River, where Margaret grew up as one of the Astor Orphans.

OPPOSITE Alice and Mrs. Lewis Iselin sitting on the running board of the Dowses' car. Lewis is in the driver's seat. The Iselins were also visiting Jekyll Island in 1916.

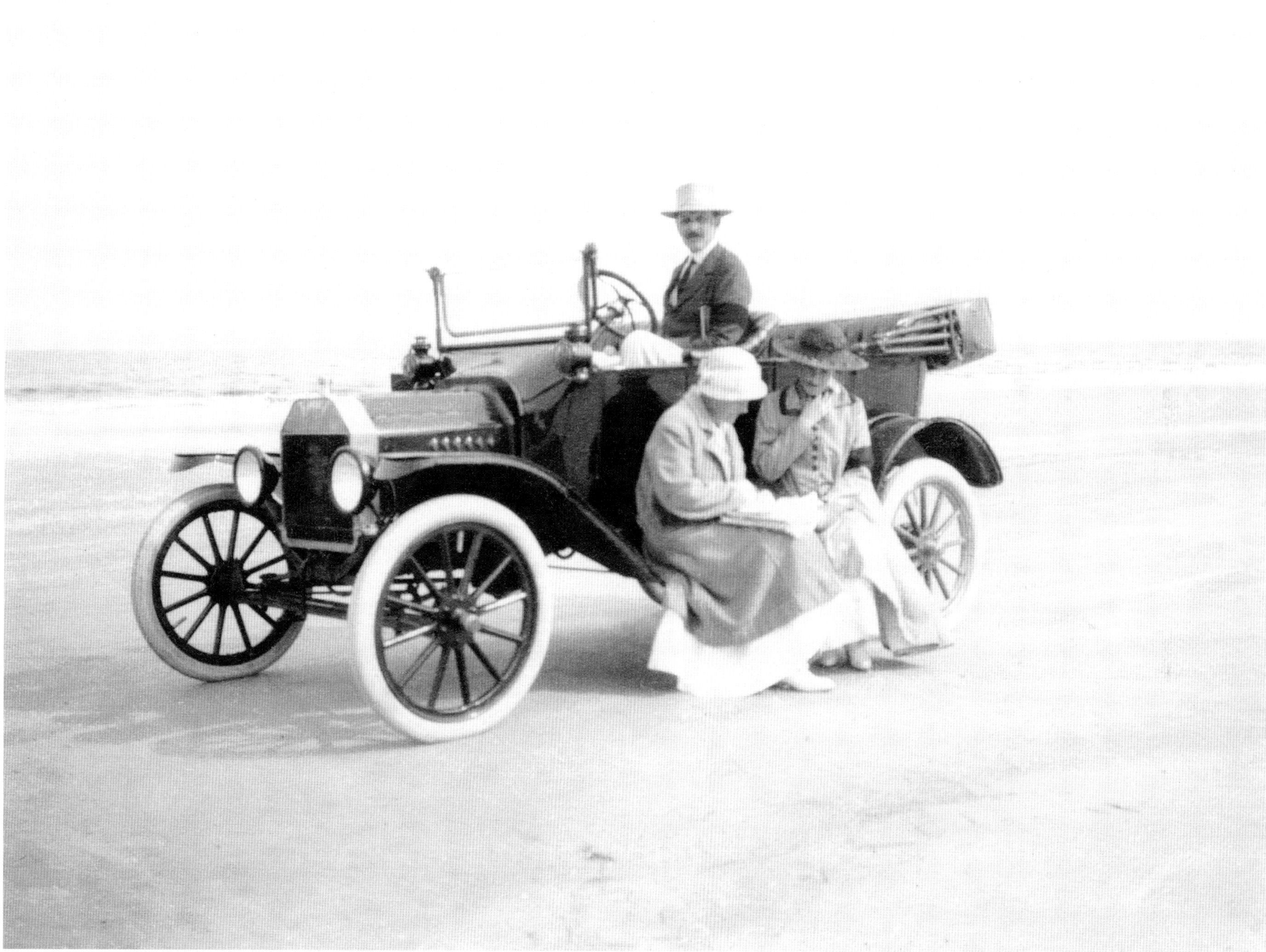

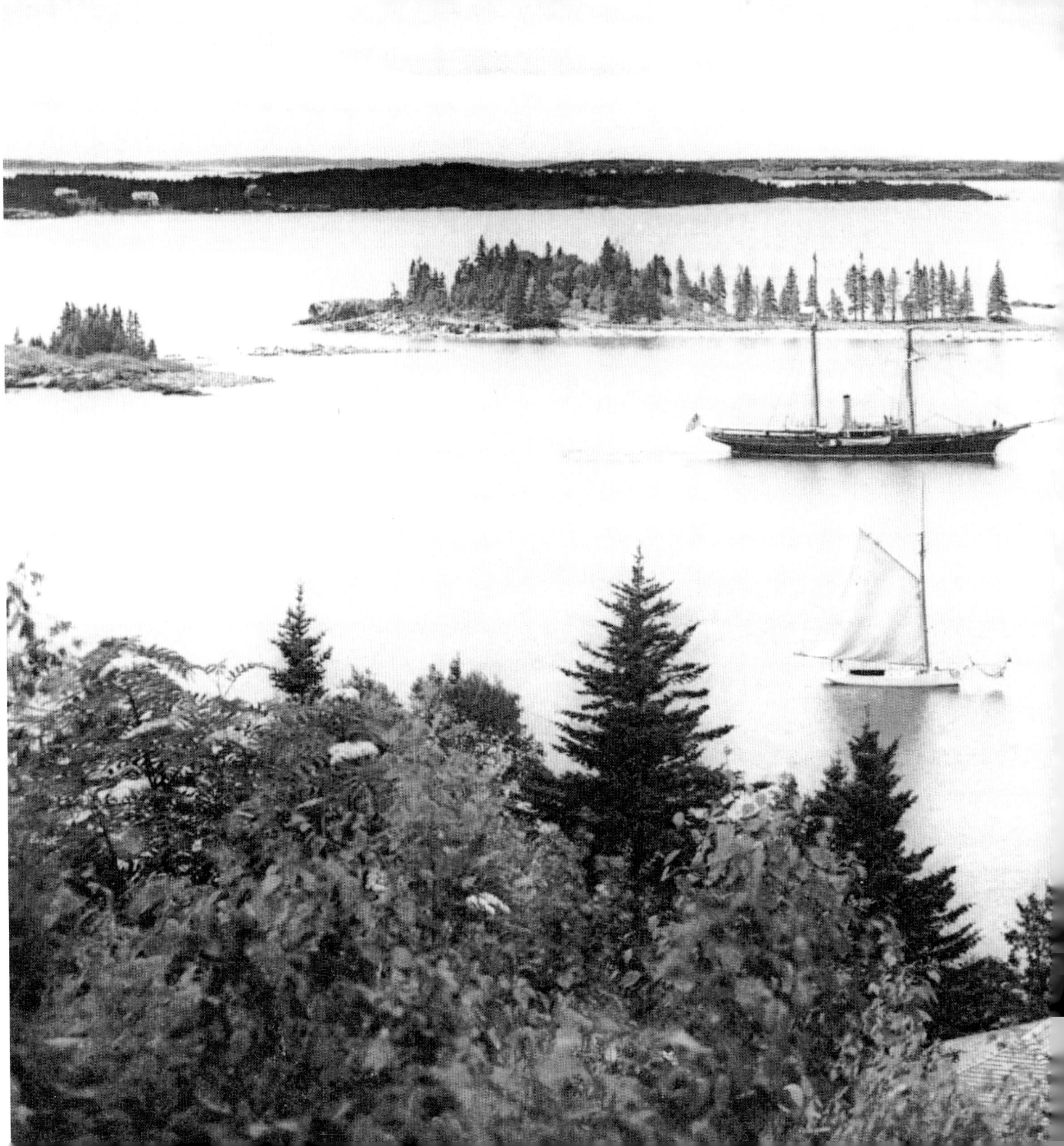

RIGHT A view of Seal Harbor, Maine, in 1903 when Tracy sailed there on the *Mohican*, which is seen anchored in the water. Situated on beautiful Mount Desert Island, Seal Harbor attracted visitors seeking the clean mountain air and beautiful vistas. The island's terrain influenced the Shingle style of the cottages built by the prominent owners, many of them choosing established architects. Four of Tracy's sisters and brothers-in-law had large and comfortable cottages there, and the Dowses were frequent visitors throughout the 1910s and 1920s.

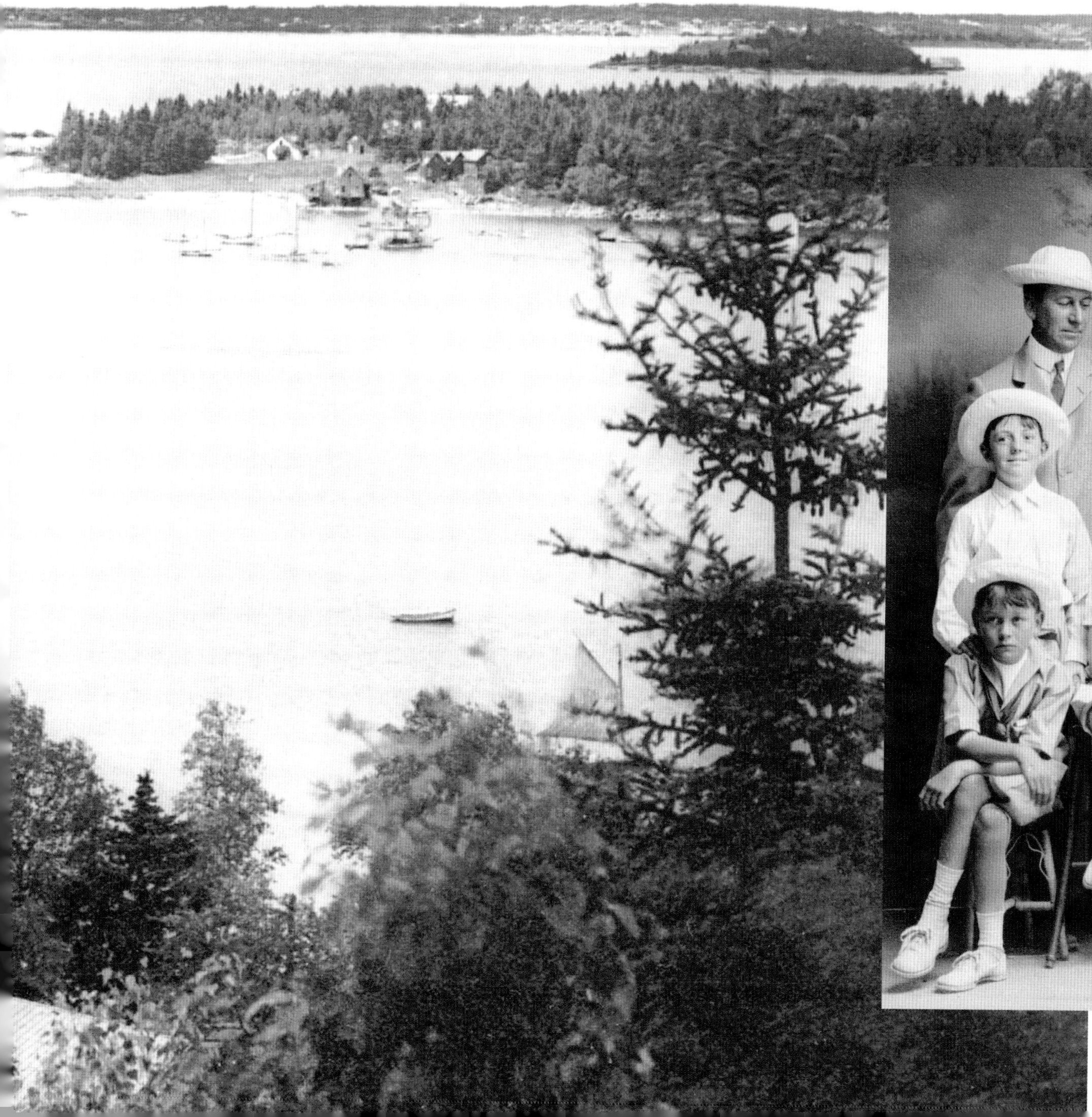

BELOW A family photograph taken in 1912 by commercial photographer I. T. Moore in his studio at Northeast Harbor. Standing are Tracy and Duncan Fuller, the children's tutor. Olin, Margaret, Alice, and the family dog are in the front. The child standing in front of Tracy is his nephew, Edward Kellogg Dunham, Jr.

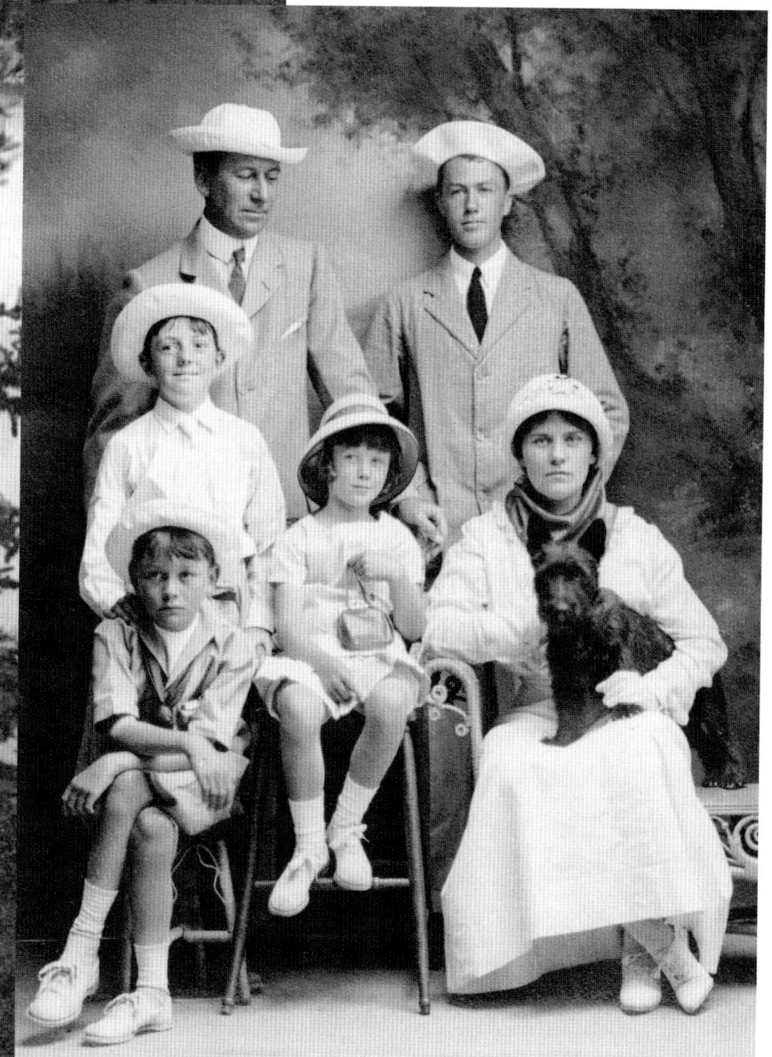

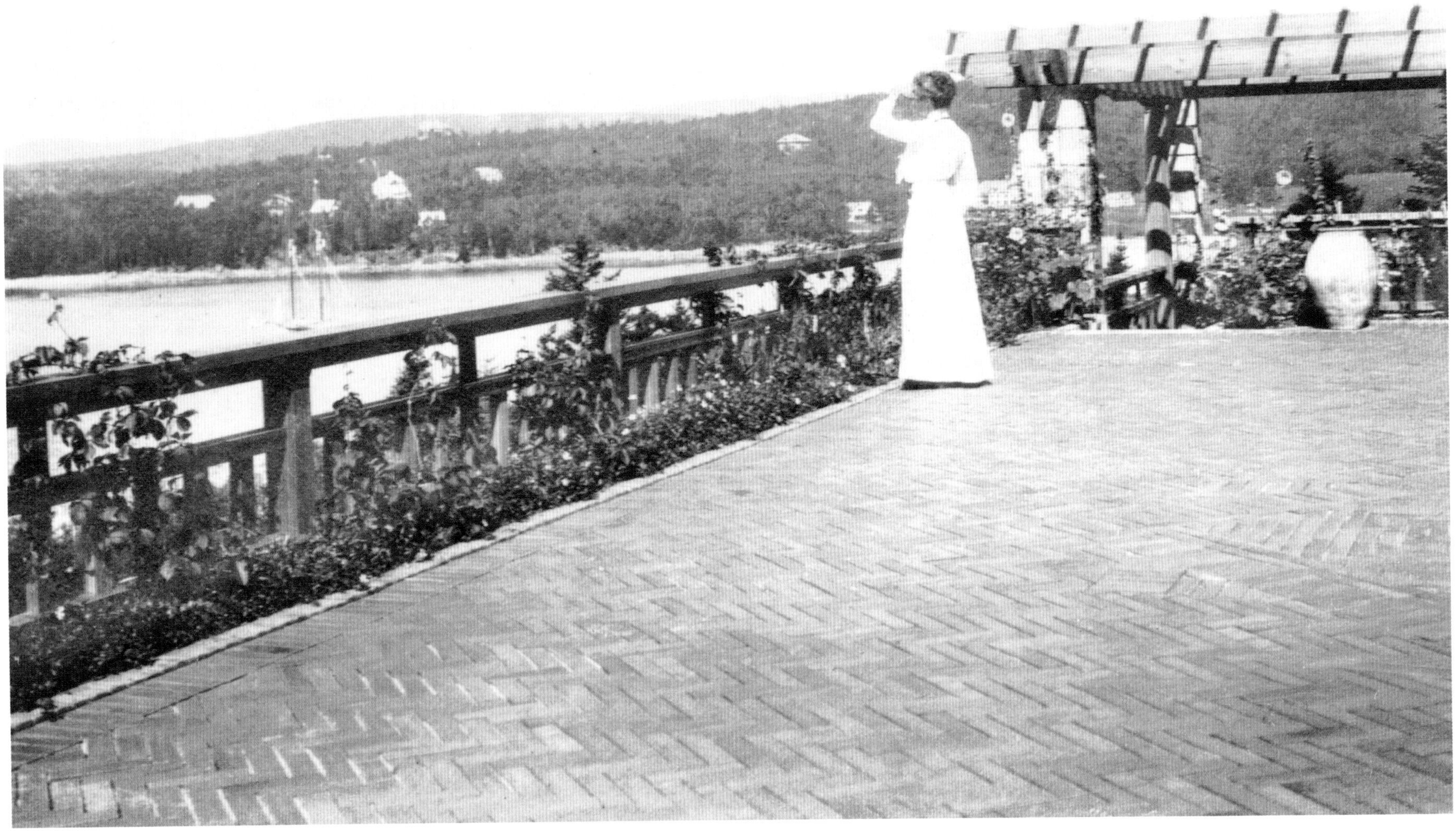

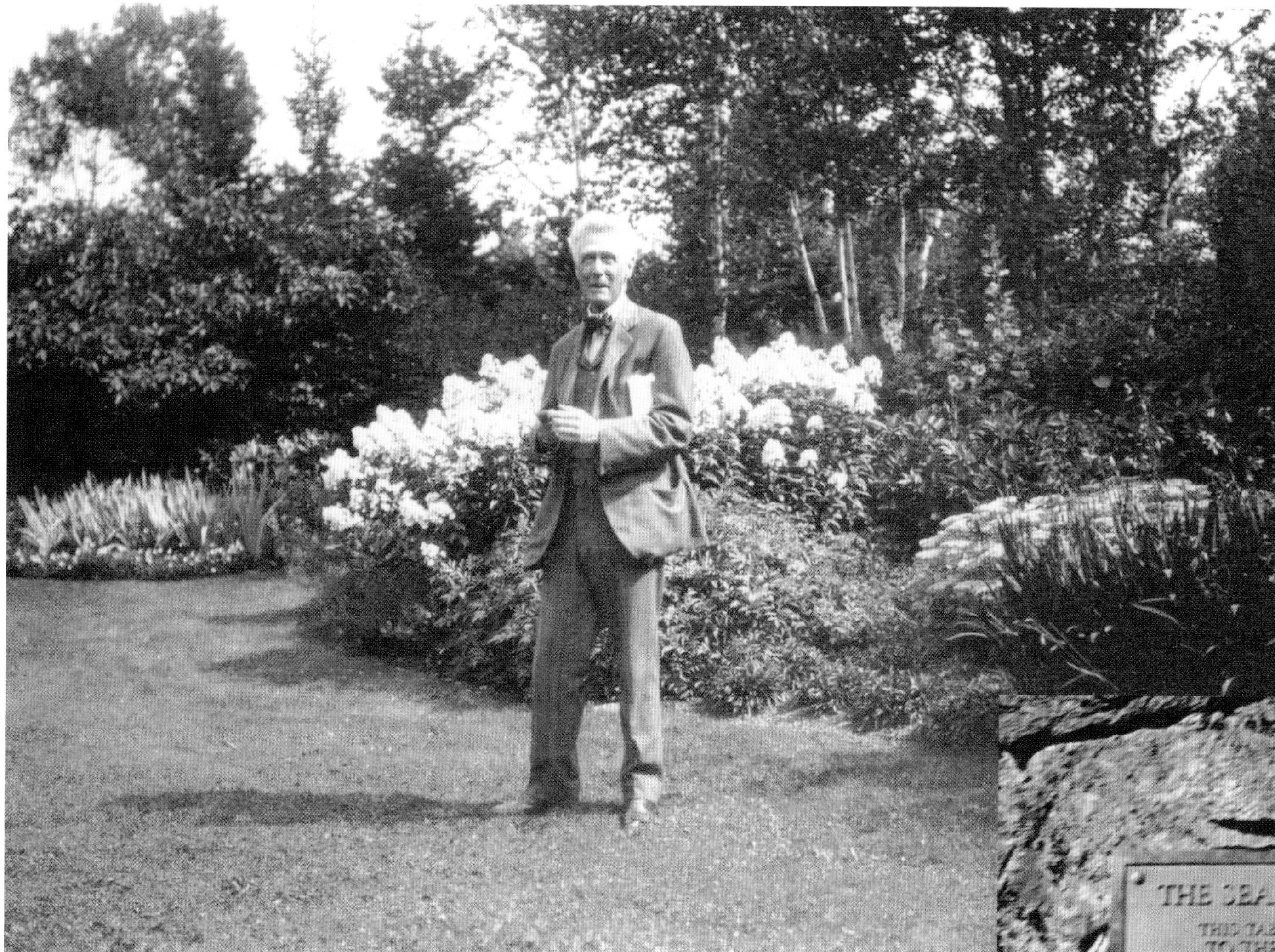

LEFT George Borwick Cooksey in the gardens at Keewaydin, 1919. Seal Harbor resident Beatrix Farrand designed the gardens in 1898 and went on to become an accomplished landscape architect. Cooksey was an important figure in the establishment and expansion of Seal Harbor. The son of a prominent Englishman, Cooksey immigrated to the United States in 1875, where he worked as an apprentice with David Dows & Company in New York City. He married David Dows's daughter, Linda Dows, and became a prosperous grain merchant himself.

BELOW Cooksey convinced family members to build cottages at Seal Harbor and saw an opportunity in the development of the harbor for others. He was responsible for the building of Sea Cliff Drive, and a memorial tablet was erected in his name after his death in 1922.

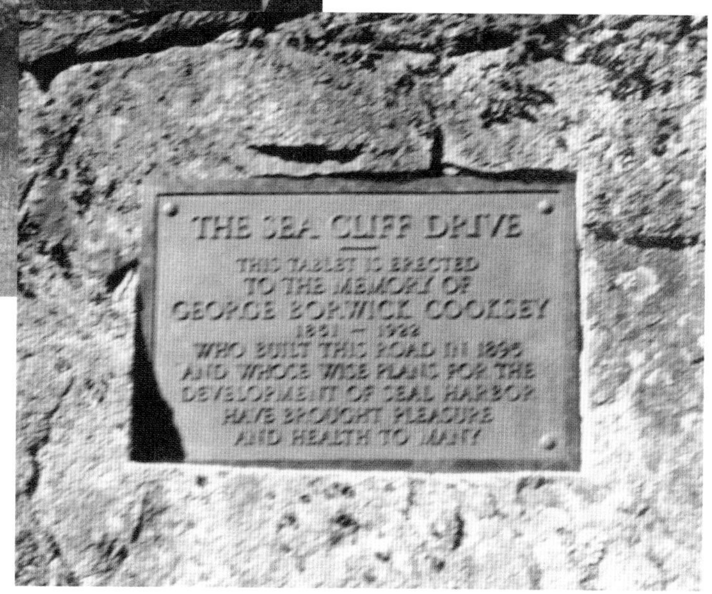

OPPOSITE Tracy's sister Mary Dows Dunham (called Polly) on the terrace of her cottage, Keewaydin, in the summer of 1911. The brick terrace was designed by architect Duncan Candler to take advantage of the picturesque view of the harbor and the vista beyond.

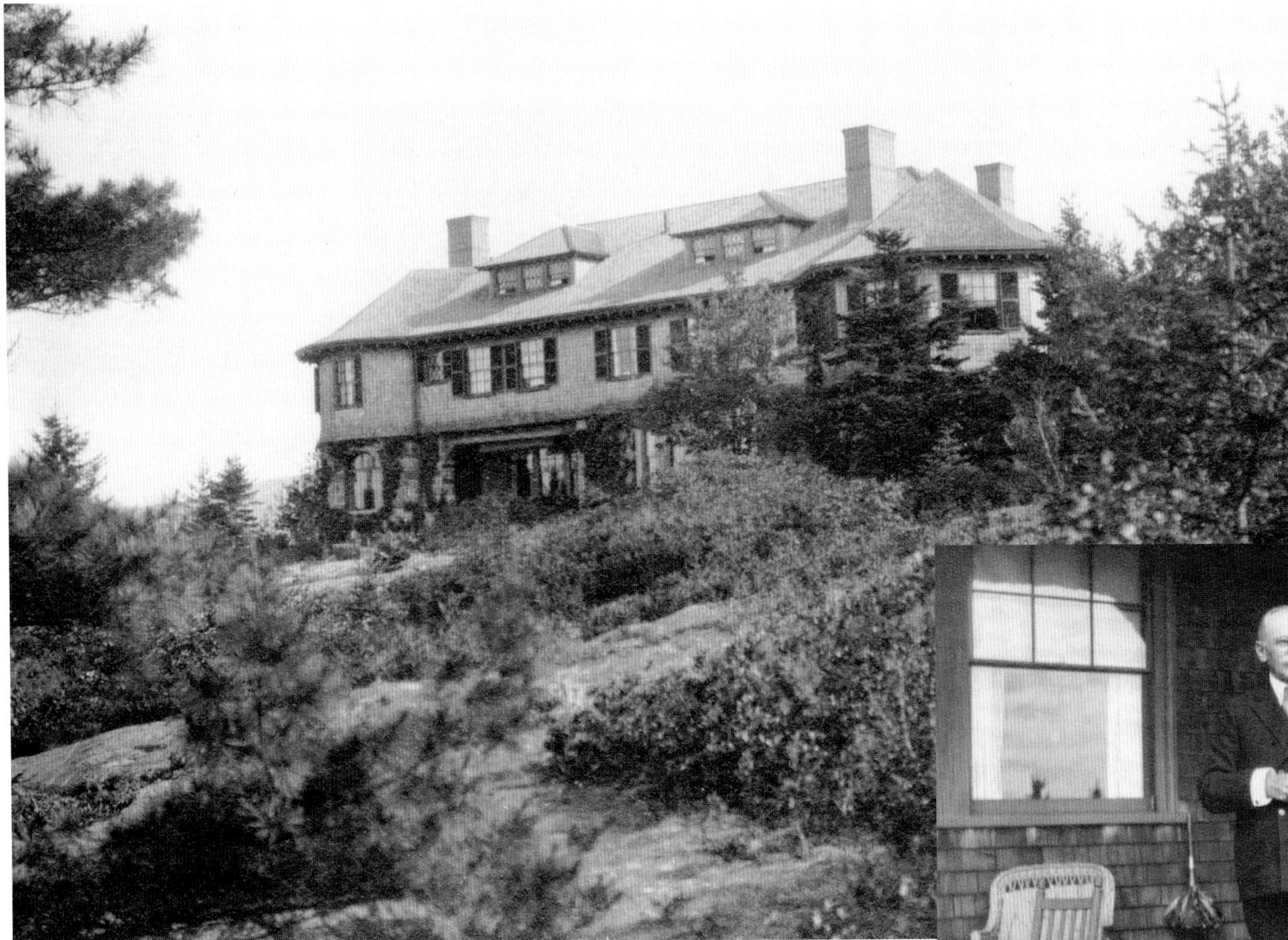

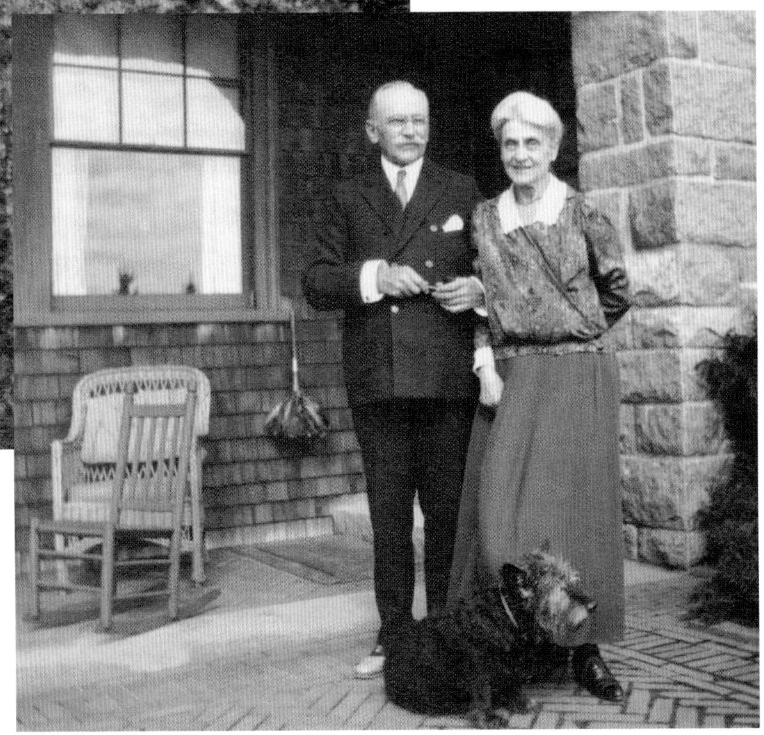

BELOW The Hoes at Eastholm in 1924. Richard March Hoe worked as a banker and grain merchant for David Dows & Company. His grandfather, also named Richard March Hoe, was a successful publisher who invented the rotary printing press. Annie Louise Dows Hoe was one of Tracy's sisters.

OPPOSITE Alice on the terrace at Miradero, the Herters' cottage, in 1912. The Arts and Crafts style cottage was designed by noted architect Grosvenor Atterbury for Christian Archibald Herter and Susan Dows Herter in 1901. Susan was also one of Tracy's sisters.

ABOVE Eastholm, the cottage of Richard March Hoe and his wife, Annie Louise Dows Hoe, in 1912. The shingled cottage was designed by the Boston firm of Andrews, Jaques & Rantoul in 1901. The Hoes's limestone mansion in New York City was designed by Carrère & Hastings in 1891.

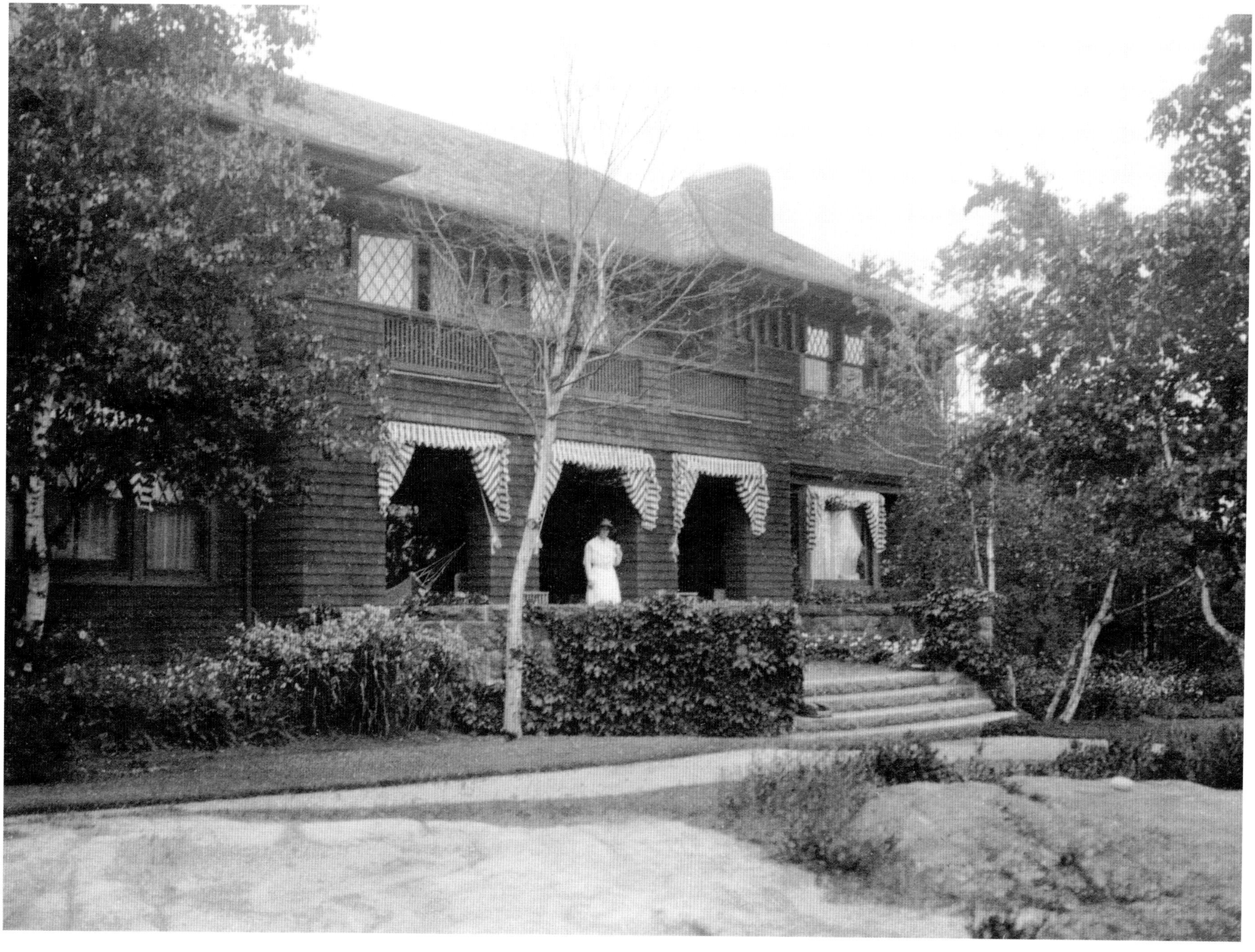

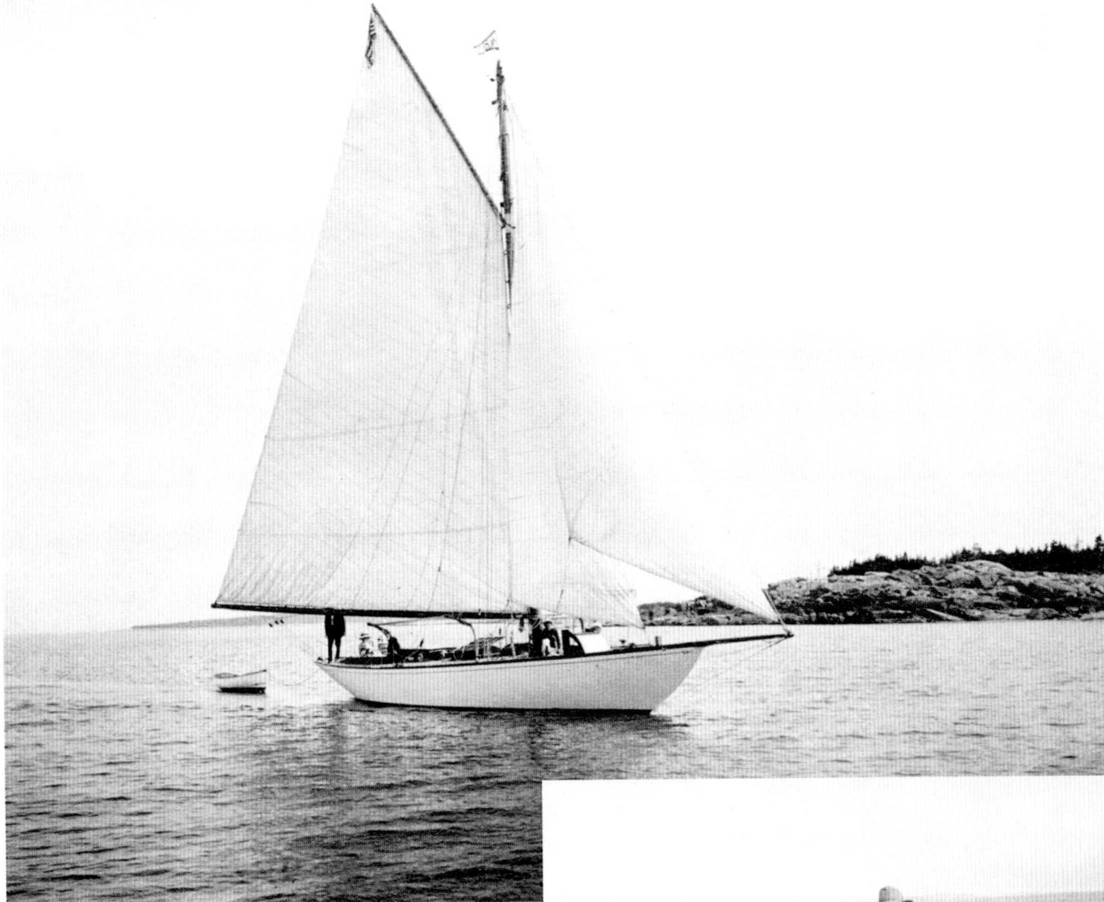

ABOVE The *Neith* sailing in the waters of Seal Harbor in 1912. The fifty-three-foot sailing vessel was designed for Tracy's brother-in-law, Dr. Edward Kellogg Dunham, by Nathaneal Herreshoff in 1907. Dunham was Herreshoff's personal physician. After Dunham sold the boat, she passed through several owners' hands and spent most of her time abroad in England, Scotland, and South Africa. After a meticulous renovation along the way, the *Neith* is still sailing today.

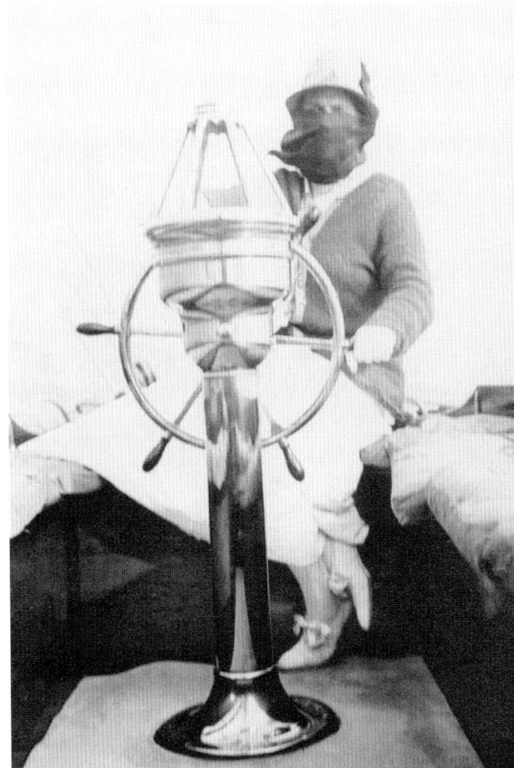

ABOVE Alice at the wheel of the *Neith* in 1912.

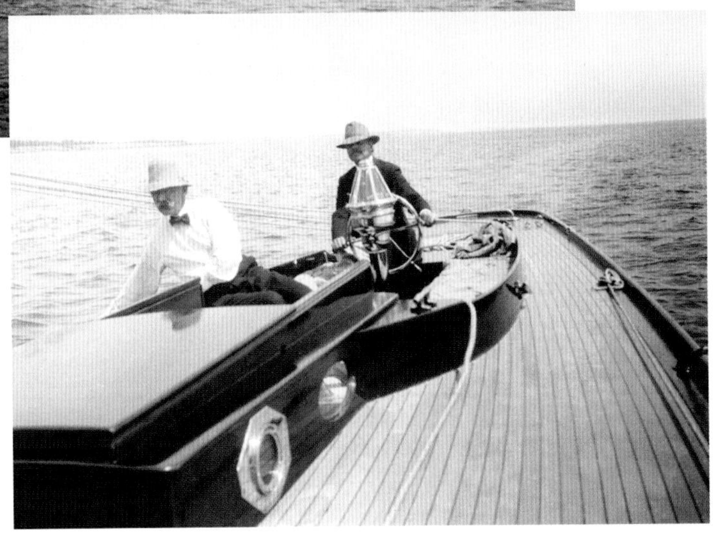

LEFT Out for a sail on the *Neith* are Dr. Edward Kellogg Dunham, at the wheel, and Richard March Hoe, 1911.

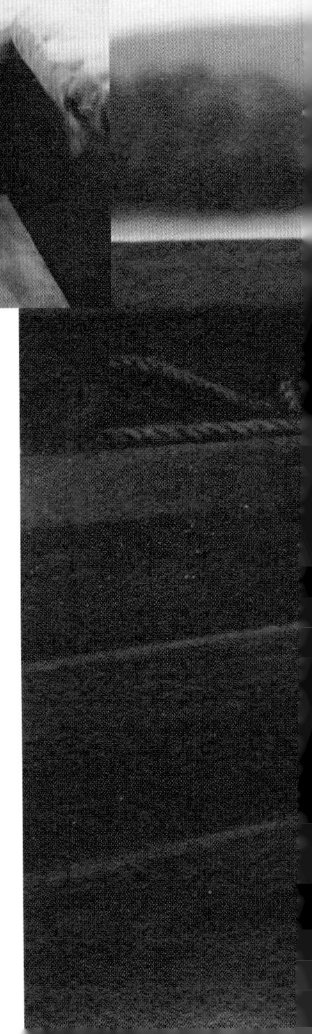

RIGHT Tracy commanding the rudder in one of the other boats used for sailing excursions, 1913.

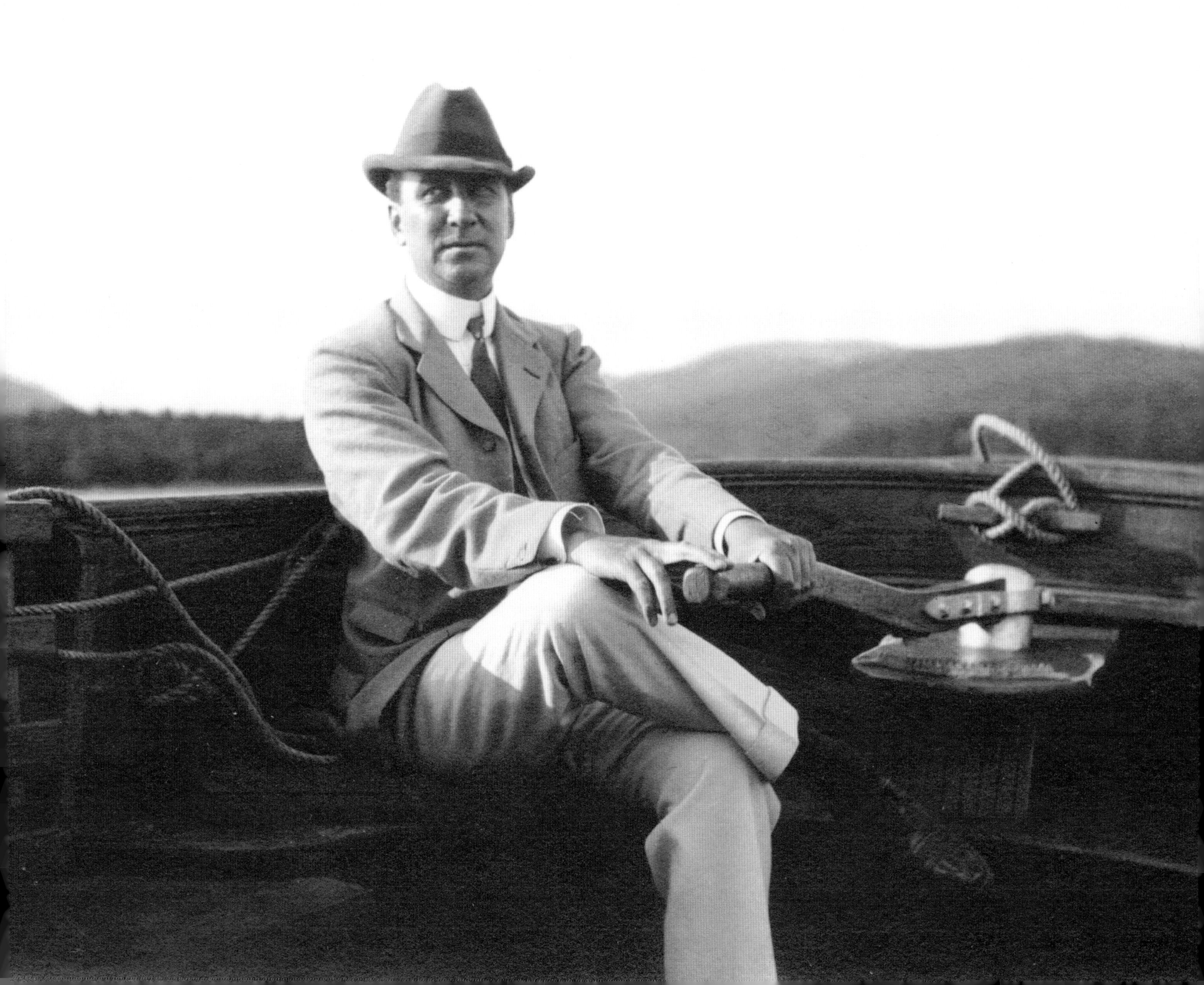

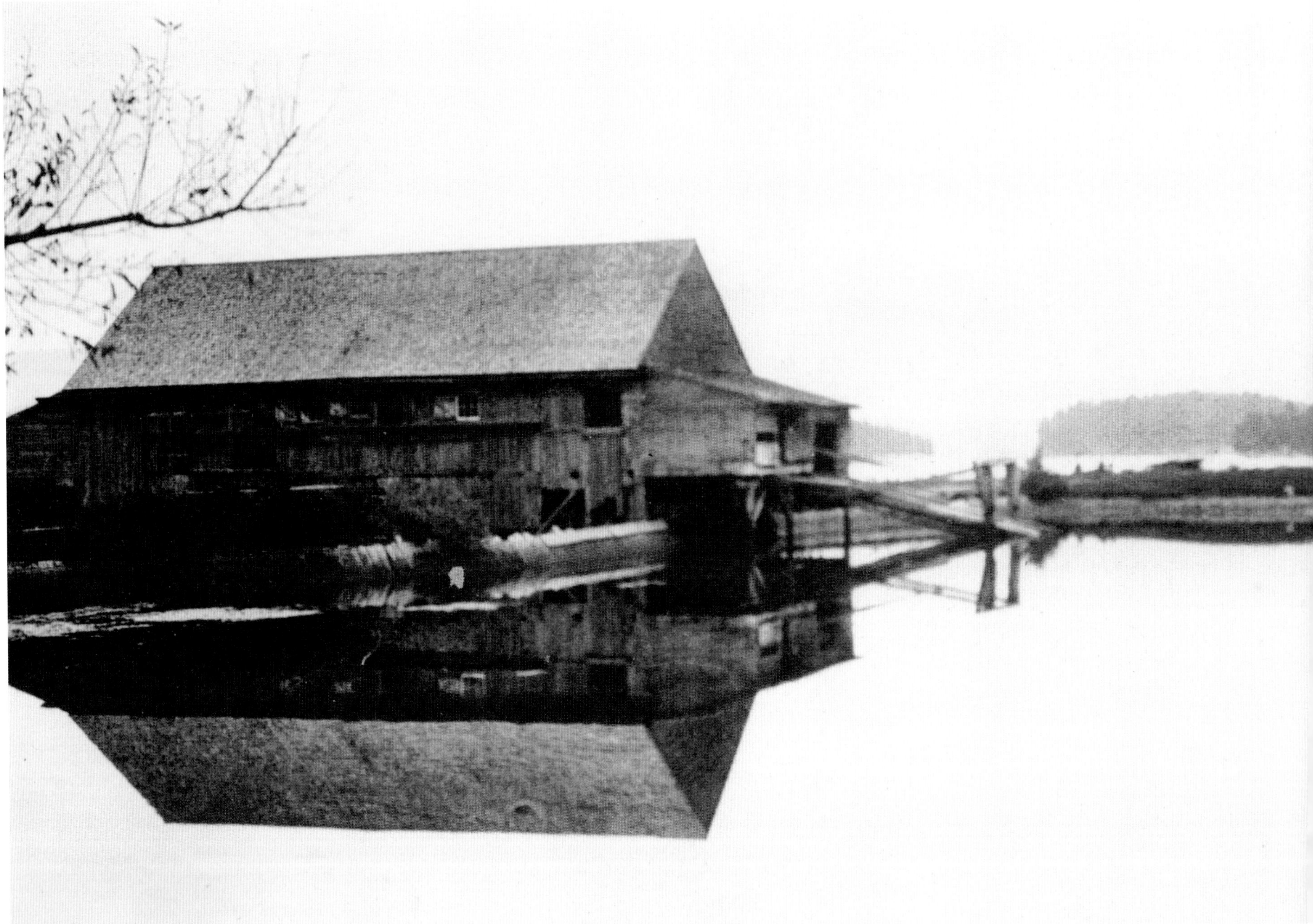

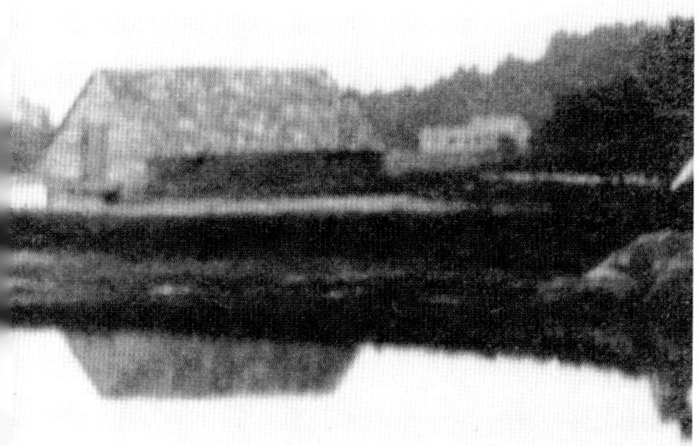

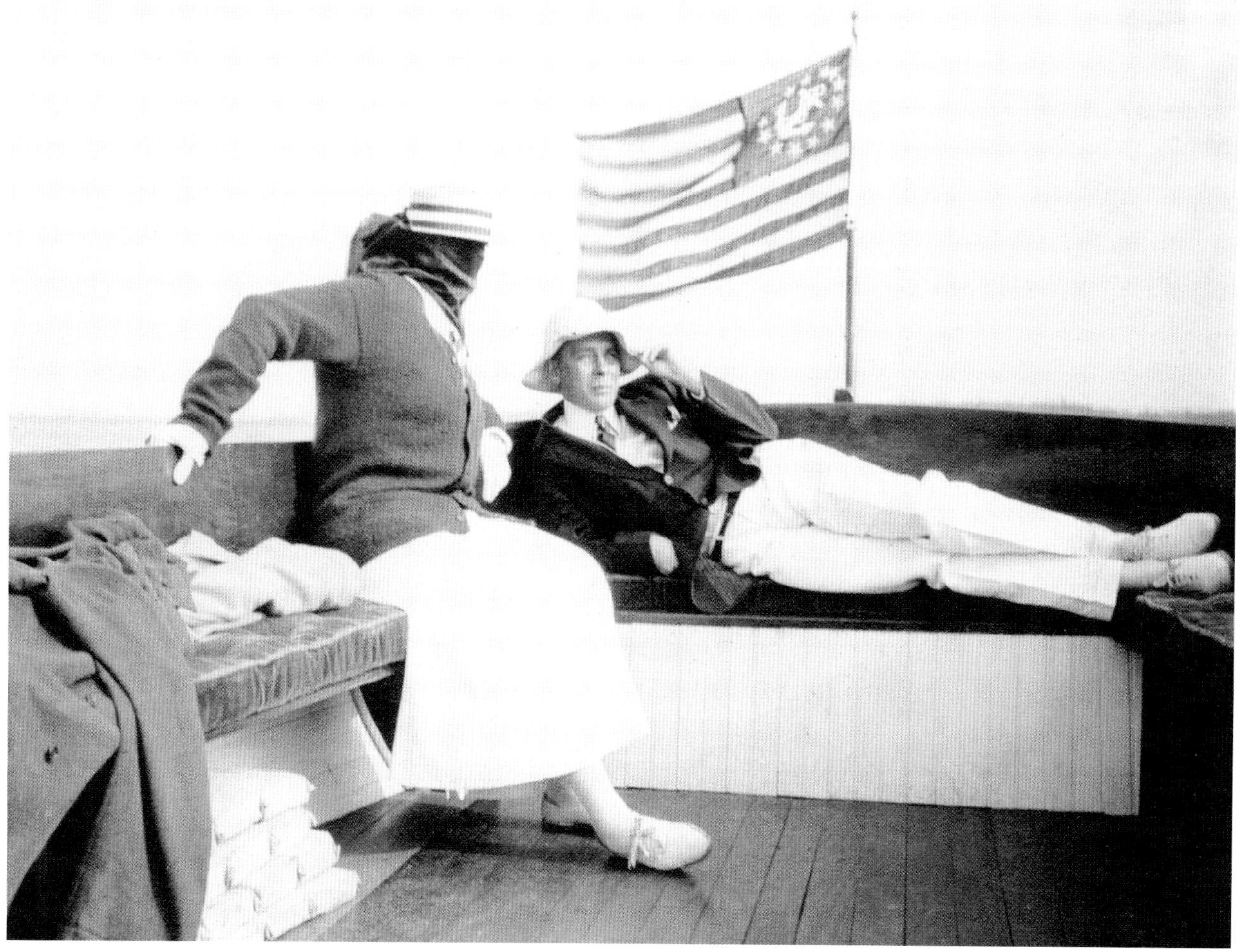

ABOVE Alice and Harrie T. Lindeberg relaxing while sailing. He joined the Dowses on a trip to Seal Harbor in 1913. Alice has a scarf over her face to protect her from the wind.

LEFT A serene view of a boathouse and pier reflecting in the water in 1919.

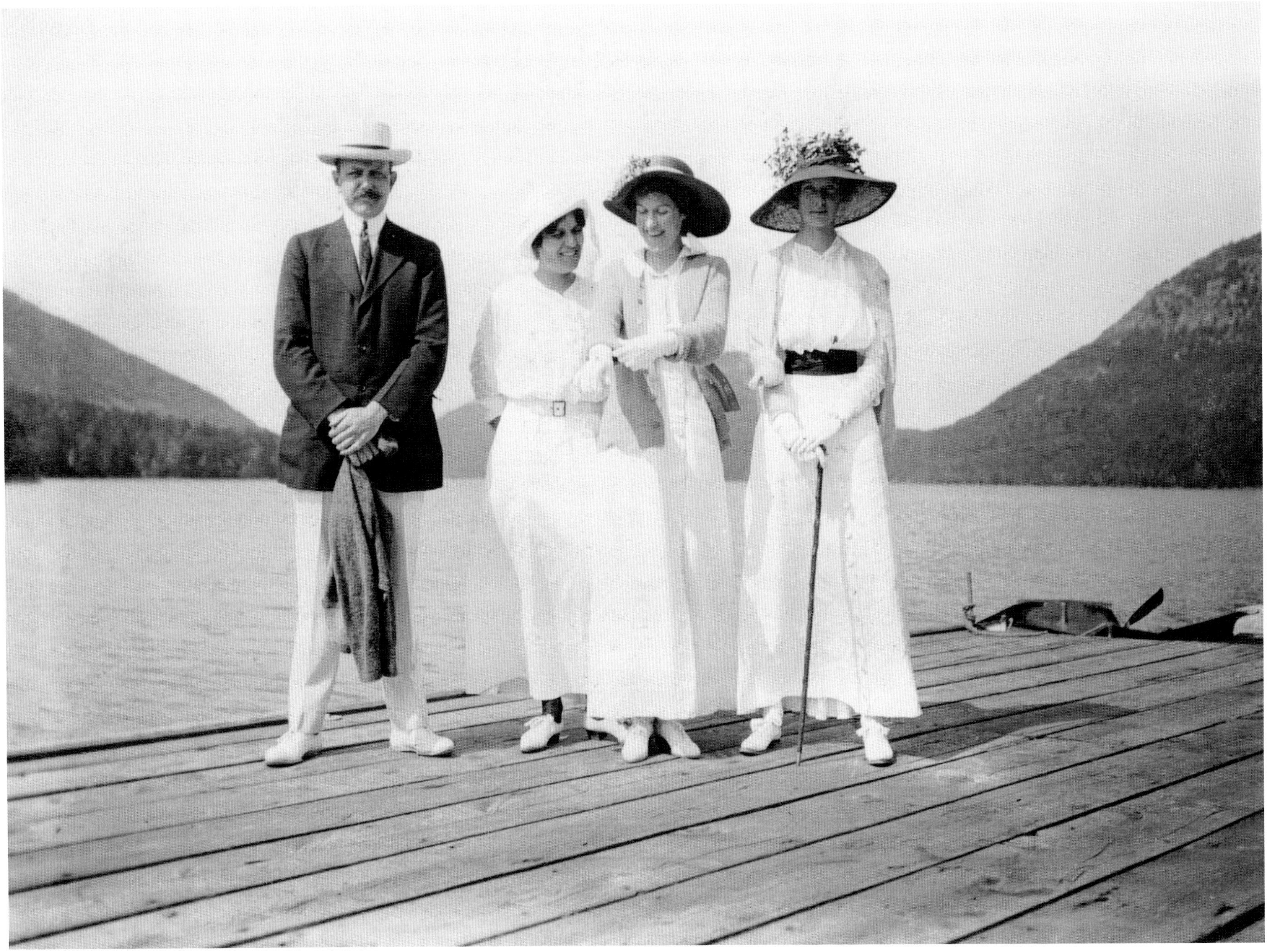

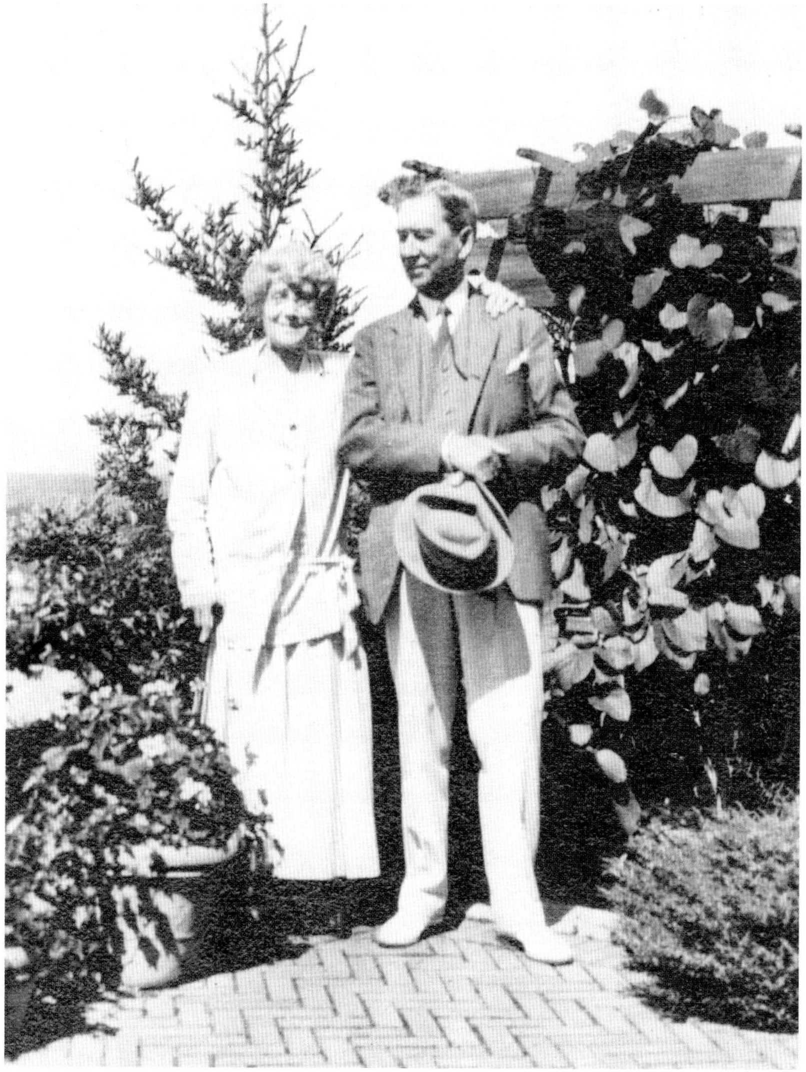

OPPOSITE Standing on a pier at Jordan Pond near Seal Harbor in 1913 are Lewis Iselin, Alice Dows, Mrs. Lewis Iselin, and Helen Dinsmore Huntington, a year before she married Vincent Astor. The mountains in the background are known as "The Bubbles."

LEFT Tracy and Polly at Keewaydin in 1928. He was fifty-seven and she was sixty-three. Tracy continued to travel to Seal Harbor to visit his sisters, even if he went alone.

RIGHT Deb proudly showing off the fish she caught while out on a boat in 1924.

BELOW The Seal Harbor Club in 1928, two years after it was constructed. The club was financially backed by residents Edsel Ford and John D. Rockefeller, Jr., and designed by architect Duncan Candler.

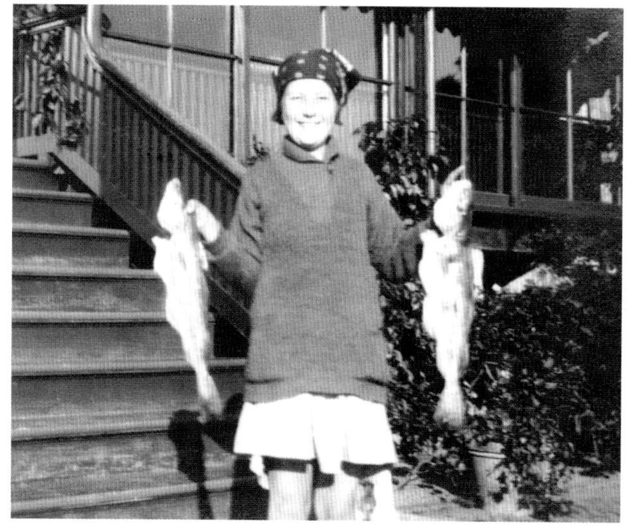

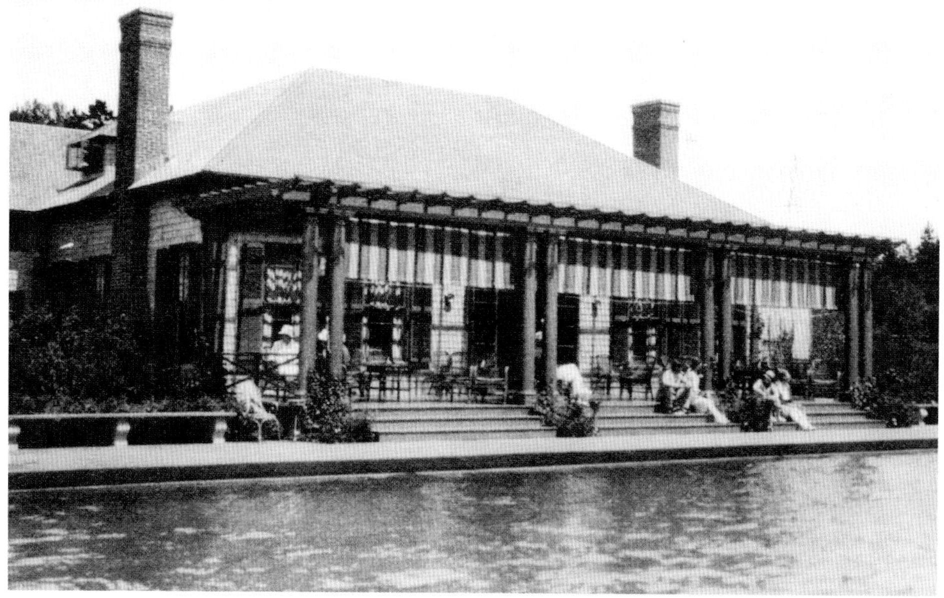

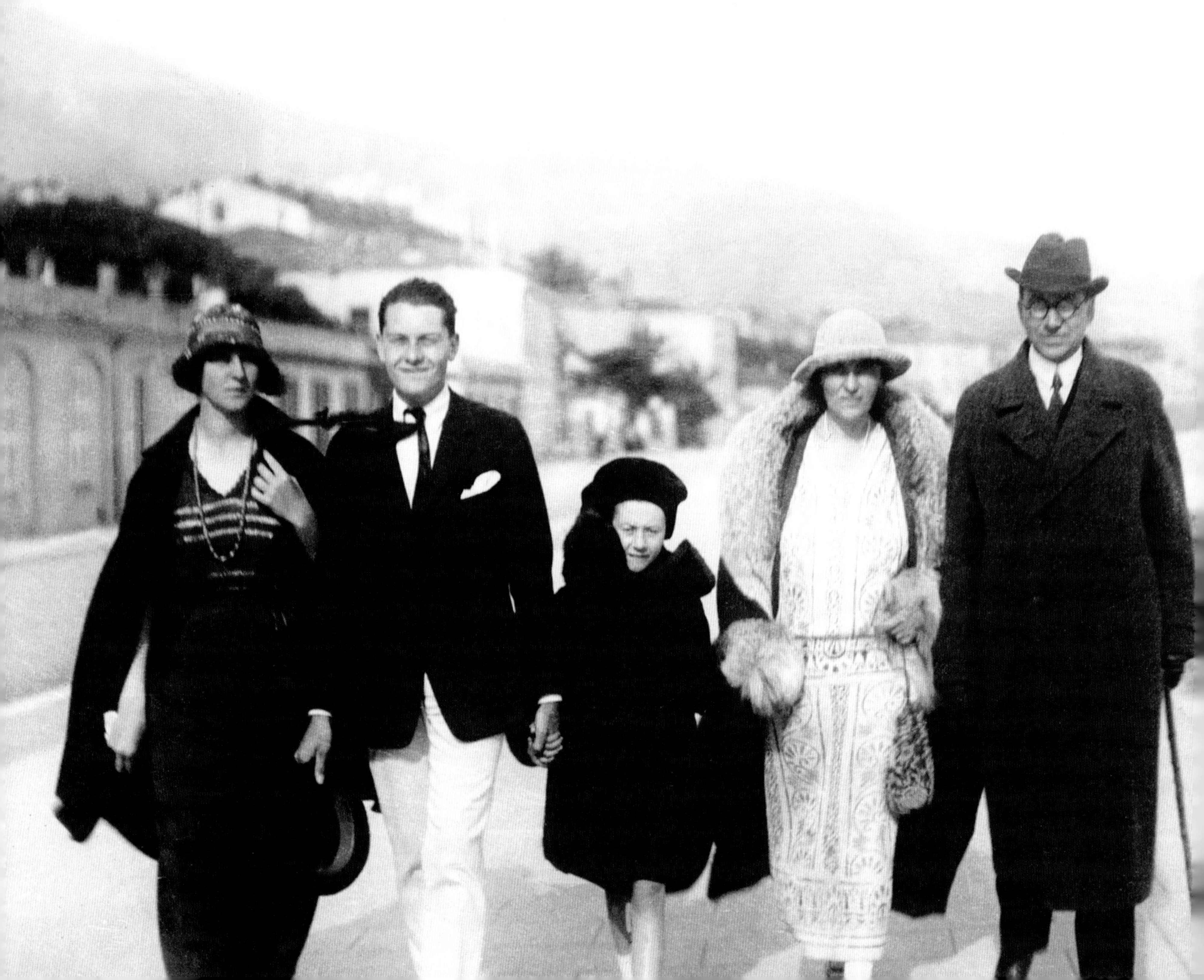

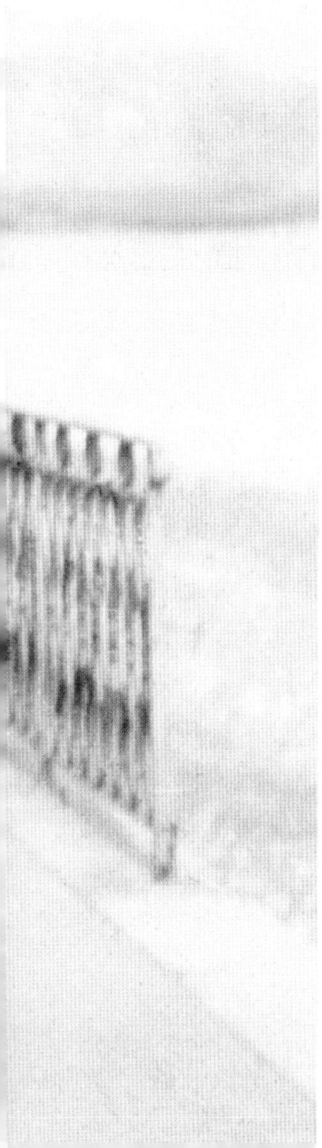

CHAPTER NINE

A YEAR in EUROPE

1921–1922

PREVIOUS PAGES The family walking along the promenade in Menton, 1922. Tracy closed Foxhollow Farm for a year to take the family on a tour of France and Italy.

RIGHT A view from the bow of the *Olympic*, October 1921, as it heads for France with the Dows family on board. The *Olympic* was the lead ship of the White Star Line's luxury transatlantic liners, alongside the *Titanic* and the *Britannic*.

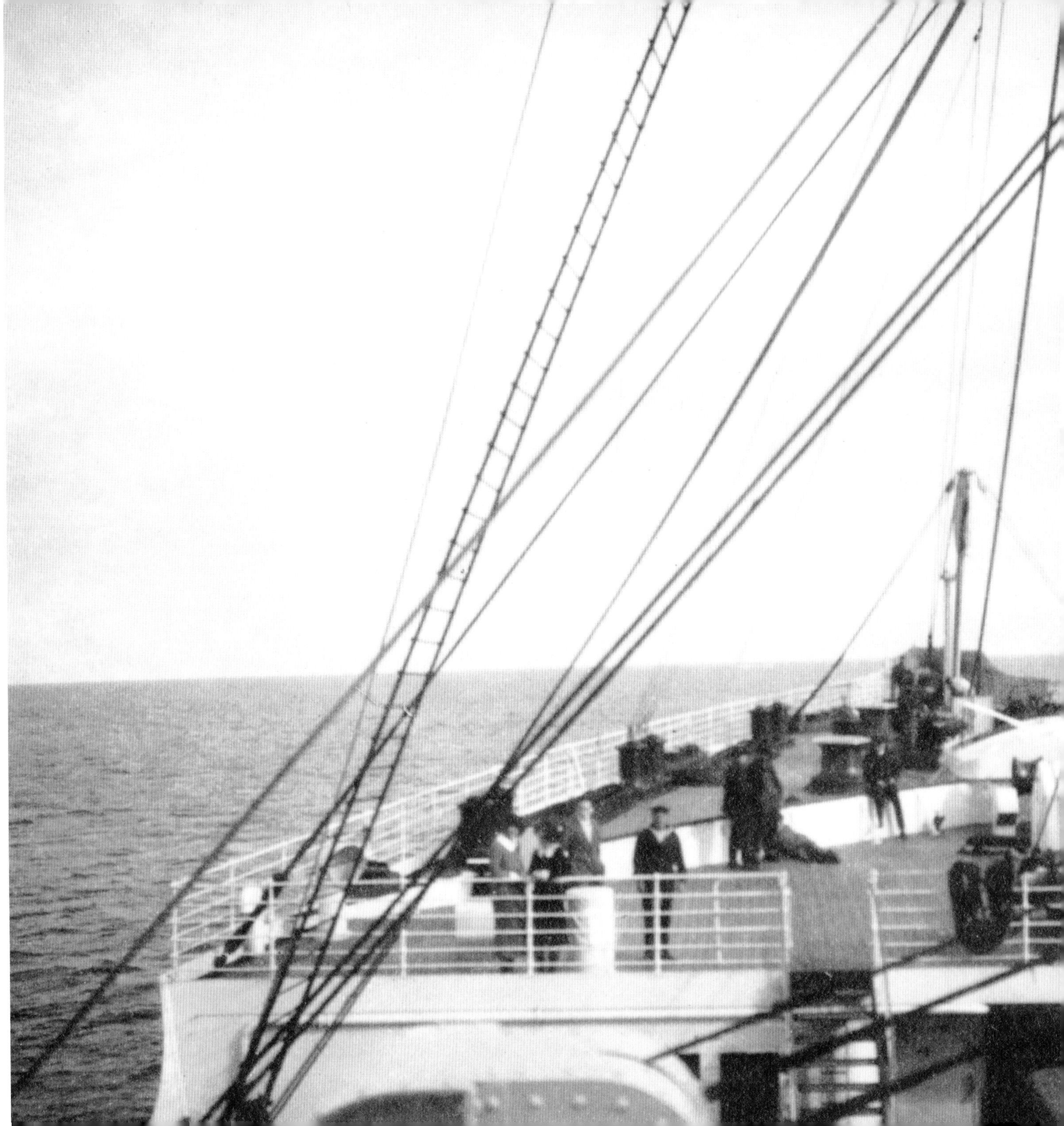

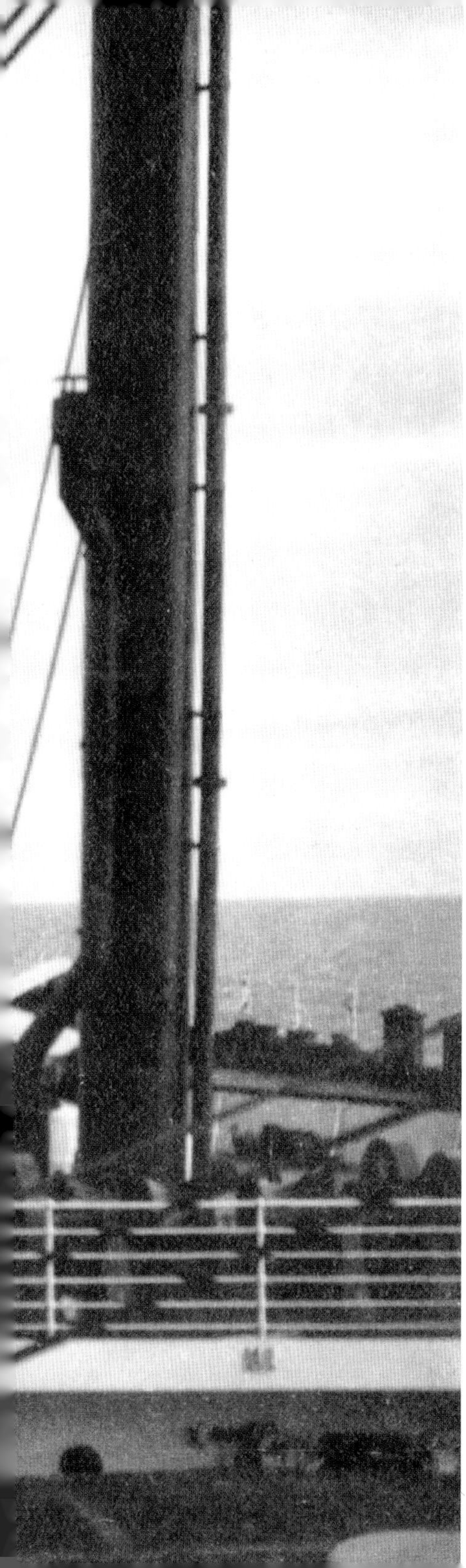

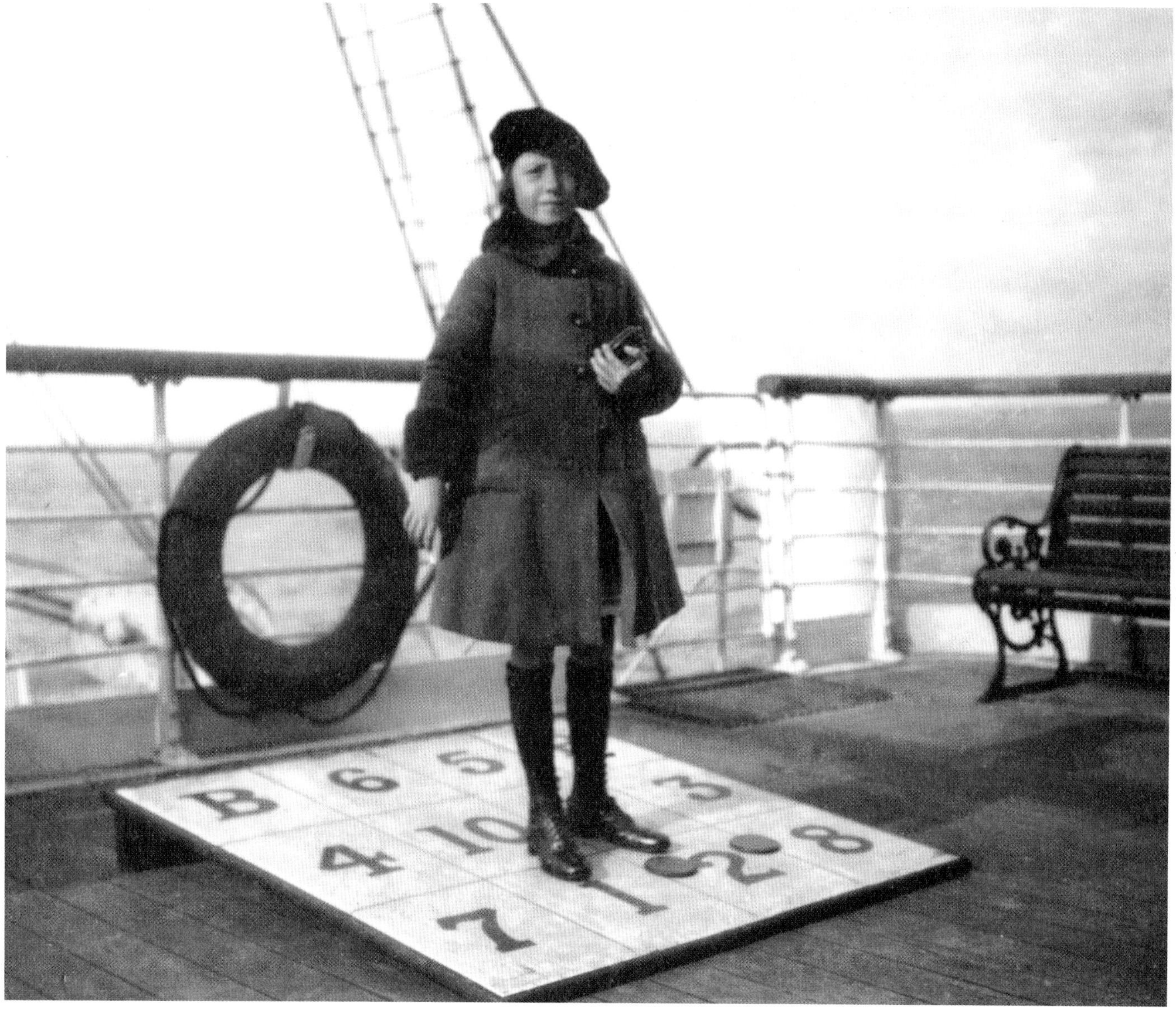

ABOVE Seven-year-old Deb standing on the game board on the deck of the *Olympic*.

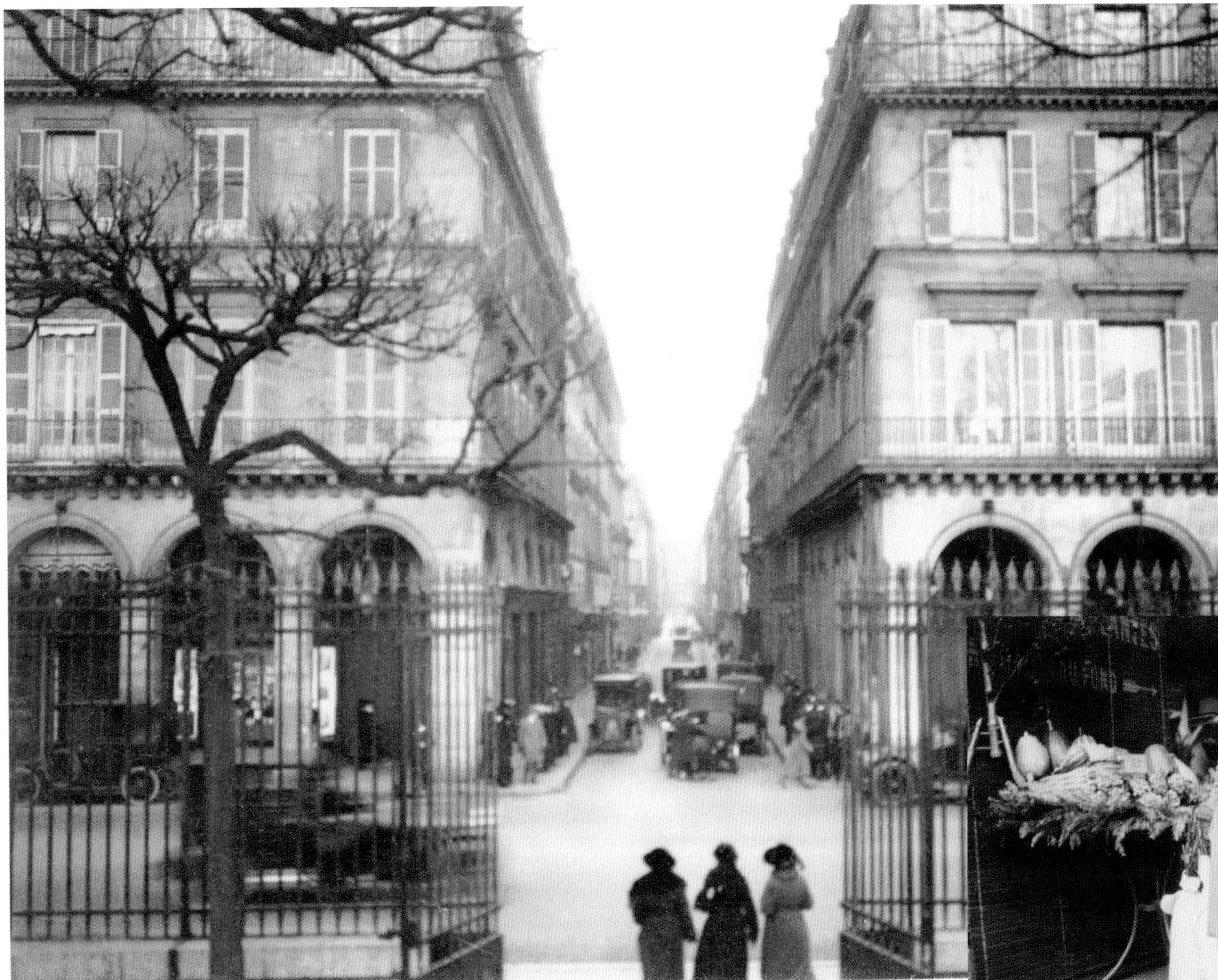

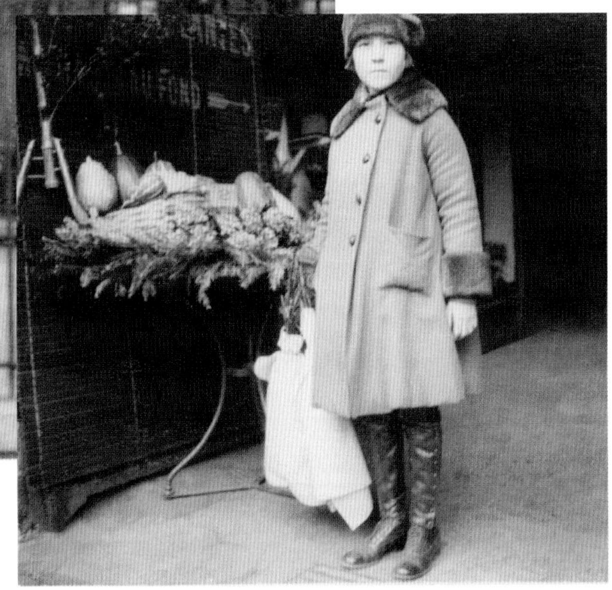

LEFT The streets of Paris, fall 1921. The family spent three months there while Olin studied painting at the École des Beaux-Arts.

BELOW Deb at a local Parisian market.

OPPOSITE Margaret, Alice, and Olin at the Grand Trianon at Versailles on a day trip in November.

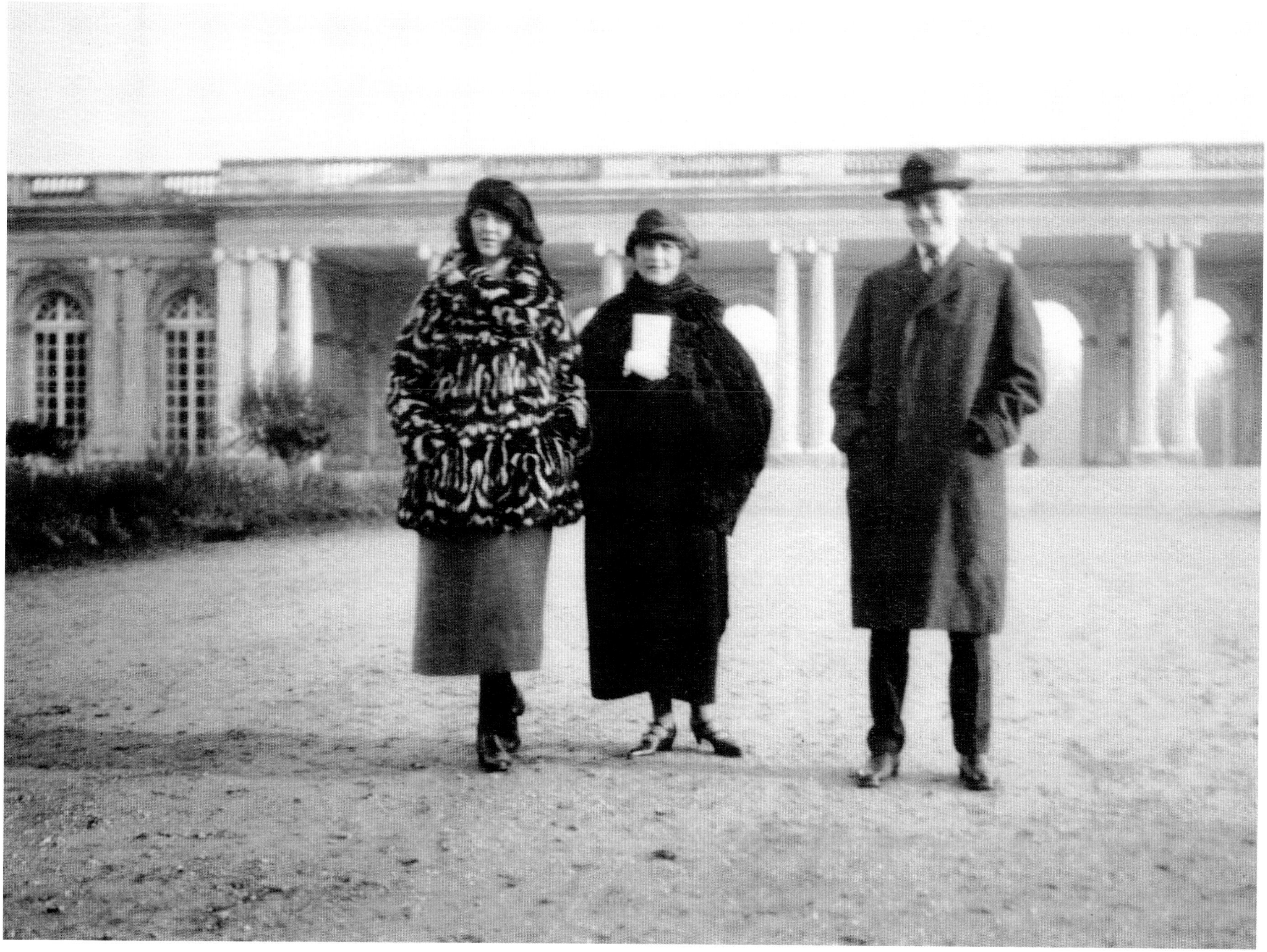

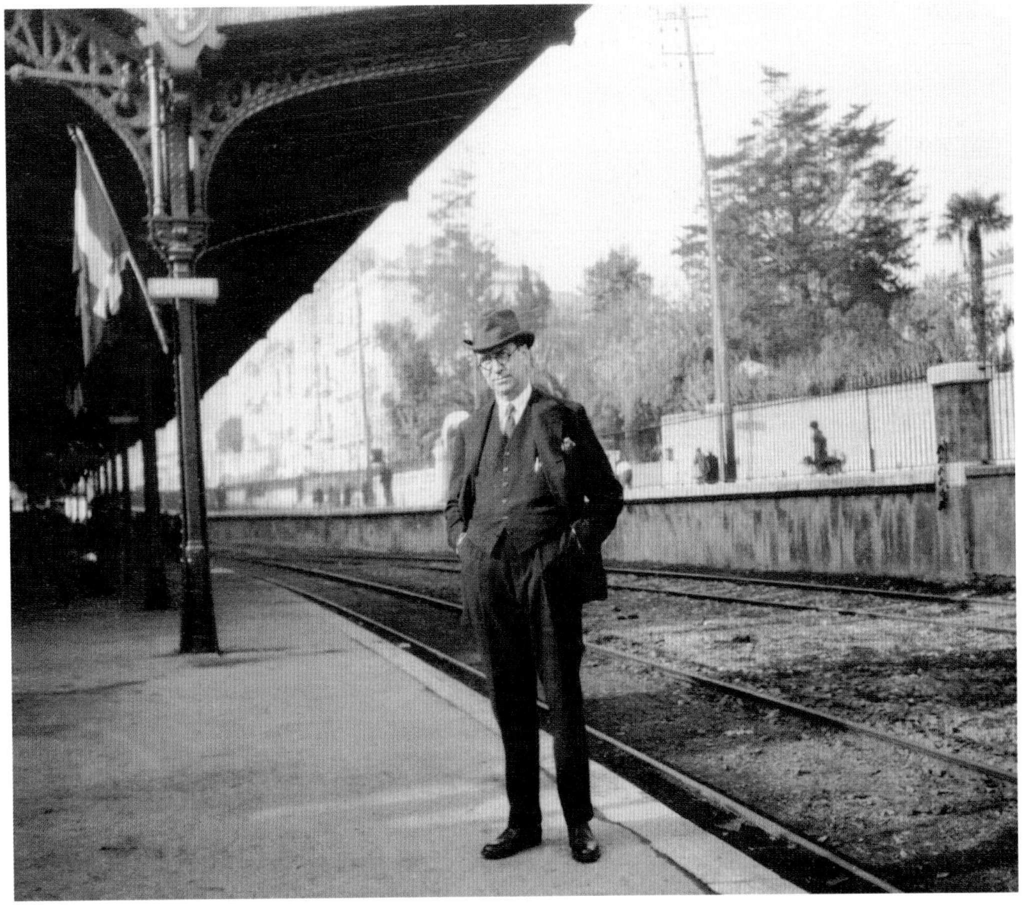

ABOVE Tracy at the Cannes train station, January 1922. The family traveled to Monte Carlo and Menton and spent a month on the French Riviera.

RIGHT A view of Menton. The area, situated along the border of France and Italy, is known as the "Pearl of France" because of its warm climate, beautiful gardens, and lemon groves.

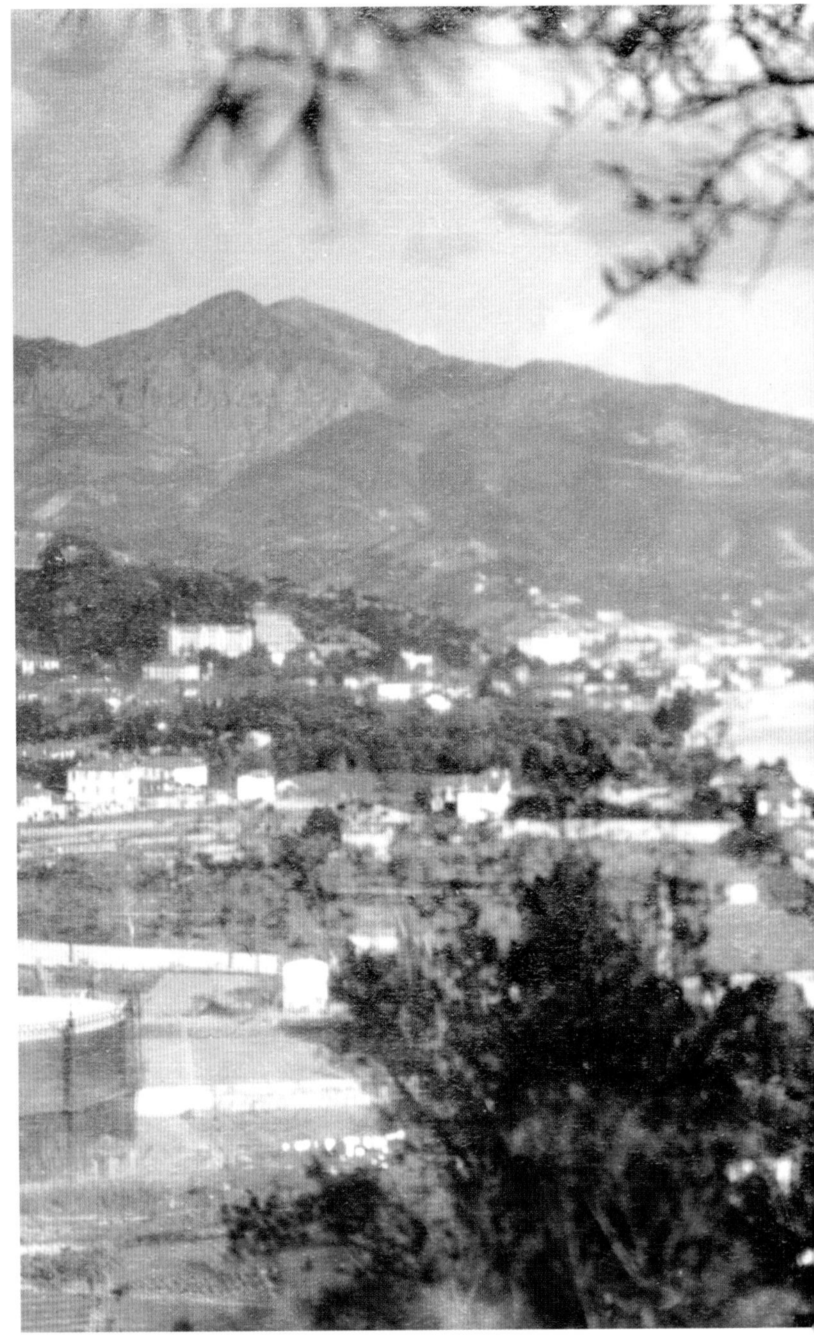

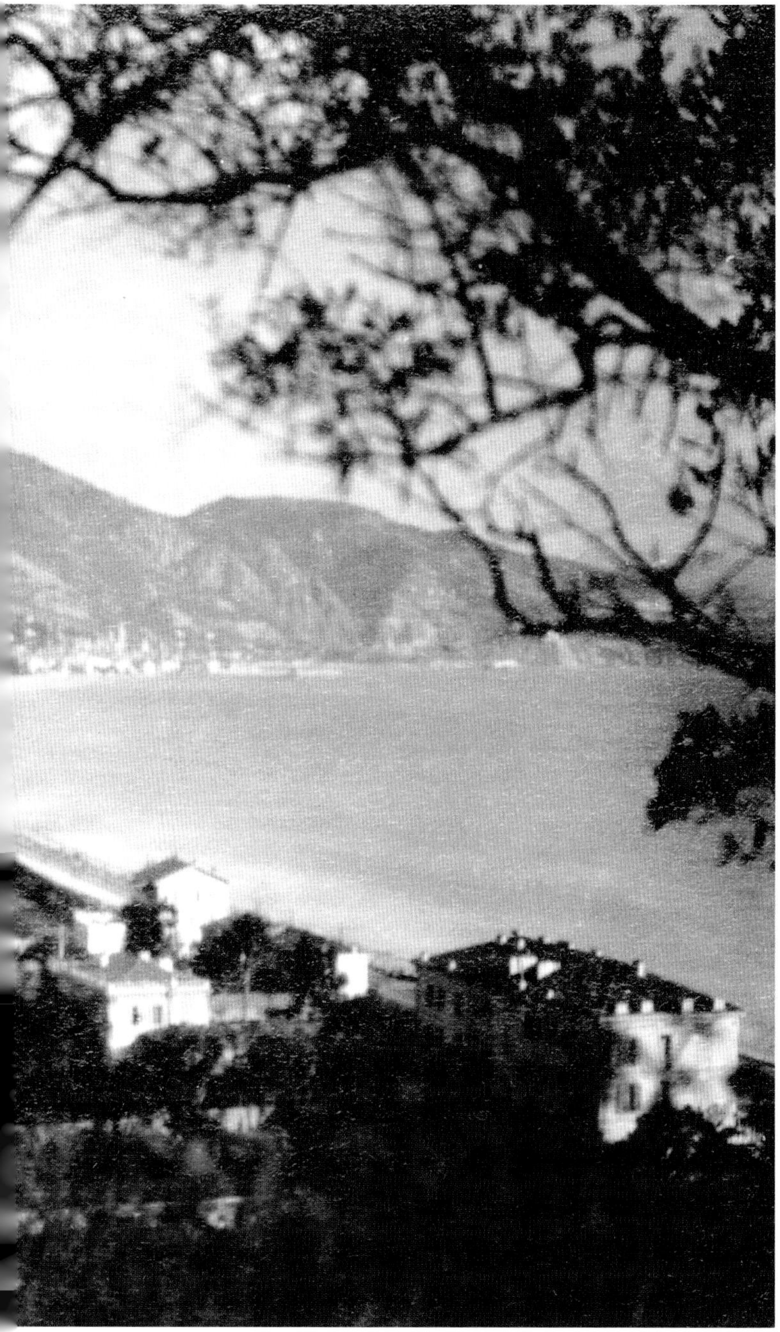

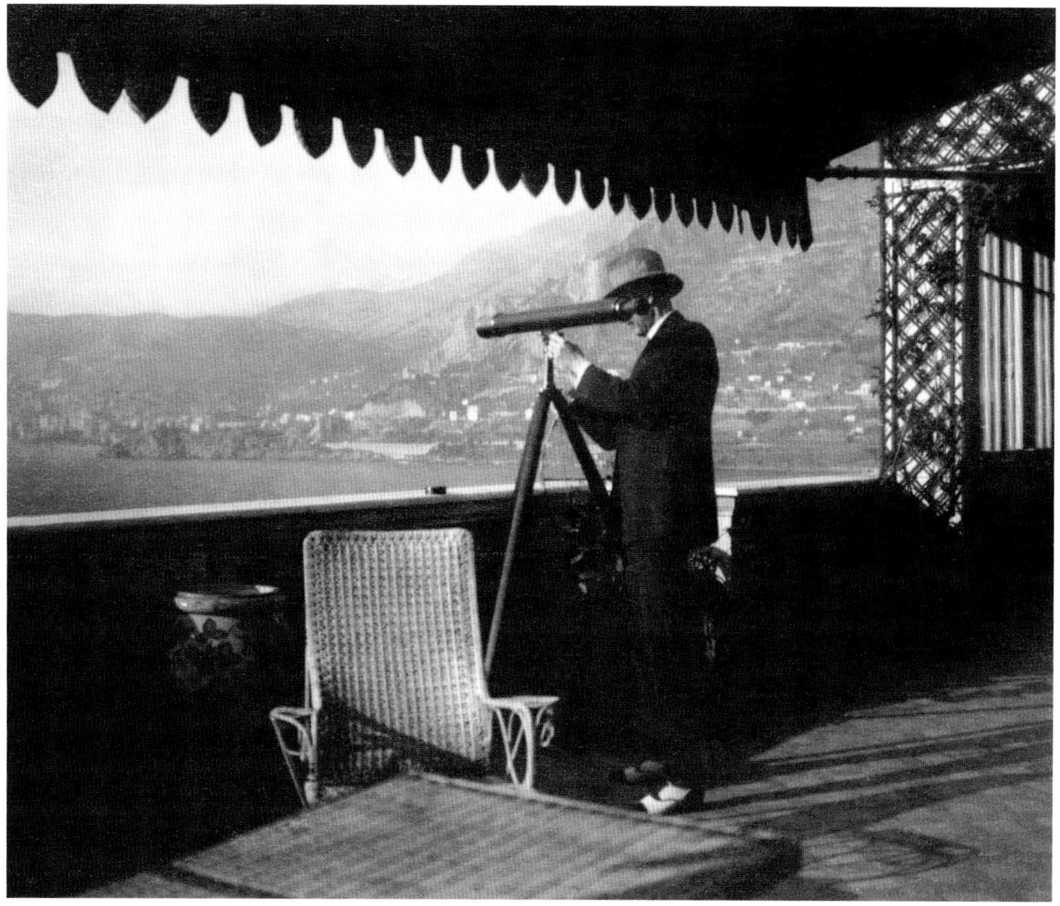

ABOVE Frank Blake adjusts his telescope on the terrace of his Roquebrune-Cap-Martin villa, Les Rochers, designed by Danish architect Hans-Georg Tersling, with a view of Monaco in the distance. The Dowses were visiting the Blakes, who had left America in 1902 to live full-time at Les Rochers. In 1914, the Blakes sailed on one of their yearly visits to the United States aboard the *Lusitania* but canceled their return passage to France in order to help with wartime aid. The *Lusitania* was torpedoed and sank on that voyage. The Blakes later returned to France and Frank secured a position with the American Red Cross.

BELOW Olin on the Simplon-Orient Express in February of 1922. The family returned to Paris to travel on the train to Venice, where they stayed for six days. The main route ran from Paris to Istanbul, with travel to Venice on a branch line.

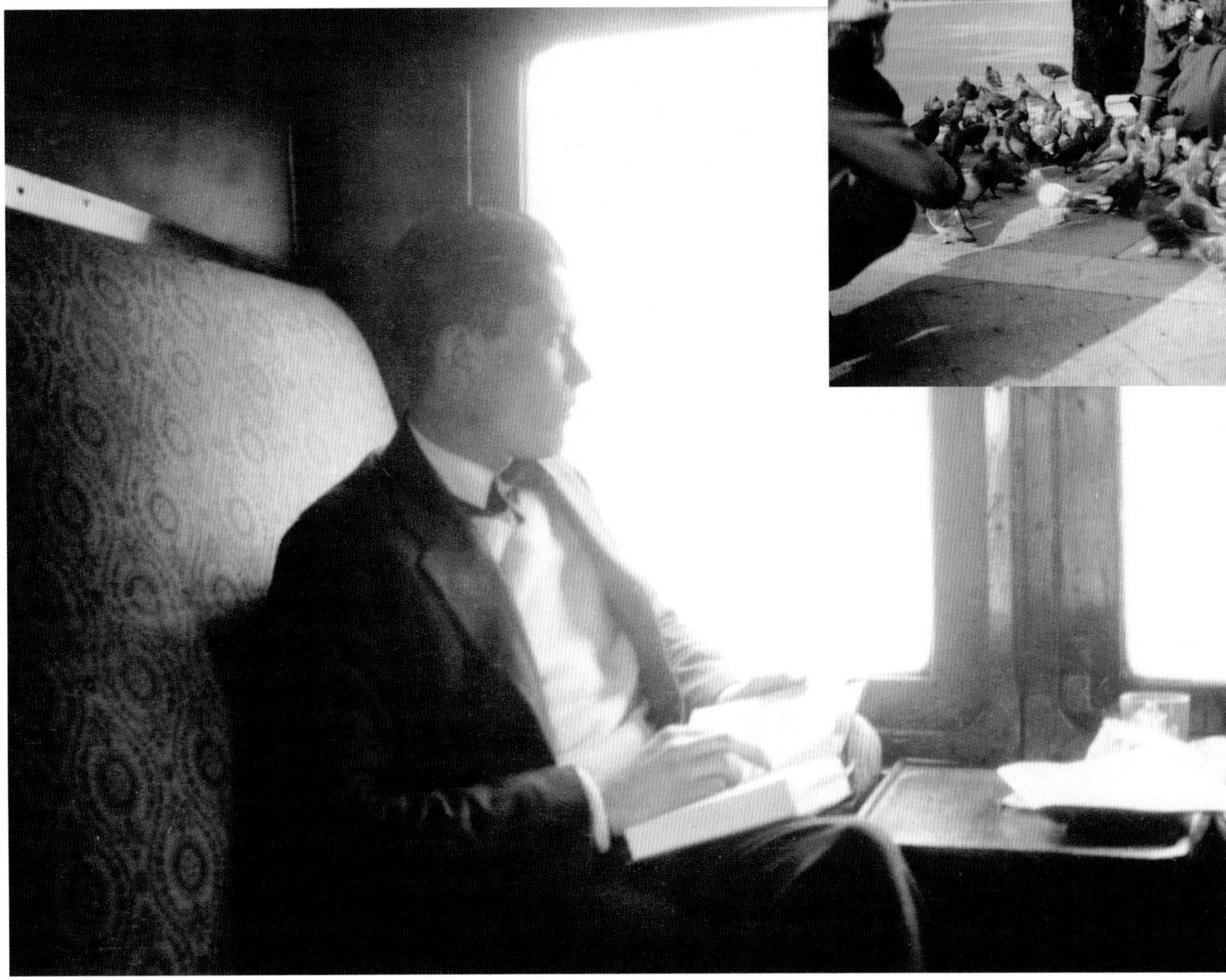

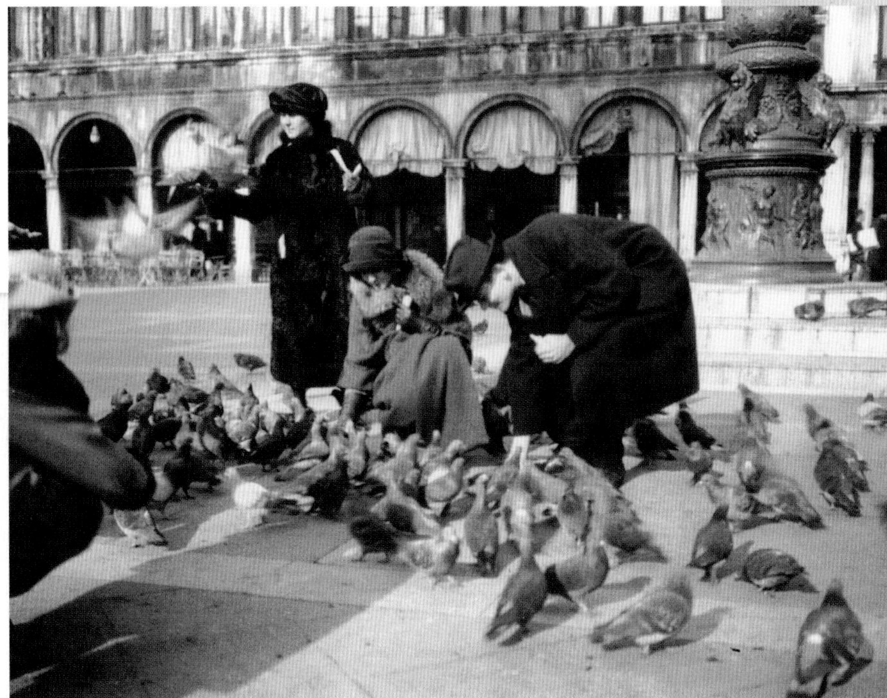

ABOVE Margaret and Olin feeding the pigeons in Piazza San Marco, Venice.

RIGHT A serene late-afternoon view of gondoliers at work.

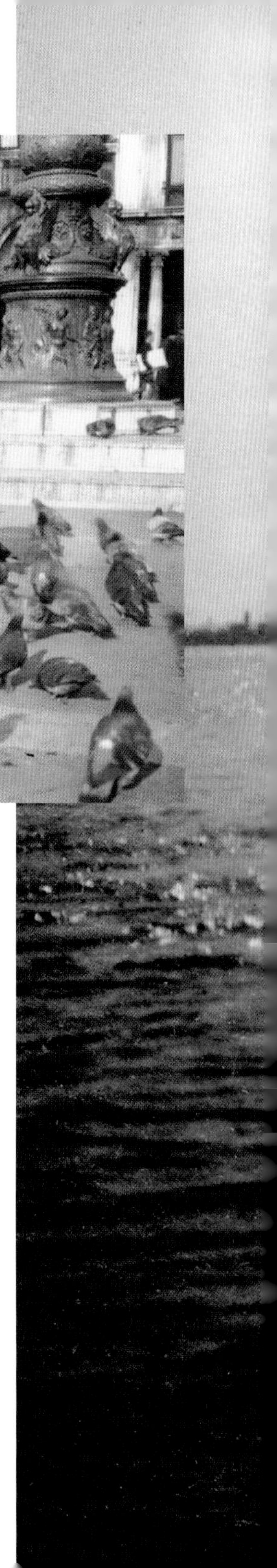

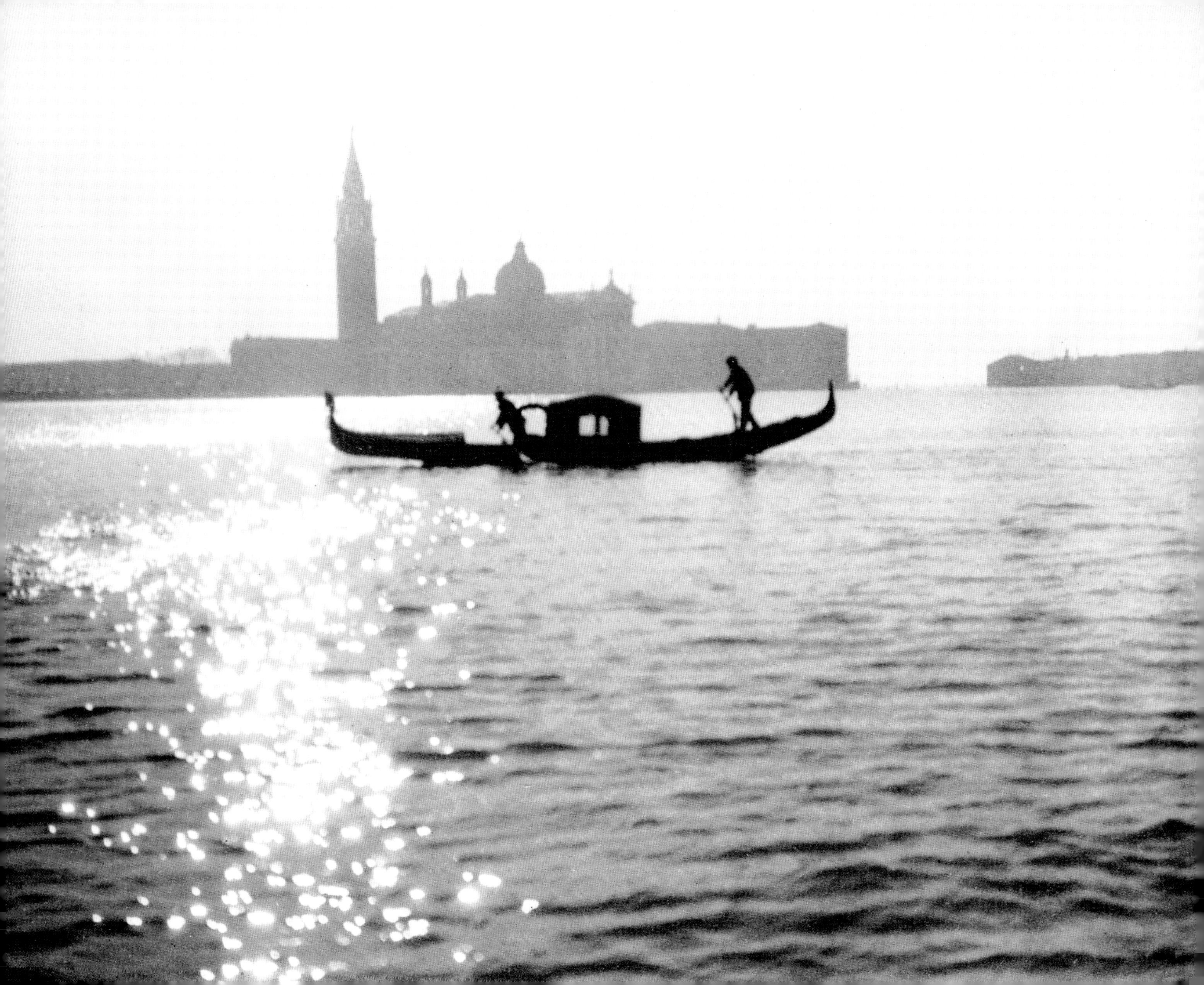

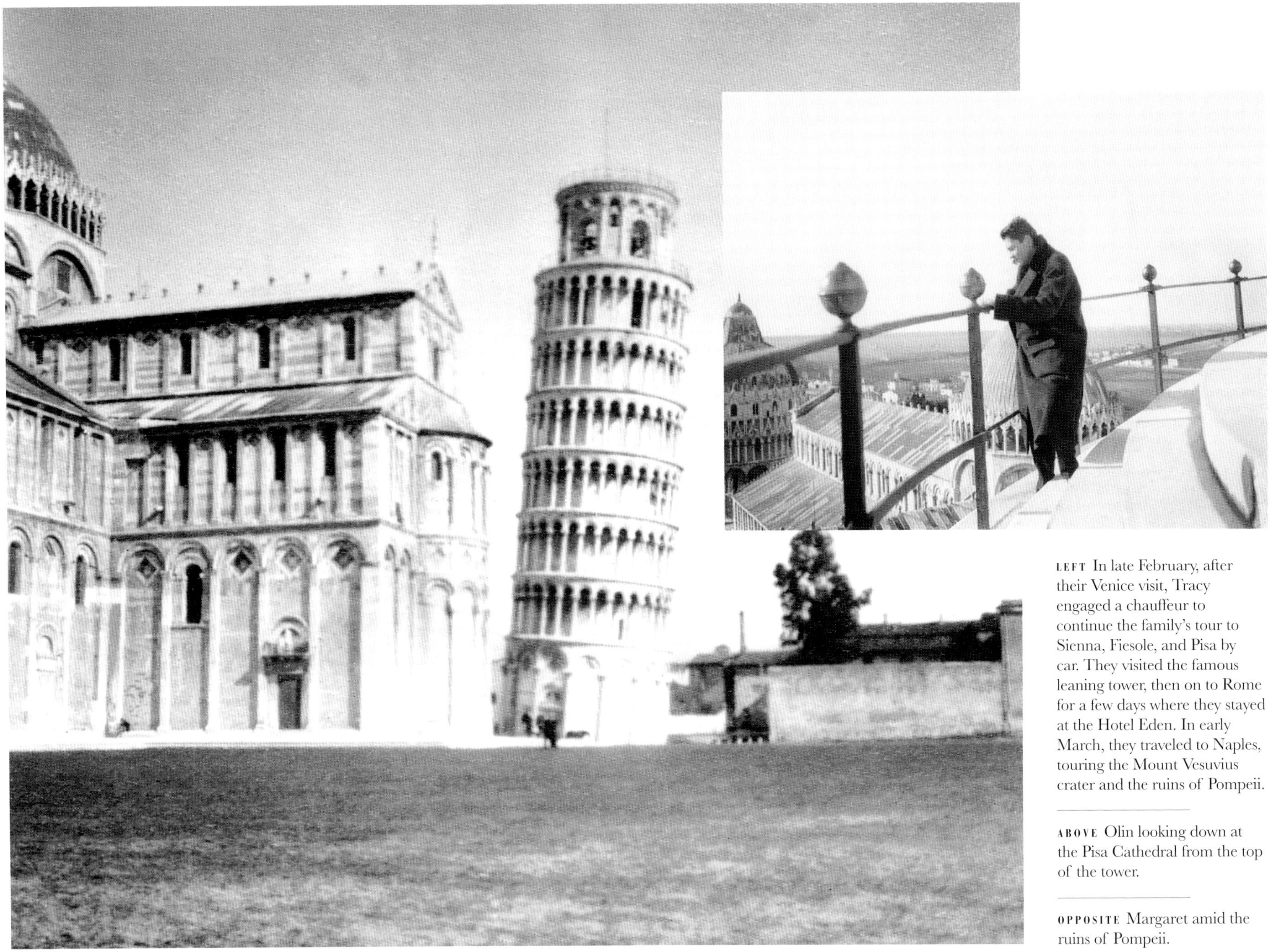

LEFT In late February, after their Venice visit, Tracy engaged a chauffeur to continue the family's tour to Sienna, Fiesole, and Pisa by car. They visited the famous leaning tower, then on to Rome for a few days where they stayed at the Hotel Eden. In early March, they traveled to Naples, touring the Mount Vesuvius crater and the ruins of Pompeii.

ABOVE Olin looking down at the Pisa Cathedral from the top of the tower.

OPPOSITE Margaret amid the ruins of Pompeii.

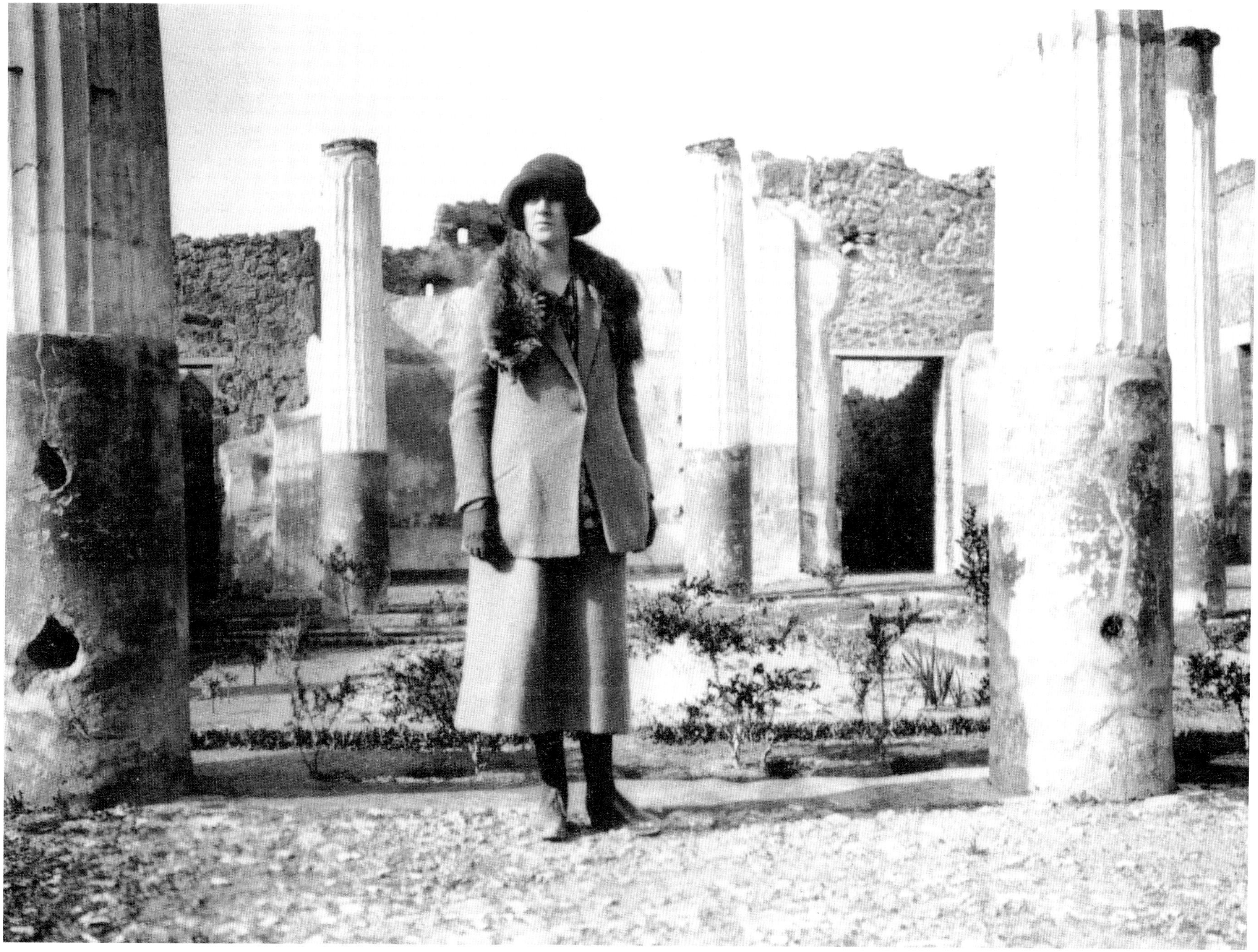

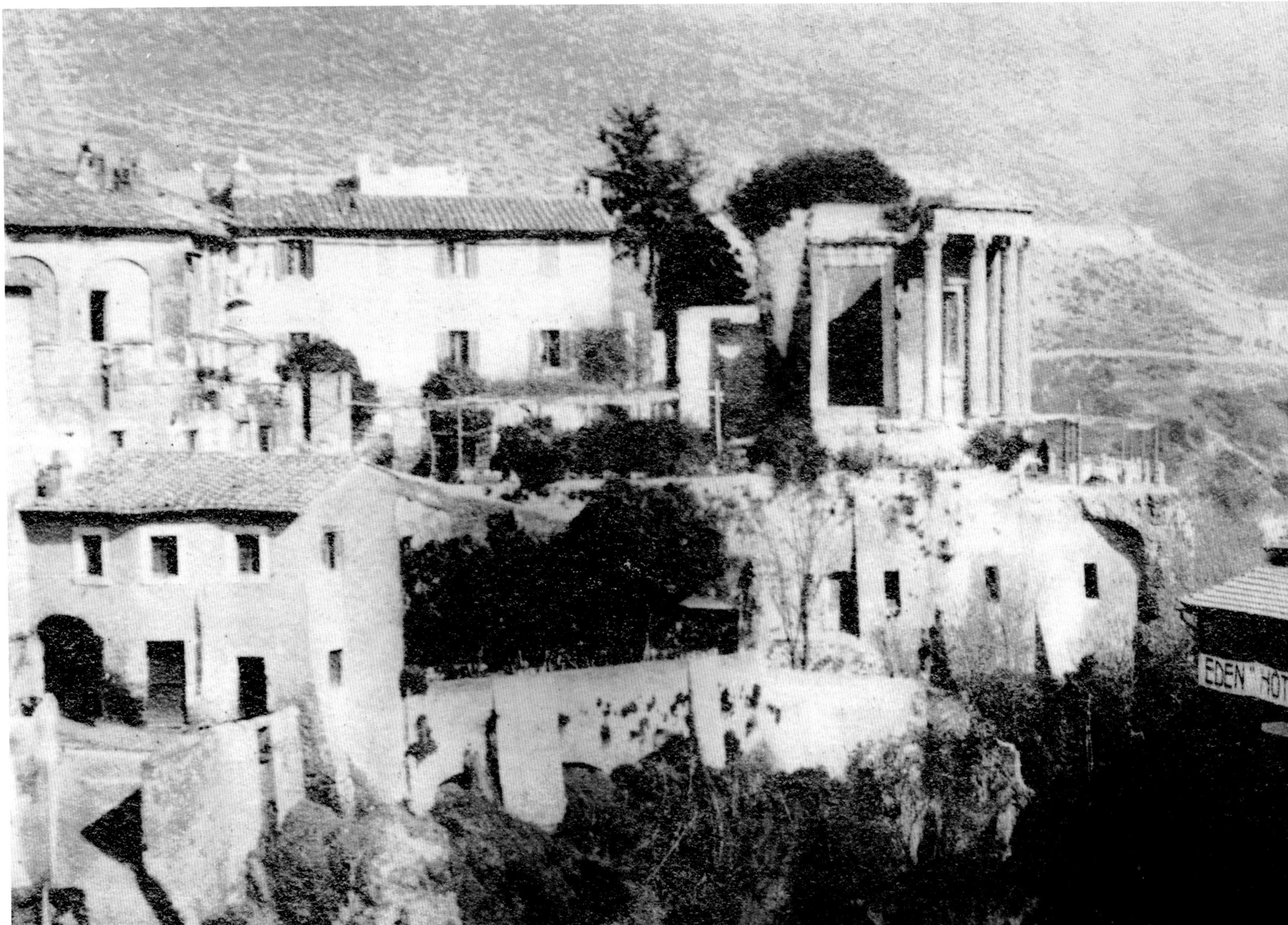
EDEN HOTE

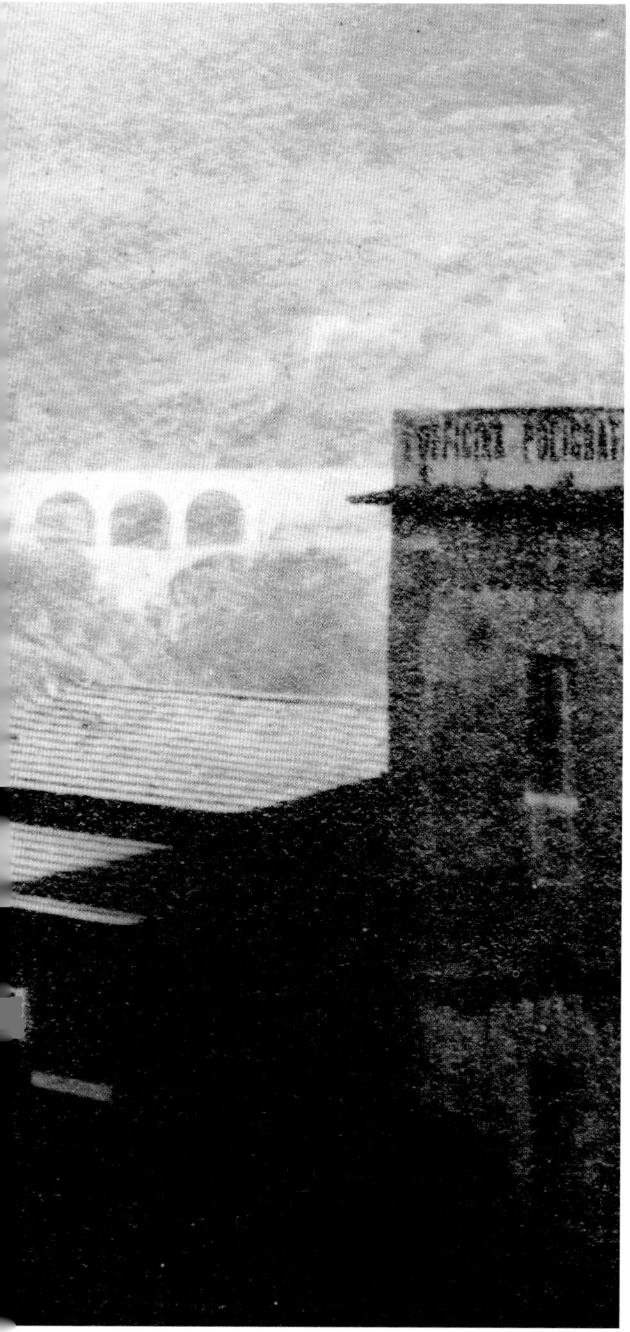

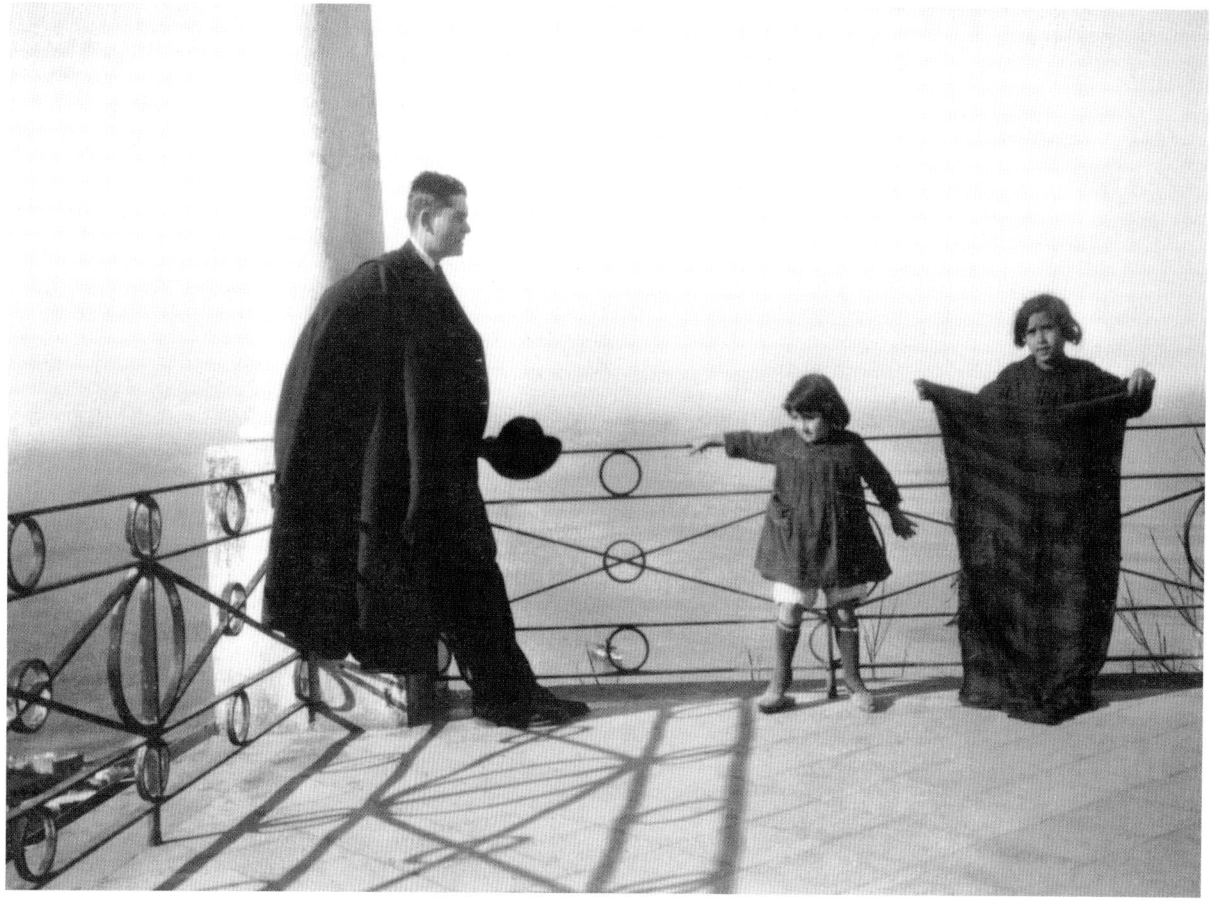

LEFT From Naples, the family motored to the picturesque hillside town of Sorrento before boarding a ferry to Capri.

ABOVE Olin, with two children from the village, on the terrace at the top of the Funicolare in Capri, March 15, 1922. The funicular cable car was built in 1911 to take passengers up a steep incline from the Marina Grande to Piazza Umberto.

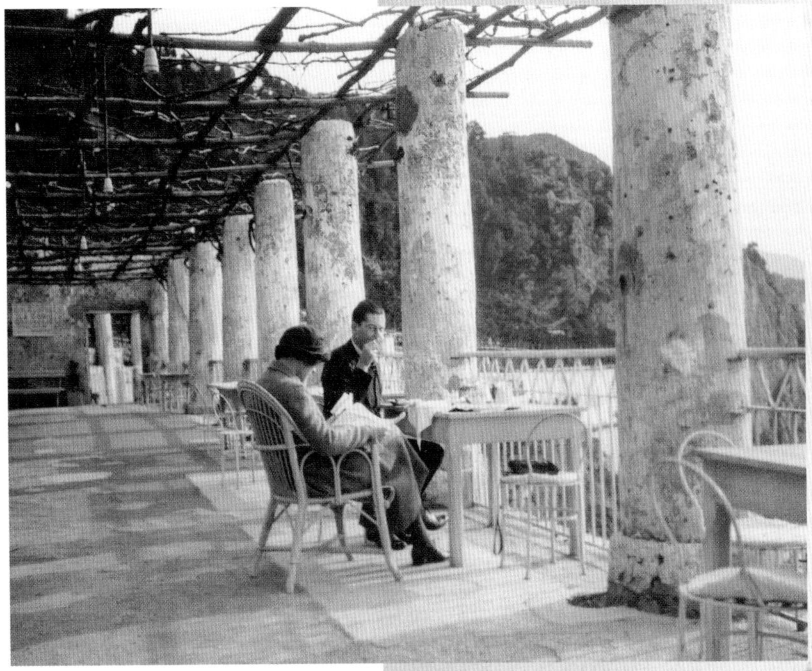

ABOVE Margaret and Olin having breakfast at Hotel Cappuccini in Amalfi. The family had continued their journey along the coast by car, visiting the towns of Amalfi and Ravello.

RIGHT A view of Amalfi showing its jagged coastline and winding streets. Hotel Cappuccini, with its colonnaded terrace, is seen on the hillside. Originally a thirteenth-century monastery, it is considered to be one of the most important monuments on the Amalfi Coast, and is now known as the Grand Hotel Convento di Amalfi.

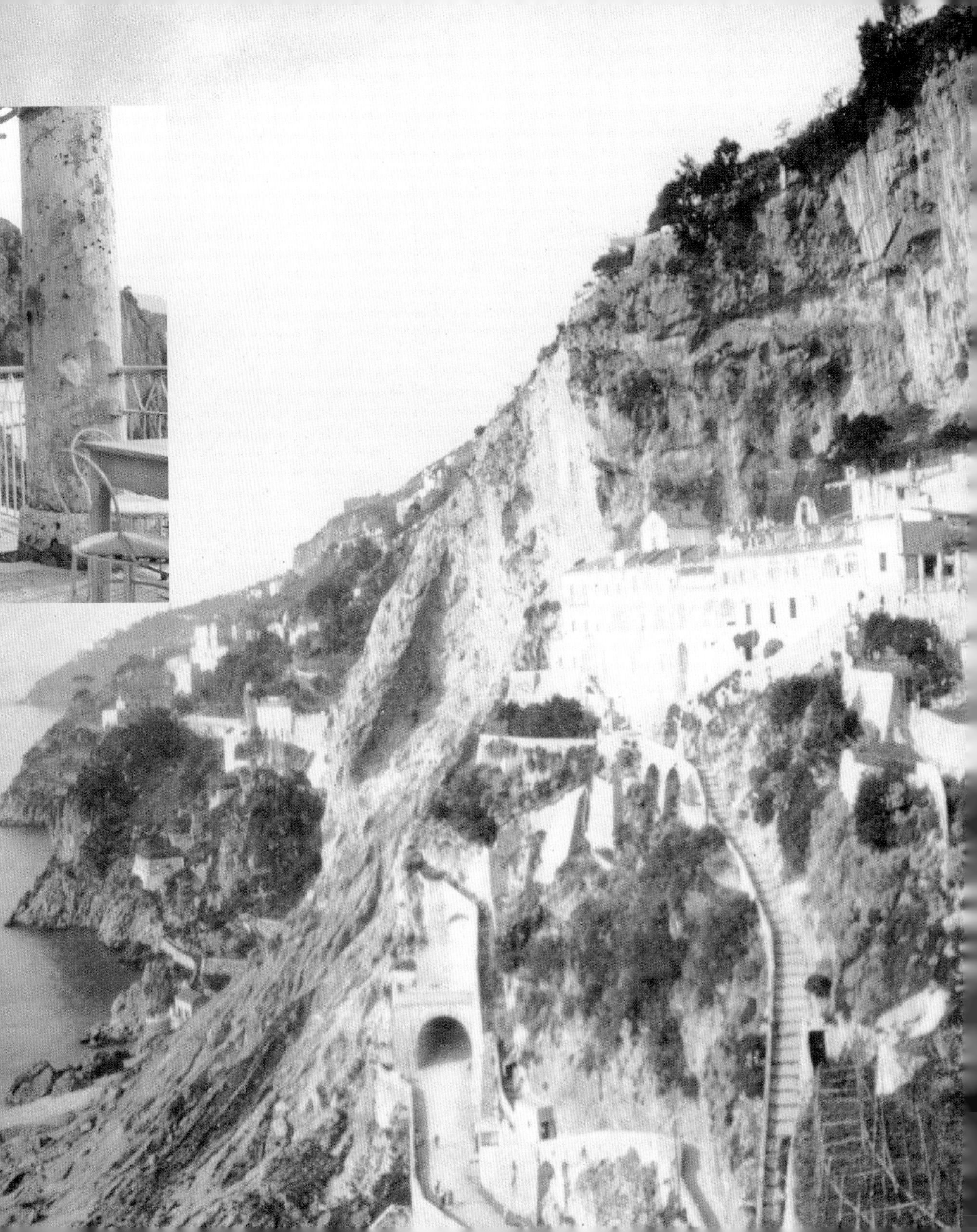

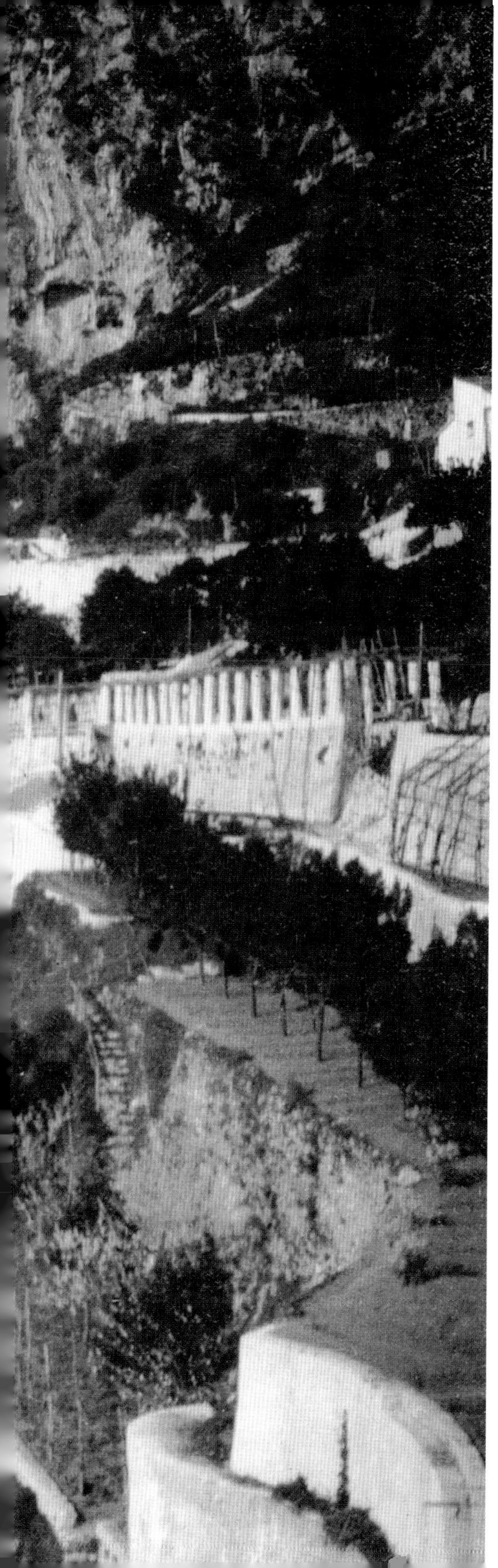

BELOW The Terrace of Infinity at Villa Cimbrone in Ravello, famous for its eighteenth-century marble busts and breathtaking views. Gore Vidal, who spent three decades living in the town, described the views as the most ravishing he had ever seen. The villa dates back to the eleventh century. After Amalfi and Ravello, the Dowses returned to Naples and sailed on the *Adriatic* to Menton, where they spent another three months in France.

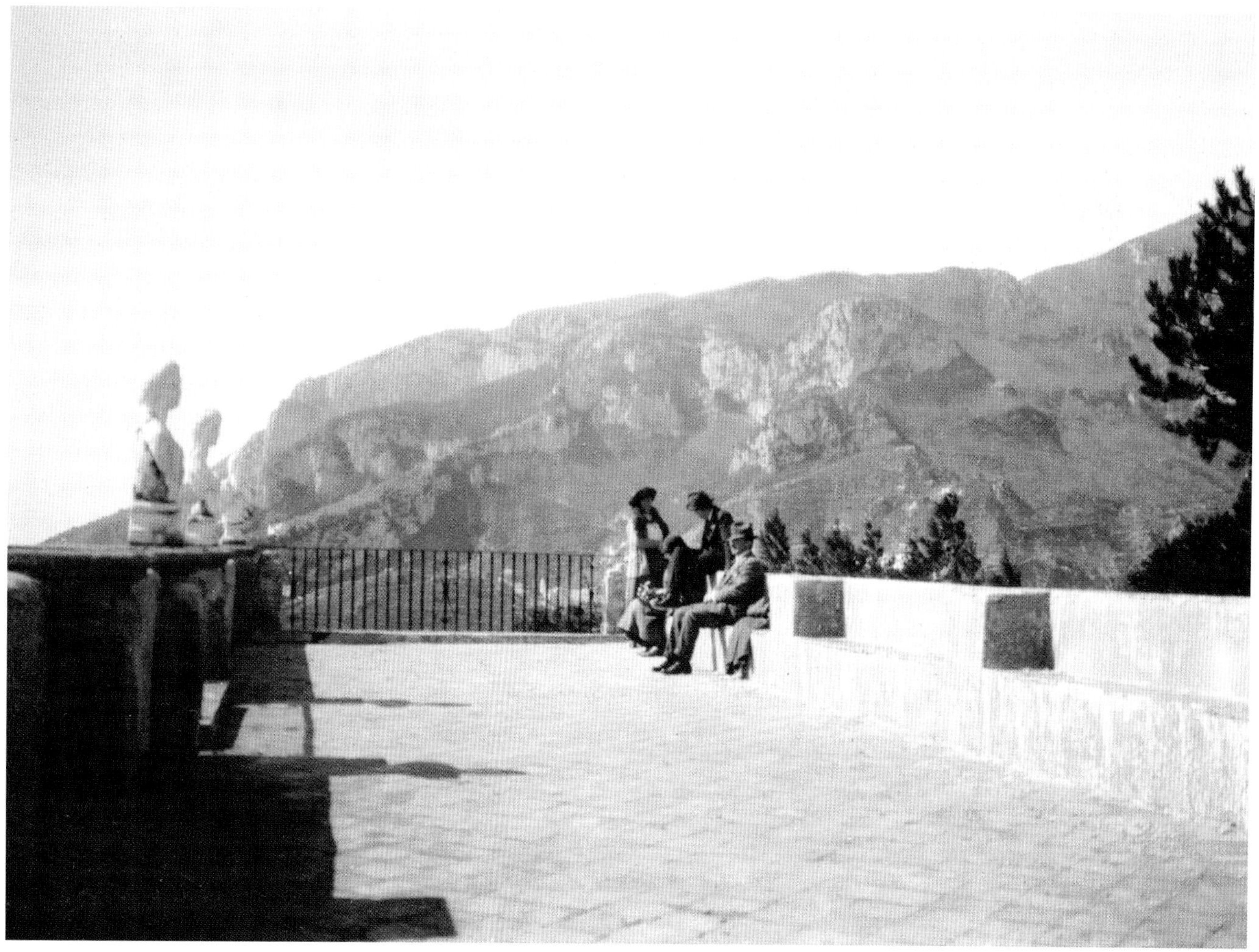

RIGHT Villagers gather around Deb in her decorated donkey cart at the Battle of Flowers Parade in Menton, March 21. She is dressed in a Pierrot costume.

BELOW Olin, Alice, and Tracy, captured by a local photographer as they watch the parade from the grandstands.

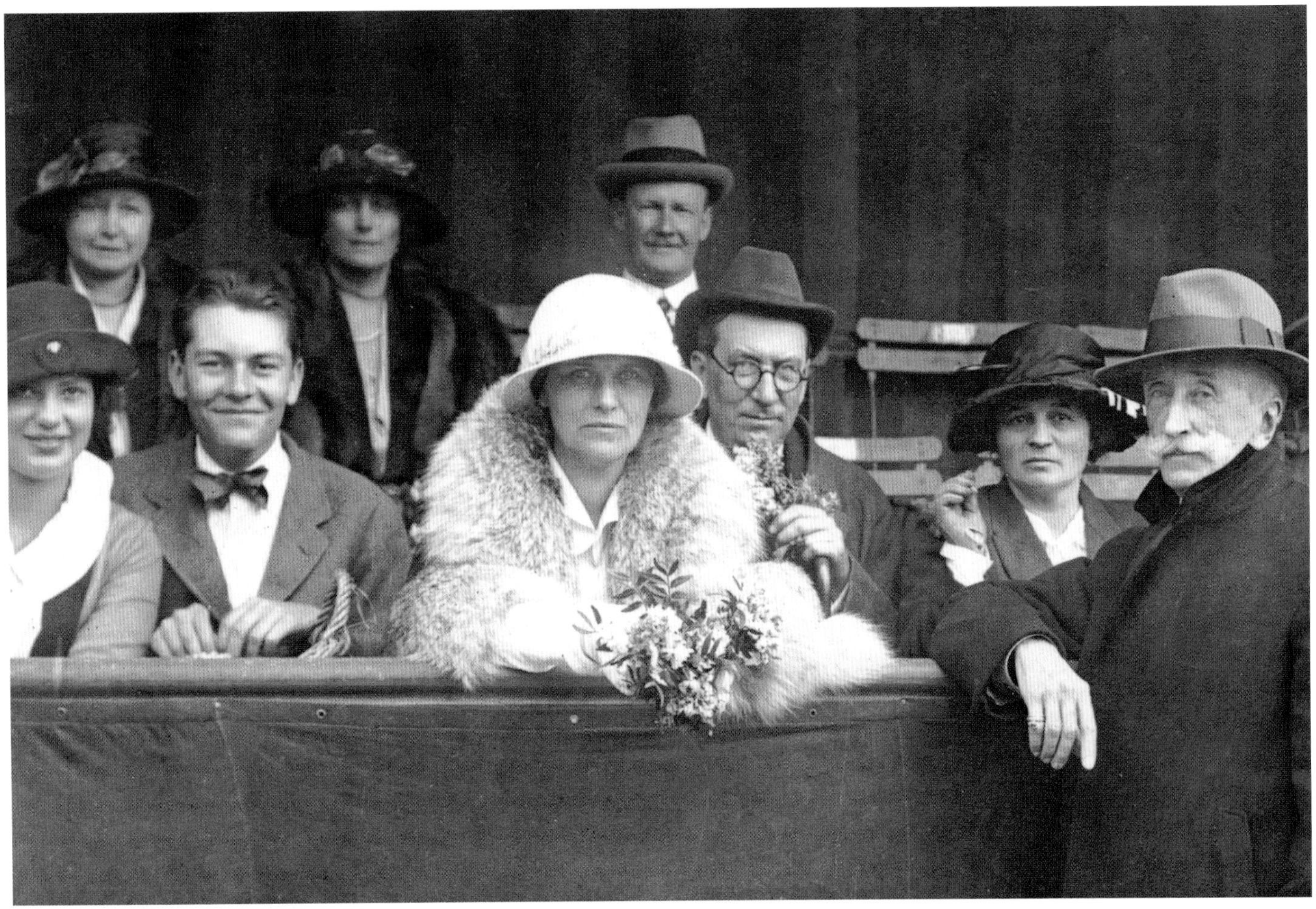

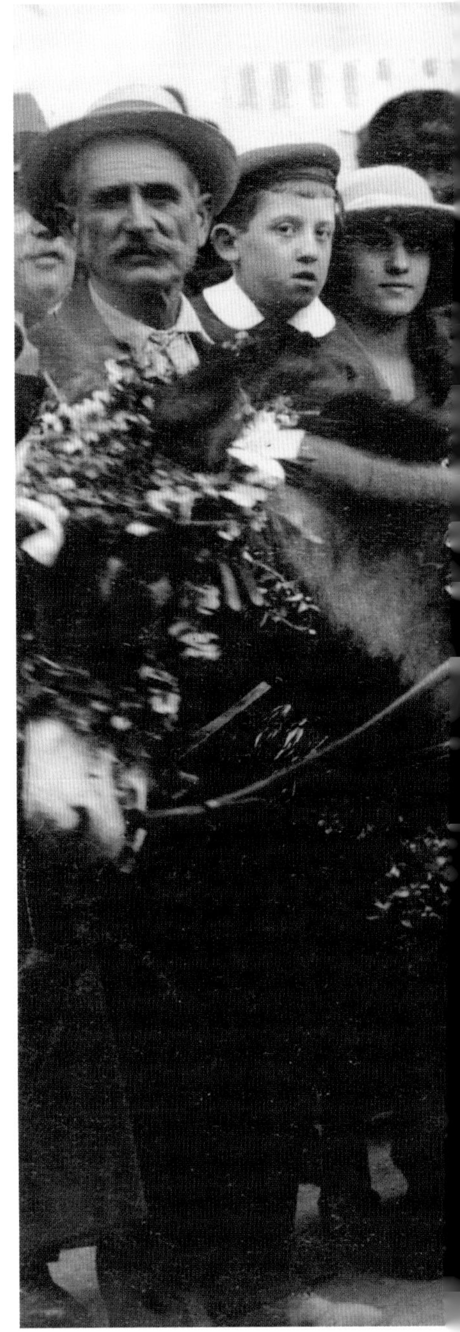

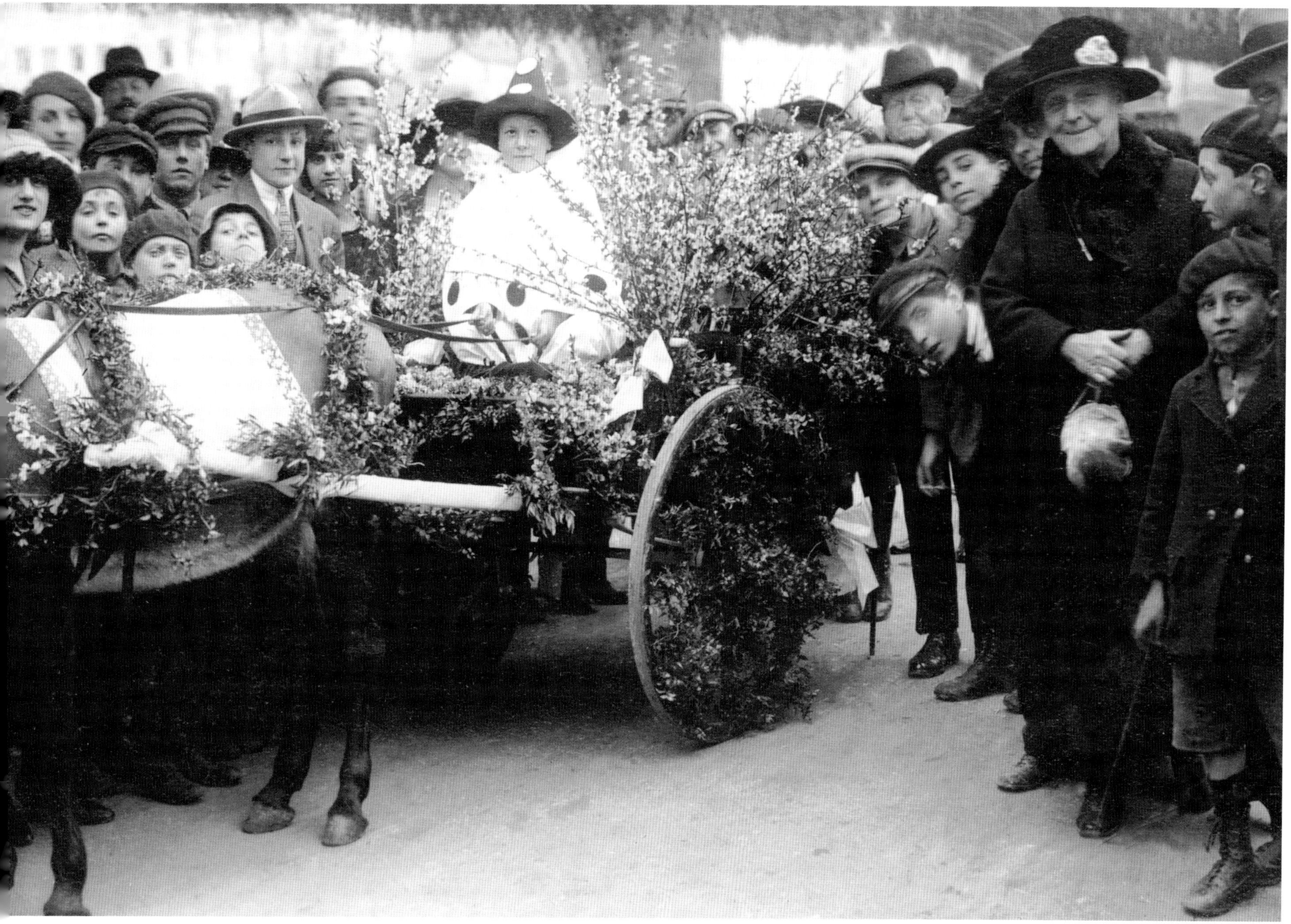

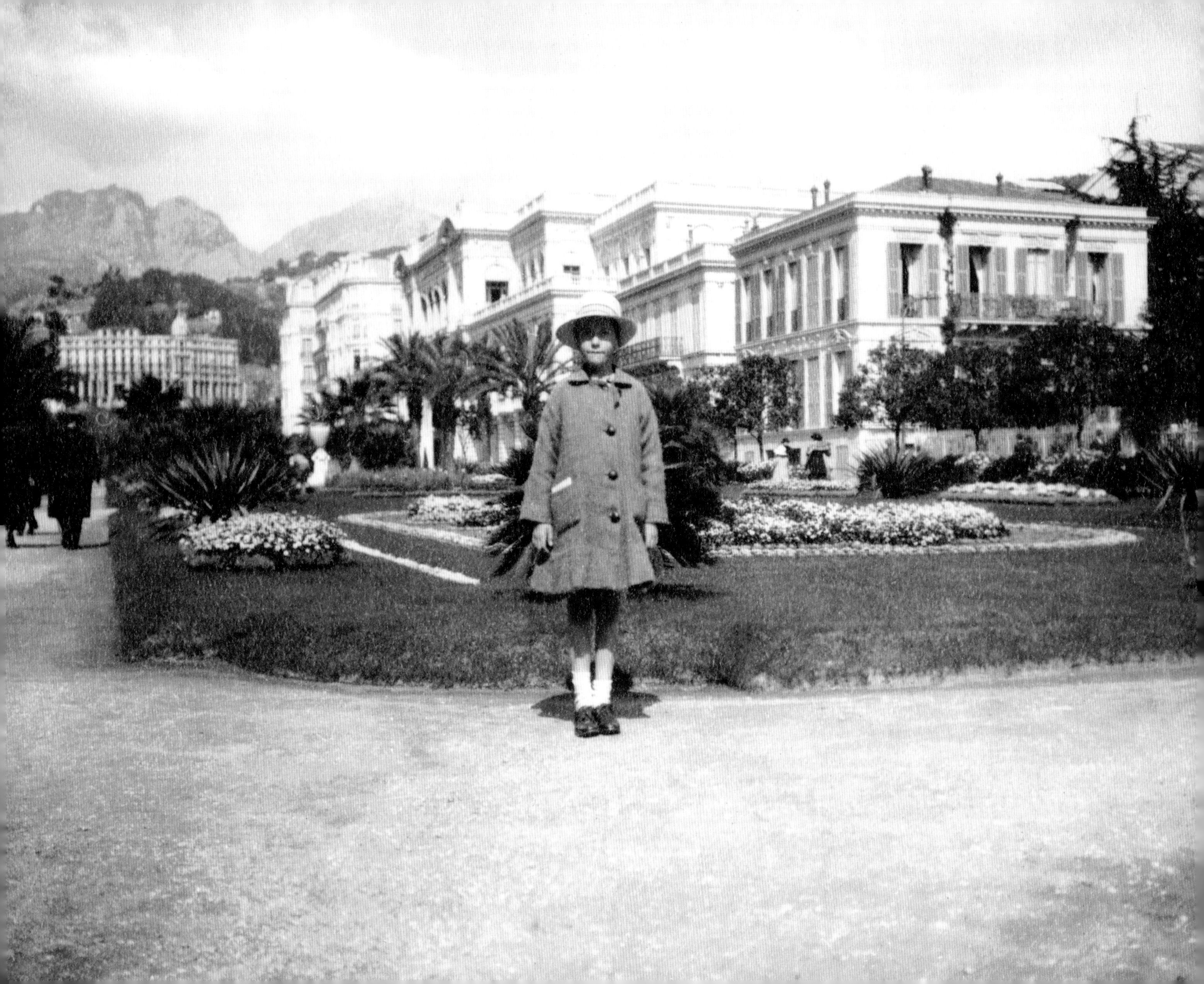

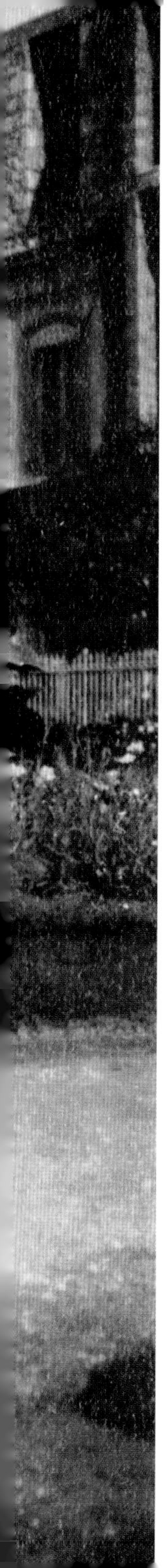

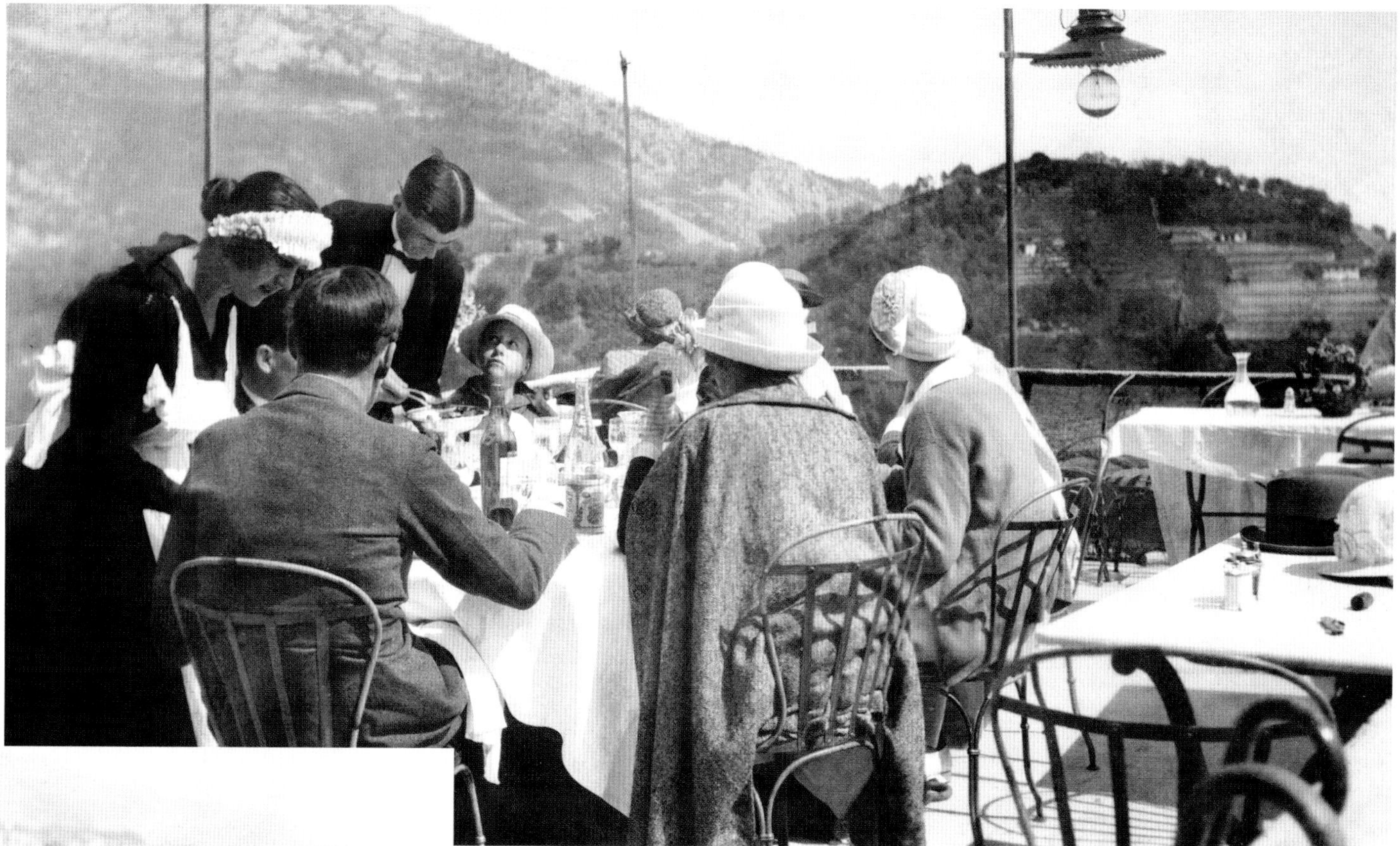

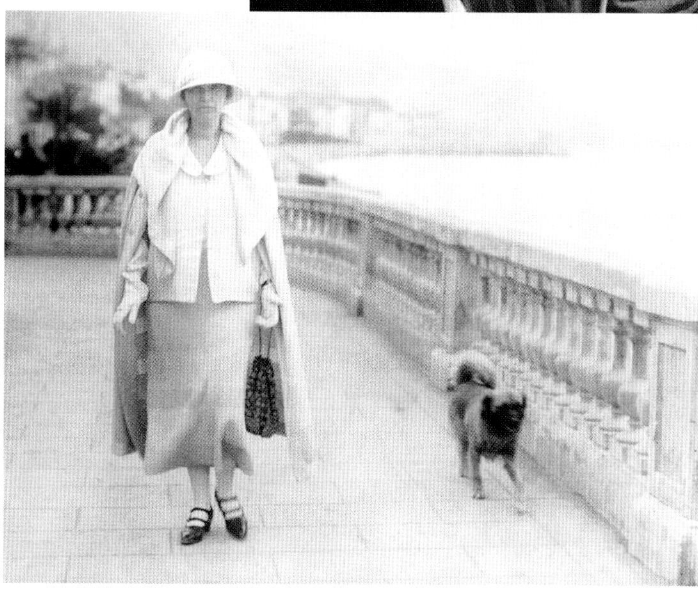

ABOVE Lunch on the terrace of a Menton restaurant.

LEFT Alice and a friendly local dog strolling along the promenade in Menton.

OPPOSITE Deb in front of The Casino (now the Palais de l'Europe.) Known for its beautiful gardens, it was built in 1908 and designed by Hans-Georg Tersling, the architect of Frank Blake's villa, and of Menton's Hôtel Impérial.

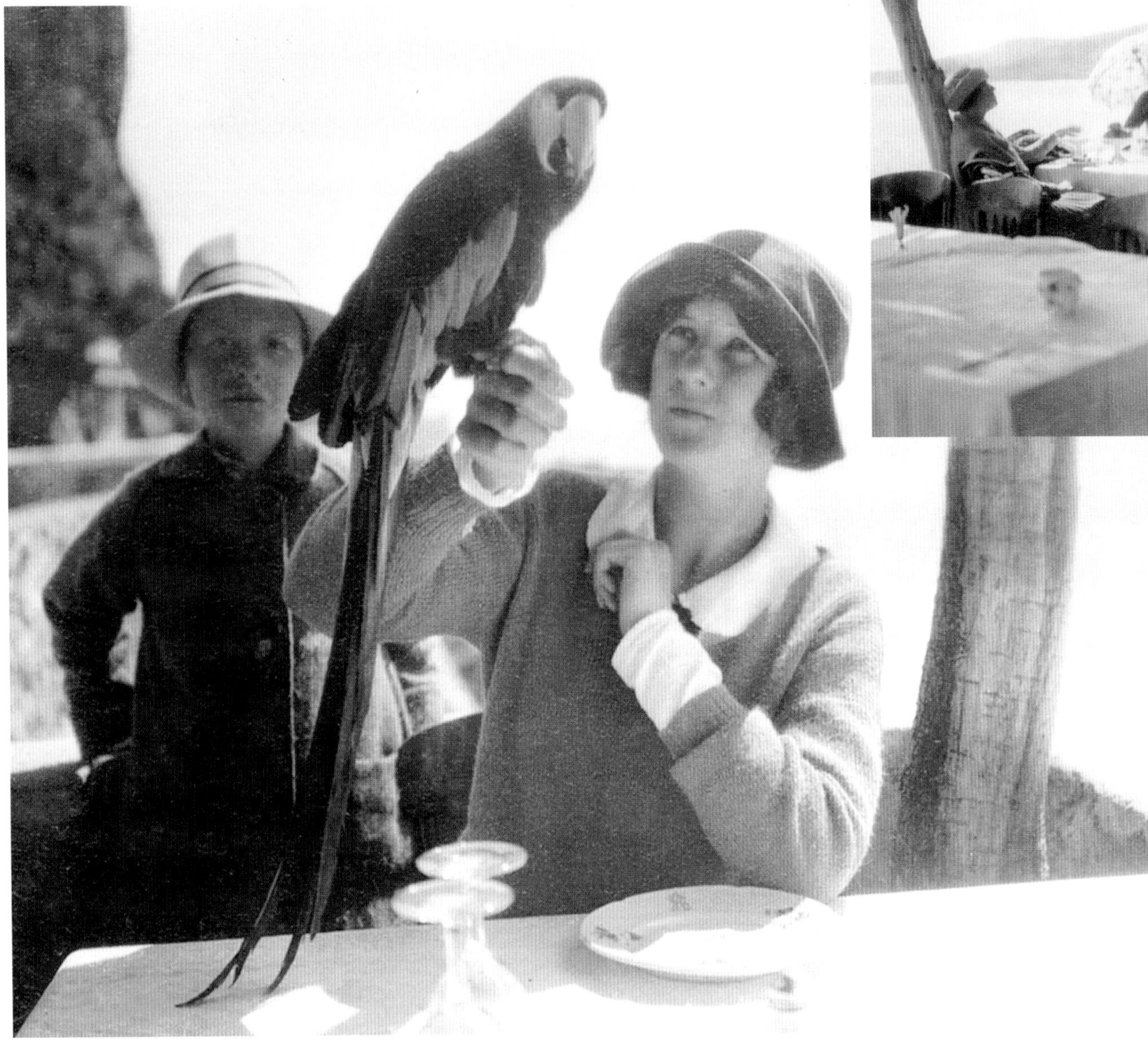

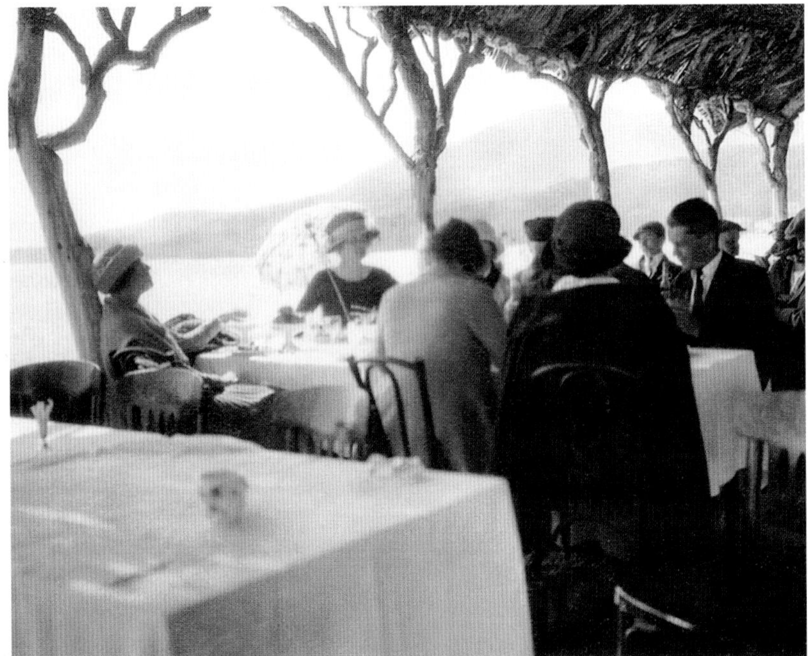

ABOVE The family having lunch at a seaside cafe at Les Rochers Rouges (also known as Balzi Rossi), the area just over the Italian border, not far from Menton. The pink-colored rocks and cliffs date back to prehistoric times. Helen Huntington Astor, who joined them from Paris, is seated at the table with a parasol. Many newspaper society columns reported that Helen had taken an apartment in Paris for an indefinite time due to marital strife. In November, Vincent joined her in Paris and they both returned to New York on the *Mauretania*, which seemed to dispel the rumors.

LEFT A friendly parrot pays a visit to the table during lunch. Deb watches as Margaret allows the bird to perch on her hand.

OPPOSITE Helen waving goodbye to the Dows family as she pretends to be a passenger in a painted backdrop of a Savoia plane set up for souvenir photographs at Les Rochers Rouges.

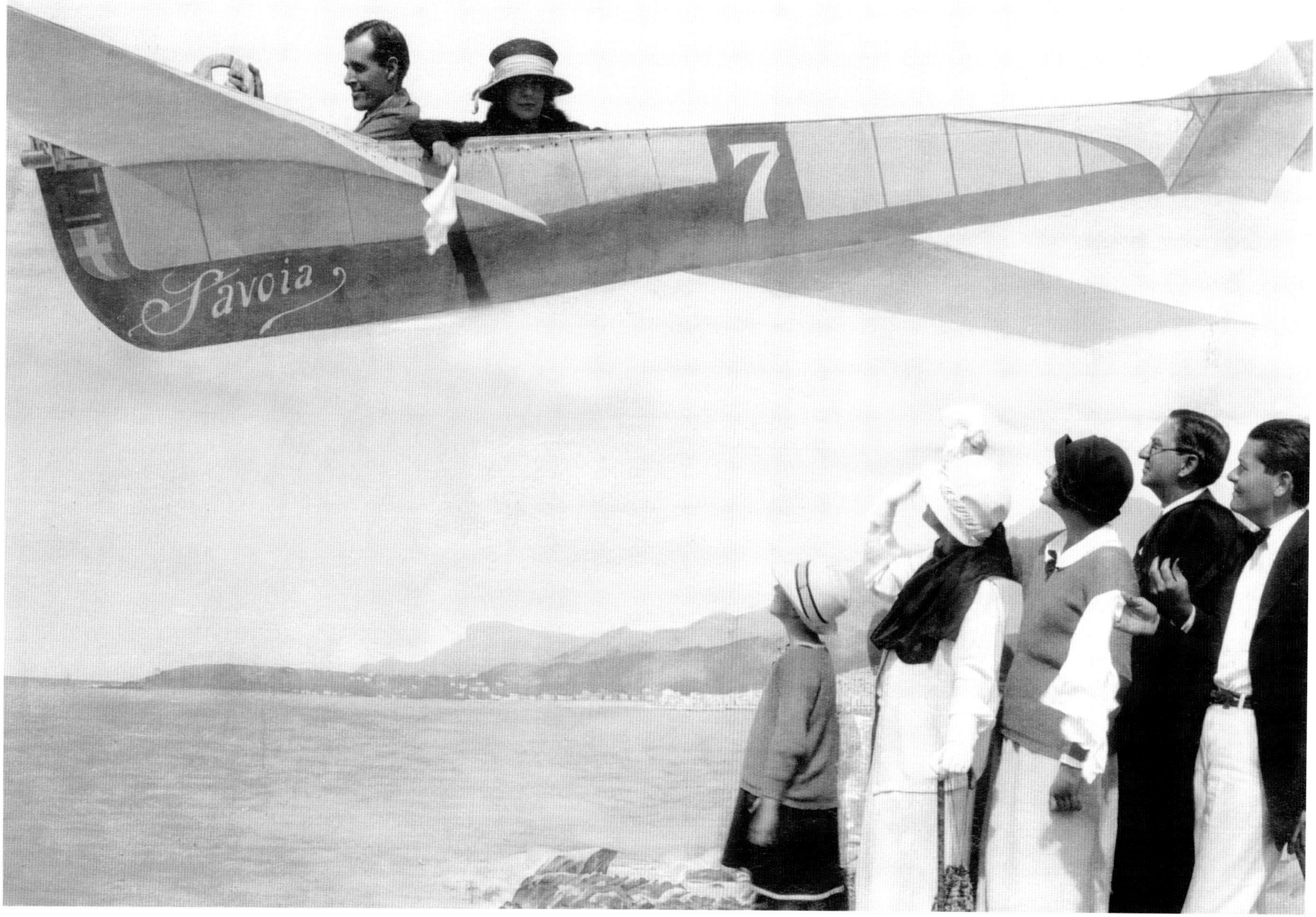
7
Savoia

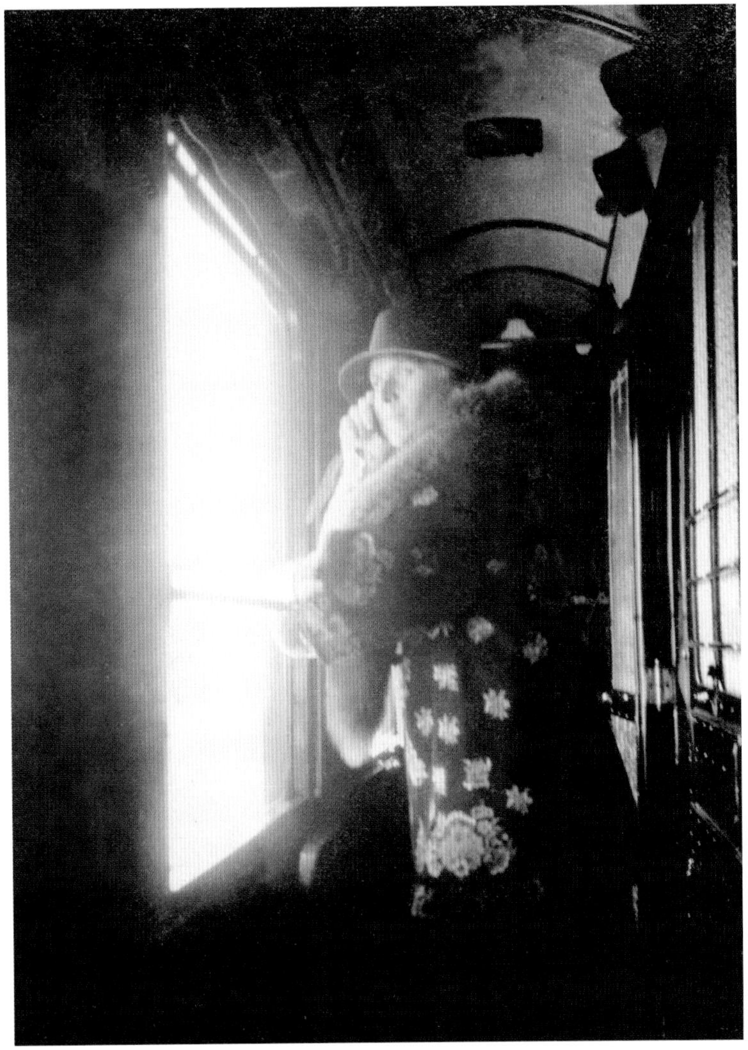

ABOVE Alice on the train from Menton to Paris, where the family returned at the end of April, staying through May. Using this as their base, they took trips by car to the chateaux and villages of the Loire Valley.

BELOW A view of the imposing sixteenth-century Château de Chambord, the largest in the Loire Valley.

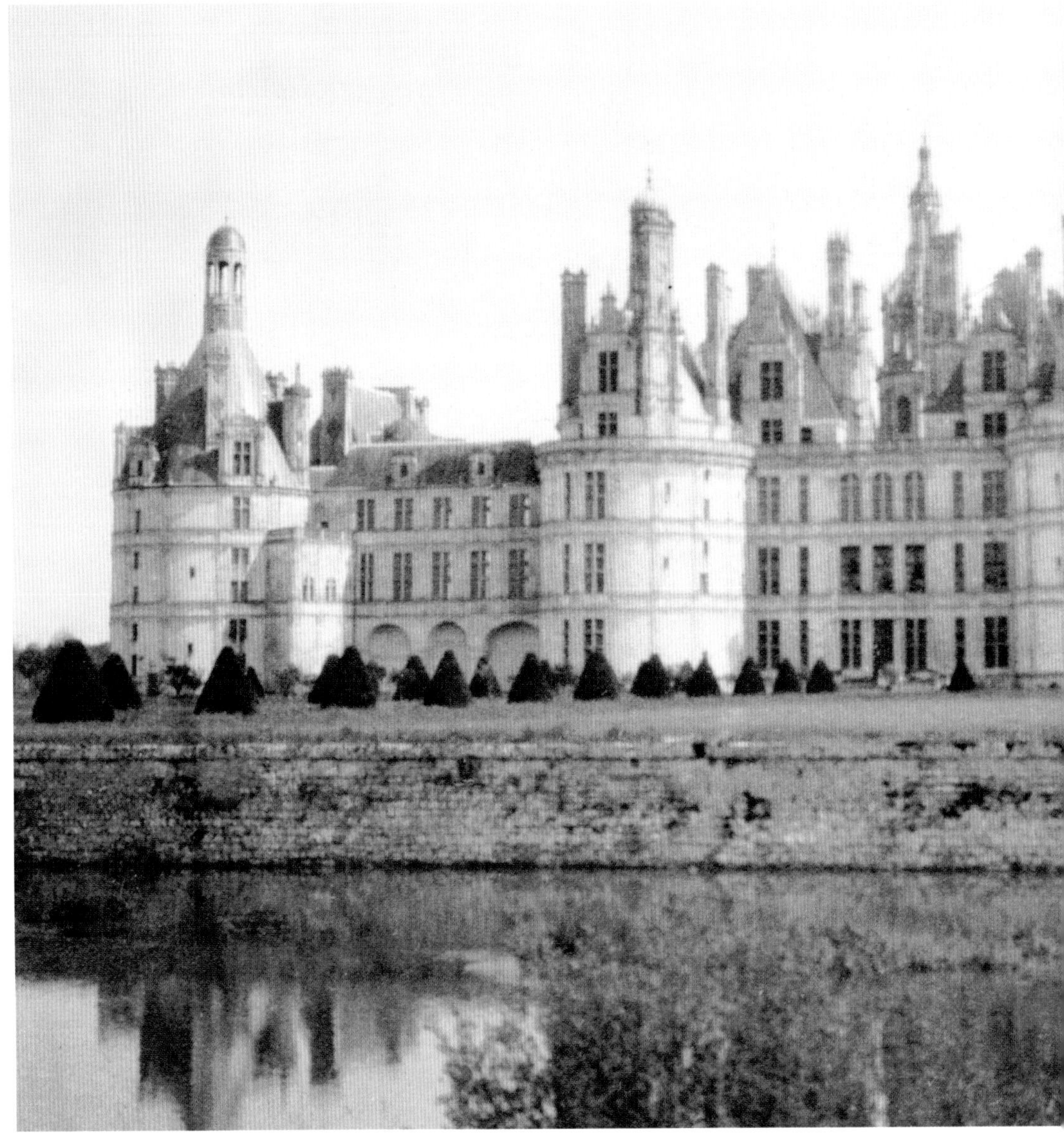

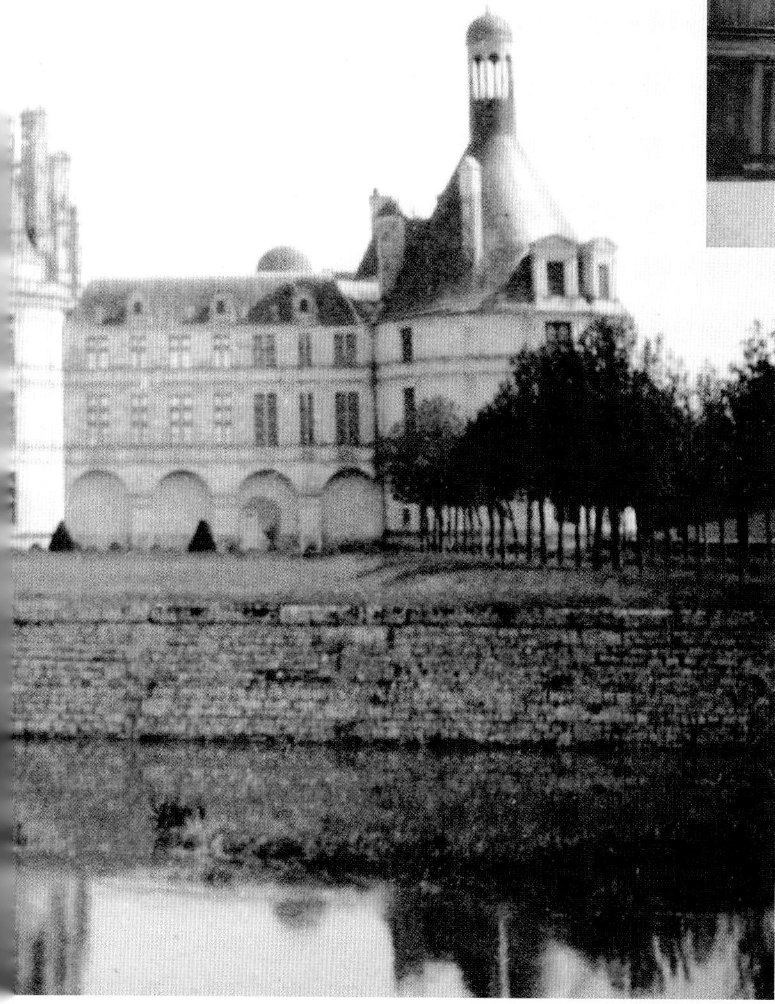

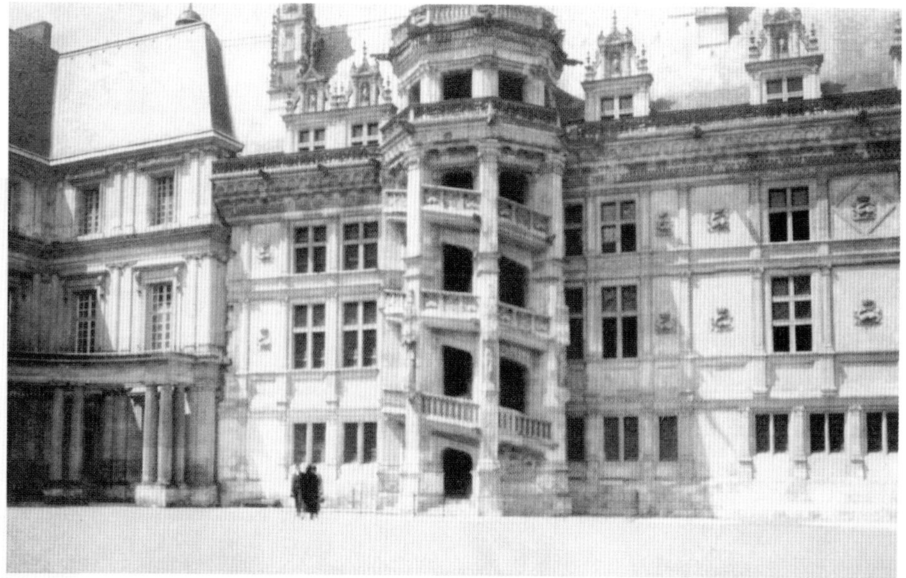

LEFT The famous spiral staircase at the Château Royal de Blois, which dates back to the fourteenth century and was the residence of several kings and queens.

BELOW The car and chauffeur in front of the main façade of the Louis XII wing of the Château Royal de Blois.

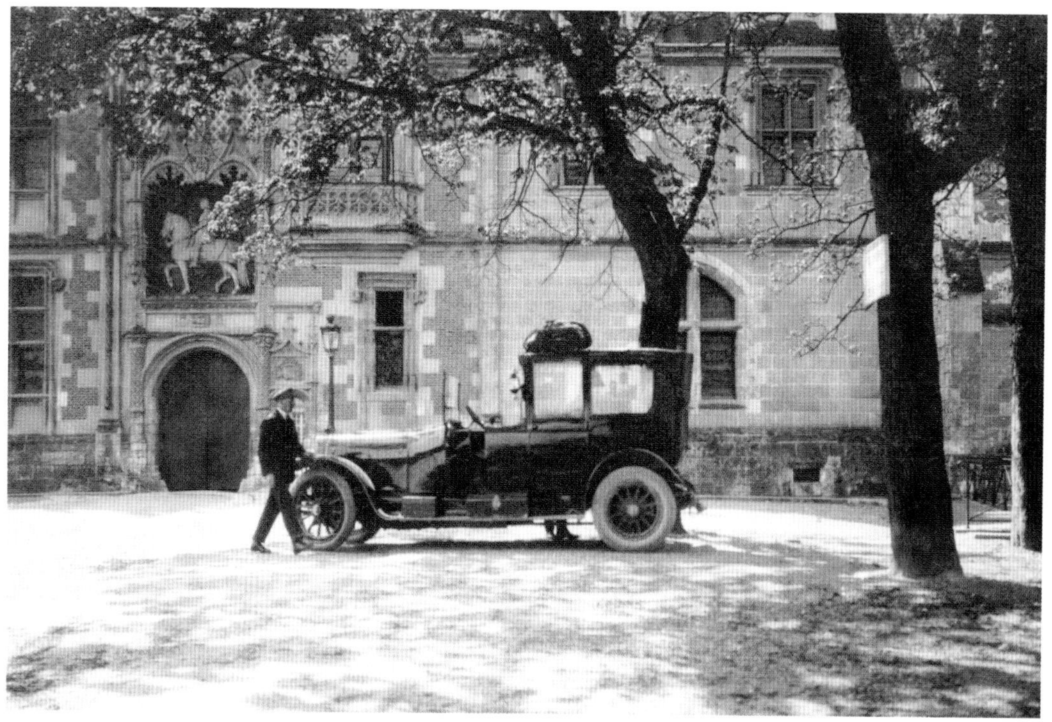

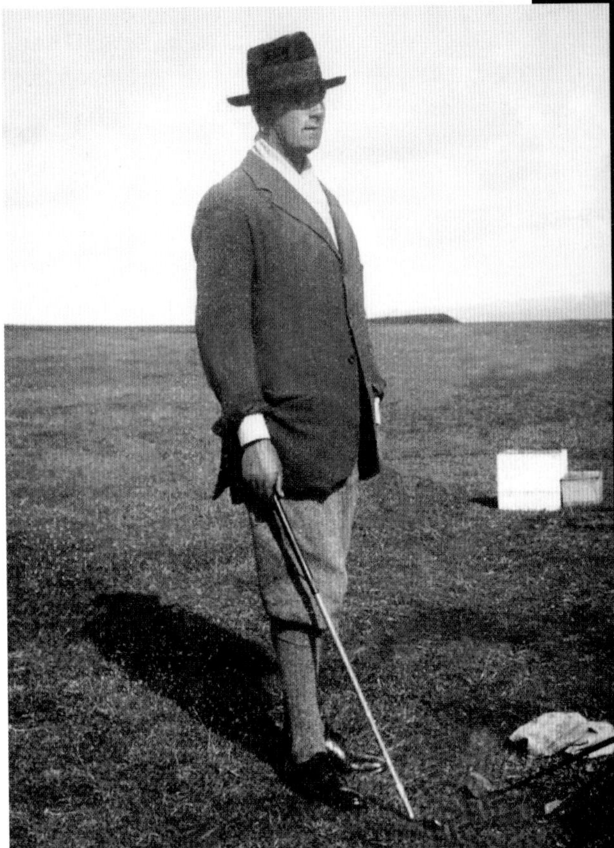

ABOVE Alice's cousin, Samuel L. M. Barlow II, playing golf in the summer of 1922 at Étretat, on the Normandy coast. Tracy had returned to Rhinebeck while the rest of the family continued their travels. When Alice heard that her cousin had taken a house in Étretat for the summer, she decided to do the same. Barlow was a talented musician and in 1934 was the first American composer to have a performance staged at the Opéra-Comique in Paris. He was married to the Philadelphia beauty Aimee Ernesta Drinker, who later changed her name to Ernesta Beaux. In the early 1920s, Barlow purchased several crumbling dwellings along a cliff in the medieval hiFrench village of Èze and fashioned them into one large exquisite house whose walls were elaborately decorated with frescoes painted by Jan Juta.

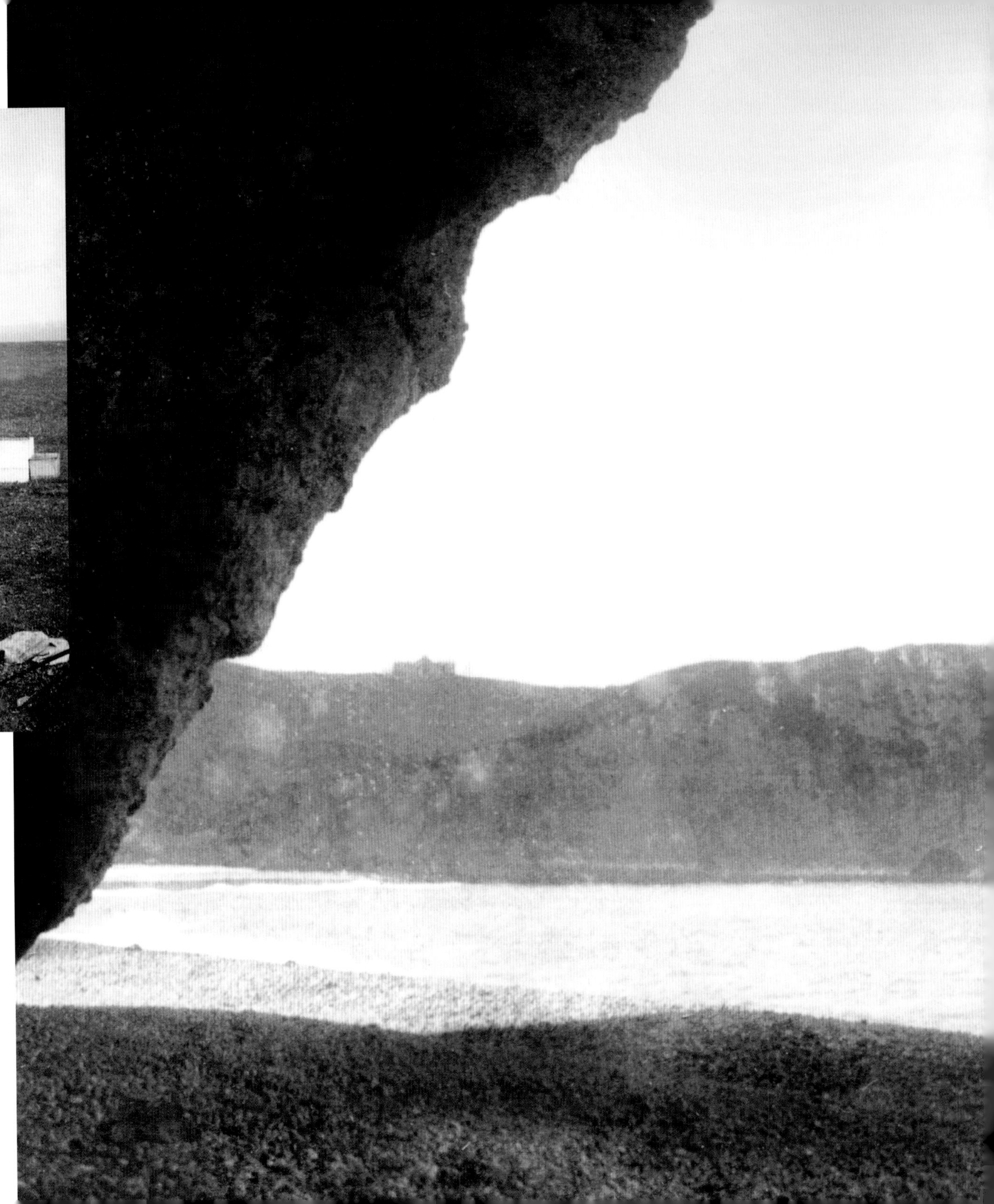

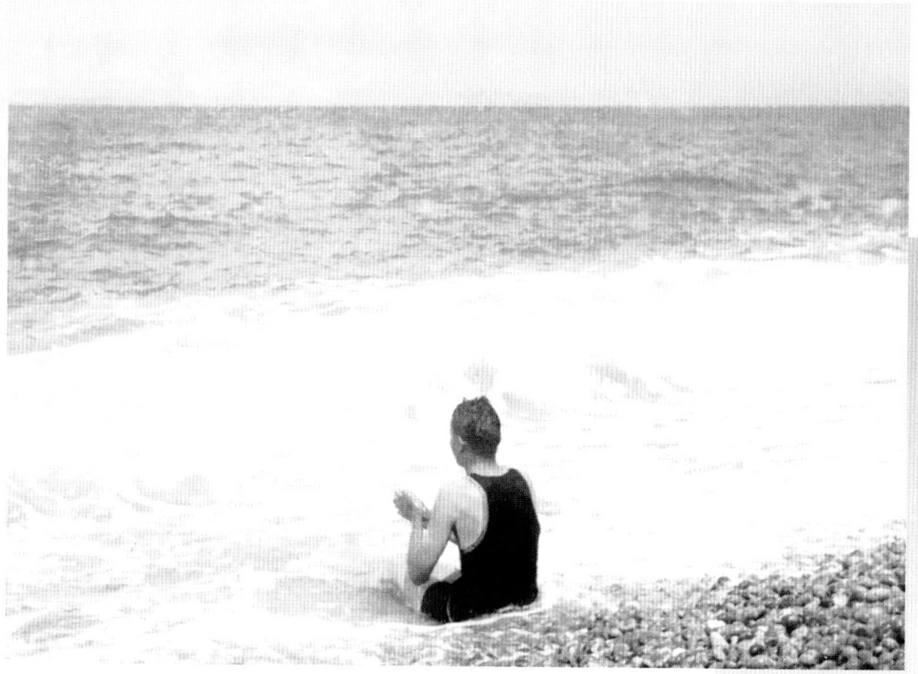

LEFT Olin at the surf's edge on the pebble beach, which was directly in front of the house where they were staying. The family enjoyed watching the local fishermen drag their boats and nets up onto the beach.

LEFT Best known for its dramatic cliffs and natural arches, Étretat attracted such French artists as Eugène Boudin, Gustave Courbet, and Claude Monet who painted the landscapes.

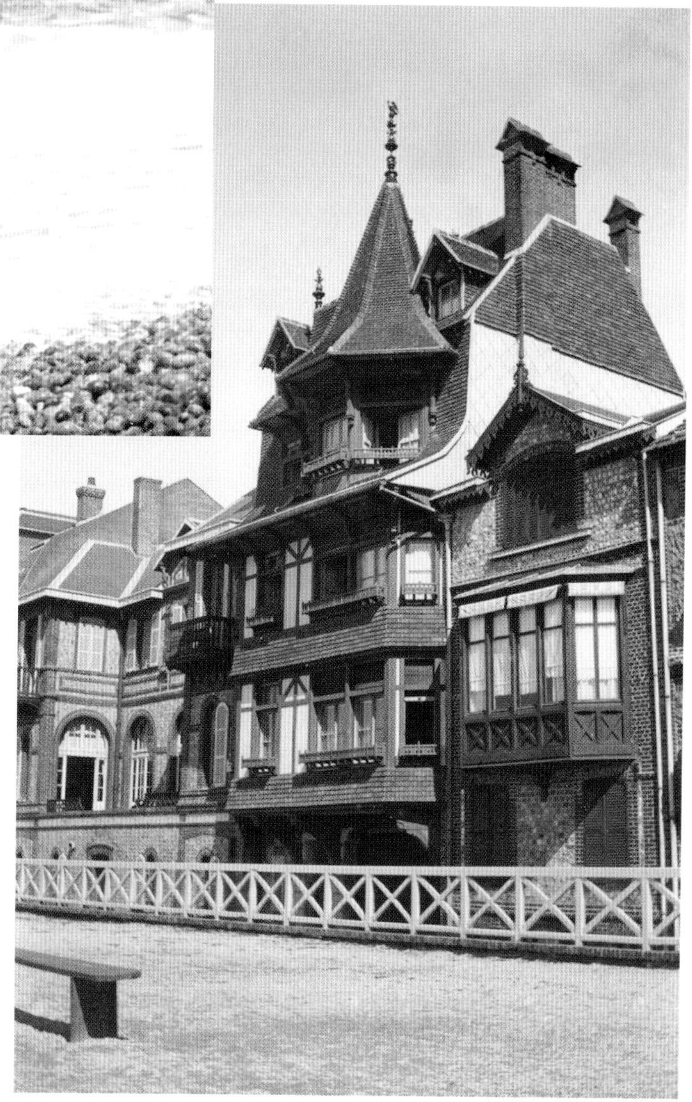

RIGHT The house, with its amusing architectural style, that Alice rented for the summer. In September, Olin sailed home to attend Harvard, while Alice, Margaret, and Deb traveled back to Paris to stay in Helen Astor's grand apartment on Rue Marbeau for two months. They returned home aboard the *Olympic* in October. The trip was particularly memorable for Alice as she met the famed soprano Lucrezia Bori, who became one of her closest friends for the rest of her life.

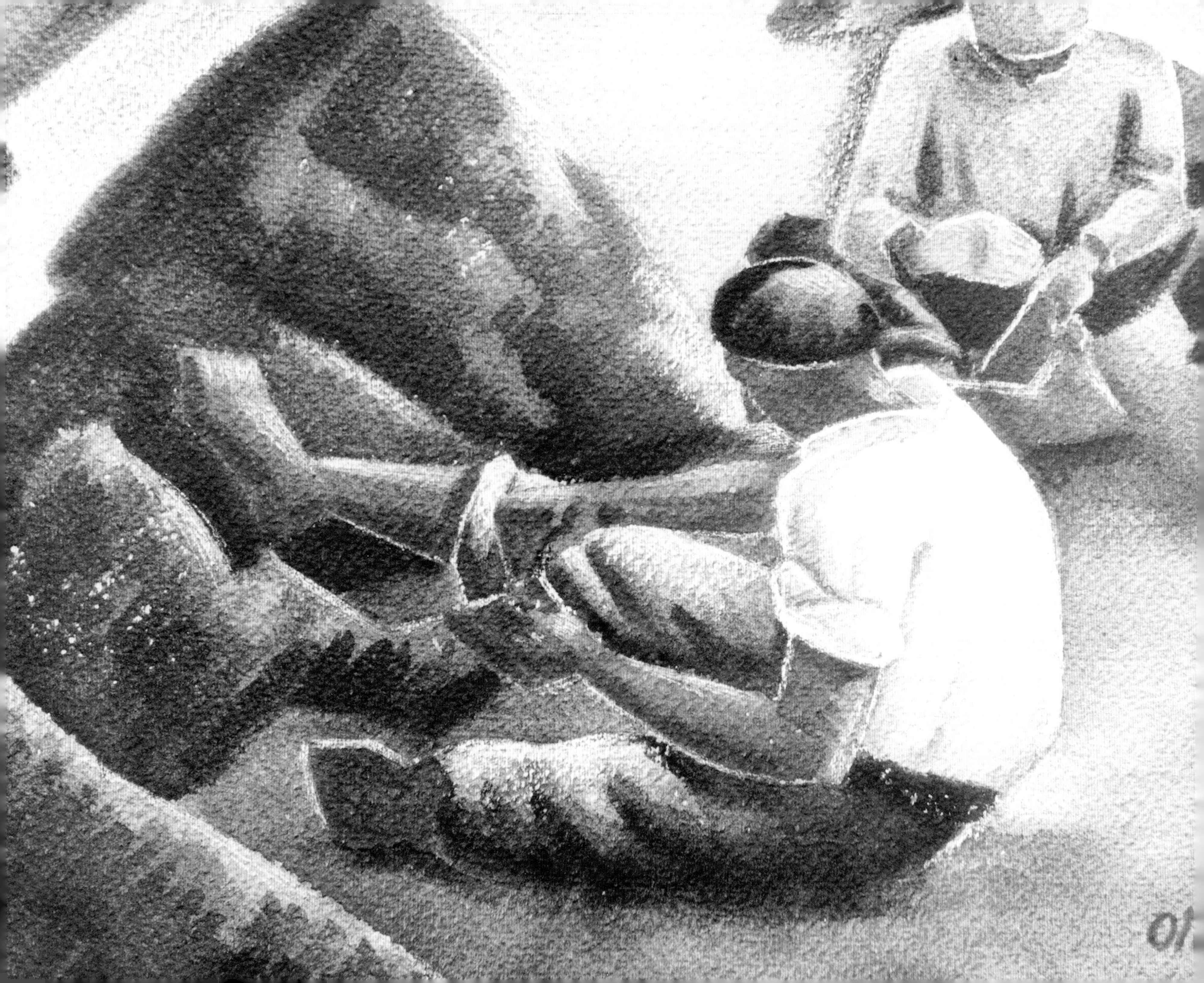

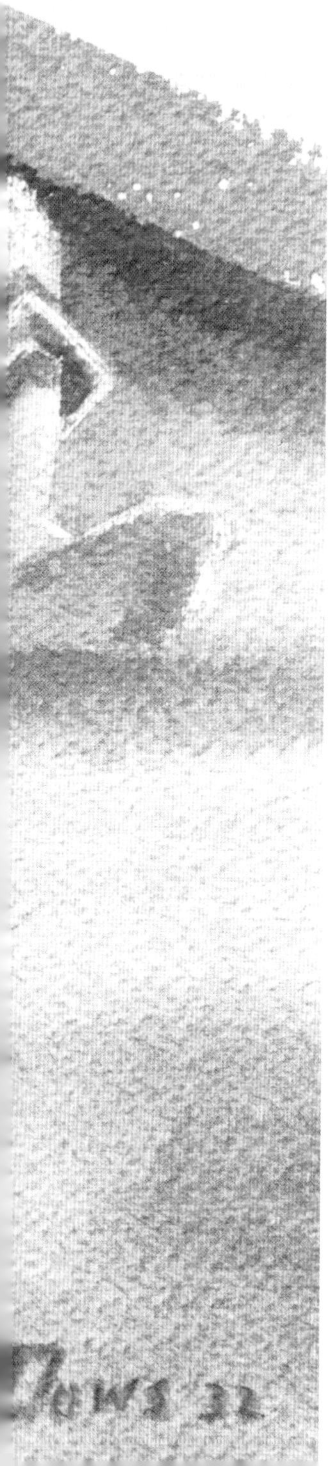

CHAPTER TEN

The ARTIST

PREVIOUS PAGES A 1932 watercolor of fishermen by Olin Dows titled, *Mending Net*. It was commissioned by Olin's cousin Edward Kellogg Dunham, Jr. (Courtesy of William Holman Gallery/Estate of Olin Dows)

RIGHT A young Olin in 1911 on the front porch of the Southampton cottage the family had rented for the summer. Olin began drawing at the age of two. By the age of seven, his mother and father realized his destiny was to be an artist. As a young boy Olin was tutored in drawing by C. K. Chatterton of Vassar College, who was a figure in the realist movement. He entered Harvard College in 1922 and studied art. A few years later, he attended the Yale Art School, where he studied with Eugene Savage and Edwin Cassius Taylor. In 1928 he spent time at the Art Students League in New York City. His classmates there included David Smith, Clyfford Still, and Jackson Pollock. Olin was recruited by President Franklin D. Roosevelt for the mural work of the Works Progress Administration, which led to his fine murals in the Rhinebeck and Hyde Park post offices. Olin worked with several programs under the WPA, including the Treasury Relief Art Project. With his administrative work he reviewed hundreds of submissions for the many buildings constructed across the United States, and approved contracts for such artists as Milton Avery, Thomas Hart Benton, Rockwell Kent, and Grant Wood, who would go on to become famous. Olin continued to paint and draw his entire life.

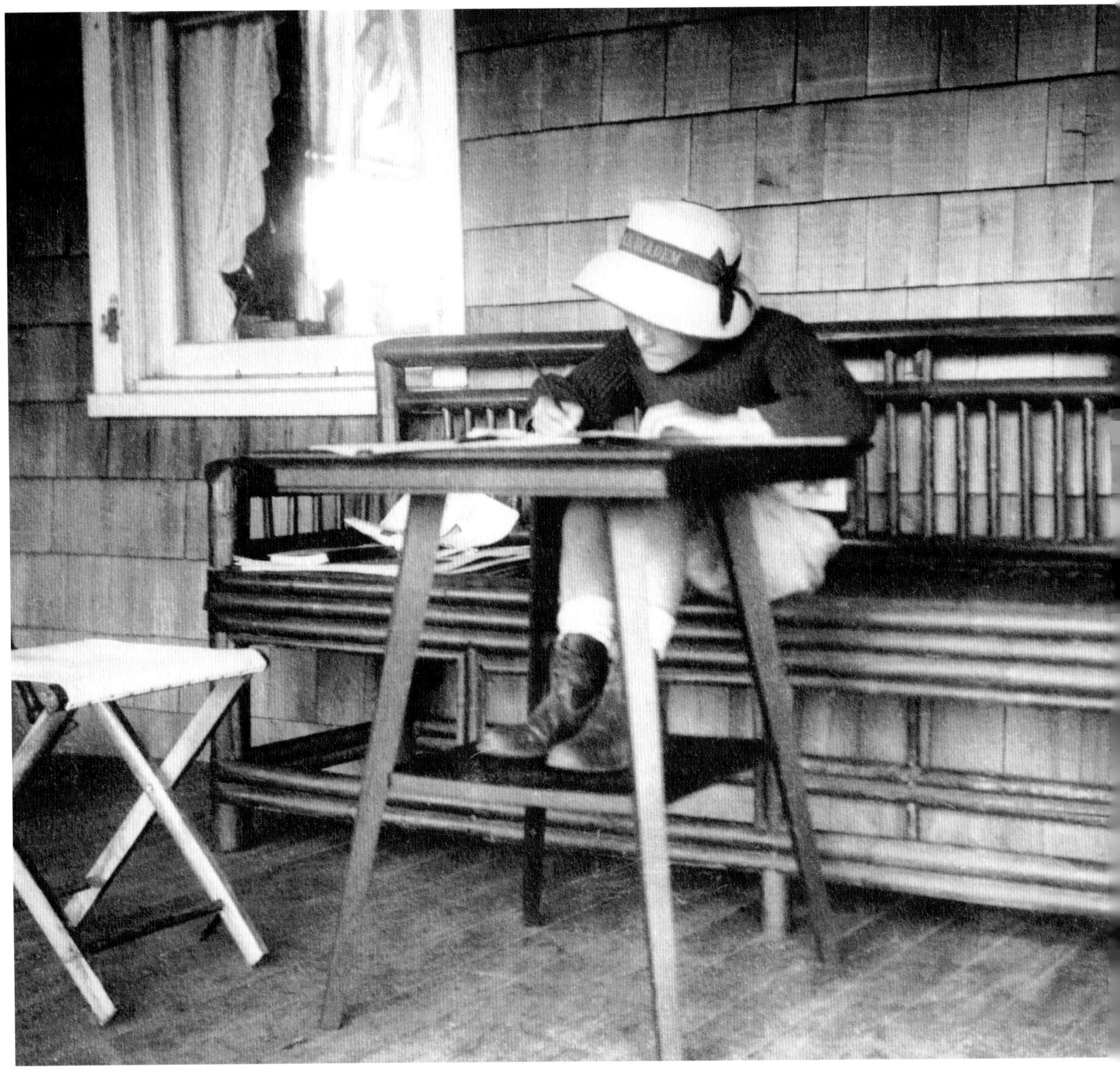

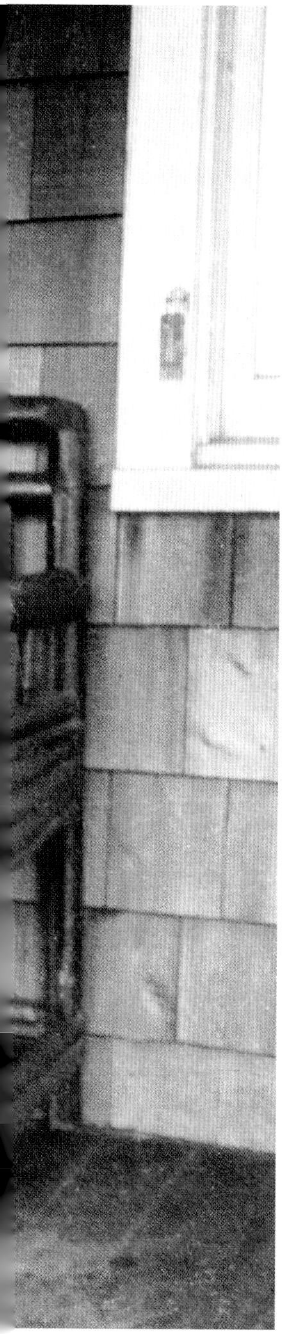

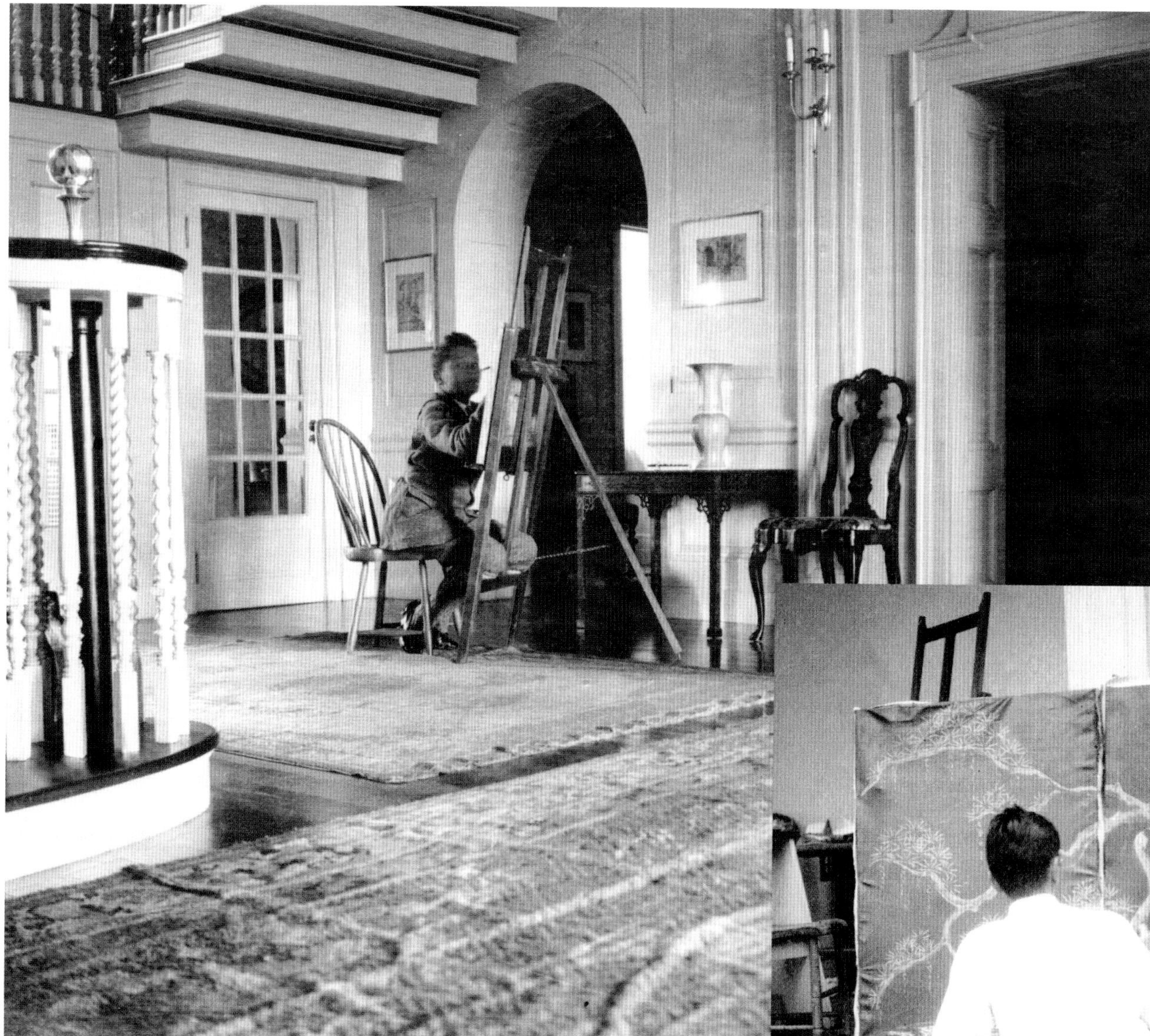

ABOVE Olin painting in the entryway of the house at Foxhollow Farm in 1918. During this time, he was painting views of the house inside and out.

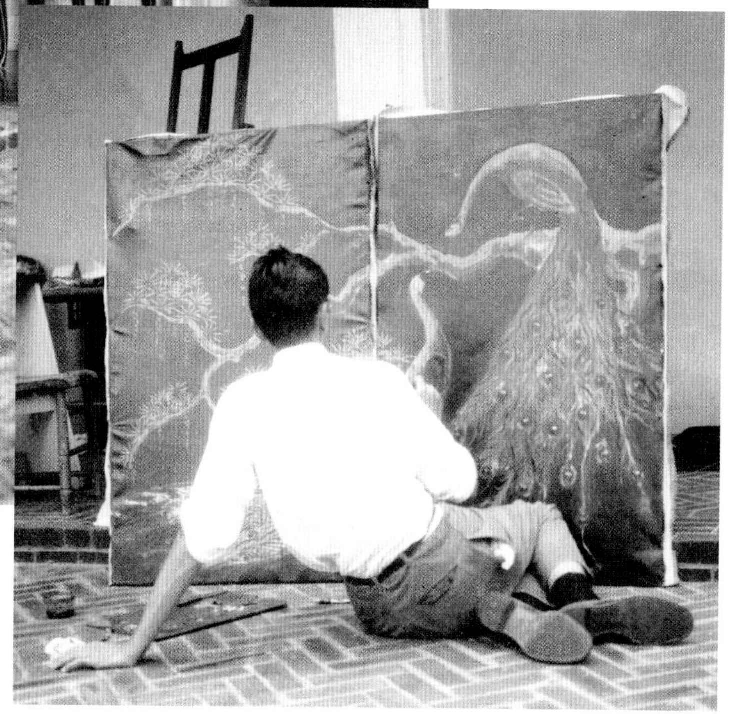

BELOW Working on a canvas in 1921. Olin's work often featured elements of nature as seen with the pheasants and pine trees in these paintings.

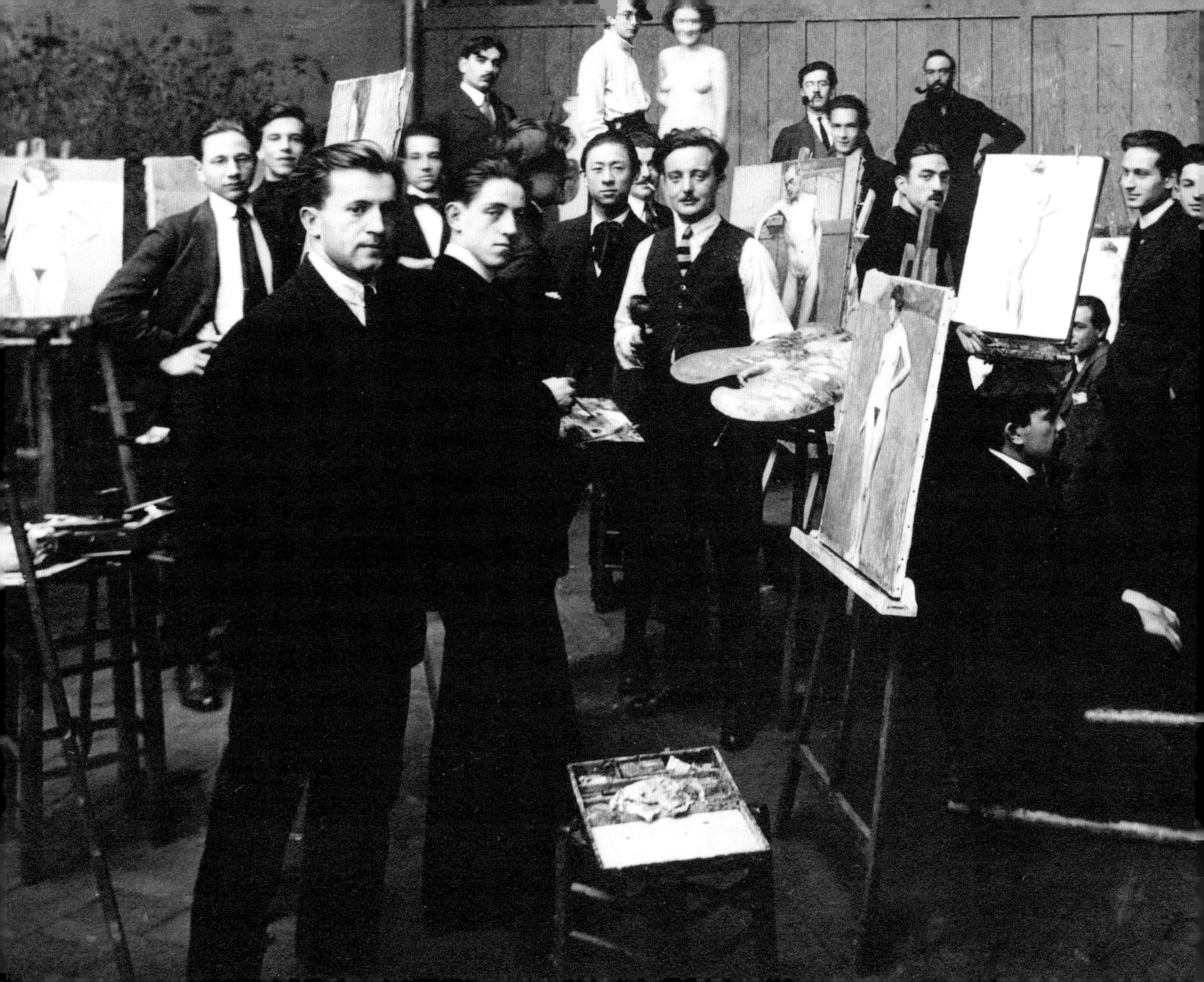

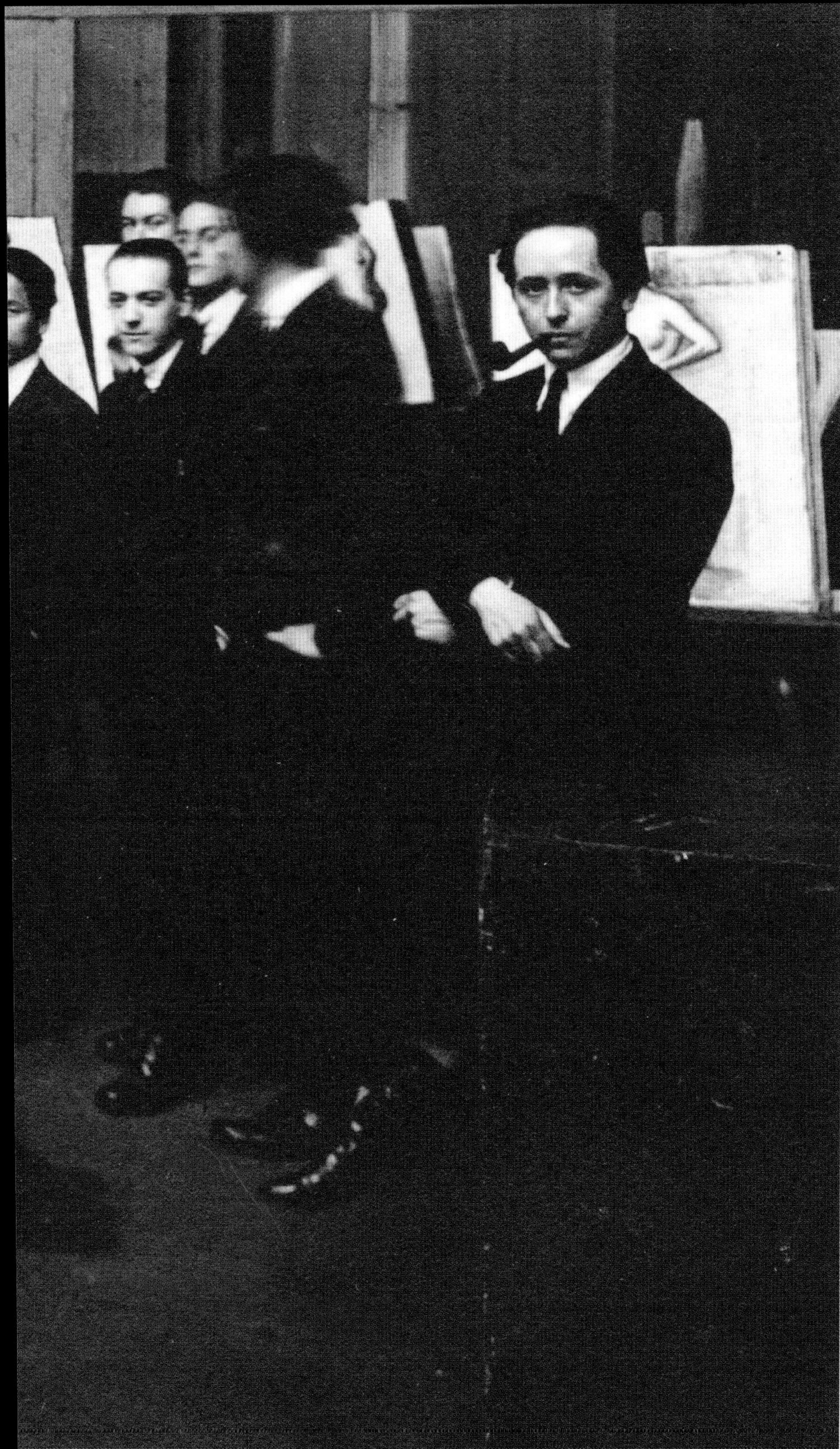

LEFT Olin at a figure drawing class at the École des Beaux-Arts which he attended while the family was staying in Paris during the fall of 1921. He is seen fourth from the right, in the very back, his mouth covered by the gentleman in front of him. While there, he studied with noted artist François Flameng.

BELOW Olin painting a portrait of his father in 1923 in Sonning, England, where the family had rented a cottage for the summer.

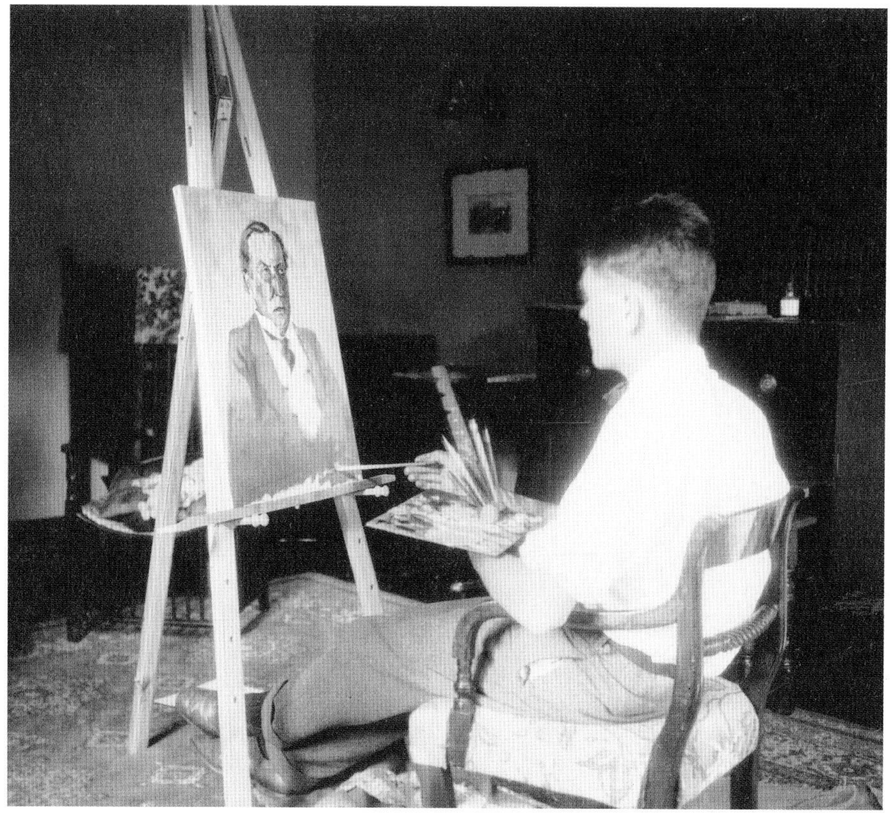

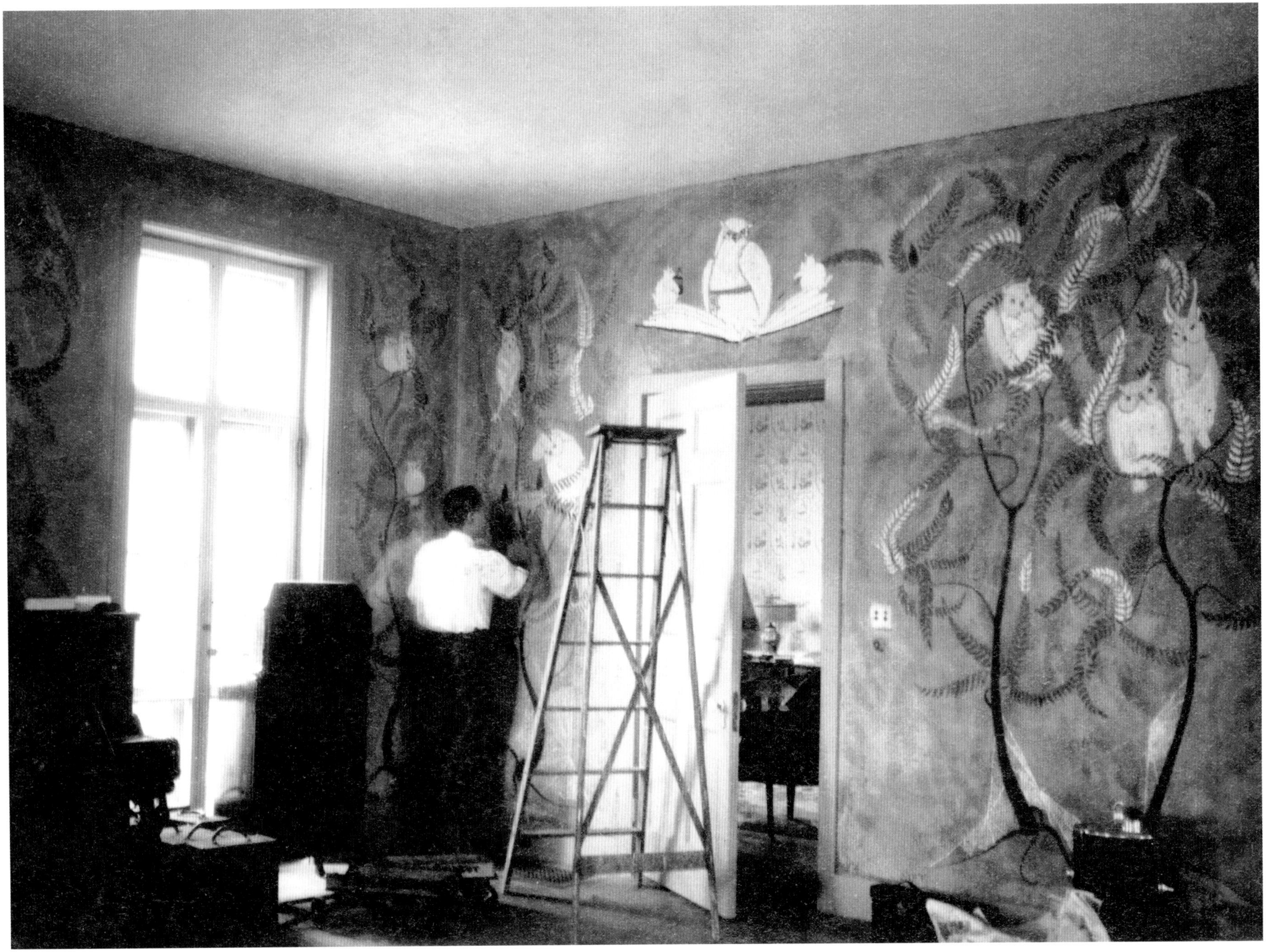

OPPOSITE In 1924, Mrs. Johnston Livingston Redmond commissioned Olin to paint the murals in the living room of Callendar House, her country home in Tivoli, up the river from Foxhollow Farm. The murals were wildly decorated with owls and sumac trees. Callendar House dates back to 1794 and was built by Henry Gilbert Livingston with renovations by McKim, Mead & White in 1910. The property was at one time owned by Johnston Livingston, one of the original directors of American Express.

RIGHT A folding screen painted with dancing fawns, along with other works of art as seen in Olin's bedroom at Foxhollow Farm in 1927.

BELOW A passport photograph of Olin taken in 1921, at age 17, when the family spent a year abroad.

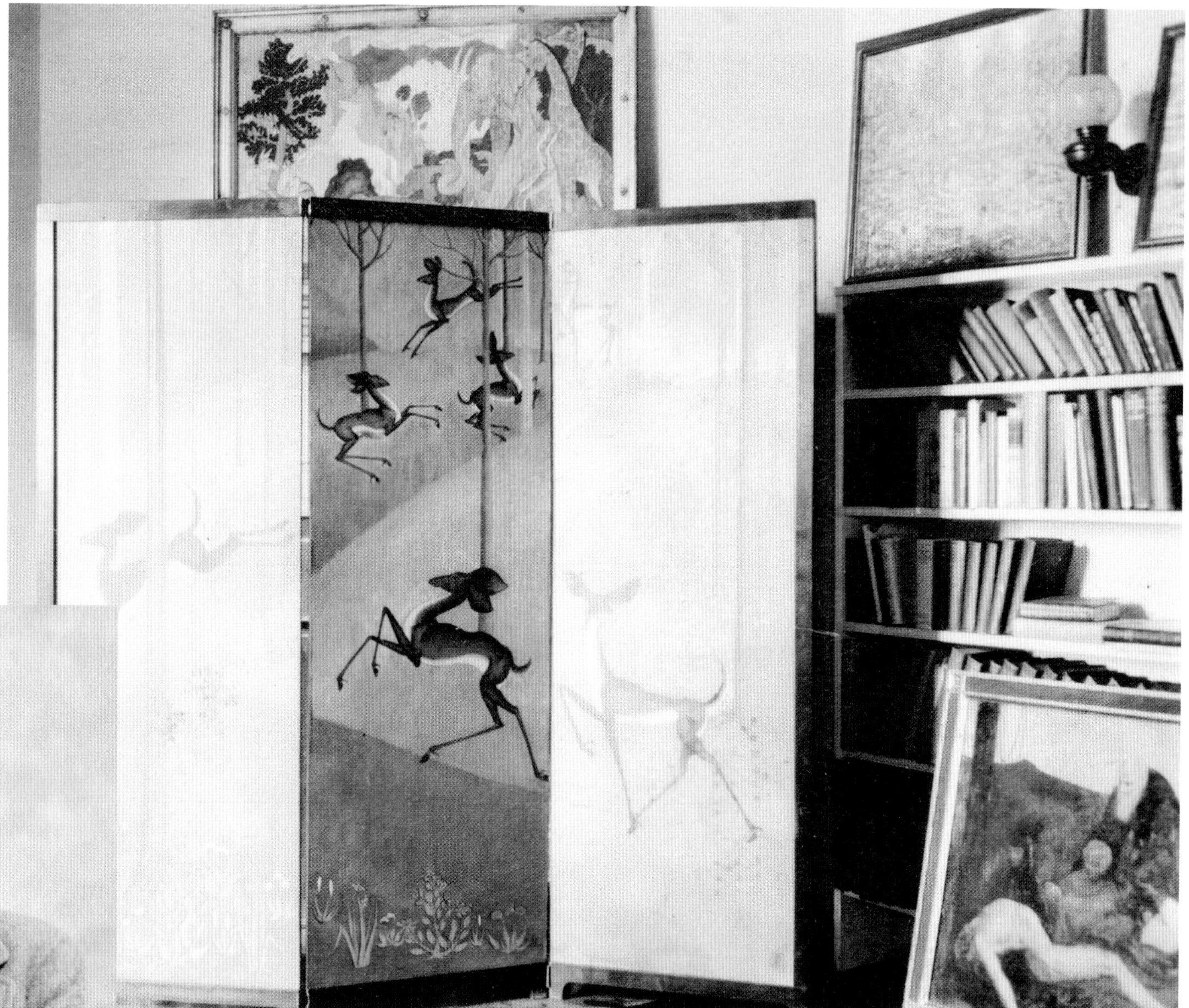

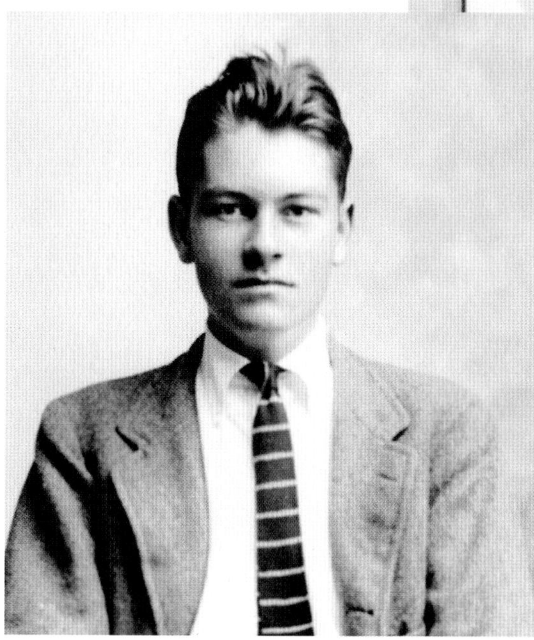

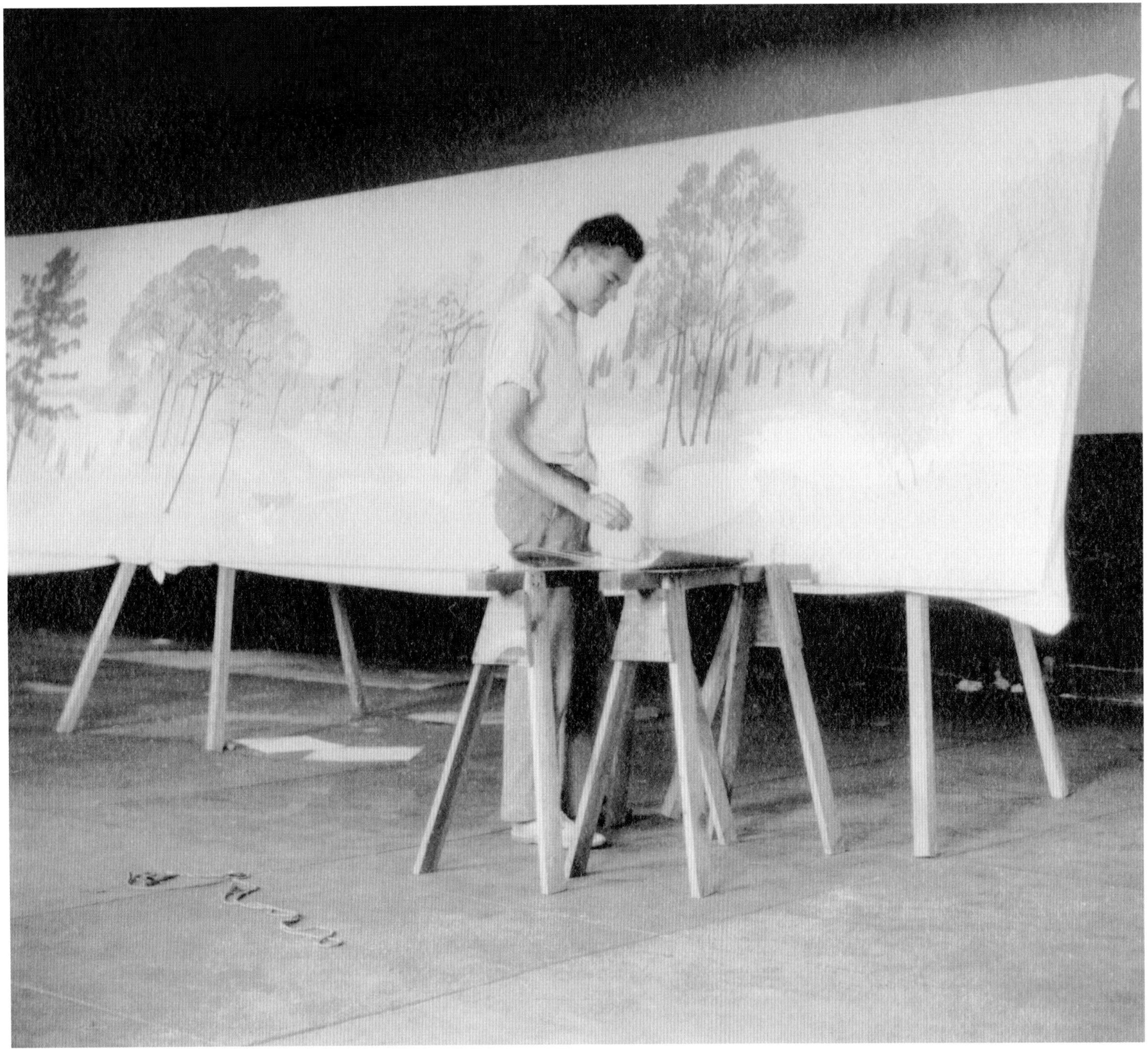

LEFT Olin painting canvases in 1927 for Alice's townhouse in Washington, D.C. By the mid-1920s, Alice was residing most of the time in Washington with trips to Rhinebeck periodically. The canvases, which depict the countryside around Foxhollow Farm and Glenburn, were installed on the walls of her library. By this time Olin had been attending the Yale School of Art.

OPPOSITE The library in Alice's house showing the finished canvases on the walls. (Courtesy of William Holman Gallery/Estate of Olin Dows)

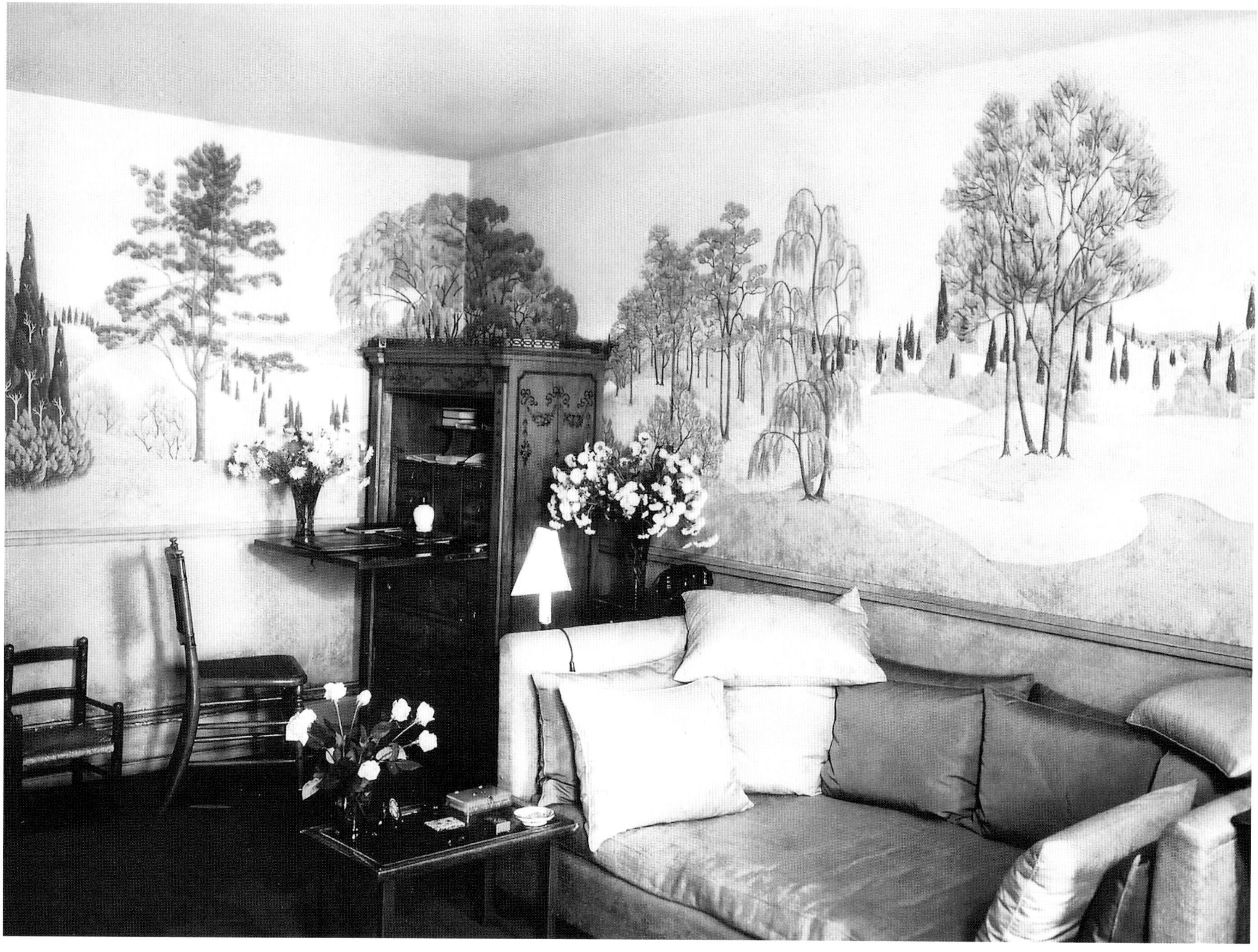

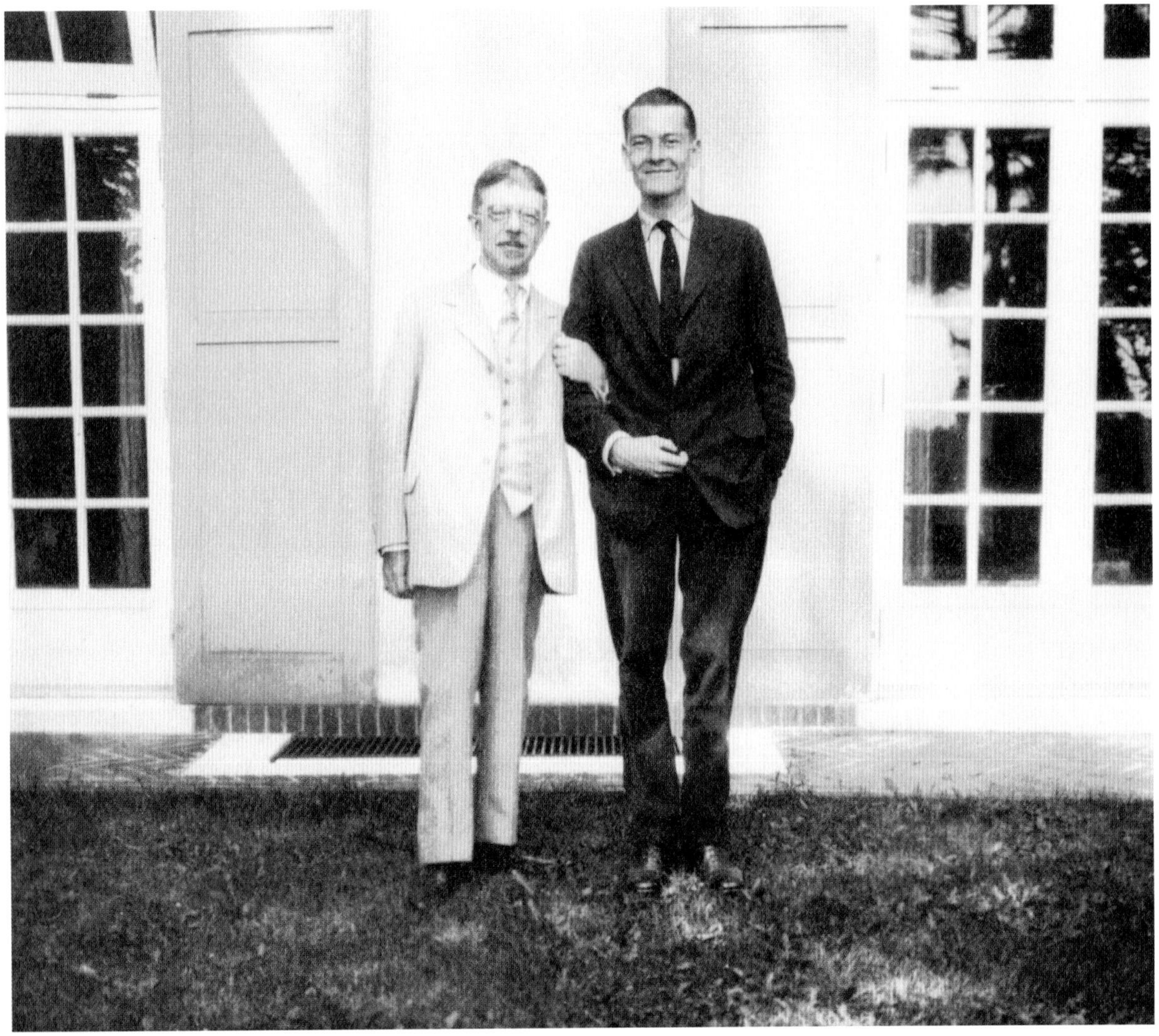

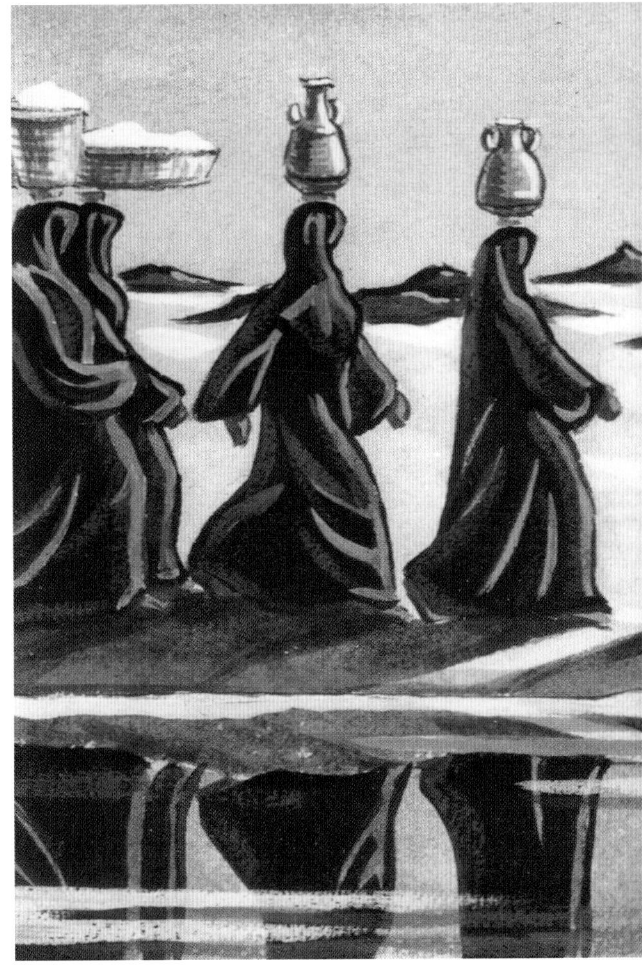

"Olin Dows has an unmistakable decorative talent and his art has a definite point of view."

Royal Cortissoz, art critic,
New York Herald Tribune, 1934

LEFT Royal Cortissoz standing with Olin while visiting Foxhollow Farm in 1924. Cortissoz was a longtime art critic for the *New York Tribune* and the *New York Herald Tribune* from 1891 until 1948. He trained as an architect for McKim, Mead & White before becoming a writer and art editor. He was a staunch traditionalist who rejected modernism. Cortissoz wrote the introduction to Harrie T. Lindeberg's 1940 monograph, *Domestic Architecture*.

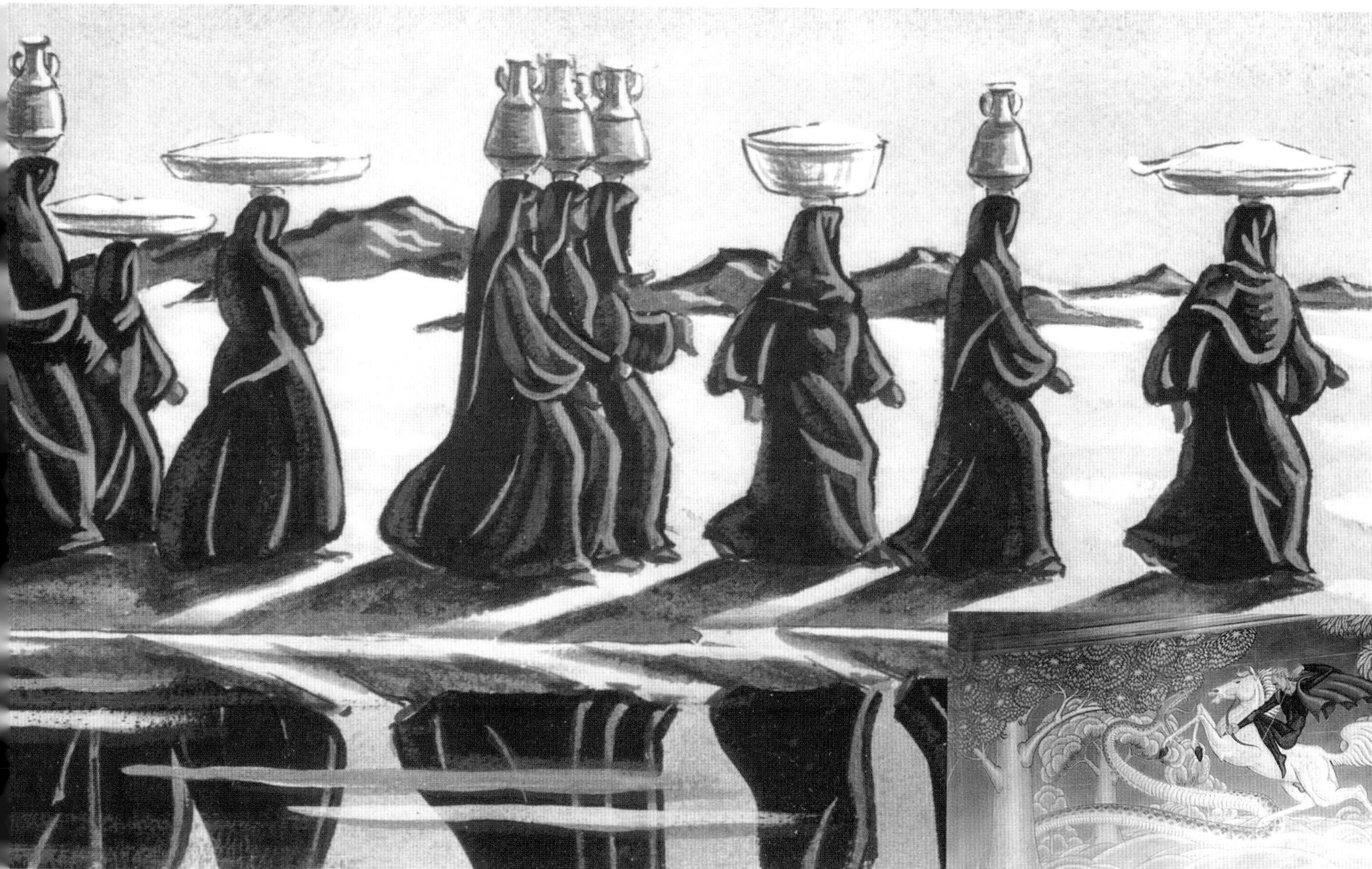

LEFT *Nubian Frieze*, painted in gouache, was commissioned in 1937 by Mr. and Mrs. Robert Woods Bliss, enthusiastic collectors of art and ardent supporters of music. They spent time traveling and living in South America and Europe, finally moving to Washington, D.C., in 1920. Their Georgetown home, Dumbarton Oaks, was one of the most outstanding estates in the city. Alice was a close friend of the Blisses and a frequent guest at their home while she lived in Washington. (Courtesy of William Holman Gallery/ Estate of Olin Dows)

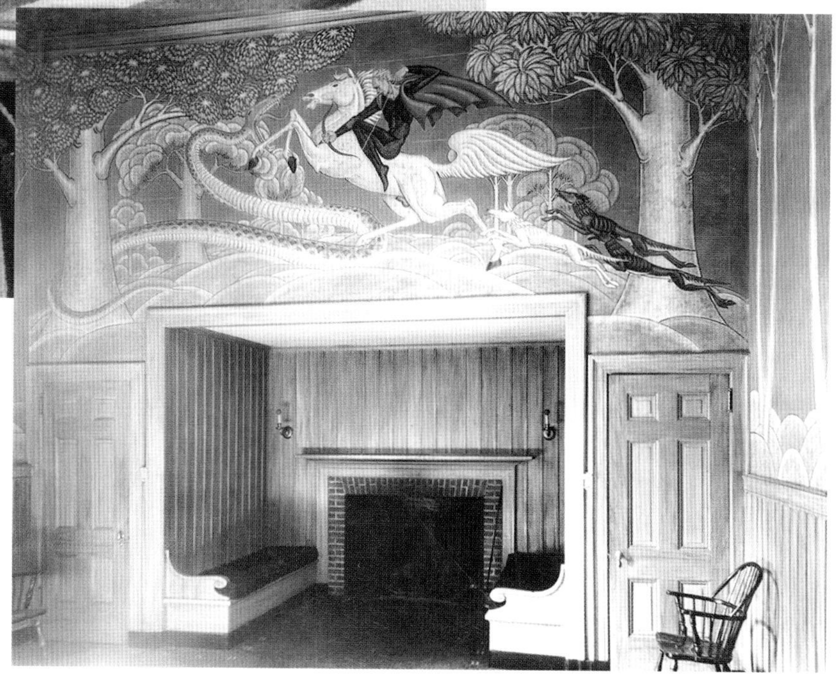

RIGHT In 1929, Olin was commissioned by the Skull and Serpent Society of Wesleyan University (his grandfather's alma mater) to paint murals on the walls inside their chapter house, which was designed by his grandfather's friend, architect Henry Bacon, in 1914. The area above the alcove depicts *Saint George and the Dragon*. (Courtesy of William Holman Gallery/Estate of Olin Dows)

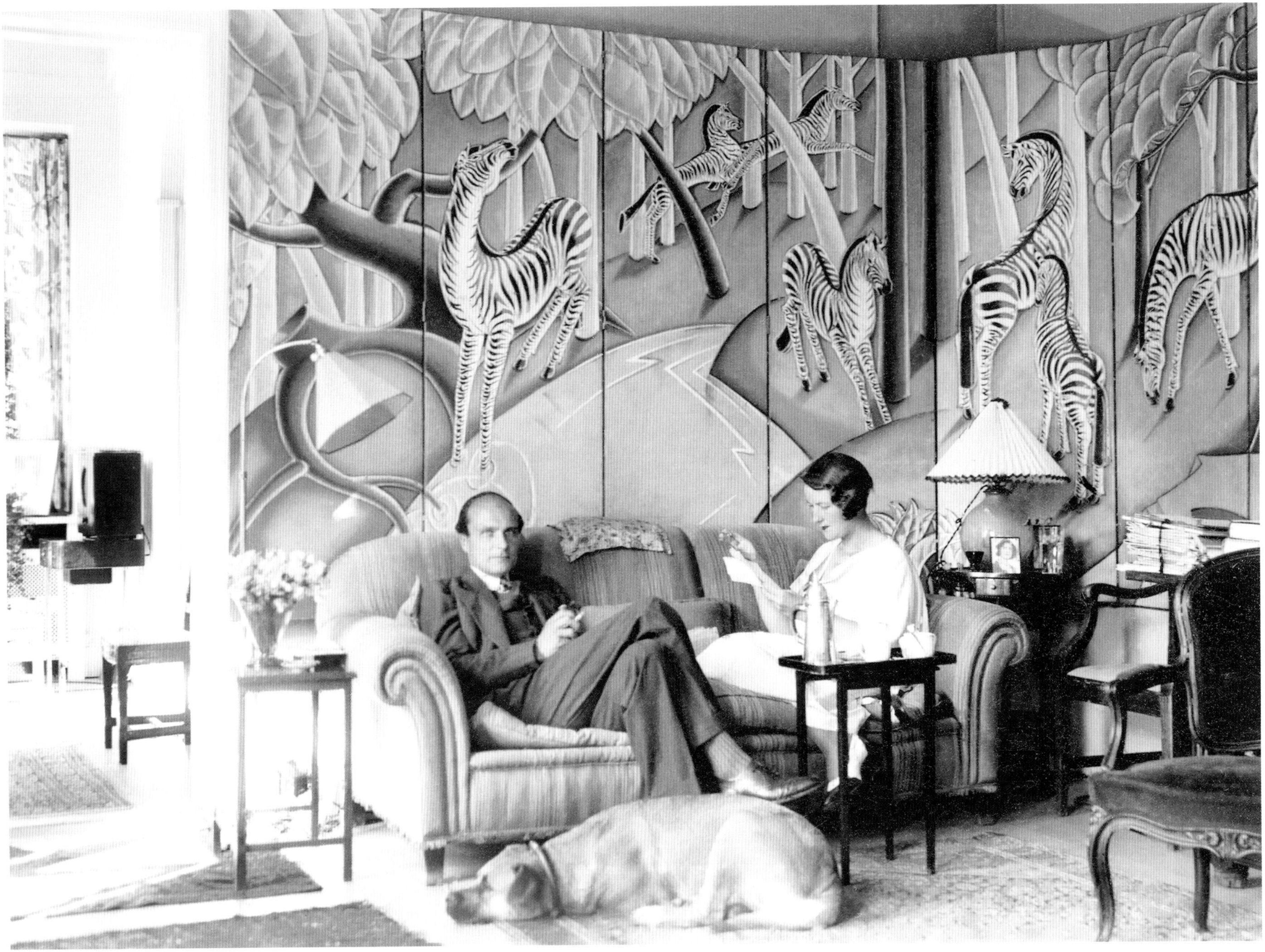

OPPOSITE Margaret and her husband, Knut Richard Thyberg, with Antoinette, their Bullmastiff, sitting in front of an extraordinary eight-panel screen of zebras, painted by Olin in 1932. During this time the Thybergs were living in Copenhagen. Margaret had married the Swedish diplomat in 1925 at Foxhollow Farm.

BELOW A photograph of Olin taken in Mexico during the summer of 1931. He was traveling and painting with fellow artists Thomas La Farge and Deane Keller. The trip left a lasting impression on him.

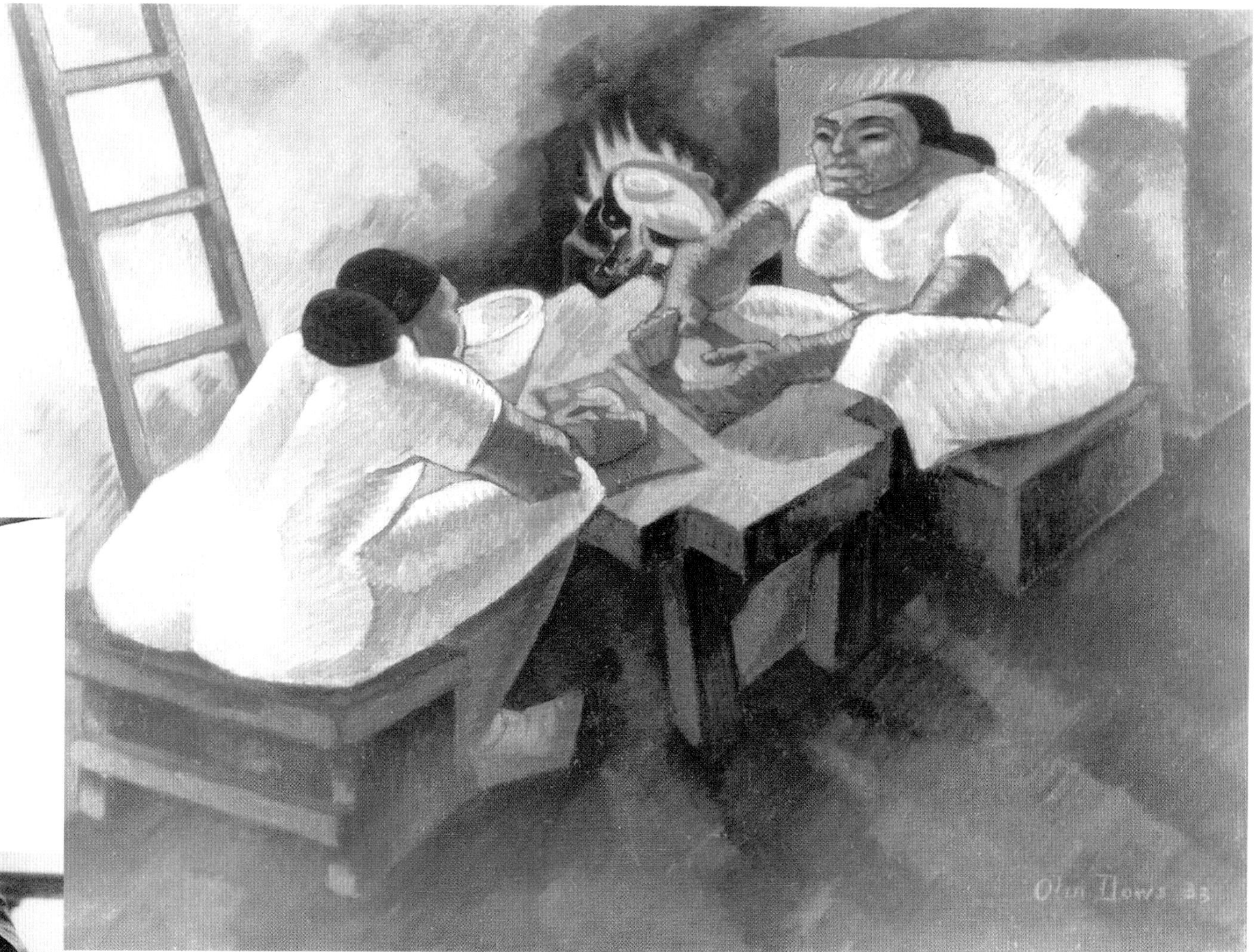

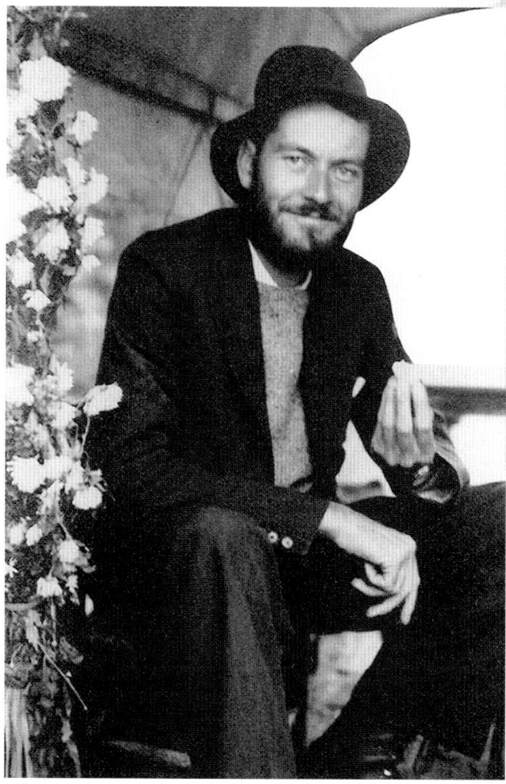

ABOVE *The Tortillieras*, one of Olin's works shown at Ferargil Galleries in New York in 1934. Influenced by his summer trip, Olin produced woodcuts and paintings with scenes of Mexican people and landscapes. (Courtesy of William Holman Gallery/ Estate of Olin Dows)

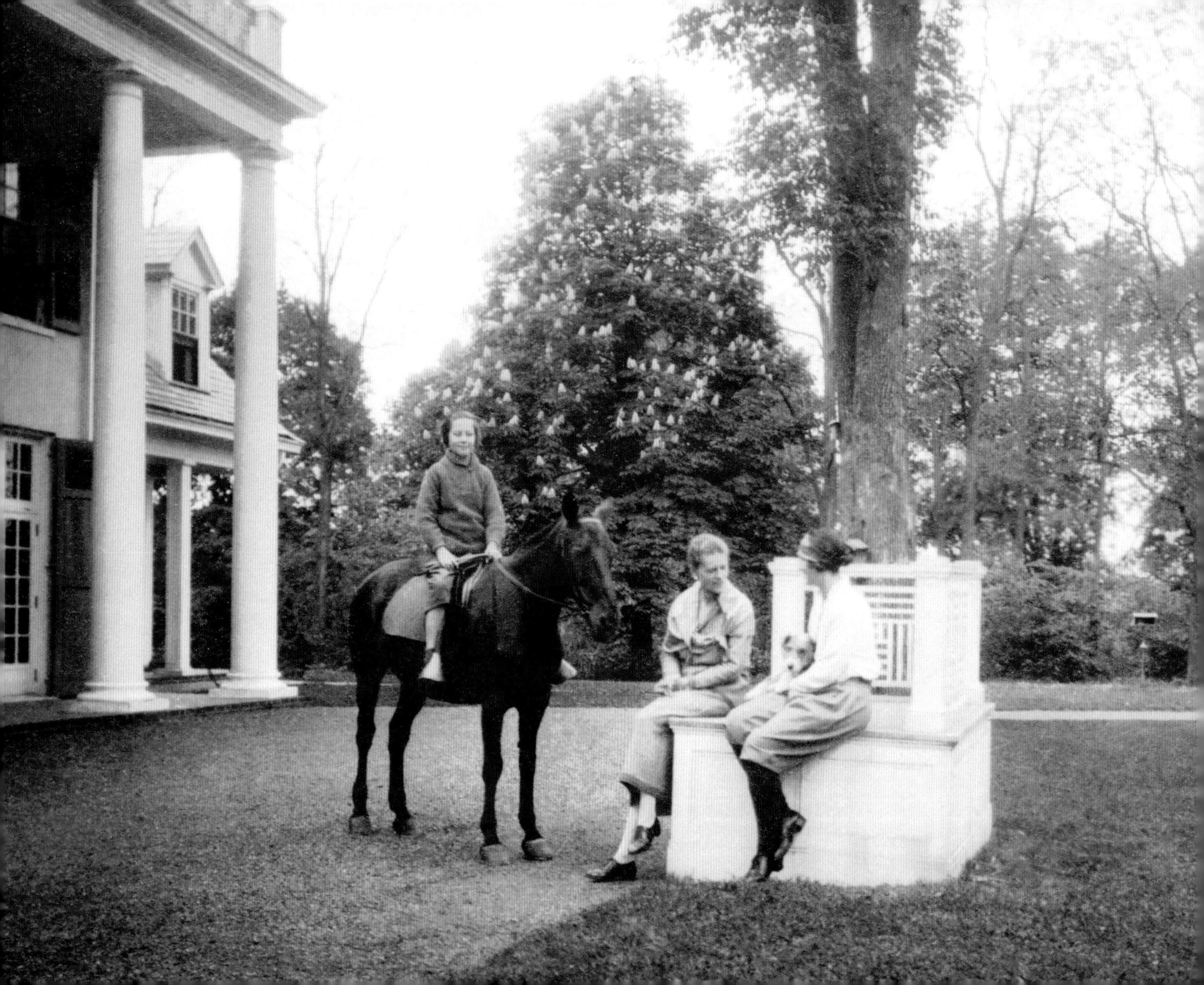

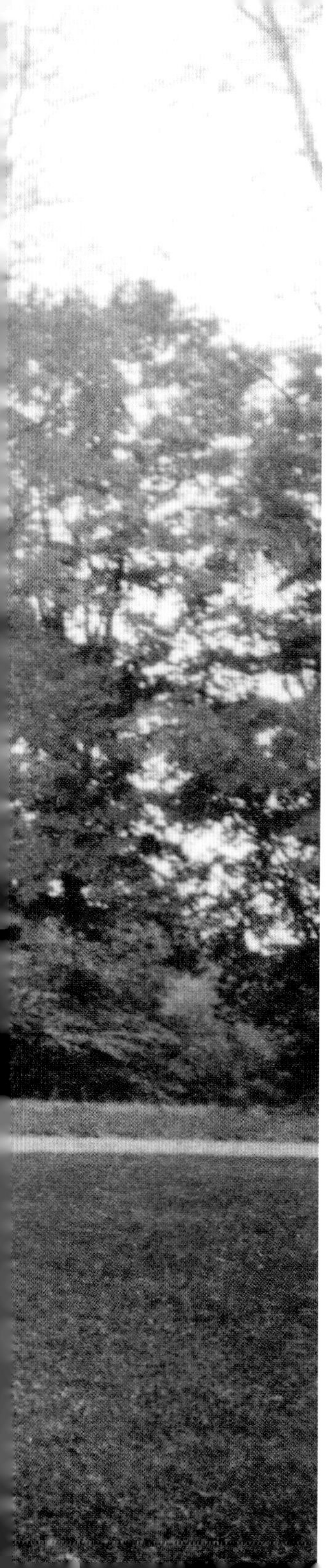

CHAPTER ELEVEN

A SENSE of CHANGE

The 1920s

PREVIOUS PAGES Deb on her horse in front of the Foxhollow Farm house, 1924, with Alice and Margaret sitting on the mounting block. The family was still living there, but, as the 1920s progressed, they began moving in different directions, coming together for trips, holidays, and summers. Olin left for Harvard, Margaret was married and moved abroad, Alice decided to live part-time in Washington, D.C., taking Deb with her, and Tracy remained at the farm.

RIGHT Alice walking with Olin during his senior year at St. Mark's School, the prestigious boys' boarding school in Southborough, Massachusetts, established in 1865. Olin attended from 1917 to 1921.

BELOW The familiar entrance to the brick and Tudor-style buildings on the school's campus.

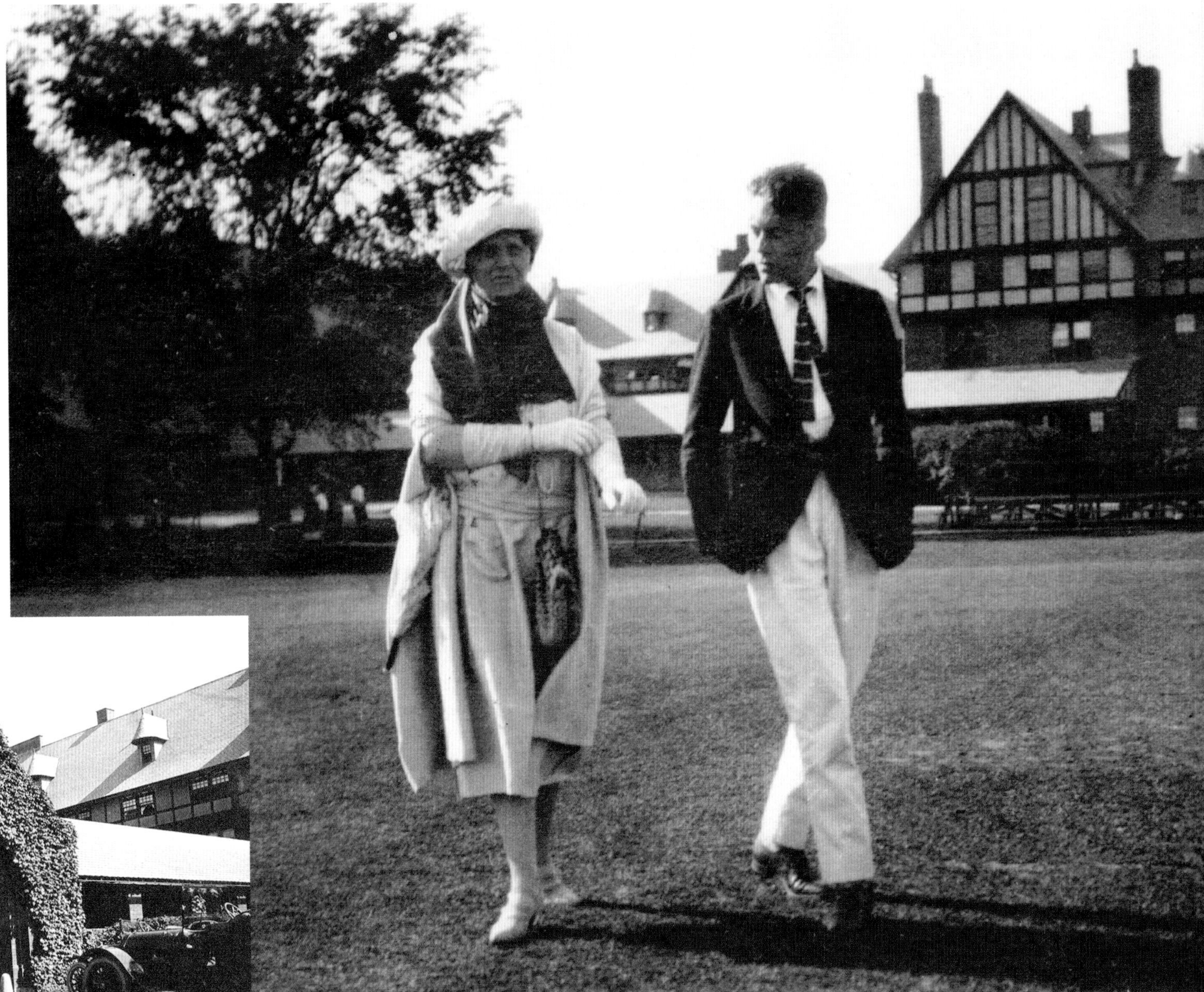

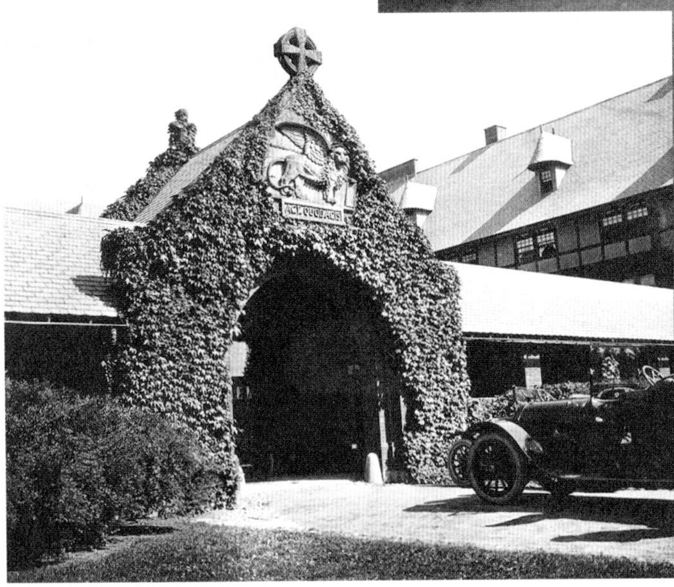

BELOW The family on the platform at the Staatsburg railway station, 1921, on their way to New York City to begin a trip to Seal Harbor.

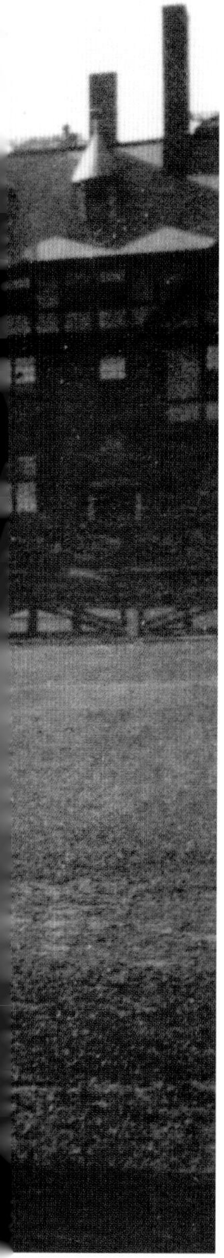

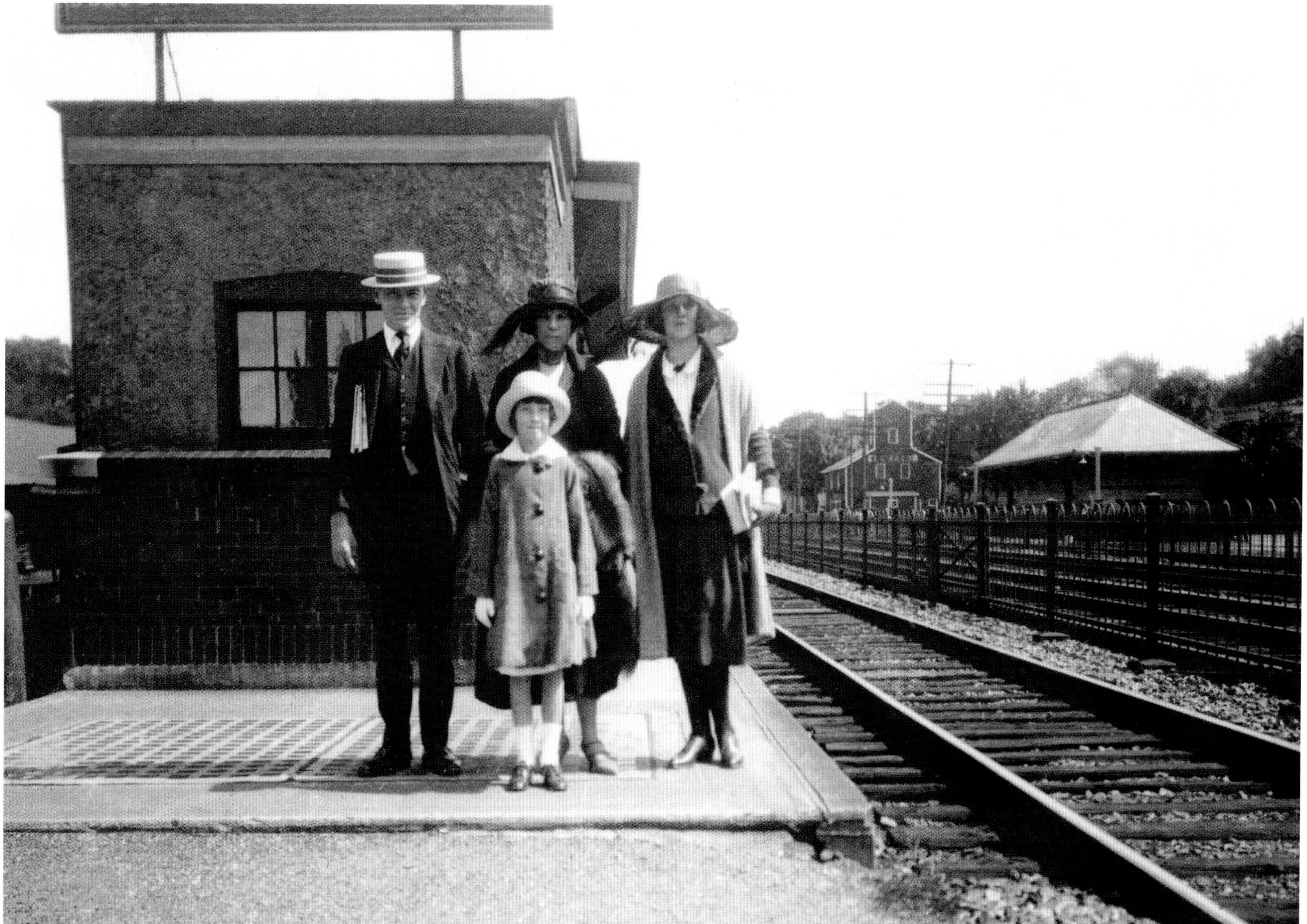

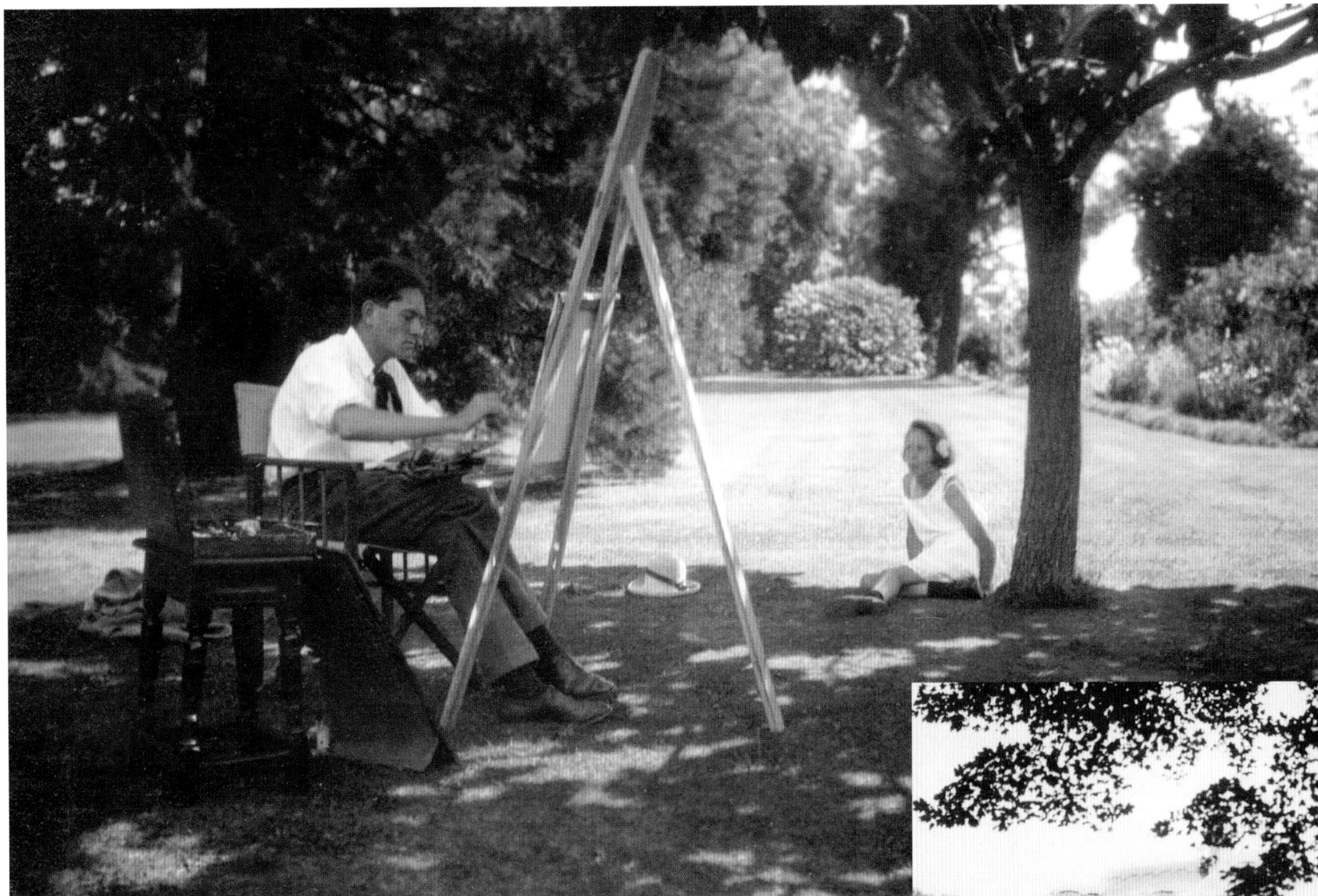

ABOVE In July 1923, the family traveled to England for the summer, spending two weeks in London and three months at a large cottage Tracy rented on the River Thames in Sonning, Berkshire. Mr. and Mrs. Stephen Olin joined them. Olin is seen painting a landscape as Deb looks on.

OPPOSITE Deb, at the Sonning Lock on the River Thames, watching the lock keeper as he maneuvers the mechanism. The original lock dates back to 1773.

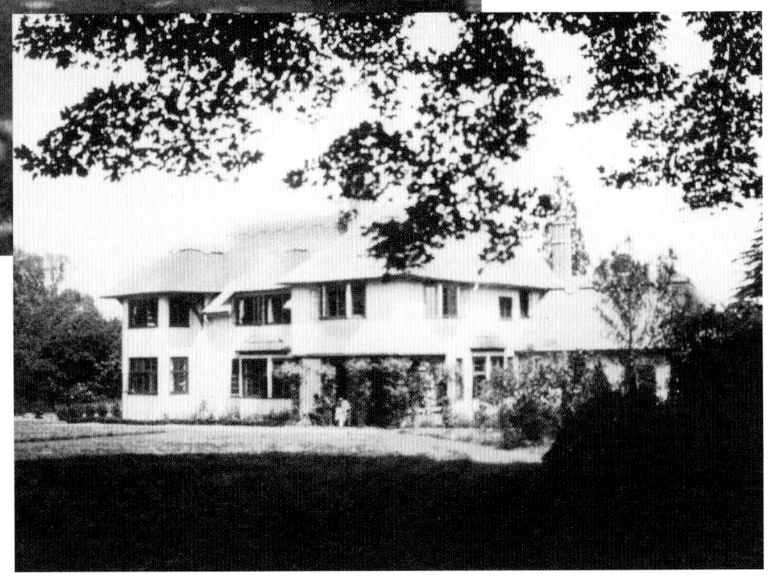

BELOW The cottage in Sonning. While there the family visited the Devonshire coast and villages in the countryside. Olin painted, and Deb had goats and rabbits to entertain her.

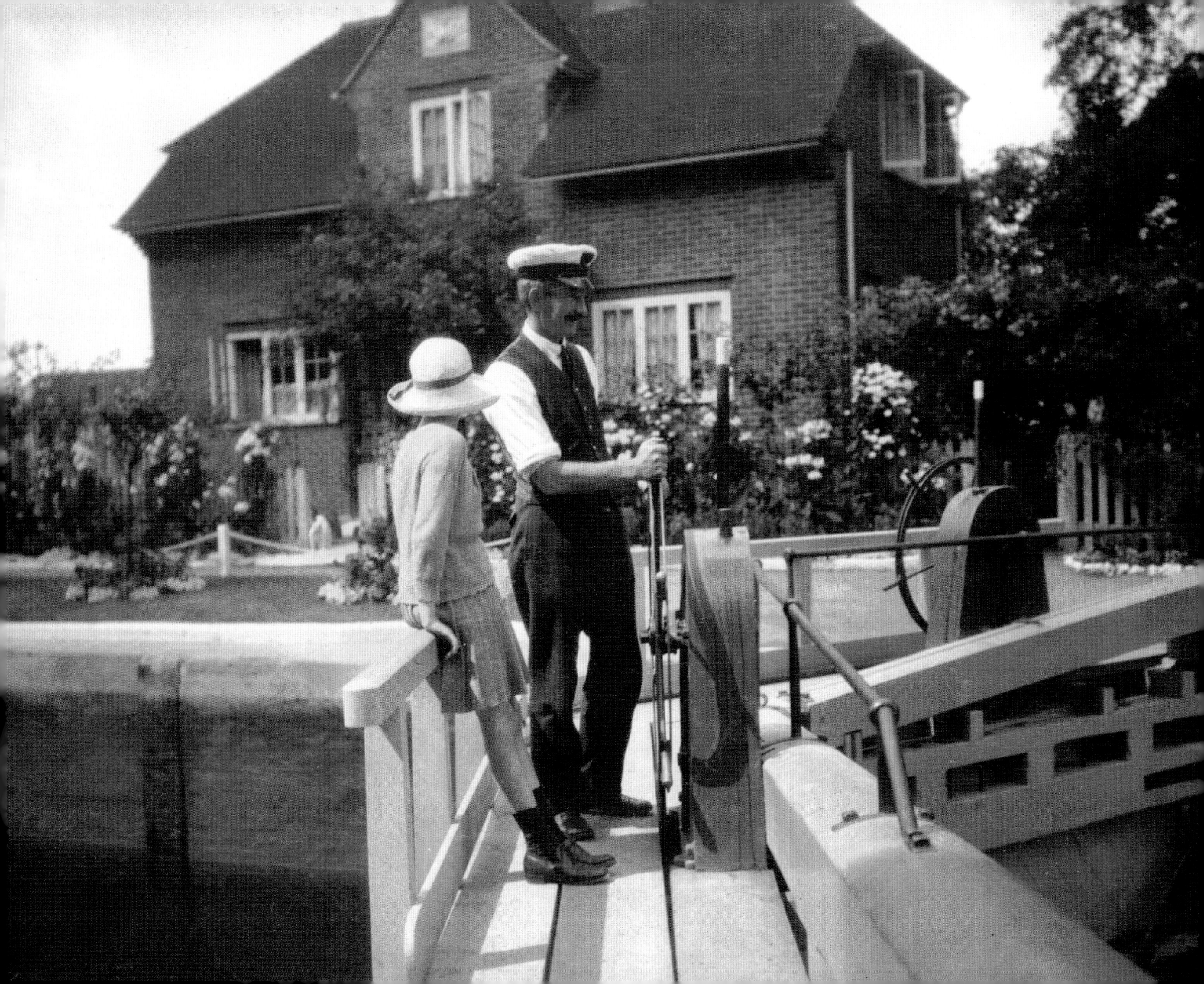

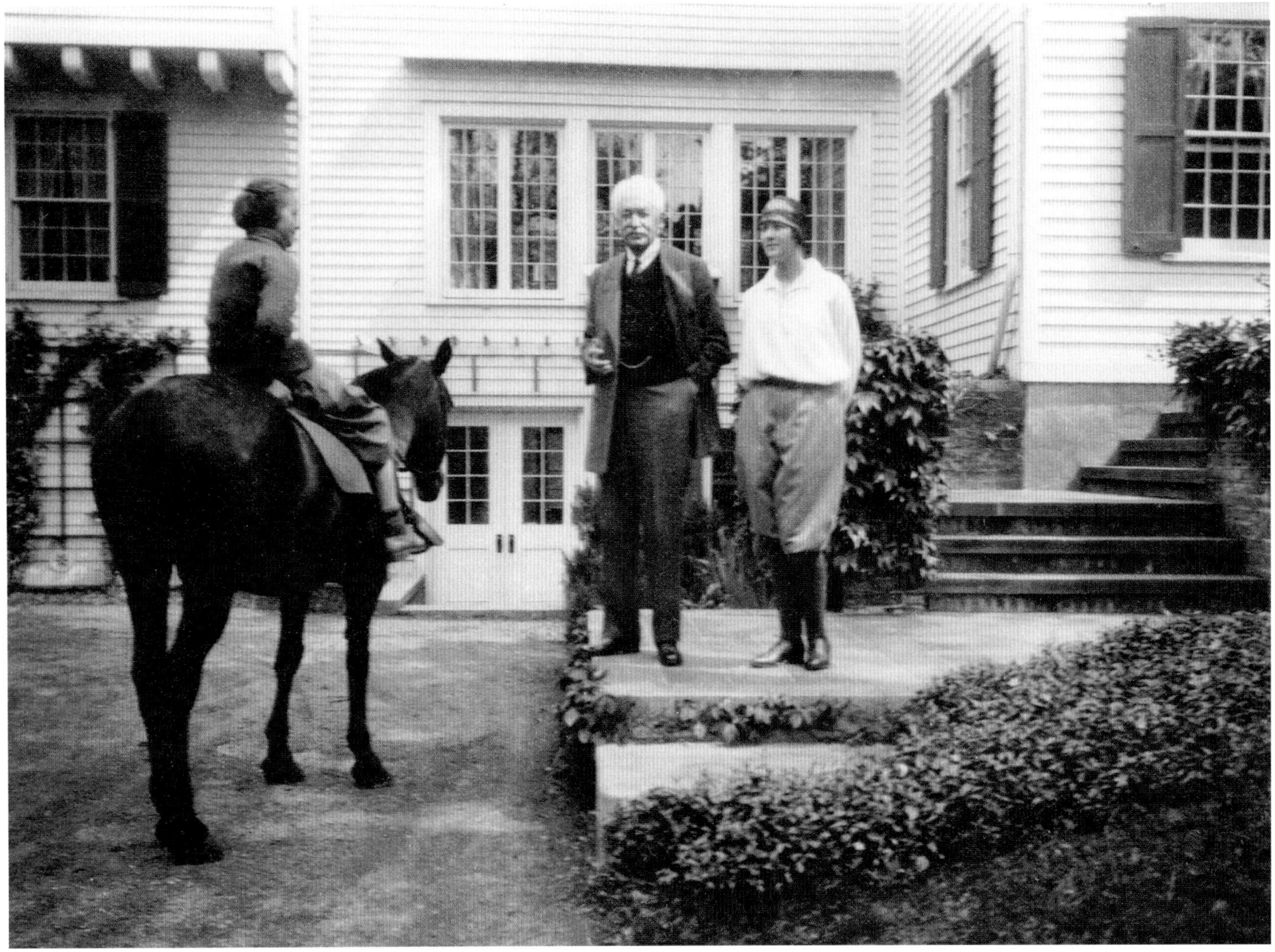

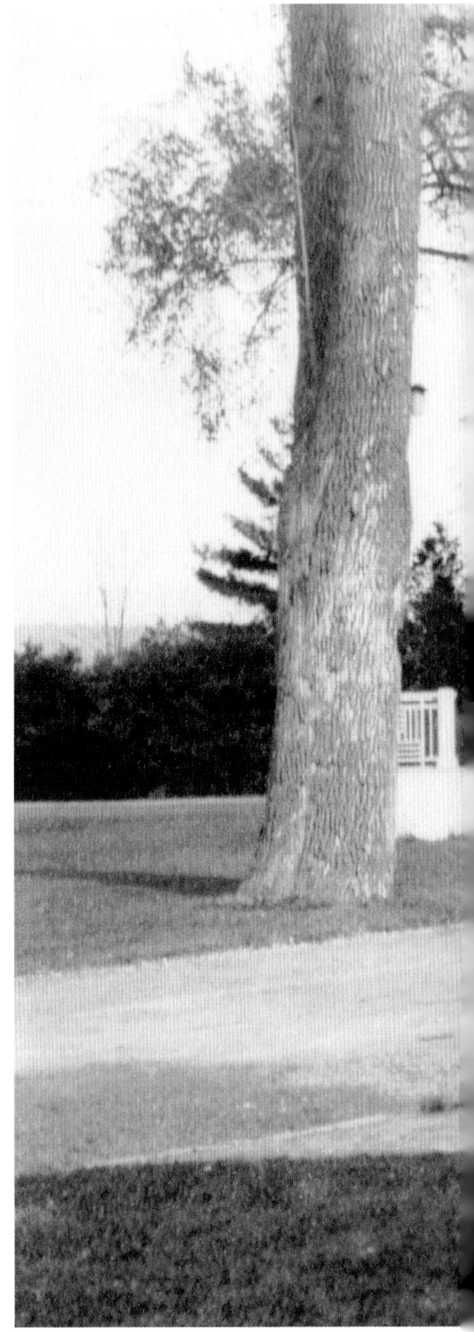

ABOVE Deb, age 10, on horseback with Margaret, age 18, and their grandfather, Stephen Henry Olin, on the front steps of Glenburn, 1924. That summer Margaret was introduced to the Swedish diplomat Knut Richard Thyberg, whom she married a year later. Stephen Henry Olin died in August 1925, just two months before the wedding.

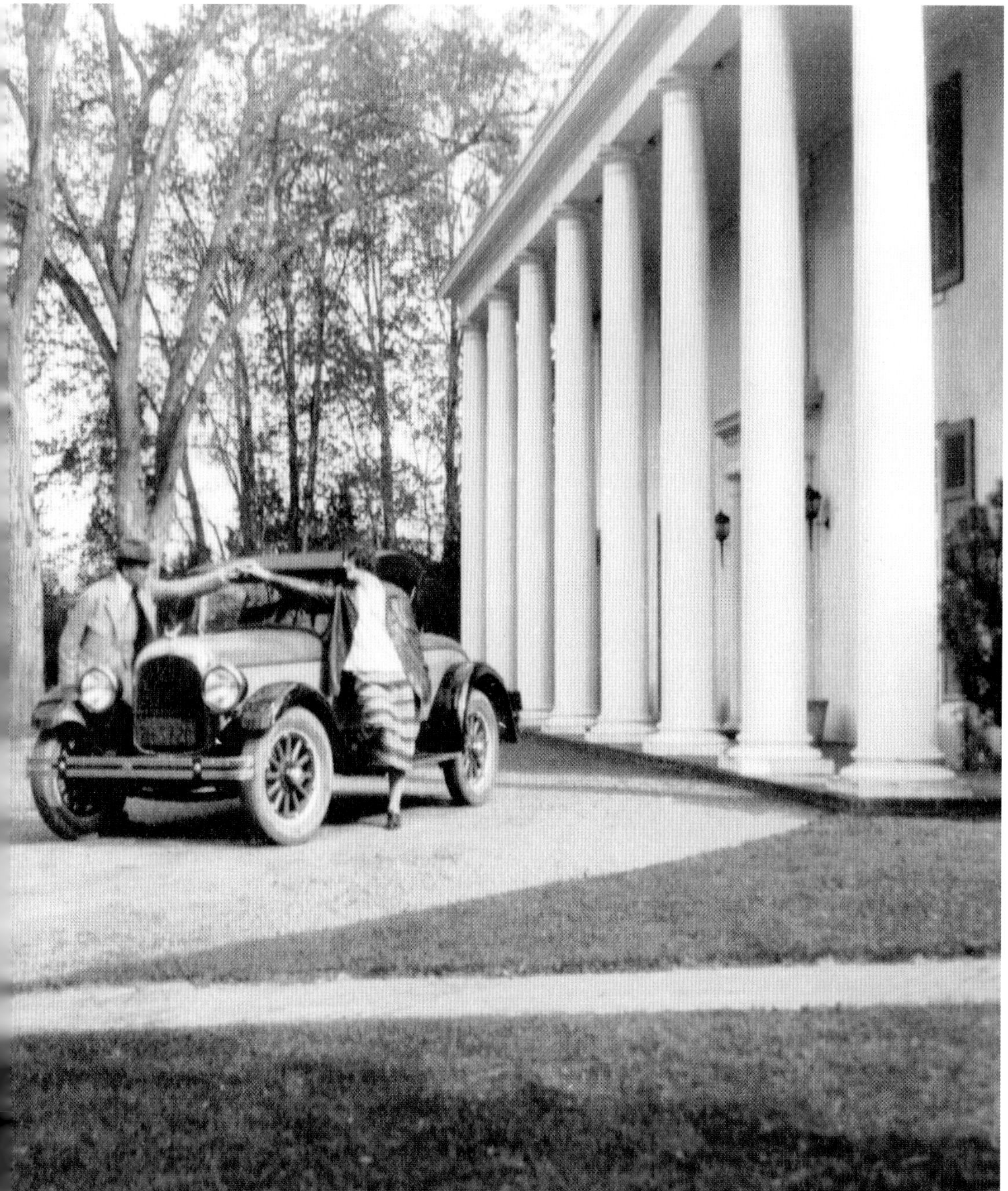

LEFT Tracy ceremoniously presenting Margaret the keys to a 1926 Chrysler Imperial Roadster, the first year the car was introduced, for her nineteenth birthday in 1925.

BELOW Tracy and Deb having breakfast on a summer morning on the roof of the Foxhollow Farm house, 1925. The Swedish flag celebrates the recent engagement of Margaret to Knut. Oddly, the blue and yellow colors of the flag look reversed in the photograph.

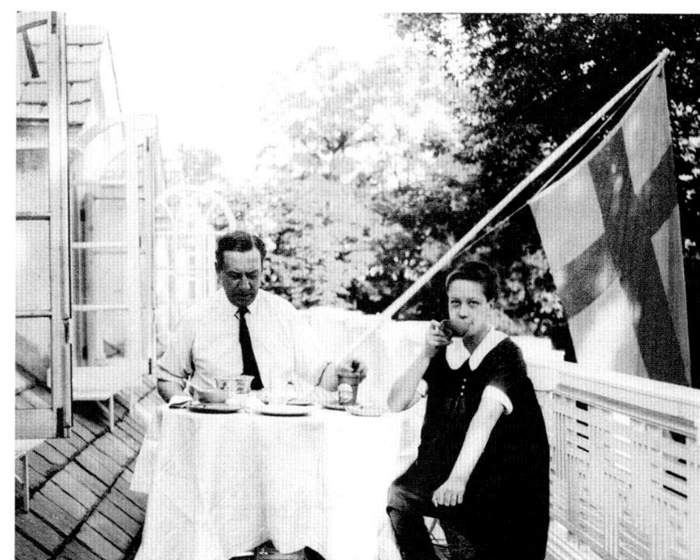

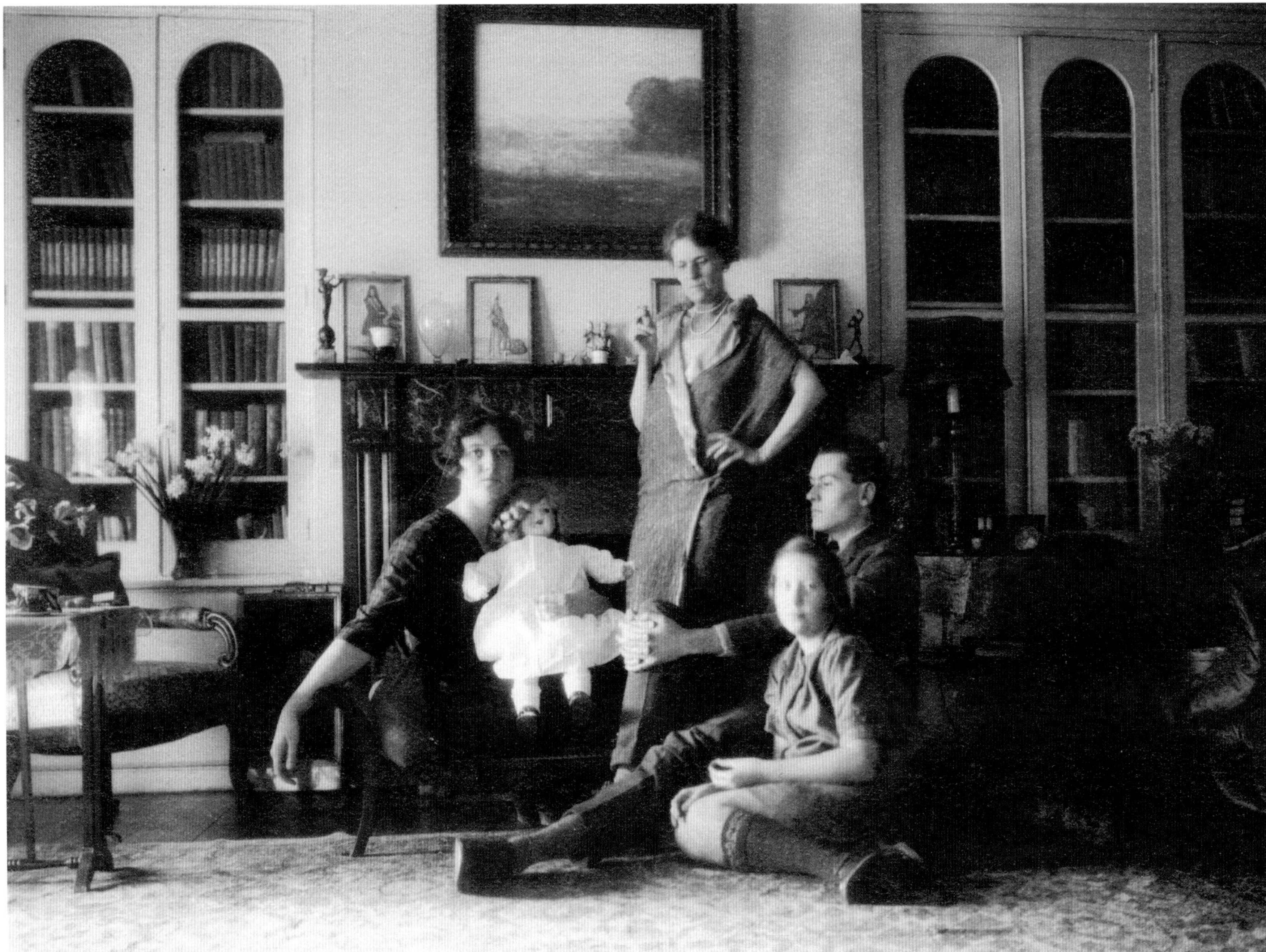

OPPOSITE The family in the library at Greyholm in Washington, D.C., 1924. Drawn to the culture and social life of the city, Alice decided that she wanted to have a house in Washington and divide her time between there and Rhinebeck. In 1924, she rented Greyholm, a large, historic house on the corner of R and 30th streets that had been the home of lawyer James Mandeville Carlisle. At Greyholm, Alice entertained guests with performances by accomplished violinists such as Nicholas Longworth (Speaker of the House), Efrem Zimbalist, and Paul Kochanski, along with the opera singers Nina Koshetz and Lucrezia Bori. The parties often lasted until the early hours of the morning. The home, later known as the Beall-Washington house, was purchased by Katharine Graham, longtime publisher of the *Washington Post*, who lived there from 1946 to 2001. During her time it was the epicenter of parties attended by heads of state, politicians, and Washington society.

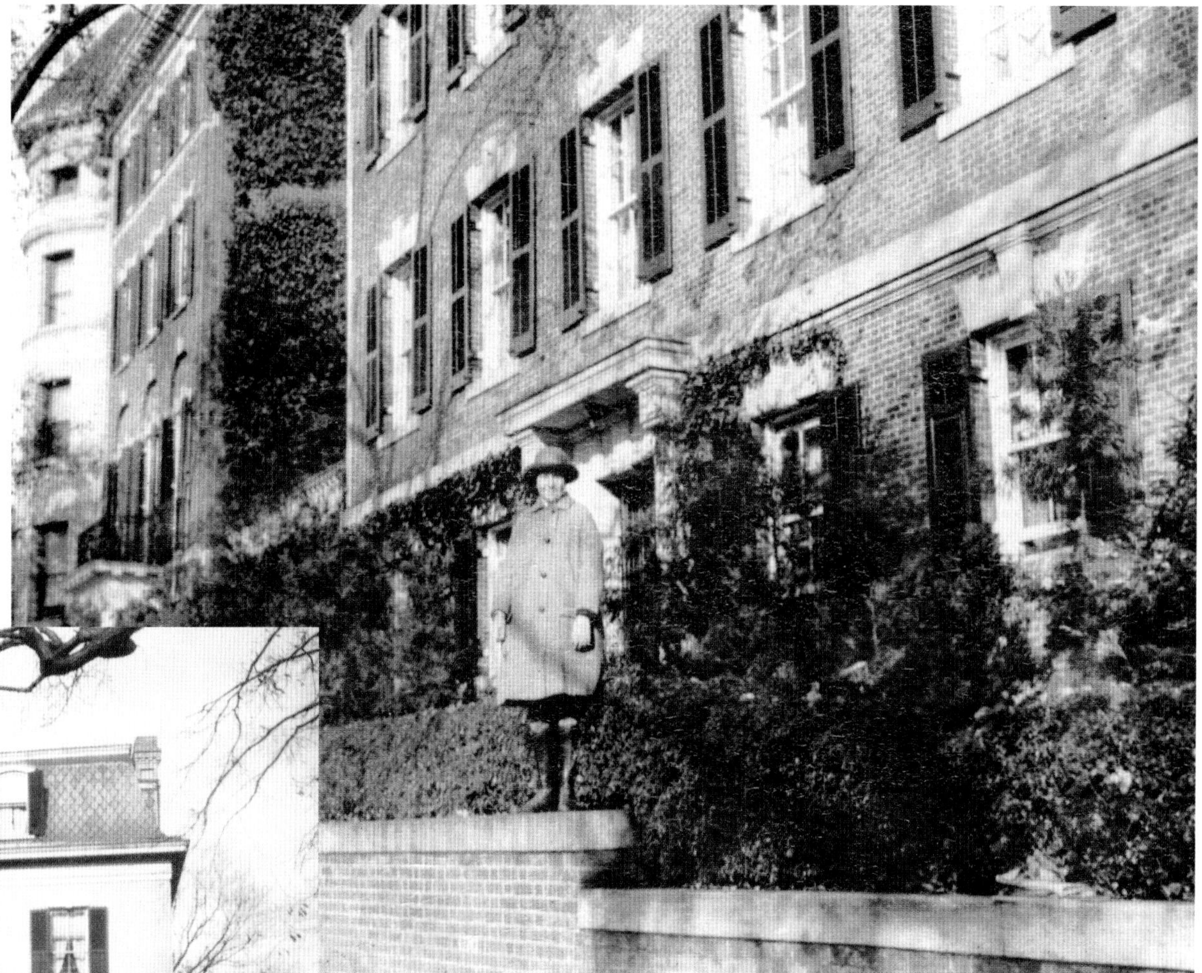

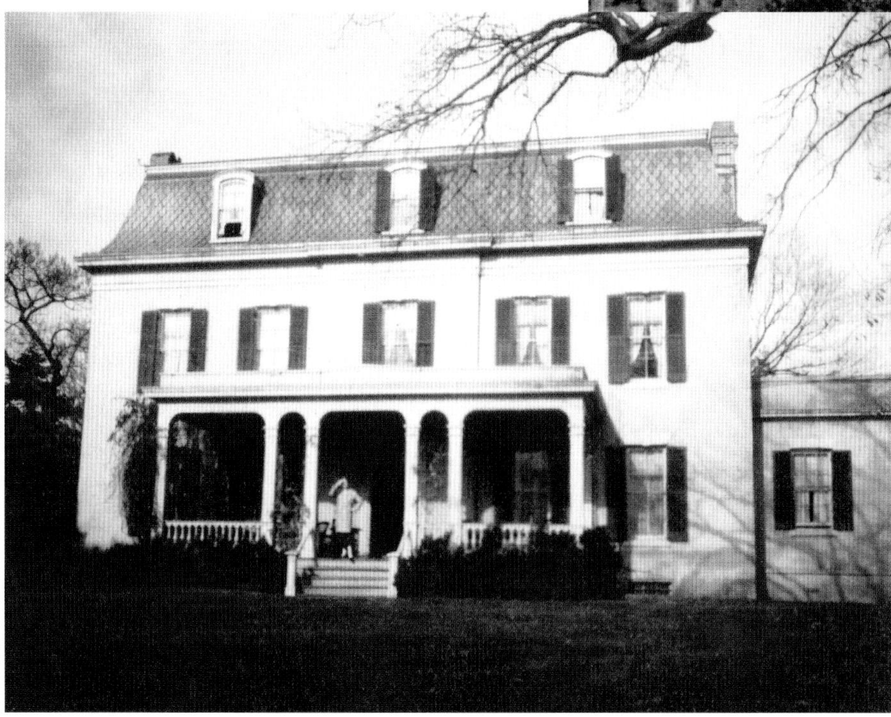

ABOVE Deb, age 10, in front of Holton-Arms School in 1924. She was enrolled there for three years. Later she attended the boarding school Foxcroft.

LEFT Alice on the steps of Greyholm. The family gathered there for the Thanksgiving and Christmas holidays in 1924.

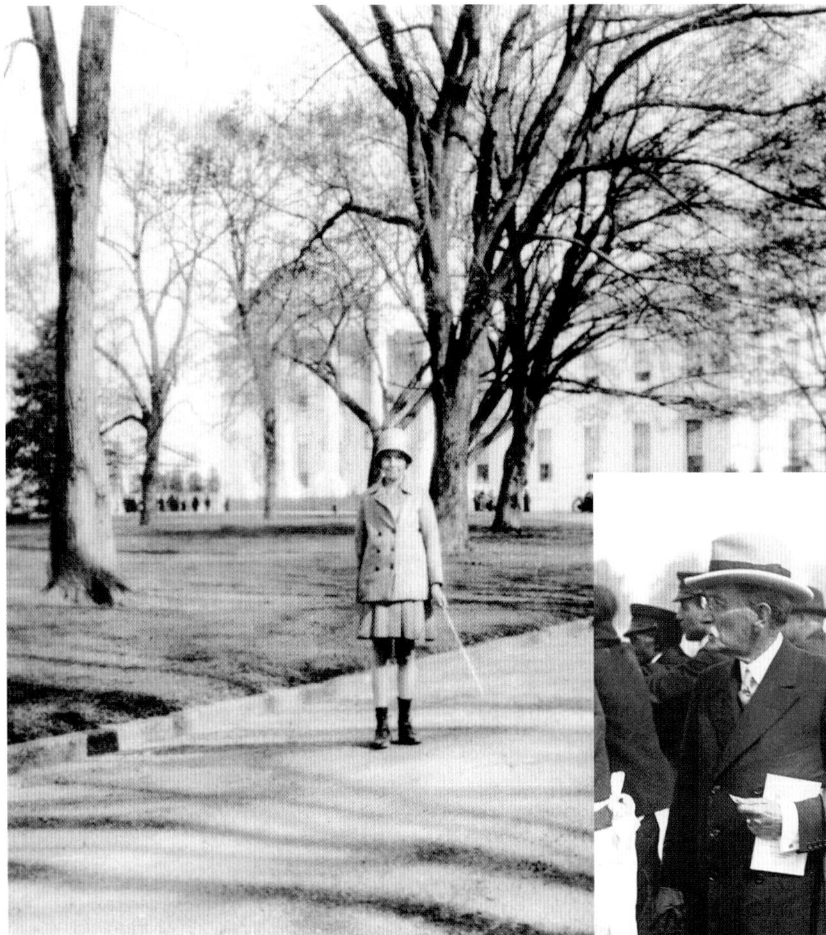

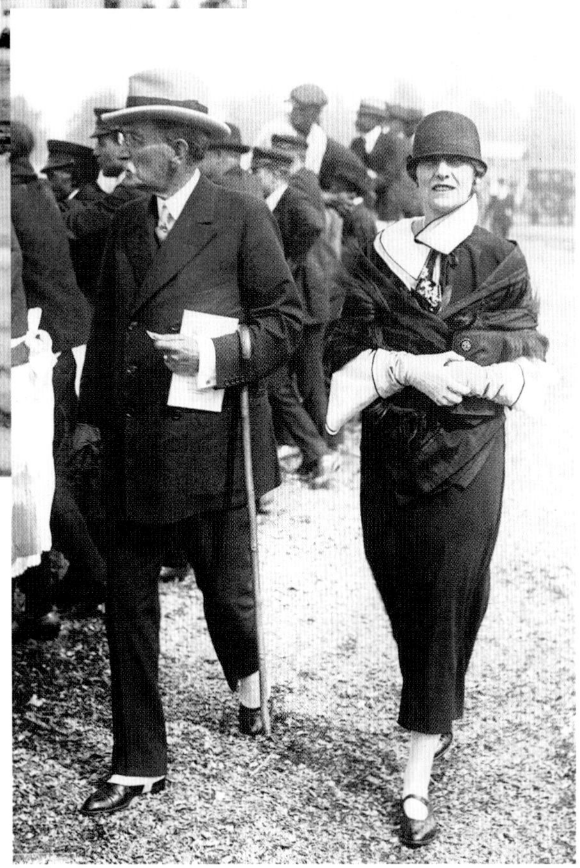

LEFT Deb with her stick on the lawn of the White House, 1924, getting ready for the annual Easter Egg Roll. Dolley Madison, the wife of President James Madison, is said to have inaugurated the event, though some historians dispute this.

BELOW Alice and a friend captured at an event in Washington by a photographer from the Harris & Ewing agency which appeared in the society pages of *Vogue*.

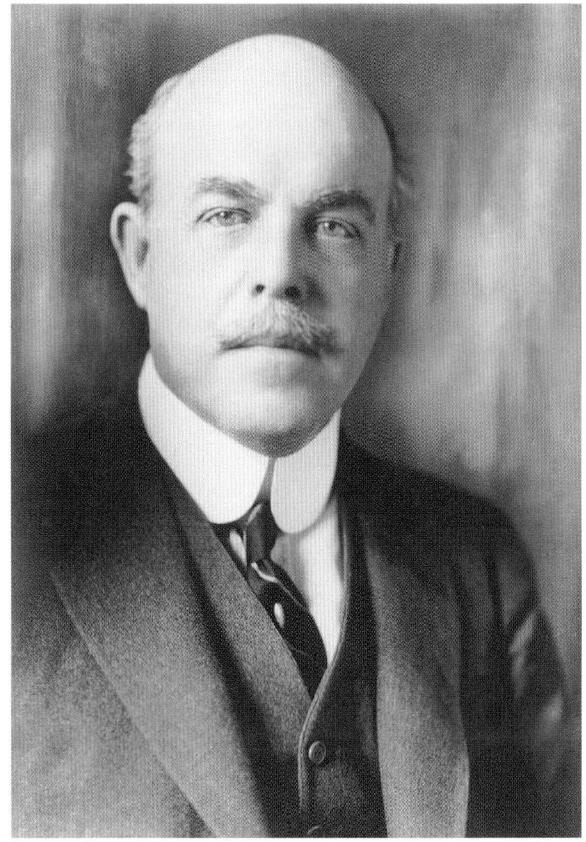

ABOVE A portrait of Nicholas Longworth taken by the Clinedinst Studio in Washington. It was given to Alice in 1926 during the time he was Speaker of the House. Alice enjoyed a close friendship with Nicholas and his wife, Alice Roosevelt Longworth. (Courtesy of Rhinebeck Historical Society)

OPPOSITE Alice may have taken this photograph on the steps of Greyholm in April 1925, during the Easter holiday. Deb and Margaret are pointing to Olin while Tracy looks on.

"Mrs. Tracy Dows is one of the most distinguished of the New York visitors of the national capital where she is always cordially greeted by a host of friends."

Vogue, July 24, 1924

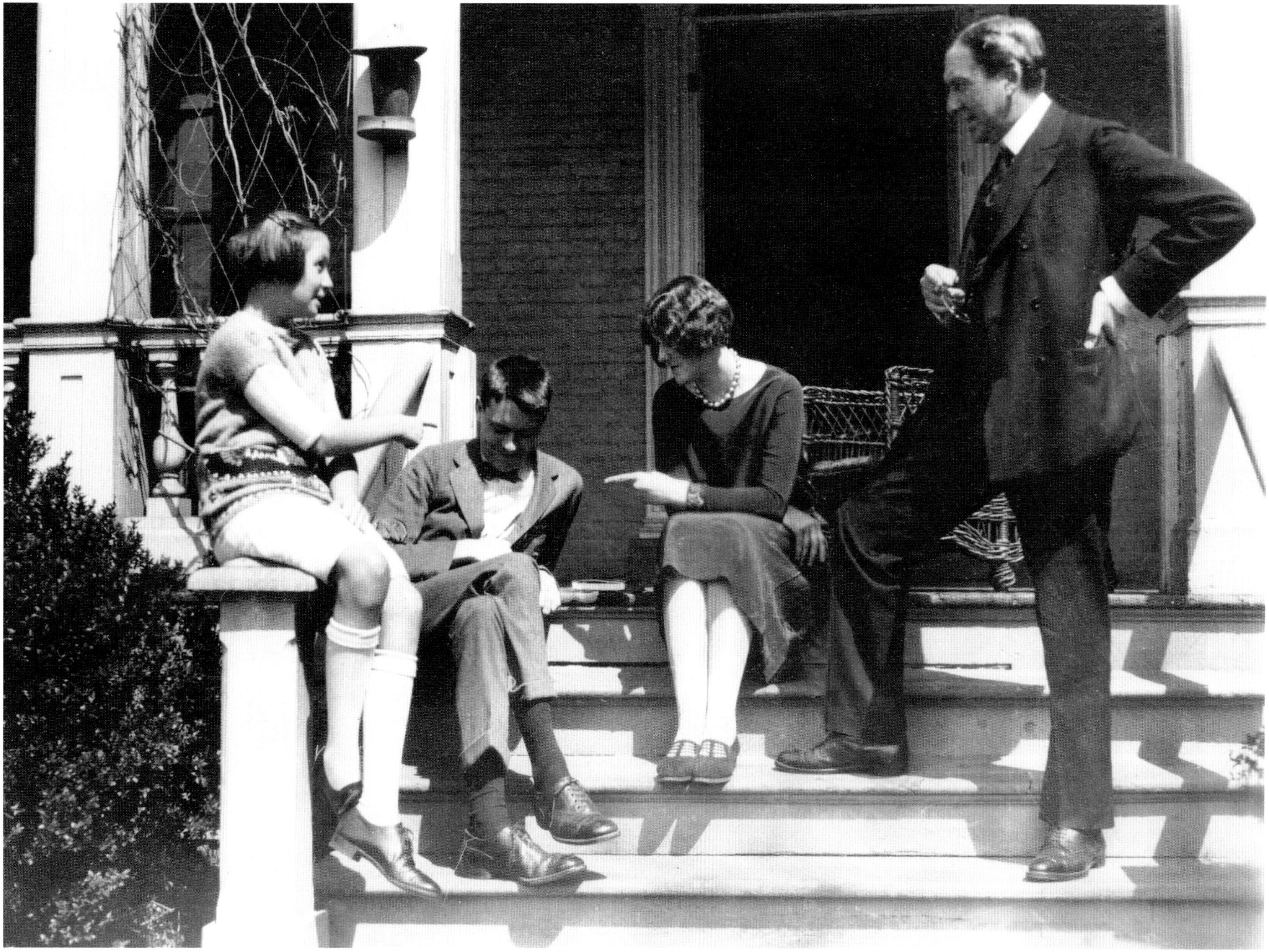

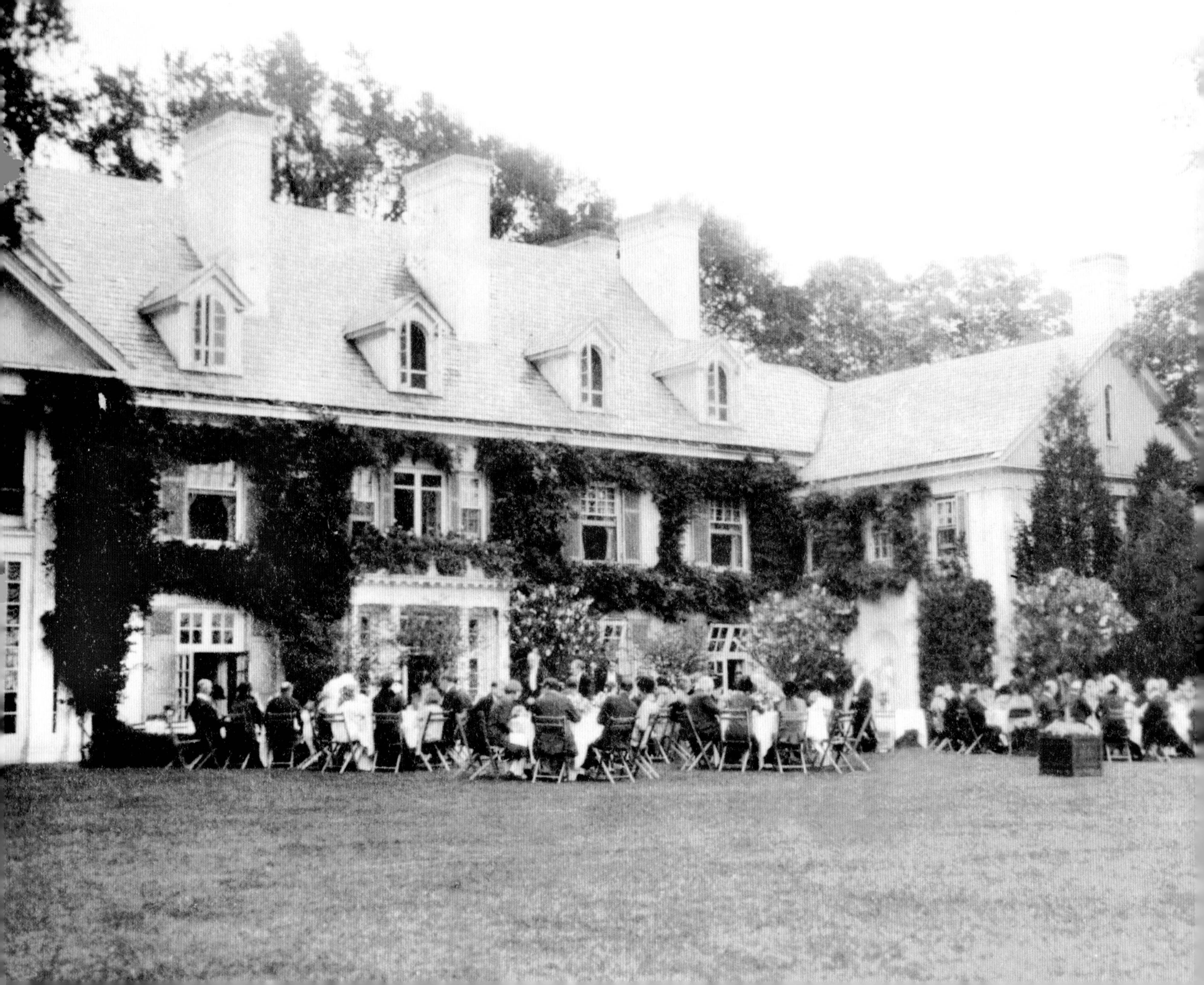

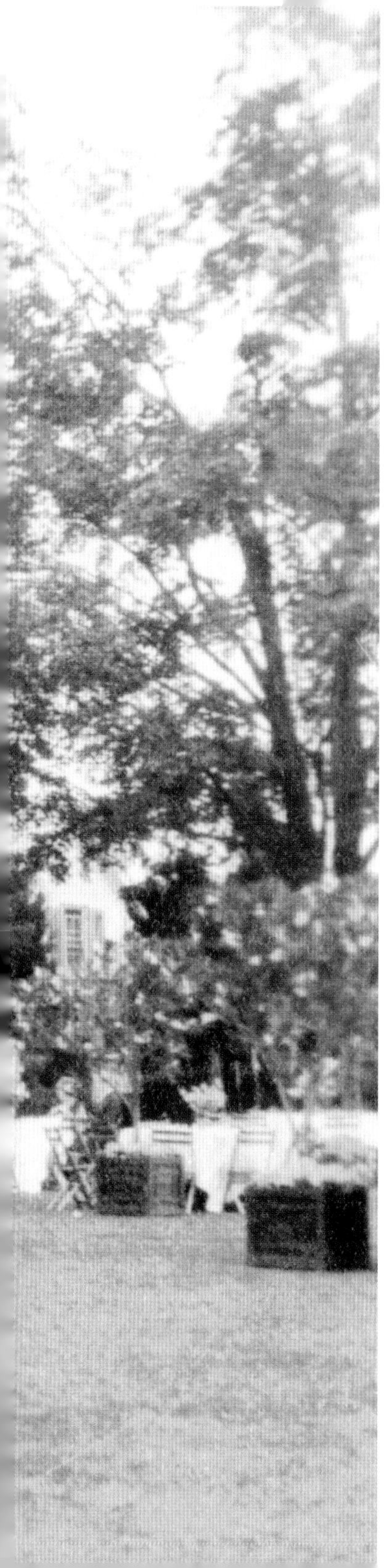

LEFT Guests at the wedding of Margaret Dows to Knut Richard Thyberg at Foxhollow Farm, October 3, 1925. Deb was Margaret's only attendant. The original wedding plan, with several bridesmaids, was scaled back in light of the recent death of Margaret's grandfather, Stephen Henry Olin. According to Alice, it was a stressful day since the food and supplies from the caterers, Sherry's restaurant in New York City, arrived too late to provide the wedding breakfast. Events had to be reordered, with the ceremony first, followed by dancing and champagne before the meal. Despite these complications, it was a lovely wedding.

RIGHT Margaret with Deb and Olin on her wedding day. The photograph was taken by Ira L. Hill, whose fashionable society portraits appeared in *Vogue* and *Vanity Fair* in the 1920s.

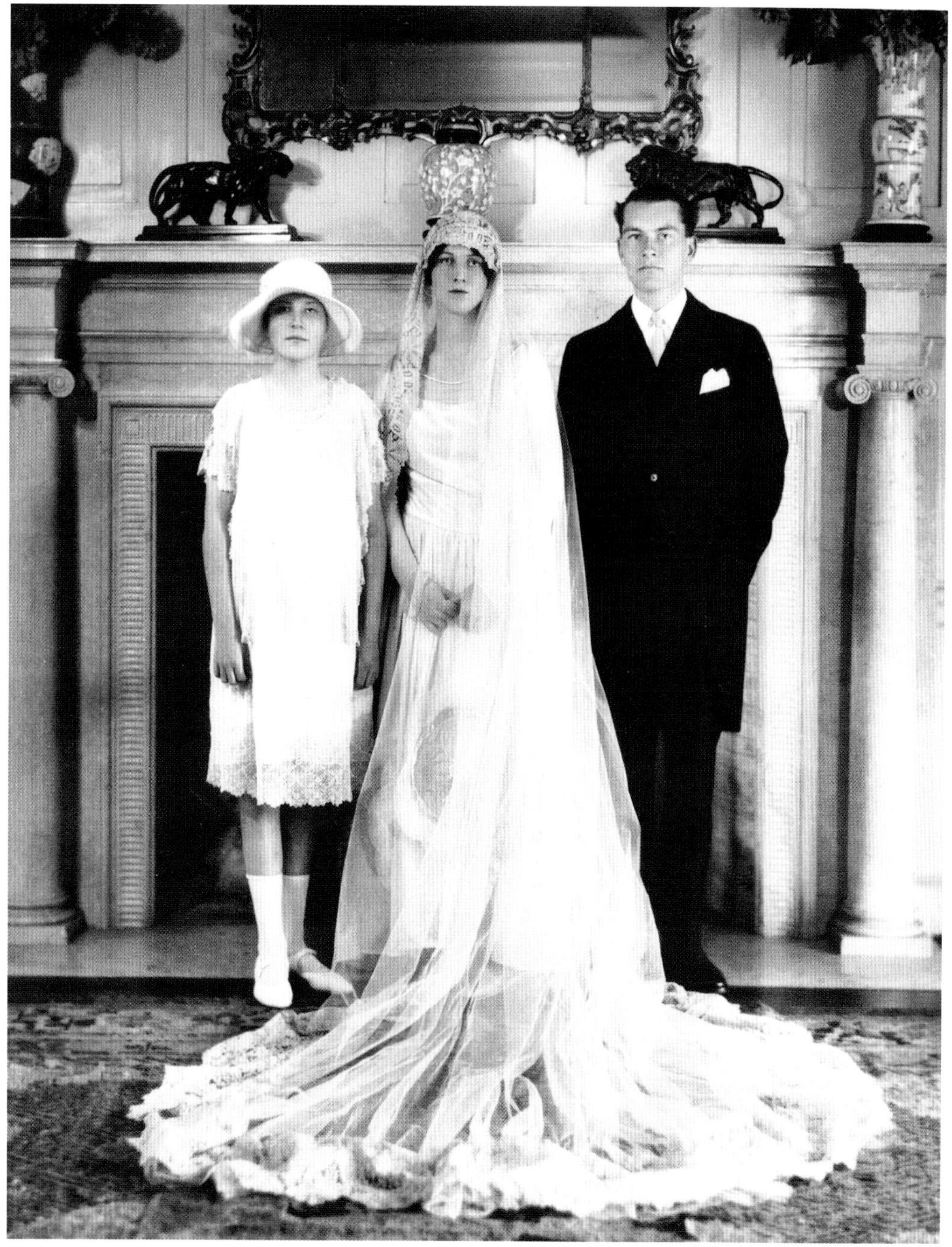

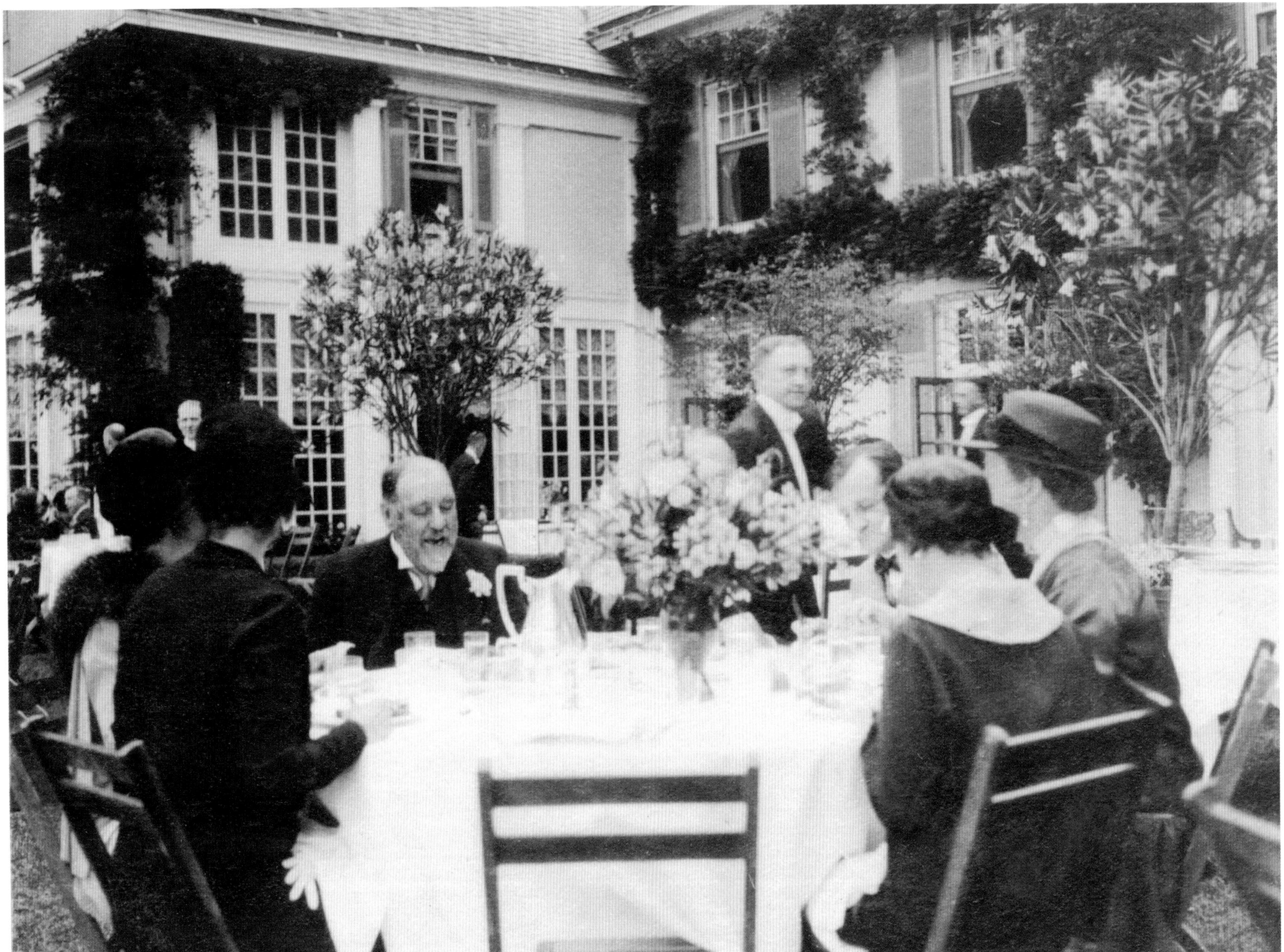

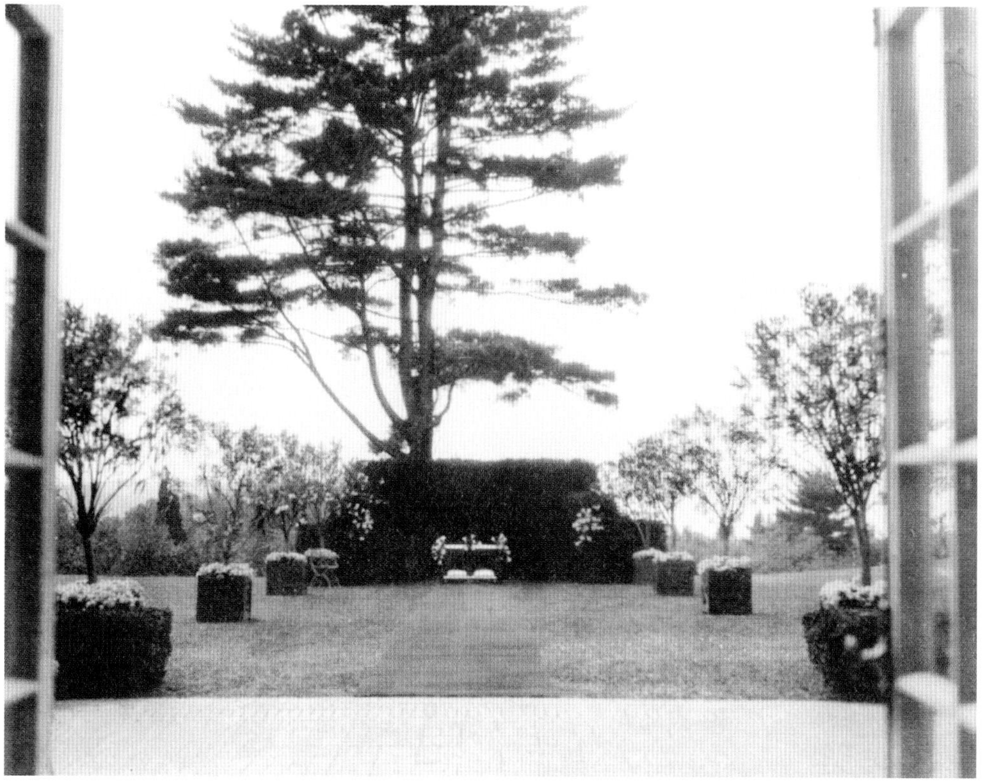

LEFT A view from inside the loggia of the aisle set up for the wedding ceremony, with potted oleander trees and flowers on each side of the aisle. A hedge was created in front of the altar, next to the large pine tree.

OPPOSITE Guests at the table entertained by James R. Roosevelt, Franklin D. Roosevelt's half-brother, known by his friends as "Rosy."

RIGHT A dashing Knut in his diplomatic uniform, 1924. Born in 1896, Knut grew up in the village of Sunne, Sweden. He was commissioned as a lieutenant of the Life Grenadier Regiment of Sweden in 1916 and graduated from the law school of the University of Stockholm in 1918. He entered the Foreign Service the following year and was sent to the Swedish Consulate General in New York as vice-consul in 1923. Knut was introduced to Margaret while visiting his Rhinebeck friend, John Langdon, in 1924.

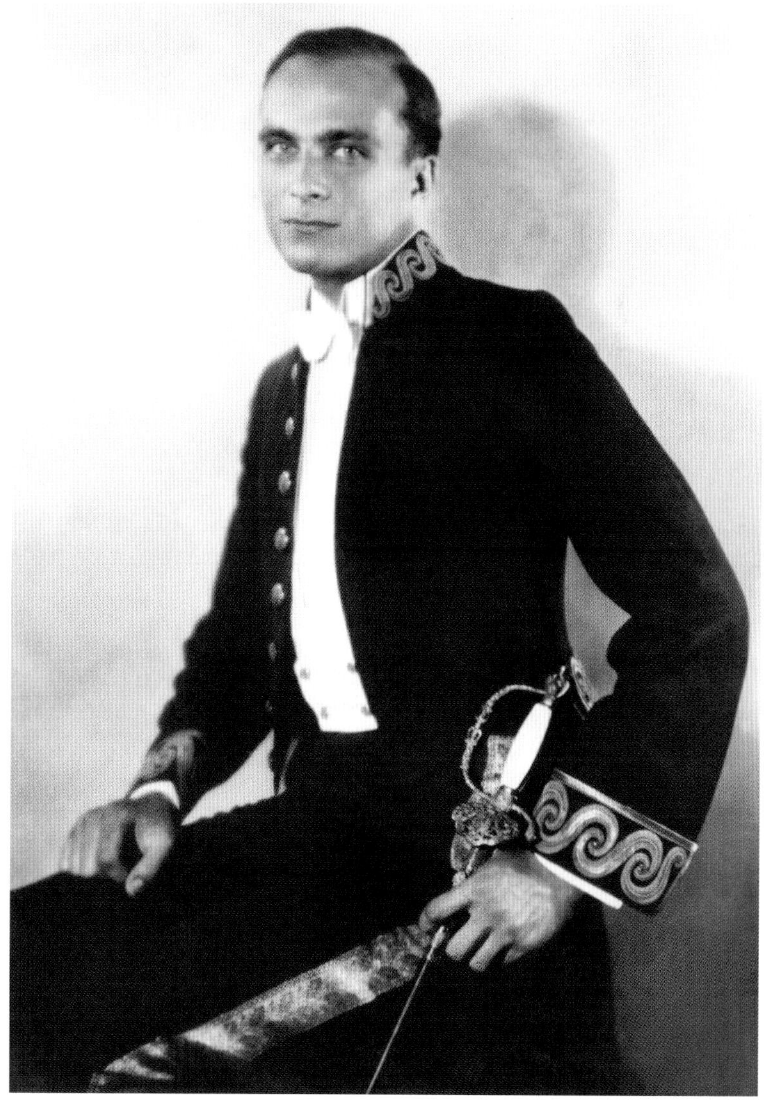

RIGHT Knut in the Thybergs' apartment in Stockholm, 1927, where he and Margaret began their married life. At that time, Alice's friend, Robert Woods Bliss, was the U.S. Minister to Sweden, and he and his wife, Mildred, were helpful to Margaret in adjusting to life there. Alice traveled to Stockholm for the birth of Margaret and Knut's first child, Olin Knut (affectionately known as O.K.).

BELOW Margaret with Knut's parents, Edvard and Thyra Thyberg, who were admiring their American daughter-in-law during a visit in 1927. Knut's father owned a country store in Sunne, located on Lake Fryken in western Sweden.

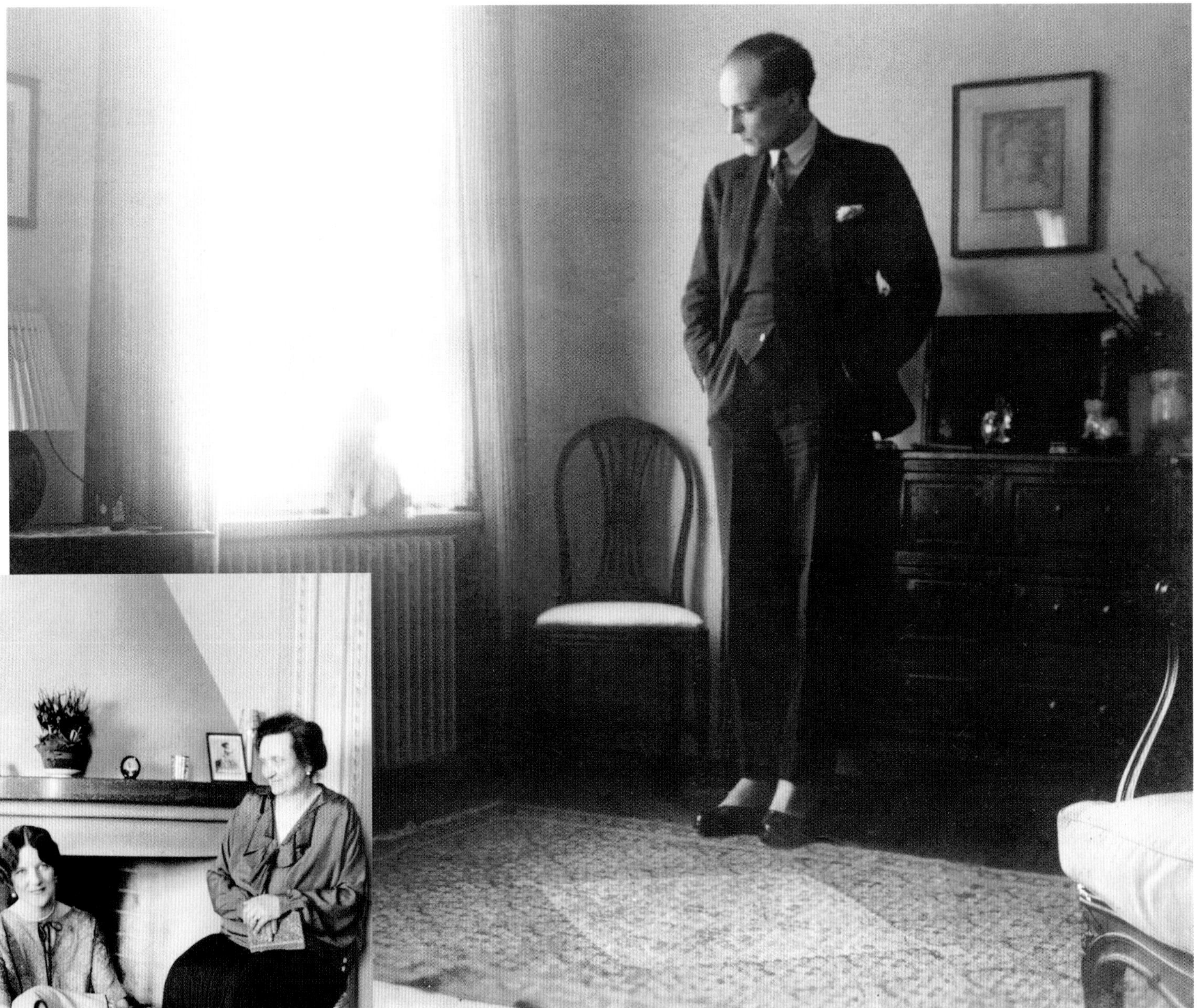

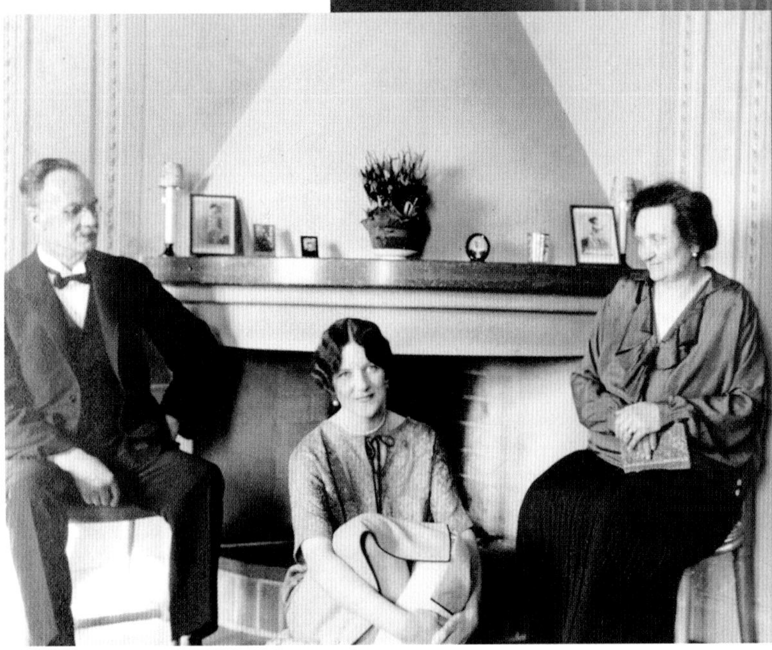

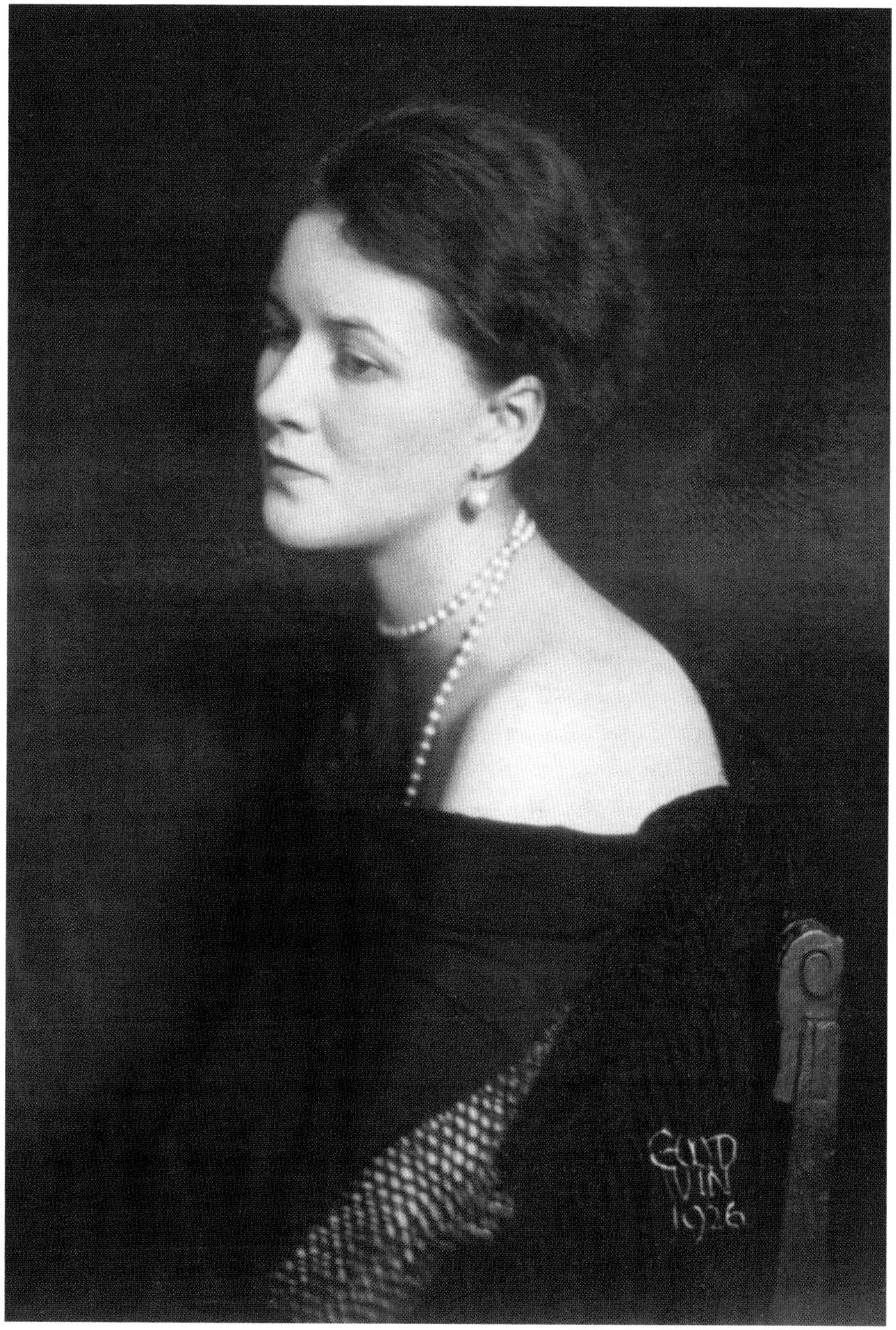

LEFT A portrait of Margaret taken by Henry Buergel Goodwin in Stockholm, 1926. Born in Germany, Goodwin became Sweden's foremost portrait photographer in the early 1900s. This photograph appeared in the February 15, 1927, issue of *Vogue*.

RIGHT AND BELOW Tracy and Alice photographed by Goodwin while they were visiting Margaret in Stockholm in 1926.

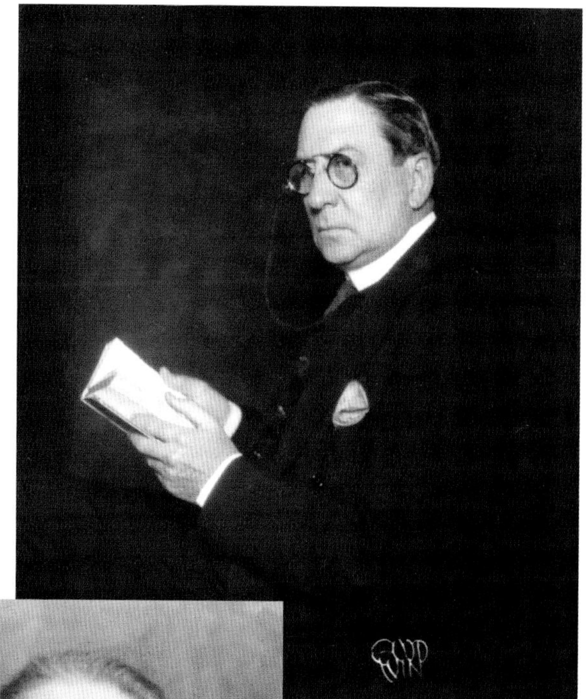

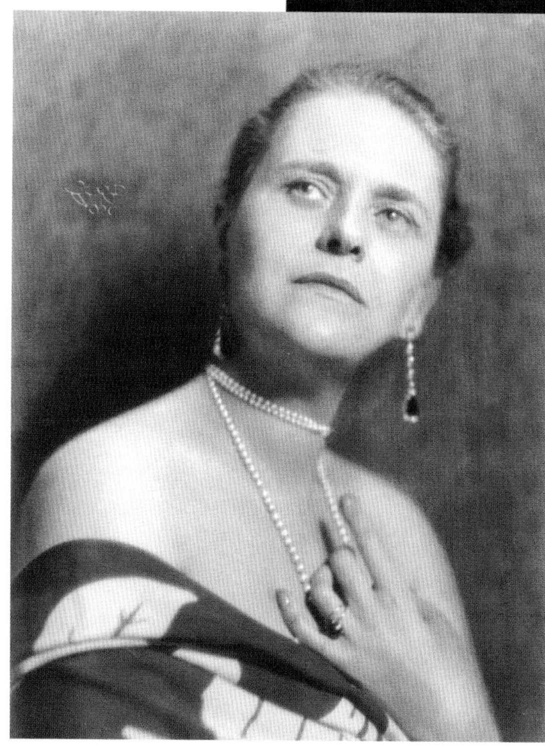

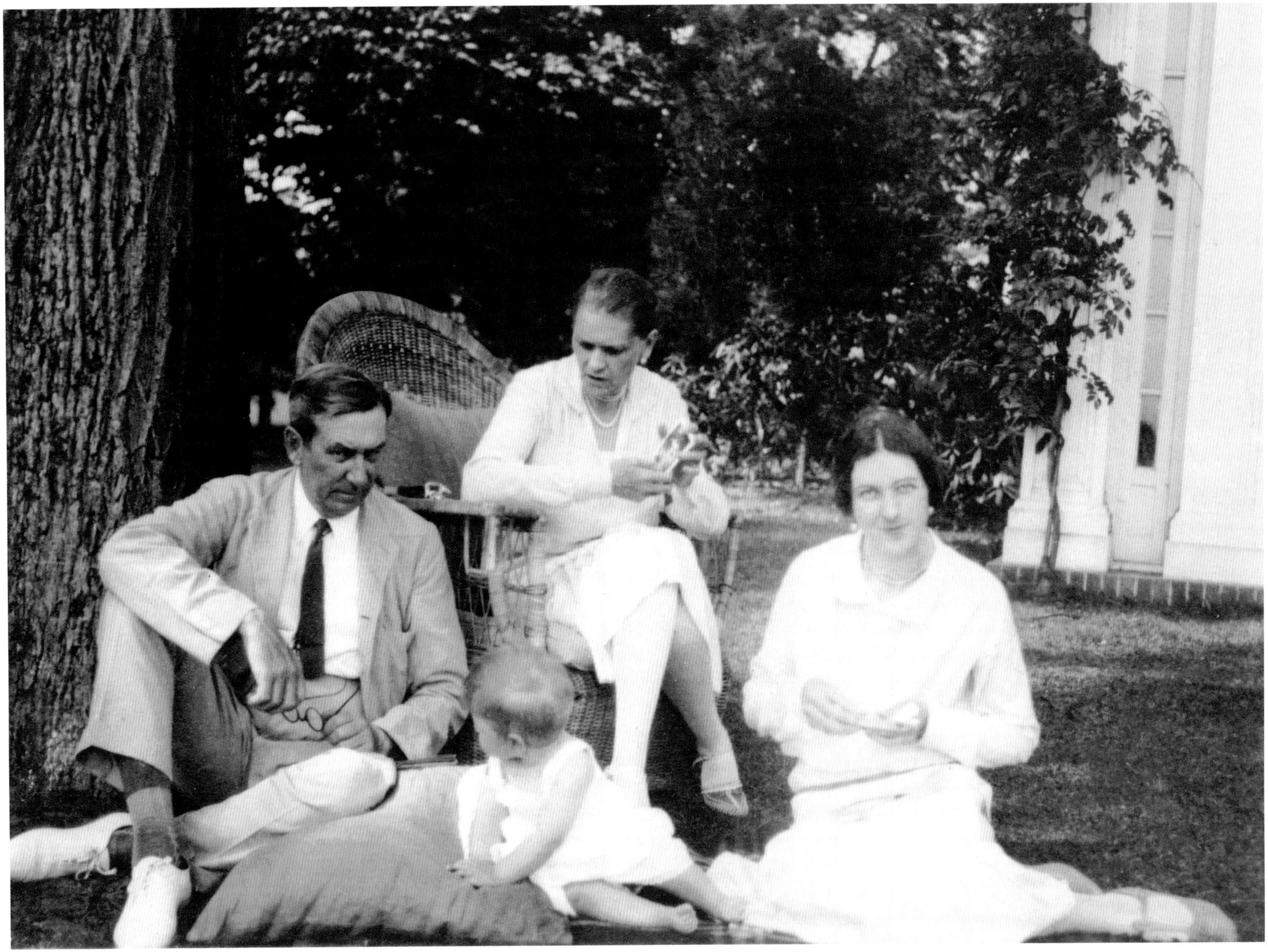

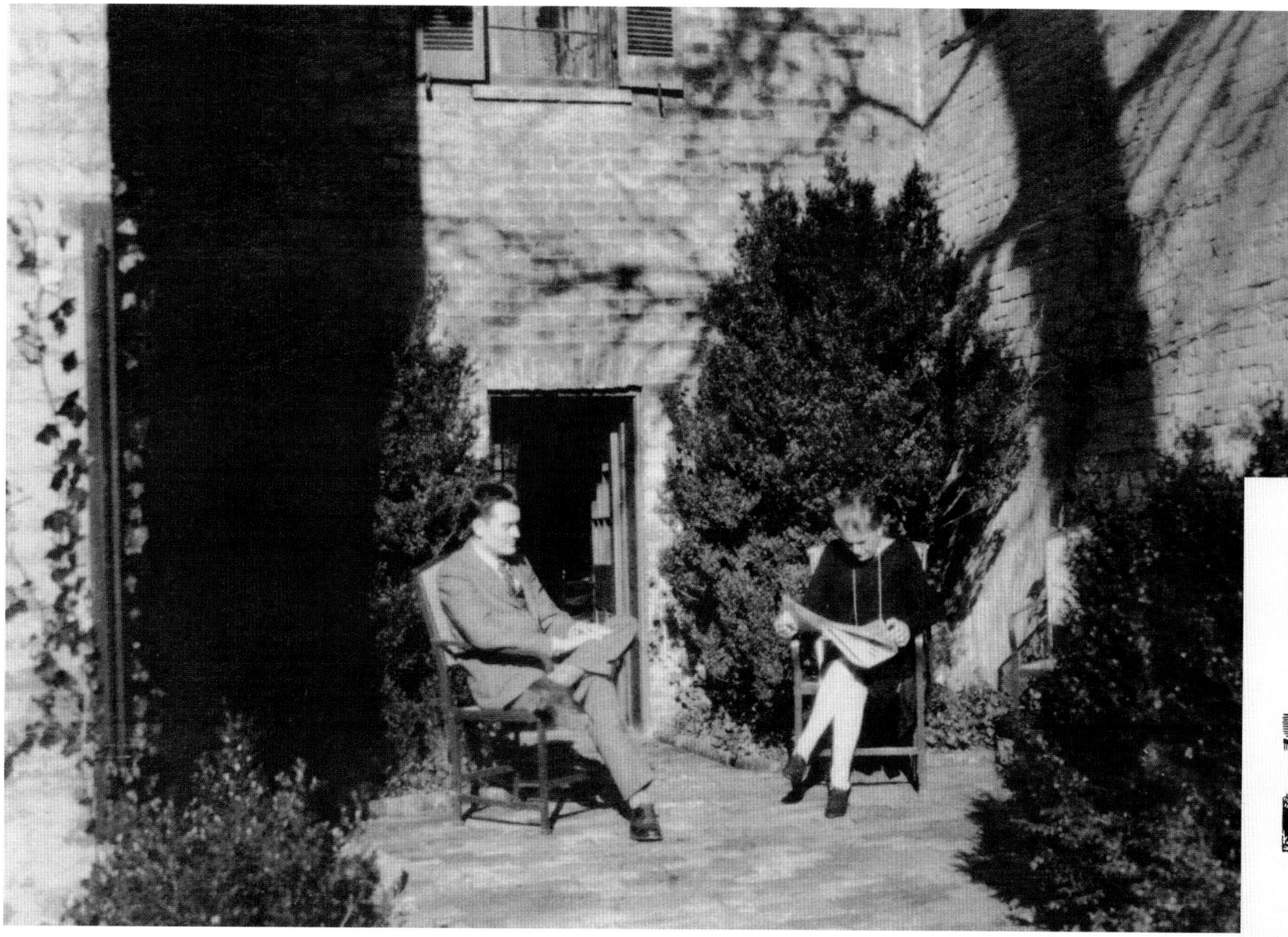

LEFT Olin and Alice on the back terrace of her O Street house in Washington, 1928. While living at Greyholm, Alice had fallen in love with the Georgetown house and in 1926 persuaded Tracy to buy it for her. It remained her home for many years. Originally built as a schoolhouse in 1811, it had a special charm with its aged yellow-painted stuccoed brick and ultramarine blue shutters. While living there, Alice began to write poetry. She published two books, *Idle Hours*, dedicated to her children, and *Illusions*, dedicated to her dear friend Lucrezia Bori.

OPPOSITE Tracy and Alice with Margaret and their ten-month-old grandson, O.K., on the back lawn at Foxhollow Farm, July 1927. Margaret and O.K. had sailed from Stockholm to spend the summer in Rhinebeck. Alice had arranged for O.K. to be christened on September 7, 1927, next to the large pine tree on the back lawn. Alice and Deb were still living in Washington but spending the summer in Rhinebeck.

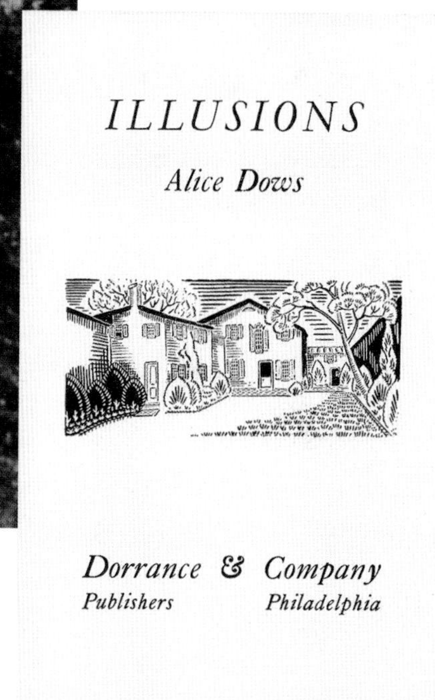

ILLUSIONS

Alice Dows

Dorrance & Company

Publishers *Philadelphia*

ABOVE Alice's second book, published in 1931, with Olin's drawing of her Washington house on the cover.

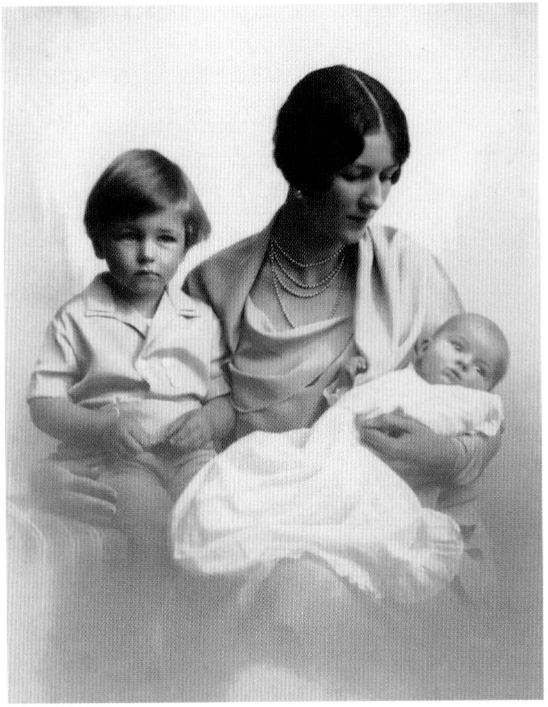

ABOVE Margaret photographed on holiday in Abbazia, Italy, with her children, O.K. and Birgitta, 1928. Knut's job had moved the family from Stockholm to a year-long posting in Riga, Latvia, where Birgitta was born.

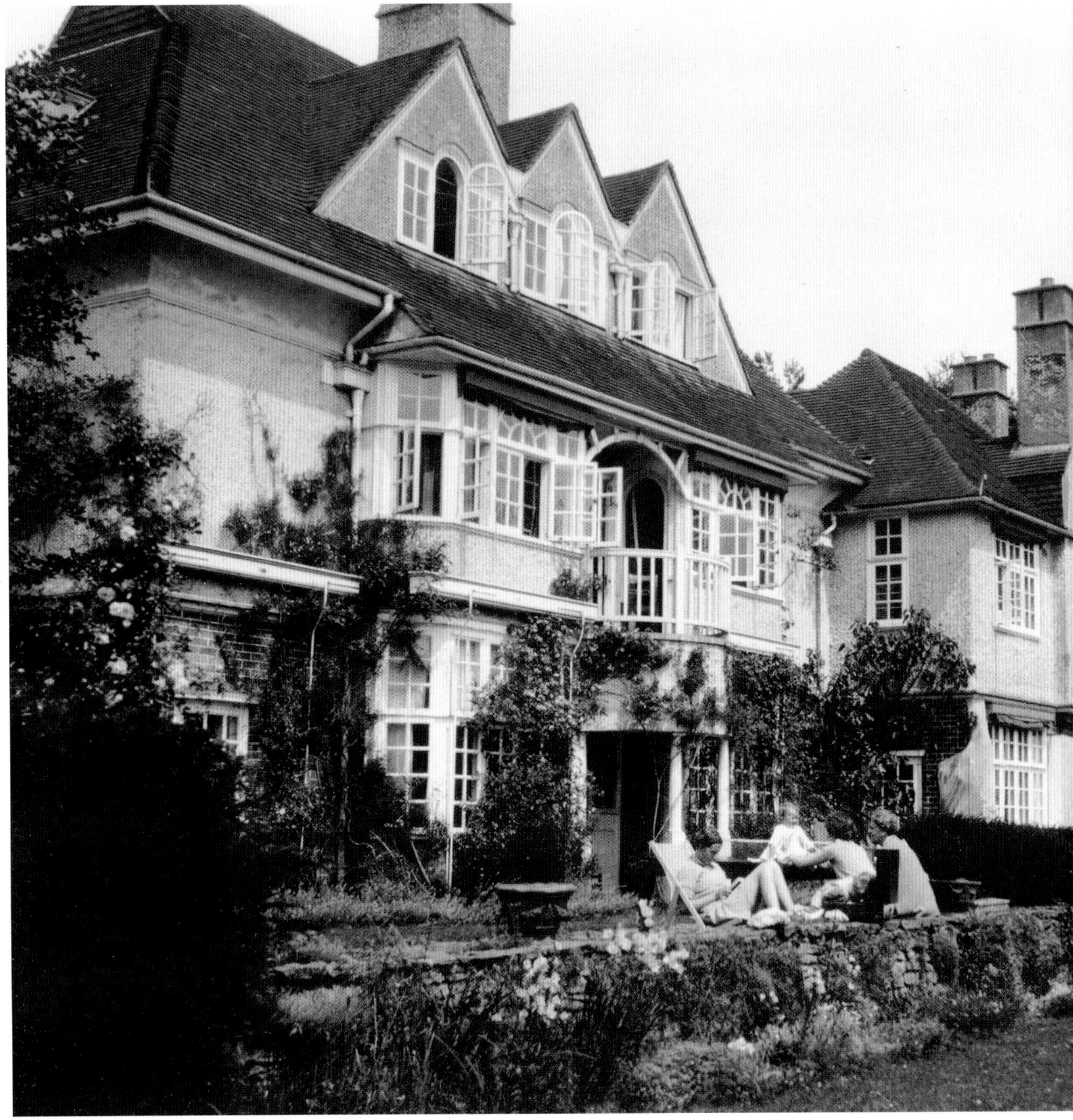

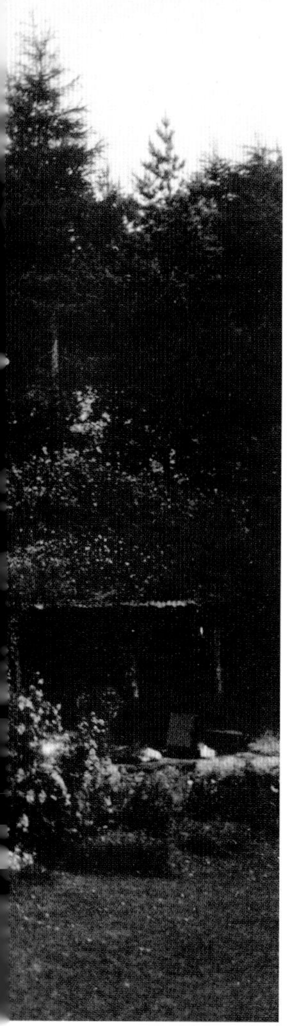

LEFT Kingsmead, the large house in Godalming, Surrey, where the Dowses and the Thybergs spent three months in 1929. The Thybergs had relocated to London from Riga, and Tracy decided to rent a house where the entire family could spend time together while Margaret and Knut looked for a house of their own.

BELOW The Blakes on a visit that summer to Godalming. On the terrace are Knut, Alice, Eugenie Blake, Margaret, Deb, and Frank Blake. The gentleman behind Margaret is unknown.

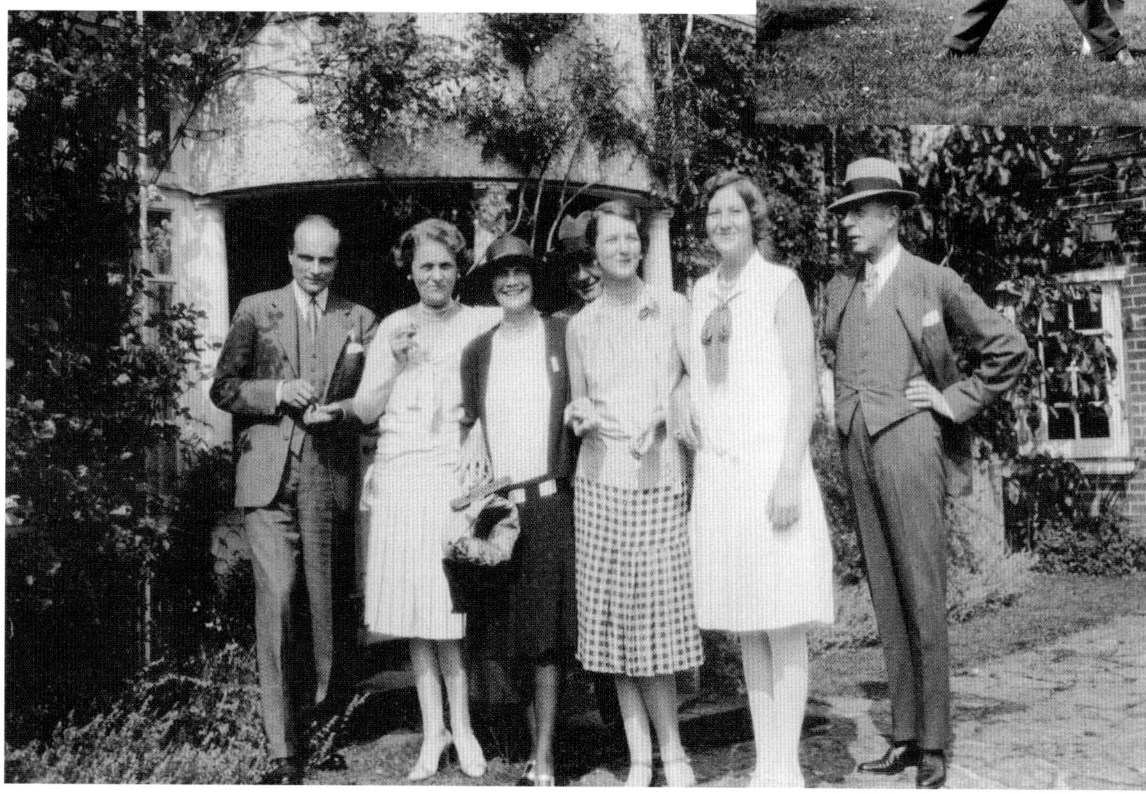

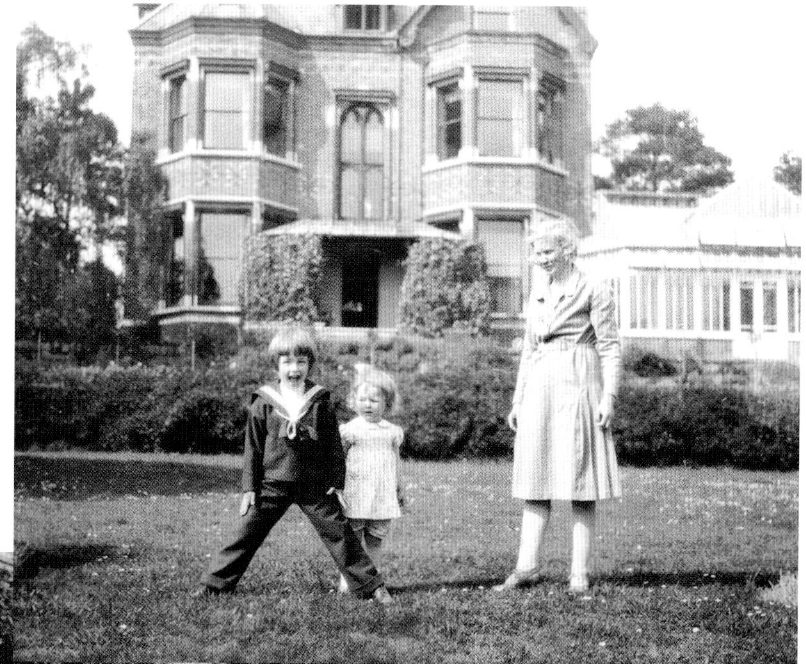

ABOVE O.K. and Birgitta with their Swedish nurse, Anna, at Cornwall Lodge, in Kingston Hill, the next house where Margaret and her family lived. Alice and Deb spent the summers of 1930 and 1931 at Cornwall Lodge, which were memorable for Alice. She visited her friends Alice and Serge Obolensky at their elegant Regent's Park house, as well as Rhoda and Oswald Birley in St. John's Wood. Alice also went to Diana Vreeland's house to see the panel of cats that Olin had painted above her fireplace mantle in the dining room, which was daringly decorated in scarlet and chartreuse.

BELOW A 1928 portrait of Deb drawn by Jean Negulesco, who was probably visiting Foxhollow Farm as a guest of Olin's. The Romanian-American began his career as a painter and scenic designer, moving to New York from Paris in 1927. In the early 1930s he moved to California and began working in the film industry, first as a sketch artist then later as a successful director. Some of his well-known movies include *The Rains of Ranchipur*, *Three Coins in the Fountain*, *How to Marry a Millionaire*, *Humoresque*, *Johnny Belinda* and *The Best of Everything*. Known to be a Hollywood charmer, and a favorite of Darryl Zanuck, he had a flair for melodrama and film noir. (Courtesy of Gale and Paul Schaefer)

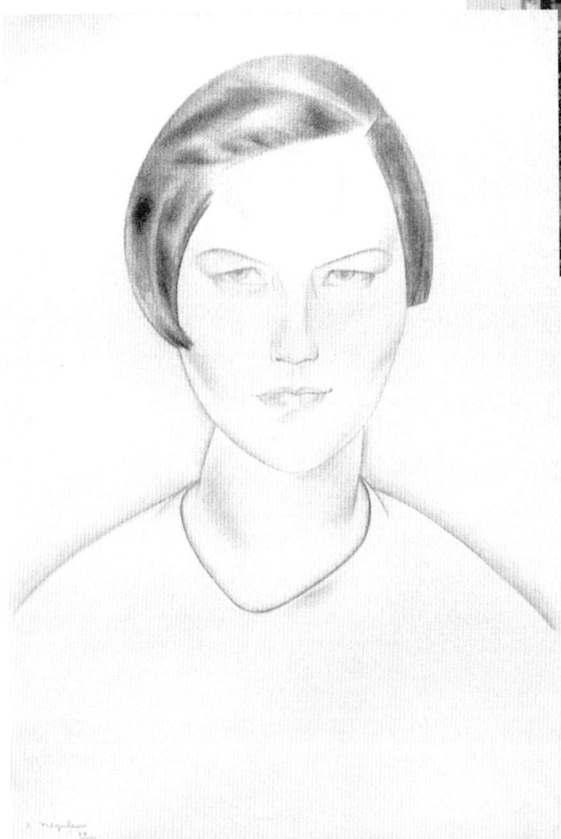

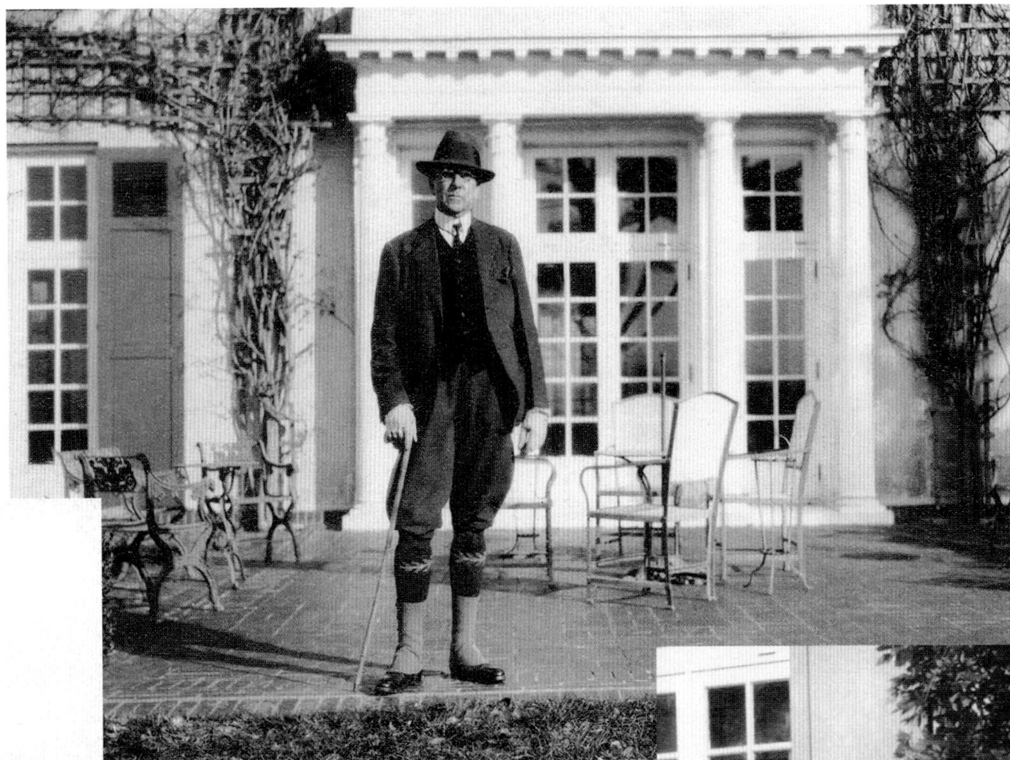

LEFT Tracy on the back terrace, 1929. He was still managing Foxhollow Farm, but with a smaller staff.

OPPOSITE A quiet moment for Deb in 1930 during the last days of living at Foxhollow Farm. She was always most comfortable in riding clothes.

RIGHT Deb's tutor, Miss Aileen Farrell, in 1929. Alice thought it best to send Deb back to Foxhollow Farm and hired Miss Farrell, a British citizen who had been a teacher at Foxcroft School, to spend eight months as a private tutor to prepare Deb to reenter Foxcroft the following year. In 1930 the Dows family left the estate for good and Tracy turned the house over to Miss Farrell as a girls' preparatory school, establishing it as the Foxhollow School. She continued as the headmistress when it moved to Grasmere a few years later. In 1939, the school relocated to Lenox, Massachusetts, where Miss Farrell purchased Holmwood, the home of Mrs. Alfred Gwynne Vanderbilt. In 1942, Miss Farrell purchased The Mount, the former home of Edith Wharton, to expand the campus where the school continued to operate until the 1970s. Miss Farrell was responsible for The Mount being placed on the National Register of Historic Places.

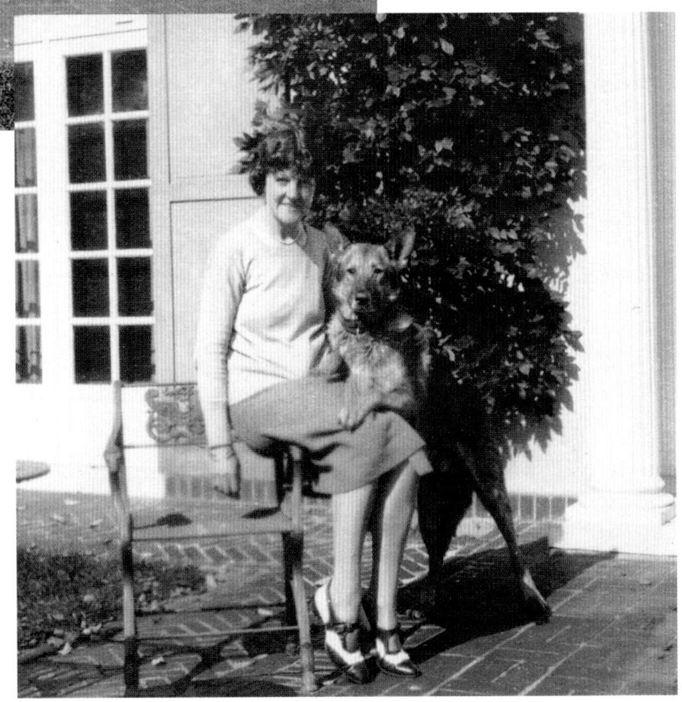

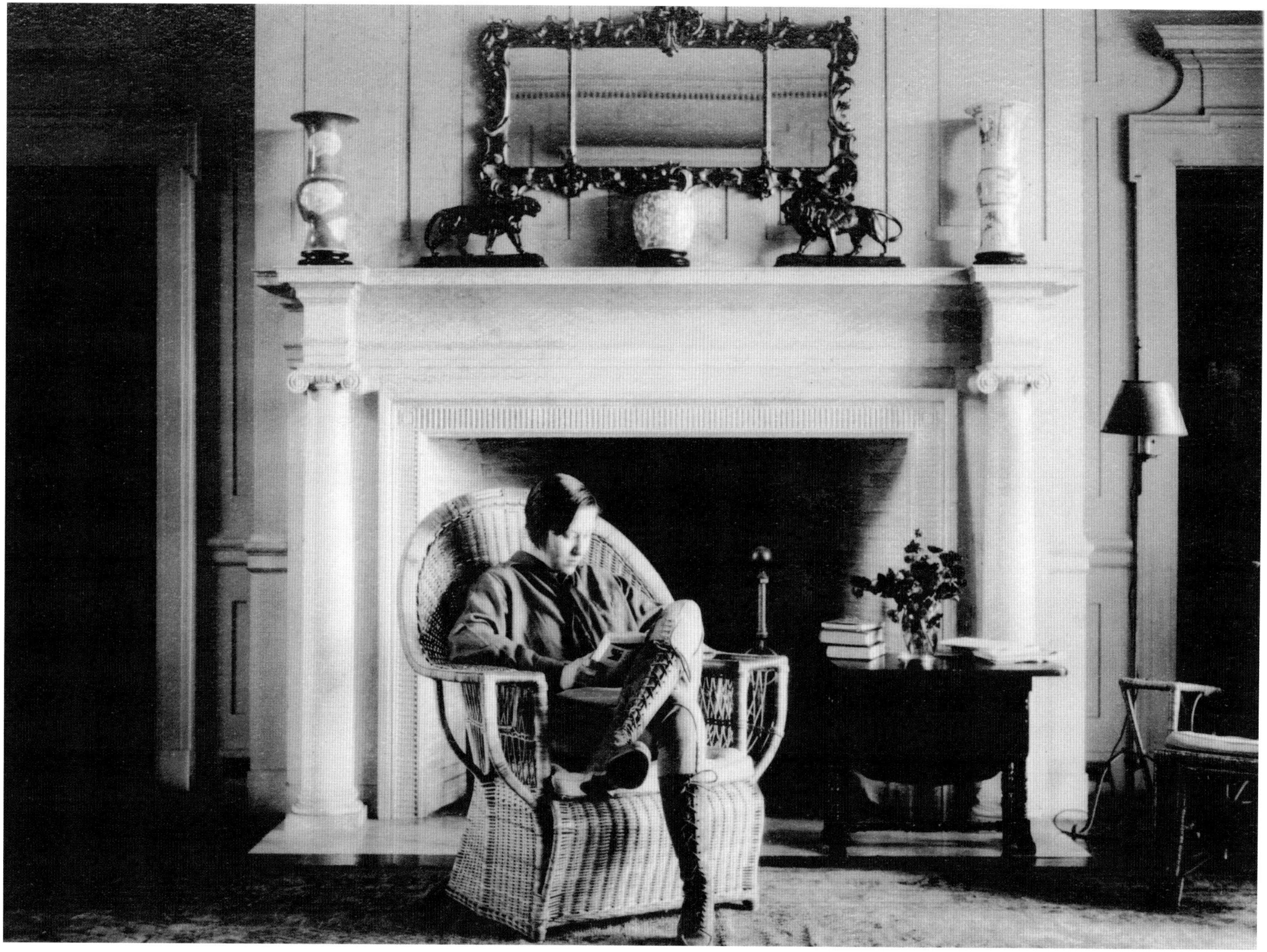

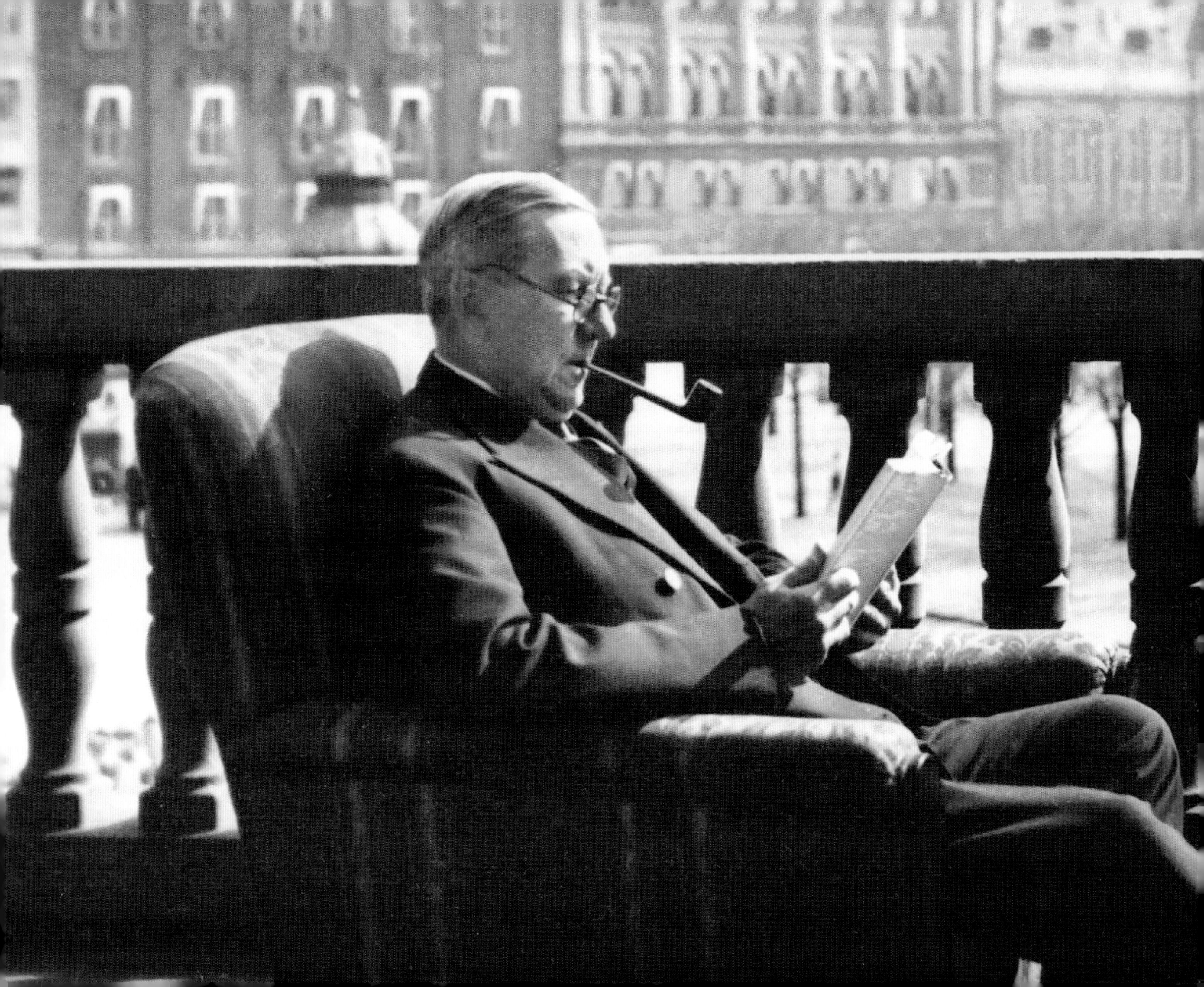

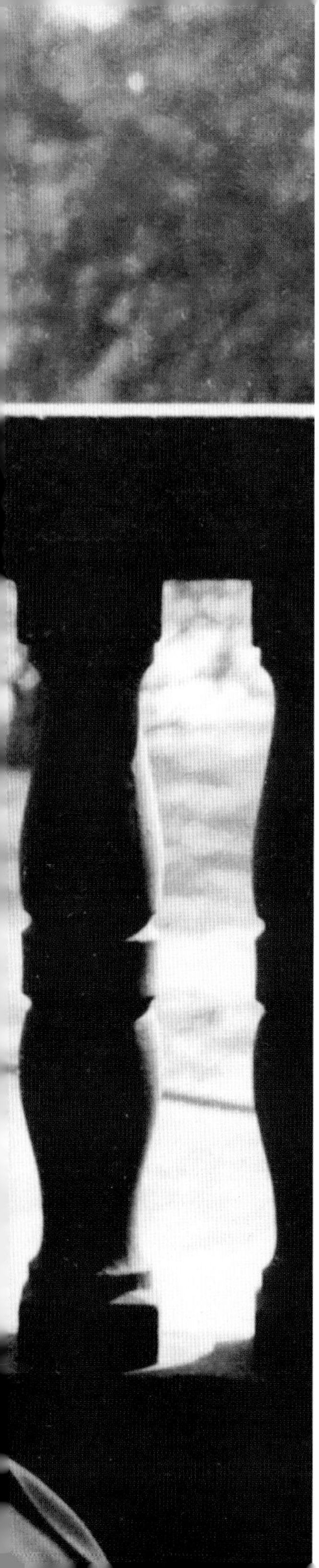

CHAPTER TWELVE

THE END of AN ERA

The 1930s

PREVIOUS PAGES Tracy sitting on his balcony at Hotel d'Angleterre, Copenhagen, 1932. Margaret and her family spent the 1930s living in London, Copenhagen, Cairo, and Belgrade.

RIGHT One of the last photographs of the house taken by Tracy in 1930, the year the family left Foxhollow Farm for good. After maintaining the property for many years, and following the stock market crash of 1929, Tracy decided it was time to move on. In 1930, after the house became a girls' school, he left for Europe, essentially leaving the house intact. Alice, Deb, and Olin continued living in Washington, where Olin set up a studio, and they all traveled abroad frequently.

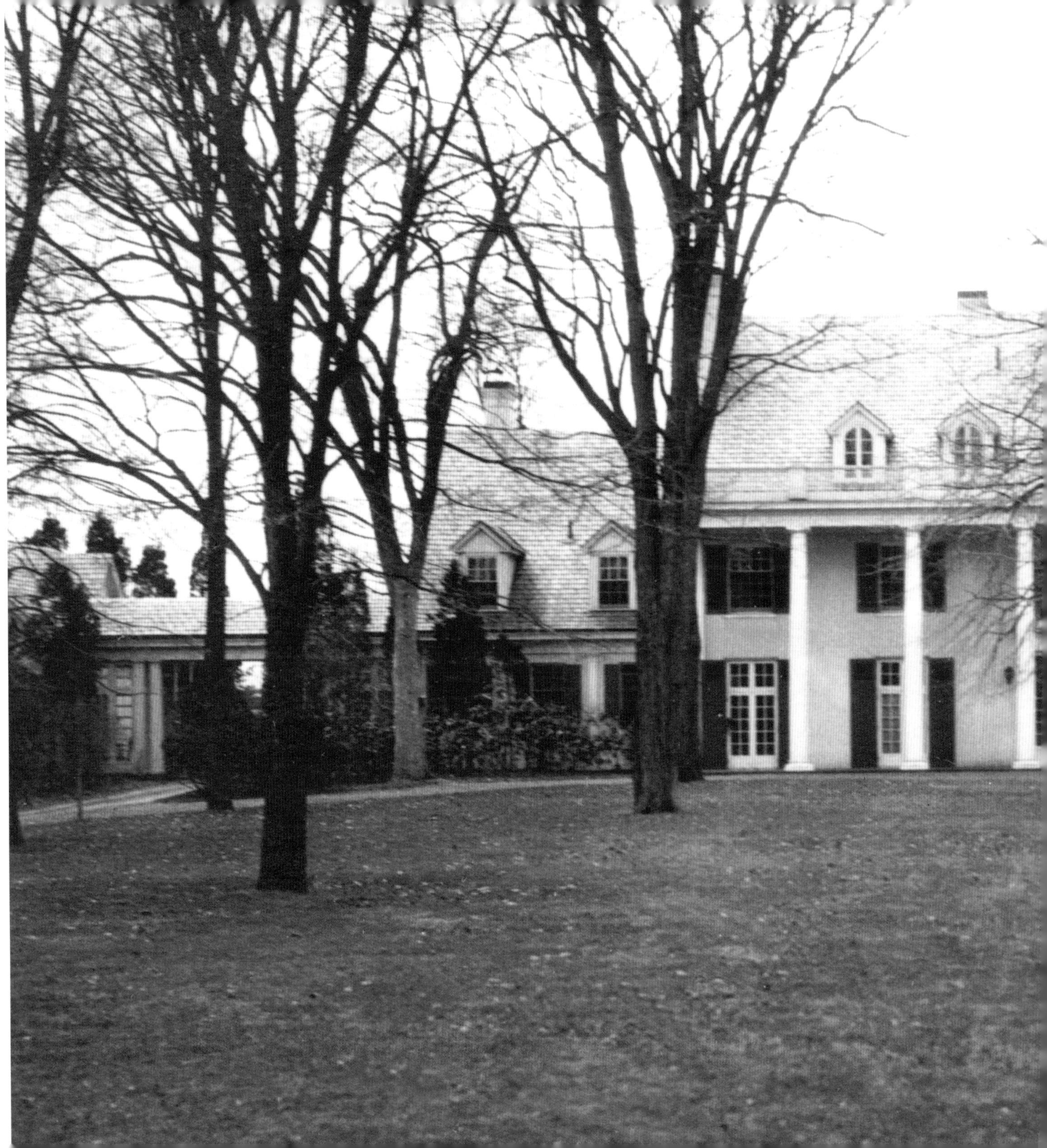

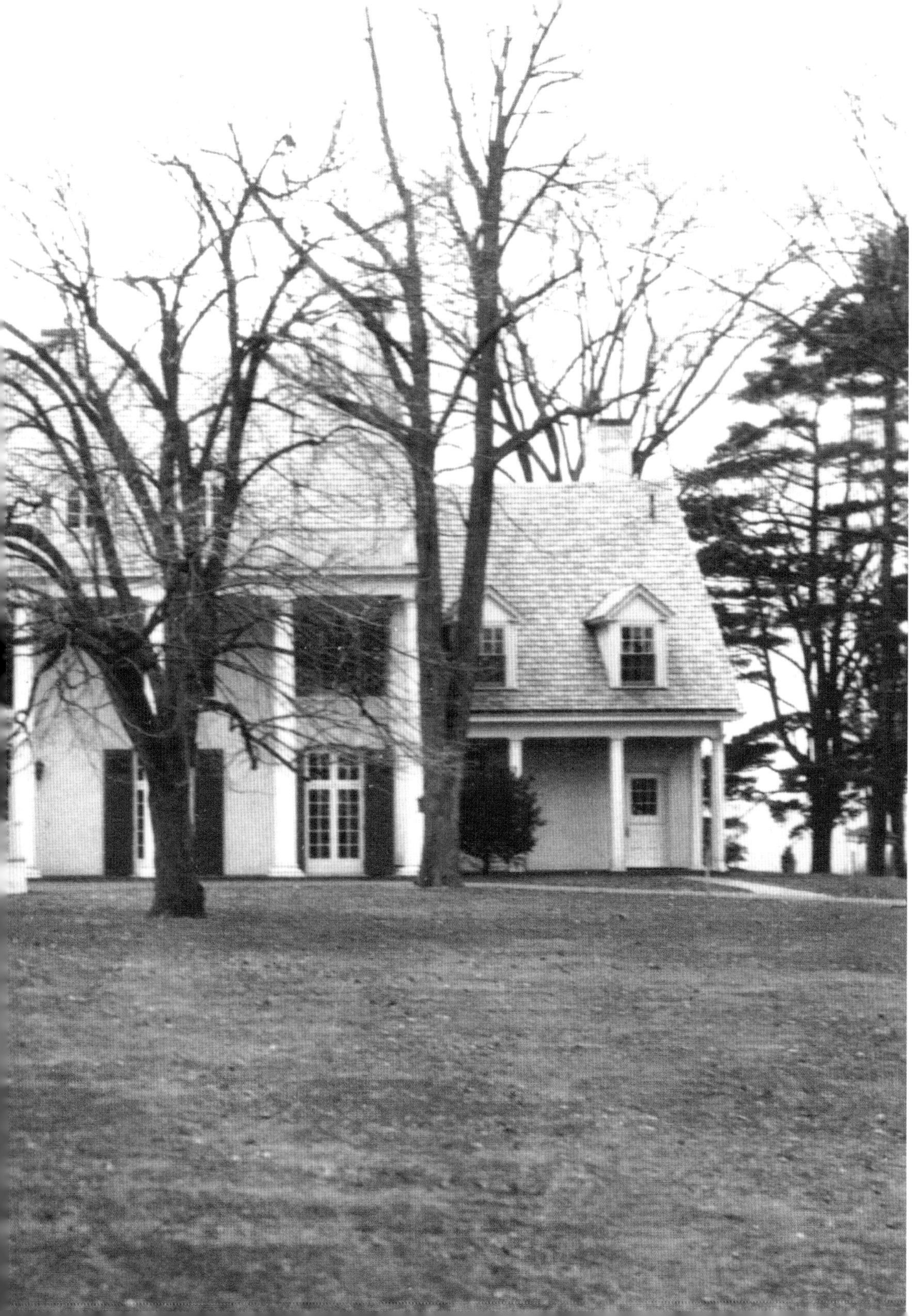

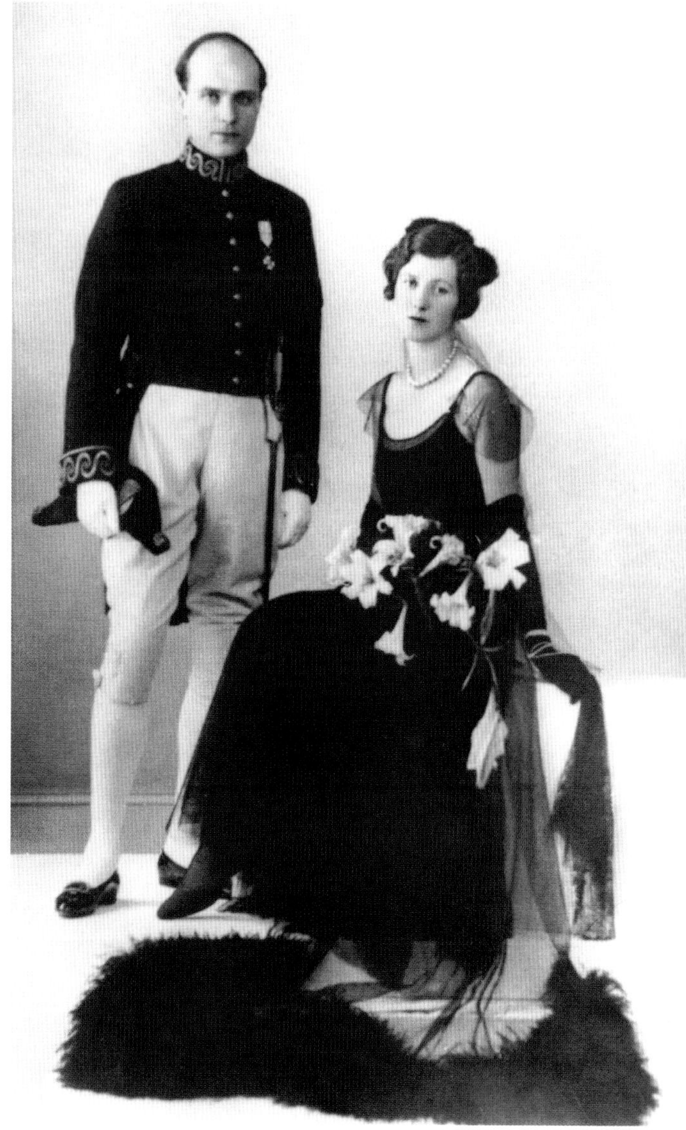

ABOVE Knut and Margaret in 1930, while living in London. They were attending a memorial service organized by the Swedish Legation for Queen Victoria, the wife of King Gustaf V, who had died that year.

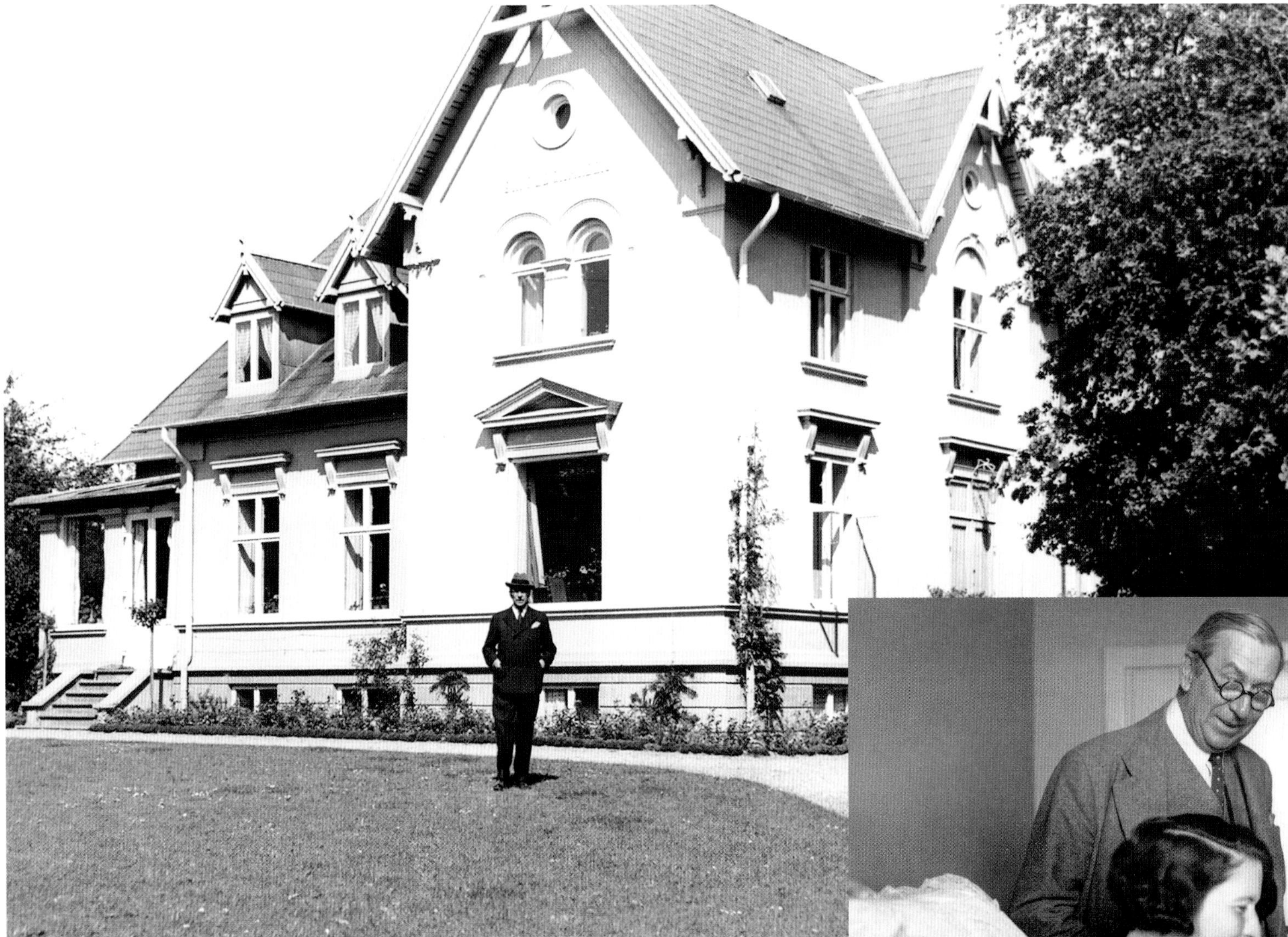

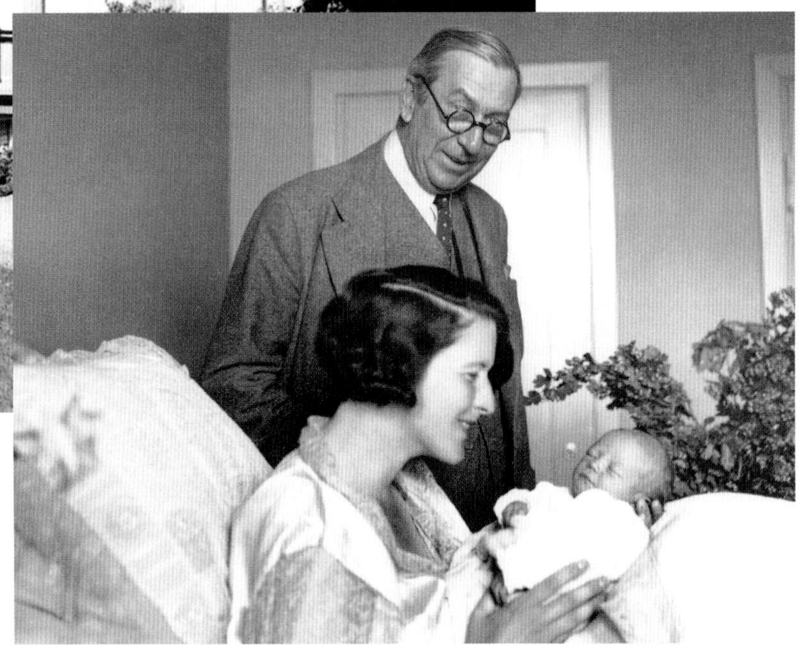

BELOW Tracy, in 1933, admiring his newest grandson, Jan, Margaret's third child.

OPPOSITE Knut enjoying a restful moment with Margaret and Tracy on the steps of their house. Tracy had taken up residence at Hotel d'Angleterre in Copenhagen.

ABOVE Tracy in front of the Thybergs' charming house in Copenhagen, where Knut was transferred from London in 1932. The family lived there until 1936.

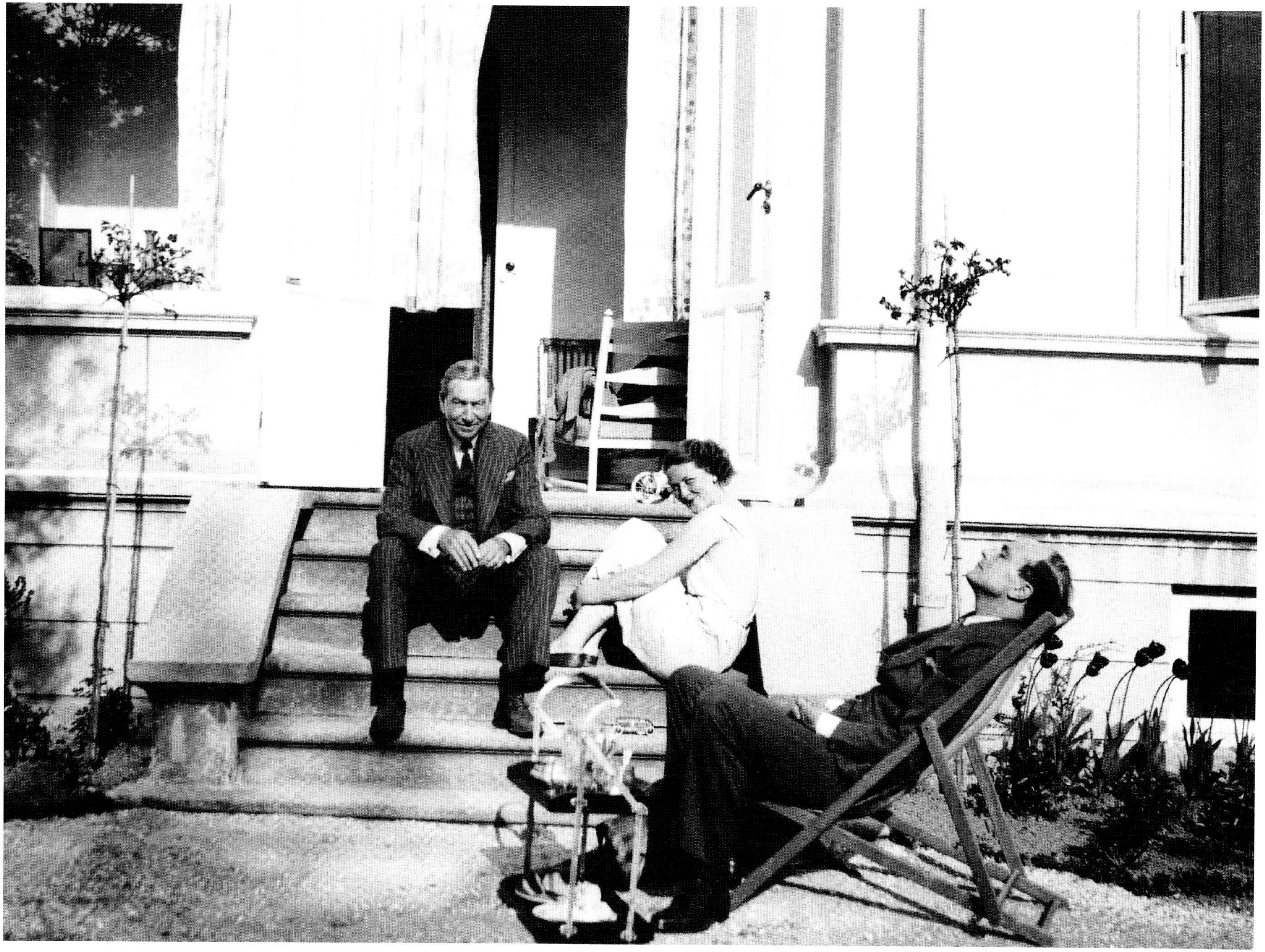

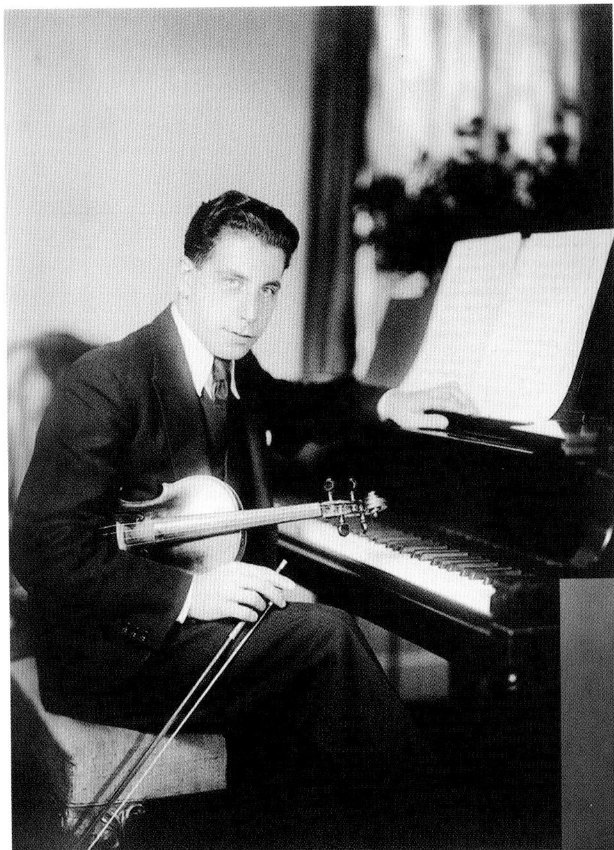

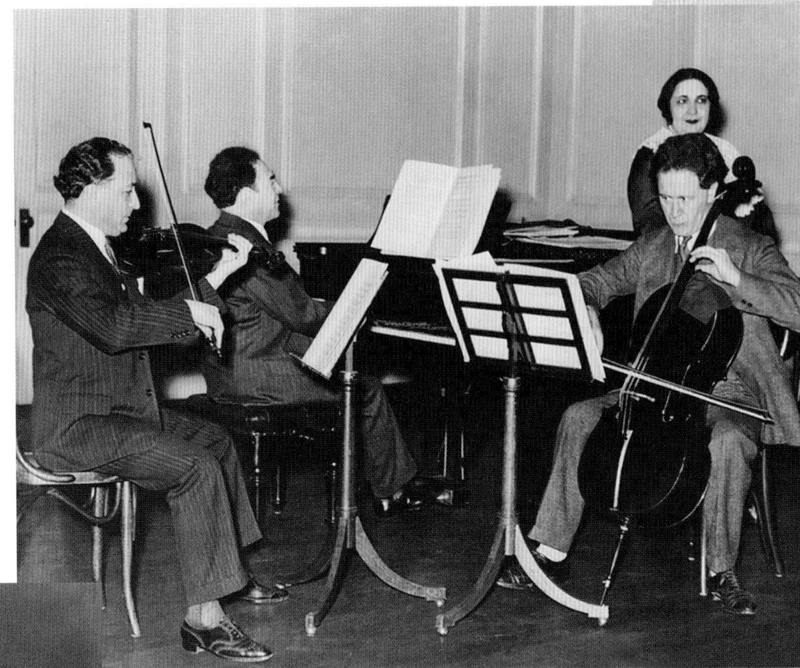

RIGHT An ensemble of Alice's Washington friends that included violinist Paul Kochanski, pianist Harold Bauer, cellist Hans Kindler, and opera singer Nina Kochetz, in a photograph taken by Underwood & Underwood. When in town for concerts, the talented musicians would often give impromptu performances at Alice's home. Kindler was a brilliant cellist who later devoted his life to conducting. He was the conductor at Totenberg's 1935 performance in Washington.

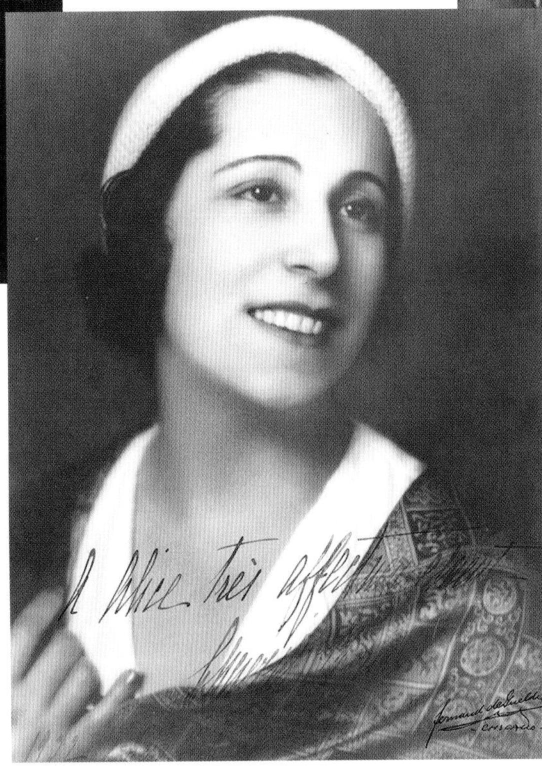

ABOVE Roman Totenberg, photographed by the Harris & Ewing agency in the late 1930s. The violin virtuoso made his debut with the Warsaw Philharmonic at age 11. He met Alice in Berlin when she, Deb, and Olin were staying there. In 1932, Alice convinced him to move to Paris to escape the approaching wrath of Hitler. It was at Alice's persuasion that Totenberg began his first tour of America in 1935, opening in Washington, D.C. In 1938, with the help of Alice's best friend, and fellow musical patron Helen Huntington Astor, Totenberg was granted a visa and permitted to stay in America, where he lived to the age of 101. One of his three daughters is Nina Totenberg, a noted correspondent for National Public Radio.

LEFT A signed photograph given to Alice by her close friend, soprano Lucrezia Bori, taken in 1932 by Chicago photographer Fernand de Gueldre, who was known for his portraits of operatic performers. (Courtesy of Rhinebeck Historical Society)

RIGHT A portrait of Alice painted by Sir Oswald Birley in 1923. It was exhibited by the Duveen Brothers gallery in New York that same year, and appeared in the October 15, 1924, issue of *Vogue*. Throughout the 1930s Alice maintained a close friendship with Birley and his wife, Rhoda. A favorite of the British royal family, many of whose portraits he painted, Birley generously gave Alice the portrait afterward as she was very fond of it. The Birleys' daughter was the fashion model Maxime de la Falaise, and their son, Mark, founded the famous London nightclub, Annabel's, in the 1960s.

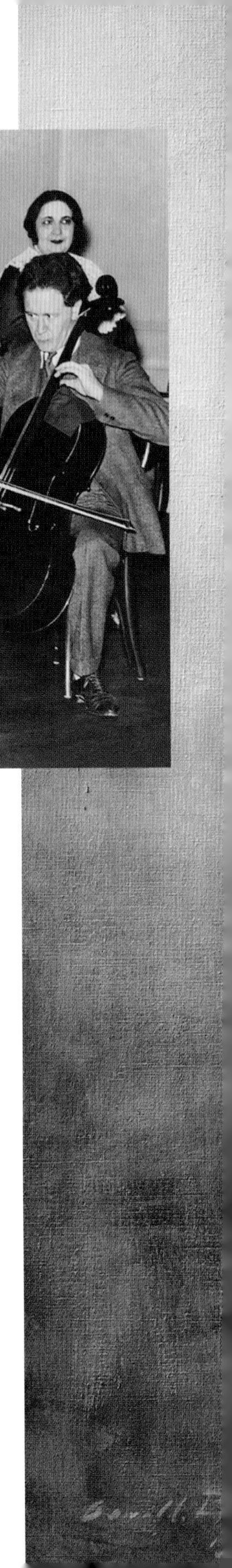

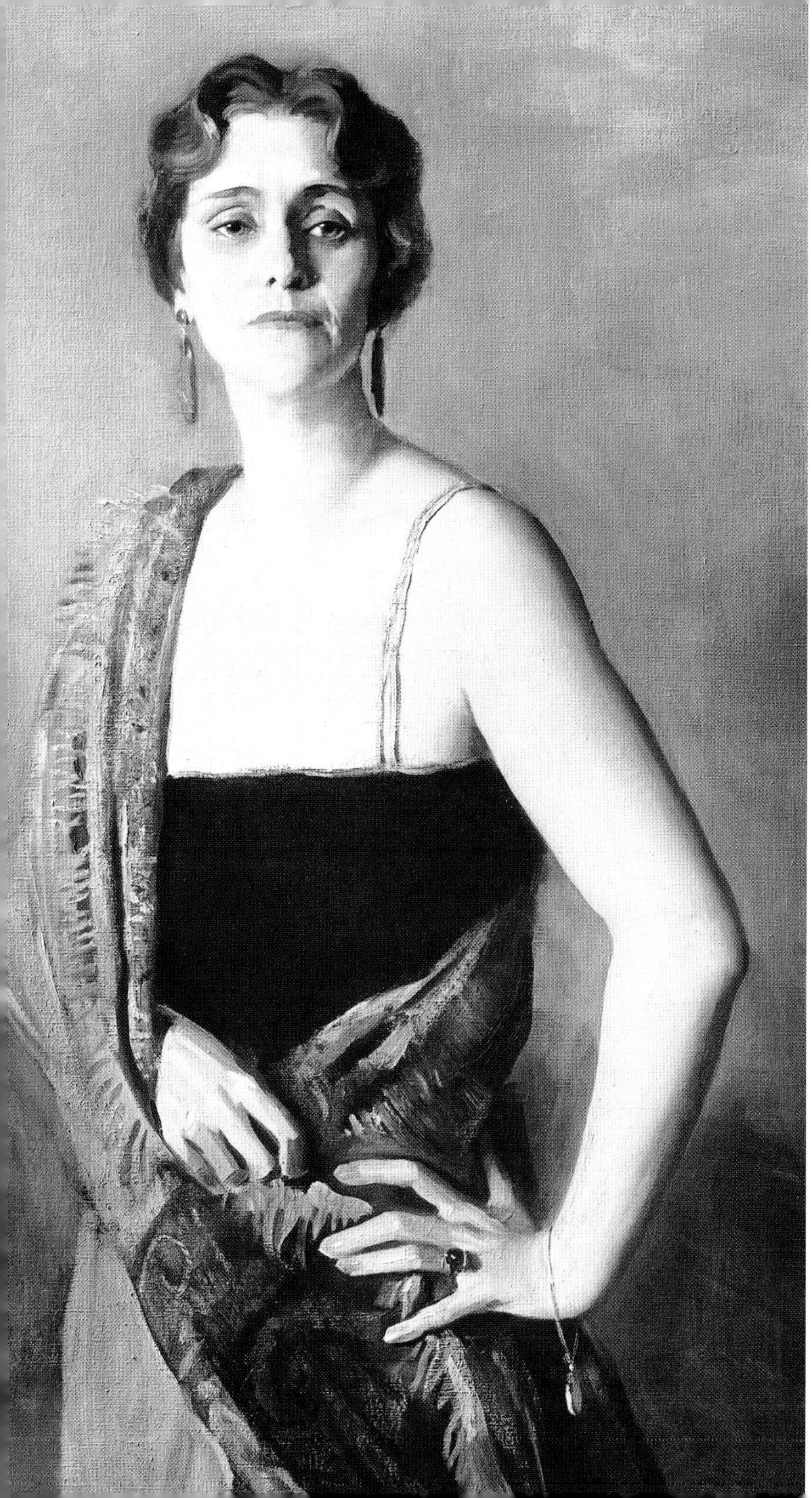

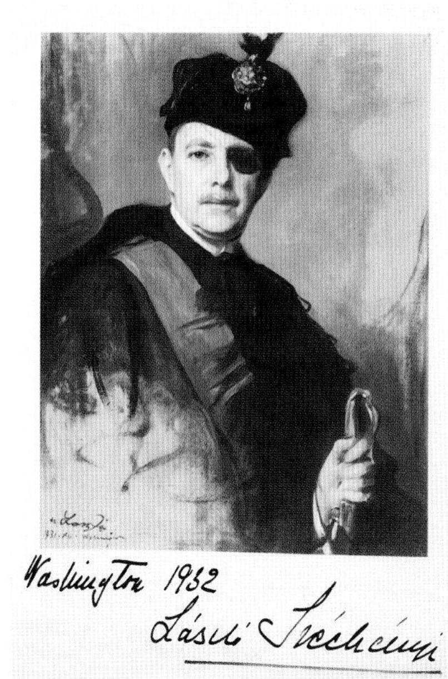

LEFT Included in Alice's social circle during the 1930s was Count László Széchenyi de Sárvár-felsővidék, the Hungarian Minister to the U.S. The signed photograph is a portrait of him by Hungarian artist Philip Alexius de László. In 1912, Széchenyi invented the submarine wireless telegraph after successfully testing sound vibrations in the ocean near Newport. In 1908, he married socialite Gladys Moore Vanderbilt, daughter of Cornelius Vanderbilt II. (Courtesy of Rhinebeck Historical Society)

BELOW A photograph given to Alice by Mildred and Robert Woods Bliss taken in their music room at Dumbarton Oaks in the 1940s. Mildred Bliss, along with Mrs. Truxtun Beale and Mrs. Robert Low Bacon, were Washington's ruling hostesses, and all dear friends of Alice's during her years living there. (Courtesy of Rhinebeck Historical Society)

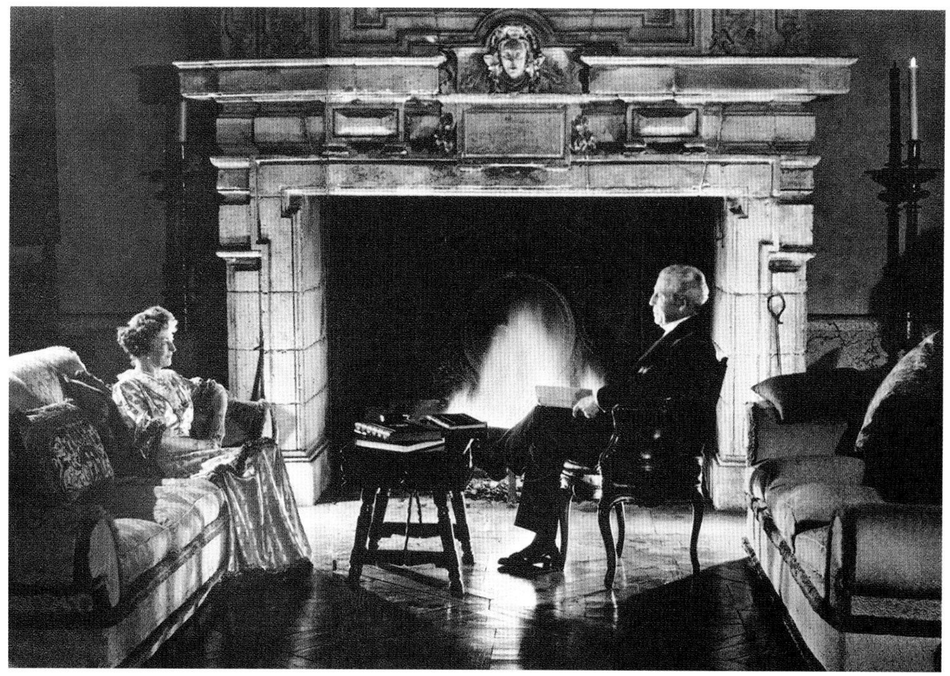

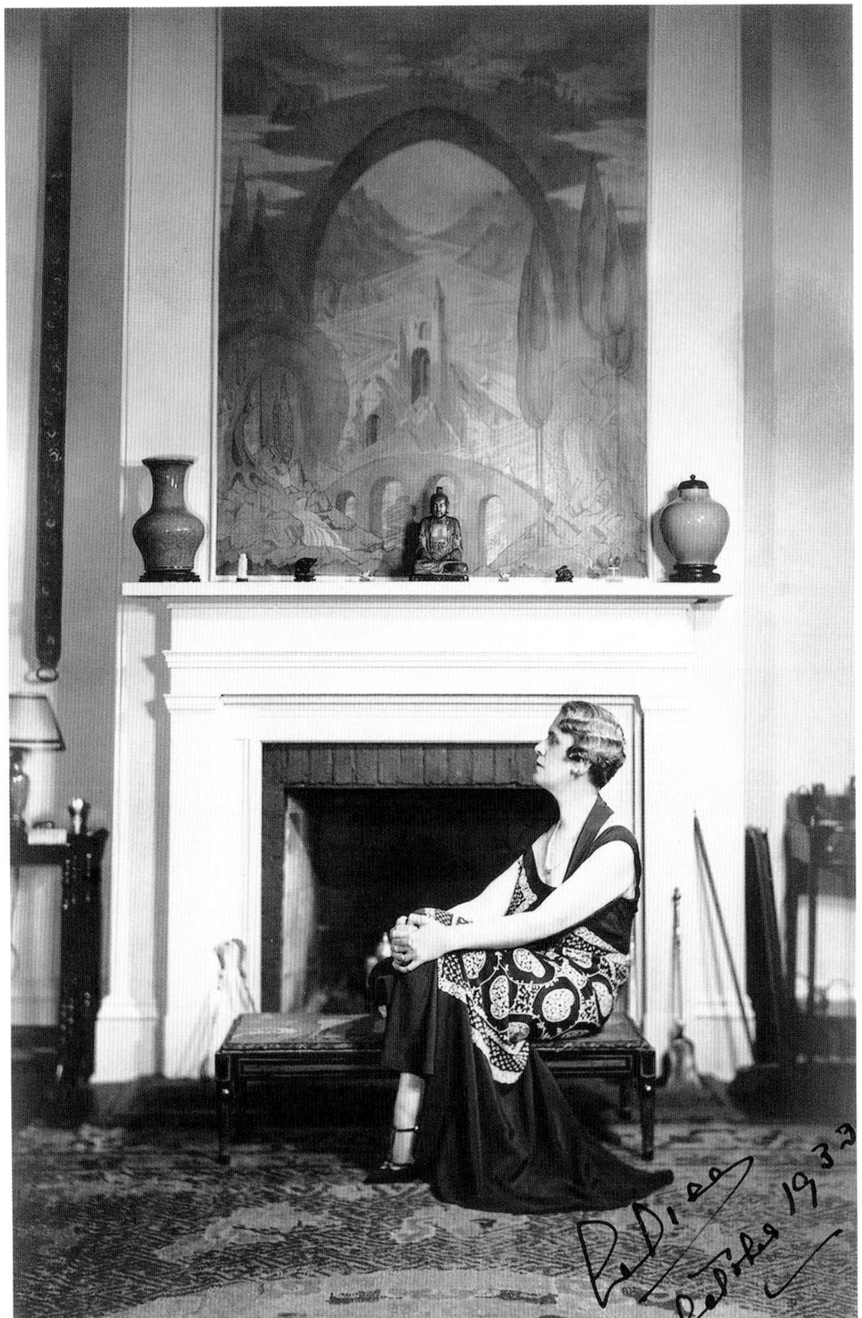

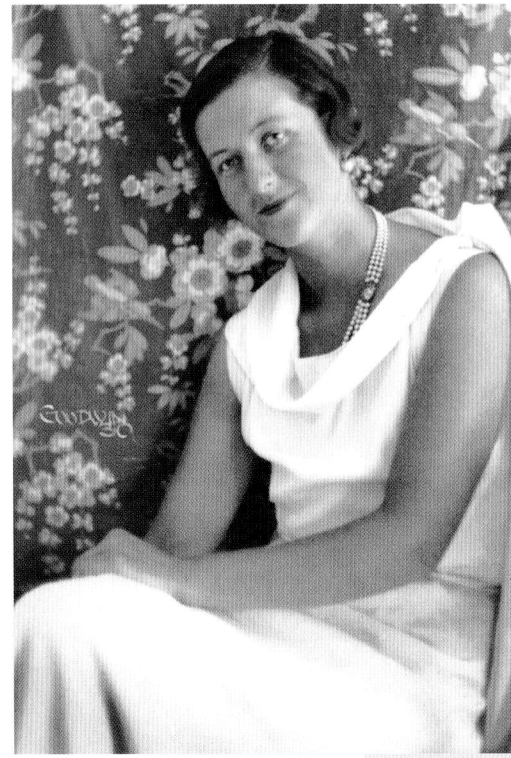

LEFT Margaret in Sweden, 1930, taken by the family's favorite portrait photographer, Henry Buergel Goodwin.

BELOW Tracy aboard the *Arandora Star* in April 1932, while traveling from London to the Mediterranean. The ship, a first-class luxury liner, was complete with a tennis court and swimming pool. Tracy spent most of the 1930s traveling on steamers.

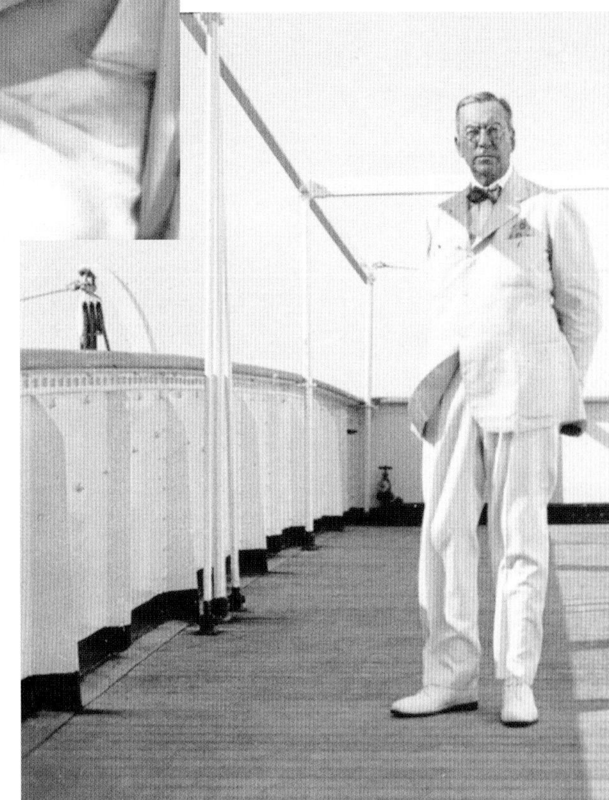

LEFT A 1933 signed photograph of Alice in her Washington house. The whimsical mural above the fireplace was painted by Jan Juta.

RIGHT Alice, Olin, and Deb in a photograph from 1932 sent to Daisy Suckley as a Christmas card, probably taken when the three of them were spending time in Germany. A framed picture of Alice's grandson, O.K., is on the mantle. (Courtesy of Wilderstein Archives)

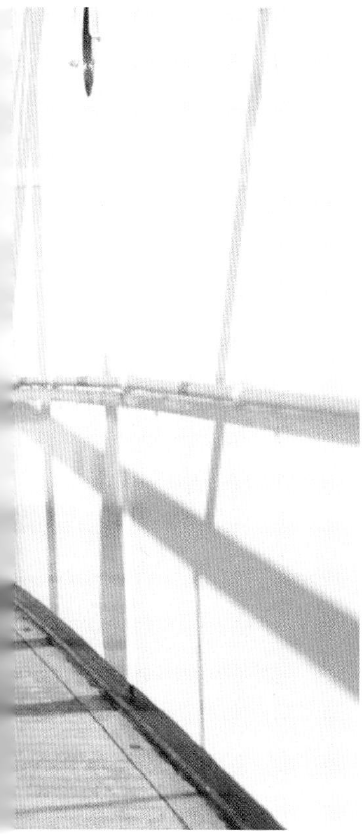

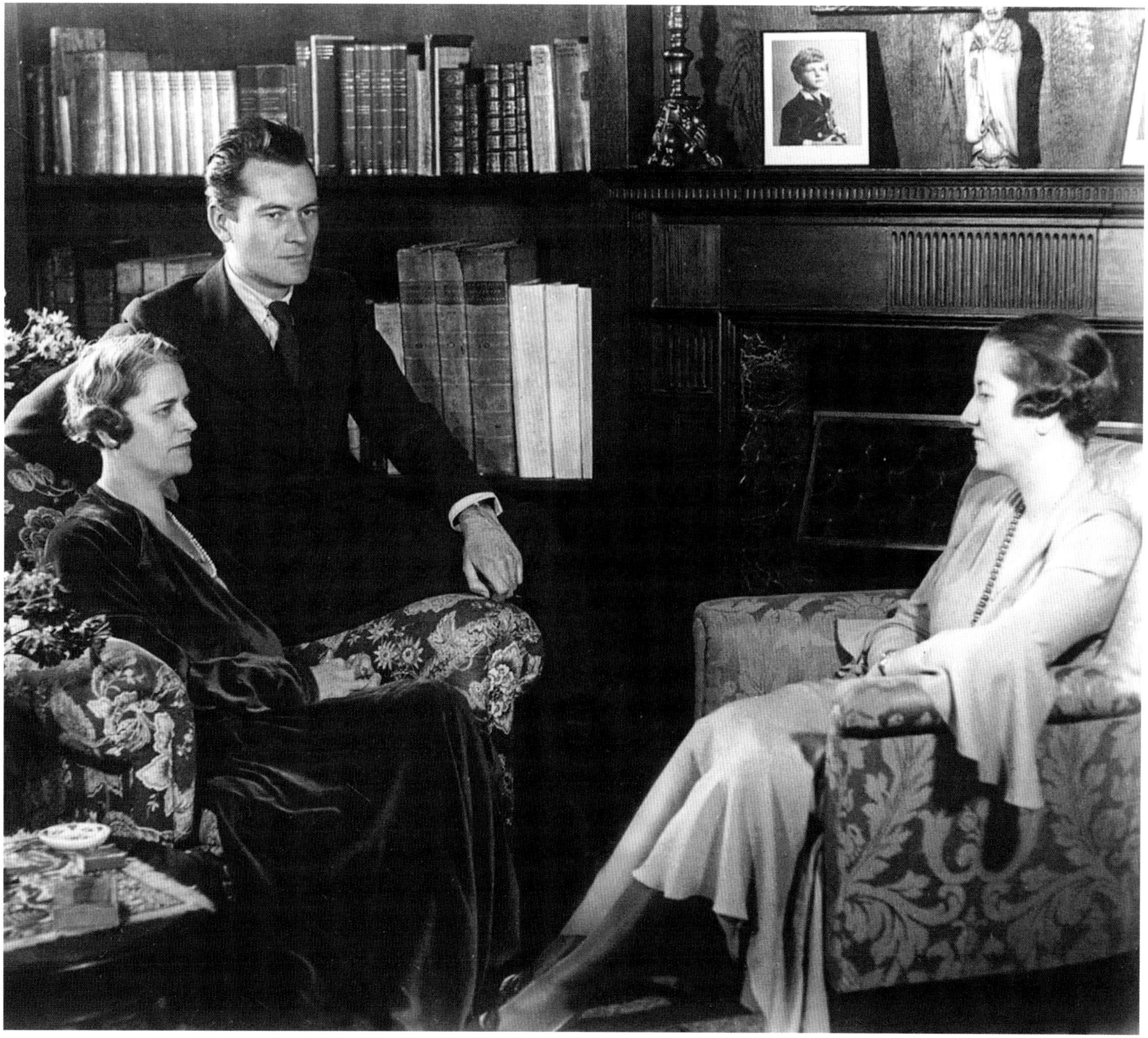

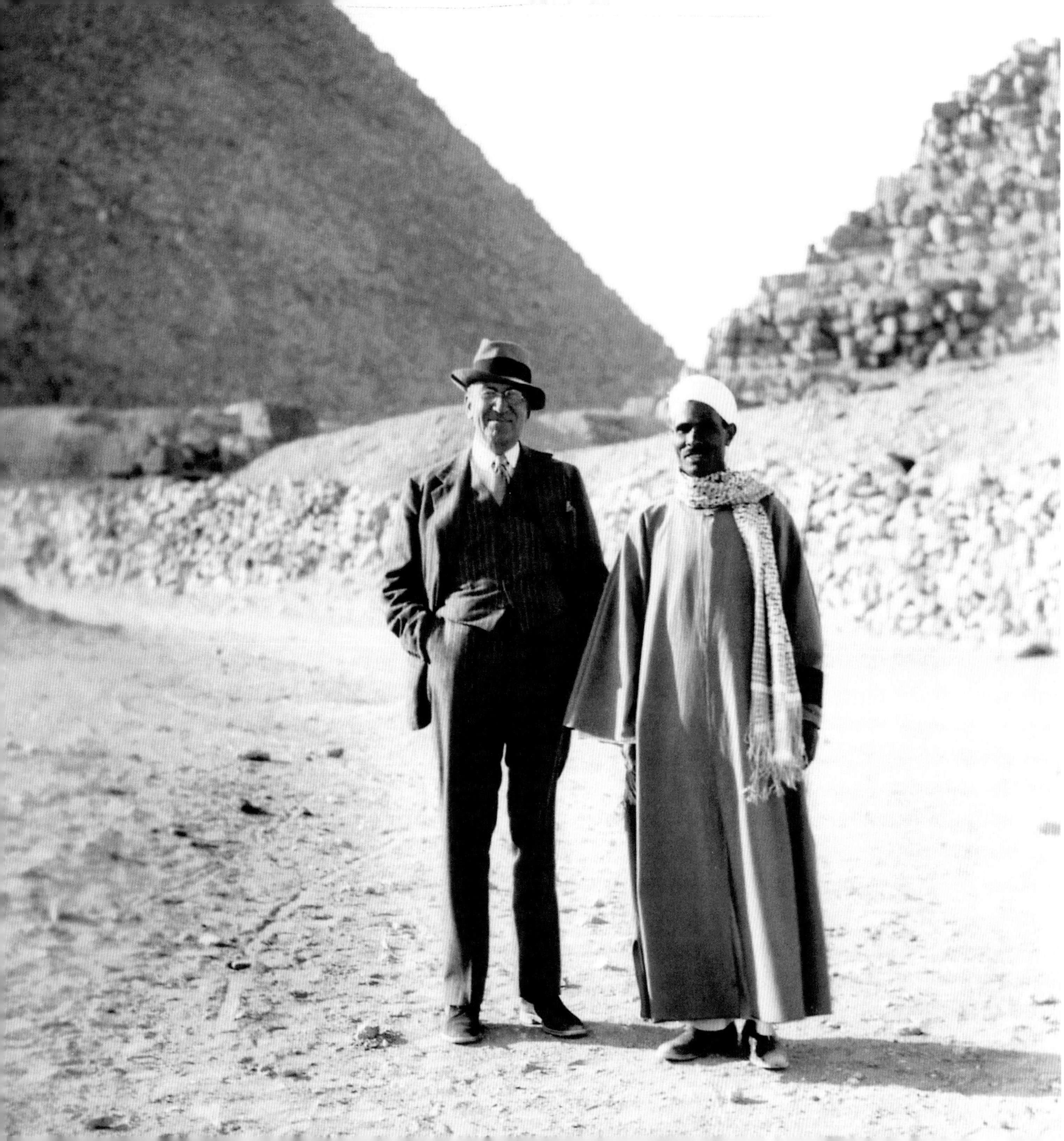

LEFT Tracy and his dragoman at the Great Pyramids of Giza in January 1937. The Thybergs had recently relocated to Egypt from Copenhagen when Knut was appointed chargé d'affaires in Cairo. The family members traveled from all directions to be together and celebrate the Christmas and New Year's holidays there. Alice and Deb came from Hamburg, Tracy from London, and Olin from Washington. They stayed at the luxurious Mena House, built in the shadows of the pyramids, where heiress Barbara Hutton was also a guest. While there, the family took a traditional Nile cruise. This was to be the last time they would be together, as Tracy died unexpectedly while living at the Connaught Hotel in London later that same year on July 3, 1937.

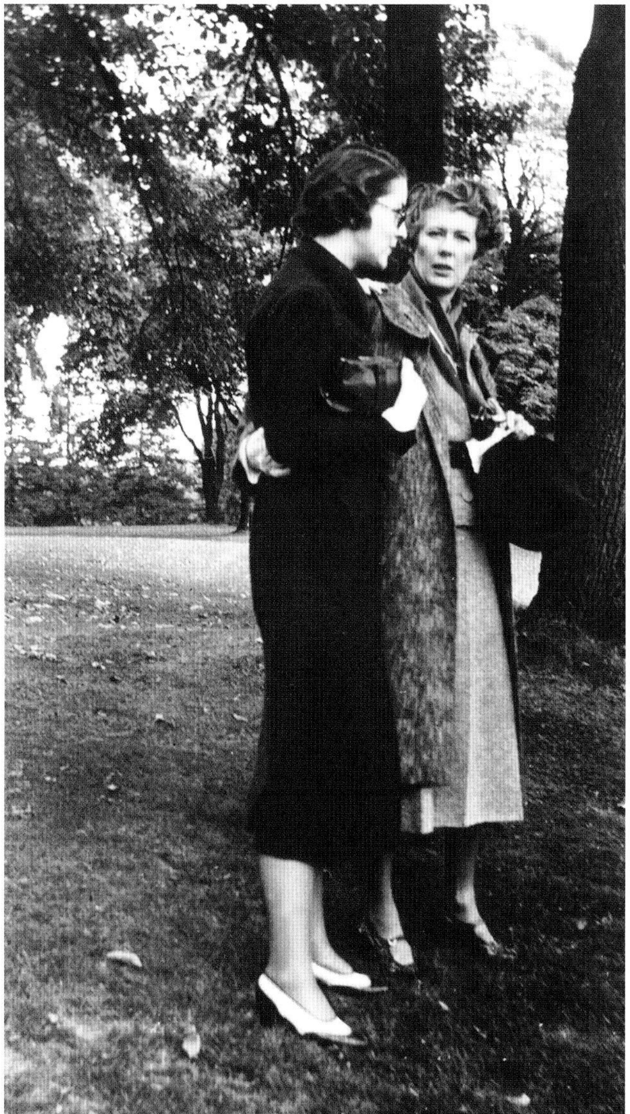

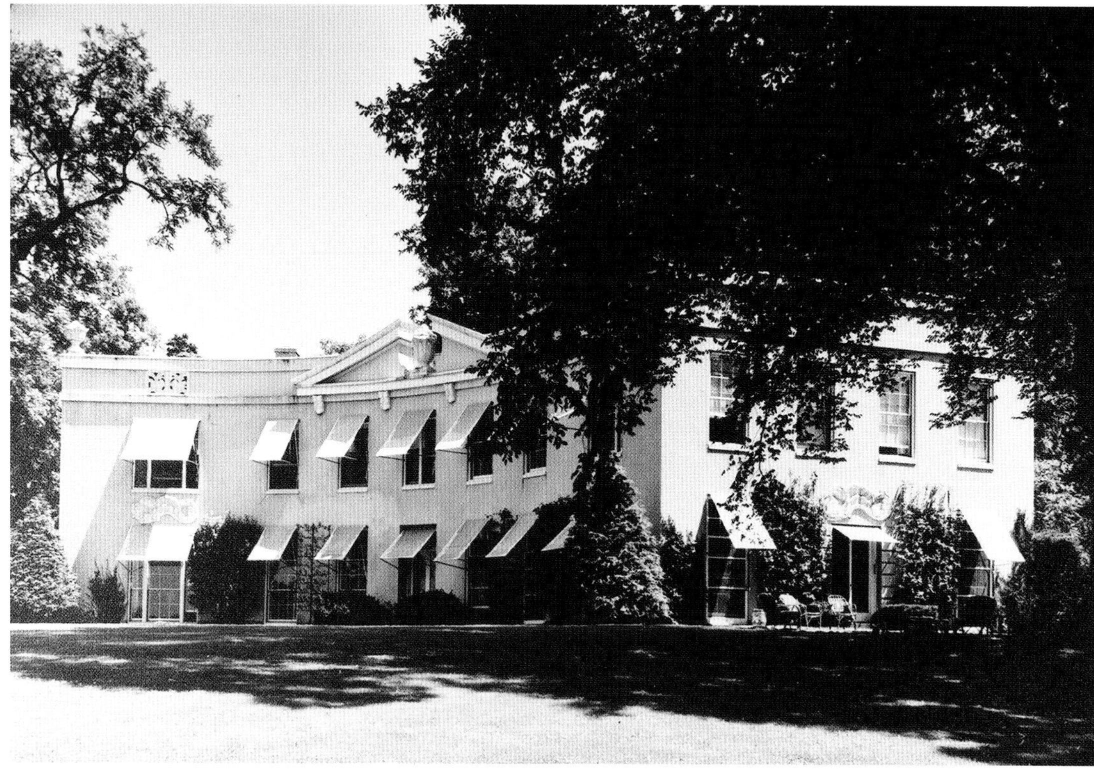

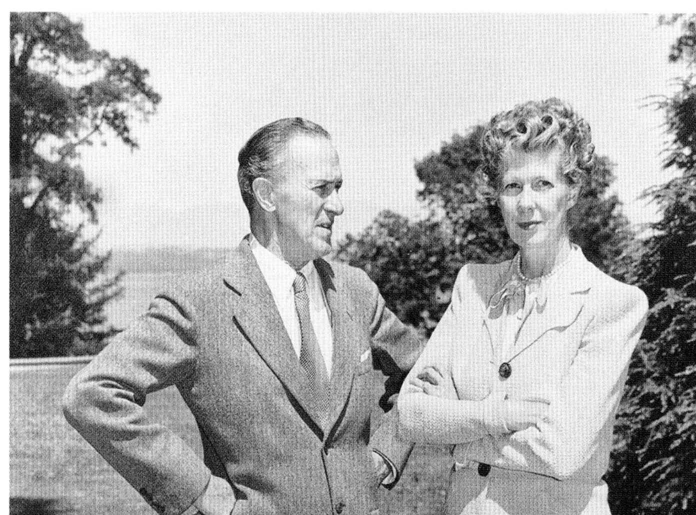

ABOVE Margaret with Helen Huntington Astor at Ferncliff, in the fall of 1937. Margaret had traveled to Rhinebeck from Egypt after the death of her father.

LEFT AND ABOVE After Helen's divorce from Vincent Astor in 1940, she married an old friend, Lytle Hull, in 1941. She took possession of her great-grandfather's house, The Locusts, and had it razed to build her own Neo-Baroque villa on its site, designed by John Churchill, also calling it The Locusts. Helen's devotion to music continued throughout her life and for many years she and Lytle happily entertained guests at the villa such as Cole Porter and Leonard Bernstein. Both photographs were taken by Charles Eggert, a landscape photographer and filmmaker who lived in nearby Barrytown. (Courtesy of Dinsmore & Huntington Family Archives)

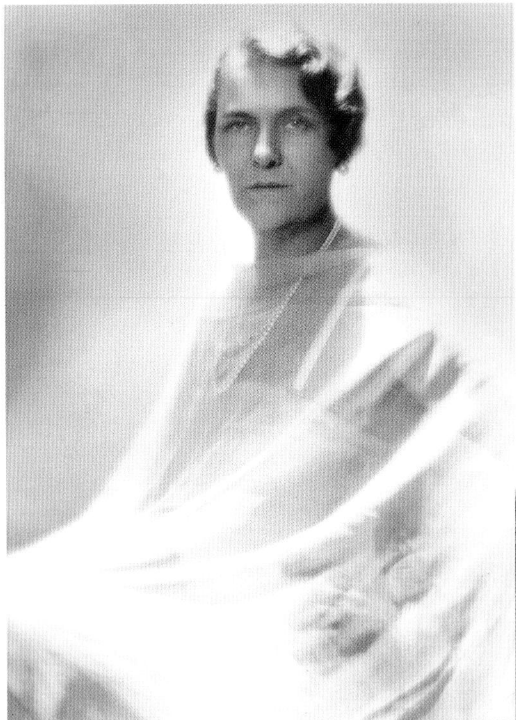

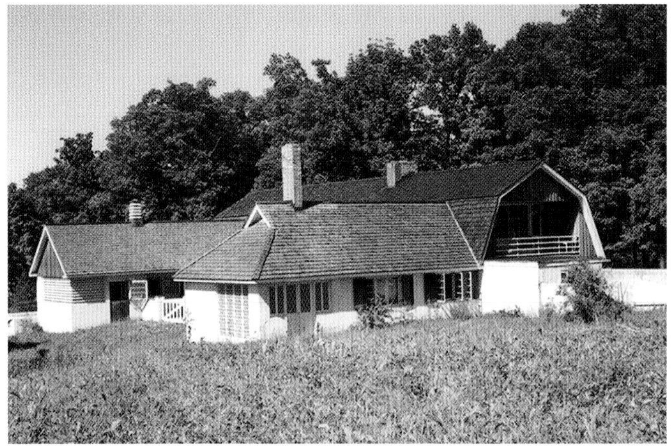

LEFT In 1938, Deb built her own house on the Glenburn property, naming it The Barn. She had the architect model it after her memory of a Baltic fisherman's cottage, where she spent several days after a sudden squall caused her sailboat to wash ashore at Hiddensee off the coast of Germany in 1936. After traveling the world, she found happiness at home living with her horses and animals, and opened a riding school that still exists today.

ABOVE A studio photograph of Alice in the 1930s. After Tracy's death, Alice, Olin, and Deb returned to Rhinebeck and moved into Glenburn after having it restored. It had been vacant for over a decade. She kept the house in Washington, but spent most of her time in Rhinebeck. When Olin married Carmen Vial de Senoret Browne, in 1950, Alice moved out of the house and settled in a cottage next to the property, which she had renovated and painted pink. She called it Garden House and lived there until her death in 1963.

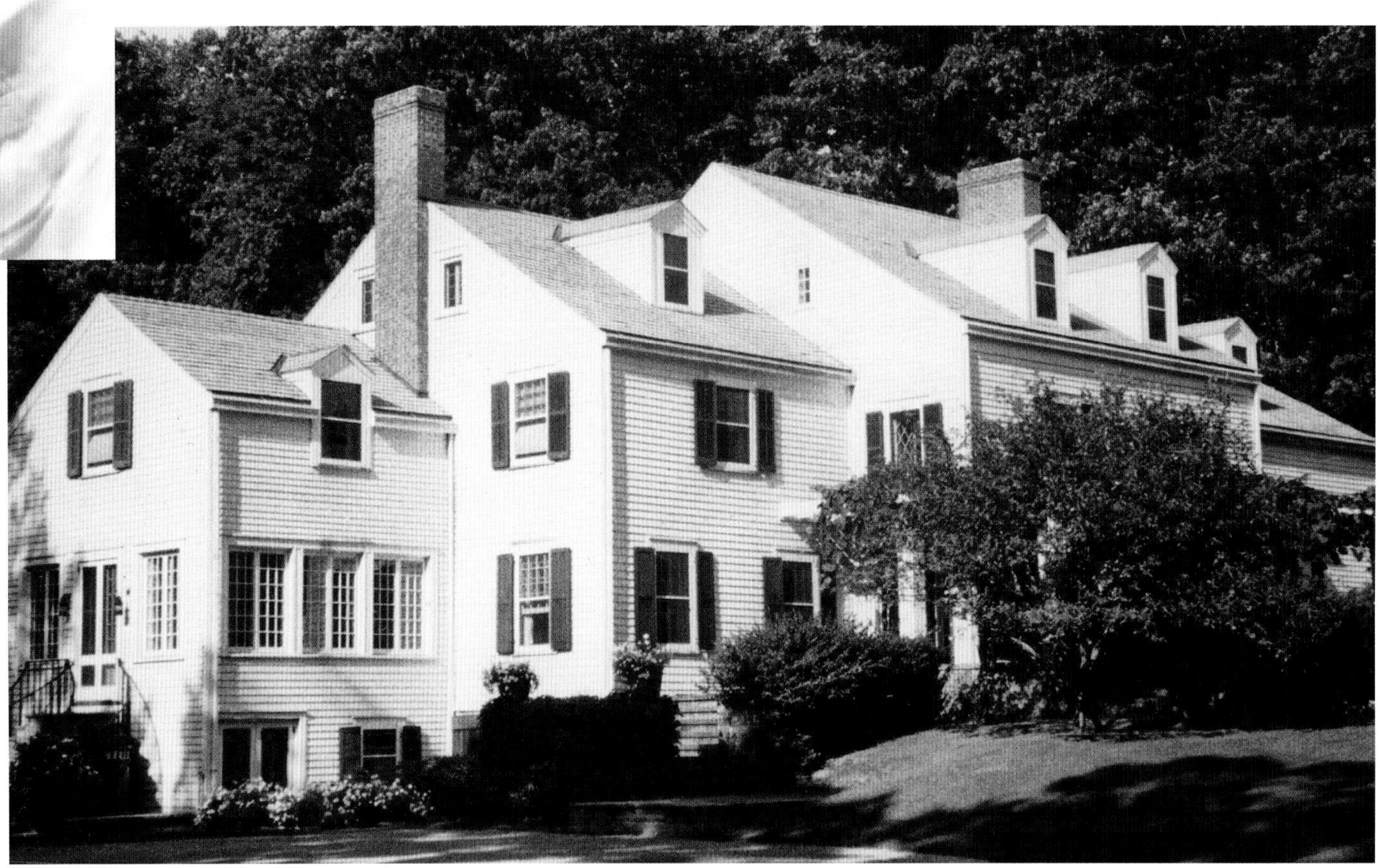

RIGHT Glenburn, in the late 1930s, after its renovations and alterations throughout the years. (Courtesy of Rhinebeck Historical Society)

BELOW President Franklin D. Roosevelt with Olin at Glenburn. His 1936 Ford Phaeton was equipped with special hand controls that allowed him to drive without the use of his legs. (Courtesy of Rhinebeck Historical Society)

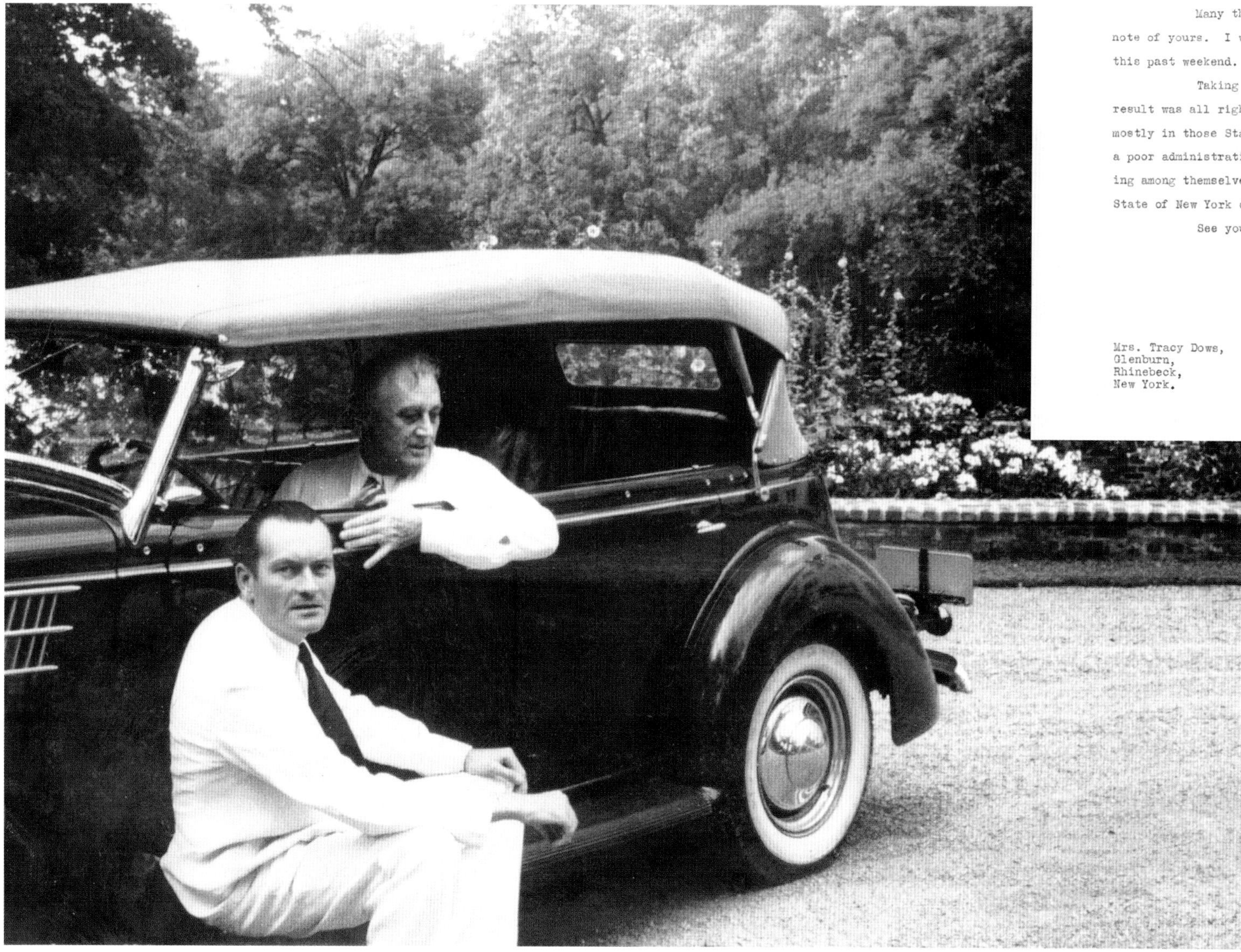

THE WHITE HOUSE
WASHINGTON

November 12, 1938.

Dear Alice:-

Many thanks for that mighty nice note of yours. I wish I could have seen you this past weekend.

Taking it by and large the election result was all right -- the Democrats lost mostly in those States where they had given a poor administration or had fallen to fighting among themselves. Thank the Lord the State of New York came through in good shape.

See you soon in Washington.

Affectionately,

Mrs. Tracy Dows,
Glenburn,
Rhinebeck,
New York.

ABOVE A note sent to Alice from Roosevelt, in 1938. He remained a good friend of the Dows family throughout his life. In 1949 Olin wrote and illustrated his personal memoir of the president, titled *Franklin Roosevelt at Hyde Park*. (Courtesy of Rhinebeck Historical Society)

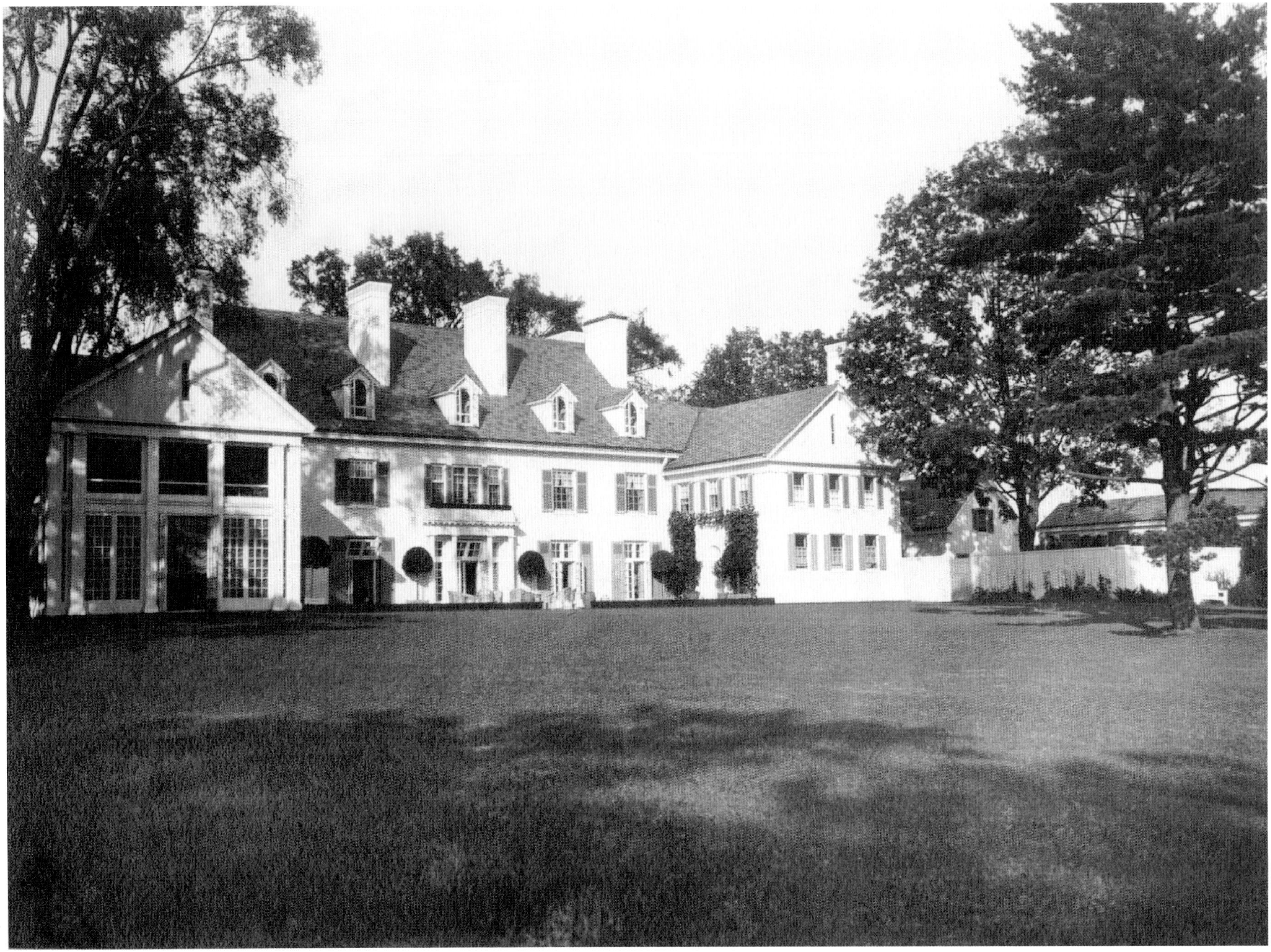

Epilogue

By the end of 1930, schoolgirls were running up and down the halls of the great Colonial Revival mansion that was once home to Tracy Dows and his family. In 1925 it was reported that Tracy and Alice had already transferred most of their property over to the Foxhollow Development Corporation, a new holding company established by Tracy and his businessmen friends, to manage the estate. The intention was to build moderate-priced homes, which were in demand at the time, on the land. Thankfully, this did not happen. In 1930, the Dows family left the estate for good, turning the house into the Foxhollow School, which continued in this location for several more years. An advertisement appearing in the classified pages of the September 4, 1936, edition of the *Rhinebeck Gazette* offered Foxhollow Farm for sale at "great sacrifice" by the Foxhollow Development Corporation. The estate finally sold to Vincent Astor's company, Harbor Acres Realty Corporation, in February 1938. During that time, John Jacob Astor V, half-brother of Vincent Astor, used the house as his country home. Also in 1938, a deed for Southlands was executed for Deb Dows, who continued to own her beloved land for the rest of her life. In 1941, Duncan G. Harris, a New York City businessman involved in real estate, and a good friend of Franklin D. Roosevelt, became the next owner of Foxhollow Farm, maintaining it as his country home. Dr. Victor Vance Anderson, who in 1924 had established the Anderson School in Staatsburg, purchased the estate in 1944 to expand the school's campus for the treatment of emotionally disturbed children. He utilized the existing buildings on the property as classrooms and staff offices and kept the mansion as his family residence. The property next sold in 1953 to Hyde Park supervisor Elmer Van Wagner, who bought the land for speculation and development. This did not happen. A year later, Leonard Zneimer, who had worked for Dr. Anderson, purchased the estate, and it once again became a school for troubled children. His organization, the Rhinebeck Country School, ran successfully for many years. In December 1986, Mr. Zneimer negotiated the sale of the school to Daytop Village (Samaritan Daytop Village as of 2015), the compassionate drug-rehabilitation organization that is the property's current owner. This caused an outcry in the Rhinebeck community, and town meetings were held in an attempt to stop the plan. The sale went through, cheered on by Deb Dows herself, who by that time had traveled widely and met people from all walks of life. Now the Dowses are gone, along with the world they lived in. But, more than a century later, the wonderful buildings designed by Harrie T. Lindeberg for Foxhollow Farm remain, a legacy of their vivid embrace of life.

My American Family

BY OLIN KNUT THYBERG

Of my grandfather Tracy Dows's offspring, only his daughter Margaret had children, and, as she married a foreigner, a Swede in fact, none of Tracy's still living descendants—twenty-three at present—are American citizens. Although we are now settled in Sweden, Switzerland, and Germany, certainly his three grandchildren—my sister Birgitta, my brother Jan, and me—are very conscious of their American heritage. I was only ten when Tracy died and too young to be aware of the influence this kind and extremely generous man had on the Rhinebeck community, his love of the land and its preservation. However, I well remember how he implored us children to be still while he took our photograph and how it irritated him when we, obeying strict parental orders, had to refuse his offers of toys we secretly coveted.

I came to know my grandmother Alice quite well—she survived her husband by more than a quarter century. Alice was in many ways the dominant member of the Dows family, who seemed, most of the time, to have things pretty much her way. She was undoubtedly a character. Her circle of friends was impressive, including personalities as diverse as Franklin D. Roosevelt and Gore Vidal. She told me once that "like the Aga Khan, I am never bored." Having lived in great comfort at Foxhollow Farm, so well depicted in the photographs of this book, she never complained when circumstances made it necessary to accept a much reduced lifestyle in her old age. She still seemed to enjoy life just as much, and her numerous friends continued to value her company as they had done during her years at Foxhollow Farm.

Her son, my Uncle Olin, continued to paint all his life. He was fortunate to be able to do so in just the way he liked without having to conform to current fashions and trends in the art world. Olin drew and painted what he saw and had little interest in abstraction. He is well remembered for his work during the New Deal as a successful administrator of several federal programs for the relief of artists. In 1942 he enlisted in the U.S. Army and served as a technical sergeant and war artist in Europe, carrying a rifle and camera as well as his watercolors and charcoals. Olin, the least martial of men, was in active combat in the battle at St. Lô in Normandy, where he was awarded the Bronze Star Medal for the outstanding display of courage on a particularly dangerous voluntary mission. Later during the campaign in France he single-handedly captured a squad of fifty-six German soldiers using his knowledge of German to talk them into surrendering. He celebrated the liberation of Paris in September 1944 with Picasso in the artist's studio. The following winter Olin was in Bastogne recording the fierce Battle of the Bulge. He was with the Third Army in the final drive through Germany and was present at the historic junction of American and Soviet forces at Torgau on the Elbe in April 1945. And all this time he was recording what he saw, leaving an impressive collection of paintings, drawings, and photographs. But he never talked about any of this. I didn't know that he was awarded the Legion of Merit after the war for his service in the army. He never showed me any of the numerous photographs he took during the war, probably because he found them too gruesome. I remember Olin as a gentleman in the very best sense of the word, modest, hard-working, and serious—my siblings and I would at times, none too fairly, call him Uncle Earnest. He was respected and liked by everyone who knew him.

Deborah, the youngest of the Dows children, had as a teenager been something of an *enfant terrible*—among her pranks was a failed attempt to steal a chair during a party at the White House when Franklin D. Roosevelt was president. Later she came to devote her life to horses. There was nothing elegant about the rather tumultuous activities at The Barn, the house she built in 1938 near the entrance to Glenburn. Deb had no social pretensions whatsoever, and her own looks were probably what mattered least of all to her. At times the number of horses, ponies, mules, donkeys, and cows exceeded one hundred, not to speak of all the dogs, cats, goats, geese, chickens and even a small pig that roamed the premises. It was a rather hard life driving horses to shows and auctions around the country, and Deb was never one to shirk the tough and dirty work involved. She is well known as the founder of The Southlands Foundation, established from the riding school she started after her father's death, aimed to teach young and old respect and love of the land and its animals. The girls and boys whom she taught how to ride, and who helped her

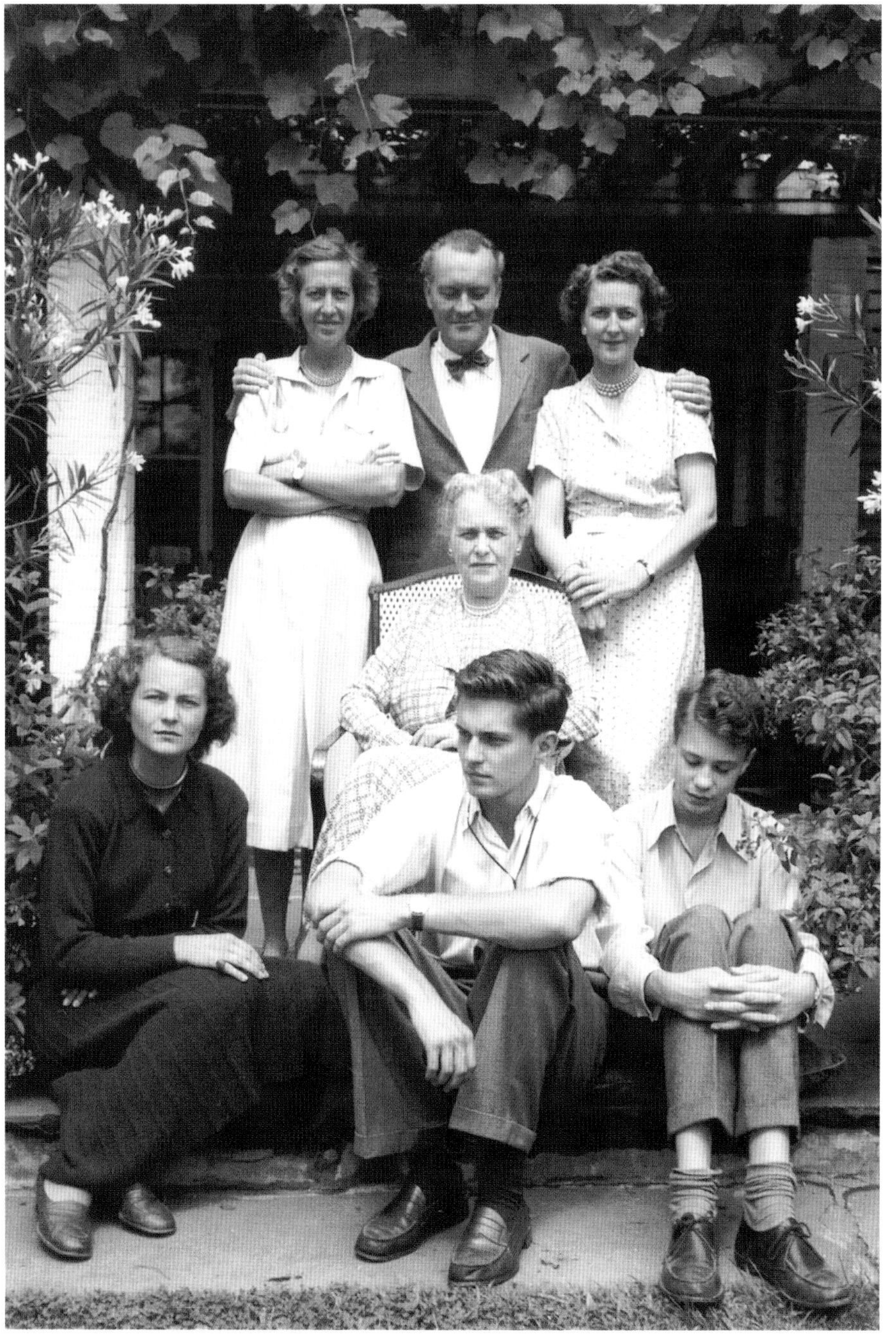

PREVIOUS PAGES A view of the back of the house in 1911, a year after it was built.

LAST PAGE Tracy Dows, the man who documented his life with a camera, in 1930.

around the place, adored her—and probably feared her a little, too. For Deb was exacting and could be very outspoken, even a little brutal at times. But she was also genuinely kind to anyone who she felt was underprivileged or needed her help, be it animal or human. A number of her pupils have testified that the experience gained at her riding school actually helped them in dealing with problems later in life. In our younger days, Deb's house was undoubtedly the place that my siblings and I enjoyed the most during our visits to Rhinebeck.

Since my mother Margaret had married a member of the Swedish foreign service, she came to spend most of her life in such cities as Stockholm, Riga, London, Copenhagen, Cairo, Belgrade, Ankara, Athens, Rio, and Lisbon. I shall make no attempt here to characterize our beloved American mother. Although her Swedish was perfect, my siblings and I never spoke anything but English with her. The books she read to us as children were all in English, *The Wizard of Oz* and *Sherlock Holmes* were favorites. Mother's accounts of her upbringing and her youth, so different from our own, fascinated us. Her trips with us to Rhinebeck were highlights in our lives, and our American relatives came to be very dear to us. Not only we, but also our children, now deplore that we have no cousins to visit in the United States. When in later years I was privileged to serve in New York and Washington as a Swedish diplomat, this made me even more aware of my American roots. And, so has this fine book of my grandfather's photographs, for which his numerous descendants in Europe send David Byars and Hudson River Heritage many a grateful thought.

LEFT A family gathering at Glenburn in the summer of 1948, when Margaret and her three children were visiting from Sweden. In the back row are Deb, Olin, and Margaret, with Alice in the center. In the front are Birgitta, Olin Knut (O.K.), and Jan.

Acknowledgments

When I had the idea of doing this book, I began by combing through thousands of photographs from the Dows Collection and selecting the ones I felt offered the greatest social, historical, and regional interest. It was my goal to feature as many images from the collection as possible. It will be no surprise to those who know me that I went through a great many layout revisions along the way.

First, I would wholeheartedly like to thank Tracy Dows's grandson, Olin Knut Thyberg, for his exceptional help with the book. He provided many wonderful stories, as well as additional photographs. He has become a delightful friend whom I had the pleasure of meeting with his family in Sweden in the summer of 2013. Kirsten Turner, another Dows descendant, also shared her extensive family knowledge, and I thank her profoundly.

I am grateful to Wint Aldrich for his encouragement and his exceptional knowledge of Dutchess County history, which was vital to the book. Fulsome thanks are also due to the board members of Hudson River Heritage, who gave me permission to use photographs from the Dows Collection and cheered me on while I worked on this project. The contributions of Emily Harding, Chip Holman, Christopher Scholz, and Linda and Duane Watson, are deeply appreciated. Conversations with Gale and Paul Schaefer helped me understand more about the Dows family. My gratitude also goes to the Rhinebeck Historical Society and The Southlands Foundation for their support. A special thanks to Joy Gross for rallying around me and to Michael Frazier for his assistance. John Craven, Eve D'Ambra, Barbara Davis, Greg Ferro, Véronique Firkusny, Kathy Hammer, Beverly Kane, Nancy Kelly, Leslie Lipton, Karen Mulligan, Brian Plumb, Joyce Rubin, and Susie Williams were each resourceful with their help. Peggy LaBelle deserves special credit for her boundless research talent. The enthusiasm of Ray Armater helped shepherd the book through its many revisions. Philip Large supplied significant help with the photographs. Derek Ostergard gave me excellent advice and kept me focused. My dear friend Leslie Daniel Rainer, who shares my love of history and historic houses, provided laughter and insight along the way.

I am fortunate to have worked with the talented team at SUNY Press: James Peltz, Jenn Bennett, Fran Keneston, Carol Reiser, and Janice Vunk, and to have benefited from the generosity of Joan K. Davidson and her foundation, Furthermore, in contributing a grant for the book. Barbaralee Diamonstein-Spielvogel, a true leader in the world of historic preservation, was particularly supportive.

Thank you to Robert Sullivan for his humor and words, and to Eve MacSweeney, who applied her expert editing skills. I owe her tremendously.

A special thank you to my family in Louisiana. And, to my husband, Joel Isler, and our dog, Lucas, stalwart companions during the seven years we now know as *Our Time at Foxhollow Farm*.

DAVID BYARS

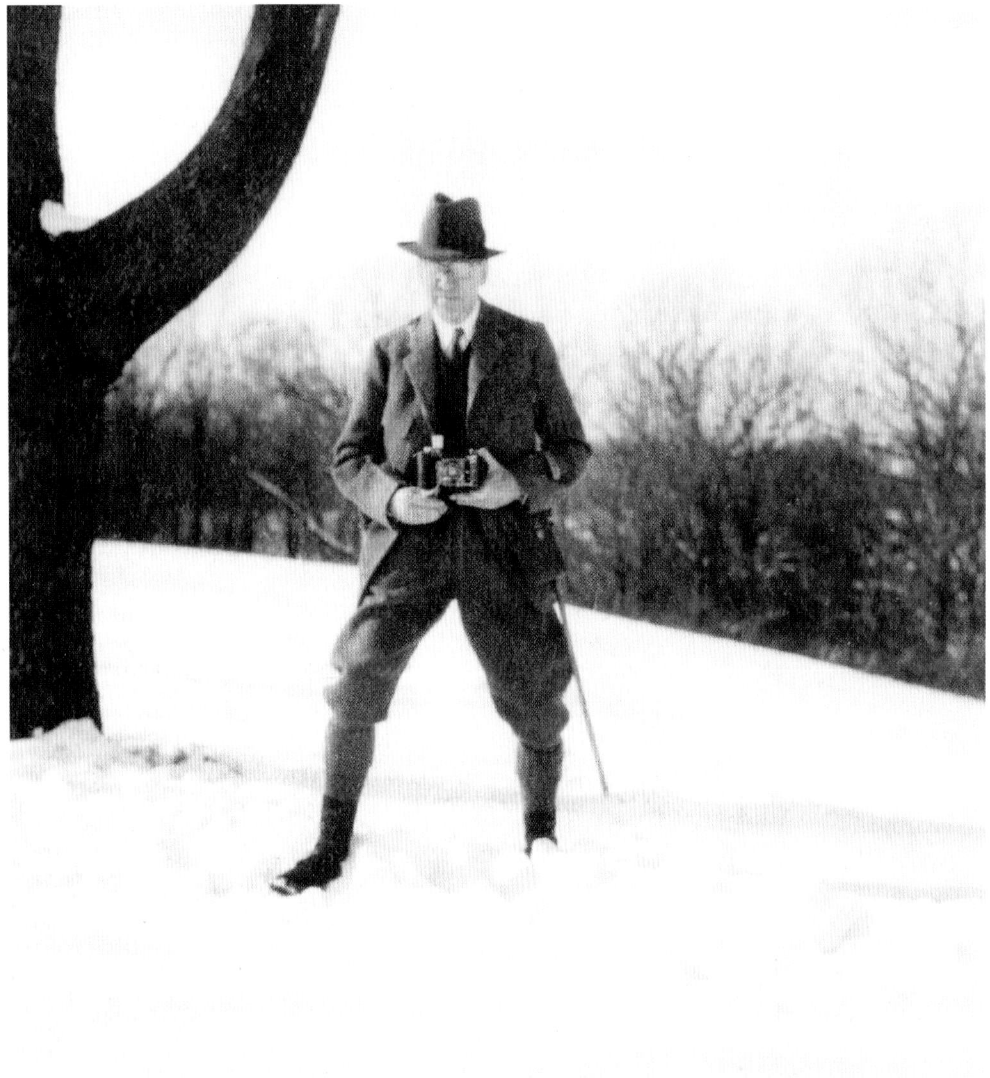